Albert J. Hoch Jr.   November - December 1981

African Insect Life

AFRICAN INSECT LIFE

S.H.SKAIFE

new edition revised by John Ledger
photographs by Anthony Bannister

Country Life Books

Published by Country Life Books
and distributed for them by
The Hamlyn Publishing Group Limited
London · New York · Sydney · Toronto
Astronaut House, Feltham, Middlesex, England

First published by Longman Green & Co. Limited
Revised edition published 1979

ISBN 0 600 34290 9

Preface to the second edition

I first read *African Insect Life* as an undergraduate biology student. We were instructed to make a collection of at least 200 insects as part of our course on the invertebrate animals. Far from being a chore, the collecting of insects opened up a new world of discovery, of hiking and camping adventures in wild and beautiful places in pursuit of flying, jumping, crawling and swimming creatures, which we impaled upon long pins and arranged neatly in cork-lined boxes. Then came the difficult part of working out the identity of our victims, and here *African Insect Life* really came into its own, for there were very few insects that could not be traced to family or order by a quick look at 'Skaife'.

Later when I joined the staff of an institute for medical research I was surprised to find that our copy of 'Skaife' was extremely well-used, quite battered in fact, by medical entomologists who had been called upon at short notice to identify red worms that came out of water taps, caterpillars in French salads or cockroaches in Cornish pasties. 'Skaife' was indispensable in answering the numerous and diverse questions about insects we were constantly being asked by doctors, health inspectors and the public.

In November 1976 the Fourth Pan-African Ornithological Congress was held in the Seychelles, the beautiful Indian Ocean island group. Dr Skaife's daughter, Bunty Rowan, was there as a professional ornithologist, and I as a part-time amateur, when the sad news of his death was received. We spoke briefly at tea in the hotel and I told Mrs Rowan how valuable her father's book was to entomologists in Africa, and how a revision would maintain its usefulness. I was greatly honoured later when the task was offered to me, but more than apprehensive about tampering with Dr Skaife's book.

Because one person cannot possibly be an authority on all the African insects, my first move was to ask for the help of a number of people, each an expert on a particular group. Their advice and comments, so freely and generously given, were then incorporated in the revised text. From the venerable Dr H. K. Munro, born in 1894, to the young postgraduate students of the university, the response was positive and constructive. I think Dr Skaife would have approved of all those who have added a bit, here and there, to *African Insect Life*.

It is fitting that those who received the training in biology at school for which Dr Skaife struggled so hard – and today study chemical communication in insects, specific mate recognition systems, evolutionary genetics and other biological projects – were able to participate in revising this book.

I have modified the original sequence of chapters, added several new chapters, and incorporated the contributions of my advisers to update the text, while trying to retain the clear and concise style that was Dr Skaife's forte. The revised edition includes numerous photographs of living insects, taken over a period of 20 years by my friend and colleague Anthony Bannister. In my view he is the world's leading insect photographer, and a highly competent naturalist whose observations have found their way into the revised text in a number of places.

The result, I hope, is worthy of its inspiration, and a fitting tribute to a remarkable man.

John Ledger
April 1979

Contents

Acknowledgements

I am most grateful to the following, who advised and assisted in the revision of the text:

J. D. Agnew, J. Bowden, H. D. Brown, W. G. H. Coaton, B. H. Cogan, W. R. Dolling, J. Heeg, S. F. Henning, M. E. Jackson, M. J. F. Johannsmeier, B. Levey, J. G. H. Londt, M. W. Mansell, H. K. Munro, N. I. Passmore, R. J. Phelps, M. D. Picker, E. C. G. Pinhey, A. J. Prins, M. J. Scoble, K. F. M. Scott, B. R. Stuckenberg, J. G. Theron, J. van Reenen and L. Vári.

Professor J. Metz kindly sanctioned and encouraged the project, and my colleagues in medical entomology are thanked for their help and advice. Lynn Walker typed the text, and she and Joyce Segerman assisted with proof-reading. I am very grateful to the publishers and their staff for their meticulous production of this book.

John Ledger
April 1979

Most of the photographs in this book were only made possible through the kind and generous assistance of various individuals and organisations, to all of whom I am most sincerely grateful. In the limited space available here I would particularly like to thank the following: Daba and Helen Wolff, Maudanne Bannister, Armin Nüñlist, Daphne and Bernie Thruthe, Tony and Elsa Pooley, Barbara Anderson, and also the Directors and Staff of the Botswana Department of Wildlife, the British Museum (Natural History), and the National Museums of Kenya.

Anthony Bannister
April 1979

The insects in perspective 1

Insects are found in almost every conceivable situation on the planet Earth, from the poles to the equator, high in the air, deep in caves and mine shafts, in seemingly lifeless deserts, rushing rivers, snow-capped mountain peaks and on the surface of the oceans. They have a history that goes back more than 300 million years, when the first cockroach-like creature appeared on Earth, yet so successful was the insect blueprint that cockroaches have changed very little in all that time. Of course during this period other types of insects have evolved, and the diversity of these creatures is another reason for their tremendous success; they range in size from minute wasps of less than a fifth of a millimetre in length to giant moths bigger than many birds.

Insects have a strong, light, external skeleton, and they seem disproportionately strong in relation to their size. The majority of insects are small, and most can fly, enabling them to escape from danger and also to invade every corner of the earth.

More than 800 000 different kinds of insect are known, and it seems likely that the total number may be more than four million. Insects account for some 70% of all animal life and one writer with a flair for statistics has worked out that the combined weight of the earth's insect population exceeds that of its human inhabitants by a factor of 12!

In order to get to grips with this enormous and varied group of creatures, we should first put the insects into perspective, and see just how they fit into the overall mosaic of living things.

How animals are classified and named Linnaeus, a young Swedish scientist dissatisfied with the clumsy way in which animals and plants were named and described, developed a new method of classification which was first used in his book *Systema Naturae* in 1745. We still use this system, and call it 'binomial nomenclature' – the use of two words (often Latin or Greek) for the name of each kind of animal or plant.

Thus the house fly is known as *Musca domestica* to entomologists. It is a pity that so many people are baffled by the need to refer to something as mundane as a house fly by a strange-sounding Latin name. In fact, scientific names are quite easy to get used to, and they allow us to refer very precisely to one particular kind of animal anywhere in the world. Common names are not universal, and even in one country the same insect may be known by several different names. Four entomologists, from Japan, Nigeria, Australia and Finland, would probably not be able to have a simple conversation, yet each would know exactly what *Musca domestica* is!

It is not necessary to know the exact Latin meaning of

Phylum:	Arthropoda
Subphylum:	Mandibulata
Class:	Insecta
Order:	Diptera
Family:	Muscidae
Genus:	*Musca*
Species:	*domestica*
Author:	Linnaeus, 1761

1. How the house fly is classified and named.

Musca domestica. The last word, *domestica* (never with a capital d), is the name of the 'species', or kind of animal. We will have more to say about what a species is, but put simply, it is a group of animals that share the same features, and interbreed with their own kind. The species *domestica* is in turn a member of a larger group or 'genus' called *Musca* (always with a capital M). Flies which are related to the house fly then belong to the same genus, so we have *Musca sorbens, Musca lusoria, Musca crassirostris,* and many others, each of these names precisely defining a particular kind of fly.

The genus *Musca* belongs to a still larger division, the 'family' Muscidae, which contains several genera of flies rather like the house fly. The many families of flies belong in turn to an 'order' – in this case the Diptera, which embraces all those insects that have only one pair of wings. There are 25 orders of insects in Africa: beetles belong to the order Coleoptera, butterflies to Lepidoptera, bees and wasps to Hymenoptera, and so on.

All the orders of insects belong to the 'class' called Insecta. Other classes of animals with jointed legs, like Arachnida (scorpions, spiders, ticks); Crustacea (crabs, crayfish, woodlice); and Diplopoda (millipedes), make up the 'phylum' Arthropoda. The highest division of the animal kingdom is the phylum, and all living things are assigned to a phylum as a first stage in classification. Some examples of familiar phyla are the Protozoa (single-celled animals), Porifera (sponges), Annelida (segmented worms), Mollusca (snails, slugs and shellfish), Echinodermata (starfishes and sea-urchins), and the Chordata (animals with a nerve chord along the back, like ourselves of the class Mammalia and the birds, class Aves, and so on). It is possible to use intermediate subdivisions as well, such as subphylum, subclass and subfamily.

The actual business of recognising and describing species and giving them names is called taxonomy, and many entomologists spend their lives doing this in museums and research institutes throughout the world. The 'International Rules of Nomenclature' govern the description and naming of animals. On discovering a new species, the taxonomist must describe it in writing, make drawings or take photographs that will assist others to recognise it, give it a name that has not been used before, and then arrange for the description to be printed in a journal or publication that is available to the international scientific community. One specimen must be selected as the 'type' of the species, and it must be deposited in a safe place such as a museum, so that future workers may be able to refer to it if need be.

What is a species? Relatively speaking, it is only a short time ago that Charles Darwin shook the world with his book, *The Origin of Species by Means of Natural Selection*. When it was published in 1859 he was bitterly criticised by those who believed that each kind of animal was exactly as it had been at the creation of the world. Darwin saw instead a dynamic and ever-changing situation, with all the animals and plants engaged in a constant struggle which he called 'the survival of the fittest'. All living things on earth today are the result of millions of years of this struggle for existence – those which lost the struggle are now extinct. This 'theory of evolution' has been difficult for some people to accept as a fact, but today it is the firm foundation on which we base our understanding of the real relationships between different kinds of living things.

The discovery of chromosomes, which carry the genes (the fundamental, chemical links of inheritance between parent and offspring), and the knowledge that changes, or 'mutations' in these genes occur frequently and regularly in nature, opened new horizons. Scientists were now able to explain how slightly different individuals could arise with the passage of time, some better-adapted for existence and the struggle to pass on their genetic material than others.

In the majority of animals the sexes are separate, and male and female must meet in order to reproduce. The fact that different kinds of animals exist, implies that under natural conditions they mate 'with their own kind'. The encounter of the sexes is of fundamental importance, for the males and females of each kind of animal must be capable of meeting and recognising one another on a regular and efficient basis. It is now known that numerous adaptations, to ensure this encounter, have evolved; these consist essentially of signals and responses between males and females. Professor Hugh Paterson has called these 'specific mate recognition systems', and he defines the *species* as *a group of organisms which share a common mate-recognition system*.

The action of the specific mate recognition system (SMRS), ensures a precise choice of mating partners and mistakes are rare under natural conditions. The system ensures that genes are exchanged only between members of the same species and the species can therefore be thought of as comprising a 'gene pool'.

This definition of species, which is a new concept that you will not find in older textbooks, is biologically acceptable. It does not imply that species are inflexible units that do not change in the course of time, nor does it define the species on the basis of particular, observable characters; thus it accommodates the fact that considerable variation in appearance can occur within a single species. Humans, for example, vary considerably in

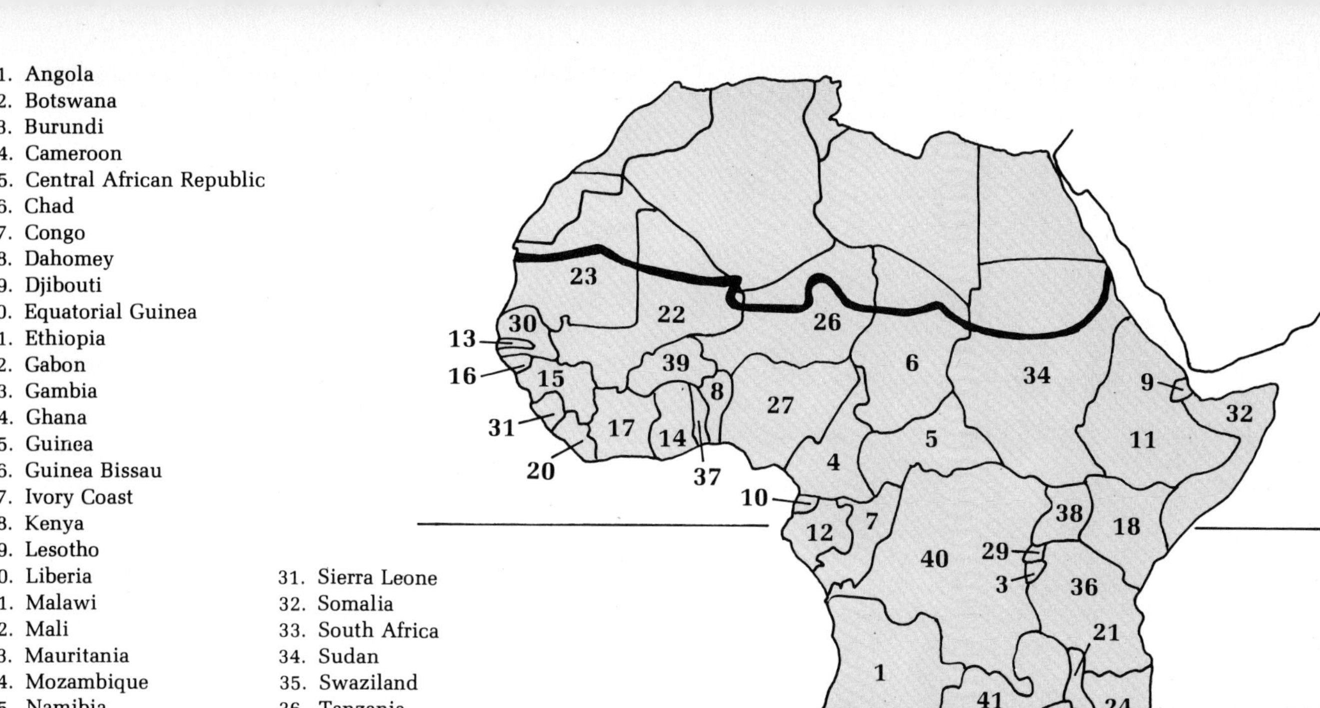

2. Africa south of the Sahara. The names of the countries corresponding to the numbers on the map are in the list. The northern limit of the Subsaharan Region is indicated by the solid line across the continent.

many aspects of external appearance, but there is no doubt they are the same species.

Conversely, there are valid biological species that are very similar and difficult to distinguish by ordinary means. We call these 'sibling species', and because of their similarity to other related species they are often discovered only by accident. There is no reason to assume that species must be vastly different from one another in their appearance. Furthermore, if we make use of the concept of mate recognition systems to distinguish species, we employ the very same methods as the animals themselves, and we are therefore more likely to make reliable decisions.

Another important attribute of the SMRS is that it is self-stabilising and therefore subject to little variability within species. This is because any individual departing from the norm would not find a mate and would leave no progeny, thus any radical genetic changes would be impossible.

The process of mate recognition is very complex, and has hardly been studied in depth in the insects. Elaborate display and courtship patterns are common, and involve chemical communication, visual recognition, touch and sound. Throughout this book you will find examples of behaviour relating to mate recognition among a wide variety of insects, but a rich field of scientific investigation still awaits future students.

The term 'subspecies' has been used in various ways, some of them inaccurate and biologically unacceptable. In brief, it is an 'extra' name, given to a population of a species that is geographically isolated from other populations and exhibits consistent differences in colour, pattern, behaviour or combinations of these. An example of a subspecies is *Musca domestica curviforceps*, which differs from *Musca domestica calleva*, and both African subspecies differ from the European *Musca domestica domestica;* but they interbreed readily when they meet. All subspecific populations would be expected to share a common mate-recognition system. These subspecies are best regarded as 'incipient species'. Depending on future events such as climatic, vegetational or topographical change, any isolated population may develop into a new species, or be reabsorbed into a single homogeneous population if the isolating barriers break down.

Zoogeography Animals living in certain regions of the world share features that, in general, allow us to separate them from those living in other regions: the marsupials of Australia, for example, are unlike any other assemblage of mammals anywhere else. We can thus divide the world into a number of zoogeographic regions, based on the kinds of animals that are found there. Most of Europe and the north coast of Africa falls into the Palaearctic Region, North America and Canada comprise the Nearctic Region, South America the Neotropical Region. The Australasian Region includes Australia and New Zealand, while China, India, Japan and other eastern countries form the Oriental Region.

The African continent has one predominant feature

Phylum:
ARTHROPODA

Class:
Arachnida (Spiders, scorpions, ticks, mites)
Crustacea (Crabs, lobsters, woodlice)
Onycophora (Onycophorans)
Diplopoda (Millipedes)
Chilopoda (Centipedes)
Collembola (Springtails)
Diplura (Diplurans)
Protura (Proturans)
Thysanura (Fishmoths, bristletails)
Insecta (Insects)

3. The major classes of the phylum Arthropoda.

that affects the distribution of animals and plants – the Sahara Desert. Although it is not very old – established perhaps only 5 000 years ago – the Sahara is today a formidable barrier to the movement of animals. The region to the south of the Sahara makes up most of Africa, and constitutes another great zoogeographical division. The choice of a name for this area is rather controversial; it was initially called the Aethiopian, or Ethiopian Region, but when Abyssinia changed its name to Ethiopia, a confusing situation arose. Some scientists then referred to it as 'Africa south of the Sahara', an accurate if cumbersome description, while the entomologist Botha de Meillon introduced the term 'Subsaharan Region', an accurate and appropriate name which is preferred by most workers on the continent. Unfortunately another term has recently been proposed, the 'Afrotropical Region'; it is inappropriate because large areas in Africa are not tropical. Readers should be aware of the various terms that might be used by different writers when referring to the Subsaharan Region.

The Arthropoda Insects belong to the phylum Arthropoda, which means 'joint-footed', and the members of this phylum all have segmented bodies bearing a variable number of paired, jointed appendages which may be modified for different purposes. Arthropods are also distinguished by having an exoskeleton made of a substance called chitin, a dorsal heart, and a ventral nervous system.

The phylum Arthropoda consists of several classes of which Insecta is but one (a further ten are discussed in Chapter 2). Insecta have further distinguishing characteristics; for instance they all have three distinct parts of the body (head, thorax and abdomen), a single pair of antennae, three pairs of legs, and most have wings.

General Structure: The insect body consists of three regions, the head, the thorax and the abdomen. The head bears the eyes, the antennae and the mouthparts. Most insects have two or three small 'simple eyes' (ocelli) on the top of their heads, and on either side two large 'compound eyes', which are often complex structures, made up of numerous 'ommatidia'. The paired antennae vary considerably in size and shape; they are used as sense organs. The mouthparts consist essentially of a 'labrum' (upper lip), a pair of jaw-like 'mandibles', a pair of jaw-like 'maxillae', a 'labium' (lower lip) and the 'hypopharynx' (a tongue-like structure). This basic design is highly modified in the different orders of insects, but even in complicated mouthparts such as those of mosquitoes or moths, their derivation from the basic structure is evident.

The thorax comprises three segments called the prothorax, mesothorax and metathorax; each segment bears a pair of jointed legs, and the last two segments each bear a pair of wings. These may be variously modified; some insects have only one pair, while others have lost both pairs.

The abdomen consists of 11 segments, but usually only ten are visible; in some insects there appear to be fewer because of fusion of the segments. Each segment consists of an upper ('tergum') and lower ('sternum') plate; there may be a lateral plate on each side (the 'pleura'). The genitalia are usually to be found at the tip of the abdomen, and the females of some insects have a specialised ovipositor (egg-laying organ) formed by structures on the eighth and ninth segments.

Internally, insects have a respiratory system made up of branching tubes (tracheae), a circulatory system consisting of a tubelike heart on the dorsal (upper) surface, a nervous system comprising a brain and a nerve cord on the ventral (lower) surface, and a digestive system running from the mouth to the rectum. The excretory system consists of a number of tubules that empty into the hind gut. The sexes are separate, and reproductive systems comprising ovaries and associated structures are found in females, and testes and associated structures are found in males.

The cockroach provides a useful example of insect structure (see further details in Chapter 4), while specific modifications and adaptations among the different orders of insects appear in the appropriate chapters.

Growth and development Insect eggs vary enormously in size, shape, ornamentation and numbers laid. Sometimes they are retained by the female inside the body until they hatch, and the young are deposited alive. Because of the restrictions imposed by the external skeleton, insects grow by undergoing a series of 'moults', when the old exoskeleton is cast off.

'Metamorphosis' refers to the changes which take place in the structure of an insect as it develops from egg to adult. Insects which have a 'simple metamorphosis' hatch from the egg into 'nymphs' that resemble their parents in most respects other than size. These nymphs then grow to adult size by undergoing several moults.

Insects which have a 'complete metamorphosis' hatch from the egg into 'larvae' that are completely different

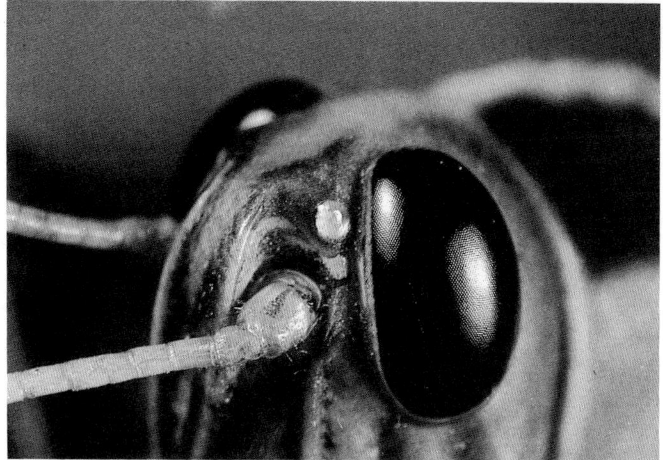

4. Close-up of grasshopper's head shows a compound eye with a simple eye alongside it above the antenna.

5. This grasshopper shows the basic insect division into head, thorax and abdomen. The thorax is divided into three segments, each bearing a pair of legs. The second and third segments each bear a pair of wings as well. The first thoracic segment forms the saddle-shaped pronotum behind the head.

from the adults. After a period of growth and several moults the larva changes into a 'pupa', which resembles neither the larva nor the adult. It does not feed, and is often enclosed in a 'cocoon' (made by the larva before it changes into a pupa) or a 'puparium' (the skin of the last larval stage). After a period, the whole structure of the pupa undergoes rearrangement and the adult emerges.

Classification and identification The class Insecta is currently represented by 25 orders recorded from Africa. The orders can be divided primarily into two groups, the first of which (the Exopterygota) have a simple metamorphosis and immature stages which are called nymphs, and the second (the Endopterygota), which have a complete metamorphosis and larval, pupal and adult stages. Each order is further subdivided into suborders, families, and subfamilies, depending on the size and complexity of the group.

At the end of each chapter a summary of the major features that distinguish the family or subfamily, is given. In a few cases a simple 'key' has been provided, that will enable interested readers to identify specimens. A key is a series of alternative combinations of characters; choosing one combination will lead to further alternatives, and so eventually to the correct group. Identification is a process of progressively narrowing down the group to which the insect belongs. In the large groups, such as flies, beetles and wasps, identification is a difficult prospect even for the professional entomologist, and no attempt has been made to provide a key. However, the combination of the description given in the text, the summarised classification at the end of each chapter, and the photographs and line drawings, should allow you to identify the family of the majority of the common African insects. For the more serious reader, a list of publications is provided at the end of each chapter, and these references will enable you to obtain further details about any group. Only the most important monographs and reviews are listed, and you may need the help of your local library, museum or university to obtain them.

Common names are provided for African insects where these are available. Scientific names are preferred, and indeed many lend themselves to use in the adjectival form as common names, for example 'hemipteran' for a

Exopterygote Insects (Incomplete metamorphosis)

Order	Common name
Ephemeroptera	mayflies
Odonata	dragonflies
Blattodea	cockroaches
Isoptera	termites
Mantodea	mantids
Phasmatodea	stick insects
Dermaptera	earwigs
Plecoptera	stoneflies
Orthoptera	grasshoppers, locusts & crickets
Embioptera	silkspinners
Zoraptera	zorapterans
Psocoptera	booklice
Phthiraptera	lice
Hemiptera	bugs
Thysanoptera	thrips

Endopterygote Insects (Complete metamorphosis)

Order	Common name
Neuroptera	lacewings & antlions
Megaloptera	alderflies
Coleoptera	beetles
Strepsiptera	stylopids
Mecoptera	scorpionflies
Siphonaptera	fleas
Diptera	flies
Trichoptera	caddisflies
Lepidoptera	moths & butterflies
Hymenoptera	wasps, bees & ants

6. The orders of Subsaharan insects.

member of the Hemiptera, or 'orthopteran' for a member of the Orthoptera. 'Fly' and 'bug' are a part of the common names of many insects. If the insect belongs to the order Diptera, the 'fly' is written as a separate word (house fly, horse fly, tsetse fly, etc.), but if the insect belongs to another order, the common name is written as one word (butterfly, caddisfly, dragonfly). The same rule applies to the use of the term 'bug', always written separately if the insect actually belongs to the Hemiptera (stink bug, bed bug, assassin bug), and as one word if it does not.

Illustrations and scales All photographs are of living insects; these are supplemented by a number of drawings. It is difficult to indicate the actual size of the insect depicted in each illustration. Individuals of the same species often vary widely in size according to the availability of food, or the insects may be larger or smaller in different parts of their range. Wherever possible, therefore, the size range of the various insects is given at the appropriate place in the text, or in the captions to the illustrations. A measurement refers to the length of the insect, from the front of the head to the tip of the abdomen, or to the tips of the folded wings if these extend beyond the abdomen.

Insects and man People seem to fall into two broad categories: those who regard insects with horror and disgust, as creatures to be eliminated at all costs and by whatever means, and those whose curiosity and objectivity enable them to appreciate and understand that man is not the only inhabitant of the planet earth. Although we may have great powers of life and death over other living creatures, our domination should be benign and humane. Tolerance and understanding of other forms of life is the first step towards similar relationships with our fellow humans. This book is dedicated to all the thoughtful, observant and tolerant men who have contributed to our knowledge of insects, and thus to our overall understanding of life.

FURTHER READING

There are many excellent general text books on entomology available throughout the world, and they tend to complement one another, for no single work can hope to cover everything there is to know about the insects.

Askew, R. R.: *Parasitic Insects*. Heinemann Educational Books, London (1971). 316 pp

Blaney, W. M.: *How Insects Live*. Elsevier-Phaidon, Oxford (1976). 160 pp

Borror, D. J. & De Long, D. M.: *Introduction to the Study of Insects*. Ed. 3. Holt, Rinehart & Winston, New York (1970). 591 pp

Borror, D. J. & White, R. E.: *A Field Guide to the Insects of America North of Mexico*. Peterson Field Guide Series No. 19. Houghton Mifflin Company, Boston (1970). 404 pp

Chapman, R. F.: *The Insects: Structure and Function*. English University Press, London (1969). 818 pp

Cloudsley-Thompson, J. L.: *Insects and History*. Weidenfeld & Nicolson, London (1977). 242 pp

Ebeling, W.: *Urban Entomology*. University of California Division of Agricultural Sciences, Berkeley (1975). 695 pp

Hanström, B., Brinck, P. & Rudebeck, G. (Eds). *South African Animal Life. Results of the Lund University Expedition in 1950-1951*. Almqvist & Wiksell, Stockholm. Vols. 1-13 (to 1967). (Contain very many important papers on African insects.)

James, M. T. & Harwood, R. F.: *Herms's Medical Entomology* Ed. 6. Collier-MacMillan Ltd., London (1969). 484 pp

Linsenmaier. W.: *Insects of the World*. McGraw-Hill, New York (1972). 392 pp

Mackerras, I. M. (Ed.): *The Insects of Australia*. Melbourne University Press, Melbourne (1970). 1029 pp (also Supplement (1974), 146 pp)

Oldroyd, H.: *Elements of Entomology*. Weidenfeld & Nicolson, London (1968). 312 pp

Passarin d'Entréves, P. & Zunino, M.: *The Secret Life of Insects*. Orbis Publishing, London (1976). 384 pp

Richards, O. W. & Davies, R. G.: *Imms' General Textbook of Entomology*, Ed. 10, Vols. I & II. Chapman & Hall, London (Science Paperbacks) (1977). 1354 pp

Romoser, W. S.: *The Science of Entomology*. MacMillan Company, New York and London (1973). 544 pp

Smit, B.: *Insects in Southern Africa: How to Control Them*. Oxford University Press, Cape Town (1964). 399 pp

Weaving, A.: *Insects. A Review of Insect Life in Rhodesia*. Regal Publishers, Salisbury (1977). 179 pp

Wigglesworth, V. B.: *Insects and the Life of Man*. Chapman and Hall, London (1976). 217 pp

Insects' near relatives: Other Arthropoda

Contrary to popular belief, spiders are not insects, although they belong to the same phylum, the Arthropoda. In order to place the class Insecta in perspective within the phylum, this chapter deals with ten other classes.

We begin with Arachnida (spiders and scorpions) for good reason: every animal phylum is arranged in an ascending order of complexity or sophistication. In the case of the Arthropoda, the spiders and scorpions are the more primitive or simple forms, going up through the Crustacea, the millipedes and centipedes, and so on, to the more advanced six-legged creatures such as fishmoths and culminating in the 'pinnacle' of arthropod success, the insects, which are the main subject of this book. This same principle applies to the way in which the book as a whole is organised: thus Chapter 3 (mayflies and dragonflies) represents the simpler forms and Chapter 23, on ants, the most advanced.

A clue to the possible ancestry and relationships of the Arthropoda is provided by the Onycophorans, peculiar worm-like creatures which have a number of jointed legs: this has led scientists to speculate that the Arthropoda evolved from the segmented worms of the phylum Annelida.

ARACHNIDA

Spiders and scorpions are greatly feared by most people, and certainly arouse stronger human emotions than the majority of insects. Their quick, scuttling movements and unexpected appearances – often at night – coupled with a reputation for biting and stinging, are responsible for considerable apprehension. The related ticks and mites are less fearsome, but they are very abundant in Africa where they cause serious veterinary problems as well as human disease.

The Arachnida are characterised by having six pairs of jointed appendages, the first of which are like jaws or fangs (the chelicerae), the second like feelers or pincers (the pedipalps), and the remaining pairs leg-like. Thus spiders, ticks and scorpions all have eight legs. The chelicerae and pedipalps may be inconspicuous (as in spiders), or the pedipalps may be large and pincer-like (as in scorpions). There are no antennae and the body is divided into two parts: the cephalothorax (combined head and thorax, with appendages), and the abdomen. The Arachnida and their relatives are placed in a special group of Arthropoda, the subphylum Chelicerata.

Scorpions belong to the order Scorpiones, and there are two important families in Africa: the Scorpionidae, and the Buthidae. The family to which a scorpion belongs can easily be determined by looking at its pincers (pedipalps) and its tail. Scorpionidae have large, powerful pedipalps, and a slender tail with a small sting. They do not have a powerful venom, and capture and subdue their prey with the pedipalps. The Buthidae, on the other hand, have slender pedipalps and a thick tail with a big sting. They have powerful venom which affects the nervous system, and they kill or paralyse their prey by stinging. There are a number of Buthidae in Africa that are dangerous to humans, and their stings can be fatal to some individuals, unless they are treated in time with anti-venom. Fortunately, most of the dangerous scorpions are restricted to very arid parts of Africa, which have low human populations, but they are a hazard to those whose occupation takes them into such regions. *Parabuthus villosus,* a large species from the Namib Desert, can squirt its venom for a considerable distance if alarmed, and since this venom is considerably more potent than that of a cobra, the result of receiving any in the eyes can be serious.

Scorpions, in general, are long-lived creatures which take many years to grow to maturity. They are active at night and hide during the day. The young, which resemble their parents in most respects except size, are born live and one may sometimes come across a mother scorpion with dozens of babies clinging to her back. They are resilient creatures, and an arid-country species like *Parabuthus villosus* can be kept in the laboratory for more than a year without food or water, provided it is well fed at the outset.

Scorpions can be divided according to their habitat into burrowing, rock-dwelling or arboreal (tree-dwelling) species, and these categories include both Buthidae and Scorpionidae. Some of the burrowers are equipped with long hairs on their legs, which increase their efficiency in soft sand; they may dig burrows as deep as 1 m below the surface. The genera *Parabuthus* and *Opisthophthalmus* contain a number of burrowing species. In hard soils the burrowing scorpions dig to a depth of only 10-30 cm, and the burrows are often located under stones.

Members of the scorpionid genus *Hadogenes* are adapted to living in narrow cracks and crevices in rocks. They are flattened and have long, slender pedipalps and tails, and cling to the rock surfaces with such tenacity that they cannot be dislodged, so that scorpion collectors have to prise open the cracks with crowbars to secure specimens.

Arboreal scorpions generally live under the bark of trees such as Acacias, and two common genera which utilise this habitat are *Uroplectes* and *Opisthacanthus.* One species of the latter genus, *O. elatus,* is the only member of the family Scorpionidae in America, and it is believed that these scorpions have crossed the Atlantic from Africa on trees washed down by rivers in flood.

Whipscorpions belong to the order Amblypygi, and though fearsome-looking arachnids, are actually harmless to humans. *Damon variegatus* is widespread in the

7. *Parabuthus* scorpions (family Buthidae) mating. In this 'dance' the male deposits his spermatophore on the ground, then moves his partner into position so that transfer of the spermatophore takes place. Note thick tails and slender pincers (pedipalps). 60 mm.

woodlands and savannas of Africa – specimens may be found under bark, in crevices in rocks, and beneath fallen trees. They are commonly found in the same cracks as the rock-dwelling *Hadogenes* scorpions and are extremely flattened, thus able to creep into very narrow cracks. The pedipalps are long, slender and armed with spines, and are used for capturing prey. In the Amblypygi the first pair of walking legs is modified into long, agile, whip-like (hence 'whipscorpion') appendages that are constantly in motion. They are used as 'feelers' and are equipped with special sensory organs. *Damon variegatus* is very agile and can move quickly and unexpectedly causing consternation and fright to people unused to their habits.

8. *Opisthophthalmus* scorpion (family Scorpionidae) eating a grasshopper. Note thin tail and stout pincers (pedipalps). 50 mm.

9. Scorpion pedipalp, showing long sensory hairs.

10. Whipscorpion *(Damon variegatus)*.

Spiders form a large and diverse order, the Araneae, of which many thousands of species are known from Africa and many more undoubtedly await description, for there are very few taxonomists working full-time on the group. Spiders vary in size from tiny species less than 1 mm across, to giants which may exceed 15 cm. They are found in every conceivable habitat, and all are predatory, generally capturing prey about their own size or slightly smaller. Male spiders are usually tiny and are seldom seen (the female often eats the male after mating). The males can be recognised by their clubbed and swollen pedipalps which are used for mating.

The spiders of Africa require a book of their own to do them justice, and this brief account will mention only a few highlights and some of the species dangerous to man.

Spiders usually have an unsegmented abdomen, strongly constricted at the base, with a group of finger-like spinnerets at the posterior end. These spinnerets produce silk, and one of the outstanding features of the spiders is their use of silk for constructing webs, snares, shelters and egg sacs. The most noticeable form in which spider silk is encountered, is in the large orb webs made by species of *Nephila, Araneus, Argiope* and *Gasteracantha*. These webs are used to capture flying insects, and in some species play an important rôle in protecting the occupants and their young from predation and the elements. Other spiders use small webs as nets, which they fling over their prey when within range. One species uses a single thread of sticky silk which it holds under tension; when a flying insect collides with this elastic thread the spider releases it, and the victim is entangled as the snare contracts.

Spider silk is also used by some species to disperse themselves: young spiderlings crawl up onto vegetation and begin releasing a silk thread into the wind; when this is long enough they are carried away by 'ballooning'. Numerous spiders are found to have a cosmopolitan distribution, and ballooning is often responsible for their widespread occurrence.

Many spiders are free-ranging and capture their prey without the assistance of a web. The large *Palystes natalius* preys on small geckos and may also, in subtropical areas of South Africa, be found searching inside houses for victims. Members of the genera *Leucorchestris* and *Carparachne* live in shallow silk-lined burrows in sand-dunes and come out at night to hunt insects. All three genera belong to the Sparassidae. Species of *Thalassius* (Pisauridae) are associated with water, into which they plunge to grasp the small frogs and fish which consitute their prey. Members of the genus *Chiracanthium* (Clubionidae) make small silk retreats in which they rest during the day, but they come out at night and wander about in search of prey. They are medium-sized, yellowish spiders with conspicuous, dark mouthparts, and are very common in houses. It is suspected that they are often responsible for biting humans, leaving a swollen, tender spot which may become ulcerated and infected.

11. Orb-web spider awaiting prey at the centre of her web, in which she hangs upside-down. 12 mm.

12. Orb-web spider (*Argiope* sp.) swathing a captured grasshopper in silk to immobilise it. 20 mm.

Another genus of spider that is of medical importance in South Africa (and probably also in other parts of the continent), is *Loxosceles* (family Scytodidae). In America these are known as 'violin spiders' because of the shape of the markings on the upper surface. They are small, brownish, inconspicuous creatures which hide in sandy or dusty places and are often disguised by a layer of debris caught in their body hairs. Their bite is pain-

13. A net-throwing spider *(Dinopus* sp.) hangs upside-down; it will drop the small web, held between its front legs, over passing prey. 20 mm.

14. *Palystes natalius* with silk-covered egg-mass. Body 30 mm.

15. 'Dancing white lady spider' *(Carparachne* sp.) in Namib Desert. 22 mm.

less and the action of their venom is cytotoxic, meaning that it causes destruction of the tissues. Victims of *Loxosceles* bites first notice a weal with a reddened centre, then the edges begin to ulcerate and a nasty, blackened lesion develops, which may take months to heal and may even require skin grafts to repair the damage.

The black widow spider is greatly feared wherever it occurs, but many people do not know that *Latrodectus mactans* is common in Africa. It is a medium-sized spider with a round, shiny black abdomen that has a crimson line or spot on the dorsal surface. The female builds her web in the base of a clump of grass, and produces a number of smooth-surfaced, white, round egg sacs. The venom of the black widow is neurotoxic – affecting the nervous system – and the bite causes excruciating pain. In the southwestern Cape Province of

16. *Loxosceles spinulosa.* This individual has lost a leg – a common occurrence which does not normally curtail an arthropod's activities. 9 mm.

17. *Latrodectus geometricus* female, showing 'hourglass' mark on underside and egg cocoon with spines. 14 mm.

South Africa, workers in the wheat fields may be bitten about the throat or chest while handling the sheaves of wheat. However, the danger of the black widow is often exaggerated and an effective anti-venom is available for the treatment of *Latrodectus* bites. The mortality figure on a worldwide basis is about 5% in untreated cases.

A second species, called the brown widow spider *Latrodectus geometricus,* is extremely common in and around buildings in southern Africa. It may be recognised by the orange 'hour-glass' mark on the underside of the abdomen, and by its egg sacs, which are covered with small spikes. The action of the venom is the same in both species of *Latrodectus,* but *L. geometricus* is much less dangerous than *L. mactans.* Both are called 'button spiders' in South Africa, and have various vernacular names in different parts of the world.

The big 'baboon spiders', which belong to the family Theraphosidae, are much feared because of their great size and hairy appearance, but they are not dangerous to humans. These tarantula-like creatures make silk-lined burrows about 30 cm deep in the ground, which are quite hard to find. Similarly, it takes something of an expert to find the lairs of the trap-door spiders (family Ctenizidae), since the lids fit tightly and are well-disguised.

There seems to be no end to the diversity in form and habits of the spiders. Some are found in the intertidal region, and their habitats are flooded by the sea with each rising tide. The spiders take refuge in cracks, crevices and empty shells, sometimes constructing a web to help keep the sea out. They draw their oxygen from a layer of air trapped in dense hairs on the abdomen. Social spiders of the genus *Stegodyphus* (family Eresidae) make communal nests in thorn trees, in which hundreds of individuals may live. Pretty little yellow, pink or green flower spiders (Thomisidae) grasp unwary victims that visit their flowers, and jumping spiders (Salticidae) with huge, headlamp eyes, make prodigious leaps to bring down their prey. The spitting spiders (Scytodidae) immobilise their victims by firing sticky blobs of saliva at them with great accuracy.

The observant naturalist in Africa will never run short of new things to discover about spiders!

Solifuges are peculiar, large spider-like creatures that belong to the order Solifugae. Some are active during the day in the hot sunshine, move quickly across the ground or on rocks, and are rather frightening in their appearance. They have large powerful chelicerae used to capture and subdue their prey, which is then passed repeatedly through the chelicerae and the body contents extracted. They lack venom glands and are not at all dangerous to humans, although the chelicerae can probably deliver a powerful bite. The pedipalps are slender and leg-like, so the solifuges appear to have five pairs of legs instead of the normal arachnid complement of four pairs.

18. Hairy 'baboon spider' (family Theraphosidae). 40 mm.
19. Social spiders (*Stegodyphus* sp.) co-operate to overpower prey. 9 mm.
20. Flower spider (family Thomisidae) with fly victim. 10 mm.
21. Jumping spider (family Salticidae), showing large frontal eyes. 10 mm.
22. Spitting spider (family Scytodidae), which has overpowered a fishmoth by pinning it down with sticky mucus. 9 mm.
23. A solifuge feeding on a caterpillar. 32 mm.

18 19
20 21
22 23

Pseudoscorpions (order Pseudoscorpionidea) are small, reddish-brown creatures with a conspicuous pair of pincer-like pedipalps which they hold out before them as they walk about. They are reminiscent of scorpions, but without tails. Although a number of species are known from Africa, hardly anything is known about their habits or ecology. They are found in soil litter, beneath stones, under bark and in birds' nests or rodent burrows.

Harvestmen are spider-like creatures with four pairs of very long and slender legs. The body is oval, compact and segmented. They are common in forests and areas of high humidity, and may be found in houses, outbuildings and gardens. They belong to the order Opiliones, and are quite harmless, feeding on both live and dead insects (particularly aphids), as well as vegetable matter. The harvestmen should not be confused with the spiders; the latter have an unsegmented abdomen with a marked constriction where it joins the cephalothorax.

Ticks and mites belong to the order Acarina (or Acari). This is a large group which is divided into a number of suborders, including the Ixodoidea for the ticks, the Mesostigmata that includes, among many others, the larger blood-sucking mites and their relatives, the Trombidiformes for a group of soft-bodied mites (some of which live in or on the skin), and the suborder Sarcoptiformes for another assemblage of mites which also includes parasite species. There are many books and publications dealing with the Acarina of Africa, and only a brief resumé is given here.

Ticks are the most important external parasites of domestic animals, and cause them untold suffering and financial loss to their owners, both directly through irritation, loss of blood and deterioration in condition, and indirectly by transmitting viral and protozoal infections and by causing toxicosis with their saliva. Man is also the victim of certain tick-borne infections. All ticks suck blood for part of their lives; some are not fussy about their choice of host, while others are much more specific and may only be found on one kind or group of animal. The mouthparts of ticks are somewhat different from those of the Arachnida already discussed: instead of a true head, the ticks have a 'capitulum', or gnathosma, consisting of a basal portion to which the piercing hypostome, the cutting chelicerae, and the palps are attached. The tips of the chelicerae have sharp digits, used to lacerate the skin and facilitate the entry of the hypostome which is then anchored by its rows of backward-projecting spines.

Ticks lay large numbers of eggs, which hatch into six-legged larvae. After their first blood meal they moult into eight-legged nymphs, then feed again and moult into adults, also with eight legs. There are differences in the life cycles of various ticks that will not be discussed in detail. Some require one, two or even three different hosts in order to complete their life cycle.

We recognise two families of ticks: the Argasidae

24. A pseudoscorpion gets a free ride by clinging to an ant, a phenomenon known as 'phoresy'. 1 mm.

25. A harvestman (order Opiliones) on a leaf in the Tsitsikama Forest, South Africa. 9 mm.

('soft ticks', or 'tampans'), and the Ixodidae ('hard ticks'). The Argasidae contains flat, leathery, grey and wrinkled creatures whose mouthparts are not visible from above (except in larvae). Argasid ticks attack a wide variety of animals, especially birds, bats, humans, and rodents. *Ornithodoros moubata*, the 'eyeless tampan', is widely distributed in Africa; it lives in huts and transmits human relapsing fever, caused by the spirochaete *Borrelia duttoni*. The same species is found in warthog burrows and seems to be important in the spread of swine fever virus.

The hard ticks (family Ixodidae) are a much larger group and most species of veterinary importance belong here. They have a hard dorsal shield, or 'scutum', that covers the whole upper surface of the male, but only a small area behind the capitulum in the case of the larva, nymph and female. The scutum bears a pattern that is characteristic for each species of tick, and can be used as an important aid to identification. Sometimes the pattern is made up of pits, grooves and bumps, but on occasions the scutum bears a distinctive colour pattern. The rest of the body is very elastic, allowing the tick to swell up enormously with the vast quantity of blood imbibed. The fat, grey, engorged ticks we find on our dogs are fully-fed females; males of the same species are reddish-brown ticks, much smaller than their buxom mates.

The list of diseases transmitted to domestic animals by hard ticks is extensive – here are a few, with the causative organism mentioned in brackets: heartwater (*Cowdria ruminantium*), redwater (*Babesia bigemina* and *B. bovis*), gallsickness (*Anaplasma marginale* and *A. centrale*), corridor disease (*Theileria lawrencei*), east coast fever (*Theileria parva*), biliary fever of horses (*Babesia equi*), and biliary fever of dogs (*Babesia canis*). The ticks responsible for transmitting these diseases belong to the genera *Boophilus* (the blue ticks), *Amblyomma* (the bont ticks), *Rhipicephalus* (the brown ticks), and *Haemaphysalis* (the eyeless ticks).

African tick bite fever, or 'tick typhus' as it is also called, results from infection with *Rickettsia conori*. The rickettsias are a group of micro-organisms about the size of small bacteria, that lie somewhere between viruses and bacteria in evolutionary terms. Many small mammals are reservoirs of the infection, and when a tick feeds on an infected rodent, and then on a susceptible human, tick bite fever is the result. The bite of the infective tick becomes swollen and tender, with a characteristic black crater in the centre. There is high fever and a splitting headache, and often a rash. The infection is quickly brought under control by the administration of modern antibiotics, although before these drugs were discovered, many people suffered severely from African tick bite fever. The disease is not as dangerous as the American equivalent, called Rocky Mountain Spotted Fever, caused by *Rickettsia rickettsi*, which often has a 20% mortality rate.

One of the features of the rickettsial diseases is that they are transmitted trans-ovarially (from infected female to her eggs and thence to the offspring), thus infecting a high proportion of ticks. Most people who live in Africa are exposed to tick bite fever at an early age, and then become immune to further infection. Overseas visitors are very vulnerable, however, and may show severe symptoms. A wide variety of hard ticks are known to transmit tick bite fever, among them species of *Rhipicephalus*, *Hyalomma*, *Amblyomma* and *Haemaphysalis*.

The various kinds of mites are mostly so small that they remain unnoticed and unknown to everybody except a small group of acarologists. In order to study these tiny creatures they must first be mounted on slides and examined under a microscope to see their diagnostic features. Many are parasitic on man and his domestic animals, or affect us in indirect ways. The house dust mite, genus *Dermatophagoides*, lives and reproduces in

26. Female hard tick laying eggs. 8 mm.

27. Hard tick bites human; this could result in tick-bite fever. 5 mm.

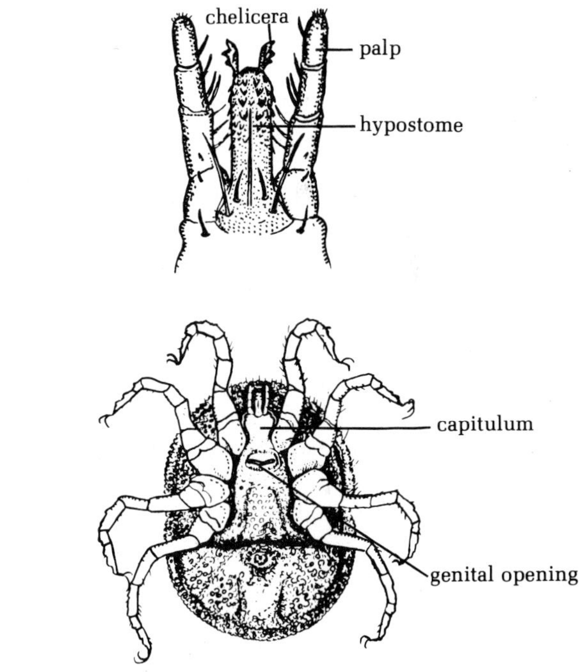

28. The soft tick, *Ornithodoros moubata*, showing the mouthparts and the underside of the female.

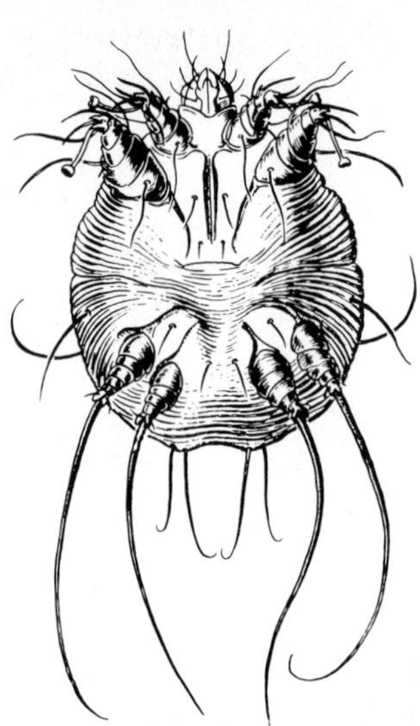

29. The human scabies mite (*Sarcoptes scabiei*). 0,4 mm.

the dust in our homes. Antigens present in the tiny particles from the bodies of millions of dust mites float in the air and are inhaled by the householders; this may cause asthma. Not all mites are tiny, and after showers of rain one may often see beautiful bright red 'velvet mites' crawling on the ground. They belong to the family Trombiculidae.

The larger, parasitic Mesostigmatic mites look a bit like unfed ticks, have piercing mouthparts, and undergo the same sort of development, with a six-legged larval stage that moults into an eight-legged nymph before changing into an eight-legged adult. Species of *Dermanyssus* and *Macronyssus* suck the blood of birds and rodents; both will attack man if their preferred hosts are unavailable.

The Sarcoptiform mites are skin parasites of mammals, burrowing in the horny layers and causing intense irritation to their hosts. Infection with these mites is called 'sarcoptic mange' in animals, and 'scabies' in man. A number of different mites cause sarcoptic mange in different kinds of animals, including dogs, cats, pigs, rabbits, goats and poultry. Humans are infected by *Sarcoptes scabiei,* and epidemics often occur among school-children, or people living in crowded and deprived conditions. The mites burrow in the skin and cause intense itching; they occur primarily in skin folds, between fingers and toes, and scratching of the mite-infested areas results in secondary sores infected with bacteria. Treatment with an appropriate lotion containing insecticide is usually successful.

By contrast, the Trombidiform mites of the genus *Demodex* seldom betray their presence to humans, despite the fact that most people harbour a few specimens. These tiny, cigar-shaped mites are less than half a millimetre long, and live in the hair follicles in our skin. They seldom develop large populations, and cause no discomfort unless they are irritated by the application of too much cream or make-up by ladies intent on beauty care. Some of the other *Demodex* mites may cause mange in a variety of domestic animals, while *Psorergates* species infest sheep and rodents, and heavy infections can cause serious symptoms, with loss of wool and hair by the intensely irritated animals.

CRUSTACEA

The class Crustacea of the phylum Arthropoda contains animals which are predominantly marine. There is tremendous variation in the size and shape of the different crustacea, ranging from lobsters, crabs, prawns and shrimps, to the peculiar barnacles and microscopic waterflea-like creatures. The chitinous exoskeleton is often calcified, forming a hard 'crust' that gives the Crustacea their scientific name.

Despite the variation, a common structural plan may usually be found in the Crustacea. The body is segmented, the head and thorax fused into a cephalothorax and covered by a fold of the exoskeleton, the 'carapace' in most of the larger forms. The abdomen may be tucked beneath the thorax (as in crabs), or extended as a tail (as in prawns). Each segment of the cephalothorax and abdomen bears a pair of jointed appendages, the general structure of which may be modified for different purposes, such as sensory functions (eyes on stalks and antennae), feeding (mandibles), creating a respiratory current (maxillipeds), walking and swimming, holding prey or fighting, carrying eggs, or copulation.

The Crustacea are classified according to differences in the number and shape of their legs, and the names of the various orders often reflect some feature of the legs. The largest order is the Decapoda, meaning 'ten-legged', and here are found the largest and most highly organised of the Crustacea. Because so many deliciously edible species of crabs, lobsters and prawns belong to the Decapoda, most people are quite familiar with their general appearance.

The Isopoda ('similar-legged') are small crustaceans which have no carapace and in which all but one pair of the thoracic legs are used for walking; they are mainly marine creatures, but a few are adapted to life on land. These terrestrial Crustacea are quite often found by gardeners and householders, who mistake them for insects.

The most common Isopoda are members of the genus *Porcellio* (family Porcellionidae), sometimes called 'woodlice' or 'sowbugs'. They are grey in colour, with about ten segments visible from above, those of the thorax and abdomen not clearly demarcated. Underneath they are paler, with seven pairs of legs. These land crustaceans cannot control their water loss efficiently; this is because their breathing tubes, or pseudotracheae, lack the spiracular closing device found in insects. The sowbugs are thus always found in moist, damp places – under stones, flower pots, piles of decaying vegetation, and so on – often huddled together in groups. They sometimes enter houses, especially if it is damp, and may be found under mats or carpets. They do no harm, and cannot survive for long indoors. Sowbugs appear to scavenge on decaying organic matter.

Pillbugs look something like sowbugs and their habits are similar, but they can be distinguished by their ability to roll up into a tight ball when disturbed. They belong to the family Armadillidiidae, which is a very descriptive term in its own way.

Few people know that the barnacles, order Cirripedia, are members of the Arthropoda, and that inside that hard, sharp shell of the adult are hidden six pairs of jointed appendages. A barnacle has a free-swimming larval stage, which anchors itself on the rocks and lays down the calcareous 'carapace' that forms the shell. The animal never moves again; it has a pair of plates that close the top of the shell tightly when the tide is out. When submerged, the six pairs of thoracic legs sweep rhythmically, producing a current that brings oxygen and food particles, which are filtered out and transferred to the mouth by three pairs of smaller limbs.

ONYCOPHORA

These strange worm-like animals are in some respects a 'link' between the segmented worms (Annelida) and the Arthropoda. They have a very soft exoskeleton, although it does contain chitin, and the legs are lobe-like extensions with terminal claws. The presence of tracheae (breathing tubes), salivary glands, jaws, and other features confirm that the onycophorans belong with the Arthropoda.

There are two families of Onycophora, the Peripatidae, which have a tropical distribution, and the Peripatopsidae, which are found only in the southern hemisphere. South Africa has a rich onycophoran fauna, and 12 species of Peripatopsidae are known from the coastal belts of the south and east coast.

Because they cannot close their spiracles (the openings of the tracheae), onycophorans are extremely susceptible to desiccation, and occur only in very humid situations, such as in moist coastal forests and in caves. They should therefore not be collected unless adequate facilities for keeping them are available, for they will die within a few hours at low humidities. Some species are threatened with extinction because of unscrupulous collecting and habitat destruction.

When disturbed or threatened, onycophorans squirt a sticky liquid from glands situated in the head; this can immobilise most small creatures, and the onycophorans probably capture their food in this way, cutting open the victim with their sharp serrated jaws, and sucking up the liquefied body contents. They may also be scavengers to some extent.

DIPLOPODA

Millipedes are very common in Africa, and come in a wide variety of sizes and colours. They are long, cylindrical, many-jointed arthropods, and most of the body segments have two pairs of legs each, hence the scientific name of the class, Diplopoda. The 'diplosegments' are actually derived from the fusion of two single segments. There is a definite head, which has a pair of short, seven-segmented antennae, at least two pairs of mouthparts, and usually eyes. Millipedes walk slowly but with great purpose and thrust.

30. 'Big fleas have little fleas . . .' Tiny mites cling to the antennae and legs of a grasshopper. Mites 1 mm.

31. Woodlouse or sowbug (order Isopoda) scavenging at night. 11 mm.

32. Onycophoran (*Peripatopsis* sp.) in the Tsitsikama Forest of South Africa, one of the few places where these creatures are abundant. 40 mm.

33. Millipede (class Diplopoda) feeding on detritus. 60 mm.

34. Centipede (class Chilopoda) in Kenyan coastal forest. 100 mm.

35. Springtails (class Collembola) massed on surface of rainwater pool. 1 mm.

Most African millipedes are reddish-brown, black, or black with yellow stripes. They sometimes appear in great numbers, trekking across roads, entering houses or falling into swimming-pools. They may writhe vigorously, or roll themselves up into tight spirals when disturbed. Like some of the other classes of terrestrial Arthropoda, they cannot control their loss of water in dry environments, so they are normally found in moist places. They will sometimes attack crops like potatoes to obtain moisture, and normally feed on both living and decomposing vegetation.

Millipedes cannot bite people, and most are harmless to humans. However, they have various glands that produce chemicals such as hydrocyanic acid, iodine and quinone; these substances give millipedes a distinctive odour, and apparently protect them from attack by predators. Few birds will go near them, although some animals (such as civet cats, *Hadogenes* scorpions, hedgehogs and one kind of assassin bug) seem to specialise on millipedes as prey. Some of the tropical species are reputed to have secretions that can blister the human skin, or damage the eyes.

CHILOPODA

Centipedes are long, flattened, soft-bodied, many-segmented Arthropoda with one pair of legs, short or long, on each segment. They run swiftly when disturbed, and are found primarily in damp places under leaves, logs, or stones. They sometimes occur in houses in humid situations. The Chilopoda are nocturnal and prey on insects, earthworms, snails and other small creatures which they kill with their maxillipeds. These are the modified first pair of legs behind the head, which have sharp piercing points, each with a hollow duct leading from a venom gland.

Many African centipedes can bite humans, and cause a burning pain of about the intensity of a bee sting. People get bitten when carrying firewood, or at night when touching or brushing against the centipedes. There are reports that certain individuals have died following a centipede bite, but these have not been verified. Secondary infection can occur following the bites of Chilopoda, so the wounds and any scratches made by the claws should be disinfected.

COLLEMBOLA

This class of Arthropoda, together with the three following (Diplura, Protura and Thysanura) have in the past been regarded as 'primitive wingless insects' (Apterygota), and that is how you will see them arranged in most entomology textbooks. Like insects, they have three pairs of legs. However, modern opinion is that they are not especially close to the insects, and all deserve the status of separate classes. You may also come across the term 'Hexapoda', which refers to the five classes of Arthropoda which have six legs.

The Collembola, or 'springtails', are small, active arthropods that may be very abundant at certain times of the year. They are found in soil, where they constitute a large proportion of the animals which convert dead organic material into humus, as well as in vegetation and under bark. Several species live with ants and termites. Some are found on snow on the tops of mountains, while others occur on water, supported by the surface film. Sometimes a bluish-grey powder may be seen on a pond or a swimming-pool – close examination will reveal that it consists of many thousands of tiny springtails.

Most springtails can jump well, but they do not use their legs in leaping. As their name implies, they carry a spring in their tail, a forked appendage called the 'furca' that is carried bent forward under the body, reaching almost to the head in some species, but shorter in others. When the springtail jumps, the furca is jerked downwards and backwards, and this strikes the surface on which it is resting, propelling it forward and upward.

On the underside of the abdomen, near the front, there is a short ventral tube – its function is not clear, but in some Collembola it acts as an adhesive organ, used to anchor the springtail to smooth or steep surfaces.

DIPLURA

These arthropods have no common name; they are small and go unnoticed by most people because they live concealed in the soil, under stones and in rotting vegetation. The largest family is the Campodeidae, and the genus *Campodea* is cosmopolitan and widespread. Its members are small, white, delicate creatures with two long projections, or cerci, at the end of the abdomen. The other main family is the Japygidae, containing Diplura that are elongated and have a pair of pincer-like cerci at the tip of the abdomen.

PROTURA

The Protura are totally unknown to all except specialist entomologists; they are minute, from 0,5-2,5 mm long, and live in soil, under stones and beneath bark.

THYSANURA

Because members of this class often come into our homes, they are familiar and known to us as 'fishmoths', 'silverfish', or 'bristletails'. The common species found in houses in Africa is *Ctenolepisma longicaudata.* About 15 mm long when fully grown, it is silvery-grey in colour and has two long, slender antennae and three bristly 'tails' at the hind end of the body.

These arthropods are found in drawers and cupboards where starched linen is kept, on bookshelves, among stored papers that have been left undisturbed, behind pictures on the wall and underneath wall paper that has become loose. They feed on starch, glue, and similar substances and may do considerable damage to the bindings of books and to valuable papers, prints and photographs by gnawing holes in them. They are active at night and may often be seen running swiftly over the walls, their hairy antennae and tails held out to warn them if they come into contact with enemies.

The fishmoth has eyes, but they are not very good and it has to depend mainly on the sense of touch, hence the long feelers and the dense coating of hairs on the head and the sides of the body. If one is examined under a microscope, the eyes can be seen as a group of about a dozen small, round lenses, placed close together on each side. With such eyes the little creature must be very short-sighted and able to do little more than distinguish light from darkness.

The gleaming, metallic appearance of the fishmoth, and the greasy feel of its body are due to the dense coating of tiny scales that clothe its body, grey above and a beautiful creamy-white below. There are thousands of these scales, neatly arranged in overlapping rows and looking very much like the scales on a fish's body. If some of the scales are rubbed off on a glass slide and examined under the microscope they are seen to be flattened, rounded, and delicately ornamented with

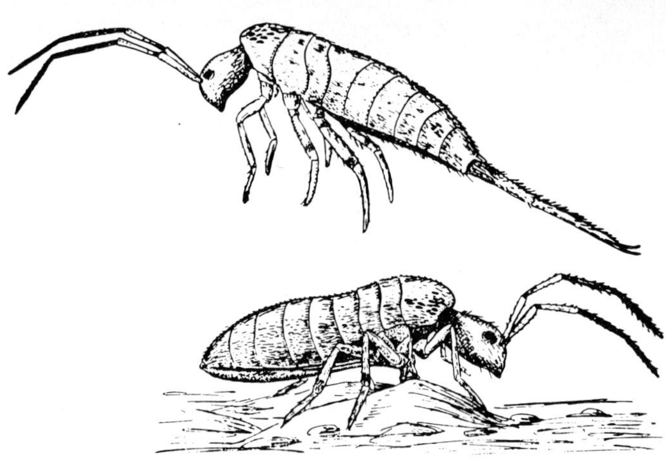

36. The springtail leaps by means of the 'furca', which is flicked downwards to throw the little creature into the air.

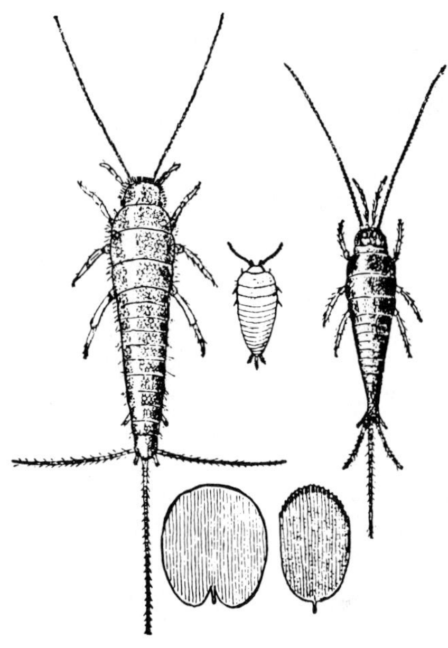

37. The common fishmoth found in houses, *Ctenolepisma longicauda* (left); a small bristle tail found in termites' nests (centre); a bristletail found in forests, *Machiloides* sp. (right); and two scales of the type found on the Thysanura (below).

regular ridges. Formerly, owners of microscopes used these scales to test the quality of their lenses: a lens capable of revealing clearly the ornamentation on a fishmoth scale was regarded as a good one.

Each scale is a modified bristle and has a tiny peg that fits into a socket in the insect's skin and together they form an elaborate protective coat. There is no difference in the appearance of the two sexes, except that the female is slightly larger and stouter than the male. She lays her oval, white eggs in cracks and crevices in batches of six to ten. These hatch out in one to three or four months, depending on the temperature, into tiny creatures similar to their parents, but without the dense coating of scales. The young fishmoths feed and grow and cast their skin at intervals; after moulting five or six times they are adults. This may take five months to two years, according to the amount of food that is available and the temperature.

Fishmoths have been widely spread over the earth by man's commerce. *Ctenolepisma longicaudata* is one of Africa's less popular exports to Australia, where it is now very common, and another well-known species, *Lepisma saccharina* ('the scaly insect that likes sweet things'), thought originally to have been a native of North America, is today spread throughout Europe. The success of fishmoths in establishing themselves in libraries, map stores and similar places (where they do considerable damage), is a result of their not needing drinking water in spite of living on a totally dry diet. They can absorb their total water requirement from water vapour in the atmosphere whenever the humidity is high.

Many relatives of the household fishmoths are found out of doors; they are small, inconspicuous creatures that are seldom noticed. These bristletails (*Machiloides* species) are usually brown in colour with a sheen like bronze. They are found on rocks and the bases of tree trunks in indigenous forest, and under stones in more exposed localities. Those investigated all seem to feed on lichens and algae growing on rocks and tree trunks. Their life histories are similar to that of the common fishmoth, but, since they lack the latter's independence of drinking water, their distribution is restricted. The scales of these insects are very beautiful when viewed under the microscope.

Another species of bristletail, silvery-white and only about 3 mm long, is found in ants' nests. When a stone is turned over and an ants' nest exposed, several of the little creatures may sometimes be seen darting about among the ants. The ants take no notice of them at all. If, for some reason or other, the ants trek to a new home, the bristletails go with them. They are never found in isolation from ants, and they do not seem to be able to live without the protection and support of their hosts. They appear to rely on the liquid food which they steal from ants while the latter are feeding each other. Several different species of bristletail are found as guests in termite nests in Africa, but practically nothing is known about their ways or their life histories.

FURTHER READING

Bristowe, W. S.: *The World of Spiders*. New Naturalist Series, Collins, London. (1958). 304 pp

Hoogstraal, H.: *African Ixodoidea. I. Ticks of the Sudan*. Department of the Navy, Washington. (1956). 1101 pp (Also numerous important works on African ticks by this prolific author).

Krantz, G. W.: *A Manual of Acarology (Ed. 2)*. O.S.U. Book Stores, Inc., Corvallis, Oregon (1979). 335 pp

Levi, H. W. & Levi, L. R.: *Spiders and their Kin*. A Golden Guide, M. S. Zim (Ed.) Golden Press, Western Publishing Co., New York (1968). 160 pp

Savory, T.: *Arachnida*. Academic Press, London (1964). 291 pp

Walker, J. B.: *The Ixodid Ticks of Kenya*. Commonwealth Institute of Entomology, London (1974). 220 pp

Yeoman, G. H. & Walker, J. B.: *The Ixodid Ticks of Tanzania*. Commonwealth Institute of Entomology, London (1967). 215 pp

Zumpt, F. (Ed.): *The Arthropod Parasites of Vertebrates in Africa south of the Sahara. Vol. I (Chelicerata)*. Publications of the South African Institute for Medical Research Johannesburg (1961). 457 pp

3

Mayflies, damselflies and dragonflies

Winged insects are divided into those which can flex their wings when at rest and those – regarded as primitive – which cannot. Only two orders of living insects cannot flex their wings when at rest – the Ephemeroptera (mayflies) and the Odonata (damselflies and dragonflies). Both groups are very ancient, and a fossil dragonfly recently discovered dates back 300 million years. This makes it one of the oldest flying creatures known – preceding the pterodactyl by some 100 million years, and the bird by 150 million.

Mayflies People living near lakes, streams and rivers are familiar with mayflies because of the sudden appearance of large numbers of these delicate insects at certain times of the year and their equally sudden disappearance. Because of their very short life as adults mayflies have been given the name Ephemeroptera, which means 'winged creatures of but a day'. Many emerge in the evening and are dead by the next morning, their mating and egg-laying having been completed within this brief period. Some species can, however, live for several days as adults although all are short-lived because they cannot feed. The mouthparts of the adult are degenerate and its alimentary canal is filled with nothing but air which gives it buoyancy but is certainly not sustaining.

Mayflies have two pairs of wings, the first pair larger than the hind pair, although some have lost this second pair of wings altogether. Usually there are three long, slender feelers (called cerci) on the tail, but some species have only two. All spend their immature stages in water, some taking six to nine months to reach full size, others longer.

Anglers know these insects well for they form an important part of the food of trout and other fish, and many of the artificial flies used by fishermen are made to resemble mayflies as closely as possible. Even in South Africa, where few small insects have popular names, various kinds of mayfly are known to fly-fishermen by such names as 'red border wing', 'yellow dun', 'Worcester dark blue', 'September brown', 'blue-winged orange', 'bronze spinner', and so on.

Ephemeroptera have been studied in depth only in South Africa, and little is known about the mayflies of the rest of the continent. Apart from their importance in fish biology, the mayfly nymphs are very sensitive to various pollutants in water and are therefore good indicators of the purity of streams and rivers.

As an example of the life history of a mayfly, let us take *Adenophlebia peringueyella* of the family Leptophlebiidae. It is called the 'September brown' because it is during this month that it appears along the banks of

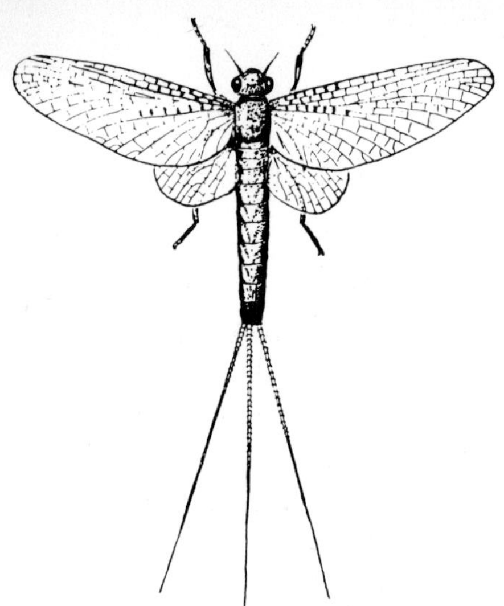

38. The 'September brown' mayfly, *Adenophlebia peringueyella* (Leptophlebiidae). It is about 30 mm across the outspread wings.

stony mountain streams in the southwestern Cape Province. Very similar and closely allied species are found further north. The adult has a brown body, mottled with pale yellow on the abdomen, and about 12 mm long. Its three slender tails are a little longer than the body and the outspread wings measure just over 12 mm across. The female is slightly larger than the male and lacks the pair of claspers that he has on the end of his abdomen.

The adults of this species are rather long-lived for mayflies; it has been found that specimens reared in captivity live for ten or 11 days, although, like the rest of their kind, they cannot take any food and their stomachs are filled with nothing but air. Mating follows a graceful aerial dance above the water, and soon after this the female lays her eggs in batches. The eggs are very small – 100 of them placed end to end would not measure 25 mm – oval in shape and covered with small pits. To drop them, she dips down and just touches the surface of the water with the tip of her abdomen.

The eggs sink to the bottom and lie on the sand amongst the stones for three weeks before they hatch into white, very small nymphs about 0,5 mm long. They creep about on the bottom of the stream, generally keeping under stones for protection, but they can swim fairly well in still water, or with the current, by jerky motions of their bodies. Their food seems to consist chiefly of any dead and decaying animal and vegetable matter which they can pick up on the bottom. In an aquarium they thrive and grow if given a little mud from time to time from the bottom of a pond: they swallow the mud which contains organic fragments which nourish them.

At first the nymph obtains all the oxygen it needs by absorption through its thin skin but, as it grows bigger, its needs increase and seven pairs of gills appear along the sides of its abdomen. These are what are known as tracheal gills because they do not contain blood-vessels, as the gills of a fish do, but tracheae, or air-tubes. The air dissolved in the water passes through the thin skin of the gills into the respiratory system of the insect. Often the gills may be seen moving rapidly, with a quivering motion; this does not help the insect to swim but keeps a current of fresh water flowing over the gills to renew the air-supply.

The insect casts its skin several times in the course of its growth: it is said that some mayflies moult 23 times or more, but the exact number is not known in the case of the September brown. By about April the nymph is approximately two-thirds grown and the buds of the future wings are clearly visible on its back. By July it is fully grown and the earliest adults may emerge towards the end of this month, although the majority do not come out until a few weeks later in September, as their name suggests.

The change from a life in the water to a life in the air is fraught with great danger for the mayfly; it must leave the shelter of the stony bottom of the stream and make its way up to the surface, and any hungry fish that sees it will at once snap it up. This passage is made therefore with remarkable speed. The full-grown nymph of the September brown usually creeps out of the water onto a stone or tree-root or other object that projects above the surface. If it cannot find a suitable resting-place, it will simply swim up to the surface and there change to an adult, supported only by the surface tension of the water. A split appears in the skin on the back and the insect struggles out and flies away in a few seconds.

At this stage the mayfly is known as a sub-imago and differs from the adult, or imago, in that it is duller in colour and still has a thin coat which must be shed. This final moult from the sub-imago to the imago is unique to mayflies. After resting for a brief period, the sub-imago creeps out of this last thin skin and flies away on the final stage of its career. The anglers' 'duns' are mayflies at the sub-imago stage, the 'spinners' are imagos.

The immature stages of various species of mayfly are to be found in almost every type of stream in Africa, and the different forms are well adapted to the conditions under which they live. Some are burrowers which live in tunnels they dig for themselves in muddy banks; these have strong forelegs. Others, like the Worcester dark blue, *Tricorythus discolor* (family Tricorythidae), adapted for life in swift-flowing streams, have flattened bodies and strong legs for clinging to stones. These nymphs do not swim much but run rapidly over and under the stones. In the case of the nymph of the Worcester dark blue, long bristles that project on either side of each mandible like a handsome moustache serve, apparently, to catch any tiny creatures or fragments of other food that the current sweeps by. Some nymphs living in swift water do not come to the surface to emerge as adults: they cling to a stone a few centimetres below the surface, their skin splits and the adults shoot to the surface enclosed in a bubble of air which bursts and projects them, quite dry, into the atmosphere. They fly immediately to the bank, where they rest until they cast their last skins.

Some of the smaller kinds (*Baetis* species) are very abundant in clear, strong-flowing streams and they are a particularly important source of food for trout. The nymphs are agile swimmers, the rows of stiff bristles on their tails together forming an efficient paddle. The adults may be recognised by their having only two tails, instead of the usual three. The females generally creep just below the surface of the water in order to lay their masses of tiny eggs.

Amongst most mayflies the adults emerge by day but some species hatch at night and are attracted to lights. Usually they may be seen on the wing from sunset to dusk, sometimes dancing in clouds like gnats. Also like gnats, these swarms consist mainly of males. Females ready to mate enter the swarm, and are approached from below by the males. The male's long forelegs have a reversible joint which he bends backwards over the female's wings to hold her while mating, a process which lasts no more then a few seconds and is completed in the air. A further adaptation for this mating behaviour is found in the eyes of the males, which are always larger than those of the female. They are often divided into lower and upper portions, the latter sometimes on column-like outgrowths of the head (as in the family Baetidae).

Although the adult mayflies are short-lived the nymphs live longer. Some of the smallest species, under very favourable conditions, may mature in a little over a month, others take four months, others nine months and some of the largest of the burrowers may take nearly two years to reach full size.

In some species each egg has a bundle of tiny threads attached to it which spreads out in the water and serves to anchor the egg to weeds or other objects below the surface. The females of a few species, such as the common two-winged mayfly, *Cloeon lacunosum,* retain their eggs in their bodies until they are ready to hatch. These are, naturally, the mayflies which have a comparatively long life of several days in the adult state. The female hides for a few days after mating while her eggs develop inside her body, then she flies back to the water and drops on to the surface. As soon as oviposition is completed, she dies. The nymphs emerge from the eggs immediately they are laid.

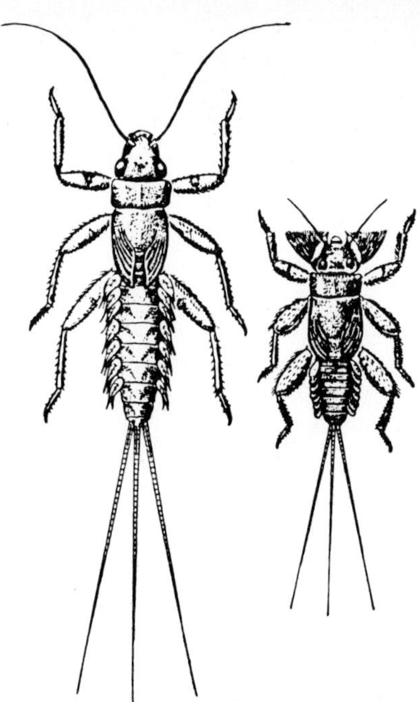

39. Two mayfly nymphs, *Adenophlebia peringueyella* (left) and *Tricorythus discolor* (Tricorythidae). The body of the larger is about 25 mm long.

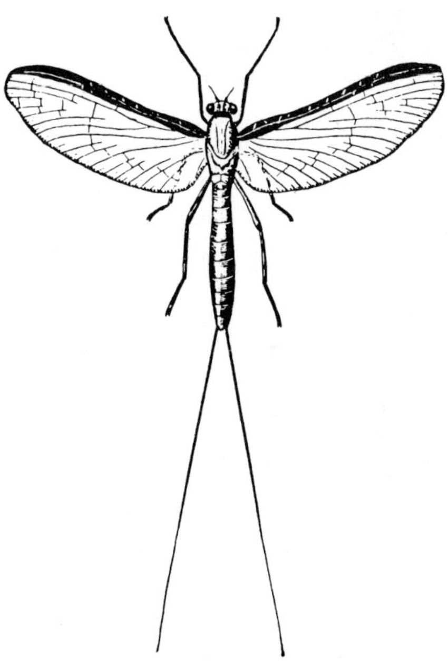

40. The 'red border-wing', a common two-winged mayfly *Cloeon lacunosum*, (family Baetidae) whose body length without the tails is only about 6 mm.

ORDER **Odonata**

The order Odonata contains some of the most handsome and striking of insects because of their beauty, their size and their powers of flight. With their large, well-developed eyes, they are among the most keen-sighted of all insects and rely mainly on their powers of vision in their pursuit of prey, the antennae being reduced to small hairlike organs.

There are probably some 6 000 species of Odonata in the world, of which about 1 000 have been described from Africa. The group falls naturally into two suborders. The larger and more stoutly-built Odonata – the dragonflies – belong to the suborder Anisoptera. It is easy to recognise most of them by their swift flight, and by the fact that when they rest they hold their wings stiffly outspread at right angles to the body. The hind wings are larger than the front pair – Anisoptera means 'insects with unequal wings'.

The damselflies belong to the suborder Zygoptera; they are smaller, with slender bodies, and all four wings are virtually the same size. When settling they mostly hold their wings together above their backs, but members of two families keep theirs half open.

Odonata means 'toothed', and seems to refer to the sharp teeth on the jaws of these voracious insects. The shape of the thorax is peculiar in all the Odonata as an adaptation to their highly specialised mode of life: the first segment (the prothorax) is quite short; the second and third segments are elongated obliquely downwards and forwards so that the legs are all brought forward to near the mouth. In keeping with their special function, the legs are armed with stiff bristles which together form a basket-like trap in which the insect scoops up its prey as it darts through the air. But because of the position of the legs, damselflies and dragonflies can scarcely walk at all – they can only cling. The wings are carried somewhat further back than is usual with most insects.

41. On the lookout for passing prey, a dragonfly reveals the structure typical of the Odonata. The first thoracic segment is very short, and the second and third segments are angled obliquely downwards and forwards so that the legs are brought close to the mouth. 45 mm.

Damselflies Damselflies are smaller, more slender and weaker than their robust relatives, the true dragonflies. Their narrow, delicate wings are not suited for swift darting flight and for the most part they rest on reeds and bushes beside the water in which they spent their immature stages. However, many damselflies, especially newly-emerged males and the females, hide from predators in scrub or bush often at some distance from the water – even on hilltops. Most of them are brightly coloured, metallic green, or azure blue or blood-red, or a combination of these. Mature males often differ in colour and markings from the females, but immature males generally resemble the female more closely in these respects.

As our example of this group we may take the common conspicuous damselfly, *Chlorolestes conspicua*, found in the southwestern Cape. Related species with similar habits occur in other parts of southern Africa. This insect is about 50 mm long, with a dark brown body and narrow yellow stripes at the sides, the male being of the same colour but slightly smaller. The wings are clear in both sexes, but in some other *Chlorolestes* the male has black or brown bands across them.

The adults may be seen on the wing in the second half of summer (January-February), making short flights along the banks of mountain streams and returning again and again to the same perch. Their mating takes place in the extraordinary manner characteristic of all the Odonata and found in no other insects. The male damselfly has a pair of claspers on the tip of his abdomen by means of which he seizes the female by the prothorax, immediately behind the head. The pair may be seen flying over the water linked tandem fashion, with the male always in front, holding his partner securely in his claspers. After a time they settle and the female then bends her abdomen forward, bringing it beneath the male until the tip reaches the underside of the second segment of his abdomen. Here his copulatory organ is lodged and the male cells are transferred to his mate at this point.

42. A damselfly, showing the slender body and the two pairs of narrow wings, held together over the abdomen at rest. 32 mm.

The internal reproductive organs of the male are of the usual type found in insects and he has a genital opening on the lower surface of the ninth abdominal segment.

But, externally, he has a peculiar special apparatus on the second segment of his abdomen, which comprises a receptacle for his sperm and an elaborate arrangement for transmitting it to the female. Just before he seizes her in his claspers he turns the tip of his own abdomen forward and injects the contents of his testes into the receptacle from where, later on, he passes it on to his mate. It is not known how or why the Odonata have evolved this unique method of mating.

The female's ovipositor is armed with two pairs of slender, sharp saws with which she makes small slits in the tender green shoots of trees or bushes overhanging water. She then deposits her oval white eggs, one in each slit. The punctures are one below the other, about 3 mm apart and generally she lays five or six eggs in a row before leaving to lay another batch of eggs in another twig later on. The tissues of the twig swell slightly round each hole and small gall-like knobs form, marking the spots where the eggs have been inserted.

As soon as it hatches the tiny nymph drops into the water where it remains until it is ready to change into a winged adult. When fully grown it is nearly 35 mm long, brown, and mottled with darker and lighter patches. It has a pair of prominent round compound eyes, two slender antennae and the buds of wings on its back. At the end of its tail there are three flattened tracheal gills, paddle-shaped, with a dark band across the middle of each. It is an active insect, swimming and running about between the stones on the bottom of the stream, hunting for the mayfly nymphs and other small water creatures that are its prey.

On the underside of its head is the curious organ known as the 'mask', characteristic of all Odonata nymphs and not found in any other insects. It is the lower lip, or labium, elongated and jointed and armed with a pair of pincers at the tip, wonderfully adapted to form a very efficient weapon for the capture of prey. It is called a mask because when not in use it is held so that it hides the lower part of the head. When the nymph sights any small creature that might serve as food it stalks its victim until it is near enough to shoot out this lower lip, grip the prey in the pincers and then, folding the lip back again, bring its captive within reach of its jaws.

When the nymph is fully grown it creeps out of the water, up onto a reed or other plant, and there it affixes itself firmly by means of its claws. Then the skin splits and the adult damselfly slowly and laboriously pulls itself free of the nymphal skin. When its head, thorax, legs and wings are free, it hangs head downwards, held in position only by its abdomen still in the old skin. Then, after its skin has hardened sufficiently, it jerks itself upright and grips the stem by its feet, finally drags its abdomen free and creeps up the stem a little way, leaving the empty husk still clinging to the stem below it. When its wings have expanded and hardened, it flies away, a living flash of light, to enter on the last stage of its career. The mask and the tracheal gills are discarded with the nymphal skin since these organs are no longer of any use to this winged creature of the air.

43. Mating completed, a male damselfly clasps his mate behind the head while she uses her ovipositor to lay eggs in a submerged stem. 35 mm.

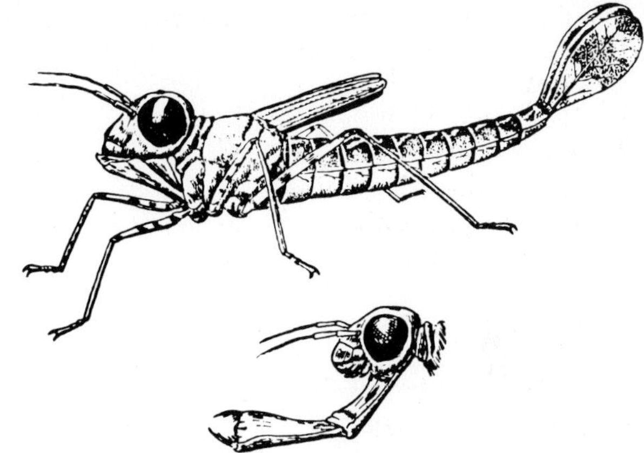

44. A damselfly nymph of the genus *Chlorolestes*, showing the 'mask' extended (below). The nymph is about 35 mm long.

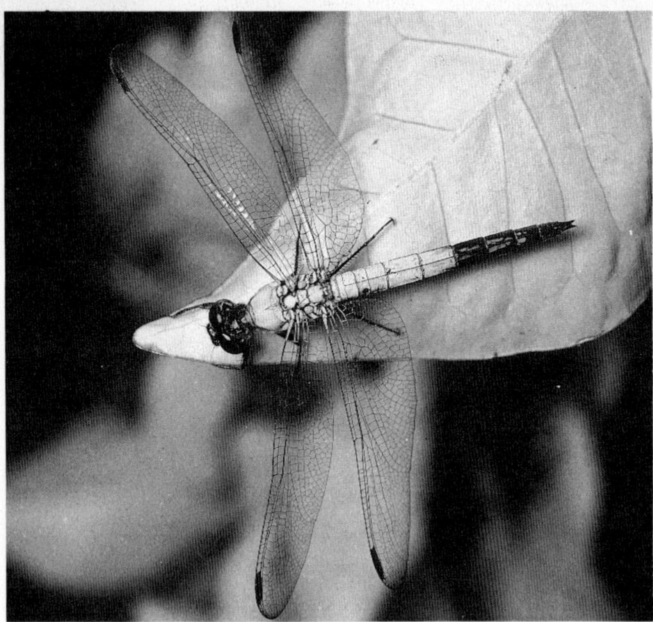

45. Dragonfly, showing the somewhat wider hind wings, with both pairs of wings held open at rest. 50 mm.

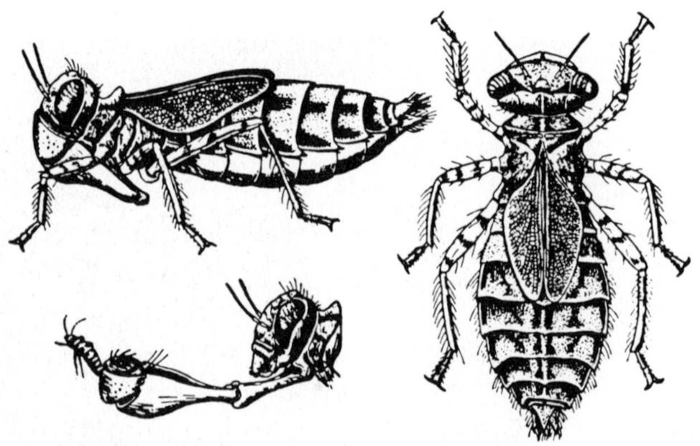

46. Nymph of the sky-blue dragonfly, *Orthetrum caffrum* (seen from the side and from above) with mask extended to capture prey.

A large number of different species of damselfly have been described and named in Africa. We still have a great deal to learn about their life histories but some of them, such as the *Lestes* species, seem to be well adapted to live in regions where the rainy season is short and uncertain and where droughts are long. The eggs of these damselflies lie dormant, protected in the slits in the stems, and only hatch after good rains. The nymphs grow with astonishing rapidity, reaching full size in a few weeks, so that they are ready to change into adults before the stream or pool dries up.

The nymphs of some species of damselfly are almost transparent and are difficult to see as they swim about in the water. Others are greenish and mottled and are well hidden among the water-weeds they choose as their hunting ground. Still others are brown and mottled and live partially concealed by the mud on the bottom.

Dragonflies Dragonflies, in the conventional sense, are the strongly-built, swift-flying, larger members of the order. They include some of the most beautiful and most conspicuous of all insects. Many of them are very wary and exceedingly difficult to catch. Unfortunately the brilliant colours fade when the insects are killed and pinned in collections and the dried specimens do not reveal anything like the full beauty of the living insect. However, there are ways of preserving the colours, and some hints on how to do this are given in Chapter 24.

In some places the gaily coloured giants of the order are feared and regarded as dangerous, but they are all completely harmless to man and do not possess any sting or other weapon with which to do any damage. Most of the species are widely distributed, some being found from the Mediterranean down to the Cape, and quite a number are found throughout the continent south of the Sahara.

The sky-blue dragonfly, *Orthetrum caffrum,* is common in East Africa as far north as Ethiopia and is also abundant in South Africa as far south as the Cape of Good Hope. About 50 mm long, the male is blue with a bloom reminiscent of the hue of a ripe plum; his mate is of about the same size and usually has a reddish tinge, but without the bloom. There are very many species of *Orthetrum* in Africa, but *caffrum* is easy to identify for it has six narrow white or cream stripes on the thorax, two in front and two on each side. They mate in the manner already described for damselflies, but in this case the male grasps the female by the back of the head with his claspers and the whole act is often completed on the wing: she stretches her abdomen forward until the tip reaches the peculiar apparatus on the underside of his second abdominal segment and the transfer of male cells is made whilst the pair is in full flight.

She lays her eggs by touching her abdomen to the surface of the water, in the same manner as already described for the mayfly. In this way her oval white eggs are washed off the tip of her abdomen and sink to the bottom where they rest in the mud until they hatch. The nymph is like that of the damselfly, only more stoutly built, rounded on the back and more or less flattened on the underside; and it does not have the three paddle-shaped tracheal gills that are characteristic of the damselflies but breathes in a different manner.

Usually the dragonfly nymph creeps about the bottom or amid the water-weeds and its brown or yellow colouring, mottled with darker brown, helps conceal it. It can, however, move more quickly when disturbed and, if watched whilst doing so, it will be seen to move its legs with a rowing action, although the legs are too slender to serve as efficient swimming organs. The speed it attains is obviously due to some other form of propulsion.

If a nymph is put in a saucer of water and a few drops of ink are dropped into the water just behind the insect, the ink will be seen to swirl and eddy in a current that issues from the hind end of the nymph, even whilst the insect is quite motionless. If the water is just deep enough to cover the insect a tiny fountain may be thrown up above the surface and it will be seen that this comes from its tail-end.

If the nymph is put in a narrow glass tube of water and held up to the light and examined through a hand-lens, a bulky organ is visible through the translucent body-wall in the hind half of the abdomen. This organ is the rectum, greatly enlarged, which by its regular pulsation constantly pumps water in and out. When the nymph wishes to swim quickly, it squirts water from its rectum with some force, creating a jet which drives it forward. It uses this jet-propulsion only in emergencies when danger threatens.

Besides making use of its rectum as a means of moving about quickly, the dragonfly nymph also uses this part of its body as its chief respiratory organ. Inside the rectum, along its muscular wall, there are folds which are richly supplied with tracheae and the constant renewal of the water that bathes them supplies the insect with all the air it needs. Because of these rectal gills, the dragonfly nymph does not need the external paddle-shaped gills that are found in damselflies. At the tip of the abdomen there are a number of short, pointed processes, three in younger nymphs, and five in mature ones.

The mask is similar to that of the damselfly nymph, except that the pincers on it are much wider and the general form of the trap is more scoop-like, with stiff bristles along the inside edge to prevent the escape of small prey. The nymph does not chase its victims: it remains motionless or creeps about slowly, waiting patiently for some small creature to approach close enough for the mask to shoot out with extraordinary speed and capture it. The full-grown nymph creeps out of the water and casts its skin in the manner already described for damselflies.

Although a large number of different species of dragonflies and damselflies have been described and named from Africa, little detail is known about their life histories. All of them spend their immature stages in water, generally in pools, lakes and slow-flowing streams with muddy bottoms. The nymphs of damselflies are slender and jerky and swift in their movements and some of them may be found in fast-flowing clear streams where they prey upon small crustaceans and mayfly nymphs. The dragonfly nymphs are much more sluggish and are usually found in stagnant water, particularly in shallow weedy ponds with muddy bottoms.

The females of most dragonflies simply drop their eggs in the water while flying over the surface, but some of them alight on reeds and other water-plants and creep below the surface in order to lay their eggs. The eggs of some species are laid in strings of jelly and attached to submerged twigs.

The nymphs cast their skin 11 to 15 times in the course of their development. Some of them reach full size in a few weeks whilst others take a year or longer to grow up. They are remarkable in that they have large compound eyes whereas the larvae of most other insects have only a few simple eyes or none at all. All are predaceous and are armed with the curious mask or elongated lower lip, for the capture of their prey. Some of the larger nymphs occasionally attack tadpoles or fish

47. Having left the water and crawled up nearby vegetation, an adult dragonfly drags itself free of its nymphal skin, its wings as yet unexpanded and its body still soft.

48. The adult dragonfly rests as its newly-expanded wings and body harden. 45 mm.

fry and are consequently a nuisance in fish hatcheries, but on the whole Odonata nymphs provide a useful source of food for fish.

As already pointed out, adult females are often differently coloured from adult males. One or both sexes can sometimes show different colour forms, as in *Agriocnemis*, *Ischnura* and other genera, but these have nearly all proved to be developmental stages in maturation of the same species.

CLASSIFICATION

ORDER **Ephemeroptera**

Soft-bodied insects, with short, bristle-like antennae. Mouthparts of adults vestigial. Wings membranous, many-veined, held vertically upwards when at rest. Forewing large, hind wing small or (rarely) absent altogether. Abdomen terminated by two or three long slender cerci. Immature stages are aquatic and feed on small aquatic organisms and organic debris. Mayflies are unique among insects in having a winged sub-imago stage, which moults to become the adult or imago. Twenty families of mayfly are recognised, 12 of which occur in Africa.

FAMILY Baetidae

A very large group with many African species. The nymphs are spindle-shaped, darting forms normally found in running water, but *Cloeon* nymphs are unique in occurring in standing water. The genus *Baetis* is found throughout Africa.

FAMILY Leptophlebiidae

A large cosmopolitan family, with a number of African representatives. The nymphs usually have feathery gills and are moderately flattened. *Adenophlebia* is described in the text.

OTHER FAMILIES

Oligoneuriidae are found only in tropical and subtropical areas; nymphs large, cling to rocks and vegetation in swiftly flowing water. Euthyplociidae, Ephemeridae and Polymitarcyidae have large nymphs with biramous, fringed gills. They burrow in mud in large tropical rivers, and often have large mandibular 'tusks'.

ORDER **Odonata**

Predaceous insects with biting mouthparts. Two pairs of membranous wings with a complex network of veins; an infraction of the front edge (costa) of each wing is called a node (nodus). Near the wing tip (apex) there is nearly always a strengthening feature, a pterostigma. The head swivels freely, compound eyes very large and prominent; three small simple eyes (ocelli) on top of head; antennae very short, threadlike. The main part of the thorax (synthorax) obliquely elongated, carrying the long slender legs close to the mouth. Abdomen most frequently long and slender, always in male having special sex organs on under surface of second segment.

Nymphs live in water; predaceous and capture prey by means of a mask which is a great development of the lower lip (labium) in the form of a hinged apparatus armed with hooks and spines at the end. Respiration either through caudal gills or rectal gills.

SUBORDER Zygoptera

Head broad, eyes widely separated. Forewings and hind wings of similar shape, generally narrowed like a stalk (petiole) at base. Body usually long and slender. Wings at rest usually held together above the body except in Chlorolestidae and Lestidae. Females have an ovipositor below end of abdomen. Nymph slender, generally with three caudal gills (upper one sometimes much reduced).

FAMILY Chlorolestidae (Synlestidae)

A small family of Australasia and southern Africa. Smallish to moderate-sized, slender-bodied Zygoptera. Body usually metallic green. Pterostigma narrow or broad. Wings of male sometimes banded. At rest the wings are held half open. Nymph with elongated mask, the three caudal gills well developed, broadly rounded at ends.

Chlorolestes is typical, occurs along mountain streams, often in forest.

FAMILY Lestidae

Cosmopolitan with a few African species of the genus *Lestes*. Smaller than average Chlorolestidae but very similar in appearance and in holding wings half open at rest. Males never banded on wings. Nymphs with long masks, reaching back at least to middle legs; apex of mask narrowly cleft. Caudal gills very long, tapering.

FAMILY Protoneuridae

Small family of very slender-bodied species, mainly tropical. Pterostigma very small, about the length of one cell on the wing. Usually found in well-shaded localities under trees or in forests. Like all southern African Zygoptera (except two families) they close their wings at rest. Nymphs variable in features. *Chlorocnemis* (mountain forests) and *Elattoneura* are examples of this family.

FAMILY Platycnemididae

In tropical African species the legs in the male sometimes have coloured expansions. Very few species in southern Africa and legs not coloured. Small or smallish species with very small pterostigma. Nymphs with short mask only reaching front legs; long, tapering caudal gills, usually rather thickened. *Allocnemis leucosticta*, of shaded pools, is easily recognised by yellow wings and unusually white pterostigma. *Mesocnemis* is quite different and favours fast running open stretches of water.

FAMILY Coenagrionidae

A large family including the majority of African Zygoptera. Small to medium in size, slender-bodied, with short or very short pterostigma. Nymphs with moderately long masks and three long or longish caudal gills, gradually or abruptly narrowed to points at the ends. *Pseudagrion* is by far the largest genus of damselflies in Africa, with many colourful species, others plainer or very dark. *Ceriagrion* usually have plain red abdomens in males. *Ischnura senegalensis* is one of the most widely distributed Zygoptera. *Agriocnemis* includes the smallest southern African species, generally colourful.

FAMILY Calopterygidae

A small family, with only one species *(Phaon iridipennis)* south of the Zambezi River, but in equatorial Africa and other parts of the world with some of the most beautiful damselflies. Easily recognised by their unusually broad wings not narrowed to a 'stalk' at bases. Body long, more or less metallic green or blue. Wings with iridescent sheen (in some with brilliant wing pigments). Pterostigma small, sometimes even absent. Found in shaded places, woodland or dense forests. Fly with wings flapping slowly. Nymph with very long mask, its tip broadly cleft.

FAMILY Chlorocyphidae

Very few colourful species in southern Africa but moderately represented in the tropics. Easily recognised by the snouted face, thick abdomen, shorter than the wings, the wings slender with narrow pterostigma. Legs in some males *(Platycypha)* with flat, coloured expansions; abdomen brightly coloured in this sex. They prefer fast-moving, shaded streams. Nymph rather robust, with caudal gills reduced to two spikes, the third or upper one vestigial. Mask short and flat.

SUBORDER Anisoptera

This larger suborder contains most of our more conspicuous Odonata, the dragonflies. Small to very large, generally robust species. Eyes touching each other except in Gomphidae. Wings not 'stalked' (petioled), the hind wing distinctly broader at base than forewing and consequently more triangular in shape. Pterostigma usually elongated. Nymph with robust body, frequently short and broad but sometimes elongated; somewhat flattened on under surface. Mask most variable in length and shape, often rounded to cover the face (hence the name mask). Respiration within the rectum, the end of the abdomen with three tapering spiked appendages, to which another pair (cerci) is added in older nymph.

FAMILY Gomphidae
A family of moderate dimensions, many of the species shy and elusive. The body colours are only green or yellow, marked with brown or black patterns. Head broad, eyes well separated. In male, the inner margin of hind wing often incurved and on each side of abdomen (segment 2) there is often a small lobe called an auricle. The function of this organ is still uncertain, but believed by some authorities to aid in the mating process. The female has no special ovipositor. The most numerous species belong to the genus *Paragomphus*, mostly small or smallish in size. Largest include *Ictinogomphus*. These and others have leaf-like expansions near end of abdomen. Body of nymph varies in shape depending whether it lives in mud and debris or moves actively in the water. Mask broad and rather square; short and flat.

FAMILY Aeshnidae
Few representatives in southern Africa but many shade-lovers, active at dusk or dawn, in the more tropical regions. Large to very large, robust Anisoptera with long, slender abdomens, sometimes with auricles in male as in the previous family. Eyes very large, confluent. Female with ovipositor below end of abdomen. Powerful fliers, but some of the species favour quite small pools or streams where they are conspicuous fliers. A few are migrants. Nymph with elongated body, more or less cylindrical. Mask usually long and flat. Examples: *Anax* includes the common blue and green Emperor dragonfly *Anax imperator*, as well as the blacker *A. tristis*, one of the largest African dragonflies. *Aeshna* are found more in forests, particularly mountains. *Hemianax ephippiger*, recognisable by a broad pale blue saddle above the base of the abdomen, is, like the Emperor, a migrant, but both breed readily in open African waters.

FAMILY Corduliidae
A family of moderate size, with few species in southern Africa. Medium to large insects, with long slender abdomens, the body coloured reddish brown to black with yellow markings; thorax with metallic sheen. Eyes large, in short contact with each other. Legs rather long. Pterostigma shortish. Abdomen of male usually with auricles (see Gomphidae). They tend to fly along more or less definite beats, often at some distance from water. Nymph with body generally short and broad, the mask rounded to cover the face; legs very long and slender. *Syncordulia* species are smallish dragonflies and peculiar to South Africa in this continent. *Macromia* is the dominant African genus.

FAMILY Libellulidae
The largest dragonfly family, well represented in Africa. Small to large species, with abdomens which may be short, broad or slender, less frequently elongated; without auricles and rarely with metallic sheen on the thorax. Hind wing sometimes very broad near base. Female without ovipositor. Nymph generally short and broad, a few elongated and more slender. Eyes sometimes prominently raised. Mask rounded to cover face when not in use. Examples: *Orthetrum* and other genera usually have powdery blue opaque colours in mature males. *Palpopleura* and *Rhyothemis* are slower fliers and have dark markings on the wings. *Brachythemis leucosticta* is a gregarious species flying low over the ground or water, the mature male with black stripe across the wings. *Tramea* and *Pantala flavescens* are large powerful fliers with strong migrant tendencies.

FURTHER READING

EPHEMEROPTERA

Crass, R. S.: 'Mayflies of Natal and the Eastern Cape'. *Annals of the Natal Museum* (1947). 11: 37-110

Demoulin, G.: 'Ephemeroptera des faunes éthiopiennes et Malgache'. *South African Animal Life* (1970). 14: 24-170

Needham, J. G., Traver, J. R. & Hsu, Y.: *The Biology of Mayflies*. Comstock Publishing Co., Ithaca (1935). 759 pp

Peters, W. L. & Peters, J. G. (Eds): *Proceedings of the First International Congress on Ephemeroptera*, (1970). London (1973). 312 pp

ODONATA

Corbet, P. S.: *A Biology of Dragonflies*. Witherby, London (1962). 247 pp

Corbet, P. S., Longfield, C. & Moore, N. W.: *Dragonflies*. Collins, London (1960). 260 pp

Pinhey, E. C. G.: 'The Dragonflies of southern Africa'. *Transvaal Museum Memoirs* (1951). 5: 335 pp

Pinhey, E. C. G.: *A Survey of the Dragonflies of Eastern Africa*. British Museum (Natural History), London (1961). 214 pp

Pinhey, E. C. G.: 'A descriptive catalogue of the Odonata of the African continent' (up to December 1959) Parts I & II. *Publcoes cult. Co. Diamang, Angola* (1962). 59: 323 pp
(Other important papers by the same author).

Cockroaches 

Everybody is familiar with cockroaches, which probably rate as the insects least liked by man. They are a very old group with a good fossil record that dates from the Upper Carboniferous period, well over 300 million years ago. The most recent classification places cockroaches in an order of their own – the Blattodea – whereas previously they appeared with either grasshoppers or mantids.

Although several thousand kinds of cockroaches have been described only five species regularly live with man, appearing throughout the world as domestic or household pests. The remaining species are less commonly encountered as they live out of doors and are largely nocturnal – we call these 'wild cockroaches'.

Students of biology become intimately acquainted with the cockroach, because it is one of the 'types' of living creatures integral to their study. Furthermore, cockroaches are readily obtainable, effortlessly confined, and suitable for dissection and experimentation. They are omnivorous and will eat almost anything that is edible, from bread to old boots!

Being a rather primitive insect, the cockroach shows in a simple form the details of internal anatomy and external morphology that are found in all insects. Let us take the large American cockroach (which is very common in Africa) called *Periplaneta americana* and look at its structure.

Cockroach structure The body is divided into three distinct regions: the head, thorax, and abdomen; the name 'insect' refers to this division of the body into separate regions and segments. The outer covering of the body consists of a tough, horny substance known as chitin (pronounced ki-tin) which is durable, lightweight and resistant to the action of acids and alkalis. Chitin can be boiled in strong caustic soda for a long time without being harmed, although it does dissolve in strong mineral acids. This material forms the exoskeleton of the insect and, because it will not stretch to any great extent, must be shed by the insect from time to time.

The insect is doomed to remain small partly because of the nature of its skeleton. When it casts its skin, the new coat of chitin is initially very soft and the muscles and other organs have little to support them; the insect, therefore, is more or less helpless until the chitin hardens. If an insect were as large as a horse it would collapse in a shapeless heap when it moulted because of the softness of its skeleton and the weight of its body. Another reason why the largest of insects are only a few centimetres long stems from the nature of their breathing organs.

The simplest method of killing a cockroach is to drop it into boiling water. You can then pin the body onto a piece of cork and remove the skin from the upper surface by cutting around the edge with a pair of fine-pointed scissors. The first thing you will notice about its internal anatomy is a number of silvery threads branching in all directions through the tissues; these are the tracheae, the breathing tubes by means of which air is carried directly to all parts of its body (the blood of the insect does not play any part in its respiration, as it does in the case of vertebrates). The tracheae appear to be silvery because of the air that fills them.

The cockroach, like most other insects, has ten small round openings along each side of its body. These are called 'spiracles' and they can be opened or closed according to the need for more or less air. The air is drawn in and out through the spiracles mainly by a pumping action of the abdomen. This action can be clearly seen in many insects. Once 'inhaled', the air supply is distributed in the fine capillary tubes that form the ultimate branches of the tracheae. Renewal is accomplished by diffusion, which is rapid enough in narrow tubes over very short distances, but slow in long capillary tubes. Respiration by means of tracheae therefore is efficient in small insects, but such an air-supply would be inadequate for the needs of a larger animal. Thus we find that the longest of all insects, such as certain stick insects found in Africa (which measure 25 cm in length), are very slender so that the capillaries of the respiratory system are not unduly extended. An insect by definition could not grow to a size, let us say, of 25 cm long and 12 cm broad, as it then could not breathe properly and would need respiratory equipment similar to the lungs and blood system of a vertebrate.

The heart of the insect is situated along its back, just beneath the skin. It consists of a tube, closed at the hind end and open in front, near the head. The blood enters the 'heart' through small vents on either side of the tube, 13 in the case of the cockroach, but fewer in most other insects. These openings have valves that control the flow of blood out of the heart. When the tube expands, blood is drawn through the open valves, when it contracts, the valves close and the blood is driven forwards, through the opening in front. There are no blood vessels apart from the heart: the blood bathes all the tissues of the body and the heart is simply an organ to keep it in motion. The pulsation of the heart can most easily be seen in large smooth caterpillars. A dark line will be seen along the creature's back. This is the heart showing through the translucent skin; waves of expansion and contraction can be seen passing from back to front along this line. Pulsations are much more rapid in warm weather, less frequent when it is cold, and this is one reason why insects are sluggish at low temperatures. In some insects the heart can reverse its action, pumping the blood forward for a number of beats and then driving it backwards for a time. The principal function of the blood is to carry food to all parts of the body and to remove waste products.

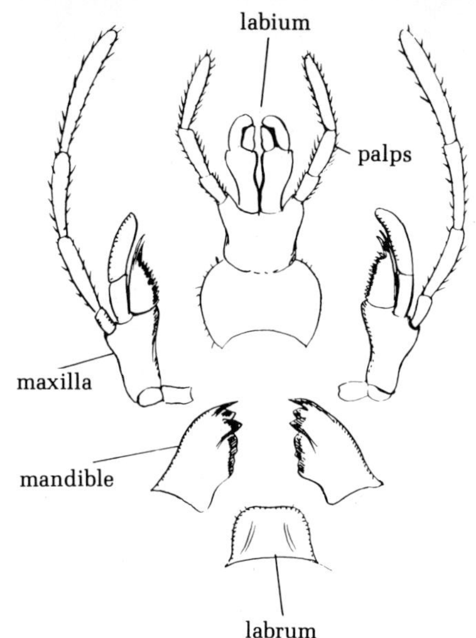

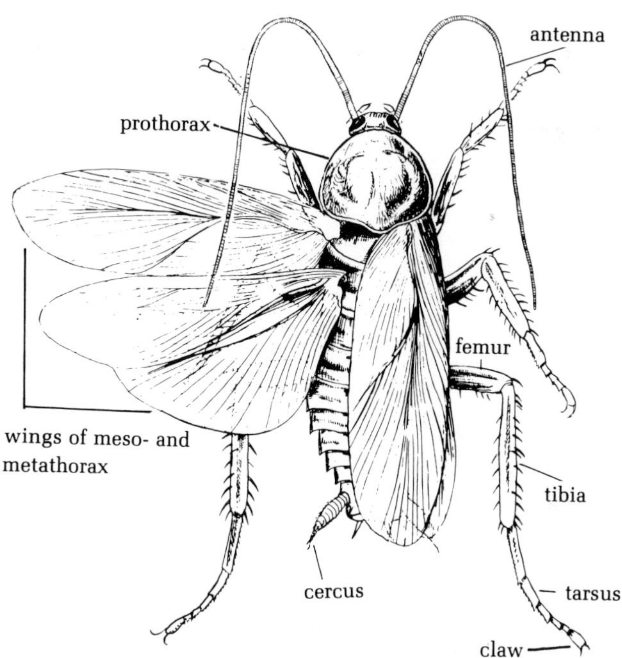

49. The mouthparts and general structure of the American cockroach, *Periplaneta americana*.

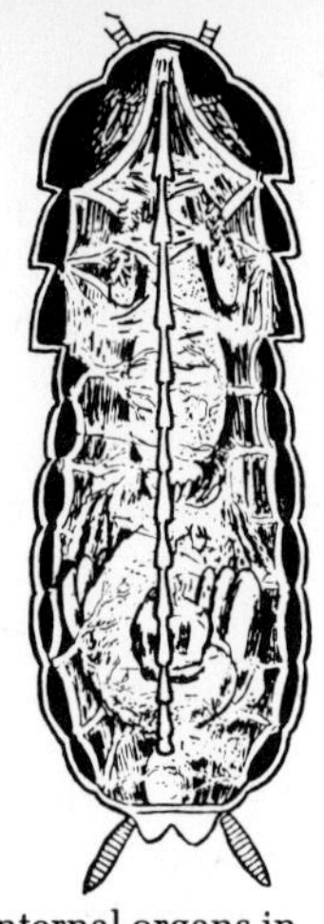
The internal organs in position, after removing the upper surface of the cockroach

The alimentary canal, showing from top to bottom the salivary glands, crop, gizzard, caeca, stomach, Malpighian tubules, intestine and rectum.

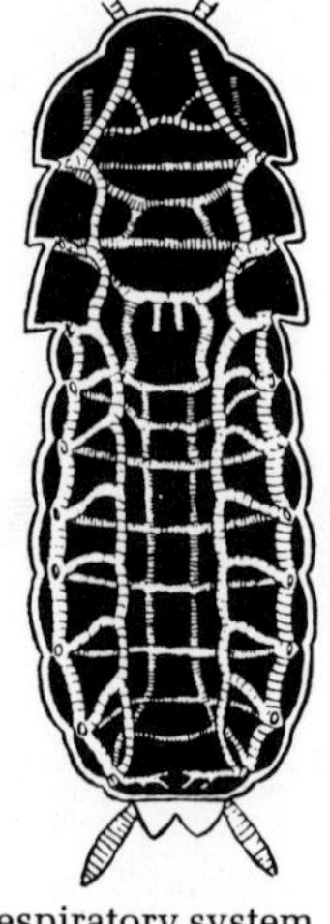
The respiratory system, showing the main tracheae; the finer branches and capillary tubes are not shown.

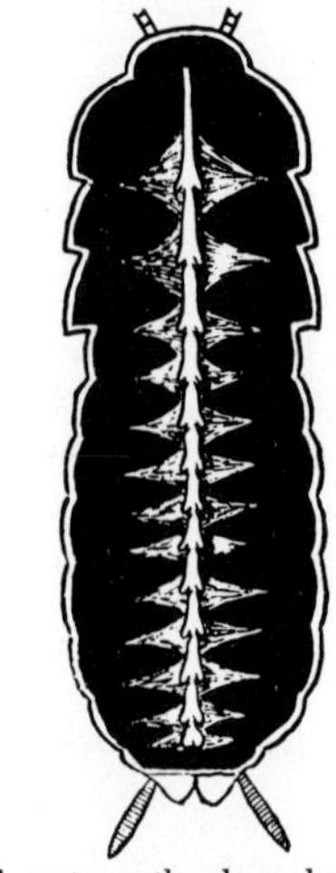
The heart, on the dorsal side, with the muscles that cause it to expand and contract.

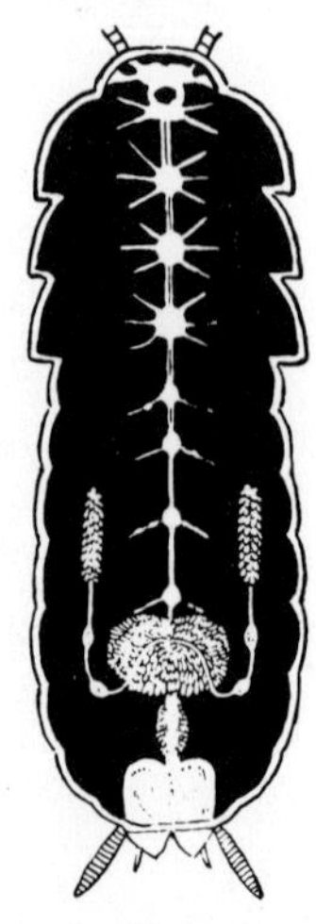
The reproductive organs of the male, showing the testes on each side and the mushroom gland in the centre. The major part of the central nervous system is shown, lying along the ventral surface.

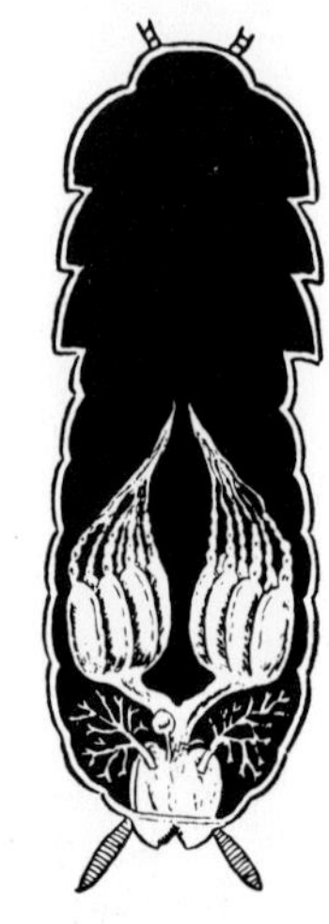
The reproductive organs of the female, showing the egg-tubes on each side, and the colleterial glands.

50. The internal anatomy of the American cockroach, as seen from above after the removal of the dorsal (upper) surface.

The digestive canal of the cockroach consists of an oesophagus that leads from the mouth and expands into a large crop at its hind end. The food is stored and softened in the crop by the salivary secretions. From the crop the partially digested food passes into the gizzard, a small muscular organ lined with thick chitin and armed with teeth on the inner surface. Here the food is ground into fine particles, after which it passes into the tubular stomach where digestion is completed and the digested food is absorbed by the blood. At the front end of the stomach there are eight short tubes, or caeca, which are prolongations of the stomach designed to increase the surface for digestion and absorption.

At the rear end of the stomach there appear a number of fine tubes known as Malpighian tubules, after Malpighi, the Italian scientist who first described them. These act as kidneys through which waste products are removed from the blood and passed into the hind intestine. The hind intestine then conveys the indigestible remnants of the food and the excretion of the Malpighian tubes to the rectum and thence to the exterior.

The reproductive organs of the female cockroach consist of eight egg-tubes on each side. These join together at the hind end to form the right and left oviducts which, in their turn, join to form the vagina. An egg-tube consists of a row of eggs, one behind the other, the oldest and largest of the eggs being the one nearest the oviduct. The eggs mature and grow as they pass along the egg-tube so that an egg is ripe and ready for laying by the time it reaches the oviduct. As the cockroach has 16 egg-tubes altogether, 16 eggs mature at a time. A pair of glands open into the vagina, consisting of fine, white, branching tubes. They produce the material that forms the egg-case which encloses and protects the eggs when they are laid.

The male cockroach has a pair of small white testes. From these, slender tubes, one on each side, convey the sperms to the wider, central tube called the ejaculatory duct, which leads to the exterior. Attached to the front end of the ejaculatory duct is a large, tubular gland, sometimes called the mushroom gland because of its shape. The function of this gland is to produce a sac-like structure called the spermatophore, in which the male cells are conveyed to the female when copulation takes place.

The central nervous system of insects lies along the ventral surface, beneath the alimentary canal. In the head, just above the oesophagus, there is a small brain from which nerves lead to the eyes and antennae. Below the oesophagus there is another mass of nerve tissue, called the suboesophageal ganglion, that gives off nerves to the mouthparts. These two are connected by nerve cords that run round each side of the oesophagus. From the oesophagus a double nerve cord runs through the thorax and abdomen. There are three swellings on this cord in the thorax – one for each segment – known as the thoracic ganglia, and nerves are given off from them to the legs and wings. Six ganglia in the abdomen give off nerves to the various abdominal organs.

The muscles of an insect are far too complex to be described here: there are about 2 000 in a caterpillar, and more in a winged insect. The strength of insects is remarkable; it has been shown that a small insect can lift something like 25 times its own weight, whereas many men could not lift their own weight. However, these feats are actually illusions and the efficiency of insects' muscles is related to their small size: if an insect were as large as a horse it would not be any stronger than the latter, if as strong.

The head of the cockroach bears the antennae, eyes and mouthparts. The antennae are regarded as the principal olfactory organs, but many insects can smell with other parts of the body as well – some butterflies, for example, can detect odours with their feet. There are many minute pits and sensory hairs on the antennae which are apparently delicate organs of smell and touch.

The mouthparts consist of an upper lip, or labrum; a lower lip, or labium; and two pairs of jaws between them, the hard jaws or mandibles, and the soft jaws, or maxillae. The jaws open sideways, and not up and down as do those of vertebrates.

The compound eyes of the cockroach, if examined under the microscope, are seen to consist of several hundred hexagonal facets so that the cornea, or outer covering of the eye, looks like a piece of honeycomb. Each facet marks the position of a separate lens and the number varies greatly with different insects: there are two to three thousand in each eye in the case of the cockroach, 20 000 or more in some dragonflies and only a dozen or so in certain ants. With eyes so very different from our own it is difficult to understand exactly what an insect sees, but it is generally accepted that insects have what is known as mosaic vision: each facet of the eye receives a small portion of the picture so that the image that reaches the insect's brain is something like a stained glass window. Due to the shape of the eyes and the absence of an efficient means of focusing, insects must be short-sighted. However, their eyes are eminently suited to detect movement, even at some distance, because the image of the moving object shifts from facet to facet in the eyes.

Insects cannot close their eyes and it is therefore difficult to know whether or not they sleep in the same manner as we do. It is very likely that they do, however, although they are much more easily aroused because of their wide-open eyes.

Simple eyes are found in many insects in addition to their compound eyes, but these are absent in the cockroach. The simple eyes, generally three in number and situated on top of the head in adults, each have one lens only and as they are very small cannot be very efficient organs of vision. It has been suggested that light falling on them serves as a stimulus to the compound eyes and other organs of the body.

The thorax consists of three segments and each bears a pair of legs. Each leg consists of five parts: the coxa, a short, stout joint connecting the leg to the body; the trochanter, a small joint connecting the coxa and the thigh or femur; the shank, or tibia which follows the femur; and the foot, or tarsus, consisting of five joints and ending in a pair of claws. The cockroach, like most winged insects, has two pairs of wings on the second and third segments of the thorax (the first segment of the thorax never bears wings). The first pair of wings are more or less stiff and leathery, while the larger second pair are thin and membranous and are the principal organs of flight. The abdomen consists of ten segments and at the hind end there are a pair of sixteen-jointed tail feelers, known as cerci.

And now, having dealt briefly with the anatomy of the cockroach, let us return to its life history. The female lays her eggs in a curious brown, leathery case that looks very much like a tiny purse with a zip-fastener along one edge. The egg-case is divided longitudinally by a thin membrane into two chambers. Within each of these chambers there is a row of cylindrical pockets, generally 16 in number, eight along each side of the purse. Each pocket contains a cigar-shaped egg.

This striking egg-case is not the calculated product of the female's skill and volition. The eggs pass into it, two by two, each into its own receptacle, as the case is slowly formed and extruded. Finally, when the batch of eggs is complete, the purse-like case sticks out at the rear end of the cockroach.

She carries it about with her for some time, though sooner or later she drops the case in some hiding place and leaves her young to fend for themselves. When the eggs hatch the purse splits open along one edge and the young cockroaches struggle out, feeble and white, but otherwise very much like their parents. Soon their skins harden and darken and they are able to run about and forage for themselves. They moult six or seven times before they are fully grown.

Household cockroaches Although the various household cockroaches have names which would seem to indicate their origins, such as 'American', or 'German', or 'Oriental', this is misleading since it is likely that

51. Female German cockroach carrying an egg-case behind her.

most of them originally came from Africa. In fact what most clearly distinguishes the household cockroaches from their 'wild' cousins is that they have become domesticated, and are today found only in buildings.

The most abundant household cockroach in Africa is the large American cockroach, *Periplaneta americana*, which is about 30 mm long and dark reddish brown in colour; both the male and female have wings. This variety is very common indeed in the coastal areas of Africa, but less abundant inland. The cockroach most commonly found in inland dwellings is *Blattella germanica*, the so-called 'German cockroach', which is only about 15 mm long, pale greyish-brown in colour and has two parallel dark stripes on the thorax. Again both sexes are winged. The third species that may occasionally be encountered in houses in Africa is *Blatta orientalis*, the so-called 'Oriental cockroach'. This is about 20 mm long and blackish in colour. The male has short wings that reach only halfway down its abdomen; the female is wingless. The German and American cockroaches are certainly the most commonly encountered household pests in Africa.

Although capable of flying, domestic cockroaches seldom do so. They rely instead on being transported in sacks, cartons, packages, laundry, furniture and so on. They frequently occur in abundance in the walls of refrigerators or behind wooden panels, surviving if necessary for months without access to their usual food, by feeding only on cast skins and their own dead. They find refuge in dark and damp places from where they may enter rooms along pipes, drains, ducts and ventilators.

Cockroaches will feed on just about anything – including animal and plant material, glue, hair, wallpaper, fabrics and bookbinding. They spread bacteria and viruses mechanically by walking over contaminated surfaces, and can harbour and spread many harmful organisms. It is thus easy to understand why cockroaches should be controlled in our homes. This can easily be done by a combination of good housekeeping and insecticidal control. As long as regular measures to combat cockroaches are taken it should seldom be necessary to call on the services of pest control firms.

Wild cockroaches Besides the cosmopolitan species that are household pests, there are a large number of 'wild' cockroaches native to Africa. These are commonly found under the bark of trees or fallen logs, beneath stones, amid decaying vegetation, in hollow stems and so on. They are easily recognised because they are nearly all brown or black, have flattened bodies and the head is bent down under the thorax so that it is scarcely visible from above.

The large brown mountain cockroach, *Aptera cingulata*, is particularly interesting. The female is a rich shiny brown colour. Flat on the underside but rounded and obese above, she is about 40 mm long when fully grown and has no wings. She is nocturnal, hiding during the day and creeping forth to hunt for food at night.

52. Cape mountain cockroach feeding on the petals of a flower. 52 mm.

These cockroaches are apparently vegetarian, and have been observed feeding on the berries of the parasitic plant, *Cuscuta*.

If a female is picked up she makes a squeaking sound by rubbing the roughened edge of one segment of her body against the surface of the segment behind. The male is quite different in appearance. He is winged, slender and looks very much like the American cockroach. Like the rest of their kind, this couple can produce an unpleasant smell if disturbed, by giving off a fluid from glands on the back.

The female of this species does not lay eggs, but retains them inside her body until they hatch. Then she deposits the living young, some 18-24 of them, in a batch. At first all the little ones are white but they soon turn black. They remain with their mother for a time, as chicks do with a mother hen. During late summer and early winter family parties of these insects may sometimes be found, beneath loose bark, under stones and amid dead leaves. Each party consists of a number of black young ones, together with one, two or more adult females and perhaps a winged male or two. Later on they scatter and live more or less solitary lives until the next breeding season – that is if they survive for more than one season.

We still have a great deal to learn about these interesting insects.

CLASSIFICATION

ORDER **Blattodea**

Antennae long, threadlike, with numerous segments. Head nearly or completely concealed from above by the large, shield-like pronotum. Mouthparts mandibulate, body flattened and oval, wings usually present but sometimes absent in one or both sexes. Tarsi 5-segmented.

The classification of cockroaches into families is controversial, some authorities recognising up to 28, and others only four. The latter are the Polyphagidae, Blaberidae, Blattidae and Epilampridae. *Blatta* and *Periplaneta* belong to the Blattidae, while *Blattella* belongs to the Epilampridae. The cockroaches of southern Africa have been well studied, and details are available in the specialised publications mentioned below.

FURTHER READING

Cornwell, P. B.: *The Cockroach*. Hutchinson, London (1968). 391 pp

Guthrie, D. M. & Tindall, A. R.: *The Biology of the Cockroach*. St. Martin's Press, New York (1968). 408 pp

Princis, K.: 'Revision der Südafrikanischen Blattarienfauna'. *South African Animal Life (1963)*. 9: 9-318

Princis, K.: 'Ordnung Blattariae'. In: Beier, M. (ed.): *Orthopterorum Catalogus*, W. Junk, The Hague (1962-1971). Parts 3-14. 1224 pp

Termites 5

Termites, often wrongly called 'white ants', are placed in an order known as the Isoptera, or 'insects with similar wings', the name referring to the fact that both pairs of wings are alike. Termites are among the most interesting and fascinating of insects. They are widespread and abundant in Africa, where hundreds of species are found – the richest termite fauna in the world. A few are of economic importance because of the damage they do to wood. The fortress homes of termites, the so-called 'ant-heaps', or termitaria, are a characteristic sight in Africa.

The structure of their bodies, their development and several other features place termites rather low down in the evolutionary scale of insect life – they are certainly far removed from ants and any similarities between the two are merely coincidental. Yet the termites have evolved an amazingly complex and efficient social life, with hundreds of thousands of individuals living in close, interdependent association in colonies that are run on absolutely totalitarian lines. They are very ancient insects, and probably existed one hundred million years ago in very similar form to that which we see today. The oldest fossil termite discovered is a harvester termite from the Cretaceous period. It seems that termites evolved from cockroach-like ancestors which began to adopt a social form of life.

The termite mound is by far the oldest type of organised community found on earth. Ants, bees, wasps and humans are modern upstarts by comparison! No known termites are able to live solitary lives; all are social insects and perish quickly if they are removed from their fortress homes.

There are five families of termites in Africa south of the Sahara, and of these the Termitidae is the largest. It is divided into four subfamilies of which the Termitinae, containing 71 genera of which 35 are represented in Africa, is the largest. As an example of this group of wood- and humus-eating termites, we shall take *Amitermes hastatus*, a common and abundant species in temperate and subtropical parts of Africa, where it constructs prominent domed mounds.

Black mound termites *Amitermes hastatus* is small, the full-grown worker being only about 4 mm long. It lives in mounds which are often blackish in colour, about 50 cm in diameter at the base and about 35 cm high. The mound is built of soil particles bound together with a cement that consists of the insects' excrement. It is a strong, weather-proof structure capable of keeping out most of the termites' enemies. Ants are the bitter, age-long enemies of termites and these soft-bodied, slow-moving insects would have no chance of survival against their agile, aggressive foes if they did not live within the shelter of their fortress homes.

Compared with the size of the puny creatures that make it, the mound is a colossal structure and the architectural wonders of man, such as the pyramids of Egypt or the skyscrapers of New York, are relatively speaking, feeble efforts. A large mound may contain a population equal to that of some of our largest cities. As a general rule, the inhabitants never venture out into the open air. They live in perpetual darkness and, in consequence, the great majority are blind. The sun never shines on them, no breeze ever stirs the still atmosphere of their corridors and the rain never reaches them. Their home is air-conditioned in a way that we can never equal.

Termites move from one part of the nest to another according to changes in temperature. If you break open a mound on a blazing hot summer afternoon you will find the cells near the surface are all empty because they are too warm and the inhabitants have crowded into cooler parts of the nest. On the other hand, these same cells near the surface are all densely occupied at night during the summer and by day during the winter. The air inside the nest is invariably humid and always contains a higher percentage of carbon dioxide than the outside atmosphere, because of the many thousands congregated in their home.

Because they have lived for countless generations in these air-conditioned homes, where there are no extremes or rapid changes, termites are very delicate creatures when removed from their normal environment. Consequently it is extraordinarily difficult to confine termites under artificial conditions in a laboratory, for observation purposes. That is the main reason why, although many volumes have been written about termites, we have still a great deal to learn about them and their strange, totalitarian ways. An artificial nest that has been found suitable for maintaining *Amitermes hastatus* is described in Chapter 24.

The great majority of the inhabitants of the termite mound are workers, males and females that are stunted in growth and whose sexual organs have failed to develop. They are, in consequence, sterile and can thus devote all their time and attention to unremitting labour for the State – without the distractions of sex. Among ants and social bees all the workers are females. In the case at least of bees the workers develop from eggs similar to those that produce queens, but the larvae are fed in a special way that stunts their growth and prevents the development of sexual organs. We do not know whether this occurs with termites, or whether the queen lays different types of eggs that give rise to workers, soldiers and sexed individuals.

Another baffling problem about the termite mound is the means by which discipline is maintained in this complex, crowded home. How are the termites' manifold activities organised? Who or what decides that this or that must be done and who should do it? None among the multitude has any authority over the others, as far as we can see, yet everything is done in an orderly fashion.

When more inhabitants are needed and when conditions are appropriate, the queen is given special food so that her ovaries are stimulated and she lays the required number of eggs. These and the young that hatch from them are treated in the manner appropriate to attaining the requisite number of workers, soldiers and sexed individuals. When the mound has to be enlarged the requisite number of workers undertake the labour. Food-gathering goes on unceasingly. It is all regulated with the utmost precision, but how, or by whom, nobody knows. The whole colony is dependent on the workers, for they do nearly all the work and without them the others would soon perish; yet all are on a footing of complete equality. A human city run on the same lines would soon be in a state of chaos.

There are runways under the ground – narrow tunnels radiating in all directions from the mound – which the workers excavate and use in their search for the decaying wood and humus (and frequently sound dead wood) that constitute their food. As soon as a source of food is exhausted, the runway leading to it is left to cave in, and workers drive new tunnels in other directions. Only the adult workers gather food.

Cellulose, the chief constituent of wood, cannot be digested by the higher animals, including insects, without the aid of micro-organisms in their intestines: the protozoa and bacteria break down the cellulose into constituents that can be digested by their host. Wood-eating termites generally have large numbers of intestinal protozoa and bacteria that help them to digest their food, but the family Termitidae is peculiar in having hardly any of these organisms in the digestive tract.

The abdomen of the adult worker is brownish-grey because the dark-coloured contents of its alimentary canal show through the translucent body-wall. Inside the nest the worker passes on this partially-digested food to any of its companions that may be hungry. The transference of food takes place from either end of its body: it may feed another termite by regurgitating some of the food from its mouth, or it may present its tail end and the second termite swallows its excrement. In this way the food passes through the alimentary canal of several individuals until all the nourishment is extracted from it and nothing but an indigestible dark-brown paste remains. This is used by the termites as the cement for building their home. Consequently there is no sewage problem in this crowded community. Furthermore, all corpses and all cast skins are devoured, so that the inside of the nest, despite being densely populated and shut off from the exterior, is always spotlessly clean.

The workers are active throughout the 24 hours of the day: in the impenetrable darkness of their surroundings there is no distinction between night and day. In the winter all activities slow down. There is no breeding and little food-gathering and the termites spend the greater part of their time doing nothing.

Early spring is the time for building, for enlarging the

mound. This work is carried out after it has rained – when the surface of the mound is moist and soft. Patches of black, crumbly material appear on the surface and, if you break away a little of this material, you will see large numbers of workers toiling away, each bringing up particles of soil from below and adding them to the ceiling above its head. Silently and unseen the workers build from the inside outwards, and the additions, frail and easily broken at first, are quickly strengthened by their strange cement until the extension to their premises is as strong as the rest.

If you break a hole in the side of the mound, the termites will be thrown into a state of great excitement because they know that their enemies, the ants, are ready to pour into the breach to slaughter them and carry them off as food. They will behave in a manner that is common to all termites when alarmed, jerking their bodies backwards and forwards, seeming to tap their heads and their tails on the ground as they do so.

The rapid restoration of the broken wall is a matter of life and death. After the hole is made, you will see soldiers come up, ready to defend the breach with their lives whilst the workers get on with the urgent work of repair. Usually this is done below the surface and you cannot see much, but sometimes the workers close small holes on the outside of the mound. Each worker, as it appears at the opening, shakes its head from side to side in a peculiar manner and then vomits a gobbet of dark-coloured slimy material which it deposits on the side of the hole; it withdraws immediately, to be replaced by another worker that carries out the same operation. Before your eyes, in a matter of seconds, the barrier is erected; damp and soft at first but rapidly hardening and drying. From this we deduce that each worker carries a supply of building material with it that can be used in an emergency. This material seems to consist of partially-digested food, soil particles, humus and chewed wood, mixed with digestive juices. If the hole is too large for this quick treatment, the workers carry up fragments of building material from below – sand grains or bits broken from the inside of the mound itself – and fasten them in position with the regurgitated 'cement'.

The hole is walled-up as quickly as possible, regardless of the fact that a number of workers and soldiers may be running about outside in confusion: these are ruthlessly shut out and left to their fate. The safety of the colony as a whole demands this sacrifice.

Another major responsibility of the tireless workers is the care of eggs. The workers collect the eggs as they are laid by the queen and carry them to that part of the nest where temperature and other conditions are appropriate. Here the white eggs are placed in heaps and carefully tended and licked by the workers. If they are removed from the nest, the eggs invariably fail to hatch: without the workers to look after them they die and go mouldy or if the air is dry, they simply shrivel up. The eggs hatch in about a month, into tiny six-legged creatures similar to the workers in form, but pure white in colour. Here we see one of the biggest differences be-

53. Not uncommonly, the termitaria of *Macrotermes* have twin spires; such a colony numbers many tens of thousands of individuals.

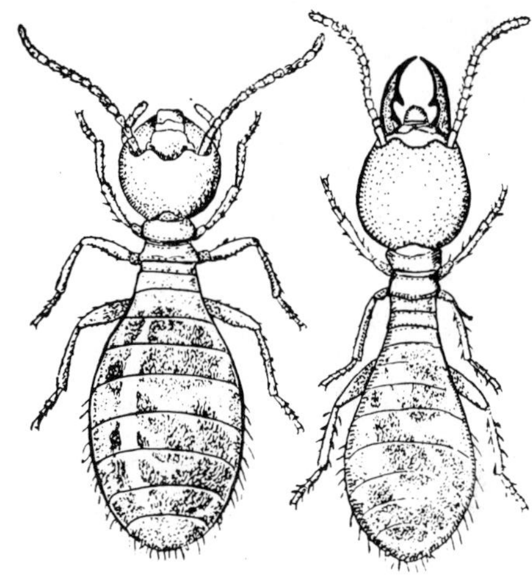

54. Adult worker (left) and soldier of *Amitermes hastatus*. They are about 5 mm in length.

tween termites and ants. The eggs of ants hatch into legless grubs, but the young of termites, like other primitive insects, are rather like their parents when born.

It is impossible at this stage to tell whether any particular young are destined to develop into workers, soldiers or sexed individuals: initially they all appear to be alike and the differences show only later in life, when they are about two-thirds grown. The young are fed by the adult workers on digested food, and their bodies, therefore, remain pure white until they are nearly fully grown (as there is no decayed wood or humus in their intestines to show through the translucent body-wall). Newly-hatched termites cast their skin five or six times and are mature when they are three months old. It is not known how long the workers live but it seems likely that, barring accidents, they have a life-span of perhaps four or five years.

Much has been made by some writers of the problem of the termites' water-supply: they point out that these insects must live in a humid atmosphere and that they quickly die in dry air. Yet many species are found in arid regions where temperatures are high and rainfall is low. It has been suggested that such termites must burrow deep into the earth in order to reach water far underground. The problem is not as difficult as it seems – at least not in the case of the black-mound termite. The workers are most active collecting food immediately after rain and so they obtain much moisture from the sodden wood and humus.

Inside their crowded, sealed home the loss of water must be very small and the air is saturated with vapour from the bodies of the insects themselves. Thus, in this particular species, the termites obtain all the water they need from their damp food and they do not burrow in search of some deeply-hidden source of water.

The soldiers, like the workers, are males and females that have failed to develop fully. They are sterile and unable to feed themselves, relying for food on the workers. Their job is to defend the colony, principally against their main enemies, ants. They have huge jaws and a swollen head in which is lodged a large gland that produces a sticky, irritant fluid. When the *Amitermes hastatus* soldier bites it grips like a bulldog and you may have to pull off its body before it will let go. If you tease a soldier with a piece of thread and get it to grip the thread in its jaws you will find that it can lift a stone much larger than its body using only its legs, whilst suspended by the jaws. As the soldier bites it gives off a fine stream of the irritant fluid from the pore between the base of its jaws. If this fluid gets onto an ant it causes the ant to curl up and may even kill it.

The soldiers are blind, like the workers, and they seem to detect friend or foe by smell and touch. When the mound is broken they come running out of the breach, their jaws wide open and antennae waving in the air, quite ready to sacrifice their lives in defence of the colony. A few soldiers always accompany the workers when they go out foraging for food, although the soldiers take no part at all in the food-gathering. Their job is to defend the workers if ants or other enemies should happen to break through into the tunnel. The workers themselves are also quite capable of fighting and will defend themselves and their home as doggedly as the soldiers. However, their first concern is to keep the enemy out by repairing any holes. Only about 5% of the inhabitants of a mound are soldiers.

Among ants, bees and wasps the males die soon after mating, but this is not the case with termites. Male termites survive with their mates to become the so-called 'kings' of the colonies. The titles, 'king' and 'queen', are misleading, however, because as far as we can see they do not rule in the accepted sense of the word, but are simply the parents of the teeming horde. Technically they are rather spoken of as 'reproductives'.

The king is much smaller than his mate because, unlike her, he does not increase in size after he has cast his wings. He is brown and easily recognised although difficult to find, being a timid creature. If the nest is disturbed he hides under the bulky abdomen of the queen or in some crack or crevice. His only function is to mate with the queen from time to time so that she maintains a regular supply of fertile eggs. It is believed that mating takes place tail to tail, with the heads of the pair pointing in opposite directions.

Normally there is only one pair of reproductives in a mound. This couple is the founder of the colony, and is known as the primary king and queen. Both king and queen have a pair of well-developed compound eyes, although these are used only once – during the brief wedding flight. They each retain the triangular stumps of their discarded wings on their backs. The abdomen of the queen swells up enormously when her ovaries begin to develop so that she looks something like a bloated sausage, with a small head and thorax in front. The black-mound termite is a small species; the queen is only about 18 mm long when she is fully grown, and the king about 6 mm.

The queen of *Amitermes hastatus* does not lay at all during the winter months. Her food-supply is reduced at this time of the year and she becomes comparatively slender. But when spring arrives the workers give her more food and she begins to bulge in a peculiar fashion. Her abdomen does not swell uniformly, but a bulge that looks like a deformity appears on one side and this is a sign that her numerous egg-tubes are beginning to function again. The workers pay her increased attention and there are always a number around her, licking her assiduously for the fatty exudation given off from the thin, distended skin of her abdomen.

The saliva of the black-mound termite has the peculiar effect of blackening anything it touches. In this way termites will blacken the wood upon which they feed and the light-coloured soil of which the mound is made turns black because it is cemented both with saliva and excreta. The young queen has a pure white abdomen but, as she grows older, her distended body slowly turns yellow and then a chocolate brown. This change of colour is apparently due to the staining effect of the workers' saliva and provides an easy way of distinguishing old queens from young ones: a white queen is young and a brown queen may be ten years of age or more.

The queen starts laying in the spring and she lays several hundred oval, white eggs that are carried away by the workers as fast as they are laid. She then rests for a period, lays no more eggs and her abdomen returns to its normal shape. But if all is well with the nest and plenty of food is coming in, she soon begins to bulge again and another lot of eggs are laid. And so it goes on throughout the summer: spurts of egg-laying with rests in between. If conditions are unfavourable and there is little food, egg-laying may cease altogether and the eggs that have already been laid may be eaten by the workers.

When the queen grows too old and her fertility wanes, the workers kill her by licking her to death. She is surrounded day and night by as many workers as can get at her. Gradually she grows thinner and thinner until finally only a shrivelled skin is left. This is covered with mound material and hidden from sight.

If you break open a mound in the Cape Province of South Africa in January you will find, in addition to the workers and soldiers, a large number of white individuals with four white wing pads on their backs. These are called nymphs –immature males and females that are being fed and treated in such a way that they will grow up into fully-developed sexual individuals. The nymphs reach full size at about mid-summer and, after their last moult their wings expand and their colour darkens. The four fully-developed wings are all the same size and much longer than the body. They are membranous and greyish-blue in colour. As these insects are destined to leave their sheltered home and face the hazards of the outside world, their skin hardens and turns black. They have a pair of compound eyes, as well as two simple eyes. These will be used only on the brief wedding flight, as both before and after this they will live in total darkness.

From about the middle of January these winged individuals can be found inside the nest. They seem to spend all their time clustered together in specific cells, where they are fed and groomed by the workers. They are kept prisoners for several weeks, for they are not allowed to leave the mound until the climatic conditions are just right for the wedding flight. Then some time in March or April the first winter rains arrive at the Cape and upon a day when the weather is clearing after a good rain has soaked the ground, when the air is still and the temperature rising, the long-awaited signal is given for the great event of the year to begin. We do not know who or what decides that the time is auspicious. Nor do we know how the termites, hidden in the blackness of their air-conditioned home, learn what the weather conditions are like outside. But simultaneously in all the mounds in a given area, generally about ten or eleven o'clock in the morning, a great activity begins.

The workers pierce a number of small round holes in the top of the mound, each hole being about 3 mm in diameter, so that the apex of the mound resembles the

55. Development of the worker of *Amitermes hastatus*, from the egg to the penultimate stage.

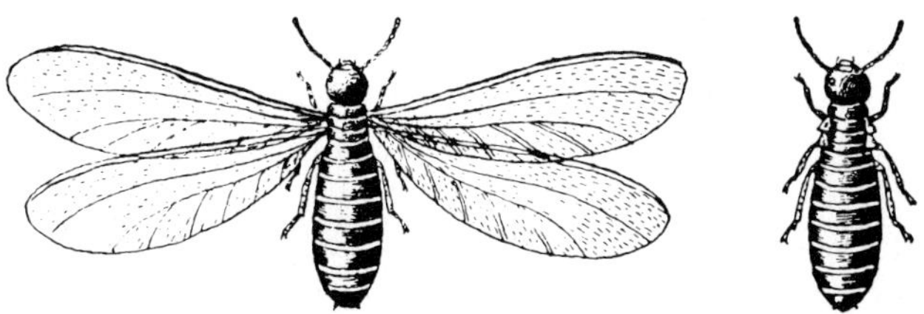

56. Winged adult of *Amitermes hastatus*, before and after shedding the wings.

lid of a pepper-pot. This is the only time that the termites deliberately make openings in their bastion walls: under no other circumstances do they run the risk of allowing enemies access to their home.

Soldiers appear at the holes, their jaws wide open and antennae waving, and then a number of workers come out into the open and these are followed by the winged males and females. There is great bustle and excitement on top of the mound for a few minutes, with the insects milling around apparently in confusion. Then the princes and princesses take to flight, fluttering away from their home in a straggling swarm. When they have all gone the soldiers and workers retreat inside, the holes are quickly closed and all is still once more. Not all the winged individuals are allowed to leave at once: some are kept back to form a second, or even a third swarm later in the season. Often the workers may be seen pulling some of the eager princes and princesses back into the mound and it seems obvious that the workers control the flight and decide how many may go and how many must be kept back.

The flying termites do not, as a rule, travel very far. They are feeble fliers and easy prey to all kinds of insect-eating animals. Birds, frogs, lizards, praying mantids, spiders and many other enemies have a great feast when the wedding flight is on and indeed very few of the fliers that leave the nest survive for long.

The female termite, if she is not caught and killed, is the first to settle. Usually she alights on the ground and runs around for a little while, then she pauses, seems to shrug her shoulders, as it were, and all her wings drop off. There is a line of weakness near the base of the wing and it is here that they break off, leaving only four small triangular stumps on her back. After shedding her wings she remains still, with the tip of her abdomen raised in the air. She gives off a scent called a pheromone that attracts the male and soon a winged male flutters down and settles on the ground just behind her. Then he gives the curious shrugging movement and all his wings drop off. After this the pair moves off together, tandem fashion, with the female leading the way and her mate keeping close behind her, tapping his antennae on her tail.

She chooses a suitable spot, the two dig a hole in the ground and then quickly disappear. Some 25 mm or so below the surface they construct a small cell in which they start the new colony. She lays four or five eggs and the pair together rear dwarf workers, feeding their young on secretions from their own bodies. They do not leave their cell or feed during this period. Reproduction is a slow business and at the end of the first year the young colony consists of only some six undersized workers, the king and the queen. Many of the new colonists may die before reaching this stage, killed by drought, cold, excessive rains, hunger, or enemies that come upon them and devour them. The colonies that survive grow slowly: a four- or five-year-old mound is only about the size of a man's fist; a full-sized colony may be ten years old or more.

If the newly-established queen dies or is killed, the workers immediately set about feeding some of the nymphs in the nest so that they are able to take her place as secondary queens. A dozen or more nymphs are selected and given special food (about which we know nothing). This treatment causes their sexual organs to develop before the insects themselves are mature; they swell up and become secondary queens, slightly smaller than their mother, and with four small, white, undeveloped wings on their backs. Their eyes are also smaller than they would have been were the nymphs allowed to grow up normally. Hence it is easy to distinguish a secondary queen from a primary one: the original mother of the colony has four triangular stumps, remnants of the wings she used on her wedding flight (the wing scales, as they are called). She has also two large compound eyes. The secondary queen has four white pads, or wings that never developed properly, and two small eyes.

If there are no nymphs present in the nest when the old queen dies the colony is not necessarily doomed to extinction, because the termites have yet another method of rearing sexual individuals that can take her place. The workers themselves, as stated before, are males and females that have failed to develop sexually. In a colony that has no queen and no nymphs, some of the immature workers may be fed in a special way so that their sexual organs develop and become functional. Such workers are converted into tertiary kings and queens, capable of mating and laying eggs.

These tertiary reproductives are not only smaller than both the primary and secondary reproductives, but have no eyes and no traces of wings on their backs, and are thus easily identified. Their fertility level is not high and they appear not to keep pace with the normal mortality rate in the colony, thus the numbers dwindle and the colony slowly dies out. Furthermore, the tertiary queens cannot lay eggs that will produce nymphs; their young are exclusively workers and soldiers and consequently such a colony cannot send winged individuals out on a wedding flight. Colonies with tertiary kings and queens are rare.

There is a belief common in Africa that if you destroy the queen of a termite colony the whole community will perish. But this is not so: a colony that has lost its queen can still survive by means of secondary or tertiary reproductives.

The above account of the biology of *Amitermes hastatus* gives some idea of the complexities of termites, with their various castes, intricate homes and interesting habits.

Fungus growers The subfamily Macrotermitinae of the Termitidae contains those termites responsible for the huge mounds which are such a spectacular feature of the African scenery. In northern Namibia and southern Angola the massive termitaria of *Macrotermes michaelseni* (formerly *mossambicus*) are typical. In southern Africa *Macrotermes natalensis* is widespread, and will serve as an example of the group.

The mounds built by this species may reach a height of 2 m or more. They may be conical or domed or of an irregular shape with pinnacles. A well-established nesting site may appear as a grass-covered hump with a newly-constructed clay mound on top. If the hard outer crust of such a mound is removed, a number of passages from 12-75 mm in diameter will be seen running down through the clay towards the nest below. The width of these 'chimneys' is due to their function as ventilation shafts.

The nest cavity is usually at the base of the mound, just below the soil surface, but it may be situated higher up in the mound, above ground level. The position seems to depend upon the water table in the soil: if there is water near the surface then the nest cavity is located in the mound itself, so that it remains dry even when the ground is water-logged. The cavity is more or less spherical, about 60-90 cm in diameter. This consists of a large number of arched clay shelves on which the fungus gardens are placed, and of irregular chambers in which the termites live. Many of the shelves are moist and fragile, little thicker than paper and easily broken. The fungus gardens are created from excreta which is moulded into spongy heaps or combs. Inside the cells these combs look similar to walnut kernels in their shells. They are reddish brown and, when the fungus begins to grow, they are dotted with tiny white spheres about the size of a pin's head. These little white fungus balls form the food of the young and the royal pair. Ultimately the fungus breaks the comb down into digestable material and the centre comb, now 'ripe', is consumed by the workers who then replace the combs.

The termites are in their limited way extremely skilful gardeners, for only the specific fungus they require is permitted to grow on their beds and all other kinds are carefully weeded out. The fungus is not allowed to develop normally and it is not known how those curious spherical bodies are produced instead of the more normal growth. The beds are carefully tended so that there is a continuous crop to meet the needs of the colony. Sometimes, after rains, the termites may bring material from the fungus beds and spread it in the shade on the surface near their nest. Numerous small, white mushrooms on slender stalks, with caps about 25 mm across, quickly develop from this material and produce innumerable spores in the ordinary way. These are dispersed by the wind and then die. This appears remarkably like a deliberate action on the part of the insects to ensure the normal development of the fungus from time to time, and to bring about its spread by means of spores. However, such foresight and intelligence on the part of these lowly creatures is incredible and it is undoubtedly an instinctive action; they can know nothing of the consequences. It is possible that they collect the spores to re-infect their beds, but this is merely surmise.

The common fungus grower, *Odontotermes badius*, is perhaps the worst pest among all termites, for it is the one which is most frequently found attacking timber in buildings and, as it is numerous and widespread, the

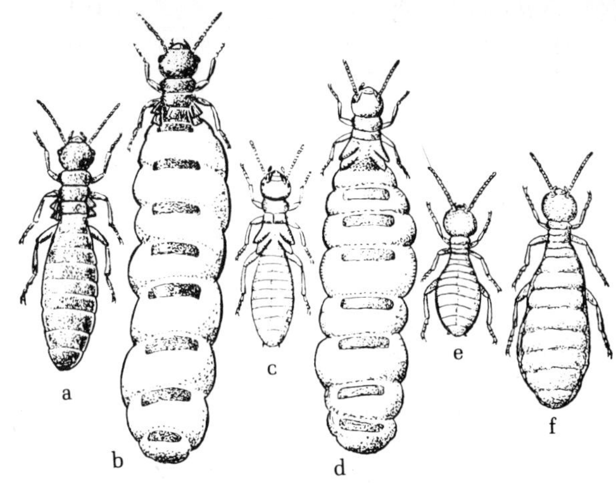

57. Queens of the black mound termite: **a.** adult female after shedding wings; **b.** primary queen that develops from **a;** **c.** a white nymph in the nest; **d.** secondary queen that develops from **c; e.** a worker about two-thirds grown; **f.** tertiary queen that develops from **e.**

58. A *Macrotermes* soldier sinks its jaws into a man's finger. They will fearlessly attack anything which threatens the colony.

damage it does is considerable. The mound above its nest consists initially of a low, rounded heap of soil particles loosely bound together. As the nest increases in size more heaps are added around the first one and these are worn down by the weather to form a low, grass-covered hump with heaps of recently excavated soil on it. This species does not make the conspicuous ventilation shafts typical of the nests of the Transvaal fungus grower, *Odontotermes transvaalensis.* Another species that does make wide ventilation shafts from the interior of its nest to the surface of the soil is the lesser fungus grower, *Odontotermes latericius.*

The fungus-growing termites *Macrotermes natalensis* usually builds covered runways when it comes out on the surface to feed and it will carry back to the nest supplies of dry grass, dead leaves, twigs and dung, but its chief food supply consists of any dry timber it can find. If it gets into a building it will build covered runways of mud up the foundations and walls to get at the joists, flooring boards, and so on. The timber is attacked from within, and the termite leaves only a thin, outer protective skin. Alternatively it is devoured on the outside surface under a cover of soil particles glued together by the insects. The wood that is removed is replaced by mud so that though it appears solid, most of it may have been destroyed.

The food is chewed off in fine fragments and swallowed by the workers, but it is only partially digested because these termites, as already mentioned, have not got the intestinal micro-organisms that are necessary to break down the cellulose.

The enormous queen of *Macrotermes natalensis,* up to 10 cm in length, and her consort (who is only about 25 mm long), are prisoners in a thick-walled royal cell situated in the heart of the nest cavity, below the fungus gardens. The queen is constantly attended by a number of workers who lick and feed her and carry away the eggs as she lays them. The tunnels leading into the royal cell are wide enough for the workers and soldiers to pass through but far too narrow for her; perhaps an academic observation only, because she is immobilised by her obese abdomen.

Altogether there are about a dozen species of fungus growers that attack timber in buildings, besides a number of others that restrict their attentions to dead wood on the veld. All have habits similar to those described above.

Snouted termites The small- to medium-sized domed or conical mounds of the various *Trinervitermes* species are a familiar sight on grasslands throughout Africa. There are about 12 different species and they are placed in the subfamily Nasutitermitinae of the Termitidae. All of them are grass eaters and feed chiefly on grasses that are most valuable as food for stock. In sufficient numbers they may do great damage to grazing.

If you break open a mound you will see that it is like a huge sponge with a very hard outer crust. The interior is filled with a maze of cells and connecting passages in which the termites live and in which they store their dried grass. The base of the mound extends 30 cm or so into the ground and from it runways radiate in all directions under the soil, like the spokes of a wheel.

The workers of this genus collect their food only at night. They make their way along the tunnels, sometimes for a considerable distance, and then surface through narrow branch passages that are scattered over a wide area around the mound. When they have finished collecting food for the night and have carried all of it below, the openings are plugged with soil and are no longer visible. By day the mound and its surroundings appear to be lifeless.

A large mound in an area more or less denuded of grass may be connected to a number of smaller mounds in the vicinity by underground tunnels. These are supplementary 'granaries' used as storage places for grass collected from far afield: they contain only workers and soldiers, besides the food, and no breeding takes place in them. When the rains come and grass grows again over the denuded area, the supplementary mounds may be deserted and the termites all concentrate in the main, central mound. That is why smaller mounds are often found to be empty when they are broken open.

The snouted termites take their name from their soldiers. These come in several sizes but they are all alike in having heads that are a reddish-yellow colour and drawn out in front into a pointed snout. Their jaws are reduced to useless tiny plates and they rely entirely on 'chemical warfare' in fighting ants and other enemies. The swollen head of the soldier consists largely of a gland which emits a colourless, irritant fluid which squirts in a sticky thread from the pore at the tip of the snout when the soldier is fighting. This can easily be seen if the mound is broken open and the soldiers that come out to defend the breach are teased. If the fluid gets onto the legs and antennae of an ant, the insect will writhe as though in pain and give up the fight.

The workers are of the usual type and they perform all the duties of the colony except defence and reproduction. The queen is smallish and can move about in the nest: she is not sealed in a royal cell but may be found in any part of the mound where conditions suit her. Her brown mate, smaller than she is, is usually found by her side. The wedding flight takes place in summer, after rains. Secondary and tertiary reproductives may be produced in a mound if the original pair die.

Harvester termites The family Hodotermitidae contains two genera (*Hodotermes* and *Microhodotermes)* that are very common and widespread throughout Africa. They are notorious for the damage they do to pastures and lawns. About five different species are found on the continent and, although they differ in size and colour, they are all very much alike in their nesting and feeding habits, and may be conveniently dealt with as a group. The commonest species are *Hodotermes mossambicus* and *Microhodotermes viator.* They flourish in regions of grassland with a fairly low annual rainfall, and are not found in mountainous areas, or where the rainfall is heavy.

Most of the harvesters do not build a mound above the surface. The position of the nest is revealed by small, scattered heaps of loose soil, only about 25 mm high. Each has a tunnel running through the centre, through which the termites transport the soil particles they remove when excavating their home beneath the ground. The little heaps of loose soil are soon blown away by the wind or washed away by the rain and then the only sign of the underground nest is the entrance holes. When the termites are not working these holes are plugged with mud. Being deep under ground with no indications on the surface of their presence, the nests are difficult to find and few people other than determined entomologists succeed in unearthing them.

An attribute unique to this family is the fact that workers have eyes and horny, brown skin – for these workers come out to the surface to cut and collect the grass that forms their food. This harvesting may be done by day or by night: during the height of summer, when the days are hot, the insects work mostly in the mornings and evenings and during the night, but in winter they come out on warm, sunny days. Besides doing considerable damage to lawns, shrubs, young trees and crops, they will attack wallpaper, books, carpets, curtains and similar articles in their interminable hunt for food. The grass and other food is cut up and carried to the entrance holes on the veld. There it is piled in heaps until it can be carried below.

Immediately below the surface the harvesting holes lead to a maze of narrow, winding, branching tunnels that are interspersed with cellars – about 75 mm in diameter and 6 mm high. Here the termites store their food temporarily. From these storage chambers wider tunnels lead downwards into the earth, to the hives which form the actual nest and which may be 1,5-6 m or more below the surface. Surrounding the hives there are a large number of flat chambers which form permanent storage places for the food.

The home of a vigorous colony may consist of a number of hives, up to 20 or more, scattered through the earth over a wide area and connected by a network of tunnels. Each hive consists of a dome-shaped cavity, 30-60 cm in diameter, and the interior contains hundreds of narrow, flattened cells, their walls made of a black, brittle material of the thickness of paper. Here the termites live, surrounded by their stores of dried grass. A few of the hives in the central part of the infested area are larger than the others and, during the summer, these contain eggs and immature termites, as well as the adults.

The queen is little more than 25 mm in length and, like the queen of the black mound termite, can move about from one part of the nest to another: there is no royal cell as there is in the case of the fungus growers. The winged males and females leave their nest during the summer after rain and their behaviour is similar to that already described for the black mound termite.

59. A toad prepares to make a meal of *Macrotermes* soldiers and workers issuing from the mound after dark. Termites constitute an important source of food for a wide variety of animals.

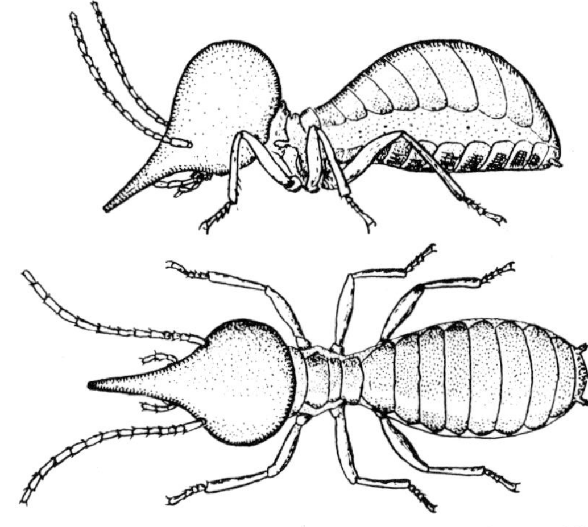

60. Snouted termite soldiers (*Trinervitermes* sp.). These soldiers have brought chemical warfare to a fine art; they squirt an irritating fluid at their enemies from a large gland in the head. 6 mm.

Dry wood termites The family Kalotermitidae is the most primitive group of the Isoptera. In Africa the family contains a number of species of termites that do not live in the soil at all but make their homes in seasoned timber, in logs, in dead branches of trees, and, in some cases, in timber used in the construction of buildings and in furniture. Several species of Kalotermitidae are indigenous to Africa but the most important of them, from an economic point of view, is the West Indian dry wood termite, *Cryptotermes brevis*. This species was introduced from overseas and is today significant in buildings along the east coast, from Natal to the Cape Peninsula. It has also been introduced to Rhodesia.

The termite reached South Africa some time around 1918, probably in crates or imported articles made of wood. Because of its hidden and secretive ways, the presence of this termite is not noticed until the damage it has done is considerable. The colonies are small, even the largest consisting of only a few hundred individuals, and the only members ever seen outside are the winged reproductives. These emerge on their wedding flight, which occurs in November and December and invariably takes place in the evening or at night.

The winged dry wood termite is small, measuring less than 25 mm across its outspread wings, and reddish brown in colour. After a brief flight the female settles on a piece of timber, almost invariably inside a building because these insects do not like timber that is exposed to the weather. She will then shed her wings and attract a male, who settles beside her and also sheds his wings. The two will then burrow into the wood and excavate a small cell not far below the surface, sealing up the entrance hole with sawdust bound together with saliva so that there is little evidence of their presence.

Mating takes place once the couple is safely lodged and, after a time, the queen's ovaries begin to function and she lays a few eggs. There are no true workers at all among termites of this family: the eggs hatch into males and females that eventually develop into winged reproductives or into soldiers. The king and queen feed the first few young but as soon as the winged reproductive nymphs are mature, they take over the work of the colony: excavating more chambers in the wood, digesting the food, and feeding and caring for the royal couple, the young and the soldiers.

The soldiers, few in number, are exclusively defenders. The soldier's head is black in front, enlarged and roughened, and sports a pair of stout jaws. The head is just the right size and shape to fit closely into the narrow passages that lead from cell to cell in the wood; a single soldier can therefore effectively close and guard one of these passages.

The inhabitants of a colony of dry wood termites thus consist of the king and queen, recognisable by their brown colour and the swollen body of the queen; the soldiers, with large black heads and white bodies; and the young winged reproductives (in various stages of growth) that eventually leave the nest on their wedding flight but act as workers when nearly full-grown.

The termites eat the wood, selecting first the softer parts, which they hollow out into cells in which they live. The cells are connected by narrow, circular tunnels about the thickness of the lead in a pencil. Eventually the harder portions of the wood are also eaten, leaving finally little but the thin outer shell of the timber. Small dark-coloured pellets of excrement, which resemble poppy seeds, are numerous in the cells. From time to time the termites make small openings in the wood and throw out these pellets. These heaps of droppings on the floor are usually the only sign that the wood is infested.

Cryptotermes brevis attacks almost any kind of wood and as the colonies are small, sometimes numbering only a few dozen individuals, they can infest small pieces of wood, such as wooden plugs in a wall or the three-ply backing on furniture, as well as massive timbers used in roof and floor construction. They have been found in South Africa in the blocks of parquet floors, skirting boards, flooring and ceiling boards, window frames, doors, picture rails, and so on, as well as in the pews of a church and compositors' desks in a printing works. The colonies increase in numbers in an infested building because of the spread of the termites by their wedding flights and the damage done may be very serious after a few years.

As with the other wood-eating termites the digestion of these insects is aided by curious parasites in their intestines. If the hind gut is removed from a nymph of the dry wood termite and the contents examined under a microscope, an amazing number of curious protozoa will be seen. These are found only in the intestines of termites and they break down the fragments of wood into constituents that can be dealt with by the digestive juices of their host. The parasites are passed from one termite to another when they feed one another with their excrement. The higher termites do not require the assistance of these micro-organisms and few if any are found in their intestines.

There are a number of wood-inhabiting termites that are indigenous to Africa, but they rarely enter buildings and are of little economic importance. They have been little studied or collected for a researcher is obliged to look upwards at dead branches on trees, rather than scratch in the ground, in order to find them.

Termitophiles and parasites In its broadest sense, the word 'termitophile' includes all the various creatures that live with termites in their nests, either as tolerated guests, obligatory members of termite societies, or as predators and scavengers. Records have been collected of termitophile members of the Isopoda, Collembola, Thysanura, Psocoptera, Thysanoptera, Coleoptera, Diptera and Hymenoptera.

In addition, there are several different species of mites that are found on the termites. A little white gamasid mite *Termitacarus cuneiformis* is quite common and these may be seen riding on the backs of the insects like miniature jockeys. They can leap nimbly from one termite to another and they seem to favour the queen as

61. Harvester termites (*Hodotermes* sp.) carrying pieces of grass they have cut into one of the many entrances to their nest. 8 mm.

their mount, for a number may usually be found seated on her head and thorax. When the workers feed the queen or one another, the mites run down to steal a little of the food as it is passed from mouth to mouth. They seem to do their hosts little harm.

Another kind of mite, *Cosmoglyphus kramerii*, pink in colour and belonging to the Tyroglyphidae, lives as a scavenger in the nest. Sometimes these become very numerous and may be seen clinging to the bodies of termites in large numbers, like tiny pink ticks. This occurs during the resting stage of the mite, known as the hypopus, during which it cannot walk but simply uses the termites as a means of transport. Later, when they emerge from the hypopal stage, the mites drop off and run about in the nest.

A parasitic worm, a nematode, *Hartertia gallinarum*, spends its young stages in harvester termites. When these infected insects are eaten by such birds as the bustard or the common domestic fowl, the worms complete their development in the intestines of the birds. The amazing assemblage of microscopic organisms found in the hind intestine of wood-eating termites includes protozoa, spirochaetes and bacteria. The great majority of the protozoa are flagellates (class Mastigophora) of a peculiar type and in some cases it is possible for an expert to determine the species of termite from an examination of the protozoa taken from its gut.

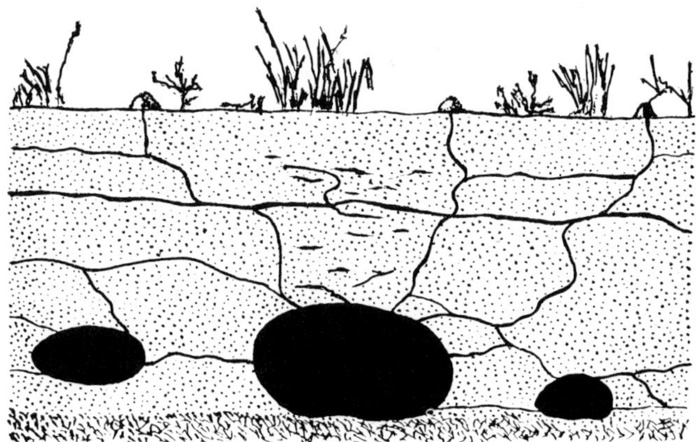

62. Diagram of the nest of the harvester termite (*Hodotermes* sp.).

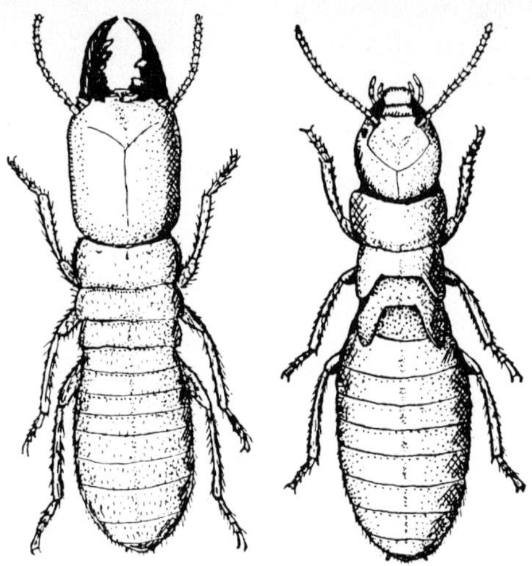

63. Wood-inhabiting termites, *Kalotermes* sp., with soldier on the left and nymph on the right. The nymphs take the place of workers in this group.

64. While a worker *Macrotermes* removes eggs from the hind end of the queen, a minute white termitophile (probably a Psocopteran) rides on its back.

CLASSIFICATION

ORDER **Isoptera**

Small, soft-bodied, usually pale-coloured social insects living in communities composed of winged and wingless forms, together with numerous sterile males and females, workers and soldiers, of different types. Antennae generally short, threadlike. Winged forms with two pairs of wings, very similar in size and shape, relatively long and narrow, membranous and held flat over the back at rest. Wings are shed by breaking off at a basal fracture. Tarsi 4-segmented. Mouthparts chewing (vestigial in nasutiform soldiers).

FAMILY Kalotermitidae
Fontanelle (pale depressed spot on front of head) absent in all castes, simple eyes usually present. Pronotum (first thoracic segment) flat, usually broader than head in all castes; anterior wing scales large, overlapping smaller posterior ones. No true workers, the well-grown nymphs of the reproductive caste act as workers. *Epicalotermes*, *Bifiditermes* and *Cryptotermes* are widespread genera; some species of the latter are economically important.

FAMILY Termopsidae
Fontanelle and ocelli absent, pronotum flat and narrower than head, anterior wing scales large. A small family represented in Africa by only two species from the southern coastal belt.

FAMILY Hodotermitidae
Fontanelle and ocelli absent. Pronotum saddle-shaped and narrower than head in all castes. Front wing scales short, do not overlap posterior ones. Harvester termites do not build nests above ground; the workers have compound eyes and collect grass on the surface.

FAMILY Rhinotermitidae
Fontanelle present in all castes. Anterior wing scales large. Soldiers have flat pronotum, frontal gland almost always present. Nearly all make nests in soil and do not cultivate fungus. Members of *Coptotermes* may be readily transported in infested timber; *C. formosanus*, the 'Oriental dampwood termite,' was accidentally introduced to Simonstown (Cape Peninsula) where it has become established and is responsible for considerable damage to seasoned timber both in and removed from buildings; also present in Komatipoort (Eastern Transvaal) where it survives but is not thriving. A number of indigenous Rhinotermitidae occur in Africa – the desert termite *Psammotermes allocerus* thrives in sandy deserts, while the golden tree termite *Schedorhinotermes lamanianus* is found in warm and moist subtropical areas.

FAMILY Termitidae
Fontanelle present. Anterior wing scale never large. Pronotum of soldier and worker narrow, with a raised median lobe in front. This family contains the vast majority of the termites and is divided into four subfamilies, the Apicotermitinae, Termitinae, Macrotermitinae and Nasutitermitinae, the last three of which are dealt with in the text. Members of the family differ widely in nesting and feeding habits: some build surface mounds or large termitaria, others nest below the surface. Some cultivate fungi for food, some feed on grass, others wood, dung or other decaying organic matter. The fungus growers are important as destroyers of wood. The Termitidae generally lack the complex intestinal fauna that is characteristic of the other families, and aids their digestion of cellulose.

FURTHER READING

Bouillon, A. (Ed.): *Etudes sur les Termites Africains.* Masson et Cie, Paris (1964). 414 pp

Coaton, W. G. H. & Sheasby, J. L.: 'National Survey of the Isoptera of southern Africa'. 1-13. *Cimbebasia,* Windhoek (1973-1977). (Also many other important papers by Coaton)

Harris, W. V.: *Termites: Their Recognition and Control.* 2nd Ed. Longmans, London (1971). 187 pp

Howse, P. E.: *Termites: a Study in Social Behaviour.* Hutchinson & Co. Ltd. London (1970). 150 pp

Hicken, N. E.: *Termites – a World Problem.* Hutchinson & Co. Ltd. London (1971). 232 pp

Krishna, K. & Weesner, F. M. (Eds.): *Biology of Termites.* Academic Press, London & New York (1969 & 1970). Part I, 597 pp; Part II, 643 pp

Lee, K. E. & Wood, T. G.: *Termites and Soils.* Academic Press, London & New York (1971). 252 pp

Sands, W. A.: [Papers on Termitidae in *Bulletin of the British Museum (Natural History)* 1959, 1965, 1972.]

Skaife, S. H.: *Dwellers in Darkness: an Introduction to the Study of Termites.* Longmans Green & Co., London (1956). 134 pp

Snyder, T. E.: [Catalogue of world termites; annotated bibliography of termites. *Smithsonian Miscellaneous Collections* (1949-1968.]

Wilson, E. O.: *The Insect Societies.* Harvard University Press, Cambridge, Mass. (1971). 548 pp

Mantids and stick insects

Few people in Africa are not familiar with the interesting insects known as 'praying mantids' or 'hottentot gods'. They are abundant, frequently come to lights at night and many are striking in form or colour. Members of the order Mantodea are all carnivorous and are easily recognised by the peculiar form of the front legs, which are adapted for seizing and holding their prey.

The stick insects, order Phasmatodea, are not closely related to the mantids, and in fact it is rather a puzzle just where they belong among the insects. They are so well disguised as sticks or twigs that these interesting creatures are easily overlooked by untrained observers. Unlike Mantodea the Phasmatodea are all vegetarian.

Mantids If you watch a praying mantid hunting (and this can often be observed near outside lights in the evening), you will see her small, triangular head, with the two bulging compound eyes and the three simple eyes between them, swing round on her flexible neck as she watches the movements of her intended victim. This ability to turn its head, to look over its shoulder, as it were, is a curious characteristic of all praying mantids. By way of contrast, the great majority of insects have short, stiff necks and cannot twist their heads round to look in another direction. However, the praying mantid can cock its head in an engagingly pert and intelligent-looking manner.

She stalks her prey, slowly, moving cautiously with a slight swaying motion on her four hind legs until she is close enough for her deadly front legs to make a lightning grab at the insect. Once grasped, the victim has no chance of escaping from those legs, which are armed with double rows of spikes. The mantid proceeds at once to nibble at it with her small jaws, reducing it to a pulp and swallowing it, except for the tough legs and wings, in an amazingly short time.

The name of the order, Mantodea, comes from a Greek word meaning a prophet or soothsayer. It was given to the insects because of their deceptively meek appearance when they are at rest, their front legs lifted as though in an attitude of prayer. The South African name, 'hottentot god', seems to have been given for a similar reason.

If you examine a praying mantid you will see that the front part of its body, between its head and the base of its wings, is long and slender. The first pair of legs are articulated to the front of this elongated segment and the first joint of the legs, the coxa, is much longer than is usual in other insects. Thus equipped the mantid has a very long reach which allows those grappling irons, toothed like a saw, to strike swiftly and surely from some distance.

65. A praying mantid cautiously stalks her intended victim, a day-flying moth.

Anybody who has caught hold of a praying mantid will recall how it claws at the fingers of its captor with its long front legs. Indeed, some of the larger varieties can draw blood if they rake their legs downwards over the skin in self-defence. One has the impression that it is a fearless, impudent little creature: it certainly does not hesitate to attack insects as big as itself and it will tackle spiders, honey bees and other armed foes if they come its way.

The female mantid has special glands inside her body which consist of a number of twisted tubes that secrete a gummy liquid something like the silk produced by silkworms. When she is about to lay her eggs (always in the dark), she pours out the liquid from her genital opening and it turns into a foam on contact with the air. She shapes the foamy mass, using only the tip of her abdomen and the two cerci on her tail as tools.

Down the middle of the mass, before it hardens, she forms a series of neat little receptacles into which she deposits her eggs, side by side, the head-end uppermost. Each of the 60-or-so eggs is enclosed in a separate compartment and there is a valve at the top of each receptacle that affords an easy exit for the young when they hatch. This arrangement prevents the entry of enemies from outside. These valvular openings can be seen in a double row along the middle of the egg-mass.

This is an extraordinary feat for an insect. The work is performed in the dark, with a foamy material that hardens quickly on contact with the air, and she uses as instruments only the tip of her tail and her hind legs. If you put a match to the egg-mass you will find that it burns with a smell like that given off by burning silk.

The hatching of the eggs presents another curious feature of the mantid's life history. When the young emerge from the eggs, after about a month, each is enclosed in a tight-fitting membrane so that they resemble tiny fish without fins. Each young mantid wriggles its way out of the cell, passing easily through the valve at the top that opens only outwards and stops when its body projects about half-way out of the opening. There it remains motionless for a time as blood is pumped into its head so that it swells and pulsates as though about to burst. However, only the membrane splits as a result of the pressure, and the little creature struggles out of the hole, leaving its cast skin behind it. Now it can be recognised as a miniature mantid, without wings. The young scatter soon after hatching, each to make its own way in the world.

The newly-hatched young are black and each carries its abdomen curled up over its back, a peculiar custom that seems to be common to all young mantids, but we do not know why they adopt this posture. The process of hatching is further complicated in some species because the young, whilst still enclosed in their swaddling membrane, drop from exit-holes in a suspended egg-case and hang for some time by silken threads before moulting and dropping to the ground. With this complication excepted, the above account applies in general to all the Mantodea, of which there are a large number of different species in Africa. Most resemble their surroundings in a remarkable manner, offering excellent examples of what is known as cryptic colouration.

The large green mantid (*Sphodromantis gastrica*), is common, and is always found on bushes and trees where the green foliage hides it; its food consists chiefly of caterpillars and it must therefore be regarded as a beneficial insect. Another common genus in Africa containing predominantly pale green species is *Miomantis*. The common brown mantid (*Tarachodes perloides*), on the other hand, is dull brown, speckled with darker brown, and is always found on the trunks and branches of trees where its colouring and markings match perfectly those of the bark.

Some mantids are marked and coloured in a more elaborate way and may easily be mistaken for flowers as they rest on a plant. The yellow, green and red mantid, *Harpagomantis tricolor*, is green and yellow with a dark red patch on the hind wings. The projecting points on the sides of its abdomen, together with its colouration, make this insect resemble the flowers among which it likes to rest and hunt. Some mantids have a quaint appearance because of the flattened areas on their limbs and the strange projections on their bodies. The mantids belonging to the genus *Empusa* are of this type. These display a conical projection on the front of the head that looks something like a miniature bishop's mitre and the knobs and projections on their legs and abdomen give the appearance of pieces of gnarled bark. The males of this genus have striking plumed antennae.

When threatened, some mantids spread their wings, and some species, like *Pseudocreobotra wahlbergi*, have spectacular eye-like patterns on their forewings that apparently frighten off attackers when suddenly displayed.

The male mantids are in every case more slender and somewhat smaller than the females and the females indulge in the practice of eating their mates: sometimes they chew off the heads of the males even as copulation is in progress!

Stick insects Members of the order Phasmatodea are among the most helpless of insects. Most of them cannot fly and they cannot jump; they can only creep slowly about on the plants upon which they feed. As they are highly edible they are eagerly sought-after by birds and other insect-eaters and their sole means of protection from their many enemies is their close resemblance to their surroundings, which makes them difficult to find.

When at rest, the stick insects, as their popular name implies, closely resemble sticks or grass stems; when disturbed, they remain stiff and motionless, shamming dead. Consequently it requires a keen eye to detect them amid the foliage. The scientific name comes from the Greek word for a ghost. The insects do not feign death as a calculated response to a threat; they are quite incapable of reasoning that they are hard to see as long as they remain quite still. When disturbed they fall quite instinctively into a cataleptic state and remain with body rigid and long front legs held stiffly out in front for some time until the fit passes and they can creep about once more.

Some of the largest stick insects in Africa may reach a length of 25 cm and they are among the longest of all insects but their bodies are slender. Much of their length is due to the elongation of the middle segments of the thorax. Some species have wings but in all cases the first pair is always small and often reduced to useless scales. The second pair can serve for flight, or in an intimidating defensive display. All are vegetarians and usually the male is smaller and more slimly-built than the female.

The common green stick insect of the Cape (*Macynia labiata*) may be taken as our example of this group. The fully-grown female is about 60 mm long and the male is a little shorter and slighter in build. Both are green, matching the colour of the foliage amid which they live, and both have pink mouthparts and a pink tip to the tail when mature. The male has a pair of claspers on the end of his abdomen, whereas the abdomen of the female ends in a blunt point.

These insects remain still and rigid for hours at a time during the day, looking like a piece of green, leafless twig. They are active and feed at night. What looks like a pair of antennae on the front of the head is really the first pair of legs: the antennae are comparatively short and inconspicuous.

Egg-laying starts in late spring, at the end of October, and goes on until January, after which the spent insects die. The process is as careless and casual as it is possible to find among insects: most female insects show remarkable instincts and labour prodigiously to provide for their offspring, but the female stick insect simply drops her eggs light-heartedly behind her, one at a time, letting them fall unheeded to the ground which may be far below her. Her maternal responsibilities are treated lightly indeed, and she hardly seems to be aware that she is laying eggs as she goes on nibbling at a leaf.

66. A grass-mimicking mantid lying in wait for a victim (above). A passing fly is successfully ambushed by the mantid (below) and then consumed. 35 mm.

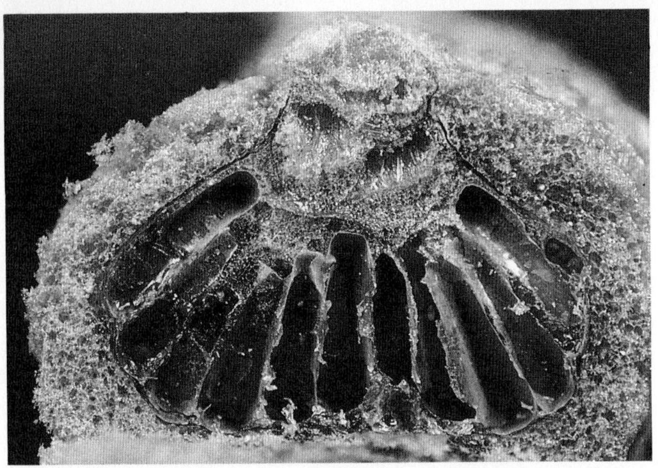

67. Section through praying mantid egg-mass, showing the separate compartments in which the eggs develop. 15 mm across.

68. Praying mantid nymphs emerging from egg case, some still dangling on silken threads. 8 mm.

69. Praying mantid drinks rainwater drops from a leaf. 45 mm.

Each female seems to lay at the rate of about one egg every 24 hours, and, as oviposition extends over three months or longer, she may lay 100 eggs before her ovaries are exhausted. The egg is a remarkable object, about the size of a cabbage seed, and looks exactly like a hard, shiny green seed. It has a beautiful and ornamental white cap at one end, which is pushed off by the young insect when it hatches. Down one side of the egg there is a white mark, similar to the mark left on a pea or bean where the stalk held it in place inside the pod. Most people, if shown some of these eggs, would unhesitatingly declare them to be seeds.

The eggs lie on the ground all through the hot southern summer, sheltered perhaps by the bush on which the mother lived, or by dead leaves. They take six months to hatch, the young emerging the following autumn, late in April and during May. The baby stick insect is exactly like its parents, a long-legged green thread about 12 mm long. As its parents did before it, it rests motionless during the day and feeds at night on the tender young leaves brought out by the autumn rains.

After feeding and growing for a few days, its tough outer skin will not stretch any more and the little creature rests, preparing for the difficult and trying process of moulting. It hangs, head downwards, clinging by its four hind legs. A split appears in the skin along its back, just behind the head, and slowly and laboriously the insect pulls itself out of its old skin, emerging clad in a new suit a size larger than the one it discards.

It is not only the outer skin that it casts off, but also the lining of the front and hind parts of its alimentary canal, of its main tracheae and of certain glands. If you watch a stick insect whilst it is moulting (and they are easy to keep in captivity), you will see two crystal globules of liquid at the bases of its front legs. This is a lubricating fluid produced by special glands to aid in the difficult task of extracting itself from its old skin. Once completed, the creature rests for a while beside its cast-off skin and then, before moving off, it frugally eats the empty husk. It has to moult in this way five or six times before it is fully grown.

In the course of its perambulations, the stick insect may lose a limb – perhaps as a result of an attack by an enemy. This is no serious matter if the insect is still immature, because a new limb grows out to replace the lost one, appearing as a stump at the next moult and rapidly increasing in size with the succeeding moults. If, however, the insect is adult when it loses a limb, a new one cannot grow because it does not cast its skin again.

Ants, frogs, lizards and birds are among its many enemies. The red-winged starling is a particularly formidable foe: this bird feeds its young mainly on stick insects and destroys them in large numbers. A fly that looks like a small, hairy house fly, but belongs to the family Tachinidae, lays its eggs on stick insects and the maggots burrow into the living victims and devour them.

Parthenogenesis, or 'virgin birth' is known to occur

among some stick insects. Parthenogenesis applies to cases where unfertilised eggs develop and hatch in the normal way. It occurs among many insects, such as bees, aphids and some moths. The males of some species of stick insects are very rare and, with these species, parthenogenesis must be common.

CLASSIFICATION

ORDER **Mantodea**

Front legs raptorial, head mobile, three ocelli usually present. Mouthparts mandibulate. Predatory insects. The mantid fauna of Africa is the richest in the world. The main families are the Amorphoscelididae, Hymenopodidae, Mantidae and Empusidae. Of these the Hymenopodidae often have the pronotum laterally expanded and coloured bands or spirals on the forewings (like *Pseudocreobotra wahlbergi*); the Mantidae never have such markings and the inner ventral spines of the fore tibia are alternately long and short. Most of the commonly-seen green mantids like *Miomantis* and *Sphodromantis*, as well as the brownish types resembling grass or bark like *Pyrgomantis* and *Tarachodes* species, belong to this family. The Empusidae have the inner ventral spines of the fore tibia alternately one long and two to four short; often bizarre forms, usually with a pointed projection on the head; the genus *Empusa* is widespread in Africa.

ORDER **Phasmatodea**

Large, elongated, cylindrical insects that often resemble foliage or sticks and twigs. Mouthparts mandibulate; all are vegetarian insects and active at night. Prothorax short, meso- and metathorax elongated, wings present or absent; when present the forewings are usually small, hind wings folded fanwise. Forelegs usually held together in front of head. There are about 2 500 known species of Phasmatodea, the majority from the Oriental region. The stick insects all belong to one family, Phasmatidae, and some of the larger species can reach 25 cm in length.

FURTHER READING

Beier, M.: 'Mantidae'. *South African Animal Life*. (1955). 2: 234-265
Beier, M.: 'Mantodea von Angola'. *Publcôes cult. Co. Diamang, Angola*. (1969). 8: 13-44
(Many other important papers on Mantodea and Phasmatodea by the same author.)

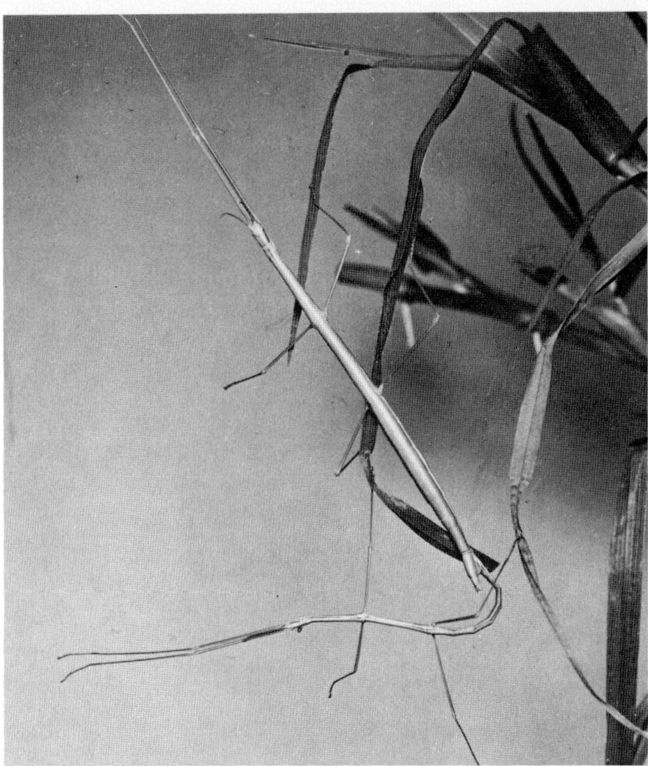

70. Stick insects mating. Female 100 mm.

71. Newly hatched stick insect, alongside the egg from which it has just emerged, after pushing off the tiny cap. 35 mm.

72. Stick insect feeding on leaves of an Acacia tree. 70 mm.

Earwigs 7

The small order, Dermaptera, includes about 1 000 species of insects commonly known as 'earwigs'. Dermaptera means 'skin-winged' and this refers to the membranous second pair of wings which is carried neatly folded beneath the small, leathery pair of front wings. The popular name earwig is said by some to be derived from 'ear-wing' and to refer to the hind wing which, when it is spread out, has something of the shape of the human ear. But in several European languages the insect is referred to as an ear-worm or ear-borer; the completely unfounded belief that these insects creep into ears seems to be ancient and widely spread.

The characteristic mark of an earwig is the curious pair of pincers on its tail: these correspond to the cerci of the cockroach but, in the case of the earwig, they have been modified to form nippers. Many people are alarmed by the appearance of earwigs, thinking that the pincers are 'stings' – especially as these little insects have the habit of raising the tip of the abdomen in a threatening manner. Earwigs are quite harmless, however, and their forceps, used only in defence, to catch and hold prey, and in courtship, are too weak to harm humans in any way. In most species the males have bigger pincers than the females.

In the winged species the second pair of wings is carried neatly folded beneath the short, protective first pair. They are folded first like a fan and then back upon themselves twice, so that they occupy very little space and are covered by the small, square first pair. No other insects fold their wings in this complicated manner.

African earwigs The European earwig, *Forficula auricularia*, has apparently been introduced to South Africa, but failed to spread widely or become numerous. In Europe it is regarded as a garden pest, but the local species, such as *Forficula senegalensis*, do not have this reputation in Africa. It would seem that they are largely scavengers, feeding on rotting fruit, other organic debris and dead insects, but they are also reputed to capture live insects with their forceps. They are nocturnal, and rest during the day in damp and dark places, under stones, in rotting logs, among leaves and under the bark of trees.

The female earwig behaves maternally towards her eggs and young: she lays her eggs in a heap in a burrow beneath a log or stone, and watches over them until they hatch. It is said that if the eggs are scattered, she will carefully collect them again, one by one, and replace them in a heap. The newly-hatched young are like their parents, except that they are white and wingless, with fewer joints to their antennae (eight instead of 14) and two simple cerci instead of the forceps. They remain with their mother for a time and then scatter to look after themselves.

Although most African earwigs have been collected and described, virtually nothing is known of their habits, and this promises to be a fruitful field of study.

Parasitic earwigs The order Dermaptera is divided into three suborders, two of which contain insects that are quite remarkable in having become parasites of vertebrates. The one group parasitizes bats in the Far East, and will not concern us further, while the other suborder contains the African genus *Hemimerus*.

Nine species of *Hemimerus* are known; they are about 10 mm long, orange-brown in colour, and lack both eyes and wings. They have paired cerci at the tip of the abdomen, but these are long, straight and quite unlike those of the free-living earwigs. Most of the parasitic earwigs are found on giant rats (genus *Cricetomys*), and they live among the fur, apparently feeding on skin scales, debris and other material.

73. Earwig raises its abdomen in a threatening manner. 22 mm.

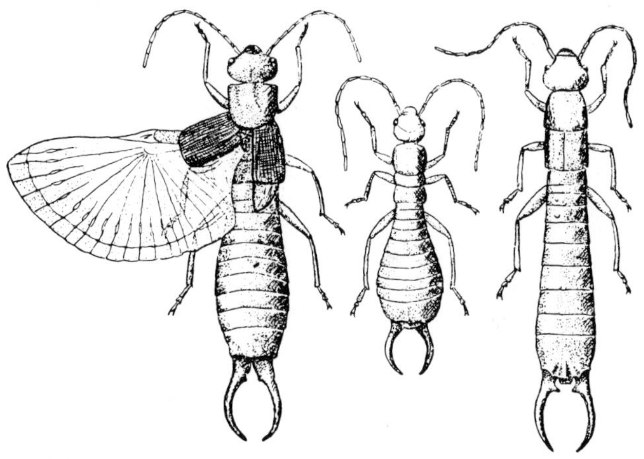

74. The European earwig, *Forficula auricularia* with left wing expanded (left), and two African earwigs, *Esphalmenus* sp. (centre) and *Apterygida* sp. (right).

CLASSIFICATION

ORDER **Dermaptera**

Elongated insects with biting mouthparts. In winged members the forewings are modified into very short leathery tegmina devoid of veins; the hind wings are membranous, have radially arranged veins and are folded in a complex fashion. Abdomen with paired cerci at tip.

SUBORDER Forficulina
Eyes well-developed; cerci unjointed and modified into heavily sclerotised forceps. Free living; wings usually present but may be wingless. This suborder contains the typical earwigs, and is divided into some six families.

SUBORDER Hemimerina
Eyes and wings absent; cerci long, straight and not forcipate. Ectoparasitic on *Cricetomys* and *Beamys* in Africa only.

FURTHER READING

Giles, E. T.: 'The comparative external morphology and affinities of the Dermaptera'. *Transactions of the Royal Entomological Society of London* (1963). 115: 95-164

Hincks, W. D.: 'Dermaptera. The earwigs of South Africa'. *South African Animal Life* (1957). 4: 33-94

Sakai, S.: *Dermapterorum Catalogus Preliminaris.* Parts I-VIII. Daito Bunka University, Tokyo (1970-1973). 1134 pp

Stoneflies 8

Stoneflies belong to the order Plecoptera and are an extremely isolated group, having branched out on their own evolutionary limb at an early stage. Africa as a whole, in comparison with the temperate regions of the world, has very few species, so few people in Africa south of the Sahara notice this interesting group. Adult stoneflies are short-lived and inconspicuous which further accentuates their rarity.

They are medium-sized insects with two pairs of wings, a pair of long, slender antennae, weak biting mouthparts and paired cerci at the end of the abdomen. The name 'Plecoptera' (folded wings) refers to the hind wings of the adult, which are larger than the forewings and are folded fan-wise beneath them when the insect is at rest. They are feeble fliers and spend most of their time resting near water – on stones, the trunks of trees and amid foliage; however they can, if necessary, run quickly.

During the nymphal stage, the insects are dependent on cold, swift-flowing and well-oxygenated water. Hence the female drops her numerous eggs into water where they are dispersed by the current before they fall to the bottom. The eggs hatch into nymphs which have six or seven tufts of gills, and oxygen in the water passes through their thin walls into the insect's respiratory system. Nymphs are actually easier to find than adults and often if you lift a rock from a fast-flowing stream and examine the undersurface you may see a few dark grey insects, rather like small shrimps scurrying around. The best chance of finding stonefly nymphs is underneath rocks that project above the water and have fallen leaves adhering to them.

The stonefly nymph can be differentiated from the mayfly nymph which closely resembles it, in that the stonefly has divergent cerci at the end of the abdomen while the mayfly has three hairlike tails. The aquatic nymphal life may last for up to two years, during which time the nymphs may moult 30 times. By contrast, as adults their lifespan is short and most survive for no more than a few days.

When fully grown the nymph leaves the water and creeps up on to a stone above the surface. Here, while it rests for a time, a split appears along the back of the thorax and the adult fly pulls itself out of the nymphal skin. The cast skin that is left behind is a fascinating object for study under the microscope: the imprints of the eyes, legs, jaws, wing-sheaths, the great airtubes and the front and hind part of the alimentary canal, including the gizzard, can all be clearly seen in the transparent husk.

Two families of Plecoptera occur in Africa. Members of family Perlidae are found from the Cape to the Sahara.

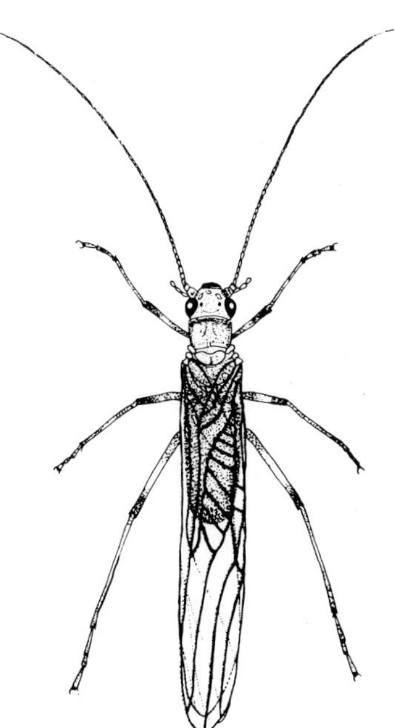

75. A male stonefly, *Neoperla kunensis*, (family Perlidae).

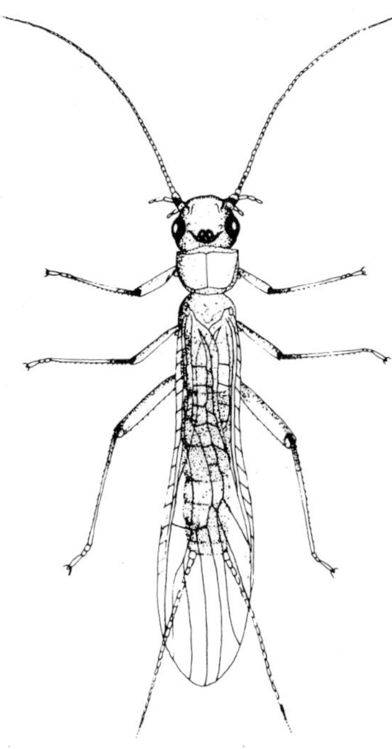

76. A female stonefly, *Aphanicercopsis* sp. (family Nemouridae).

There is only one genus, *Neoperla*, containing a number of species which look very much alike as adults: all are nondescript and greenish-brown, nocturnal in habit and attracted to light. The nymphs can reach a length of 25 mm and are voracious predators, creeping about among the stones on the stream-bed, and devouring any small creatures they capture. A microscopic examination of the eggs is revealing: they bear a number of adhesive papillae by which they are attached to the stream-bed after the female lays her eggs on the surface.

The second family found in Africa is the Nemouridae whose members occur only in southern Africa, where four endemic genera with 21 species have been recorded so far. Most of them are from the clear, cold mountain streams of the southern and southwestern Cape, but some are from the northern and northeastern Transvaal. They are small, elongated stoneflies with silvery-grey wings that, in contrast to the Perlidae, are furled around the abdomen at rest. They differ also in their life habits since both the adults and the nymphs feed only on vegetable matter. The adults are generally active early in the day or when it is dull and drizzly.

CLASSIFICATION

ORDER **Plecoptera**

Elongate, flattened, soft-bodied insects with four wings, usually found near streams. At rest wings are folded flat over abdomen; hind wing with a large anal lobe that is folded fanwise. Antennae long and threadlike, tarsi 3-segmented, long cerci present. Mouthparts chewing, sometimes reduced. Metamorphosis simple, nymphs aquatic.

FAMILY Perlidae
Comprises the single genus *Neoperla* in Africa; nymphs carnivorous, adults non-feeding.

FAMILY Nemouridae
Four endemic southern African genera, *Aphanicercella*, *Aphanicera*, *Aphanicercopsis* and *Desmonemoura*. Adults and nymphs both vegetarian.

FURTHER READING

Hynes, H. B. N.: 'Biology of the Plecoptera'. *Annual Review of Entomology* (1976). 21:135-153

Illies, S.: 'Phylogeny and zoogeography of the Plecoptera'. *Annual Review of Entomology* (1965). 10:117-140

Zwick, P.: 'Insecta: Plecoptera. Phylogenetisches system und Katalog'. *Das Tierreich* (1973). 94, 465pp

9

Grasshoppers, locusts and crickets

The order Orthoptera contains some of Africa's most striking forms of insect life, and the night-sounds, so typical of this continent, are predominantly those of the field crickets, tree crickets and the long-horned grasshoppers. By day short-horned grasshoppers are ubiquitous, and the dreaded dark cloud of a swarm of migrating locusts is a sight feared by most of Africa's peoples. The name Orthoptera means straight-winged, and an examination of a grasshopper will reveal a pair of straight, leathery forewings, called the tegmina. The hind wings are broad and membranous, folded fanwise under the tegmina at rest. Most orthopterans can jump and fly well, but there are many that are wingless, or have very reduced wings.

The sounds made by the various Orthoptera are produced by mechanical means: the apparatus usually consists of a sharp or serrated edge (the scraper) which is rubbed against a file-like surface or ridge (the file). The file and scraper may be located on the wings only, or on the legs and the wings, or on the legs and the abdomen. Some orthopterans employ remarkable means to amplify their sounds, and details of a few will be given later.

The order is divided into two groups: the suborder Caelifera, which contains the familiar locusts and grasshoppers, sometimes called the short-horned grasshoppers because of their stubby antennae; and the suborder Ensifera, which includes the crickets and the long-horned grasshoppers, which have antennae at least as long as the body. We shall deal first with the families of the Caelifera.

Bladder grasshoppers The interesting family Pneumoridae is endemic to southern Africa, although two members of the genus *Physophorina* do occur as far north as Uganda and Tanzania.

The bladder grasshoppers are mostly green in colour but some have a pinkish tinge and others may be beautifully marked with silver or red mottling and stripes. Their colouring is such that they harmonise very well with their surroundings and are difficult to find.

The sound that the male bladder grasshopper makes is so loud and so unlike that made by any other insect that few people hearing it during the night would recognise it for what it is – (most would declare without hesitation that it is the croaking of a large and noisy frog). It is difficult to describe the sound, but the call may best be explained as a long, loud rasping noise, with deep resonance, repeated every few minutes. The volume suggests the owner of such a voice must be at least as large as a bullfrog, yet it is the call of a puny grasshopper about 50 mm long – albeit an insect which looks as if it has been pumped up with air to the point of bursting. It sometimes flies into rooms at night and circles lights. It may be picked up and handled freely as it is quite harmless and cannot bite.

If the insect is held up to the light it will be seen that its body is almost completely hollow and filled with air. A dark line along its belly, about the thickness of a match-stick, marks the position of the digestive organs, the reproductive organs and the nervous system, while a thin line along the back indicates the position of the insect's heart. The rest of the body consists of nothing but air contained in the enormously dilated tracheae. The whole structure of the insect has been profoundly modified so that its body may act as a resonance box to amplify its call. The sound-producing apparatus, or stridulating organ, as it is called, is lodged on each side of the bloated body and consists of a row of raised, hardened spots. These are yellow in colour and resemble a miniature fish backbone when viewed through a hand lens.

Projecting from the inner side of each hind leg is a tiny comb consisting of about a dozen stiff points. This is so situated that when the insect moves its hind legs up and down against the sides of its body the combs rub against the raised dots located there and set up the vibrations that are magnified by the hollow body. This produces the loud call. The male might well be called a perambulating love song, for his loud, far-reaching call is apparently meant to attract his fat, wingless mate.

The female is quite different. Her stout, solid body is of the ordinary grasshopper type, except that her hind legs are not adapted for leaping and her wings are reduced to small stumps. Consequently she can neither jump nor fly. She creeps about in the bushes, not far from the ground, and her colour harmonises so closely with the foliage that she is extremely difficult to find. It is not known where the eggs are laid and the general habits and life histories of these interesting insects have still to be investigated.

Toad grasshoppers The family Pamphagidae contains some remarkably well-camouflaged insects that so closely resemble stones, branches or dead leaves that they are usually only discovered when they move. Some species, like *Trachypetrella andersonii* (found only in South Africa) are short, squat creatures that look very much like little toads, hence the common name of the group. In this and many other species of Pamphagidae, the females are wingless, whereas the males, only half the size of their mates, nearly always have wings.

Members of the genus *Lamarckiana* include some large grasshoppers that are rather less well-camouflaged than most of the family, but their wings and bodies have a bark-like appearance and texture which enables them to blend with the branches upon which they sit.

Pyrgomorphid grasshoppers The family Pyrgomorphidae contains a number of strikingly coloured grasshoppers, which are common throughout Africa, especially in rather dry areas. The bright colours are a warn-

77. Male bladder grasshopper, showing the row of raised bumps that constitute the 'file' on the side of the body. A thin hard ridge (the 'scraper') projects from the inner side of each hind leg, and a loud noise is produced by rubbing the scraper across the file. 50 mm.

78. Wingless female toad grasshopper, showing the hearing organ midway along its body. 52 mm.

79. Contrasting patterns and bright colours of pyrgomorphid grasshoppers that warn predators of their foul taste. 34 mm.

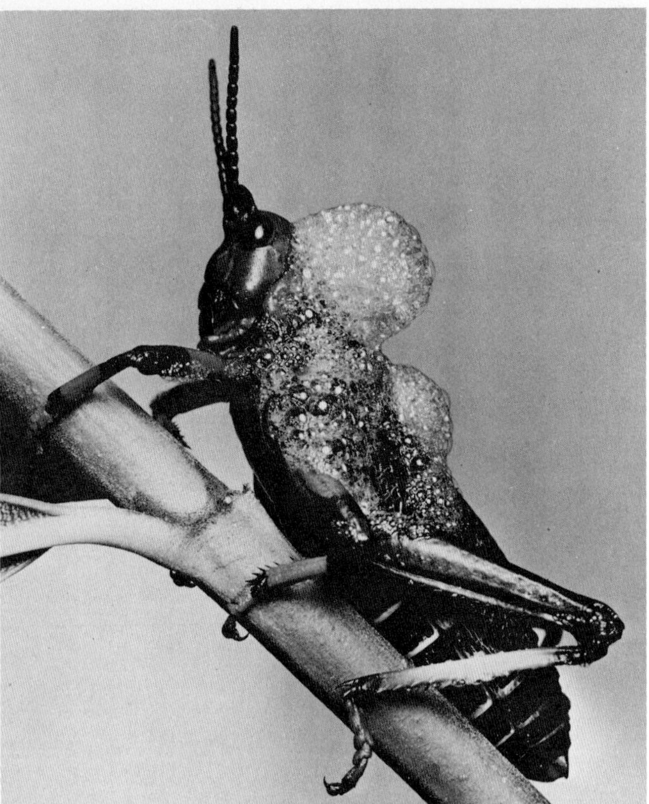

80. A pyrgomorphid grasshopper emits a foul-smelling foam in response to being disturbed. By means of repugnant fluids, these grasshoppers render themselves immune to most predators. 42 mm.

ing to enemies that the pyrgomorphids are evil-tasting and foul-smelling, protected by glands that produce repugnant secretions. An indication of their poisonous potential is illustrated by the case of a child in South Africa who died after eating a *Phymateus leprosus*.

As an example of the group we may take the common milkweed locust, *Phymateus morbillosus*. This heavily-built insect can scarcely hop and is a weak flier. Its favourite food is plants of the milkweed family (Asclepiadaceae). It goes about in small bands when young, but the insects do not travel far and the bands soon break up.

The bright red head, thorax and legs, the purple, yellow-spotted wings and the yellow and purple abdomen of the adult combine to make it one of the most striking and conspicuous of the Orthoptera. It is an excellent example of the phenomenon of aposematic (warning) colouration. A young and inexperienced bird or baboon might be tempted to seize such an easily-caught victim, but it would quickly drop it because of the evil taste, and the predator would soon learn to associate the nauseating smell and flavour with those bright colours.

The milkweed locust, and indeed most of the 'bush locusts', belonging to the genus *Phymateus*, exaggerate the impact of their warning colours by suddenly spreading their brightly coloured wings. They are also protected by a frothy liquid that exudes from openings situated near the bases of the hind legs. This liquid is in fact the insect's blood and it has the same distasteful properties as the rest of its body, but to a greater degree. The froth is given off only if the grasshopper is roughly handled.

The female *Phymateus morbillosus* lays her eggs in the ground. She has four hard, horny points on the tip of her abdomen, present in females of most grasshoppers and locusts. The male has a soft, rounded tip to his abdomen. When the female is ready to lay her eggs she presses the tip of her abdomen against the soil and by steady pressure and a slow turning movement she forces it into the ground. Her abdomen is more or less telescopic and she can elongate it to about one and a half times its normal length. When she has thrust her abdomen right into the soil, so that only her head, thorax, legs and wings are above the surface, she lays her large, yellow, cigar-shaped eggs at the bottom of the hole. Then she emits a frothy fluid that binds the soil particles together and forms a case or pod enclosing the 50-or-so eggs. Finally she scrapes a little soil into the top of the hole and the egg-laying is complete.

A week or so later the female may lay another batch of eggs, and so on until three or four egg-pods complete her contribution to the next generation. She may linger for a time after this, more sluggish than ever and feeding very sparingly, but the cold weather and rain of the late autumn put an end to her existence.

The egg-pod is about 35 mm long and 12 mm thick and is buried 50-75 mm deep in the ground. The eggs are yellow at first but soon turn brown. They lie in the soil all through the winter and hatch only the following spring, or early in the summer. The eggs begin to develop as soon as they are laid, but after a time development stops and there is a long dormant period of five or six months. Development recommences in the spring and then proceeds without check until the young hatch. This embryonic diapause, as it is called, is common among many short-horned grasshoppers; it is a provision of nature to enable the eggs to pass unharmed through prolonged periods of unfavourable weather conditions.

The eggs are placed head-end downwards when they are laid in the soil, but as embryonic development proceeds, a remarkable change takes place: the embryo inside the egg slowly creeps round, as it were, until its head is uppermost and in the best position for hatching. This slow movement inside the egg-shell can be observed if some egg-pods are kept on damp soil in a box. The black eyes of the embryo, which are visible through the thin, translucent covering of the egg, betray the movement.

When the embryo is fully formed and ready to emerge a swelling called the 'egg-burster' appears in the joint between the head and the thorax in the back of its neck. This swelling throbs and eventually bursts the egg-shell, allowing the young grasshopper to wriggle its way out.

At this stage the grasshopper is still enclosed in a thin membranous covering, and it has to struggle up through the frothy plug and then through the soil until it reaches the surface. The first to emerge has the hardest task as the others usually follow its route. The membranous coat is shed as soon as the little insect reaches the outer air and the cast-off membrane shrivels up at once. The tiny white objects strewn around the hole after the young have emerged are their discarded first coats, intended only to protect them during their struggle to the surface. The skin of the larva soon hardens and turns black and it is then ready to move off and feed in company with the rest of the family. It moults six times in the course of its growth and is fully-grown when about three months old.

The elegant grasshopper, *Zonocerus elegans*, is another brightly-coloured member of the family Pyrgomorphidae that is found throughout most of Africa south of the Sahara. Normally it has short, non-functional wings, but occasionally long-winged forms are found. Despite its elegant appearance, it has a disgusting smell, produced by a yellow fluid that it exudes when threatened. In certain areas it is a destructive pest which attacks various crops. Other members of the family that occasionally damage crops are the bush locusts, *Phymateus leprosus* and *Phymateus baccatus*.

An interesting point about all the Pyrgomorphidae is that they lack stridulatory apparatus in the form of a file and scraper, and therefore cannot produce the sounds that are so characteristic of most grasshoppers. Despite this, like most grasshoppers, they have well-developed 'ears', or more correctly, tympanal organs. These are not situated on the head, but on the abdomen, just above the base of each hind wing. If the wings are lifted they are clearly visible to the naked eye as circular depressions on the body. Each is about 3 mm in diameter and is covered by a tightly-stretched membranous eardrum.

Locusts and other acridid grasshoppers Strictly speaking, the term 'locust' should be applied only to those members of the family Acrididae that gather in swarms and migrate from place to place doing damage to crops. Using the name in this restricted sense, there are fewer than a dozen species of locusts in the whole world. On the other hand, there are probably 10 000 different species which belong to the same large family, few of which have common names, and are generally called 'grasshoppers'.

The Acrididae found in Africa may be divided into some 16 subfamilies, and it comes as no surprise to find that much remains to be learnt about the group. The largest subfamilies are the Acridinae, Gomphocerinae and the Catantopinae. Most can jump well and can fly strongly, often revealing brightly-coloured wings when they do so. Many have well-developed spines on their powerful hind legs that are used for self defence, and which will draw blood from the hand of an unwary collector who grapples with a large specimen.

Turning now to the locusts proper of Africa, there are four species to consider. The desert locust, *Schistocerca gregaria*, is the insect referred to in the Bible as one of the plagues of Egypt, and to this day it occurs in vast

81. Fearsome spines on hind leg of large short-horned grasshopper (*Cyrtacanthacris sp.*), which it effectively uses to defend itself.

82. Tropical migratory locusts (*Locusta migratoria*) mating. 54 mm.

83. Female tropical migratory locust forcing her abdomen into the earth as she prepares to lay an egg package. 54 mm.

swarms and may do great damage to crops in north Africa and Asia Minor. A subspecies (called *flaviventris*) is also found in South Africa and Namibia, but swarms only after exceptionally good rains. However the swarms are comparatively small and are soon scattered.

The tropical migratory locust, *Locusta migratoria*, breeds in West Africa and frequently gives trouble in Nigeria and Mali. Scattered individuals of this species are widespread and can appear unexpectedly anywhere. Occasional swarms have formed in recent years in Rhodesia and in the northern Orange Free State in South Africa.

The permanent home and natural breeding-ground of the brown locust, *Locustana pardalina*, is mostly within the borders of South Africa. It is the most important species in the south; when it is abundant and migrates in swarms it often spreads into Namibia, Botswana and Rhodesia.

The red locust, *Nomadacris septemfasciata*, is the most important locust, a well-known pest of tropical Africa, including Mozambique, Malawi, Rhodesia, Angola, Zambia, Zaïre, Tanzania, Kenya, Uganda, Sudan and Ethiopia. Its permanent home is in the region of Lake Rukwa and other shallow central African lakes, but when it is swarming it may extend its range as far as the equatorial area in the north, and Natal and the eastern Cape Province of South Africa in the south.

Let us take this species as our example to describe a locust life history. The red locust is one of the largest species, the adult reaching a length of 70-80 mm from the front of the head to the tips of the folded wings. The full-grown, winged insect lives for about nine months, from April to December, and during this period its colour changes quite considerably. At first it is brown, with transparent wings; later its body turns reddish, the front wings displaying seven distinct brown stripes on them (hence the scientific name *septemfasciata*), and the hind wings turning red at their bases. Later still, in November when the eggs are being laid, the colour changes again to yellow.

When overcrowded in their permanent homes, red locusts form huge swarms and migrate in the direction of the prevailing winds (there have been reports of flying swarms that were 30-60 km in length and 3-8 km wide). As a rule, the swarms fly during the daytime, pausing in dense clusters on trees and bushes to rest, feed and sleep at night. The hungry hordes may travel for about eight months in this way, searching for feeding grounds and suitable climatic conditions and during the course of the search covering hundreds of kilometres.

In November or December, egg-laying begins. This takes place at night and the females deposit their eggs in the ground. Each female that is ready to lay her eggs rests on the ground and forces the tip of her abdomen, which is armed with four, hard, horny points, to a depth of 60-70 mm into the soil. She deposits a neat package of 60-80 eggs in the hole and then squirts a frothy liquid on top of them which hardens to form a plug.

After the egg-laying is over the swarm moves on again, but about a fortnight later the females are ready to deposit more eggs and the process is repeated, probably many kilometres from the spot where the first lot of eggs were laid. Before she dies, each female may lay some 200 eggs in three or four packages.

The eggs hatch in about a month. The newly-hatched hopper is yellowish and wriggles its way up out of the ground, looking very much like a small worm. Within a minute or so of emerging it casts its skin, leaving this behind as a crumpled white speck at the mouth of the hole. Slowly the little insect's new skin hardens and the colour changes, until, by the time it is a few hours old, it is brown with black and yellow markings. At this point it can hop about and feed.

The young hoppers gather together in bands and when they are a few days old begin to move farther afield in search of food. They feed chiefly on plants belonging to the grass family, such as maize, wheat, sorghum and sugar-cane, but they will also devour other kinds of plants such as citrus, cotton and ornamental shrubs.

For a period of two or three months the hoppers have partly-developed wings and can move only by walking and jumping. They grow rapidly, casting their skins six times during this period. Their colour varies, but mostly they are handsome creatures with red, black and yellow markings. After the sixth moult they have fully-grown wings, and at this stage are called 'fledglings' – they can just manage to fly. Gradually their powers of flight improve, until they are capable of extended journeys.

Like other locusts, the red locust has a number of natural enemies that readily take advantage of the rich food source provided by the swarms. Birds such as white storks, marabou storks and kestrels follow the locust swarms and eat great numbers of the insects. The larvae of many different kinds of blister beetles and of various kinds of flies destroy the eggs in the ground. Other fly larvae parasitize the locusts themselves. A fungal disease (caused by *Empusa grylli*) kills numbers of the locusts in swarms during warm, wet weather; the dying insects creep up onto grass stems and bushes where they die. Their dead bodies may often be seen hanging on the stems, covered with the furry growth of the fungus.

Modern man is the most deadly of all the locust's enemies, because he now fights them in their breeding centres as well as in the areas they invade with modern technology and insecticides. It is rather ironic that locusts are destroyed, as although they admittedly constitute a threat to crops and pastures, the insect swarms themselves are a massive food resource of exceptionally high nutritional value to man. Only cultural habits and logistical problems prevent us from utilising this potential source of food at present.

Normally locust plagues are self-limiting, as the invaded areas are unsuitable as permanent homes for such large numbers and the swarms die out after a time. However, some red locusts remain, living as solitary grasshoppers. They are scattered in small numbers and breed in most years in vleis and other grassy areas. Their habits have naturally changed: they no longer move about from place to place and even differ in colour and markings from the locusts that flew in swarms.

Within a few years, however, conditions favourable for the swarming of the red locust – abundant food and few natural enemies – may return to certain places, called the outbreak areas. These include Lake Rukwa in Tanzania and Mweru Wantiba in Zambia. Various factors result in the overcrowding of the outbreak areas, and the locusts enter what is known as the 'swarm phase'.

We know that all locusts go through these two phases, the solitary phase and the swarm, or gregarious phase. Each differs both structurally and biologically. The change from the solitary to the gregarious phase arises as a result of over-crowding in the outbreak areas.

Current locust control is based on concentrated warfare waged in breeding centres. It is designed to keep down their numbers sufficiently to prevent them from entering the swarm phase. Since migrating locust swarms have no regard for political boundaries, co-operation between the countries of Africa is a prerequisite for successful locust control. At Mbala in Tanzania, for example, an international locust control organisation was established to keep constant watch on the permanent homes of the red locust in that region, and to take steps to deal with any swarms that may begin to develop. In Pretoria, South Africa, the Red Locust Control Service has its own helicopter and full-time pilot on standby to take action against the locusts wherever necessary.

A vast amount of research has been done on locusts, and there are many books and numerous scientific papers dealing with all aspects of their biology.

Long-horned grasshoppers or katydids As their name implies, the members of the family Tettigonidae all possess long, slender antennae, which have more than 30 joints and are in fact longer than the body itself. Nineteen subfamilies are currently recognised in Africa; of these the armoured ground crickets are especially striking and are dealt with separately. The remaining members of the family can all be loosely referred to as long-horned grasshoppers, although in the absence of local common names for the African species it seems reasonable to borrow the American name, 'katydid', for the various subfamilies. This comes from the nocturnal song of certain tettigonids in the eastern United States that sounds like 'Katy-did, Katy-didn't', repeated endlessly.

The African katydids have not been studied in any detail, and we do not even know the possible number of species that might occur on the continent. Many are green in colour, they are largely nocturnal and their habit of climbing in bushes and trees makes them difficult to collect and study. The silent females, who lack the stridulatory apparatus of the males, can usually be recognised by a conspicuous sword-like ovipositor.

84. Desert locust hopper *(Schistocerca gregaria)* in its penultimate stage of growth, showing the incompletely developed wings. 36 mm.

85. Adult desert locust showing the fully-developed wings with which these insects can travel many thousands of kilometres in vast food-seeking swarms. 58 mm.

86. Typical long-horned grasshopper or katydid feeding on vegetation. Many members of this family (Tettigonidae) will also readily feed on other insects. 39 mm.

Eggs are laid in the soil, or in flattish slits cut in the bark of bushes and trees by means of the ovipositor.

The males are often loud and persistent singers. They do not stridulate in the same way as do the short-horned grasshoppers, but rub their wings rapidly one over the other. When held together closed, the left front wing usually overlaps the right one and the underside of this wing has fine teeth near the base which form a rasp. This rubs against a special roughened area on the right wing and the vibration thus set up is amplified by the wing acting as a resonator.

Katydids have tympanal organs (their 'ears'), situated in a most extraordinary place – on their front legs. On the tibia of each front leg, just below the femural joint, a slight swelling may be seen. There are usally two longitudinal slits in this swelling. These reveal the external openings of two small cavities, the membranous walls of which are connected to auditory receptors. At the base of each front leg there is an opening, the auditory spiracle, which is connected to a tube (a trachea) that runs up the femur, past the joint, and down to the auditory receptors behind the slits. This arrangement gives the insect a remarkably sophisticated hearing system. When singing, resting or feeding, the katydid is vulnerable to attack, but uses the spiracle and trachea in combination as a very sensitive omnidirectional sound receiver that will alert the insect to potential danger. The slits on the forelegs, on the other hand, are used as unidirectional sound receivers, and the females use this system with a high degree of accuracy to locate singing males.

The true katydids (subfamily Pseudophyllinae) are rare in Africa, the majority being found in tropical regions. They are vegetarian, nocturnal and most species can fly.

The shield-backed katydids (subfamily Decticinae) can be recognised by the large prothorax which extends backwards to cover part of the abdomen. This also covers the tiny wings, which are used only for stridulation and are useless for flying. The decticines are nocturnal, and spend the daytime resting in bushes and dense vegetation. After dark they climb into plants to feed and court.

Cone-headed katydids (subfamily Copiphorinae), have pointed heads, as the name suggests, and powerful, dark-coloured jaws, which contrast with the usually uniform pale-green colour of the insect. These jaws are used for cracking grass seeds, and the katydids can also bite severely if handled carelessly. The copiphorines are found in grassland and savanna; they are nocturnal and the males sing with a very loud and continuous buzz, rather like the sound made by cicadas.

In contrast to these subfamilies, which are vegetarian, the Saginae are exclusively carnivorous and are fierce predators of other insects. They are large and conspicuous katydids, and the genus *Clonia* contains the most species. Also strictly nocturnal, the males sing with a low buzz.

The bush katydids (subfamily Phanopterinae), are widely distributed in Africa and occur in very many

87. A cryptically-coloured female katydid gives a warning display upon being disturbed by suddenly raising and rustling her wings. Note the conspicuous scimitar-shaped ovipositor. 54 mm.

88. Close-up of the wing bases of a male katydid showing the circular patch of wing membrane (known as the 'mirror') which acts as a resonant loudspeaker to amplify the insect's song. Mirror 3 mm diameter.

89. A shield-backed katydid stridulating at night by means of tiny wings used only for sound production, hidden beneath the shield. 22 mm.

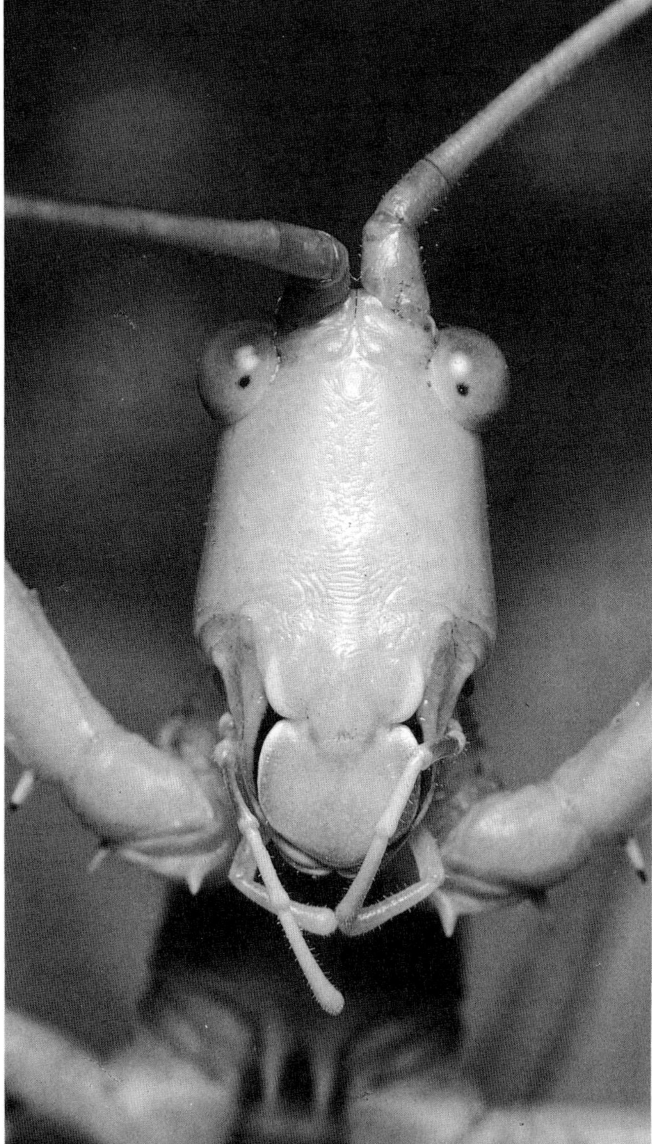

90. 'As mean as he looks . . .', 10 cm long male predatory katydid (*Clonia maculosa*) will not hesitate to sink his sharp mandibles (here hidden behind the upper lip) into a finger of anyone foolish enough to handle him. The normal prey consists of caterpillars.

habitats – they are partial to gardens and other cultivated areas, and are common in Acacia savanna. Many species are winged, nocturnal and uniformly greenish in colour although some have yellowish wing markings. The males sing with a low, rasping sound, not a continuous trill. Eggs are often laid in leaves, which are first split along the edge with the flattened ovipositor.

Armoured ground crickets The large, ungainly insects called koringkrieks, or armoured ground crickets, belong to the subfamily Hetrodinae of the Tettigonidae and thus also qualify as long-horned grasshoppers, despite their bizarre appearance. They are endemic to Africa, where about 12 species have been described. They are widespread, but most abundant and noticeable in the more arid areas of southern Africa.

A very common species, *Hetrodes pupus,* is about 40 mm long and has a stoutly-built body, dark-brown in colour, with two narrow yellow stripes and five rows of spines along the back of its abdomen. On the back of its thorax it has a strong armour-plate around which sharp spines bristle. If this insect were magnified a thousand times it would look rather like one of those fearsome reptiles that became extinct long, long ago. Koringkrieks are greatly feared by some people and have a reputation for being poisonous. However, there is nothing to suggest that they secrete anything other than the repelling fluid commonly found among the Orthoptera. Indeed, lizards have been observed to catch and eat the nymphs of certain koringkrieks. However, they can, and do inflict a sharp bite with their powerful jaws.

If the shield on the back of a male armoured ground cricket's thorax is lifted, the remnants of his wings can be seen. They form a pair of stout, membranous stumps that can move one over the other. By rubbing these stumps rapidly together he produces a loud, rasping note. The female does not display these stumps and is therefore unable to produce any sound. The tympanal organs can be seen just below the knees on the front legs.

The koringkriek has a curious pair of eyes: each is small and hemispherical and projects from the head on a short stalk – something like a crab's eye, except that the stalks cannot be moved. This gives the insect a goggle-eyed appearance, as though its eyes were popping out of its head in a state of perpetual surprise. It is difficult to conceive what view of the outside world such a pair of eyes convey to their owner; certainly the koringkriek must be very short-sighted, but the shape and position of the eyes must allow a wide angle of vision.

Koringkrieks are omnivorous and will feed on both plant and animal material. They may be cannibalistic, and often feed on their fellows that have been killed by vehicles on the roads. Although nocturnal, they are conspicuous when resting on bushes during the day. The males start singing after dark, with a loud, continuous and piercing buzz.

The female apparently uses her long ovipositor to thrust her eggs deep into the soil; these are large, measuring nearly 6 mm in length, oval in shape and white. If a gravid female is killed and dissected only about 14 of these large eggs will be found inside her. The eggs hatch into small koringkrieks exactly like their parents, but black.

It is not known how long they live or how long they take to reach full size, but it seems almost certain there is only one generation per year.

Field crickets The so-called field crickets belong to the subfamily Gryllinae of the family Gryllidae. They are related to the long-horned grasshoppers and also have long, slender antennae, a long ovipositor, tympanal organs on the front legs, and a stridulating organ – present on the wings of the male. Their feet, however, are more like those of the short-horned grasshoppers.

The most common cricket associated with human habitations in Africa is the abundant *Gryllus bimaculatus,* which ranges through Asia, Mediterranean Europe and all of Africa. This is the tireless singer we can hear on any warm evening even in the centre of our largest towns. However, if you try to locate a male cricket by the noise it is making, you will soon discover that it is a practised ventriloquist. When he is chirping, by rubbing one wing over the other, he raises his front wings so that they are free of his sides and there is nothing to interfere with the vibration – consequently the sound is loud and clear. But if he becomes suspicious, he can lower his wings so that the depressed edges touch his sides: this dampens the vibration and muffles the sound, making it seem to come from some distance.

If you listen to the chirping of crickets on several evenings and time the rate at which they chirp, you will find that temperature has a considerable effect on the speed and vigour of their song. If you record this chirping rate at different temperatures, you will be able to draw a graph that will relate the two factors: you will then be able to determine the temperature simply by timing the chirping of the cricket!

The sound of this cricket is produced exclusively by the male, sitting at the entrance of his burrow and seeking to attract a mate. Males sometimes fight with each other over disputed burrows, chirping defiance at one another.

The eggs of most species of garden and household crickets are laid singly in the ground and the young that hatch from them moult six or seven times before they reach full size – a process that takes several months. In many cases the young emerge in spring and are full-grown by the following autumn.

Crickets normally feed on plants, but at certain times of the year some species may enter houses for shelter and get into cupboards and drawers. They often chew holes in clothing and linen and may on occasion do much damage.

There are a number of grylline crickets in Africa, but their nocturnal habits ensure that they are heard rather than seen. The very large *Macrogryllus consocius* occurs along coastal southern Africa, where it burrows in sandy areas. The crickets are subsocial, living in small colonies. At night the ear-piercing songs of the males can be heard from a remarkable distance.

A further six subfamilies of Gryllidae are recorded in Africa. These are seldom encountered by the average person, and are known to only a few specialist entomologists. The exception is the subfamily containing the tree crickets.

91. An armoured ground cricket, or koringkriek, feeding on wild flowers in the Kalahari Desert. 46 mm.

92. Common cricket *(Gryllus bimaculatus)* feeding on a flower – the long ovipositor indicates that this is a female. 28 mm.

93. A pair of Namib Desert dune crickets *(Comicus* sp.) mating. 21 mm.

Tree crickets There are several different species of delicate tree crickets of the subfamily Oecanthinae, that look like pale green ghosts when they come out at night to feed. Despite their frail appearance, some are carnivorous and feed on small insects such as aphids and young caterpillars. The males are persistent and rather pleasing, although monotonous singers. The females cut slits with their ovipositors in the tender young twigs of bushes and trees, in which they deposit their eggs. The punctures are in a neat, regular row along the twig, and often they are so deep that the twig dies as a result. Fruit trees, particularly peach trees, may be injured in this way.

Only one genus is found in Africa, the cosmopolitan *Oecanthus*. The males use an ingenious method to amplify their song. You can observe this for yourself if you locate a singing tree cricket, approach as closely as you can, and then search with a torch amongst the leaves. The male will be found sitting in a pear-shaped hole he has gnawed in a leaf. The front part of his body protrudes through the hole, and when he starts stridulating the front wings are raised and pressed against the leaf, sealing the hole. The little *Oecanthus* can thus be observed employing a phenomenon well-known to acoustical engineers – the so-called sound baffle – to increase the intensity of his call.

Mole crickets Mole crickets belong to the family Gryllotalpidae, and one species *Gryllotalpa africana*, is widespread all over Africa. They are often attracted to lights at night, causing consternation to householders by flopping down on the floor and then scurrying about. At certain times of the year they may be especially numerous, but these 'plagues' do not last long and the mole crickets soon disappear.

In these insects the front legs are highly adapted as digging implements, being very stout and armed with strong teeth. They burrow in damp earth and often disfigure lawns and bowling greens by throwing up small mounds of earth during the night. A male mole cricket beneath a stone in a damp spot in the garden will keep up a shrill whirring song for minutes at a time but its source will be difficult to locate.

These insects seem to feed principally on roots but they may also be carnivorous. Sometimes they do damage in the garden by eating holes in potatoes and strawberries. The females lay their oval, white eggs in groups in holes in the ground.

King crickets Among Africa's most extraordinary and bizarre insects are the large and aggressive king crickets that belong to the family Stenopelmatidae. Males frequently have grotesquely enlarged heads and enormous mandibles. All the stenopelmatids are wingless and nocturnal; most are omnivorous, and some of the larger ones can drag away dead animals as big as frogs.

Many genera of king crickets are endemic to South Africa, and *Henicus monstrosus* is a common species. The male is a little less than 25 mm long and brown in

94. The foot of the Namib Desert dune cricket shows the remarkable modifications that increase the surface area enabling it to walk on loose sand.

95. More often heard than seen, the male African mole cricket (*Gryllotalpa africana*) uses his burrow, usually located near water, as a resonating tube to amplify his harsh and piercing nocturnal call. 36 mm.

96. A female king cricket. These insects are common pests of gardens and lawns, where they excavate their burrows. 52 mm.

97. Viewed from close-up, a male king cricket becomes a nightmarish monster.

colour. There is nothing out of the ordinary about his body and legs, but his head is quite unique, making him one of nature's weirdest-looking creations. If he were magnified to the size of a dog and you were to see him coming along the road, he would look like something out of a particularly hideous nightmare.

First of all, the head is much too large for the puny body and is armed with a pair of jaws that are quite ludicrous. They are long and curved, like a pair of bandy legs, and furnished with four small teeth at the tips. Although he looks fearsome, his jaws are so weak that he cannot even administer an effective nip with them. They are so long and rigid and their tips are so far away from his mouth, that it is difficult to understand what they are used for.

However, like all other insects, he has a second pair of jaws (the maxillae). These are smaller and softer than the mandibles; they are hidden by the large, shield-shaped upper lip that hangs down in front of the mouth, and are armed at the tips with sharp points. Possibly he used his absurdly long mandibles for holding his food while he nibbles at it by means of the second pair of jaws. This is pure conjecture, however, as we know nothing at all about the nature of his food or how he feeds.

On his forehead there are two quaint horns which curve slightly downwards and hanging below the head are two pairs of long, jointed palps, that add to his grotesque appearance. His eyes are small but prominent and he seems to have quite good sight relative to other insects. Despite this he lives in almost perpetual darkness, deep in the ground or under a large stone by day and venturing out only at night.

The female of *Henicus monstrosus* is quite unlike the male, and she looks rather like an ordinary wingless cricket. Her ovipositor is unusual in that it is shaped like a scimitar at the tip of her abdomen.

Gardeners often unearth king crickets who spend the day in burrows underground. The crickets emerge only at night in order to feed. Large members of the genus *Maxentius* live on sandy beaches along the southern African coast, where they are frequently encountered by holiday-makers taking evening walks.

CLASSIFICATION

ORDER **Orthoptera**

Forewing long, narrow, many-veined and somewhat thickened; hind wing broad, membranous, many-veined and folded fanwise under forewing. Wings may be reduced or absent. Mouthparts chewing. Female generally with well-developed ovipositor. Specialised stridulatory and auditory organs often present.

SUBORDER **Caelifera**

Antennae shorter than body, tympanal organs at base of abdomen, hind legs often enlarged for jumping. Stridulatory apparatus frequently on hind-femora and wings or abdomen.

SUPERFAMILY Acridoidea
Hind tarsi, usually also front and middle tarsi, with three segments. Ovipositor present. Important African families are Acrididae, Pyrgomorphidae, Pneumoridae and Pamphagidae. Acrididae, divided into at least 16 subfamilies, contain the majority of species.

SUPERFAMILY Eumastacoidea
Primitive caeliferans, mainly tropical and subtropical, living among bushes. Wings often reduced or absent; tympanal and stridulatory organs absent.

SUPERFAMILY Tetrigoidea
Pronotum enlarged, backward directed process covers abdomen and conceals hind wings; forewings short, scale-like. Frequently found in damp places. Commonly called pygmy grouse locusts. This group is little studied in Africa.

SUPERFAMILY Tridactyloidea
Hind tarsi 1-segmented, middle and front tarsi 1- or 2-segmented. Pygmy sand crickets are little known in Africa. They live near water where they burrow in sandy soil; some species apparently can move above or beneath the water surface.

SUBORDER **Ensifera**

Antennae long, slender, usually as long as body or longer. Auditory organs (when present) located on front tibiae. Stridulatory apparatus, when present, on forewings. Ovipositor long and slender.

SUPERFAMILY Tettigonioidea
Tarsi 4-segmented. Ovipositor sword-shaped. One family, the Tettigonidae, divided into 19 subfamilies collectively known as long-horned grasshoppers. Of these the Hetrodinae (armoured ground crickets or koringkrieks) are distinctive, many of the remaining subfamilies containing the predominantly green or brownish coloured katydids.

SUPERFAMILY Grylloidea
Tarsi 3-segmented. Ovipositor needle-like and cylindrical. Mostly drab, black, brownish, or greenish, nocturnal, ground-dwelling insects. Family Gryllidae contains the Gryllinae (field crickets), Nemobiinae (miniature field crickets), Oecanthinae (tree crickets) and at least four other subfamilies in Africa. Family Gryllotalpidae contains the mole crickets, recognisable by their highly modified forelegs, used for digging.

SUPERFAMILY Gryllacridoidea
Tarsi 4-segmented, usually compressed; usually no tympanal organs on forelegs, stridulatory organs rarely present; ovipositor usually well-developed, sometimes very long. The Stenopelmatidae are the large king crickets which are wingless, nocturnal and burrow in the ground. The Gryllacrididae are wingless or winged, often brownish in

colour and are nocturnal predators of other insects. They spend the day in shelters of rolled leaves that they tie with silk. The family Rhaphidophoridae contains only one African species, *Speleiacris tabulae*, known only from a few caves near Cape Town.

FURTHER READING

Beier, M. (Ed.): *Orthopterorum Catalogus: 1-14*. W. Junk, The Hague (1962-1970). 2160 pp. (Also other papers by the same author).

Dirsh, V. M.: *The African Genera of Acridoidea*. Cambridge University Press, Cambridge (1965). 634 pp

Dirsh, V. M.: 'Acridoidea of Angola'. *Publçoes cult. Co. Diamang. Angola*. (1966). 74: 527 pp

Dirsh, V. M.: *Classification of the Acridomorphoid Insects*. E. W. Classey, Faringdon (1975). 184 pp
(Other papers by the same author).

Harz, K.: *Die Orthopteren Europas*. W. Junk, The Hague (1969, 1975). Vol. I, 750 pp; Vol. II, 939 pp

Johnston, H. B.: *Annotated Catalogue of African Grasshoppers*. Cambridge University Press, Cambridge (1956, 1968). 833 pp. Supplement, 448 pp

Ragge, D. R.: *Grasshoppers, Crickets and Cockroaches of the British Isles*. Warne, London (1965). 299 pp. (Other papers by the same author).

Rehn, J. A. G.: *The Grasshoppers and Locusts (Acridoidea) of Australia*.
Vols. I-III, 326, 270 & 273 pp CSIRO, Melbourne (1952-1957).

Uvarov, B. P.: *Grasshoppers and Locusts: A Handbook of General Acridology*. Cambridge University Press, Cambridge (1966, 1967). Vol. I, 481 pp; Vol. II, 597 pp

10 Zoraptera, webspinners, psocids, thrips and strepsiptera

In this chapter we look at five unrelated orders of insects that are either extremely rare, or else so small as to be overlooked by everyone other than specialist entomologists.

Zoraptera The order Zoraptera is a small group, with only a few species known from Africa. This is largely because the insects are very tiny – 1,5–2,5 mm long – and because they are found only in moist, decaying, woody debris, most often in the crevices and soft rotting wood of fallen logs and stumps. When disturbed, the Zoraptera disappear into cracks in the wood, as they shun light.

The Zoraptera are thought to be related to the cockroaches in certain respects: they have mandibulate mouthparts and the legs are adapted for running. Both winged and wingless individuals may occur in the same species. As the females lay relatively big eggs, they cannot carry more than two or three fully developed eggs at the same time. The Zoraptera apparently scavenge to some extent, feeding on fungi, mites and other tiny creatures.

Webspinners The order Embioptera contains a couple of hundred described species of slender-bodied, yellowish or brownish insects, commonly called 'webspinners'. Fragile, with a very soft, thin skin, they are mostly small (4–8 mm), the males winged and the females wingless. The feature which immediately identifies them and sets them apart from all other insects, is the enlarged first joint of each front tarsus. Inside this segment is a silk gland, and the webspinners make silk-lined tunnels and galleries in which they live in colonies. These silken tunnels are made beneath the bark of trees, under stones and in other damp, dark places. Here the eggs are laid and may be attended by the females.

As the winged males are sometimes attracted to lights at night, they are better known than their wingless mates which remain concealed in the silken tunnels. The males with their smoky grey wings look superficially like miniature flying termites. The insects, which feed chiefly on dead plant material, are active and can run backwards rapidly if disturbed.

Psocids The insects placed in the order Psocoptera, which contains some 1 700 known species, are very small, soft-bodied creatures with long, slender antennae. They are commonly called booklice, barklice or psocids, but the latter name is to be preferred because the Psocoptera should not be confused with the true lice (order Phthiraptera).

Most householders are familiar with the tiny brown insects so often seen running over books and papers, particularly if they have been stored in a damp place. These are psocids of the genus *Liposcelis*, and they feed on the paste and glue of the bookbindings, and on dried cereal products. Some species are of economic significance because of the damage they do to stored grain, and *Liposcelis bostrychophilus* has been responsible for spoiling dried meat products in South Africa.

Quite a number of different species of psocid are found in Africa and some are very common, although they escape attention because of their small size and hidden ways. Some of them are winged, with two pairs of delicate, membranous wings that are carried roofwise over their backs when at rest. Others are wingless. They are to be encountered in all sorts of places – under the bark of trees, on weathered palings and walls, in birds' nests, amid moss, in chaff and straw, and so on. Although some of the species mentioned earlier may attack stored products, most are scavengers and do little harm, as they eat fragments of animal and vegetable matter, lichens, moss and fungi.

Sometimes psocids are to be found in numbers in the nests of solitary bees, feeding on the larvae that have died and on the store of honey and pollen. Most of them are gregarious and individuals at all stages of development may be found living together. Some species spin thin silken webs as a cover under which they live.

The second pair of jaws of these insects, the maxillae, is armed with a stiff rod on each side, forked at the tip. The rod is known as the 'pick' and it slides up and down in a groove. This apparatus is used to rasp off small fragments of food, and it is said the psocids' mouthparts are responsible for the faint sound of ticking sometimes heard coming from books and papers.

Thrips About 5 000 species of thrips have been described; they belong to the order Thysanoptera. These tiny insects seldom attract any attention because of their size and sober colouring: few exceed 2 mm in length and nearly all are black, brown or yellow.

They are common enough on flowers, especially those of the daisy type, and most of them feed on the juices of plants, piercing the tissues with their peculiar mouthparts and sucking up the sap. Some of them are predaceous and feed not only upon aphids but their own kind. Usually they have two pairs of narrow wings fringed all round with long hairs. The name of the order Thysanoptera means 'fringed wings' and refers to this characteristic feathery outline of the wings. The feet are peculiar in that at the tip each has a curious bladder which can be withdrawn when not in use; but if the insect is walking over a smooth surface, such as a leaf, these bladders can be extended and enable the thrips to cling securely.

A common and widely spread thrips which is a pest is the onion thrips, *Thrips tabaci*. The full-grown insect is only about 1 mm in length and varies from yellow to light brown in colour. Among other plants, it feeds on onions and if it multiplies rapidly, whitish-silvery patches appear on the leaves as a result of the damage they cause. These patches spread, particularly in dry weather, and eventually the leaves curl up and wither. The insects are difficult to detect, not only because of their diminutive size but also because they hide beneath the leaf-bases and amid the dead leaves, but the harm they do is evident enough.

Her microscopic, kidney-shaped eggs are inserted by the female into minute slits in the leaves where they hatch in about a week. The young larva is like its parents, but white, with bright red eyes and without wings; it feeds on the sap of the leaves. After the second moult, wing-pads appear on the back and the insect assumes what is known as the pre-pupal stage. It can move about, but it does not feed and usually it remains hidden. It then casts its skin again and becomes a pupa with long wing-pads and with its antennae bent back over its head. It does not feed and moves very little during this stage. Finally, for the fourth time, it casts its skin and becomes an adult.

The greenhouse thrips, *Heliothrips haemorrhoidalis*, comes from Brazil, and has been spread all over the world, including Africa. Although restricted to greenhouses as a pest in cooler countries, it flourishes out of doors in Africa and attacks many different kinds of plants. In pine plantations the female lays her eggs, ten to 20 in number, within the tissues of the pine needles. In about ten days the eggs hatch into tiny, white young which feed in colonies on the surface of the needles and cause them to turn from a healthy green to a mottled yellow, with black spots from the insects' excreta.

The larval stages last for two or three weeks, during which time the insects moult twice, changing to a prepupa at the last moult. This stage lasts but a few hours, and the insect then changes into a pupa. Some five days later the winged adult emerges, only about 1 mm in length, black and with white legs.

The insect breeds continuously throughout the year – there are some 12 generations annually – so it is not surprising that when weather conditions are favourable it can multiply very rapidly and do great harm to the trees by destroying the foliage. It has been found that the correct thinning and pruning of the pine trees, so that they do not grow too thickly, reduces the problem of thrips quite effectively.

There are very many known species of Thysanoptera in Africa, some of them confined to indigenous vegetation and others pests of cultivated crops. Citrus is especially vulnerable to damage by thrips, which feed on the tiny fruits when they have just set. As the oranges grow, the feeding marks expand as unsightly blemishes, making the fruit unattractive to buyers. Thrips are also important as the transmitters of various plant viruses.

Strepsiptera The order Strepsiptera contains about 300 known species of tiny insects that range from 1–4 mm in length, and are seldom encountered by anyone other than specialist entomologists. The sexes in Strepsiptera are quite different: the male is remarkable in that the forewings are reduced to short, club-like structures, while the hind wings are large and fanlike, with a few weak veins. His antennae are also peculiar, having one or more segments with lateral processes, which give a branched appearance. The females on the other hand are wingless, often lack legs and antennae and live as internal parasites of other insects, which they never leave.

Each female produces numerous tiny larvae, which have well-developed legs and are very active. The larva seeks out a new host – be it a wasp, bee or planthopper – and enters the body of the host to moult into a legless stage. It seldom kills the host, but does cause a certain amount of injury; sometimes the parasite protrudes from between the abdominal segments of the host.

These interesting parasites have been little studied, and only three species are known from South Africa. Several more are known from the rest of Africa, but no doubt the vast majority still await discovery and description.

CLASSIFICATION

ORDER **Zoraptera**

Minute insects, 3 mm or less; antennae 9-segmented, threadlike or beadlike. Tarsi 2-segmented. Wings present or absent; when present four, membranous, forewing slightly larger than hind wing. Wings are eventually shed to leave short stubs on thorax. Cerci at tip of abdomen short, 1-segmented.

ORDER **Embioptera**

Small insects, 4-7 mm, slender bodied. Tarsi 3-segmented, with basal segment of front tarsi greatly enlarged. Legs short, hind femora thickened. Antennae threadlike, 16-32 segmented. Mouthparts chewing, cerci at tip of abdomen 1 or 2-segmented, usually asymmetrical. Three families are recognised, Embiidae being the largest, Teratembiidae and Oligotomidae are small. Very many new species of African Embioptera are awaiting description.

ORDER **Psocoptera**

Small, soft-bodied insects less than 5 mm long; wings present or absent, if present four, held rooflike over the body at rest. Antennae long and threadlike, mouthparts chewing, face somewhat bulging. The order is divided into three suborders, each containing a number of families. A recent account of the South African fauna lists representatives of 16 families.

ORDER **Thysanoptera**

Slender, minute insects, 0,5-2 mm long, pale or dark. Antennae short, 6-9-segmented. Wings, when present, four in number, long and nar-

98. A webspinner, showing the swollen first joint of the front tarsus, in which the silk gland is housed. 19 mm.

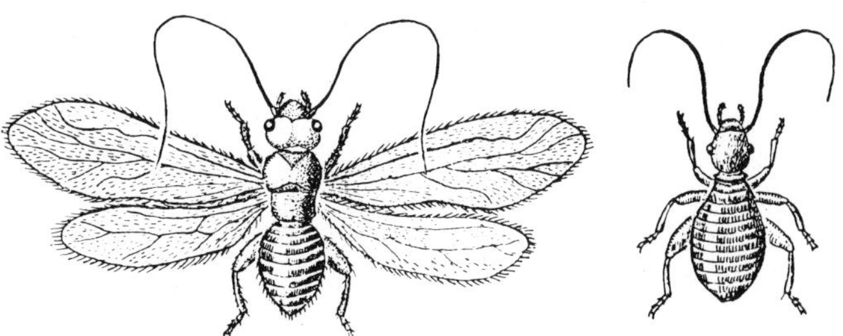

99. A winged psocid found on the bark of trees (left) and the wingless booklouse, *Liposcelis divinatorius*.

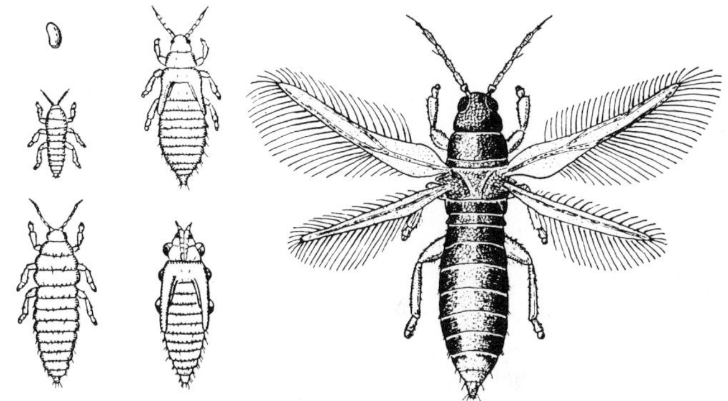

100. The development of the greenhouse thrips, *Heliothrips haemorrhoidalis*. The adult is only 1 mm long.

101. A paper wasp that has been 'stylopised', or parasitized by a strepsipteran. The parasite can be seen as a dark lump protruding between two of the dorsal abdominal segments near the rear end of the wasp.

row, fringed with long hairs and with few or no veins. Tarsi 1- or 2-segmented, with swollen tips. Mouthparts asymmetrical, in the form of a conical beak at base of head. The order is divided into two suborders, the Terebrantia and the Tubulifera. The latter contains a single family, the Palaeothripidae with more than 300 genera, while the family Thripidae of the Terebrantia contains more than 160 genera, and most of the species that are injurious to crops.

ORDER **Strepsiptera**

Minute insects, 1,5-4 mm. Males have forewings reduced to clublike structures, hind wings are large and fanlike. Eyes bulging. Antennal segments with lateral processes. Female wingless, living as an endoparasite in various insects belonging to orders Blattodea, Mantodea, Orthoptera, Thysanoptera, Hemiptera, Diptera and Hymenoptera. Nine families of Strepsiptera are recognised, of which representatives of the Elenchidae, Stylopidae and Halictophagidae have been recorded from South Africa.

FURTHER READING

Gurney, A. B.: 'A synopsis of the order Zoraptera with notes on the biology of *Zorotypus hubbardi* Caudell.' Proceedings of the Entomological Society of Washington (1938). 40:57-80

Jacot-Guillarmod, C. F.: 'Catalogue of the Thysanoptera of the world'. I-III. *Annals of the Cape Provincial Museums (Natural History)* (1970-1974). 7: 1-515

Kinzelbach, R. K.: 'Morphologische Befunde an Fächerflüglern und ihre phylogenetische Bedeutung (Insecta: Strepsiptera)'. *Zoologica, Stuttgart* (1971). 119: 1-256

Lewis, T.: *Thrips, their Biology, Ecology and Economic Importance.* Academic Press, London & New York (1973). 350 pp

Ross, E. S.: 'Biosystematics of the Embioptera'. *Annual Review of Entomology* (1970). 15: 157-172
(Many other important papers by the same author).

Smithers, C. N.: 'A Catalogue of the Psocoptera of the World'. *Australian Zoologist* (1967). 14: 1-145

Smithers, C. N.: 'The Classification and Phylogeny of the Psocoptera'. *Memoirs of the Australian Museum, Sydney,* (1972). 14. 351pp
(Many other important papers by the same author).

Weidner, H.: 'Die Ordnung Zoraptera oder Bodenläuse'. *Entomologische Zeitschrift, Frankfurt* (1969). 79: 29-51

Lice 11

Today lice are generally considered to belong to one order, Phthiraptera, although in the past their classification was different. Closely related to the booklice (see Chapter 10), they are wingless and dorsoventrally flattened, and have reduced eyes or none at all. They are permanent ectoparasites of birds and placental mammals and cement their eggs or 'nits' onto the feathers or hair of their host.

These eggs hatch into nymphs which undergo three moults before reaching adulthood and the entire life cycle is completed on the host; lice cannot survive for long away from the warm body of a living bird or mammal. They are spread mainly by close contact such as between parent and young. Furthermore, many of them are host specific; consequently merely by examining the louse, an expert can tell from what animal it has come.

Four suborders are recognised: three have chewing mouthparts and occur on birds and mammals and the fourth, the Anoplura, has mouthparts adapted for sucking blood. Many lice are important in the veterinary field for the damage inflicted on livestock and poultry, and human lice have been responsible for major disease epidemics.

Human lice Man is host to three species of lice and it is only within very recent times that he has had the chemical means to rid himself of these insects that have been his intimate companions for thousands of years.

The crab louse, *Pthirus pubis,* lives in the coarse pubic hairs, although heavy infestations may spread all over the body. Although only about 2 mm long, it is easily recognised by its crablike appearance and pale grey colour. Normally it spreads from person to person during close bodily contact and frequently people are unaware that they have been infected until some time afterwards when the eggs, which are firmly cemented onto the pubic hairs, hatch and the nymphs reach adulthood. At this point their bites become an irritation, for crab lice tend to remain attached for a long time while sucking blood, and leave characteristic marks on the skin where they have been feeding.

The application of powders containing pyrethrin or carbamates controls crab lice, but as the eggs are impervious to the insecticide, treatment must be repeated at weekly intervals. Those with whom infected people have been in intimate contact must also be treated.

The African gorilla is host to a crab louse very much like our own called *Pthirus gorillae,* but as the gorilla is so much more hirsute, the lice range over the whole body.

Pthirus pubis is not considered an important vector of human disease, nor is the head louse, *Pediculus capitis.* The female, during her adult lifespan of a month, starts to lay eggs at a rate of three to five a day until she has deposited between 100 and 200, after which she dies. The three moults occur over a 21 day period – a fairly lengthy nymphal stage.

This insect is largely restricted to the hair on the head, attaching itself firmly to individual hairs and sucking blood from the scalp. Head lice are spread easily by close body contact, stray hairs and even the innocuous 'borrowing' of brushes and combs; epidemics often occur among schoolchildren even under extremely sanitary conditions, to the consternation of parents and teachers alike. However, the lice are easily controlled by the application of shampoos containing insecticide – soap and water alone are futile.

The body louse, *Pediculus humanus,* concentrates in those areas of the body which are constricted by clothing such as the armpits, waist and shoulders. They cannot travel far from the host and as a result are spread through contact with affected people or their clothing. The females lay up to 300 eggs which take about a week to hatch. In contrast to the head louse, the nymphal stage of the body louse is only ten days and it can therefore multiply rapidly.

Continual feeding by large numbers of lice causes

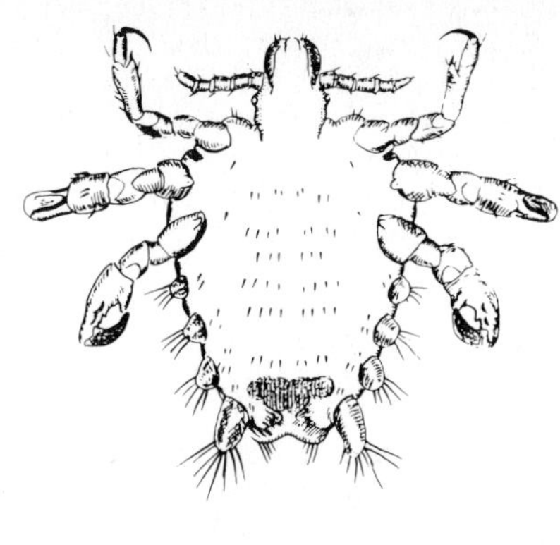

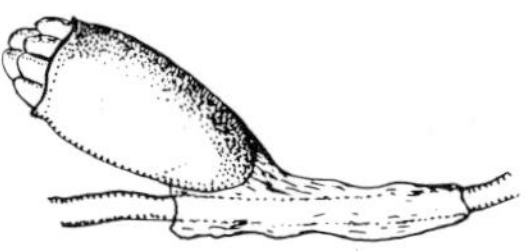

102. The crab louse, *Pthirus pubis,* and its egg cemented to a pubic hair. 3 mm.

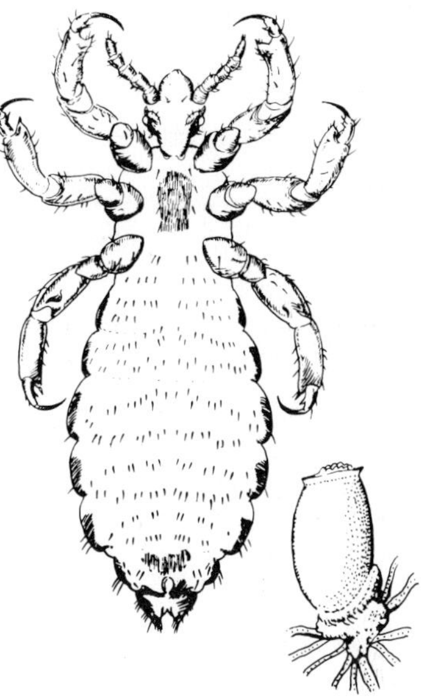

103. The body louse, *Pediculus humanus,* and its egg cemented to clothing. 4 mm.

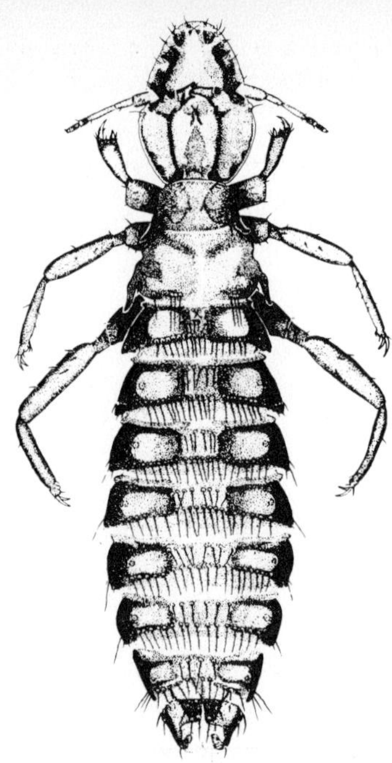

104. A bird louse of the family Philopteridae, which is a parasite of large eagles *(Falcolipeurus quadripustulatus)*. 8 mm.

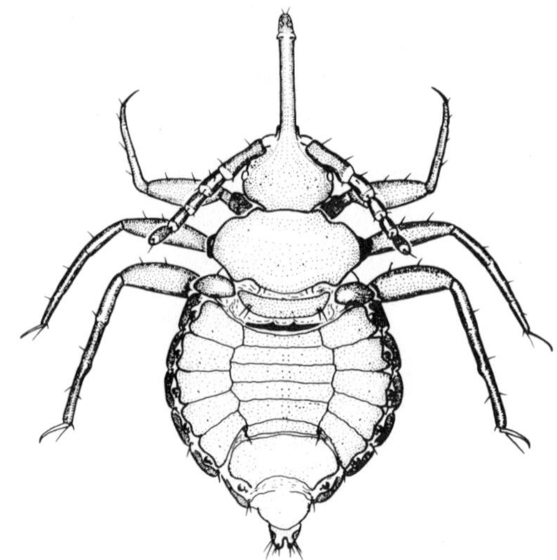

105. The elephant louse, *Haematomyzus elephantis*. 3 mm.

intense discomfort and may even lead to illness. Some individuals seem to tolerate lice fairly easily – a man examined in 1940 had more than 25 000 in his clothing which is probably a world record for lousiness.

Pediculus humanus is of the utmost medical importance because of its rôle in the spread of epidemic relapsing fever caused by *Borrelia recurrentis* and epidemic typhus caused by *Rickettsia prowazeki*. Typhus has afflicted man since antiquity and still can arise when people are crowded together under deprived conditions such as during times of war, famine or natural disaster. But the discovery of DDT, to which lice are extremely susceptible, has largely nullified their menace and it is now comparatively easy to rid whole populations of these dangerous parasites.

It has been said that prior to the discovery of DDT, lice played a far more important part in history than all the great militarists put together. During World War One, Russia alone is believed to have lost three million people to typhus but when this disease threatened during the Second World War, the timely application of DDT in large-scale 'delousing campaigns' averted disaster. Today new and equally effective insecticides are used.

Bird lice We frequently hear stories that 'lice' from birds nesting around the house are biting the human occupants. The actual culprits are invariably blood-sucking mites (Acarina) for bird lice do not readily leave their hosts nor do they have mouthparts suitable for piercing the human skin.

Most birds are parasitized by several lice belonging to the families Menoponidae and Philopteridae and close study of these insects has revealed a fascinating relationship between parasite and host that has evolved over millions of years of close association. Young cuckoos, for instance, are not infected by lice from their foster parents; they become infested only through contact with members of their own species.

Bird lice range in size from less than 1 mm to the giant *Laemobothrion* species which may be more than 10 mm long. In order to survive, the lice have been forced to make morphological adaptations, depending on which part of the bird's body they infest. For example, the stout, rounded head lice are sharply differentiated from the slender, elongated wing lice which must move fast to avoid being eaten by the bird when it preens. The head lice are not threatened in this way and selection has favoured a completely different and slow-moving form.

It is interesting to note that if a bird has a damaged or deformed beak, the number of lice increases dramatically because the bird is unable to preen effectively.

Bird lice have evolved differently to take advantage of the various niches offered by their habitat. Some of the Menoponidae which feed extensively on blood have sharp mandibles that can pierce the young growing feathers. Other Menoponidae drill holes into the wing feathers and actually live inside the quill. Members of the genus *Piagetiella* which belong to this family too, go further and live inside the throat pouches of pelicans and cormorants where they feed on blood and skin, but come out at breeding time to lay their eggs on the feathers of the head and neck. Most of the Philopteridae feed exclusively on feathers and have special digestive enzymes to break down the tough keratin of which feathers are made.

In economic terms bird lice are of particular importance when they affect poultry since irritation causes the birds to lay fewer eggs and gain little weight.

Mammal lice Most African mammals are parasitized by sucking lice of the suborder Anoplura and biting lice of the family Trichodectidae. Although there is no record of lice being found on lions, this may well be because few attempts have been made to collect them. It is unlikely, however, that they do not harbour them and they are quite possibly host to a *Felicola* similar to the species that occurs on the domestic cat. Even the elephant is not immune to attack from lice, and tiny *Haematomyzus elephantis* may be found attached behind the ears, or in folds of skin on the body. These lice are peculiar creatures with biting mandibles placed at the end of a long proboscis.

Seal lice are fascinating in that they have special valves in their spiracles to prevent water from entering when their hosts are in the sea. Their breeding is timed to coincide with that of the seals, so that this part of the life cycle takes place on land.

Bats appear to be one of the few groups of mammals that are free of lice. However, as lice are found on other insectivores, it is thought that bats may once have been infested with lice, but that these were eliminated by flies belonging to the families Streblidae and Nycteribiidae, which are very successful ectoparasites of bats.

In the same way that selection has favoured certain forms of bird lice according to the parts of the host's body they infect, so mammal lice have made similar adaptations, however, little is known about the subject. Most of the investigations so far have been on domestic animals, since infestations of lice on sheep and cattle are a serious veterinary problem.

CLASSIFICATION

ORDER **Phthiraptera**

Small, wingless flattened permanent ectoparasites of birds and mammals. Antennae short, 3-5 segmented, sometimes concealed in grooves in head.

Key to Suborders:

1 Third antennal segment pedunculate; maxillary palps present .... Amblycera
Third antennal segment not pedunculate; no maxillary palps **2**
2 Piercing mouthparts comprising a sac containing three fine stylets ....Anoplura
Biting mouthparts with conspicuous mandibles **3**
3 Mandibles borne at end of long proboscis ....Rhynchophthirina
Mandible not borne at end of long proboscis ....Ischnocera

SUBORDER Amblycera
Four families occur in Africa. The only representative of the Boopidae is *Heterodoxus spiniger*, a parasite of dogs and jackals. There are about ten species of *Ricinus* (Family Ricinidae) known from African passerine birds, while some eight species of *Laemobothrion* (family Laemobothriidae) are known to occur in Africa. The rest of the Amblycera fall into one large family.

FAMILY Menoponidae
These lice are found on nearly all kinds of birds. Approximately 300 species are known from Africa, contained in 46 genera. Many genera are confined to a single host family, like *Psittacomenopon* from parrots, *Bucerophagus* from hornbills and *Plegadiphilus* from ibises.

SUBORDER Ischnocera
Two families are recognised, the Philopteridae, which have two claws on each leg and occur only on birds, and the Trichodectidae, which have a single claw on each leg and occur only on mammals.

FAMILY Philopteridae
More than 500 species are known from African birds, contained in 75 genera. There is a high degree of host specificity in these lice, and they also exhibit a wide range of morphological types, as indicated by the large number of genera involved.

FAMILY Trichodectidae
About 140 African species belonging to seven genera are known. Four genera occur only on hyraxes and are of great interest in elucidating the relationships of their hosts. *Damalinia* is an important genus on wild antelopes and domestic stock, while *Felicola* occurs on most of the carnivores.

SUBORDER Rhynchophthirina
This contains one family, one genus and two species, parasitic on elephants and warthogs.

SUBORDER Anoplura
The latest classification divides the Anoplura of Africa into 12 families with 25 genera and about 170 species. Some of the families are small, like Hybophthiridae for the single species of *Hybophthirus* on the aardvark, Neolinognathidae for two species of *Neolinognathus* on elephant-shrews, Pthiridae for two species of *Pthirus* from man and gorillas, and Pediculidae for the three species of *Pediculus* on man and chimpanzees. The biggest families are Hoplopleuridae and Polyplacidae, mostly on rodents, Linognathidae on antelopes and important parasites of livestock, and Haematopinidae, which are very big lice found on pigs, bovines, horses and zebras.

FURTHER READING

Ledger, J. A.: *The Arthropod Parasites of Vertebrates in Africa South of the Sahara.* Volume IV. *Phthiraptera (Insecta).* South African Institute for Medical Research, Johannesburg (1979). 320 pp.

Bugs 12

Some people refer to any insect as a 'bug', but to the biologist a bug is a member of the order Hemiptera, one of the largest groups of insects, and certainly one of the most important from the economic point of view. The members of this order vary widely in size, shape, habits and life histories, but all have mouthparts that are adapted for piercing and sucking, and these mouthparts nearly always take the form of a distinctive beak-like proboscis. Bugs live entirely on liquids, such as the sap of plants or the blood of other living creatures and they have no mandibles for chewing. Many are wingless and the wings of the remainder vary in structure, consequently it is impossible to derive a general definition. The name of the order, Hemiptera, which means 'half-winged', refers only to the type of wings found among some of the bugs. This enormous group of insects includes stink bugs, twig wilters, aphids, scale insects, white flies, cicadas, bed bugs, water bugs and a host of others.

We divide this vast assemblage of bugs into two suborders, the Homoptera and the Heteroptera. In the former group the forewings, when developed, are more or less uniform and are generally held roof-like over the abdomen. However, the forewings of the Heteroptera are generally divided into a thick and horny basal part, and a membranous outer part. Furthermore, they are usually folded flat on the abdomen, with the tips of the two wings overlapping.

The Homoptera This suborder contains such well-known insects as cicadas, leaf-hoppers and aphids. Also included, however, are the scale insects and mealy bugs which are so highly modified that they would probably not be recognised as insects by the uninitiated. The Homoptera are traditionally divided into two series: the Auchenorrhyncha, with three-segmented tarsi and short, bristle-like antennae; and the Sternorrhyncha, that have one- or two-segmented tarsi and long, thread-like antennae, unless legs or antennae or both are lacking. Further details of the classification of the group may be found at the end of the chapter.

Lanternflies Some of the larger members of the family Fulgoridae are handsome insects with brightly-coloured wings and they may easily be mistaken for butterflies or moths. However, closer examination of the antennae and the jointed beak beneath the head will reveal their true character as plant bugs. In many lanternflies the front of the head is elongated to form a hollow, horn-like projection and it was once believed that this part of the body was luminous – hence the name of lanternflies (in the genus *Zanna* the head is so elon-

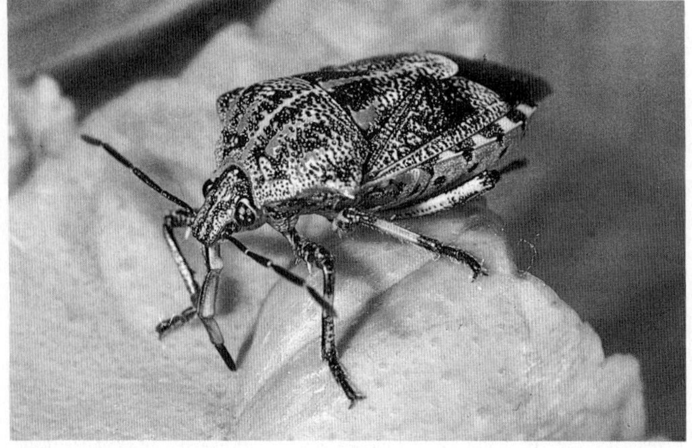

106. A shield bug, feeding on sap from a citrus leaf, showing the distinctive beak-like proboscis with which it pierces and sucks. 13 mm.

gated that the whole insect looks like a broken twig). Certain species display equally unusual attributes at their hind ends, secreting long threads of white wax which trail from the abdomen, as they fly. The young are often covered with similar long, curled, waxy filaments, which make them very conspicuous as they feed in groups on the sap of a twig or leaf.

The adults of some species of the family Flatidae occur in two quite different colours. Some may be green, others red, and when the insects congregate – as they often do – they sometimes arrange themselves with the red individuals below and the green ones above, so that they resemble a spike of red flowers with green buds. The family is well represented in Africa, the larger, showy members of this group being mainly tropical. Many smaller, less conspicuous species are found outside the tropics.

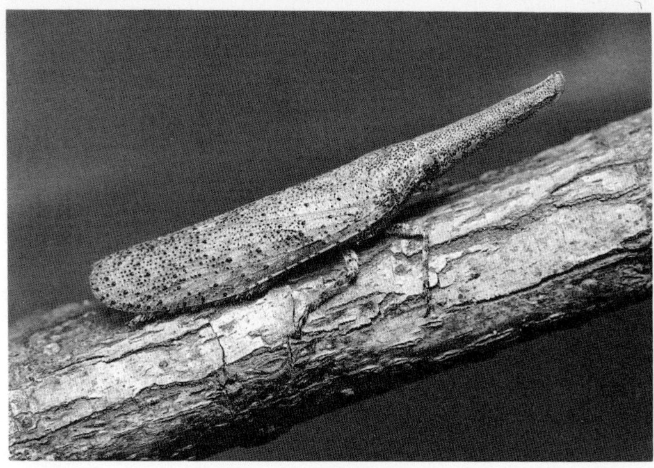

107. A fulgorid bug (*Zanna* sp.), whose resemblance to a broken twig almost certainly affords it good protection from would-be predators. 24 mm.

Froghoppers and spittle bugs Small, spittle-like masses of white foam, or 'cuckoo-spit', may often be seen on the twigs and leaves of different plants. These shelter the immature plant bugs known as froghoppers, thus named because the adult is shaped rather like a tiny frog and can leap well. Sometimes called spittle bugs, these insects belong to the family Cercopidae.

If a patch of the cuckoo-spit is disturbed with a match-stick the owner of the bubbly home will be found inside. He is a stout, soft-bodied insect, usually green in colour, though some species have dark markings. He moves sluggishly, ill at ease when forcibly removed from his watery home, and will soon die if exposed to hot sunshine and allowed to dry out.

The froghopper feeds on the sap of the plant. This is a weak solution of sugars and salts and the insect has to imbibe a great deal in order to obtain sufficient nourishment; its watery excretion, therefore, is copious. Along each side of its abdomen a membranous flap folds under the belly. These flaps meet, enclosing a space between themselves and the underside of the abdomen. This chamber contains the spiracles. It is opened and shut by a valve situated near the anus. Glands that extrude a waxy secretion are located near this valve and consequently the insect's liquid excrement is mixed with this secretion. By flexing its tail in and out, the froghopper forces both air and liquid through the valve, thus producing the innumerable small bubbles that form its foamy home. These spread round and over the insect and serve to protect the insect from the hot rays of the sun and conceal it from its enemies. The bubbles do not burst for some time because they are strengthened by the waxy secretion, and, as they are being constantly renewed by the froghopper, the foam provides a cool shelter for the insect as long as it is feeding.

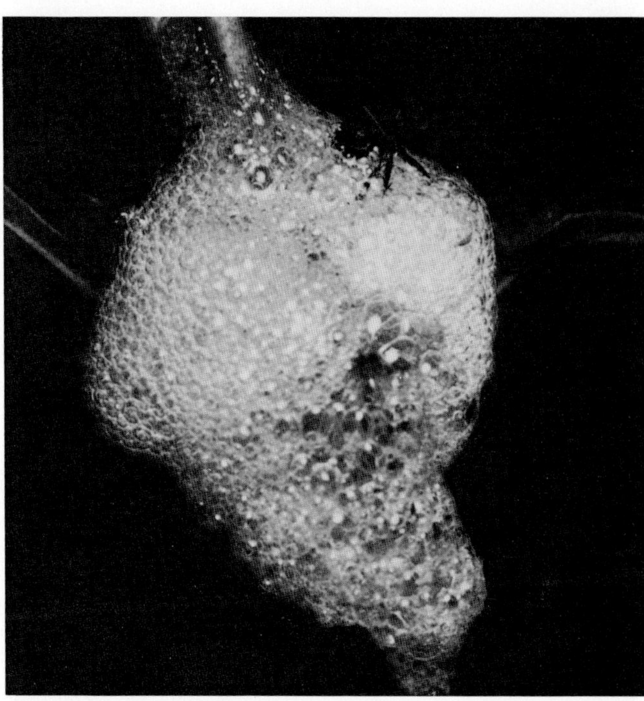

108. A mass of foam produced by a single spittle bug nymph within. Note two ants trapped in the viscous liquid.

Eventually, when it is fully grown, the froghopper leaves the foam and casts its skin for the last time. The wing-buds on its back expand into a pair of stiff wings which it holds roofwise, over its back. These have a pair of delicate, membranous wings folded beneath them. Most froghoppers are small – only about 6-8 mm in

109. Here the spittle, produced from plant juices which the nymph sucks, has been removed to reveal the froghopper nymph responsible. 7 mm.

length and dull in colour – but some are brightly coloured in red, yellow and black. The members of this family are distinguished by their shape, their leaping abilities and by the prominent spines, and the cluster of shorter spines at the apex of the tibiae of the hind legs.

Cicadas Perhaps the most characteristic feature of a hot, drowsy day in Africa is the shrill call of cicadas. Only the male cicadas sing: the females are voiceless. If one of these insects is captured it is easy to determine the sex through an examination of the insect's underside. At the tip of the abdomen the female has a sharp ovipositor which is, naturally, absent in the male who displays instead two semi-circular plates, called opercula, at the base of the abdomen, just behind the hind legs. These cover his sound-producing organ.

This organ, which is so characteristic of the cicada family, consists of a cavity on either side of the abdomen in which the 'drums' or 'timbals', the folded membranes and the 'mirrors' are lodged. The 'timbals' are folded membranes resembling miniature drums, with strong muscles attached to them. Through the contraction and expansion of these muscles the timbals are made to vibrate and so sound is produced, in much the same way as a sound can be produced by pressing the bottom of a tin vessel in and out.

The folded membranes on each side of the cavity simply act as sounding boards to increase amplification. If one of the opercula is lifted with the point of a pin, the mirror – which seems to function as an ear – can be seen at the back of the cavity as a small, white, round, shining plate. The timbal is at the side of the cavity and not so easily seen in the captive – and therefore silent – insect; the folded membrane, in front of the mirror, is also not readily detected when the insect is silent. The female lacks this sophisticated apparatus, but she does have a pair of mirrors at the base of her abdomen that serve as her ears.

By raising or lowering the opercula, the male can increase or diminish the volume of its sound. This action also has a ventriloquial effect, making it difficult for the human listener to locate the exact source of the sound.

Two or three cicadas will generally be found close together on a tree, their beaks embedded in the branch, feeding on the sap. One or more will be male, singing tirelessly, while the silent members will be female. It is believed the loud song serves as an assembly call, and that it may also have a stimulating effect on the mating instinct.

The cicada has four membranous wings, stiff and flat and held roofwise over the body. It has two large compound eyes, with three small simple eyes between them. The antennae are short, black and threadlike. Its mouthparts are of the true bug type, consisting of a grooved beak in which are lodged four slender lancets for piercing the tissues of plants and sucking the sap. Throughout its life the cicada is a sap-sucker.

The female lays her eggs in slits she makes in the bark of trees. Nobody has yet studied the life history of any African cicadas in detail but it would seem, from observations made overseas, that the eggs take about six weeks to hatch. The young cicada resembles its parents but is more stoutly built and has two curious front legs, with greatly enlarged spiny thighs and shanks that serve as digging implements. At birth the little creature drops to the ground and at once burrows beneath the surface. It spends its entire immature life tunnelling through soil

110. An adult froghopper newly emerged from its pupa, which it formed within its foam mass. 11 mm.

111. An adult cicada sucking sap from a tree by means of its piercing proboscis, which may be seen running diagonally down below the head. 45 mm.

112. A leafhopper sucking sap from a leaf.

in search of the tender young roots upon whose sap it feeds.

When the nymph is fully grown it burrows its way upwards to the surface and out into the light and air. It climbs a few centimetres up some nearby tree-trunk, digs its claws in and clings there motionless for some time. Then its skin splits down the back and the adult cicada struggles laboriously out of the nymphal skin. After its wings have expanded and dried it is ready to fly away and spend a few brief weeks revelling in the sunshine and singing its shrill, monotonous song.

In America the periodical cicadas of the genus *Magicicada* are well known: in the southern states the species take 13 years to reach maturity; those in the north take 17 years. This was first ascertained by studying the intervals between the appearance of the various broods. We do not know how long the different species of cicada found in Africa take to reach maturity. There may be some that are as long-lived as the American periodical cicada, but disconnected observations made from time to time indicate that some of our cicadas spend only two or three years underground.

There are several thousand different species of cicada, found chiefly in the warmer regions. As far as is known, all have a life history similar to that just described. Sometimes, under circumstances not yet understood, the immature cicada constructs a curious chimney, or cone of earthen particles glued together by saliva; this projects 10 cm or so above the surface of the ground, is closed at the top, and is hollow inside. The cicada lives inside this for some weeks before breaking a hole at the base and emerging. The chimney is thought to protect individuals which have been forced to come to the surface prematurely due to extreme temperatures.

Leafhoppers Aphids apart, the agile little leafhoppers of the family Cicadellidae are probably the most abundant of all plant bugs – although they do not attract much attention because of their small size and protective coloration. However, some are of considerable economic significance because they attack crops and spread certain diseases among plants, in much the same way as mosquitoes spread yellow fever among people.

The maize leafhopper, *Cicadulina mbila*, is the chief agent in the spread of streak disease in maize and sugar cane. This is a virus disease that streaks leaves with yellow stain and stunts the plant. The adult responsible is only 3 mm long, slender, and purplish-black in colour with a yellow line down the centre of its back. Like the rest of its kind, it can leap vigorously and fly well.

The female inserts her tiny white eggs into slits she makes in leaves. These hatch in about a fortnight into white nymphs with black eyes which feed on the sap like their parents. The nymphs moult five times and are fully grown in about a month. There are several generations a year, and, if weather conditions are favourable, the number of leafhoppers may increase rapidly, doing considerable damage. The increasing horde robs plants of sap and spreads the disease.

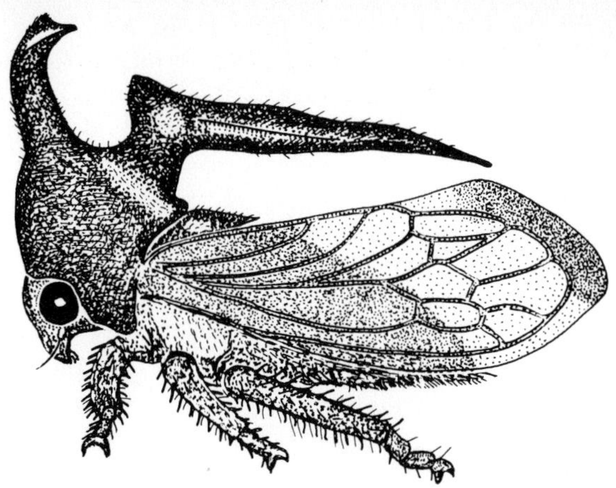

113. A treehopper (*Anchon* sp.), showing the bizarre modification of the pronotum, common in the family Membracidae.

Leafhoppers may be recognised by their delicate, slender form and by the double row of spines along the hind tibiae. The first segment of the thorax is not prolonged backwards as it is in the treehoppers.

Treehoppers The common and quaint little bugs of the family Membracidae are easily recognised by the shape of the first segment of the thorax, which is prolonged over the back and often bears hornlike projections which give the insects a bizarre appearance. These bugs are small, few greater than 6 mm long when fully grown, and are mostly brown. The female apparently lays her eggs in slits cut in twigs of trees and shrubs. The resulting young, usually black, are gregarious and feed in groups on the sap of the plant. They are attended by ants eager for the sweet liquid they excrete: the ants stroke the young treehoppers with their antennae and the latter respond by exuding liquid excrement from their long anal tube. This tube contains an eversible 'anal whip', which can be waved rapidly from side to side, probably for defensive purposes.

Psyllids The little bugs belonging to the family Psyllidae are about the size of aphids and resemble tiny cicadas. As an example of the group, we may take the common citrus psylla, *Trioza erytreae*, found throughout Africa south of the Sahara on orange trees and some related trees. They are of great economic importance as the vector of the virus which causes 'greening' disease in citrus. The adult, only about 2 mm long, is green at first but darkens almost to black as it grows older; when at rest its four transparent wings are held roofwise over its back.

The female lays her eggs at the tips of young shoots, usually on the edges of tender young leaves. These hatch in about a week into sluggish nymphs which initially creep slowly about, but soon settle down to feed after which they scarcely move at all unless they become overcrowded. Clustered on the underside of the young leaf the insects look very much like small scale insects. Where each nymph settles, a small pit forms in the leaf and, as the nymph grows, so the pit increases in size. A badly infested leaf in consequence will become stunted, discoloured and deformed. The nymphs moult five times in the course of their growth and reach full size in about three to four weeks. The hind legs of the adults are rather stouter than the two front pairs and they can jump as well as fly.

Another common psyllid forms galls on the leaves of stinkwood trees whilst yet another is found on wild figs.

Aphids Members of the family Aphididae are familiar to every farmer and gardener because of the harm they do to many different kinds of cultivated plants. Although among the feeblest and most defenceless of all insects, and although they have many natural enemies, aphids not only manage to survive but may do so in abundance. This amazing fecundity is their strength. A female aphid may begin to produce young when she is only a week old and may give birth to two or three offspring every day until she has a family of 100 or more. Indeed, if the descendants of a single aphid all survived, at the end of a single year they would reach the colossal total of 210 raised to the 15th power, a truly astronomical number.

There are species of aphid in which the males are rare or have never been traced. In other words, the countless hordes of tiny insects on peas and beans, roses, peach trees, cabbages and so on may all be 'fatherless'. Let us take the common pea aphid, *Aphis craccivora,* as an example. Very common and widely dispersed on various kinds of leguminous plants, such as peas, beans and ground-nuts, it is of great economic importance not only because of the damage it does by sucking the sap of the plants, but also because it spreads rosette, a disease afflicting ground-nuts. Should the number of aphids feeding on the underside of the leaves increase too rapidly, some proceed to grow wings. It is these winged individuals, flying from sick to healthy plants, that carry the virus with them.

The female aphid does not lay eggs. Her eggs mature and hatch inside her body. She then deposits her young singly at short intervals, generally at the rate of two or three a day if weather conditions are favourable. This interesting event can be watched with the aid of a hand lens. The tiny, newly-hatched aphid, only about 0,5 mm in length and pale green in colour, is slowly extruded by the mother, head first with its legs folded along its sides. As soon as it drops on to the plant it creeps off, while the mother continues feeding unconcernedly and takes no heed at all of her new-born youngster.

The young aphid soon begins to feed and darkens rapidly until almost black. It grows quickly, casting its skin four times before it reaches the adult stage, about a week after its birth. It has two tubes, or cornicles, on its back, projecting like a pair of horns from the rear end of the body. It was once believed a sweet liquid called honey-dew was given off by these cornicles but we now know they are the exit tubes of glands that secrete a waxy fluid, which helps to repel enemies. The honey-dew that is so eagerly sought after by ants is simply excreted plant sap. Sugars, salts and proteins are absorbed by the insect but the passage of sap through the body is so rapid and copious that enough nourishment remains in the excretion to make it attractive to ants. The ants can be observed tapping successive aphids with their feelers. If ready to excrete, the aphid lifts its tail in response to this enquiry and a drop of clear liquid appears at its vent which the ant greedily laps up before passing to another of its 'cows'.

Initially all the aphids on a leaf colony are wingless and they live amicably and peacefully side by side. However, as numbers increase the leaf begins to wither and curl as a result of the numerous tiny beaks robbing it of sap. Over-crowding and the diminishing food supply provokes some change in form among several young aphids: more slender than their siblings, and with four wing-buds on their backs. At the last moult these wing-buds expand into four gauzy, transparent wings with dark veins. This amazing change enables the winged individuals to fly to other plants to start new colonies. Sometimes, on a warm, still day the air is filled with these flying aphids seeking new homes for themselves. The offspring of the winged individuals are wingless, until population pressures cause more winged aphids to appear.

So the cycle goes on throughout the year in warm areas, generation after generation of virgin females giving rise to countless numbers of young like themselves, without the intervention of any males at all. There may be 40-50 or more generations a year, all fatherless, all produced parthenogenetically.

In cooler parts this asexual breeding continues during the summer months, but with the approach of winter a remarkable change occurs that does not occur in warmer climates.

In late autumn both males and females appear among the offspring. Usually the males have wings. They die soon after mating, and each female lays a single egg, large relative to the size of the insect, and thick-shelled. These eggs are generally placed in cracks and crevices in the bark. With the onset of cold weather the progenitors die, but the eggs survive and hatch into females in the following spring. These are the virgins that sustain the pest's population growth throughout the summer until with the onset of cool weather and shorter days, the males appear once more.

Besides temperature, the amount of daylight seems to affect the appearance of males. It has been found by experiment that no males are produced and no eggs are laid in autumn if the aphids are kept in a greenhouse and exposed to artificial light at night. On the other hand, if they are shut up in the dark at the height of summer, after being exposed to only eight hours of light, males and eggs are produced.

There are a large number of species of Aphididae in Africa, found on all kinds of plants. All are small, soft-bodied and feeble and all suck sap. It is not easy to distinguish one species from another because they are much alike, and their colouring is not constant. Furthermore, the winged forms differ from the wingless individuals and, in some cases, the aphids feeding on one plant differ from individuals of the same species feeding on another kind of plant. Microscopic features are used in determining the species, such as the arrangement of the sense organs on the antennae and the length and shape of the cornicles and the tip of the abdomen. The species that are of economic importance and that are widely distributed include the green peach aphid, *Myzus persicae,* which transmits potato leafroll disease; the cotton aphid, *Aphis gossypii,* dark in colour and found on garden plants as well as cotton; the dark green maize aphid, *Rhopalosiphum maidis,* a pest of grain crops, particularly maize and grain sorghum; the sugar-cane aphid, *Aphis sacchari;* the cabbage aphid, *Brevicoryne brassicae;* the black peach aphid, *Anuraphis persicaeniger;* the woolly aphid of apple, *Eriosoma lanigerum;* the wheat aphid *Schizaphis graminum;* the vine phylloxera, *Viteus vitifoliae;* and many others. The last mentioned species belongs to a separate family, the Phylloxeridae.

As a counter-balance to their prodigious reproduction, aphids have many natural enemies, including ladybirds, hover flies, lacewings, parasitic wasps and others.

Whiteflies The insects known as whiteflies, family Aleyrodidae, have four wings dusted with a characteristic white powder. They are minute (only about 3 mm across the outspread wings), and attack plants in greenhouses, as well as potplants, tomatoes, beans, pumpkins, oranges and others. A severe infestation will make the leaves turn yellow, dry up, and drop off.

The female generally lays her oval white eggs in a semi-circle, each attached by short stalks, on tender young leaves. These hatch into oval, flattened young that can creep about at first, but once attached to the leaf, and after the first moult, their legs become degenerate and they can no longer move.

The nymph moults three times and then enters the pupal stage. During the first part of this stage it feeds, but after a time it becomes quiescent and the adult wings and legs develop, enclosed in sheaths. At this point the insect is very like the pupa of one of the higher insects, hidden within its old skin. Finally a T-shaped slit appears in the back and the adult emerges. The adult is a rather sluggish insect and lives for only a few days. Males are frequently rare in some generations and parthenogenesis, or the development of unfertilised eggs, is known to occur.

Scale insects and mealy bugs Scale insects and their relatives (superfamily Coccoidea) are often such insignificant-looking objects, mere specks adhering to fruit, leaves and twigs, that it is difficult to believe they can do harm. However, some of them are amongst the worst pests with which the fruit-grower and gardener have to contend. Many hundreds of species of scale insects are already known from Africa, but many more

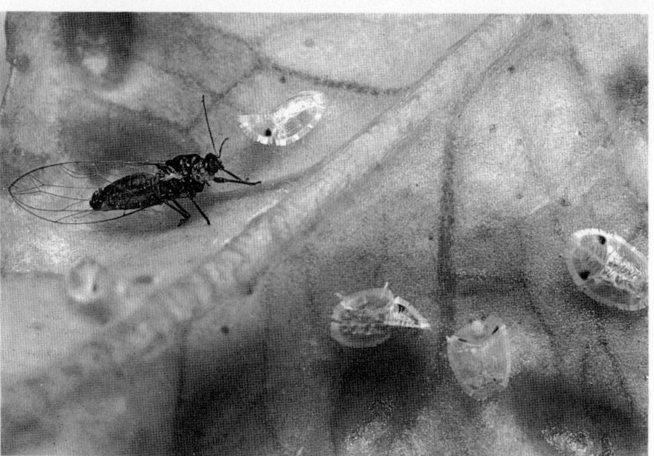

114. Winged adult citrus psyllid with nymphs on a citrus leaf, showing the characteristic pits made by the nymphs. 4 mm.

115. Aphids clustering on the stem of milkweed, each with its proboscis embedded in the tissue of the plant as it sucks sap. Note the pair of dark, tubular cornicles projecting from the hind end of each insect, which secrete a waxy fluid. 3 mm.

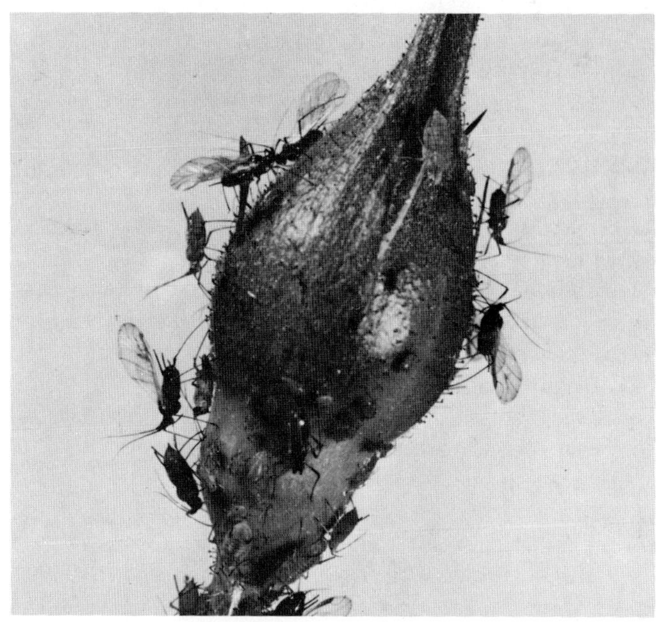

116. Aphids clustering on a rosebud, showing both winged and wingless individuals. 3 mm.

117. A mother aphid surrounded by her offspring feeds on the underside of a leaf. To the left lies the egg of a hover fly which will soon hatch into a predaceous, aphid-eating larva.

118. Aphids feeding on a leaf. The area is littered with their white, moulted skins, and the pale, bloated bodies of several individuals that have been parasitized by tiny braconid wasps.

119. Whiteflies (family Aleyrodidae) feeding on the underside of a leaf. 3 mm.

await discovery and description. About 70 different kinds have been imported from overseas, and many of these are significant pests.

One of the commonest and most troublesome of the scale insects is the red scale, *Aonidiella aurantii.* It is a member of the family Diaspididae, known as the hard, or armoured scales. It is not a native of Africa and we do not know how or when it was first imported. But we do know this occurred a long time ago – perhaps a century or more – and probably by the agency of imported fruit trees. The red scale is widespread throughout the world today and is of extreme economic importance because of the damage it does and the difficulty of controlling it. These little sap-suckers attack all parts of the tree: fruit, leaves, twigs and branches. Leaves that are badly infested turn yellow, die and drop off. This may be followed by the dying back of the twig. Later on the branches become thickly encrusted with the scale and they also may be killed. If the pest is not controlled it is capable of destroying a well-grown tree within three or four years.

A close examination of a scale infestation on an orange, or on an infected twig, will show that the insects range in size from tiny dots to fully grown females that are at most about 2 mm in diameter. Two types may be seen among the scales: there are circular ones and smaller, oval scales. The larger, round scales indicate full-grown females, while the oval scales indicate males.

The adult female lacks legs, wings or even a recognisable shape because it is not necessary for her to move about. Her body consists of a flattened bag, with a long, threadlike beak on the underside which she thrusts deep into the plant upon which she is feeding. The round, hard scale that covers and protects her body consists of her cast-off skins; the outer rim of the scale is a hardened exudation. If the insect is examined through a hand-lens, a nipple of sorts can be seen protruding slightly from the middle of the scale. This is a remnant of skin that the insect cast when she moulted for the first time. This nipple projects from a slightly raised area, resembling a miniature watch-glass which is the second cast skin. The scale insect moults only twice, therefore the scale encircling this central area consists of the hardened exudation given off after the insect is mature.

If the scale is lifted up with a needle point the body of the female generally comes away attached to the scale. However, the bodies of certain scale insects – such as the pernicious scale, which resemble the red scale – remain on the plant when the scale is removed. In the case of the red scale, the edge of the scale is turned in under the body, completely enclosing it except for a circular opening on the underside. This explains why the whole insect comes away when the scale is lifted.

The long and slender beak of the scale insect consists of four very thin threads, much finer than a human hair and much longer than the insect's body. It is believed that the ring of muscles at the insect's mouth holds these four lancets just behind the tip, so that the points can be pushed a little way into the plant. Once secured, the hold is shifted a little way further back and the lancets are thrust a little deeper in, and so the process continues until the whole beak is inserted. This process needs to be carried out only once in the insect's lifetime, since it never moves once it has settled down and fixed itself in position.

The male scale insect is quite unlike the female. If you lift up a number of the smaller oval scales that cover the body you will find that some are empty, but under others you may come across a tiny little winged insect, so small that the details of its structure can be distinguished only with the aid of a hand-lens. It has a pink body, two gauzy wings, well-developed eyes, long feelers and six legs, but it has no mouthparts and cannot feed. Its life as an adult lasts two or three days at most and its sole function is to creep from under its protective scale when weather conditions are favourable, seek out a female and mate with her; it then dies.

The female red scale does not lay eggs. She retains her eggs inside her body until they hatch and she gives birth to her young at the rate of about one a day over a period of about three months. The number of young, and the rate at which they are produced, varies according to the climatic conditions. More young are produced over a shorter period during the summer when it is warm, than in the winter. The newly-hatched insect (called a crawler) is a tiny yellow creature, about 0,25 mm in length. It has six legs and a pair of feelers. Quite blind, it creeps out from under its mother's scale and wanders about on the plant until it finds a suitable spot where it can insert its beak and settle down. If the wind is blowing at the time, it may be blown away to another plant, and this seems to be the principal way in which scale insects are dispersed. The tiny crawlers, roaming restlessly about on the tree, may also creep onto larger insects, such as beetles, flies and bees, or onto the feet of birds, and in this way they may be carried far afield.

When the young crawler settles down and begins feeding, it grows a hard skin on its back – the beginnings of the scale. In two to three weeks it casts its first skin and this forms the nipple already mentioned. At this stage there is no visible difference between a male and a female; the second stage lasts for about six weeks, after which the female moults for the second and last time. The male then changes into a pupa and about ten days later the adult emerges. The entire life cycle of the red scale lasts three or four months.

Of the many other hard-scale insects found in Africa, the following may be briefly mentioned: the pernicious scale, *Aspidiotus perniciosus,* which was introduced into South Africa in 1905 and caused great alarm because it is one of the most harmful of all scale pests. However, strict control measures have prevented its spread. It infests various kinds of fruit trees as well as oak, poplar, willow, rose and pepper trees. The scale of the young female is black with a central grey dot; the adult female has a grey scale with a central black area and dot. Once infested, twigs and fruits often show red discoloration in the area surrounding the insects. The aloe red scale, *Furcaspis capensis,* is a large, striking insect found only on aloes. It is dark red in colour, with much smaller oval scales covering the males. The mussel scale, *Lepidosaphes beckii,* may be recognised by its shape and its bluish-brown colour. It is found on citrus and other plants.

The soft scales, family Coccidae, differ from the armoured scales in that they are not covered by a definite scale: they are protected only by their own thickened skin. The best known and most common of these is perhaps the black scale, *Saissetia oleae,* very widespread in Africa and other parts of the world and found on citrus, olives, oleander and a wide range of other

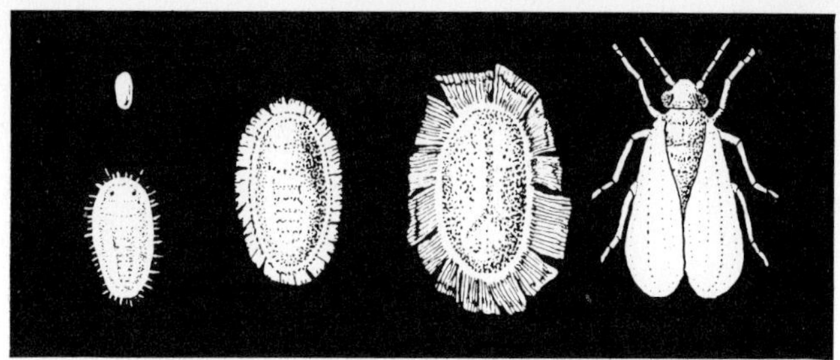

120. The development of a whitefly, from the egg to the adult.

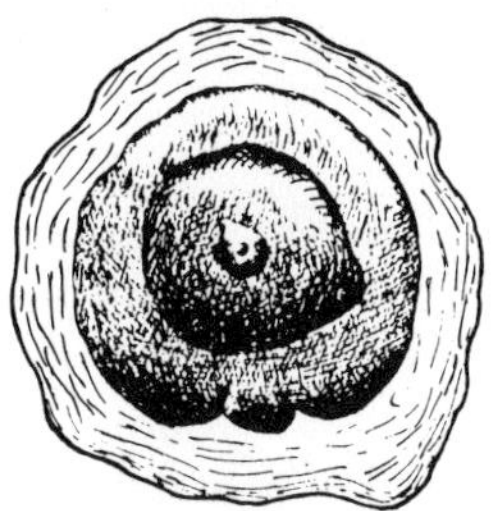

Adult female scale, from above

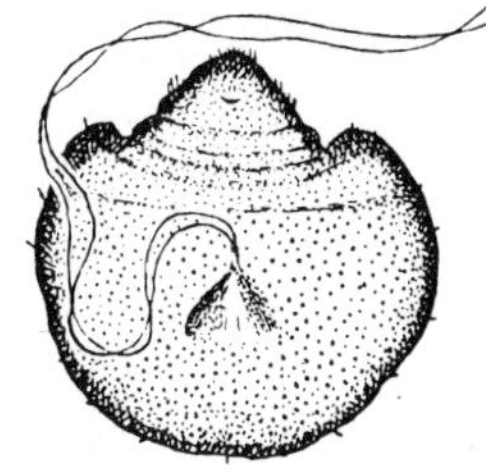

Female removed from scale, from below

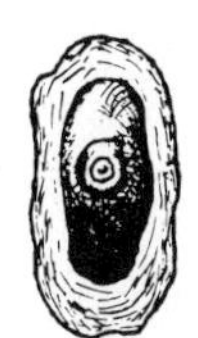

Male scale, from above

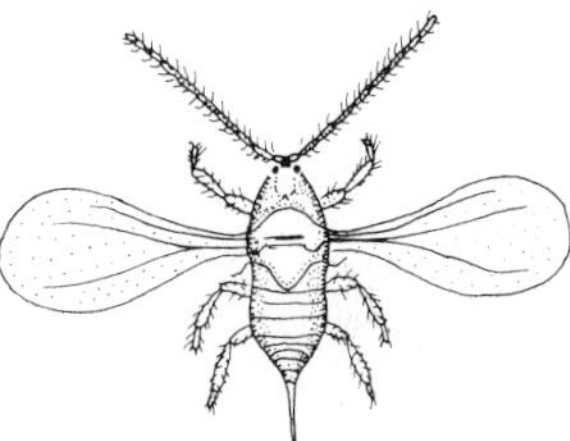

Winged male

121. The red scale, *Aonidiella aurantii.*

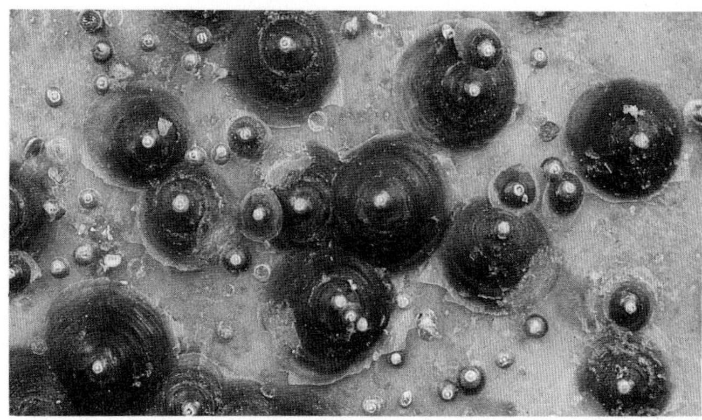

122. Circular purple scales on a melon, in various stages of development. Up to 4 mm.

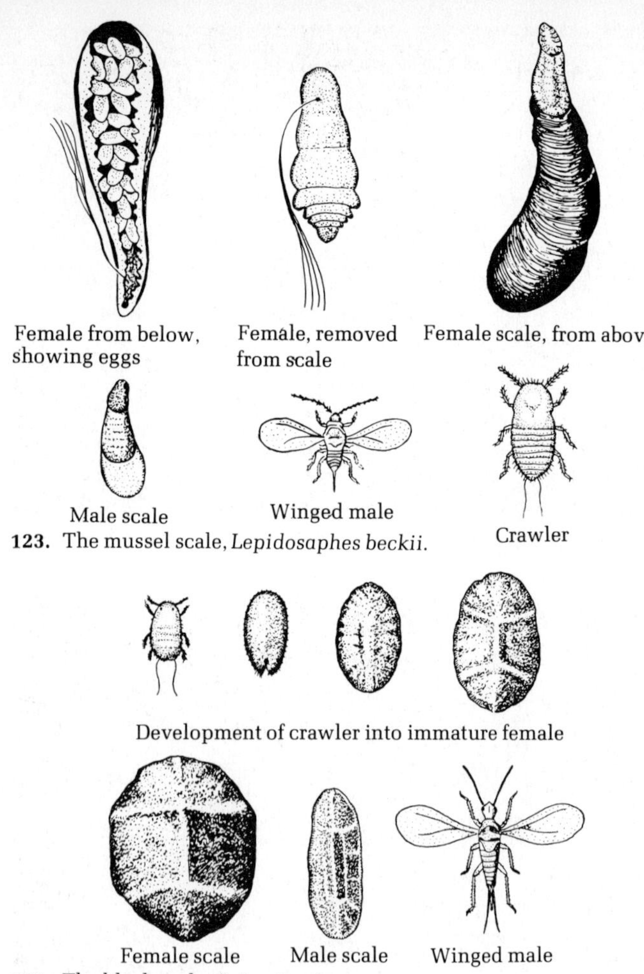

123. The mussel scale, *Lepidosaphes beckii.*

124. The black scale, *Saissetia oleae.*

plants. The harm done by this pest on fruit trees is not so much due to the loss of sap as to the growth of an unsightly sooty mould fungus. Soft scales give off a good deal of the sweet excretion known as honey-dew, and if not removed by ants, this forms a favourable medium on which the fungus can grow. Fruit and twigs infested by the black scale are often blackened by the sooty mould growing around and over them.

The female black scale is rounded, dark brown or black with a distinct H-mark on her back. She may be up to 5 mm in length but many are smaller. She grows slowly, taking about nine months to reach full size, whereupon she begins laying numerous tiny eggs, about 40 a day, and up to 2 000 or more before she dies. Her oviposition lasts for about two months, the tiny young creeping out from under her body as they hatch. The newly-hatched nymph is barely visible to the naked eye, oval, flat and brown, with two small black eyes, long antennae and six legs. It creeps about until it finds a leaf or tender twig on which to settle. After moulting twice over about three months, it reaches the adult stage when its back becomes arched and it darkens in colour.

The male black scale is rare, sometimes absent altogether, and the eggs of the females develop parthenogenetically. When present, the male scale is similar to the female until after the first moult; he then becomes oval, elongated, flat and pale brown. At the end of the second stage he forms a glassy covering for himself under which he changes into a pupa. Finally, when about three months old, the tiny winged adult male emerges. He is only about 1 mm in length, yellow in colour and lives for only two or three days.

Numbers of black scales may often be found with small round holes in them. These have been destroyed by small parasitic wasps, mostly of the families Encyrtidae and Aphelinidae. Many years ago certain of these parasites were sent from South Africa to California, to help combat the black scale, which is a serious pest in citrus orchards. The parasites flourished in their new home and have played an important part in controlling the pest.

The wax scales (*Ceroplastes* species) are soft scales, belonging to the family Coccidae, the females of which secrete a waxy covering over their bodies. In some species the wax is thin and hard, whilst in others it is soft, thick and watery. Certain species of white wax scales are common on thorn trees, others on wild figs, avocado pears and syringa trees.

Mealy bugs are small insects, belonging to the families Pseudococcidae and Eriococcidae, the largest being only about 3 mm long, pink or purplish in colour but appearing white because of the waxy powder which covers their bodies. Along each side of the body are projections consisting of bundles of waxy threads. Over 90 different species have been identified in South Africa alone, several of which were introduced from overseas. These include serious pests of citrus, pineapples, vines, pears, guavas, sugar-cane and many other cultivated plants.

The citrus mealy bug, *Planococcus citri,* may be taken as a typical example. It is widely spread and often does serious harm in citrus orchards, particularly to navel oranges. It infests young fruits in spring and may cause many of them to drop off. Later in the season the bugs migrate to the navel end of the fruit, where they find shelter. They secrete fluffy masses of white waxen threads that may fill the navel cavity and produce much honey-dew on which sooty mould develops. The honey-dew also attracts ants which feed on it, and at the same time protect the bugs from ladybirds that would otherwise destroy them.

The female mealy bug, when ready to lay her eggs, produces a mass of fine waxen threads, like cotton wool, at the hind end of her body and in this she deposits her numerous, tiny yellow eggs – up to 1 000 or more. The egg-laying extends over two or three weeks and, when it is completed, the bug shrivels up and dies. The eggs hatch in 10 to 30 days, depending upon weather conditions, into tiny yellow young that creep out of the sheltering mass of threads and seek a suitable spot on a fruit or leaf where they can settle down and feed. Many get blown or carried away at this stage to settle on other trees.

During the first stage of their career the young males and females are alike. After the first moult, however, they are quite different. The female does not change her form but casts her skin four times in the course of her growth; she may reach the adult stage in about two months during summer, but this takes much longer in winter. The male makes a cocoon for himself when he is three or four weeks old and inside this he changes into a pupa. Two or three weeks later a winged adult emerges, very similar to the males of all this family, a feeble little creature that cannot feed and which lives for only 3-4 days. There are three generations a year and the bugs can be found on the trees at all times of the year.

Cochineal insects (family Dactylopiidae) are mealy bugs that were formerly cultivated for the colouring obtained from them and are today important because of their rôle in the control of prickly pears. They are natives of America but some species have spread to other parts of the world. Two or three species are found on prickly pears in Africa and are easily identified by the fluffy masses of white waxen threads beneath which the insects shelter. If they are crushed a rich purple colour is seen.

In 1938 a species of cochineal, *Dactylopius opuntiae*, was deliberately introduced into South Africa to be used in the fight against the pest prickly pears that covered so much fertile land, and rendered it useless for farming. Although indigenous to America, this cochineal came originally from Australia where it had proved useful, together with other insects, in destroying prickly pears. It has flourished and spread in Africa, where it now plays an important rôle in helping to control certain kinds of prickly pears. Unfortunately, it also attacks spineless prickly pears that are grown for fodder; like the other cochineal insects, it will not infest any plants other than those of the prickly pear family. The life history of the cochineal is very similar to that described for the citrus mealy bug, but, in the case of *Dactylopius opuntiae*, the female retains her eggs inside her body until they hatch. Their distribution has been restricted by ladybirds (which feed on the insects), a fungus disease, hail, heavy rain and winter frost. Consequently they have not proved as effective in killing off the pest prickly pears in South Africa as they were in Queensland. Nevertheless, they have done good work, in conjunction with the cactoblastis moth and the prickly pear beetle.

The Australian bug, *Icerya purchasi*, belongs to the family Margarodidae and was accidentally introduced into South Africa in about 1872. It became a very serious pest of citrus trees, roses, acacias and other plants, but was eventually controlled by the introduction of the Australian ladybird, *Rodolia cardinalis*. This was the first and perhaps the most famous example in the history of agricultural science of what is known as biological control – that is to say, the control of a pest by the introduction and encouragement of its natural enemies.

The fully grown Australian bug is about 10 mm long, with a fluted white bag making up the greater part of its body. Because of this characteristic bag, made of waxen threads, the insect is known in America as the cottony-cushion scale. The bugs are usually females, which are

125. Soft scales on hibiscus bush being tended by ants for their sweet excretions.

126. Wax scales; the sedentary females have a thick coating of soft wax to protect them.

127. Australian bugs *(Icerya purchasi)* feeding on the underside of a leaf. 6 mm.

functional hermaphrodites. Males are rare. The body of the female is a flattened yellow disc at the front end. She is attached to the twig only by her slender beak, which is deeply embedded in the woody tissues. The yellow colour of her body is more or less hidden by the white waxy material that oozes from glands in her body and forms a powdery coating. If the white bag is torn open it will be found to contain some 200 oval pink eggs that look like little coral beads in their soft bed of waxy down. The eggs hatch in about 14 days.

The newly hatched bug is pink, about the size of a pinhead, with six black legs, a pair of black feelers and two well-developed eyes. Once it has settled down to feed and has sunk its beak into a twig it never moves again. The wax glands in its skin begin to secrete the powdery covering and slowly the little insect assumes adult form.

Some members of the family Margarodidae are perhaps the most remarkable of all scale insects. They are adapted for a life underground: the young of both sexes have strong legs and claws suitable for digging in the soil; they feed on the sap of various roots. The females go through a curious resting stage enclosed in a yellow glassy case. Thus protected, they may remain in the soil for a long time during a period of drought. After rain the females emerge from their cases looking somewhat like mealy bugs. The brassy-looking cases of some of the Margarodidae are called 'ground pearls'. They are rather large, about 7 mm or more in diameter, and are sometimes strung on thread as beads. The adult males are winged and free-living.

The Heteroptera Although some are wingless, most members of this suborder can be identified by the nature of their forewings, which are leathery and thickened at the base and membranous at the tip. At rest, the wings are held flat over the body with the tips usually overlapping. The suborder is large, containing many species of economic importance. Most are terrestrial, but quite a few families are aquatic, and some are parasitic on vertebrates. There are differing views on the classification of the Heteroptera: the old system of dividing them into the Cryptocerata ('short-horned') and Gymnocerata ('long-horned'), is unsatisfactory and a more practical arrangement is to recognise three groups – the Geocorisae (terrestrial); Amphibicorisae (semi-aquatic); and Hydrocorisae (aquatic). Further details may be found at the end of the chapter.

Bed bugs The small family named Cimicidae comprises a group of wingless bugs that are parasites of certain vertebrates. A number of Cimicidae are bat parasites, and prehistoric man probably first encountered prehistoric bed bugs in caves that he shared with bats. The bed bug, *Cimex lectularius,* is found throughout the world today, living in association with man, its preferred host. Another species, *Cimex hemipterus,* found in the tropics, is also a human parasite.

The female lays her eggs in cracks in bedsteads, wall panels, behind skirting boards and other sheltered places. The eggs hatch into young bugs which look like small copies of their parents. All stages feed only on blood, coming out at night to feed on sleeping people, and hiding by day in any convenient cracks in furniture or walls.

Some people suffer from severe allergic reactions to bed bug bites, while others hardly notice any effects at all. Because of their blood-sucking habits, bugs have long been under suspicion as possible transmitters of human disease, but until fairly recently no adequate proof of their involvement had been found. Entomologists in West Africa and South Africa have now gathered evidence that suggests bed bugs may be responsible for transmitting serum hepatitis from infected to healthy persons. Since hepatitis infection seems linked with liver cancer, which is invariably fatal, bed bugs may yet prove to be prominent among Africa's many insects of medical importance.

Other African Cimicidae are nearly all bat parasites; on this continent only one species, *Paracimex africanus,* is found in association with birds whereas bird bugs are common in other parts of the world. The very closely related family of Polyctenidae contains bugs that are all bat parasites.

Leaf or plant bugs Although abundant in Africa, the Miridae tend to be small, delicate, shy insects, with the result that this very large family is often overlooked. The leaf and plant bugs are soft-bodied, and many are brightly coloured. Most feed on plants, but some are predators; while a few even favour a mixed diet of vegetable and animal matter.

Many of the vegetarian Miridae are of agricultural importance. The West African *Salhbergella singularis* is a pest of cocoa, and *Kiambura coffeae* attacks coffee plants in East Africa. Species of *Pleurochilophorus* in Central Africa feed on peas, cotton, maize and various wild plants; while members of the genus *Helopeltis* may do severe damage in tea plantations by attacking the young leaves and shoots, shrivelling the entire leaf and rendering it useless for the manufacture of tea.

Lace bugs The lace bugs, family Tingidae, are pretty little bugs that feed on the sap of various plants and are sometimes numerous enough to do harm. There is little remarkable about these insects when they are young, but the mature bugs have curious flattened projections on their thorax and abdomen. These are marked with ridges that form a network which gives the insects their popular name. Some species have long spines on these flattened projections. All lace bugs are very small and feed on plants. Some species defoliate their host plants.

Assassin bugs Members of the family Reduviidae may be recognised by the short, curved, three-segmented beak. When not being used as a weapon, this usually fits into a groove in the ventral surface of the thorax. The majority of species are predators of other insects, which they grab and then stab with their beaks, which are armed with four sharp lancets. They suck the juices of their victims and discard the hollow remains. Some species attack warm-blooded animals, and even man himself. In South America, members of the subfamily Triatominae bite sleeping humans and transmit the trypanosome that causes Chagas's disease (*Trypanosoma cruzi*).

In Africa the worst one can expect from an assassin bug is a painful bite, and indeed to handle one of these insects carelessly is to invite trouble. The bugs bite in self-defence, but the effects can be serious; excruciating pain is normally experienced, while allergic reactions and secondary infections may occur.

Pirates lugubris is a pretty little bug, often attracted to lights at night. Should one land on a person and be roughly brushed away, it will probably administer the burning bite that gives this species the name 'night bee'. Other assassin bugs that have been identified after biting people in Africa belong to the genera *Rhinocoris, Acanthaspis, Platymerus* and *Pantoleistes*.

A common species that is often found if stones are lifted is *Ectrichodia crux*. These are robust, yellow and black assassin bugs that prey on millipedes, which seem to have few natural enemies because of their hard shells and chemical secretions. Sometimes a whole family party of *Ectrichodia* bugs will be seen gathered around the body of a millipede, the bright red nymphs contrasting with the yellow and black adults.

Twig wilter bugs These dull-brown elongated bugs, about 25 mm long, that suck the sap of plants and cause tender twigs to wilt are well known to all gardeners. They belong to the family Coreidae. The odoriferous glands – those that secrete a stinking fluid – are particularly well-developed in members of this family. The slits through which the liquid pours can be seen with the naked eye on the underside of the adult body near the bases of the hind legs. They are surrounded by a slightly raised, roughened border, called the evaporating surface; here the liquid is retained so that it evaporates slowly. The immature stages have the slits on their backs and these too can be seen with the naked eye. The change in position of the glands is apparently necessary because the bug acquires two pairs of wings when it casts its skin for the last time and, if the glands were still on the back, their openings would be covered by the wings and the smell would then not be so widely or freely diffused. In the southern African species, *Carlisis wahlbergi*, the bugs gather in thousands on gardenia and azalea shrubs. If disturbed, they emit a rain of repugnant fluid, the smell of which makes humans feel ill and will burn the skin or eyes on contact. This fluid seems to be poisonous to other insects, and is used as a defence mechanism.

One of the most widely spread of the African coreids is *Anoplocnemis curvipes*, which can be encountered in virtually every country south of the Sahara. The bugs vary in colour from pale grey to dark brown. The hind

128. A bedbug's body is almost fully distended as it takes a meal of human blood. 6 mm.

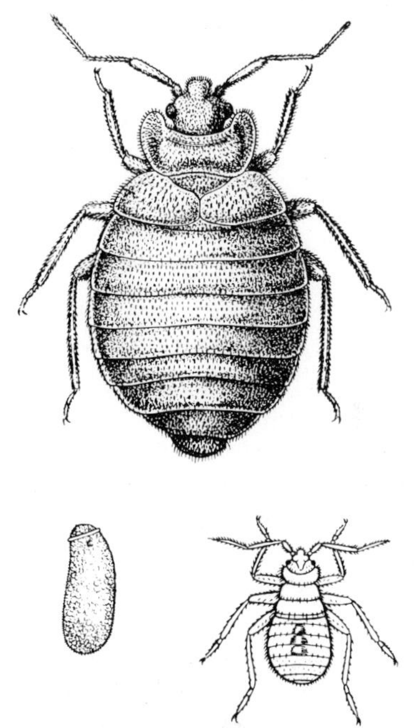

129. The egg, newly hatched nymph and adult male of the bedbug, *Cimex lectularius*.

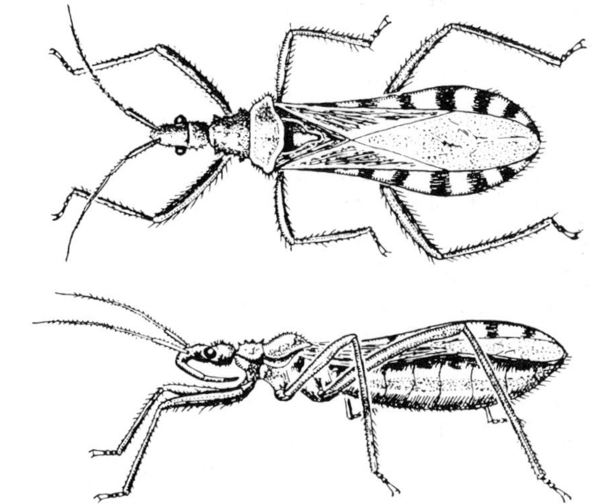

130. An assassin bug – note the strong beak extending below the head.

131. An assassin bug feeds on a caterpillar. 38 mm.

132. A twig wilter bug (*Anoplocnemis* sp.) newly emerged from its nymphal skin, seen attached to the leaf at lower left. 26 mm.

133. A twig wilter bug (*Anoplocnemis* sp.) with its proboscis embedded in a plant stem as it feeds.

femora are enlarged, and the males have especially inflated femora with a broad, inwardly pointing projection on each. The area around the repugnatorial glands is often bright orange. *Anoplocnemis curvipes* feeds on the stems, buds, shoots and leaves of a wide variety of plants – over 100 different species were recorded in a South African study. In most cases the host plant shows severe wilting of the tender parts beyond the bug's initial point of attack.

The eggs are cylindrical, barrel-shaped objects, deposited in rows of about 15 each on the stems of young and healthy plants. They hatch after one to two weeks, and the nymphs moult five times before they turn into adults. This takes about four to six weeks. In South Africa there are two, three or four generations of these bugs a year, depending on the climatic conditions and the type of host plant chosen.

Another common coreid is *Elasmopoda valga,* which has horn-like projections on either side of the prothorax. It is an abundant species in southern Africa, and attacks a variety of plants. The female twig wilter lays her oval brown eggs in a row, generally fixing them along a twig of the food plant. They are about as large as cabbage seeds and hatch in a fortnight. Each egg has a lid at one end, and, in order to force its way out, the young bug is armed with a sharp T-shaped egg-piercer on top of its head. After it has burst open the lid of the egg, the youngster, halfway out of the shell, takes a rest. It casts its skin in this position and leaves the egg-piercer behind in the empty eggshell. This T-shaped instrument can be seen if the eggshell is examined through a hand lens. All the coreids have this special means of breaking out of the egg.

Seed bugs Members of the family Lygaeidae are plant feeders, and as their common name suggests, they favour seeds for their diet. Most are small bugs of around 10 mm; their colour varies from dull brown in many species, to bright colours in a few. Some seed bugs are of economic importance in Africa, especially members of the genera *Nysius, Oxycarenus* and *Blissus.* For example, *Nysius ericae* and *N. binotatus* are very common in southern Africa, and may destroy fruit and vegetable crops. They sometimes invade houses in great numbers. The large, striking, black and white milkweed bug of tropical and subtropical Africa, *Oncopeltis famelicus,* is known to damage cotton and sweet potatoes. In South Africa it has damaged fig trees, to which the bugs had migrated from milkweed.

Red bugs or cotton stainer bugs The family called Pyrrhocoridae contains bugs that are robust and usually brightly coloured in red, orange and black. They differ from the Lygaeidae insofar as they lack ocelli (the two small simple eyes on the top of the head). These bugs are important because they include such pests as the cotton stainers (various species of *Dysdercus),* so-called because they pierce the bolls of cotton and introduce fungi which stain the fibre. They can be recognised by their contrasting colours of red and black. The males are smaller than the females, and mating couples may often be seen, walking about tail to tail. Several species of red bugs feed on wild plants of the same family as the cotton plant, but when the cotton appears they turn their attention to this crop and may do great damage.

Shield bugs or stink bugs Shield bugs form a large family called the Pentatomidae, of well over 4 000 known species. They receive their popular name from the shape of their flattened bodies. Many are brightly coloured, some are well-known pests of crops and garden plants and all have the power to emit an unpleasant smell that serves to protect them from enemies.

As our example of this important group we may take the antestia bug, *Antestia variegata*, which is very widely spread in Africa and a serious enemy of coffee-growers in East Africa and of fruit-growers in the Cape Province. It is a rather pretty insect, about 10 mm long, usually yellow marked with dark brown and red, but its colouring is variable and specimens may be found that are green, marked with red and blue. If roughly handled it gives off a strong 'buggy' odour that comes from a fluid produced in special glands lodged on the underside of the abdomen. The fluid is secreted from a pair of slits just behind the bases of the hind legs.

Many of the shield bugs might at first sight be mistaken for beetles, but a glance at the underside of the head should serve to distinguish them. Beetles are armed with biting jaws, but the bugs all have a slender, tubular beak which is carried folded back against the underside of the body and between the bases of the legs when not in use. The beak, or proboscis, consists of a grooved sheath – the labium – in which four slender lancets are lodged. These lancets correspond to the mandibles and maxillae of other insects and are highly modified to serve as piercing and sucking organs. The labium does not enter the puncture made by the lancets: it serves only as a protective covering and guide for the lancets. Assisted by a pumping action of the pharynx, food passes up the capillary tube formed by the four lancets.

The female *Antestia* bug is slightly larger and more robust than the male, but otherwise she is similar in coloration and markings. She lays her eggs on the twigs and leaves of the food plant in clusters of 10-14. They are about 1,5 mm long, pearly white when first deposited and shaped like short, stout barrels, with a clearly marked circular lid on top of each. In about a week the eggs darken to a slate colour and they hatch in 10 to 14 days. The young bug emerges from the egg by pushing off the lid. For about 24 hours the little creatures, black and similar to the parents but wingless, remain clustered round the empty eggshells, but after this they move off and scatter in search of food.

The young bug feeds on the sap of the plant for about 12 days and then rests and moults to the second stage. The colour now changes and the second stage nymph is gaily spotted with yellow and black. It feeds again for a

134. Cotton stainer bugs (*Dysdercus* sp.) feeding on a cotton boll. To the left is an adult, and to the right is a final stage nymph. Adult 11 mm.

135. Mating pyrrhocorid bugs (*Probergrothius sexpunctatus*). 14 mm.

136. Bright red pyrrhocorid bug nymphs feeding on a plant stem. Largest 6 mm.

fortnight and then casts its skin for the second time and the first sign of wings appears on its back. In all, the skin is cast five times; after the fifth moult the adult stage is reached. The female deposits several batches of eggs before her ovaries are exhausted and she dies. The whole life cycle from egg to the death of the adult, extends over about 100 days; and there are three generations a year, as the development during winter is slower than that during summer.

The *Antestia* bug is avoided by insect-eating animals because of its unpleasant smell, but it does have one enemy that destroys a large number of eggs. This is a tiny black parasitic wasp that may infest as many as 90% of the eggs in some seasons, making them turn black. The parasite's offspring then emerge from the eggs instead of the young bugs.

Antestia feeds on several veld plants including *Rhus* species (taaibos), some composites and species of *Psoralea*. When fruit or coffee berries are ripening, the bugs find their way into the orchards and plantations and attack the fruit. The punctures made by the bugs cause the fruit to become misshapen: as they ripen, the area round each puncture fails to develop and depressions remain, marking the sites of the punctures. Just below the skin hard little lumps form and the value of the fruit is greatly depreciated. Quinces and pears are particularly vulnerable to this type of damage. When stone fruits are attacked, gum oozes from the punctures and the fruit becomes misshapen and 'furry', and many of the fruits drop off prematurely. Furthermore, the tiny holes made by the bugs undoubtedly serve as a means of entry for various disease-causing organisms.

Another common African stink bug is the green *Nezara viridula*, which is found all over the world. It is often seen in vegetable gardens, and may do much damage to tomatoes and other plants.

There are a number of other species that the gardener and farmer will come across and they can all be recognised as shield bugs by the shape of their bodies and the nature of their wings. The Bagrada stink bug, *Bagrada hilaris*, is one of the most troublesome. Not quite 6 mm long, black with a few bright orange or yellow spots, it attacks all kinds of plants belonging to the cabbage family. When congregated in sufficient numbers the bugs may completely destroy the young plants. The female lays her small, oval, cream-coloured eggs in the soil and these hatch into little black bugs that go through the same stages as those described for the *Antestia* bug.

The large, pale-green shield bug, *Eucosternum delegorguei*, is found in considerable numbers at the end of the rainy season in some parts of Africa. The young stages of this bug are apparently unknown, but the adults – about 25 mm long – are strong fliers and gather in swarms on certain kinds of bushes and trees. Despite their strong buggy odour, local Africans cook and eat them, regarding them as great delicacies.

Two small families of distinctive African bugs are the Plataspidae and Scutelleridae, both related to the Pentatomidae. The former are short, rounded 'pill bugs' that might be mistaken for beetles. *Plataspis* species are gregarious and may be found in clusters on their host plants. The nymphs are grey, tortoise-like creatures with dark dorsal plates.

The Scutelleridae are commonly called shield-backed bugs. They are also very beetle-like, but the underside reveals the slender proboscis that identifies them as bugs. Many are brightly coloured in metallic green, yellow and blue, like members of the genus *Calidea*.

Water striders Water striders belong to the family Gerridae, and are common everywhere in Africa. They are small, slender, dark-brown insects about 10 mm in length and wonderfully adapted for their way of life on the elastic film that constitutes the water surface. The underside of the body is clothed in a coat of dense, white, scale-like hairs that give the insect a silvery appearance – in sharp contrast to its dark upper side. These hairs prevent the bug from getting wet. Even though it may be pushed under the water with a stick, it bobs up again immediately, quite dry.

At first sight the water strider seems to have only four legs, but it actually has six, like the rest of its kind. The first pair of legs are short and usually tucked away beneath the front of the body. They are placed so as to form efficient grasping organs by means of which the bug can hold any prey floating on the water. A timid creature, it does not normally hunt healthy prey but contents itself with the juices of insects that are struggling on the surface and cannot defend themselves. When the water strider finds a victim, it seizes the body in its front legs, brings its beak forward and thrusts the four lancets deep into the tissues.

The bug's middle and hind legs are long and thin and stiff brushes of water-repellent hairs are present on the feet and on part of the hind legs below the knee joint. These are the only parts of the insect that come into contact with the water surface. These modifications support the insect on water, enabling it to skim swiftly over the surface, held up only by surface tension.

The body itself does not touch the water. When something happens to break the surface film, such as a shower of rain, the striders rush to shore and hide under fallen leaves until the water is calm again.

A number of different species of water strider are found in Africa; most are winged so that when the water of a pool dries up they can fly away (usually at night) in search of fresh abodes. However, there are a few kinds that are wingless and certain other species in which two or even three different types are found. Among these exceptions are certain individuals which may have fully developed wings, while others have only half-wings and still others are wingless – despite the fact that all these individuals belong to the same species.

Water striders use the surface film as a means of communication, as well as a means of support: if an insect falls into the water from an overhanging tree, its struggles set up vibrations in the surface film; these vibrations are picked up by the strider, which has special sensory areas in its feet, and very soon the prey is located, stabbed with the beak, and sucked dry.

Water striders also use these surface vibrations to send messages relating to their courtship and mating: the male will hold onto a suitable floating object and send out a series of high-frequency ripples by moving his legs up and down; a responsive female who receives these vibrations through the surface film will approach the male, sending out answering signals at a lower frequency. As soon as he picks up this message, the male responds by changing his high frequency vibrations to low frequency replies. Further specific messages and responses result in mating taking place, after which the female lays her eggs in or on the object that the male used as his base for the whole courtship procedure. Meanwhile, the male sends out another type of surface vibration at a different frequency, which serves to mark his territory and thus keep other male water striders away.

Two genera of water strider are found throughout the world: *Gerris,* on freshwater surfaces, and *Halobates* on the surface of the sea. The latter live very much like their freshwater relatives, but the only objects that the females are known to fix their eggs to are feathers. These may be either floating on the surface of the ocean, or still attached to birds asleep on the sea at night!

Backswimmers In contrast to the water striders that live just above the surface film, the backswimmers, family Notonectidae, live just below it. They are remarkable in that they always swim with their backs on the underside and the ventral side uppermost. The back is generally strongly ridged, so that it is shaped like the bottom of a boat, although it is smooth and shiny and snow-white in some species. The surface of the abdomen (the upper side of the swimming insect), is dark-coloured and has four rows of hairs along it: a double row down the middle and a row down each side. These hairs, overlapping on each side, enclose air so that the bug is able to breathe while below the surface. Like their water-striding cousins, backswimmers also obtain information from tiny ripples and vibrations on the surface of the water.

The front and middle legs are carried tucked away against the sides, so that they offer little resistance when the insect is swimming. Its hind legs, long and fringed with stiff bristles, project from the sides like a pair of oars. It swims with a vigorous rowing motion of the hind legs, 'feathering' its oars on the return stroke by folding the bristles along the legs in order to offer less resistance. When it dives it carries a layer of air between its wings and its back and this gives it a silvery appearance. It can leap from the surface of the water and take to wing.

About 50 different species of backswimmer have been recorded from Africa, but doubtless many more still await discovery and classification. They are common in shallow, stagnant water and are fiercely predaceous insects, feeding on any small creatures they can capture. The backswimmer attacks its prey from below,

137. Shield bug feeding on a caterpillar. Though predominantly plant feeders, many shield bugs will also prey on small soft-bodied insects. 11 mm.

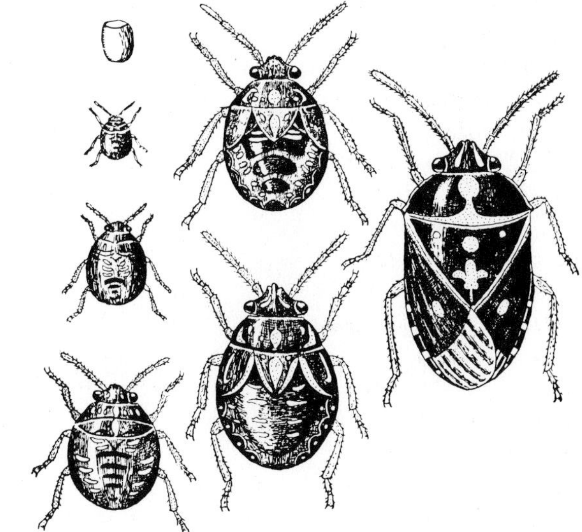

138. Development of the Bagrada bug, from egg to adult. The adult is about 6 mm long, black with orange spots.

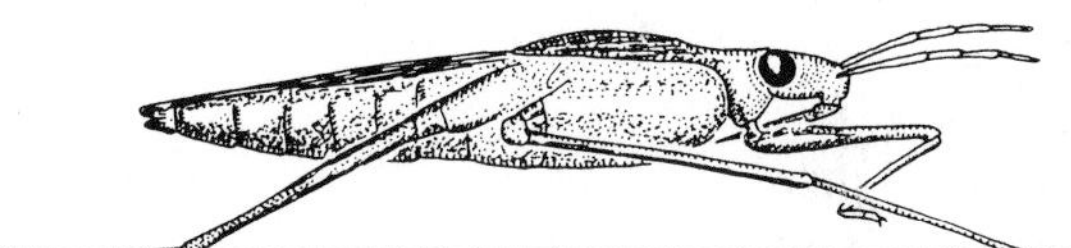

139. A side view of a water strider, showing how the bug is supported on the surface film by the tarsi of the middle and hind legs.

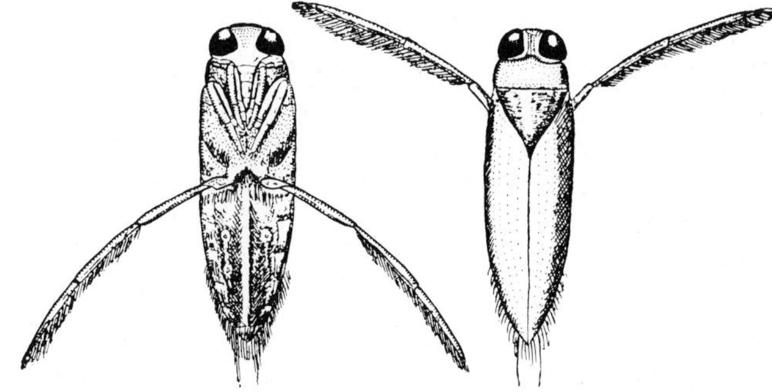

140. A backswimmer, *Anisops varia,* as seen from above the water surface (left) and from below. One of Africa's common backswimmers, it is found in slow-moving streams, muddy ponds and puddles left in drying river beds. The insects are about 6 mm long, bluish white on their backs, with a bright orange triangle at the base of the wings.

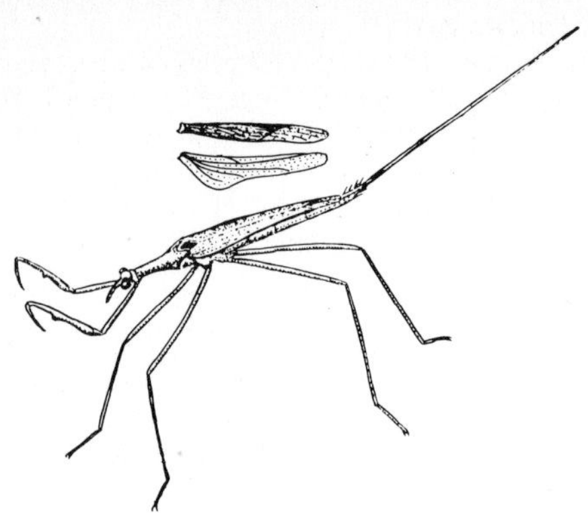

141. A water scorpion, *Ranatra grandicollis*, showing a forewing and a hind wing (above). Its length is about 12 cm, including forelegs and tail.

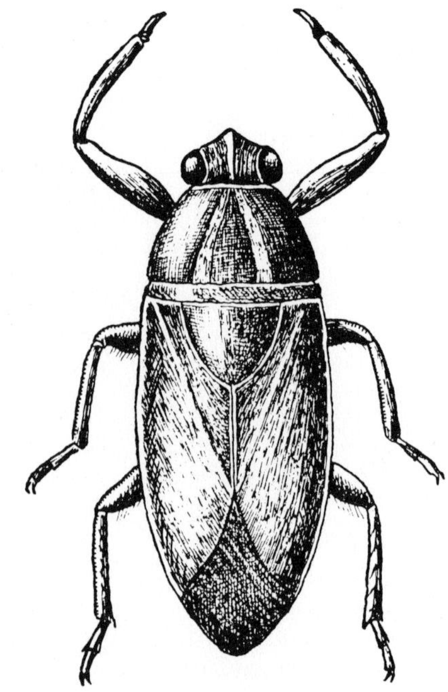

142. Giant water bug, *Lethocerus cordofanus*, about 80 mm long, is often attracted to lights at night. It gives off a disgusting odour if handled, and can inflict a painful bite. Some of the giant water bugs are among the largest insects in the world, reaching almost 12 cm in length.

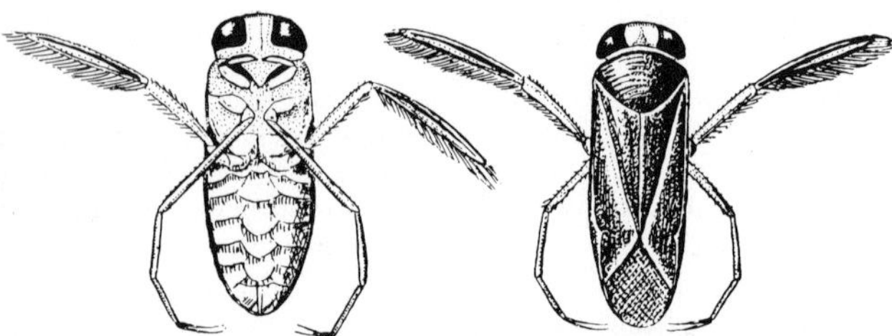

143. A water boatman, *Sigara meridionalis*, as seen from above the water surface (right) and from below. It is about 6 mm long and brown in colour. It is mainly southern African, and occurs on small ponds everywhere.

stabbing it with the powerful beak, then sucking out the body contents. The Notónectidae are not sociable, and when prey becomes hard to find the backswimmers become cannibalistic, the bigger and stronger ones consuming the rest. The males have stridulatory combs on their front legs by means of which they can produce a chirping sound. The females of some species lay their eggs in slits they make in the stems of water-plants, while the females of other species lay their eggs on the surface of submerged stems and other objects. The nymphs live in water and have habits similar to those of their parents. There are five nymphal stages before the adult form is reached.

Water scorpions Members of the family Nepidae are aquatic bugs in which the front pair of legs are adapted for seizing their prey. The slender brown water scorpions (*Ranatra* species) are quite common although they are not often seen because they spend their time creeping slowly about amid water-weeds and on the muddy bottoms of shallow pools. Here they hunt for mayfly and dragonfly nymphs, crustaceans and small tadpoles. They may also feed on mosquito larvae, and play some part in controlling their numbers.

The beak of the water scorpion is short, curved and strong, well equipped to pierce the body of its victim and to suck the contents (it can also deliver a painful bite to a careless insect collector). Antennae cannot readily be seen because they are hidden in special cavities on the underside of the head. The first segment of the thorax is elongated, as well as the coxa, or basal joint of the front legs, so that its grasping legs have a long reach for seizing prey. It is a sluggish, slow-moving creature, remaining motionless until a victim comes within range of its legs.

The female water scorpion lays her eggs in slits she cuts in the stems of water plants by means of her sharp, toothed ovipositor. From each egg a pair of threads or filaments protrudes though the hole in the stem, and it is believed these filaments help the embryo inside the egg extract air from the water. The young are like their parents.

The long, slender thread on the tail is the respiratory tube, which consists of two grooved appendages, locked together by stiff bristles projecting from the edges of each groove. In order to breathe, the insect simply brings the tip of the tube to the surface. The wings are of the usual type but small and narrow, and it is surprising that the long, ungainly insect is able to fly at all. However, it does migrate from one pool to another at night. Often small red water mites may be seen clinging to the legs and respiratory tube of the water scorpion, but they do not seem to do any harm to their host and use it only as a means of transport. After a time the mites cast their skin, become free swimming, and leave the insect.

The broad water scorpions, *Nepa* species, have similar habits to *Ranatra*, but their bodies are flat and broad and their breathing tube is short. The female lays her eggs in chains in the water, the eggs linked one to the other by means of seven slender threads.

Giant water bugs The Belostomatidae include among their number some of the largest of all insects. Certain species found in Africa are more than 10 cm in length and they are formidable insects that attack tadpoles and small fish. The lancets in the strong, curved beak are capable of inflicting a painful wound if one of these bugs is held in the hand. They can fly quite well and move from one sheet of water to another at night, sometimes attracted to lights. Their favourite haunts are the muddy bottoms of weedy pools, where they lurk, well concealed by their dull colours, in wait for their prey. They can swim very well because their hind legs, flattened and fringed with stiff hairs, form efficient swimming organs.

Two appendages on the tip of the abdomen can be withdrawn or extended at will: each is grooved, and, when they are closely applied one to the other, form a tube down which air can be drawn when the tip is thrust above the surface of the water. The back of the abdomen is hollowed out so that a space is enclosed between it and the wings and this forms a reservoir for air. Consequently the insect can remain for long periods beneath the surface. In some species of giant bugs the eggs are carried by the male, glued to the upper surface of his first pair of wings. They are placed here by the female and it is believed that she often is obliged to hold him by force whilst she imposes them upon him. He carries them about with him until they hatch and often the young bugs prey upon one another for their first meal before leaving the paternal back.

Water boatmen The last of the aquatic Hemiptera to be considered are the common inhabitants of shallow pools in Africa, the Corixidae. They are small insects, brown in colour, with short front and middle legs, and long, fringed hind legs that are used as oars. Superficially, they resemble backswimmers, but have flattened backs, short, scoop-shaped front legs, and swim right side up.

Water boatmen are not found in deep water, or in the open water of large lakes. Their feeding habits have been the subject of much speculation in the past, but it is now reliably known that they are mainly predaceous, although there is no doubt that some may utilise bottom ooze containing protozoans, rotifers and diatoms, while a few species feed on the cell contents of filamentous algae.

CLASSIFICATION

ORDER **Hemiptera**

Mouthparts piercing and suctorial, consisting of a grooved sheath, the labium, in which four stylets, the mandibles and maxillae, are lodged. The mouthparts usually in the form of a beak, or rostrum.

SUBORDER **Homoptera**
Forewings, when present, of uniform consistency throughout their length and usually held rooflike over the abdomen. Rostrum usually short and rising at back of head, close to front coxae.

SERIES **Auchenorrhyncha**
Tarsi 3-segmented, antennae generally short with a terminal arista. Rostrum 3-segmented, arising from the head and extending backwards between coxae. Active bugs, often able to jump or fly.

SUPERFAMILY **Fulgoroidea**
Antennae arising on sides of head beneath eyes; two ocelli near eyes. Middle coxae elongated and separated. A very large group consisting of some 20 families. Of these the Delphacidae, Fulgoridae, Dictyophoridae, Cixiidae and Flatidae are the most commonly encountered in Africa. They are usually jumping insects; some species have mixed short- and long-winged individuals, or different colour phases.

SUPERFAMILY **Cercopoidea**
Small jumping insects. Hind tibiae with one or two stout spines, and usually a circle of small spines at the apex. Adults called froghoppers, nymphs called spittle bugs because of the frothy foam that surrounds them. Some authorities recognise three African families, while others place all species in the Cercopidae.

SUPERFAMILY **Cicadoidea**
Large insects, with three ocelli and membranous, transparent forewings. Males with sound-producing organs (tymbals) at base of abdomen. Nymphs are subterranean, and many species have exceptionally long life cycles. Cicadas are very well known, and all the African species belong to a single family, the Cicadidae.

SUPERFAMILY **Cicadelloidea**
Small insects, often brightly coloured, which jump and fly when disturbed. Hind tibiae are elongated, with one or more longitudinal rows of spines which are diagnostic of the group. Many species are economically important through damage to plants, or by transmitting plant virus. Classification of the group is controversial, some authorities recognising up to 16 African families, others placing most species into the Cicadellidae (formerly called Jassidae).

SUPERFAMILY **Membracoidea**
Members of the family Membracidae are immediately recognised by the shape of the pronotum which extends upwards and backwards over the abdomen, giving the insect a hump-backed or thorn-like appearance. They are common in Africa, the genus *Oxyrhachis* being widespread. Some membracids are of very minor economic importance on wattle, lucerne, coffee, tea and cocoa.

SERIES **Sternorrhyncha**
Tarsi 1- or 2-segmented, antennae long and threadlike (sometimes absent). Mostly rather inactive insects, the females of some groups incapable of moving.

SUPERFAMILY **Psylloidea**
The family Psyllidae contains small active jumping insects with 2-segmented tarsi and 10-segmented antennae; wings held rooflike over the body at rest. A few are gall-makers, and one species is a serious pest on citrus.

SUPERFAMILY **Aleyrodoidea**
Minute insect with 2-segmented tarsi, 7-segmented antennae and wings held shallowly rooflike over body at rest. Body and wings dusted with white powder. Only one family, the Aleyrodidae, which sometimes attack citrus or greenhouse plants.

SUPERFAMILY **Aphidoidea**
Small insects with 2-segmented tarsi; wings, when present, membranous and not covered with white powder; hind wing much smaller than forewing. Abdomen oval or pear-shaped, often with a posterior pair of fingerlike cornicles. The majority of the aphids belong to the family Aphididae; they have a complicated life cycle, and highly developed polymorphism. A small family, the Phylloxeridae, also occurs in Africa and contains a few economically important species.

SUPERFAMILY **Coccoidea**
Tarsi 1-segmented, or legs absent; males midge-like and minute, with 1 pair of wings and vestigial mouthparts. Females wingless, often also legless, and usually with a scale-like or waxy covering. At least 10 families can be recognised from Africa; the Margarodidae include the Australian bug *(Icerya purchasi)* and the 'ground pearls', which are

waxy cysts of female *Margarodes*. The Pseudococcidae comprise the mealy bugs, and the Coccidae contain the soft scales. The cochineal insects that live on cactus belong to the small family Dactylopiidae. Some of the most destructive and economically important members of this group are hard-, or armoured scales of the family Diaspididae.

SUBORDER **Heteroptera**
Forewings, when present, thickened at the base, membranous at the tip, held flat over the body at rest with the tips overlapping. Hind wings membranous, shorter than forewings. Beak generally rises from anterior part of head, comprises four stylets in a segmented sheath. Tarsi with three or fewer segments.

SERIES **Geocorisae**
Mainly terrestrial bugs; legs not modified for swimming; antennae usually longer than head.

SUPERFAMILY **Cimicoidea**
Antennae not geniculate, 2nd segment longest. This group contains some 8 families, of which the bed bugs (Cimicidae) are well known; they have very reduced wings and are blood-sucking ectoparasites of man, bats and birds. The closely related Polyctenidae occur only on bats. The damsel bugs (Nabidae) are mainly small, dull insects, with the body in the shape of a tear drop. They are predaceous and rather like assassin bugs, from which they are distinguished by their 4-segmented rostrum. The family Miridae is the largest in the order, comprising the small and delicate leaf bugs. The minute pirate bugs (Anthocoridae) are small, mostly brown or black and white bugs, usually predaceous. Some prey on harmful insects like thrips and scale insects. One of the jumping tree bugs (*Letaba bedfordi*) of the family Isometopidae feeds on citrus red scale in South Africa.

SUPERFAMILY **Tingoidea**
Upper side with a lace-like, reticulate sculpture over the thorax and forewings. Only one African family, the Tingidae, commonly known as lace bugs. They are small, flattened bugs of a great variety of strange forms.

SUPERFAMILY **Reduvioidea**
Predaceous bugs with long head, 3-segmented rostrum and large eyes; antennae usually geniculate. There are three families, of which the Reduviidae is the largest and contains the well known assassin bugs. They are fierce predators and can inflict painful bites. The ambush bugs (Phymatidae) frequent flowers and are often brightly coloured; they capture other insects which visit the flowers.

SUPERFAMILY **Saldoidea**
A small group with one important family, the Saldidae or shore bugs. These are recognised by the four or five long, closed cells in membrane of forewings; the eyes are large and prominent. Generally oval in shape, they occur along grassy shores and are predaceous.

SUPERFAMILY **Aradoidea**
The Aradidae are called flat bugs or fungus bugs. Wings are well-developed but small, and do not cover the entire abdomen. Wingless forms are known. Antennae and beak are 4-segmented, tarsi 2-segmented and there are no ocelli. They are extremely flattened, dull-coloured; they live concealed under loose bark or in crevices in dead and decaying trees, where they feed on fungus sap.

SUPERFAMILY **Coreoidea**
Medium to large, elongated bugs usually of brown or grey colouration, 4-segmented antennae and rostrum, and strong legs, the hind tibiae sometimes expanded. The most important family is the Coreidae, containing the twig wilter bugs. They are all plant feeders, sometimes causing serious damage to crops, and produce repugnant fluid from their conspicuous scent glands.

SUPERFAMILY **Lygaeoidea**
A large group of medium-to-small, strongly sclerotized, sometimes brightly coloured bugs, most are plant feeders and some are of economic importance. Rostrum and antennae both 4-segmented. The Pyrrhocoridae (red bugs, cotton stainer bugs) are sometimes placed in their own superfamily. They lack ocelli which are present in the other two important families, the Lygaeidae (seed bugs) and the Berytidae (stilt bugs). The latter are small and delicate, the body elongate and linear, the legs and antennae long, and they occur in dense herbaceous vegetation.

SUPERFAMILY **Pentatomoidea**
Body strongly sclerotized, antennae usually 5-segmented, pronotum often 6-sided, the scutellum large, reaching at least to middle of abdomen and sometimes covering entire abdomen as in the Scutelleridae (shield backed bugs) and Plataspidae (pill bugs). Members of these families may be convex, metallic, plain or patterned species. The Pentatomidae or stink bugs are well known insects, the Cydnidae (burrower bugs) less so. The latter are mostly black or brownish, with a shining and usually punctate surface. They have stout spines (diagnostic) on the tibiae, live mostly in soil and feed on roots or animal matter.

SERIES **Amphibicorisae**

SUPERFAMILY **Gerroidea**
Aquatic Heteroptera, living on the water surface; antennae longer than head, underside of body with water-repellent hairs, claws not at apices of legs. The Gerridae (water striders) occur on water surfaces all over the world. Their relatives, the Veliidae (ripple bugs) and Mesoveliidae (water treaders) are similar in having short front legs, with long middle and hind legs, used for locomotion. Shallow ponds with partly submerged vegetation provide suitable habitat for the Hydrometridae (water measurers), which resemble tiny stick insects as they walk on water and vegetation in search of prey. The Hebridae (velvet water bugs) are tiny, hairy, broad-shouldered bugs of the water surface. *Hebrus violaceus* is common in Africa, found on reservoirs, muddy brackish pools, or fast running streams.

SERIES **Hydrocorisae**
Aquatic or (less often) semi-aquatic Heteroptera; antennae shorter than head and usually concealed beneath it; hind legs modified for swimming in some families.

SUPERFAMILY **Notonectoidea**
Aquatic, rostrum elongated and 3-4 segmented; front tarsi not spatulate, ocelli absent. The Notonectidae (back swimmers) are easily recognised by their swimming habits; the Nepidae (water scorpions) by the long breathing tube at the end of the abdomen; and the Belostomatidae (giant water bugs) by their large size and raptorial front legs. Less well-known in Africa are the Naucoridae (creeping water bugs), which are small to medium, rounded, and flattened, with thick front femora. They crawl about on aquatic vegetation, hunting various aquatic animals.

SUPERFAMILY **Corixoidea**
This group contains a single family, the Corixidae (water boatmen), that are recognised by their short, scoop-shaped front tarsi, elongated oar-like hind legs and their habit of swimming with the dorsal surface uppermost. They are not predaceous.

FURTHER READING

Capener, A. L.: (Papers on Membracidae and Psyllidae. Most in *Journal of the Entomological Society of Southern Africa.*) (1962-1970)

Carvalho, J. C. M.: (Papers on Miridae, including a world catalogue, published in Rio de Janeiro, in Spanish.) (1952-1960)

De Lotto, G.: (Papers on Coccidae, Pseudococcidae and other Homoptera, published in *Bulletin of the British Museum (Natural History)* and South African journals.) (1958-1978)

Drake C. J. & Ruhoff, F. A.: 'Lace bugs of the World, a Catalog (Hemiptera: Tingidae)' *Bulletin of the United States National Museum* (1965) 243: 634 pp (Also various other important papers by Drake and co-workers.)

Eastop, V. F. & Hille Rislambers, D.: *Survey of the world's Aphids.* W. Junk, The Hague. (1976) 573 pp (Also other important papers by Eastop.)

Hesse, A. J.: 'A list of the Heteropterous and Homopterous Hemiptera of South West Africa.' *Annals of the South African Museum* (1925) 23: 1-190

Metcalf, Z. P.: (Many important papers on Hemiptera, including series of catalogues published by the United States Department of Agriculture.) (1927-1968)

Miller, N. C. E.: *Biology of the Heteroptera.* E. W. Classey Ltd., Hampton (1971). 2nd edition, 206 pp (Also papers by the same author on Reduviidae.)

Mound, L. A. & Halsey, S. M.: *Whitefly of the world.* British Museum (Natural History), London (1978). 340 pp

Munting, J.: (Papers on Diaspididae, mostly in *Journal of the Entomological Society of Southern Africa.*) (1965-1971)

Poisson, R. H.: Papers on aquatic and semi-aquatic families (1924-1966). Major work with P. Pesson on the Hemiptera in Grassé, P.P. *Traité de Zoologie* (1951). Vol. 10, pp 1385-1803

Slater, J. A.: *A Catalogue of the Lygaeidae of the World.* University of Connecticut, Storrs (1964). 1668 pp (Also other important papers by Slater and co-workers.)

13

Alderflies, lacewings and antlions

This interesting group of insects was formerly regarded as a single order, but today researchers recognise three: the Megaloptera (alderflies), the Neuroptera (lacewings and antlions), and the Raphidioptera, known as 'snake-flies' which do not occur in Africa south of the Sahara and do not concern us here.

Alderflies The order Megaloptera occurs almost world-wide, but in Africa has so far been found only in the southern part of the continent. The family Sialidae comprises but one species found in South Africa's Cape Province; seven species belonging to the family Corydalidae have been described from the mountainous regions of the Cape and Natal.

The common Cape alderfly, *Taeniochauliodes ochraceopennis* is one of the largest, measuring 60 – 80 mm across the outspread wings. It is found at an altitude of 700 m or more along the mountain streams of the south-west Cape. The adult alderfly is brown with transparent wings that are tinged with grey or brown and dotted with darker brown along the veins. It may be found during the summer months in shady kloofs where it settles on the bushes beside streams or on rocks jutting out of the water. When disturbed, the insect flies swiftly and erratically but when at rest it folds its wings round its body.

The female lays her numerous brown eggs in masses on rocks near the water. Each egg is about 2 mm long and has a curious club-shaped projection at the upper end: the entire mass may measure nearly 25 mm in diameter. The newly-hatched larvae make their way into the water where they live under stones and in moss,

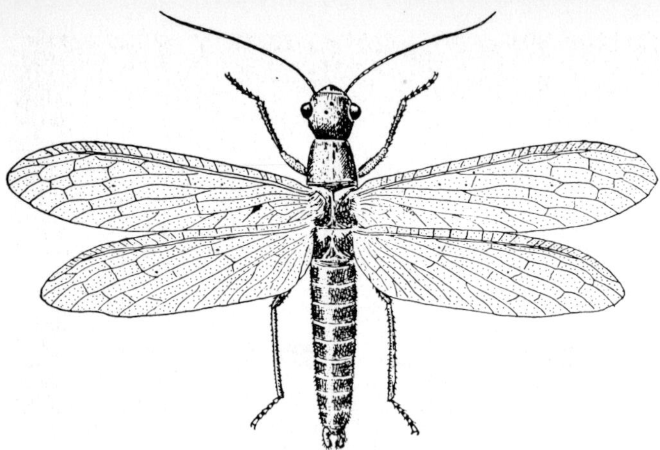

144. A male alderfly, *Taeniochauliodes ochraceopennis.* The outspread wings are about 80 mm across.

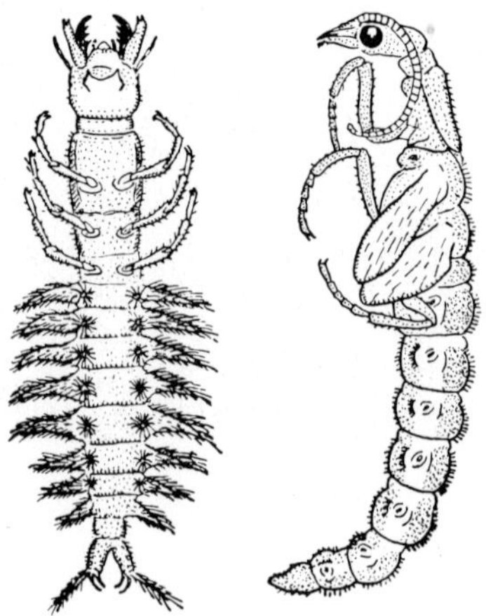

145. Larva (left) and pupa (right) of the alderfly *Chloroniella peringueyi;* both are about 30 mm long.

hunting for the aquatic insects and crustaceans upon which they feed. The fully-grown larva is about 40 mm long and armed with a pair of powerful jaws with which it attempts to bite fiercely if it is handled. Along each side of its abdomen it has six legs and eight hairy lateral gills. At its posterior end are a pair of double hooks with which it clings to submerged objects in order to prevent itself from being washed away by swift currents. If disturbed, it will curl up, but soon uncurls and creeps to safety under a stone or anchors itself by its abdominal hooks.

When ready to pupate, the larva creeps out of the water and burrows into sphagnum moss beside the stream. The pupa is about 25 mm long, yellow, with the antennae, compound eyes, legs and wing-buds of the adult clearly evident. Just before the fly emerges, the pupa wriggles its way to the surface of the moss. The adults may be found on the wing during the southern summer months and are commonest in January and February.

Neuroptera The order Neuroptera contains a number of families of insects that are mostly slender, soft-bodied and rather weak fliers. The scientific name, Neuroptera, refers to the network of so-called veins or nerves on the wings and means 'nerve-winged'. The adults have two pairs of these wings, both alike and held roofwise over the body when at rest. Some are large and showy and might easily be mistaken for dragonflies whilst others are medium-sized or small. The larvae are predaceous, feeding on other insects. All the members of this order have a true pupal stage, often enclosed in a silken cocoon spun by the larva.

Lacewings The pretty little green insects with eyes of a yellow, metallic lustre, popularly known as 'lacewings', or 'golden-eyes' belong to the family Chrysopidae and are often found on aphid-infested plants. There are a number of different species but all look very much alike and they are mostly about 12 mm long. Some have a pair of glands on the thorax which gives off an unpleasant smell when the insect is handled, giving rise to their other common name 'stinkflies'.

The eggs of the lacewings *(Chrysopa* species) are remarkable objects and easily recognised. Each is mounted on top of a slender stalk and looks something like a miniature balloon on the end of a string. The female generally chooses the underside of a leaf on a plant that is infested with aphids and, when she is laying, she touches the leaf with the tip of her abdomen and ejects a drop of sticky fluid from the glands associated with her ovaries. She then lifts the tip of her abdomen and the gummy substance is drawn out in a thread which rapidly hardens in the air. On top of this she deposits her egg. The eggs are, as a rule, placed in a group where they look like a tuft of clubbed hairs projecting from the surface of the leaf.

Mounted on these stalks, the eggs are less liable to be found by enemies and furthermore the young insects, which are fiercely cannibalistic, cannot get at one another easily when they first hatch; there is, therefore, more chance for their survival than if the eggs were simply laid on the leaf, side by side, as is the case with most insects.

The larva is six-legged, active and armed with a pair of sharp jaws with which it pierces and sucks the juices of the aphids. Some species cover themselves with the wax or empty skins of their victims; others fix fragments of bark, dead leaves and other material to the hairs on their backs, but many do not conceal themselves in any way. The larvae of lacewings might be mistaken for the larvae of ladybird beetles which they resemble, but can be recognised by the curious trumpet-shaped appendage – its function unknown – between the claws on each foot; this is so small that it can only be detected through a hand-lens.

When the larva is fully grown it seeks out a sheltered spot and there it spins a spherical silken cocoon inside which it pupates. Two or three weeks later the adult emerges.

Some male lacewings have scent glands and they attract their mates simply by sitting on a twig and emitting the odour that guides the females to them.

The brown lacewings, family Hemerobiidae, are very similar to Chrysopidae but their eggs are not laid on stalks. The silky lacewings of the family Psychopsidae, their wings broad and mothlike, are usually very well camouflaged as they sit motionless on trees during the day. They are generally seen only at night when they come to lights.

The mantidflies or mantispas belong to the family Mantispidae. The adults look like small praying mantids because their front legs are modified for capturing and grasping prey, with a row of sharp spines along the outer ege of the femur, and a tibia that closes down on the femur like the jaws of a trap. There are a number of different species found in Africa but we know little of their habits and life history.

The female lays a large number of small eggs that are mounted on stalks similar to those of the green lacewings. The newly-hatched larva of the mantispa is very small and slender, with six legs and runs about actively. It can endure a long fast and may even hibernate for several weeks without food if conditions are unfavourable. In order to survive it must find the egg-cocoon of a spider. If it succeeds, it burrows through the silken envelope and takes up its abode amid the ball of eggs. Here it waits patiently until the eggs hatch and then, for the first time since birth, it begins to feed, devouring the young spiders inside the cocoon until it is soon surrounded by the shrivelled skins of its victims. The larva grows rapidly on this fare and in a few days it is a bloated yellow grub that can scarcely move. When fully grown it spins a neat spherical cocoon of silk, with the dried remains of the young spiders adhering all over the outside.

Practically nothing is known about the habits of the adult. The nature of the front legs indicates that it is predaceous, feeding on small insects which it captures by stealth as it cannot run quickly and is a feeble flier. Apparently it waits on flowers for small flies, bees and beetles hunting for nectar.

The thread-wing lacewings are highly specialised insects placed in the family Nemopteridae. Common in some of the more arid parts of Africa, these striking and beautiful insects fly with a curious up and down motion, their long, threadlike hind wings trailing behind them. They are sometimes seen around lights in the evening, particularly when rain threatens. The female lays her eggs in fine, dry dust, with which the larvae subsequently cover themselves as camouflage, just inside the entrance of caves, or beneath over-hanging rocks, or on the dirty floors of buildings that are little used.

The larva has a long, narrow 'neck' and typical curved, sucking jaws. It feeds on psocids, small spiders, mites and any other creatures it can capture. When it is fully grown it makes a cocoon of silk and sand grains and the pupa is easily identified by the long, slender hind wings coiled like watch-springs along the sides.

Antlions The most commonly encountered members of the order Neuroptera are the antlions, family Myrmeleontidae, which are widely spread throughout the continent of Africa. The adults are like dragonflies in

146. Eggs of green lacewing, laid on a tree trunk. Length with stalk, 8 mm.

147. 10 mm long larva of a green lacewing feeding on aphids by means of its piercing jaws. This is one of many insects that benefit gardener and farmer alike.

148. Adult green lacewing. These insects are often attracted into houses by lights, and give off an unpleasant odour when handled. (25 mm, including antennae.)

149. A mantidfly awaiting prey on a flower. It is about 12 mm long. Note the front pair of legs, modified for seizing prey in much the same way as those of the praying mantid.

150. Thread-wing lacewing. In these insects the hind pair of wings is reduced to a pair of long threadlike filaments. Length 50 mm, including tails.

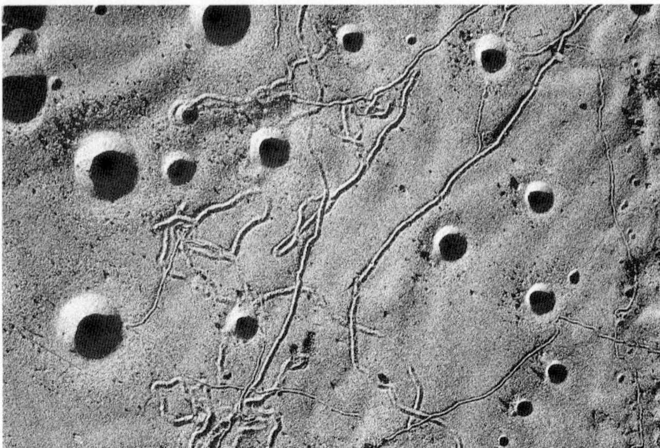

151. Pit traps (about 30 mm in diameter) of antlion larvae in fine sand, showing the trails left by the larvae as they move about at night.

general appearance but their antennae are different. The antennae of an antlion are conspicuous and clubbed at the tip, like those of a butterfly, whereas the antennae of a dragonfly are small, threadlike and scarcely visible. Furthermore, antlions are clumsy fliers compared with dragonflies and they take to the air mostly in the evening and at night.

The conical pit made by the antlion larva is familiar to anybody in Africa who takes even the slightest interest in natural history. Found in dry, sandy soil, it is usually 30 mm or so in diameter and about 25 mm deep. At the bottom of the pit, buried in the sand resides a drab, squat creature, dull brown in colour and armed with a pair of sharp, curved jaws. If an unwary ant or other insect walks over the edge of the pit and stumbles down the crumbling sides, the head of the antlion at once appears. With jerky movements of its head, the owner of the pit throws sand up at the struggling insect, making it slip further and further down the side towards the bottom. As soon as the creature is within reach of the murderous jaws it is seized and dragged below the surface, where the antlion sucks its body dry of juices and then discards the empty skin.

Although the antlion larva is such a voracious feeder, it has no mouth; either the mouth is permanently sealed by a membrane that grows over it, or the upper and lower edges are so closely joined that it is impossible for the insect to open its mouth. However, the two sickle-like jaws have a narrow groove along the inner edge and the long, slender maxilla on each side fits over the groove to form channels along which the victim's juices pass into the pharynx. All the members of this order have sucking jaws of this type.

Owing to the nature of the soil in which it is made, the pit is easily destroyed – by wind, rain, or passing animals. Such destruction does not inconvenience the larva to any great extent for it quickly excavates a new home. The insect always moves backwards, tail first, with its body just beneath the surface of the sand. As it moves round and round in circles of decreasing diameter, it tosses the sand to one side by jerking its head. In this way a conical pit is slowly sunk until, when it is deep enough, the larva conceals itself at the bottom to wait for its next victim. If the site chosen proves to be an unprofitable spot, with captures few and far between, the antlion deserts the pit and digs a new one somewhere else. This departure to a fresh site usually takes place at night.

The alimentary canal of the antlion is blind; it has no connection with the intestine at the rear end. Owing to the nature of its food there is little waste matter and what there is, is dealt with by the Malpighian tubes. There are eight of these tubes of which six are connected with the hind intestine and are extraordinary in function.

When the larva is fully grown it buries itself 50 – 75 mm deep in the sand where it makes itself an oval cell. Next it spins a spherical cocoon, the silk coming from the Malpighian tubes and oozing from the anus. As the silk is sticky when first emitted, grains of sand adhere to it and in this way the larva constructs a compact, secure shelter in which to change into a pupa. The pupa is short and stout and it is astonishing that such a long, slender, four-winged adult eventually emerges from it.

The large and rather showy adults, such as the spotted-wing antlion, *Palpares speciosus*, with yellow wings blotched with brown, and the smaller kinds with transparent wings, such as *Myrmeleon obscurus*, are common in Africa.

The larvae of the various species of *Myrmeleon* and *Cueta* build pits, but the majority of antlions do not construct pits and are free-living in sand. The larvae all have a large head with curved, toothed jaws, four or five simple eyes on each side of the head at the base of the jaws, a small thorax, six short legs, and a flattened, rounded abdomen armed with bristles. They are ugly, ungainly creatures, but they can burrow in the soil with remarkable speed; often their trails are visible as slight raised ridges on the sand, winding in all directions as the insects travel backwards in search of a suitable site for their home.

The long-horned antlions, or owlflies, are placed in a family by themselves (Ascalaphidae). The adults are more active in the air than the Myrmeleontidae and they may be seen in the evening hawking to and fro for their prey like dragonflies. When they settle they usually adopt a characteristic pose, with the abdomen held up at right angles to the thorax and the wings folded down away from the body.

The female of one of the commonest of the ascalaphids, *Proctarrelabris capensis*, lays her oval white eggs in an irregular group on a rock, generally on the underside of a projecting ledge so that they are protected from the weather and the direct rays of the sun; these may be found at mid-summer. The newly-hatched, black young remain clustered round the empty shells for a day or so after they emerge. They sit quite still, their jaws held wide open and, if you bring an aphid or other small insect into contact with these jaws, they snap shut. Unfortunately it seems to be difficult to rear these little creatures in captivity: they soon become restless and wander about until they die. In the natural state it seems that they hunt beneath stones and amid vegetation for their prey. They do not construct pits.

152. An antlion larva, shuffling backwards into sand prior to making its pit. Clearly visible are its powerful hollow jaws, with which it sucks its victims' body juices. 10 mm long.

153. An adult antlion (45 mm). They spend the daylight hours resting among vegetation. The stout antennae and gauze-like wings are characteristic of adult antlions.

154. With only its jaws visible, a large, freeliving antlion larva lies hidden beneath the sand as it sucks the body juices of a long-horned grasshopper that chanced to pass close by the lurking larva. Grasshopper length about 50 mm.

CLASSIFICATION

ORDER **Megaloptera**
Medium to large insects with two pairs of membranous wings, the hind pair slightly broader at their bases than forewings, and with the anal area folded fanwise at rest. Larvae aquatic. Two families occur in Africa, both restricted to the southern part of the continent; Sialidae (one species) and Corydalidae (seven species).

ORDER **Neuroptera**
Forewings and hind wings similar in size and shape, anal area of hindwing not folded fanwise at rest. Larvae terrestrial. Several families occur in Africa, most of them having predaceous larvae.

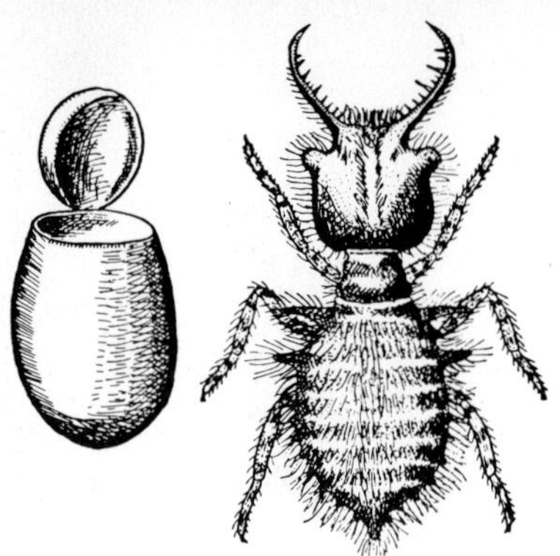

155. Newly hatched larva of the long-horned antlion, *Proctarrelabris capensis*, next to the empty eggshell, which is pure white and about 1,5 mm long.

FAMILY **Chrysopidae**
Wings usually greenish, eyes golden or copper coloured, antennae long and threadlike, may produce unpleasant odour when handled. Eggs laid on stalks. Larvae have long sickle-shaped mandibles; feed principally on aphids, as do adults.

FAMILY **Hemerobiidae**
Similar to previous family, but smaller, brownish in colour and with different wing venation. Adults and larvae are predaceous.

FAMILY **Psychopsidae**
Wings broad and mothlike with characteristic venation, antennae short. Larvae predatory with enlarged mandibles, living mostly under bark from which they emerge to seize their victims.

FAMILY **Mantispidae**
Front legs raptorial, with spines on the femur which acts against the tibia to constitute a powerful grasping weapon. Adults predatory, larvae parasitic, sometimes associated with spiders.

FAMILY **Nemopteridae**
Adults with elongated, ribbon-like hind wings. Antennae long and not clubbed. Larvae live in dust and are characterised by having a long 'neck'; they are predaceous on booklice and other small insects.

FAMILY **Myrmeleontidae**
Adults superficially resemble dragonflies but have prominent, clubbed antennae. Wings usually spotted or blotched with black or brown. Most larvae dig conical pits in the ground, trapping other insects which fall into them; a few larvae hide under stones or bark.

FAMILY **Ascalaphidae**
Antennae very long, with clubbed ends, and adults may be active fliers and predatory. Normally take up a characteristic attitude at rest, with abdomen and antennae held up almost at right angles to surface. Larvae do not construct pits, but live under stones, leaves or bark from where they emerge to prey on other insects.

FURTHER READING

Mansell, M. W.: (Papers on Mymeleontidae, mainly in *Journal of the Entomological Society of southern Africa*) (1973-1978).
Tjeder, B.: (Numerous papers on Neuroptera, including monographs in *South African Animal Life*) (1957-1969).
Wheeler, W. M.: *Demons of the Dust*. Kegan Paul, Trench, Trubner & Co., London (1930). 378 pp
Youthed, G. J. & Moran, V. C.: (1968). (Three papers on biology of Myrmeleontidae larvae in *Journal of Insect Physiology* vol. 15)

Beetles 14

Beetles make up the largest order in the whole animal kingdom – approximately 300 000 species have been described and named, and many more are being discovered all the time. They include many insects which are of economic importance: some destroyers of wood, seeds, crops and stored products, others useful predators of aphids and scale insects. The beetles include some of the largest and some of the smallest of all insects: certain long-horn beetles found in the tropics measure up to 15 cm in length, whereas there are minute fungus beetles that are less than half a millimetre long. They abound everywhere, but most do not attract much attention because of their dark colouring and their covert ways. Some are attractive, even spectacular, which makes the group the favourite of many collectors.

The most striking characteristic of beetles as a group is the nature of their front wings which are horny or leathery, and are not used in flight, but serve as a protective cover for the second pair of wings and the soft upper surface of the abdomen. The scientific name of the order comprising the beetles is Coleoptera, which means 'horny-winged', derived from these front wings or elytra. The membranous hind wings are carried folded beneath the elytra when not in use.

Many beetles have lost the ability to fly and their second pair of wings is much reduced or has disappeared completely, their elytra being firmly joined together to form a strong covering for the abdomen. Another feature of beetles is their mouthparts which are adapted for biting and chewing. The life histories of different types of beetles are extremely varied, and members of this most successful order are found living in every conceivable habitat on earth. All beetles have a complete metamorphosis, and pass through the four stages of egg, larva, pupa and adult. The order is divided into a great many families; only some of the most important, interesting and conspicuous can be dealt with here.

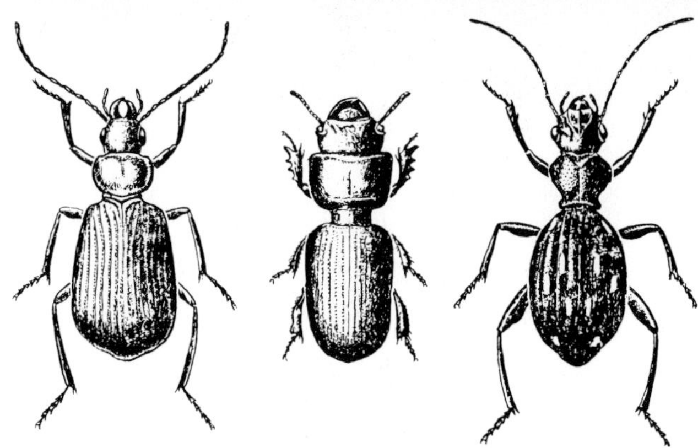

156. Three ground beetles (Carabidae), showing how the forewings are modified into horny cases (the elytra).

Ground beetles The family Carabidae contains over 25 000 described species, including many which are important predators in all terrestrial habitats. The family contains numerous subfamilies, two of which have, because of their specialised life styles, traditionally been treated as separate families. These are the tiger beetles (Cicindelinae) and the ant nest beetles (Paussinae). The remaining subfamilies together constitute the group commonly referred to as 'ground beetles'. These beetles were once thought to be entirely predaceous, but there is now evidence that many groups are at least partly plant eating, some of them specialised feeders – creatures that feed exclusively on a particular plant or other foodsource. Although called ground beetles, this is to some extent misleading since certain groups are largely found on plants or under the bark of trees.

157. A 50 mm long ground beetle of the genus *Anthia*. It is predominantly black, with two patches of yellow on the upper thorax, and usually hunts at night.

Ground beetles are renowned for their fascinating chemical defence mechanisms. Best known are the European bombardier beetles of the genus *Brachinus*, which can discharge from the tip of the abdomen a mixture of chemicals that smells foul and when released explodes audibly. This is sufficient to frighten and demoralise potential predators like toads, which would be given a nasty surprise if they tried to eat one.

In Africa the best known and most widespread bombardier beetles belong to the genus *Pheropsophus*, which produce the same chemicals and may have similar abilities to those of *Brachinus*. These beetles are black, or black and yellow, and the apical segments of the abdomen are exposed. Some *Pheropsophus* have parasitic larvae which feed on the eggs of mole crickets.

158. Ants dragging a paussid beetle about, probably in order to stimulate it into producing the secretions of which they are particularly fond. The very enlarged antennae, characteristic of this group of beetles, are a source of these secretions. 8 mm.

Another group of ground beetles noted for their chemical defence mechanisms are members of the genus *Anthia* and related genera. These are striking, large black beetles 25 – 50 mm in length, many of them with yellow or white spots on the thorax or elytra. They are found throughout Africa and may be seen running about swiftly during the day. They cannot fly as their wing cases are firmly joined and the membranous wings beneath have disappeared. Fierce hunters with strong, sharp jaws, they can inflict a nasty bite on the hand of a careless collector. The main defence chemical of *Anthia* beetles is formic acid, which they can squirt up to 35 cm in any direction when threatened. The fluid can cause severe pain if it comes in contact with human skin, and more serious problems if it gets into the eyes.

Species of *Scarites* and related genera live in burrows. Accordingly, their bodies are adapted for burrowing; they are somewhat elongated and parallel-sided, with large serrations on their flattened fore-tibia. Although they are predaceous, there is evidence that some species also eat seeds and seedlings.

Another departure from typically predaceous behaviour is seen in *Chlaenius*, beetles which occur mainly near water. They are often gregarious and numbers have been seen dismembering large dead or dying insects. *Chlaenius* species are black or metallic, and the elytra, usually densely clothed in short yellowish hairs, have a broad yellow margin.

Specialised predatory habits are seen in the genus *Calosoma*, of which *Calosoma imbricatum* is a common African species. These are handsome, shiny greenish-bronze or black beetles, about 30 mm long and with six longitudinal rows of small greenish or coppery punctures on the elytra. They may be seen running about on bushes and trees, hunting for the caterpillars which form part of their diet.

An interesting example of mimicry among ground beetles exists in the genus *Lebistina*, and flea beetles of the genus *Diamphidia* (Chrysomelidae). The larvae of the ground beetles parasitize the larvae and the pupae of the flea beetles, while the adult ground beetles closely resemble the adult flea beetles. The *Diamphidia* are used by the Bushmen to poison their arrows, and it is presumed that the ground beetles are shunned by predators such as birds because they are mistaken for the poisonous flea beetles.

Ant nest beetles The subfamily Paussinae of the Carabidae contains some remarkable beetles. The largest are not quite 12 mm long, and most are 6 mm or less. They are never found in the open, but only in ants' nests, or sometimes when they are attracted to light at night. Most species of Paussinae can be recognised by their extraordinarily shaped antennae, in which the terminal joints are fused together to form a curiously shaped club. When irritated, these beetles eject a volatile, caustic fluid, as do the bombardier beetles, and if it gets on the skin, or in the eyes, it can result in severe pain and burning.

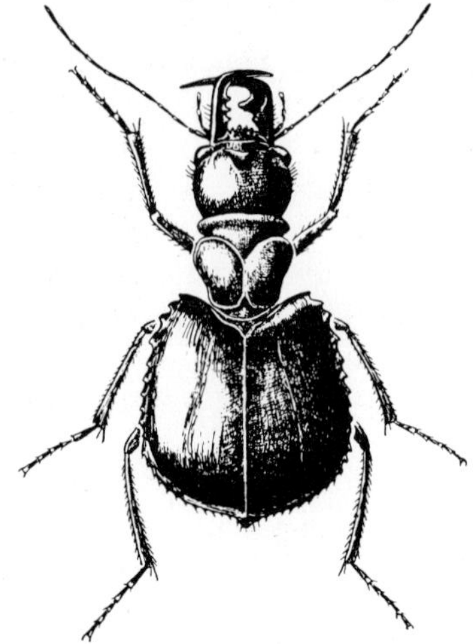

159. Some tiger beetles are very large, such as this male *Manticora* sp. which, including the large mandibles, may reach 50 mm in length. The mandibles are thought to be used for holding the females when mating.

They are tolerated as guests inside ants' nests for it is believed that the ants receive from them an aromatic secretion of which they are very fond. The glandular tissue that produces the secretion is lodged in the enlarged antennae, the head, thorax and apex of the abdomen. Tufts of yellow hair and groups of pores mark the glands and these the ants lick. When these beetles are kept in an artificial ants' nest they remain motionless most of the time, apparently asleep, and the ants ignore them. Occasionally, however, the ants drag them about, usually seizing them by the antennae. It has been suggested that the beetles feed on the adult ants and their larvae. This relationship is explained more fully in Chapter 23. Four genera are widespread in Africa, namely *Heteropaussus, Pentaplatarthus, Cerapterus* and *Paussus*.

Tiger beetles Beetles of the subfamily Cicindellinae are aptly named tiger beetles, for they are among the fiercest and most voracious of all insects, both as larvae and as adults. The adults have large, prominent eyes, strong, sharp mandibles and long legs and can run rapidly over the ground. Most of them have wings and fly readily, but some have lost their second, membranous pair of wings and are flightless.

Members of the genus *Cicindela* are found throughout Africa. Most are brightly coloured with a metallic sheen, the elytra usually having contrasting and complex patterns of white or yellow. They revel in the hottest sunshine and retire to rest, creeping beneath a stone or burying themselves in the sand, before the sun sets and reappear again next morning only after the sun is up and the sand is warm once more. They may be seen running about on open patches, along paths and on the banks of streams and vleis, at any time of the year. Their eyesight is keen and they take short flights if disturbed.

Small, neat round holes about the diameter of a lead pencil can be seen dotted about on the hard patches of sand that are the tiger beetles' haunt. If a slender grass stalk is pushed down one of these holes it will go straight down into the soil to a depth of 30 cm or more. In order to see something of the owner and builder of this tunnel-dwelling, the observer must sit down close by and remain quite still for several minutes. After a time a flat stopper, fitting the hole perfectly, appears at the mouth of the burrow. Even the slightest movement by the observer will cause the stopper to disappear immediately, but if a dead fly is stuck head downwards into the opening, after a short while it will be drawn into the hole and disappear.

The burrow belongs to the larva of the tiger beetle; a

160. A tiger beetle (*Cicindela* sp.) with a fly it has caught along its river-bank haunt.

strange white grub with a big, flat head, it is a creature as unlike its parents as could be. It has a pair of strong, curved jaws and four tiny eyes that gleam like beads on each side of its head. With its six well-developed legs it can crawl about on the ground quite nimbly if need be. On the back of its wormlike body, on the fifth segment of the abdomen, is a curious hump bearing two curved hooks. This hump, with its upward-pointing hooks, enables the larva to keep a grip on the side of its tunnel and to move up and down with astonishing speed. When it comes to the surface, its head and the hard first joint of the thorax form the plug that closes the mouth of the burrow.

Although the insect deepens and enlarges its tunnel from time to time, you never see a heap of soil at the entrance, such as betrays the work of so many burrowing insects. You will, however, see little pellets of soil scattered about 20 mm from the hole. When the insect digs, it forms the pellets of soil with its jaws, and carries them to the surface on top of its head much in the same way as a labourer carries up bricks on a hod. Once at the top, it jerks its head and flings the pellets away, to return at once to the bottom of the burrow to repeat the whole performance.

When on the look-out for food it lies for hours on end, its head plugging the entrance to its home, waiting with endless patience for some unsuspecting insect to come within reach of those murderous jaws. It then throws its head back with a jerk and seizes the victim which is dragged below to be devoured. The larvae of tiger beetles feed on many different types of arthropods and are apparently not very specific in their tastes.

The larva may take a year or more to reach full size, its rate of growth depending mainly on the number of victims that happen to fall into the trap. When fully grown it makes a cell beside its tunnel, not too far below the surface, and there it changes into a pupa. About a month later the adult beetle emerges.

Two other genera of typical tiger beetles are common in Africa, namely *Dromica* and *Prothyma*, the former being common in south and east Africa and the latter in west Africa. Less typical are members of the genus *Mantichora* which inhabit steppe and desert areas in south and east Africa. With a wide abdomen and fearsome jaws, they can inflict a severe bite if handled carelessly. The jaws of the males are exceptionally large and it is believed they are used for holding the female when mating. Although swift runners, these nocturnal large black tiger beetles are wingless and cannot fly.

Water beetles Some 18 families of beetles are more or less exclusively associated with water in Africa, although the casual visitor to a pool or stream will usually only see the bigger and more conspicuous members of three families. The first of these comprises the predaceous water beetles, the Dytiscidae, numerous species of which are found throughout Africa in all types of aquatic habitats. They vary in size from only a few millimetres in length, to over 40 mm in the case of some species of *Cybister*. The biology of this beetle is fairly typical of the Dytiscidae in general.

Strong fliers which migrate from pond to pond under cover of darkness, *Cybister* species are often attracted to lights at night. If one of them strikes the lamp and flops on to the table or floor, it can do little but writhe awkwardly because its legs are so modified for swimming that it walks clumsily and with difficulty. The hind legs are the principal swimming organs; they are flattened and the tibiae and tarsi are fringed with long, stiff, brown bristles. The insect uses these legs like oars and can 'feather' its oars much more neatly than any human oarsman. The tarsi are jointed to the legs in such a way that they can turn on their long axis and, when the water beetle kicks out backwards, the bristles stand out in stiff array to offer the maximum resistance to the water. But when it draws its legs in for the next stroke, the tarsi turn so that the bristles lie flat and there is little to impede the forward momentum.

The body itself is flat and extraordinarily smooth. If one of these beetles is picked up it is liable to shoot from between the fingers like a wet orange pip. The head, thorax, abdomen and elytra are all streamlined, so that there are no angles or projections to hinder swift progress through the water. On the underside, just behind the bases of the second pair of legs, is a strong, sharp spine that projects backwards. If the beetle is held tightly in the fingers it will probably try to wriggle its way out and the spine may pierce the skin and draw blood. While struggling to escape, the beetle also emits a white fluid from the joint between the head and thorax and, if held close to the nose, it will be found to have a disgusting odour, worse than that of rotten eggs. This fluid has been shown to have a temporary stunning and toxic effect on fish and frogs, the most common predators of dytiscid beetles. Furthermore, two anal glands secrete a fluid that smells like ammonia which can be discharged with a small explosion when the insect is irritated.

Although the water beetle spends most of its time in the water, it breathes air. The elytra fit tightly and closely over the back, enclosing a space between them and the back of the abdomen. The spiracles are situated in this space, along each side of the abdomen, the last pair, at the hind end, being the largest. When the beetle needs to renew its air supply it simply stops swimming and floats slowly to the surface, for its body is just a little lighter than water, and the hind end is lighter than the front, so that it floats tail upwards. When the tip of the abdomen projects above the surface the air-supply between the elytra and abdomen is renewed and the beetle dives once more.

It is carnivorous, capturing and devouring insects, small worms, tadpoles and other small water creatures. It is long-lived for an insect; specimens have been kept alive in captivity for over a year. The male is distinguished from the female by the swollen, circular pads on his front legs. The pads are armed with a number of tiny suckers that enable the male to cling to the smooth and slippery body of the female when they mate.

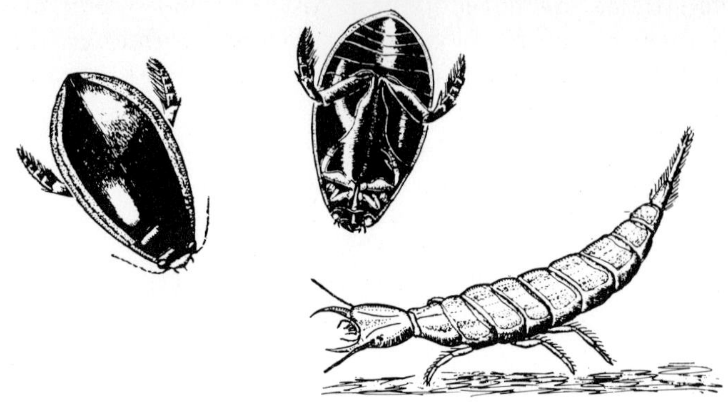

161. The larva (below) and adults of the water beetle (*Cybister* sp.). The adults are about 20 mm long.

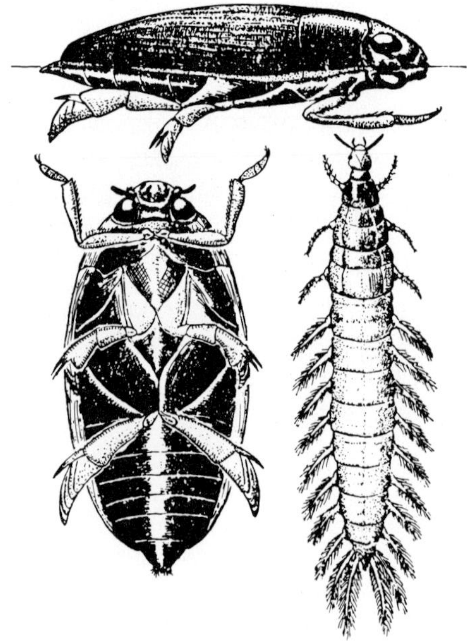

162. Adult whirligig beetles (*Aulonogyrus* sp.) seen from the side and from below, and a larva (right). Adults are about 8 mm long.

The female lays her eggs singly in the stems of different kinds of water plants, after making deep slits to receive them. In about three weeks the egg hatches into a six-legged, pale brown larva armed with a pair of sharp, curved jaws. It is carnivorous, like its parents, and is also an air-breather, rising to the surface at intervals to breathe through two spiracles at the tip of its tail.

Running through each jaw is a canal that opens at the tip, through which the beetle injects poison into its victim. After the victim dies, digestive juices from the stomach pass through these same canals into the dead body. In this way digestion takes place outside the body of the larva which then sucks in the dissolved tissues of its victim, leaving only the empty shell. The larva cannot chew and swallow in the ordinary way as its jaws are not adapted for this. When it is fully grown it leaves the water and burrows into the wet soil beside the pond and there it changes into a pupa.

Some species of Dytiscidae differ from *Cybister* in laying their eggs in heaps outside the water, or on vegetation floating on the surface. Also, in some genera, the larvae rely entirely on gaseous exchange through the body wall to renew their oxygen supply and do not rise to the surface as *Cybister* does.

While the Dytiscidae spend nearly all their time swimming under water, members of the other big family of water beetles, the Gyrinidae, live on the surface of the water. Commonly called 'whirligig beetles', they may be seen gyrating on almost any pool at almost any time of the year. They are occasionally seen on still water, but they prefer pools in gently flowing streams where the current brings them the dead or dying insects which have fallen into the water and which are their main food supply. If you stand beside a stream and watch the beetles as they glide ceaselessly over the surface you will see that they swim over to investigate every small object that comes floating past. If you drop a dead fly or other insect into the water above them, they will seize upon it as soon as it floats down to them and tear it to pieces like a pack of miniature hyaenas, each swimming away with whatever portion it has managed to secure for itself. If one of their own kind is caught, crushed and dropped among them they will devour it with impartial gusto.

When alarmed, the whirligigs speed up their gyrations until they can scarcely be followed with the eye. If further alarmed, they dive beneath the surface and career wildly about below. In this completely submerged state, each one carries a bubble of air with it which looks like a silver ball on its tail, so it can breathe for some time while under water.

Like the Dytiscidae, whirligig beetles are wonderfully well adapted for their mode of life. They are streamlined and smooth; the head is recessed into the thorax so that there are no jutting angles or corners, the hind legs are fringed with bristles and make efficient oars. The middle legs are similar to the hind ones, but not as long or powerful, while the front legs are quite different and not used in swimming at all. Long and armed with short sharp bristles, they serve as organs for grasping prey. The beetle's antennae are also peculiarly modified for an aquatic life: the basal joint is broad and serves as a lid to close the cavity in which the antennae lie, thus keeping them dry when the insect is submerged.

The most remarkable adaptation, however, is found in the structure of the eyes. Each is divided into halves and one half is on top of the head while the other is beneath. The whirligig, therefore, seems to have four eyes, two of which look upwards into the air and two which look downwards into the water. Thus it can keep an effective look-out for enemies in both elements.

A whirligig taken from the water and placed on land can only flop about clumsily, but can fly well. Interestingly, it cannot take off from the surface of the water or from flat ground: if it wishes to fly off in search of fresh hunting grounds, it must first climb up on to the stem of a water-plant or the side of a stone and only then, when well clear of the water can it stretch its wings and fly away.

It usually utters a faint squeaking sound before taking to the air and it produces this noise by rubbing the hind edges of its elytra against the tip of its abdomen. If roughly handled it gives off a white fluid from the joints of its thorax and this has an unpleasant odour.

The female lays her elongate, oval eggs in a row upon the leaves of water-plants. The larva is a slender creature that looks at first sight not unlike a small centipede. It has a small head, six long legs and a pair of feathery gills on each segment of the abdomen, with two pairs on the last segment, making ten pairs in all. It creeps about the bottom of the pool, feeding on any small creatures it can capture. According to observations made in Europe, the full-grown larva spins a silken cocoon, grey in colour and pointed at each end. This is so well hidden among water-weeds or stones that it is seldom found.

All the beetles that live in an aquatic habitat are very well adapted to their particular living space, be it the water surface, the subsurface area, stones at the bottom, or mud at the edges. A few members of the genus *Hydrophilus*, family Hydrophilidae, occur in tropical Africa. They are large, about 35 mm long, shiny black and attracted by light. They lay their eggs in silken cases which float freely in the water. Members of the genus *Helochares* carry their egg cases under the abdomen, held there by the hind legs; certain other hydrophilids attach their egg cases to aquatic plants.

While dytiscids and gyrinids are carnivores as adults and larvae, only the larvae of hydrophilids are carnivorous, the adults being vegetarian. Another group of vegetarian beetles is the family Haliplidae. These beetles are yellowish or brownish, with dark spots, and because they cannot swim well they are usually called 'crawling water beetles'. The larvae are normally found among filamentous algae and apparently pierce the algae cells and suck out the contents. The larvae do not need to come to the surface, as they are able to utilise oxygen in the water.

Hister beetles Adults of the family Histeridae are usually hard, shiny, black (or, more rarely, metallic) beetles, which retract their antennae and legs under the body when threatened, and remain still until the danger has passed. They have conspicuously clubbed and elbowed antennae, and the elytra are usually short, exposing one or two abdominal segments.

Histerids are found in a wide variety of habits, often around decaying organic matter where they feed on other insects attracted to such situations – both the larvae and the adults are predators.

Members of the genera *Hister* and *Saprinus* are usually found in dung, where they prey on fly maggots. Other members of these genera reportedly feed on caterpillars, and the larvae of leaf beetles.

The very flat Histeridae of the genus *Hololepta* are found under bark, where they prey on other insects. The small, subcylindrical *Teretrius* and *Pachycraerus* live in the tunnels of the wood-boring beetles on which they prey.

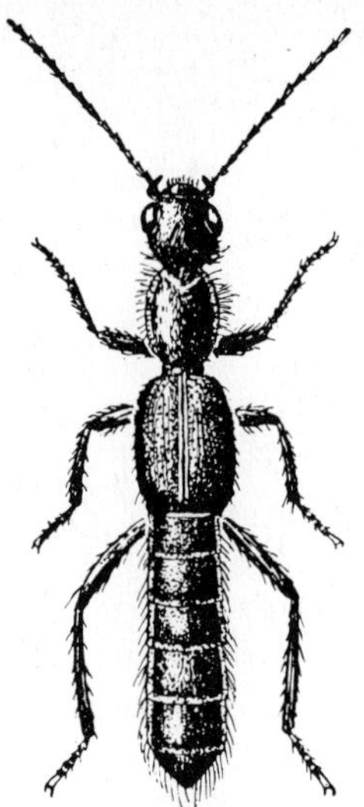

163. The blistering rove beetle, *Paederus sabaeus*, which causes painful irritation if crushed on the skin.

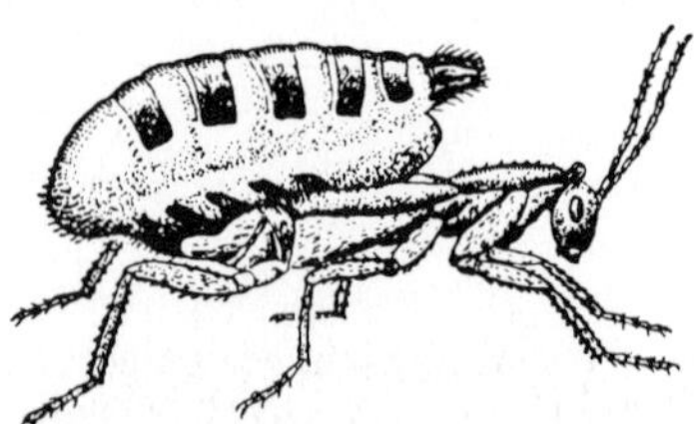

164. Termite guest staphylinid beetle, which lives in the mounds of *Macrotermes natalensis* and probably feeds on young termites. The beetle is about 3 mm long, yellow with its swollen white abdomen carried over its back. Secretions from its thorax and abdomen are eagerly licked up by the termites.

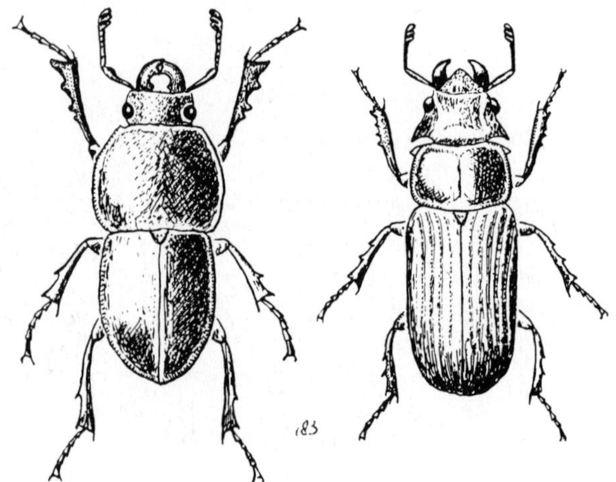

165. Stag beetles from the mountains of the Cape Province of South Africa; *Colophon westwoodi* (left) and *Xiphodontus antilope*. 30 mm.

Rove beetles Members of the family Staphylinidae are usually straight-sided and elongate and may be recognised by their short elytra which cover less than half of the abdomen. The second pair of membranous wings are large and well developed and, therefore, must be folded in a complex manner to fit under the elytra when not in use. If a rove beetle is watched you will see that just after it alights, its abdomen moves in a distinctive way and the membranous wings fold up and, in remarkable manner, disappear beneath the elytra. Contrary to what was formerly believed, the beetle does not use the tip of its abdomen to assist in this process.

This is a large family, its members being commonest in wet climates. Even in dry areas they will be found in habitats that are especially humid, such as in the nests of ants and termites, in dung, carrion and fungi, under bark or in compost heaps. It used to be thought that all rove beetles preyed upon small arthropods, but while this is true of the majority, there are many exceptions.

If you break up a piece of half-dry cow dung, you will usually find a fair number of rove beetles in it. Some, such as members of the genus *Philonthus*, prey on fly maggots in the dung, others, such as those belonging to the genus *Anotylus*, feed both as larvae and as adults on the dung itself. The related *Platystethus* also lives and feeds in dung, and is interesting for its primitive social behaviour. The female constructs a chamber in the dung in which her eggs are laid. She then looks after them, safeguarding them from other insects, and keeping them clear of fungal growths until they hatch.

Another genus which shows a degree of social behaviour is *Bledius*. These beetles live in colonies, making burrows in the sand or mud near water and feeding on algae. In one species at least, the female looks after her eggs and larvae, protecting them from intruders and brings back algae with which to feed her offspring.

Another departure from typical predaceous behaviour is seen in the subfamily Omaliinae. Certain genera frequent flowers and consume pollen and other floral parts as adults and larvae. In South Africa, *Protea* flowers often contain large numbers of these beetles.

Many rove beetles live only in the nests of ants and termites. The relationships between the beetles and their hosts are varied and fascinating: some species prey on their hosts, some scavenge in the nests, and yet others induce their hosts to regurgitate food for them. Many have special glands producing attractive substances which the worker ants or termites lick up eagerly. Although more research is needed on this subject, the function of these secretions seems to be to deter the hosts from rejecting the beetles.

Certain species of rove beetles, belonging to the genus *Paederus*, produce blisters if crushed against the human skin. One of them, *Paederus sabaeus*, is widely spread and common in many parts of Africa. It is a small black and red beetle that is often attracted to lights at night and might easily be mistaken for a flying ant. Should one of these alight on a person and then be crushed and rubbed into the skin, the blood and juices enter tiny scratches made by the hard wing covers and chitin of the insect, and after two days blisters form which leave a scar after they heal.

Similar beetles sometimes emerge in hordes and cause considerable suffering to people living in the vicinity. The painful condition known as 'Nairobi eye' in Kenya results from crushing staphylinid beetles while brushing them from the face, or wiping the eyes with hands that have been in contact with the crushed beetles.

Stag beetles The family Lucanidae is not very well represented in Africa. In Europe, stag beetles are renowned for their marked sexual dimorphism, with the jaws of the males enlarged to a tremendous extent. In west and east Africa we encounter the genus *Dorcus*, which exhibits a similar tendency. However, species of the genus *Nigidius*, widespread in tropical and subtropical Africa, do not display such sexual dimorphism: they are fairly small, black beetles with regularly striated elytra and both males and females have vertical processes on their mandibles. The larvae of most stag beetles feed in decaying wood, especially stumps and logs. The adults do not take solid food.

A very interesting genus, called *Colophon*, contains stag beetles found only in the mountains of the south-western Cape Province of South Africa. Most of the 12 known species have separate distributions restricted to the summits of different mountain ranges, and a number have been named after the various mountaineers who helped in their discovery. Their nearest relatives occur in eastern Australia and western South America, a distribution which points to a common ancestry.

Trox beetles Members of the family Trogidae occur on carcases when only the skin and bones remain. Some species frequent the nests of birds and the burrows of mammals, the larvae feeding on the feathers, or hairs, or other debris found in such places. They are 6-20 mm long and black (though usually covered with dry mud) with ridges and tubercles along the thorax and elytra. Most species belong to the genus *Trox*, and can fly, but some have lost their hind wings. When captured they emit a feeble squeaking sound, which they produce by rubbing the edges of the abdominal segments against the inner margins of the elytra.

Scarabaeid beetles The huge family Scarabaeidae contains some of the most conspicuous and abundant of all African insects, such as dung beetles, rose beetles, rhinoceros beetles, chafers and many others. They are all alike in possessing antennae that terminate in a fan of three or more flattened joints that can be folded one over the other. The family is divided into a number of subfamilies, two of which are commonly referred to as 'dung beetles'.

The Aphodinae, with the commonest African genus being *Aphodius*, are regular inhabitants of herbivore dung which they never bury but move about in freely. They are mainly small to medium beetles, 5-15 mm long and straight-sided.

The majority of Scarabaeinae, the most abundant of the African dung beetles, roll their food into a ball and bury it for themselves and their larvae. The ball-rolling habit, for which dung beetles are famous, appears to have evolved to minimise competition with other beetles which also feed on the dung of large herbivores and compete with one another for burial space beneath the dung mass. Members of the genus *Gymnopleurus* (which occurs throughout Africa) are an exception; they feed at the surface and do not make a food ball.

166. A small dung beetle (about 12 mm) rolling a ball of dung many times its own size and weight.

167. Larva of a cetoniid beetle. These large cream-coloured larvae are commonly found in compost heaps and amongst leaf litter.

168. Section through the silk and sand-grain pupal case of a cetoniid beetle, unearthed from a compost heap, showing the pupa inside.

The most famous of the ball-rolling beetles is the sacred scarab of Egypt, *Scarabaeus sacer,* although there are many other scarabs found throughout Africa that have similar ways. Its most striking anatomical feature is its complete lack of tarsi on its front legs: its middle and hind legs have well-developed, five-jointed feet, but its front legs end, as it were, at the ankles. The stout front legs, their tibiae armed with four strong teeth, are an adaptation to the beetle's feeding habits. They are used as scoops and rakes, to break up droppings left on the road or countryside by passing animals and to gather the best parts of it together in a ball. The beetle makes a ball by patting and pressing the dung with its front legs; it is obvious that a pair of slender, five-jointed tarsi on these legs would be more of a hindrance than a help and they have, over the course of time, disappeared.

In *Scarabaeus* the male makes a 'nuptial ball' which he rolls away, the female following behind. When he has buried it the female follows him down into the hole and there they mate. They then settle down to eat the ball of dung, a task which may take several days.

The honeymoon over, either the male or female now prepares a 'brood ball'. When this second ball is buried, the female alone goes underground into the chamber, which now has ample room for her to move around and over the ball.

Using her curved, toothed front legs, she now begins a long patting and smoothing process which leaves the mass of food perfectly round and smooth. Next, she makes a hollow at one side of the ball and deposits an egg in it. The egg is fairly large when compared with the size of the insect that lays it, being 3 mm long, oval and white. Finally she pats and smooths the edge of the hollow to cover the egg so that a projection forms on the ball, like the small end of a pear. Having completed the pear-shaped mass, she leaves the underground chamber, closing the tunnel behind her and goes off to repeat the same task somewhere else.

In a week or so the egg hatches into a white grub with six legs and a curious hump on its back. It lies on its side inside the ball and devours the provisions provided by its mother. The outer surface of the pear hardens to form a crust which prevents the food from drying out. Within two or three weeks the larva has devoured the whole of the contents and it lies snugly concealed in the hollow shell of dry dung. Here it changes into a pupa that later gives rise to the adult beetle.

Whereas *Scarabaeus* and its relatives roll their dung balls a considerable distance from the source, others usually bury dung below or close to the place where they find it. Typical of this group are members of the genus *Onitis*.

When preparing to lay her eggs the female first digs a tunnel in the soil beneath the dung. This tunnel is about 12 mm in diameter and may slant some 20 cm into the ground. At the bottom of the burrow she excavates a large chamber, often of irregular shape because of obstructions such as stones and roots, large enough to accommodate a mass of dung about the size of a man's fist. Having completed the laborious digging, during which the excavated soil is thrown up in a heap at the side of the dung, she now proceeds to fill the chamber with food carefully selected from the mass above. She burrows into the dung and chooses only the softest and most nourishing portions, shovelling it below with her front legs. She packs the chamber solidly with dung, laying her eggs at intervals as the filling proceeds.

The first egg is laid after a few loads have been brought down and packed tightly in the far end of the chamber. In this the female makes a neat spherical cell about the size of a pea and coats its walls with a brown liquid regurgitated from her stomach. This is food she has partially digested and which is intended to serve as the first mouthfuls for the delicate larva when it hatches. Then she lays her egg, fixing it on end inside the cell. It is very large in comparison with the size of the beetle, being about the size of a grain of wheat, white and oval.

After this, more dung is packed in the chamber, a second egg-cell is made, and so it goes on until the cavity is full and about half a dozen eggs have been laid. The egg-cells are always made near the outer surface of the mass and never in the centre; this is apparently to ensure that the eggs and larvae receive enough air. The mass of dung forms a sort of communal feast, with the inhabitants situated as far from one another as possible, but each larva's share is not separated in any way from that of the others.

The eggs hatch in about a fortnight and the hump-backed larvae feed almost incessantly from the moment of their birth, eating out large hollows, until, by the time they are fully grown, they are separated from one another only by thin walls of dry fibre. Each makes a neat cell for itself amid the remains of the food and then pupates. The pupa is a beautiful object which looks as though carved from white crystal. The curious horns on its back serve to keep its soft, delicate body away from the damp floor of its prison. The adults emerge after two or three weeks.

Three subfamilies of Scarabaeidae are commonly referred to as 'chafers'. The Melolonthinae, of which there are many species in Africa, are mainly nocturnal brown or black beetles which are attracted by lights at night. As far as is known the larval stages live in the ground and eat roots. Adults of many species eat leaves, especially young and tender ones, and when they are abundant can just about defoliate a grape vine or rose-bush virtually overnight, leaving no more than the veins of the leaves. Some species are of minor economic importance, such as those of *Schizonycha,* which are found throughout Africa and whose larvae are reported to damage the roots of many crops, and the pods of ground-nuts.

Less typical members of the Melolonthinae are those placed in the tribe Hopliini, which occurs only in southern Africa. The adults are small and hairy beetles, sometimes marked with coloured patterns of scales. Unlike most members of the subfamily, they are diurnal and frequent flowers, especially Compositae. These beetles are commonly seen with just their hind legs protruding from the surface of the flower into which they have burrowed.

The subfamily Rutelinae is a group with habits very similar to those of the Melolonthinae, but differ in that many are diurnal and therefore more brightly coloured, such as the green *Popillia* species which occurs on foliage.

The brightly coloured, diurnal and strong-flying Cetoniinae often frequent flowers as adults. The genus *Pachnoda*, coloured green and yellow, can devastate cultivated roses, hence their common name 'rose beetle'. Some cetoniids visit ripe fruit and bore into them to feed on the juices. Species of *Goniochilus* and *Oplostomus*, for example, go into beehives to feed on the honeycombs. Others are at least partly predaceous as adults; for instance, *Pseudospilophorus plagosus* which feeds on soft brown scale insects on citrus trees. A near relative, *Brachymacroma emarginicollis*, feeds on the poisonous yellow aphid *(Aphis nerii)* that occurs on milkweed plants *(Asclepias* species). The larvae of most Cetoniinae are believed to feed on accumulations of decaying vegetable matter, such as those found in compost heaps and so on.

The 'rhinoceros beetles', subfamily Dynastinae, are familiar to most people in Africa. The horns of rhinoceros beetles are apparently used as weapons in fights between males. The male of the genus *Oryctes* has a particularly large horn on his head, while the female has none. Their larvae are huge white grubs, often found in manure heaps. If the manure is spread over fields the grubs lie helplessly in the sun, providing giant meals for shrikes and other birds.

Not all the Dynastinae are as spectacular as the rhinoceros beetles, most being nocturnal brownish or blackish beetles. The larvae of some feed on the roots of living plants and can be of economic significance. Members of the genus *Heteronychus* are serious pests of cereals and sugar-cane in parts of Africa, and also damage lawns. The adults eat through the shoots of young stems just below ground level, while their larvae eat roots.

Metallic wood-boring beetles The adults of the family Buprestidae are nearly always metallic or bronzed, some being so beautiful that they are occasionally incorporated into items of jewellery. They are very active at the hottest times of the day, but extremely difficult to catch. Their eyesight is good and they fly off strongly when disturbed. The beetles often occur on flowers, where some of them feed on pollen. Others are found feeding on leaves or bark.

The larvae of the Buprestidae are often called 'flat-headed borers' because the prothorax is flattened and very much enlarged, being broader than the rest of the body. These borers gnaw wide galleries between the bark and sapwood, and often the noise of their chewing is actually audible. The larvae have no legs, but the expanded prothorax enables them to grip the sides of their tunnel as they gnaw their way forwards.

169. Adult cetoniid beetle feeding on ripe apricots. 20 mm.

170. Black and yellow cetoniid beetle feeding on sap exuding from a tree in a coastal dune forest along Africa's southeast coast. 20 mm.

171. Rhinoceros beetle from the forests of the Drakensberg mountains. Only the males possess the large horns, which are apparently used in combat with other males. 30 mm.

Not all buprestids are sapwood borers; the larvae of some genera bore right into the heartwood, and others are not borers at all. Members of the genera *Julodis* and *Sternocera*, for example, which are the largest African Buprestidae, have larvae which live freely in the soil and feed on roots.

Many species have leaf or stem-mining larvae, such as those of the small, triangular *Trachys* and *Habroloma* which mine the leaves of various plants. Usually each species attacks only one or a few related genera of plants, such as *Aphanisticus* species which mines the stems of sedges and rushes.

Click beetles, Elateridae, are elongate insects, mostly of sombre black or brown, but a few are red or have metallic colours. If one of them is placed on its back it will 'sham dead' for a time and then, with a slight clicking sound, will leap into the air, probably right itself and run off. Its prothorax is jointed with the rest of the body so that the insect can move freely but, when it is on its back, the two parts are held rigid, with the body slightly arched. There is a hard pointed projection on the underside of the prothorax that fits into a notch between the bases of the second pair of legs. This projection apparently presses down hard on the notch and suddenly slips out into the cavity below, causing the insect to jerk itself into the air.

The larvae of click beetles are found in decaying wood or in the soil. The smooth, shining, tough-skinned, yellow grubs popularly known as 'wire-worms', found in the soil feeding on the crowns and lower parts of the stems of wild and cultivated plants, are the larvae of click beetles.

Although plant-feeding tends to be the rule, the larvae of many genera are reported to be predaceous; for example, species of *Agrypnus*. Species occurring in wood appear to prey upon wood-feeding insects. Some soil-living species also feed on insect larvae and small worms. The very large members of the genus *Tetralobus*, the males of which have lamellate antennae, sometimes come to lights at night. The larvae live in the ground, and their feeding habits are unknown.

Glow-worms and fireflies Despite their misleading common names, the glow-worms and fireflies are beetles of the family Lampyridae, of which two genera are common in Africa. Both males and females of the genus *Luciola* are winged, but the males seem to be much commoner than their mates and their lights are brighter. The male firefly is easily recognised by his enormous, spherical eyes, dark violet in colour, which occupy almost the whole of his head and meet at the middle line. The eyes of the female are smaller and fairly widely separated. Apparently she does not flit about much, for, if a number of the insects are captured of an evening, they will probably all be males. The beetles each have a pair of sharp, curved jaws but they do not seem to feed at all in the adult state.

The firefly's light-producing organ is lodged on the underside of the abdomen, at the tip. If you examine this part of the body you will find that the last two segments are pale yellow in colour and peculiarly dense and smooth in appearance. The outer integument is transparent and beneath it there is a layer of spherical masses of cells well-supplied with tracheae and nerves and filled with a white substance. Behind this layer is a second layer of cells filled with tiny urate crystals and it is this layer that serves as the reflector.

The light-producing substance is lodged in the spherical white cell-masses and is called luciferin. An enzyme called luciferase, contained in the insect's blood, acts upon the luciferin and the light is due to the oxidation of the luciferin under the action of the luciferase. The process seems to be reversible – that is to say, the luciferin can be used over and over again.

The cold light of the firefly is very efficient. It contains no infra-red or ultra-violet rays: all its rays are visible, and scarcely any energy is wasted in the production of useless heat. The insect seems to be able to switch the light on and off at will, control apparently being effected by the nerves which regulate the air-supply to the layer of white cells. If a firefly is crushed between the fingers, the white cells give off a greenish glow like phosphorus, and the light slowly fades away.

Members of the genus *Lampyris* have larva-like females, commonly known as glow-worms. They can be distinguished from larvae in that they display some adult features such as multi-segmented antennae and five-segmented tarsi. Female glow-worms, about 25 mm in length and dark brown or black, may be found in damp spots at almost any time during summer. The winged males of this genus are very much like fireflies. While it is the male firefly which attracts attention with his flickering light as he flies about, it is the female glow-worm, with her steadily glowing lamp, that catches our eye among the weeds in a ditch or on a bank. Her light-producing organ is similar in structure and function to that of the firefly and it is situated on the same part of the body.

We know little about the habits and life history of African fireflies. It is probable that the female lays her eggs in the soil among dead leaves where the bush is thick. They hatch out into larvae that look very much like tiny female glow-worms: flat, segmented, dark brown, with six legs and a tiny head. They are almost certain to be carnivorous, killing and devouring any small, soft-bodied creatures they can capture with their sharp, curved jaws. The larvae probably pupate in the soil.

Firefly and glow-worm larvae seem to feed chiefly on snails and slugs. According to the French entomologist Fabre, the insect injects its victim with a poison through its mandibles. This substance serves a double purpose – it anaesthetises the prey and liquefies its tissues, to form a dark-coloured broth which the beetle then sucks up through its hollow mandibles. The adults take little or no food.

The glow-worm's flashing signal enables the male and female to find one another, and the different signals produced by different species ensure that only males and females of the same species mate with one another.

Net-winged beetles The genus *Lycus*, of the family Lycidae, is very common in Africa and may occur in large numbers in savanna areas. The wings have characteristic longitudinal ridges and the beetles are black and yellow or reddish. The adults are often seen sitting atop grass stems, or flying lazily about. When harassed they do not attempt to escape, but become comatose and 'play dead'. Their bright colours serve to warn that they are distasteful, and members of this family are mimicked by a variety of insects as diverse as long-horn beetles, moths and flies.

The elytra of *Lycus* males are often very different in shape to those of the females, and since several species may occur together in the same area, it is sometimes difficult to associate the males and females unless they are observed mating.

Little is known about the biology of this family. The larvae look similar to those of the Lampyridae, and are reported to live in rotten wood where they dissolve the material with their digestive juices and suck up the fluid.

Dermestid beetles The various members of the family Dermestidae are commonly called skin beetles, leather beetles or museum beetles, because they feed on dried animal and plant remains which have a high protein content. Some, like *Dermestes ater* and *Dermestes maculatus vulpinus*, will feed on a variety of substances, such as old bones, carcases, skins, hides, leather, dried fish, bacon and so on.

The females lay their eggs in small batches in cracks and crevices in the food material. These hatch into active black hairy larvae that feed on the dry material, moulting between six and ten times before they are mature and some 15 mm long. When fully grown the larva leaves its source of food and seeks out a place where it can pupate. It bores into anything at hand to make a sheltered tunnel for itself: even the mortar between bricks may be honeycombed with their burrows. As adults they are some 10 mm in length.

Other species of the genus *Dermestes* also breed in birds' nests, or in the nests of bees and wasps where they feed on dead insects.

The genera *Anthrenus* and *Attagenus* also occur in Africa. Adults of both genera are found in flowers, where they feed on pollen and nectar. Their larvae are found in birds' nests, or in bee and wasp nests, feeding on dry material with a high protein content. Sometimes they indulge in the seemingly dangerous practice of foraging for insect remains in and around spiderwebs. The larvae move slowly about the underside of the web so as not to attract the spider's attention. As further protection they erect and vibrate the stiff, dense hairs with which they are covered. These have spear-like tips and are easily detached, and seem to deter the spiders from attacking the scavengers.

172. A pair of buprestid beetles *(Sternocera orissa)*, with black bodies and yellowish markings, on an Acacia tree. 45 mm.

173. A click beetle showing the backward projections of the thorax which are typical of this beetle family. 30 mm.

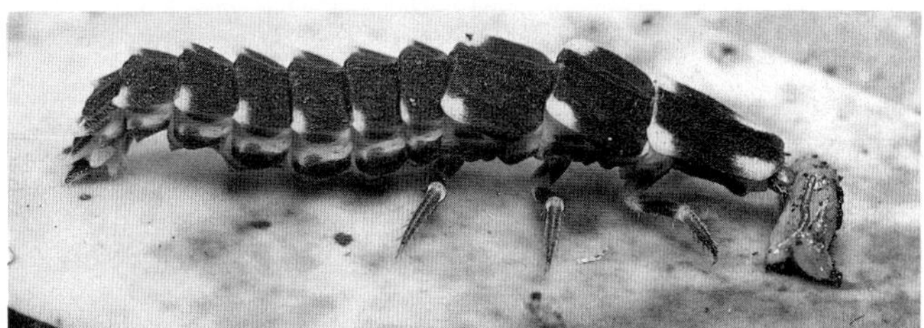

174. Larva-like adult female glow-worm, feeding on a slug in the forests of the southern Cape. 25 mm.

Anybody who collects insects is certain to have made the acquaintance of the destructive little museum beetles, which include several species of *Anthrenus*. Sooner or later small heaps of brown dust begin to appear beneath the specimens in the store-boxes and, if nothing is done to check the damage, the whole collection is eventually reduced to an unsightly accumulation of dust and fragments of legs and wings.

One of the common museum beetles, *Anthrenus verbasci*, is a pretty little insect, about 2,5 mm long, with a round, flattened body. It is black, but its body is covered with tiny scales that give it a marbled appearance – a mixture of grey, red and black. It can be seen in the insect boxes, among the ruined specimens, but it is also to be found out in the open, usually on yellow flowers of the Compositae, or daisy family.

When the female is ready to lay her eggs she seeks out any dried animal matter she can find and she is quickly attracted to skins, insects or other museum specimens that have not been protected by some poison. In her quest for a suitable spot, she will, if she can, make her way through narrow cracks into the boxes and lay her eggs directly on the specimens. If she cannot get inside, she will deposit her eggs in the crevices of the lid, or in some similar opening, and leave her young to find their own way inside when they hatch. Short of pasting paper all round to seal the lid it is almost impossible to keep the beetle or her grubs out of insect boxes and cabinets.

Shot-hole borers There are many species of the family Bostrychidae in Africa. They all bore in wood, as their common name indicates. Females lay their eggs on the cut surface, or in cracks in the wood, and the larva makes its own gallery when it hatches. Alternatively, males and females co-operate to make a gallery in which the eggs are laid. Most species feed on the wood of many different trees.

The bamboo borer, *Dinoderus minutus*, is one of the smallest of the shot-hole borers, measuring only about 3 mm in length. This insect is a native of the Far East but has been distributed in infested bamboo and cane widely through the world and is prevalent in many parts of Africa where it does considerable damage to bamboo, cane chairs and wicker-work.

The beetle bores into cut bamboo at any spot where the hard outer rind has been damaged and makes a tunnel in which mating takes place and the tiny white eggs are then laid. On hatching, the larvae burrow up and down the wall of the bamboo and their tunnels become packed behind them with a fine dust consisting of inedible fragments and excrement. When fully grown the larva is yellowish white, about 3 mm long, curved, and with a swollen thorax. It pupates in a chamber it hollows out at the end of its tunnel and a week or so later the adult beetle emerges, biting its way out of the bamboo through a neat, round hole. There are three or four generations of these beetles a year and they can, therefore, increase rapidly in number and do much damage.

The Acacia shot-hole borer, *Sinoxylon transvaalense*, common throughout Africa south of the equator, infests the wood of trees and shrubs belonging to the Leguminosae, as well as a wide range of other timbers. It is about 6 mm long, black, and has a pair of spines near the hind end of its elytra. A pair of these beetles burrows into the wood to mate and to lay eggs. The tunnel runs in for a short distance at right angles to the surface and then turns and runs parallel with the grain of the wood. It is kept scrupulously clean and the beetles remain in it for some time, apparently to guard the eggs and the newly-hatched young from parasites and other enemies. The larvae burrow, feed and pupate in the usual manner and there may be two or three generations a year.

Powder post beetles Three genera belonging to the family Lyctidae occur in Africa. Some of them are of economic significance in that they damage processed timber; for example *Lyctus africanus* in South Africa.

The female deposits her long narrow eggs in pores in the wood, generally at a sawn end. She will not lay on surfaces which are polished or protected by paint. Many different kinds of wood – limba, oak, wattle, marula, kiaat and so on – are liable to be attacked if they contain sapwood, for this outer part of the tree under the bark that contains sugar and starch is where the larvae develop. Conifers, however, are not normally favoured by these beetles.

The egg hatches in two or three weeks and gives rise to a tiny white larva that tunnels in the wood, feeding as it goes, and simultaneously reducing the wood to a fine powder which is tightly packed in the tunnel behind it. Starch and a certain amount of moisture must be present in the wood, which is why hard, dry heartwood is left entirely alone by these beetles.

Under normal conditions it takes about ten months for the larva to reach full size, but this period may be shortened if the infested wood is in a warm room and if there is more than the usual amount of food material present in the timber. Similarly, it may be considerably lengthened if the temperature is low, the wood is very dry and contains little nourishment.

The fully grown larva is only about 5 mm long, slightly curved and with the front end of the body thicker than the hind end. At this stage it bores its way towards the surface of the wood, stopping when only a thin layer remains between it and the outer air. Here it hollows out a small chamber in which it changes into a pupa and about a month later the adult beetle is ready to emerge. If the weather is warm the beetle will soon cut its way to the surface, making a small round hole about 1 mm in diameter, and leaving a small tell-tale heap of sawdust on the floor beneath the hole. But if the weather is cold and the room unheated the beetle may lie motionless in its cell for weeks before emerging. Ordinarily, the complete life cycle takes from nine to 12 months, but under favourable conditions this period may be shortened to seven or eight months, and if conditions are unfavourable the beetle may take two or even three years to reach maturity.

A few beetles in a piece of timber will do little damage but, if they are allowed to breed unchecked, they will eventually reduce the sapwood to a hollow shell of powder, and leave the surface riddled with holes.

Clerid beetles Members of the family Cleridae are mainly predators as larvae on the larvae of wood-boring beetles in whose galleries and burrows they live. The adults also feed on wood-boring beetles, and so the Cleridae may be regarded as a beneficial group. They have no common name, although some of the brightly coloured kinds are known as 'checkered beetles' in North America.

Adults of the genus *Thanasimus,* and many others which occur in Africa, have colours that predators know to avoid such as black with orange or red and white bands. They probably mimic certain wasps and derive protection from their disguise. By contrast, adults of some of the species of *Gyponyx* are cryptically coloured to resemble the lichen-covered bark on which they are found.

Less typical members of the family belong to the genus *Necrobia.* These metallic blue beetles occur on carrion and in bones, as well as in some commercial vegetable products and processed meats which have a high oil content. Larvae and adults feed on high protein material, and also on fly larvae.

The related genus *Opetiopselaphus* contains species with metallic blue elytra and head, and an orange pronotum. They are encountered in horse and cow dung but their biology has not been studied – they possibly feed on fly larvae in the dung.

Lymexylid beetles The small family Lymexylidae contains only a few known African species. One, *Atractocerus brevicornis,* would at first sight probably not be recognised as a beetle. The adult is very elongated, with tiny elytra and long, exposed hind wings that fold fanwise over the dark brown abdomen. The beetle is up to 40 mm long, and fairly common in certain places. It is attracted to lights at night. The larvae live in hardwood and are also very elongated. They are reported to feed on a fungus growing in their tunnels and brought there by the adults.

Sap beetles Most members of the family Nitidulidae are small, broad, flattened beetles with shortened elytra that leave between one and three segments of the abdomen exposed. The antennae have clubbed ends, each made up of three segments. Their biology varies, though most are associated with fermenting fruits, sap or carcases.

The 'dried fruit beetle', *Carpophilus hemipterus,* is a common pest of stored dried fruit. Only about 3 mm long, the adults are black with light brown patches on the elytra. The female lays her eggs on ripe fruit still on the trees, or inside the fruit if it is damaged and she can penetrate. She will also deposit her eggs on fruit drying in the sun, or on dried fruit in packing sheds and store rooms. The larvae feed on the dried fruit and are about

175. An adult and a larva net-winged beetle *(Lycus* sp.). These flattened, slow-moving beetles are apparently distasteful to predators.

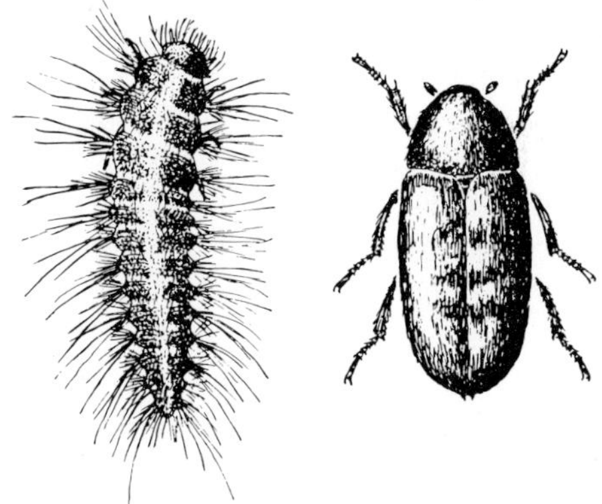

176. A larva and an adult leather beetle *(Dermestes* sp.). The larva is covered with long hairs; the adult is about 10 mm long.

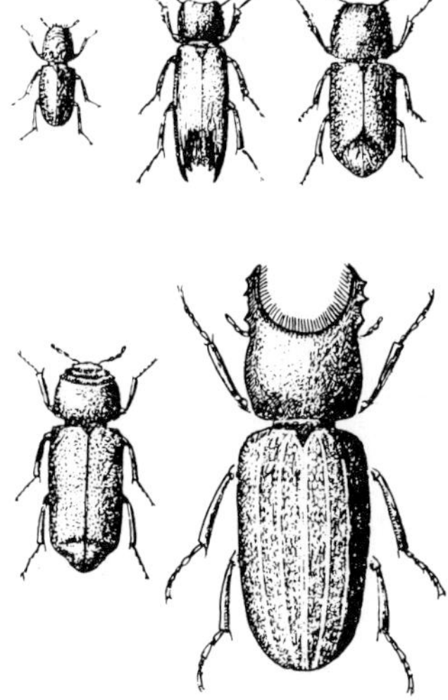

177. Various shot-hole borers (family Bostrychidae) showing the great variation in size and shape. The largest specimen is about 12 mm long.

6 mm long when fully grown, creamy white, with the head and hind end of the abdomen dark brown. They take about a month to reach full size, and the pupal stage lasts a fortnight. There are several generations a year.

A few larvae in a package of dried fruit will quickly ruin it, often bringing wrath upon the head of the shop-keeper who is merely at the end of a chain of events that started in the orchard!

Members of the genera *Pria* and *Meligethes* occur on flowers. The *Pria* are found in southern Africa; *Meligethes* are confined to the high mountains of east Africa. Their larvae feed on various parts of the flowers, such as pollen and the ovules.

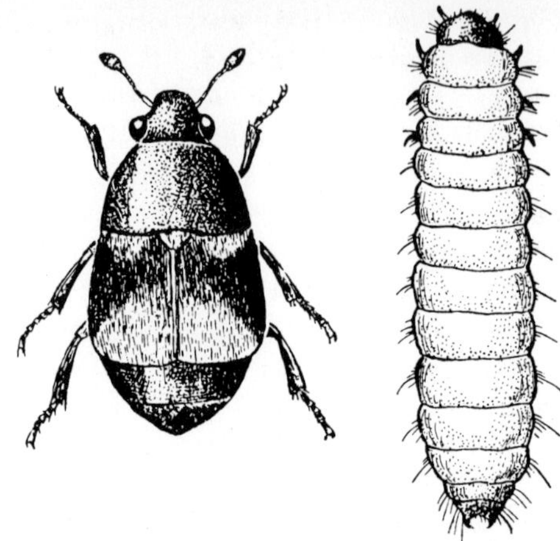

178. The dried fruit beetle, *Carpophilus hemipterus*, adult (left) and larva. The adult is about 3 mm long, black with brown markings on the elytra.

Ladybird beetles Adults and larvae of most of the ladybird beetles, family Coccinellidae, feed on soft-bodied insects such as aphids, coccids and mealybugs. However, some of them (belonging to the subfamily Epilachninae) feed on plants and may be agricultural pests at times. Many species of vegetarian *Epilachna* occur in Africa, their main host plants being members of the cucumber family (Cucurbitaceae), although many important crop plants such as potatoes, maize and others may be attacked. Both the adults and the larvae feed on leaves and fruit.

These vegetarian ladybirds are generally recognisable by their orange and black colouration, and rather dull appearance, which is due to a layer of short, fine hairs.

In southern Africa the adult *Epilachna* ladybirds hibernate over winter during which time countless thousands of them congregate in dense masses in rock crevices or small caves. Sometimes when such swarms enter houses in their search for a safe winter abode, they cause the occupants considerable alarm at this inexplicable invasion.

179. Thousands of ladybird beetles (*Epilachna* sp.) congregating under a rock ledge as they hibernate on a mountain top on the southern African highveld. 7 mm.

Predaceous ladybirds are welcomed wherever they occur. A fairly typical example is the lunate ladybird, *Cheilomenes lunata,* which is found all over Africa feeding as both adult and larva on all sorts of plants that are infested with aphids. Brightly patterned in red and black, this pretty little beetle is very shiny (as are most of the predaceous ladybird species). If one is caught and handled roughly a yellow fluid will ooze from between the joints of its legs. This fluid is extremely bitter and serves as a protection to the ladybird, making it unpalatable to birds, lizards, frogs and other insect-eaters. As it is unpleasant tasting it has no need to conceal itself and its conspicuous colours and markings advertise the fact.

180. The plant-eating larva of the vegetarian ladybird beetle (*Epilachna* sp.). The function of its spiny armour is unknown. 10 mm.

The female lays her yellow, cigar-shaped eggs in clusters of 20 or 30, generally on the underside of leaves. They are usually to be found on plants that are infested with aphids, for as pointed out above, the female herself feeds on them and she leaves her eggs where the young will not have far to search for prey.

In about a fortnight the eggs hatch into small black larvae with six legs and three simple eyes on each side of the head. They feed on the aphids, spearing them with their sharp, sickle-shaped jaws and sucking their juices. As the larva grows bigger it develops conspicuous spots of pale yellow on the black background. It casts its skin four times before it is fully grown, by which time it is about 9 mm long. At this stage the larva generally leaves the plant and seeks out a stone or wall where it fixes itself head downwards by means of a sticky secretion that oozes from its tail end. Once in position its body thickens and shortens and, after a few hours, the skin splits to reveal the yellow pupa inside. In about ten days the adult beetle emerges. It is pale yellow at first but its colour slowly darkens to red, with crescent-shaped black markings that join end to end.

Some predaceous ladybirds have more specialised feeding habits, like the genera *Pullus*, *Nephus* and *Scymnus*, which feed only on the red spider mites that are at times a serious agricultural pest.

The larvae of some ladybirds produce a covering of waxy plates, fibres or powder, which is thought to serve as protection or camouflage. Members of the genus *Ortalia* have wax-covered larvae that prey on worker ants of the genus *Pheidole*. The adult beetles are grey with brilliant green eyes, and they occur on flowering trees such as Acacias.

Certain ladybird beetles have been imported as part of programmes to assist in the non-insecticidal control of various pest insects. For example, the little Australian species, *Rodolia cardinalis*, dark crimson in colour and marked with black, is well known for the important part it played in destroying the very harmful Australian bug, *Icerya purchasi*. Many years ago the citrus industry in California and South Africa was threatened with disaster as a result of the rapid increase and spread of the Australian bug, a pest which is extremely difficult to combat with sprays because it has a protective coating of waxy threads. Then, in Australia, the little cardinal ladybird was discovered to feed largely upon their eggs, tearing open the egg bags of the females and devouring the contents. It was sent to California where it thrived and soon reduced the bugs to negligible proportions. Subsequently it was brought from California to South Africa and is now so well established that the Australian bug is no longer a threat.

Tenebrionid beetles The enormous family called the Tenebrionidae contains such diverse members as meal worms, 'tok-tokkies', flour beetles and many thousands of other African species whose appearance and habits are as varied and interesting as the continent itself. Many tenebrionids are brown or black, and some are unable to fly because they have lost the use of the second pair of wings. The family occurs in all types of terrestrial habitats, but the greatest diversity of species is found in dry areas and deserts.

The larvae resemble mealworms, and mainly live in the soil or other concealed situations where they generally feed on dead vegetable matter, although one subfamily specialises in feeding on bracket fungi. The adult beetles are usually long-lived and mostly nocturnal, but differ widely in appearance, size and behaviour.

Zophosis species are somewhat flattened, black, oval and fast-moving diurnal beetles in sandy areas. They virtually 'swim' across the sand and are very difficult to catch. By way of contrast, members of the genus *Eurychora* and its relatives are very slow-moving. These flat beetles are covered with sparse long hairs, which help to trap and hold a layer of sand and other debris as camouflage.

Perhaps the best known of the Tenebrionidae are the medium to large 'tok-tokkies' of the genus *Psammodes*

181. An adult ladybird beetle *(Cheilomenes lunata)* sinks her jaws into an aphid. By destroying these and many other plant pests, the predaceous ladybirds do untold good. 7 mm.

182. A newly hatched ladybird larva *(Cheilomenes lunata)* attacks an aphid larger than itself.

183. A tenebrionid beetle feeds on a hare dropping. These beetles tap the underside of the abdomen on the ground in a rapid rhythm – a habit which has given them the common name of 'tok-tokkie'. The sound produced is audible from several metres away, and probably serves to attract a mate. 35 mm.

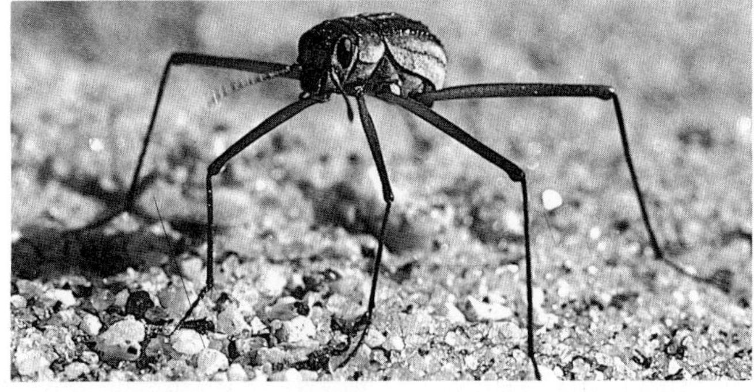

184. *Stenocara phalangium*, living on the hot gravel plains of the Namib Desert, has the longest legs, for its body length, of any insect in the world. 8 mm.

and its relatives. These heavy-bodied, wingless beetles derive their name from their habit of knocking on the ground loudly at intervals, apparently to attract the opposite sex. To produce this tapping noise the beetle raises its abdomen and brings it down on the ground several times in quick succession. Their long, smooth yellow larvae live in the soil and feed on the roots of grasses and other plants. Occasionally they occur in large numbers in fields of wheat, oats, barley and maize and may do considerable damage to the young plants.

In Africa the richest tenebrionid fauna is found in the Namib Desert, where scientists from the Desert Ecological Research Unit at Gobabeb have discovered the most remarkable habits and adaptations to life in one of the harshest environments in the world. Even the vegetationless dunes support a rich fauna of highly specialised beetles, whose main food supply is wind-borne plant and animal debris, blown from distant sources into the desert.

Certain nocturnal species show remarkable behavioural adaptations which enable them to collect moisture from the periodic fogs, so characteristic a feature of the Namib. *Lepidochora* species, for example, normally 'swim' across the surface of the sand, but when the fog comes rolling in, they dig trenches in the sand across the path of the fog-bearing wind. These trenches catch and condense moisture from the fog, and when the beetles later retrace their steps they are able to extract the water, flattening the ridges in the process.

Equally remarkable is the behaviour of *Onymacris unguicularis*. When the fog comes rolling in, this beetle climbs to the top of a ridge and stands head-down, its abdomen raised, pointing into the wind. As the fog condenses on the body of the beetle, the droplets of water run down towards the mouth and are swallowed.

There are many other equally fascinating beetles in this family, and entomologists have so far studied only a small part of it. The tenebrionid's adaptations which permit it to survive in dry environments, feeding on substances with a low moisture content, has allowed some of them to successfully invade man-made habitats such as stored cereal products. Two species of *Tenebrio* and a number of species of *Tribolium* have taken advantage of this new habitat.

'Mealworms' are the larvae of *Tenebrio molitor* or *Tenebrio obscurus*, well known to many because they are reared as food for small animals, predaceous arthropods and fish. They have been spread all over the world and are well established in Africa, where they may do considerable damage to stored grains, meal, flour and other foodstuffs. The adults are 12-18 mm long, dark brown or black. The larvae are elongate, yellowish-brown and cylindrical. Colonies of mealworms can be normally sustained on bran, slightly moistened by the addition of a lettuce leaf or a carrot from time to time.

Of the several *Tribolium* beetles that damage stored products, the flour beetle called *Tribolium confusum* is a cosmopolitan and common invader of bran, flour, rice, ground-nuts and other cereals. It is a small reddish-brown tenebrionid about 6 mm in length, with a life history similar to that of the mealworm.

Tumbling flower beetles There are hundreds of species of Mordellidae in Africa, but they have not received much attention and the biology of their larvae is virtually unknown. In other parts of the world studies have shown that the larvae are borers or miners in the stems, wood or pith of various plants, and it is probable that they do likewise in Africa. The adults are very active and are usually found in flowers. They are hump-backed beetles with their heads bent right down under the body, and the tip of the abdomen prolonged into a pointed spine. When disturbed they run and skip away rapidly. If caught they tumble about comically – hence their common name.

Blister beetles Numerous species of Meloidae are found throughout Africa. The adults feed on plant material while the larvae prey upon or parasitize the egg packets of locusts, or the eggs, pollen and honey stores of bees, chiefly of the families Megachilidae and Andrenidae. Species parasitizing locust egg masses, and some of the bee parasites, lay their eggs in groups in dry, hard soil, and the active first-stage larvae must locate their hosts on their own. Some of the bee parasites lay their eggs in flowers and the larvae then attach themselves to bees visiting the flowers and are carried back to the nest. Other blister beetle bee parasites lay their eggs near the entrance to the host's nest.

Blister beetles of the genus *Mylabris* are very common throughout Africa and are of considerable interest because they do good at one stage of their career and harm at another, and because their bodies contain a powerful drug known as cantharidin. There are many different species ranging from about 20-50 mm in size. Most of them are black and yellow, some are black and red and others are all black.

These beetles are found on flowers throughout the summer months, especially on plants of the pea and bean family of which they eat the petals, often doing harm to the crops because they destroy the flowers and in this way prevent the formation of pods. They walk about and fly slowly and deliberately, as if they have no foes, for the poisonous substance in their bodies, cantharidin, protects them from insect-eating enemies, such as birds and lizards. Their striking colours warn their enemies to leave them well alone.

Cantharadin blisters the skin, hence the family's common name. The chemical has a reputation as an aphrodisiac, and the 'Spanish Fly', *Lytta vesicatoria*, is actually a beetle belonging to the Meloidae. In fact, not only does cantharadin cause blisters but it is extremely poisonous, and may do kidney damage or cause death. *Mylabris* beetles contain large amounts of cantharadin, and there is reason to believe that some witchdoctors in Africa have used the beetles as poison.

The female *Mylabris* beetle lays her eggs in the

ground. Although she is ill-fitted for the task, she labours prodigiously for half an hour or more to dig a hole about 25 mm deep in hard soil, using her slender legs and jaws as tools. Then she turns round and backs into the hole and deposits in it some 20 or 30 fairly large eggs, oval and white. When laying is completed, she fills the hole by raking the loose soil back into it and stamping it down with her feet. Once this batch is safely buried, she goes off to repeat the process somewhere else a day or two later, and continues to do so until her ovaries are exhausted at which point she dies.

The eggs hatch in three or four weeks into tiny, active creatures about 1,5 mm long, white, with a large head, six legs and two stiff bristles on the tail. The newly-hatched larvae run about over the hot ground, seeking those spots where grasshoppers and locusts have laid their eggs. Many do not survive because the newly-hatched larva must find an egg-pod of a locust or grass-hopper within a few hours of birth, otherwise it dies of exhaustion and hunger.

By some mysterious means, perhaps by a keen sense of smell, it finds the eggs if it is anywhere near them and it bores down into the soil to reach them. As soon as it is lodged safely inside the pod it casts its skin and becomes a fat, white maggot with very short legs – quite a different creature from that which was first hatched. It no longer needs to run about, and for the rest of its career as a larva it is very sluggish, feeding on the eggs and growing rapidly. Towards the end of summer it burrows into the ground beside the pod and changes its form once more – it now enters a larval resting stage in which it passes the winter months. Its skin is tough and white, and although it has short legs it does not move about.

When the warm weather arrives it casts its skin once more and enters the next stage of its development. It may enter the egg-pod again, feeding on any eggs that are left, or it may, after a short period, change into a pupa without taking any more food. At first the pupa is white but slowly it darkens in colour and finally, after three or four weeks, the skin is cast for the last time and the adult emerges. It rests for a time in its underground cell until its skin hardens and then makes its way to the surface, to feed on flowers, to lay its eggs and to die.

The oil beetles are stout-bodied insects, with short elytra, which cannot fly as they have lost their second pair of wings. They are brown, black or dark blue and from 12-20 mm in length. When caught they exude through the leg joints a yellow fluid which contains cantharidin and it is from this habit that they receive their popular name. They are not common but are widely spread and may occasionally be seen on the veld and on flowers during the summer months.

Oil beetles belong to several genera and little is known about the life histories of the African species, other than that they are associated with various solitary bees. The female lays a large number of eggs which hatch into tiny active creatures similar to those described above and called triungulins. They creep up on to the flowers and there await the arrival of the bees,

185. More than any other desert in the world, the Namib has a great many beetle species unique to its hostile environment of wind-blown sand. Here one of the many tenebrionid beetles endemic to the area dives into a sand dune, through which it will 'swim', in much the same way that an aquatic insect would through water. 6 mm.

186. A blister beetle feeding on a flower petal. These insects are attracted to vivid colours and will often land on brightly coloured garments or pieces of paper.

187. The striking yellow and black colouration of this blister beetle (*Mylabris* sp.) serves to warn would-be predators of its poisonous properties, due to the chemical, cantharadin, contained in its body.

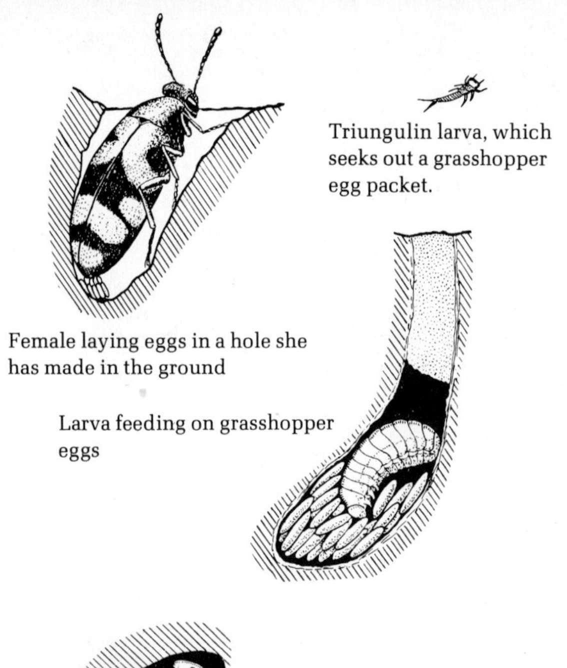

188. The life history of a typical blister beetle, *Mylabris* sp.

189. A long-horn beetle (*Ceroplesis* sp.) showing the long antennae that give these wood-boring beetles their common name. Body length 25 mm.

190. A female long-horn beetle (*Litopus latipes*) using her ovipositor to lay eggs deep within a log. Body length 25 mm.

to which they cling and are then carried to the bees' nests. Large numbers of them perish because they fail to find a suitable host, but a triungulin that succeeds in getting into a cell in the bee's nest leaves the bee on which it travelled and devours first the egg and then the store of honey and pollen provided by the bee for its young. The larva goes through changes of form similar to those of *Mylabris* species.

Long-horn beetles The very large family called Cerambycidae contains numerous wood-boring species, but also a fair number of beetles which mine the stems and roots of herbaceous and semi-woody plants, as well as some seed-eaters. Many species are pests of commercially important timber trees, and several species from Australia and Europe have been imported along with their host trees and are now well established in Africa. The eucalyptus borer, *Phoracantha semipunctata*, for example, is an immigrant from Australia.

Nearly all Cerambycidae only attack trees that are dead or dying and, commercial interests aside, serve a useful purpose in hastening the breakdown of dead wood and the return of nutrients to the soil.

Many long-horn beetles will make a feeble squeaking or creaking noise upon being picked up. This sound is produced by rubbing the hind margin of the prothorax against a roughened area between the bases of the elytra; the movement can easily be seen if the beetle is observed while it is squeaking. The functions of these noises is not known; they do not appear to be used in mate recognition, and it seems unlikely that they would deter a predator. We do not even know if the insects can hear the sounds themselves! Specialised auditory organs have not been found in any beetles, but it is possible that chordotonal organs, found scattered over the bodies of many insects, may be able to detect air-borne vibrations such as those made by long-horn beetles. 'Chordotonal' means a string or fibre for detecting sounds and a chordotonal organ consists of one or more microscopic rod-like structures, situated just beneath the skin and connected to nerve fibres.

Chordotonal organs, looking like denser spots in the thin white skin and situated just below the spiracle in each segment, are also found along each side of the fat white larva of long-horn beetles. Hearing, as we know it, would be of little use to the sluggish larva lodged in a tunnel in a log as very few sounds can reach it in such a retreat, but the organs are probably of value to the larva in enabling it to detect vibrations set up by the jaws of another larva feeding close to it.

The larvae are cannibalistic and when a number of young emerge from the cluster of eggs, they devour one another until the survivors are too widely scattered to do further damage to one another. In their subsequent tunnellings, the grubs skilfully avoid the burrows of their fellows, turning aside when approaching another burrow too closely. The chordotonal organs along their sides may therefore enable them to detect the proximity of others.

Most cerambycid larvae grow slowly, perhaps because the nutrients in wood are slowly assimilated. Some species take three or four years to reach full size. When mature, the larva usually tunnels towards the surface of the log and hollows out a chamber just below the bark in which it develops into a pupa. The larvae of *Plocaederus* species and some other long-horn beetles plaster the walls of the pupal chamber with a sort of liquid chalk, that comes from the Malpighian tubules, which forms a hard, smooth, waterproof lining to the chamber. When the pupa changes into an adult, the beetle bites its way out of the chamber and into the open.

A species which leaves interesting and characteristic signs of its presence in wood is *Batocera wyllei*, found in central and west Africa. The adult oviposits on recently felled trees and the larva feeds under the bark. When nearly mature, the larva excises a circular disc of bark between 10 and 15 cm in diameter, and then proceeds to bore deeper into the sapwood. It has been suggested that this practice may promote the more rapid drying out of the pupal cell and thus discourage fungal growths which might attack the pupa. Eventually the excised discs of bark fall to the ground, leaving circular marks on the tree.

An example of less typical feeding habits is seen in small members of the genus *Sophronica*. These species attack the seeds of a wide variety of plants, and are of some economic importance insofar as they attack coffee berries.

Pea and bean weevils Beetles belonging to the family Bruchidae are commonly called 'pea weevils' or 'bean weevils', yet these names are misleading since the true weevils belong to a different family, the Curculionidae. The larvae of Bruchidae are seed-eaters, the majority of the species attacking seeds of Leguminosae, which includes peas and beans. However, certain species attack other plant families. Most bruchids appear to lay their eggs on almost fully developed seeds, one seed supporting a single larva, but a few species lay their eggs on flowers or young fruits.

Bruchidius species, of which there are many in Africa, mainly attack Leguminosae. Some species have a single generation a year, developing in green pods, but others have many generations a year which develop in dry pods or seeds.

The large bruchids of the genus *Caryedon* attack the winged fruits of Combretaceae as well as some Leguminosae. In species attacking *Combretum*, the eggs are laid on fully formed green or dry fruits, and the species breed throughout the period when fruit is on the trees. Normally only one larva develops to maturity in each fruit, constructing its cocoon within the fruit, from which the adult emerges. By contrast, those species which attack Leguminosae leave the pod to pupate and construct a cocoon at or below ground level.

A number of cosmopolitan species of Bruchidae are important pests of stored peas and beans. The female bean weevil, *Acanthoscelides obtectus*, waits until the

191. Larva of fig tree borer *(Phryneta spinator)* revealed feeding in its burrow immediately beneath the bark of a cultivated fig tree. 35 mm.

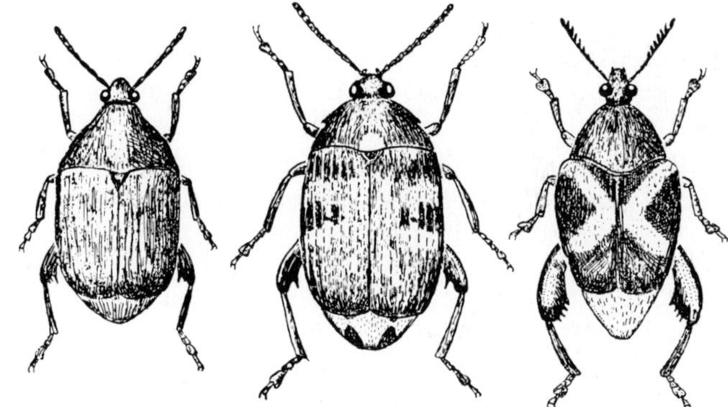

192. Seed beetles of the family Bruchidae, from left to right: the bean weevil *Acanthoscelides obtectus* (3 mm), the pea weevil *Bruchus pisorum* (4 mm), and *Caryopemon cruciger* (6 mm).

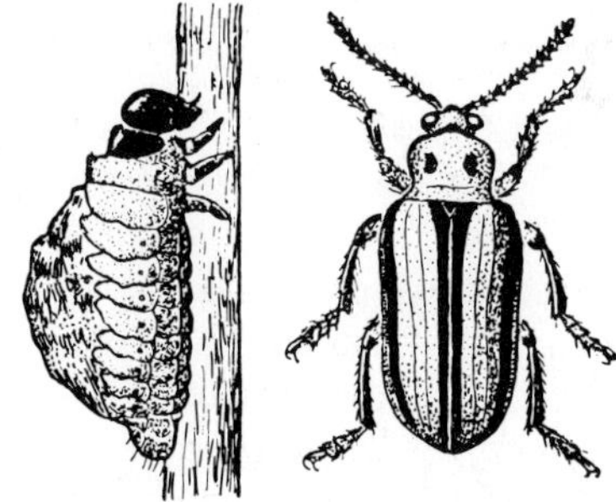

193. The leaf beetle, *Lema trilineata*. The larva (left) is covered with a layer of slimy excrement. The adult is yellow with black stripes, 6 mm long.

pods are ripe and have partially split open. She then creeps inside and lays her elongate, oval white egg loosely inside the pod, among the ripe beans. The newly-hatched larva burrows into the beans and is safely lodged inside when the beans are harvested and stored. They are so small that several can mature in a single bean. The beetles that develop from these larvae emerge in the bag of beans about three months after harvesting, and they mate and lay their eggs without leaving the bag. The beetles can go on breeding in stored beans until the seeds are riddled with holes and completely ruined.

The cowpea or Chinese weevil, *Callosobruchus chinensis*, and the four-spotted cowpea weevil, *Bruchus quadrimaculatus*, are also found in Africa and are at times serious pests of stored cowpeas. As with the bean weevil, the attack begins when the cowpeas are ripening in the field and the female glues her small white eggs on to the seeds, and continues in the store until the seeds are destroyed.

Leaf beetles The Chrysomelidae constitute another vast family of plant-eating beetles whose various subfamilies show interesting differences in their biology.

Members of the subfamily Criocerinae are found all over Africa. Both larvae and adults are leaf-eaters, and a few introduced species have become pests in southern Africa. Their life history is fairly typical of most members of the subfamily.

The pests sometimes known as tobacco slugs are the larvae of two closely allied leaf-eating beetles, *Lema bilineata* and *Lema trilineata*, natives of South America which have been introduced into South Africa and which are common on the plants of the potato family, such as potatoes, Cape gooseberries, tobacco and stinkblaar (*Datura*). The adult beetles are small, black and yellow insects, about 6 mm in length; the back is flattish and the elytra have three black stripes down the back; the underside of the body is usually black but the colour varies.

On the underside of leaves the female lays in clusters her oval, yellow eggs which are covered with a sticky substance that gradually darkens to a dark brown colour. They take about six days to hatch and the larvae feed ravenously on the leaves, reaching full size when about ten or 12 days old. They are at this stage about 6 mm long, with black heads and legs and are covered on the back with slimy excrement which serves as a protection from enemies. The larva places this repulsive substance in position by undulating its body. If the larva is disturbed it rears up its head and emits a drop of brownish fluid from its mouth.

When fully grown it drops to the ground and buries itself in the soil to the depth of about 25 mm. Here it builds a cell by cementing the particles of soil together to form walls, and changes into a pupa. About a week later the adult beetle emerges. There are five or six generations a year.

Members of several other subfamilies also have larvae which use their excreta as a means of camouflage or protection. Larvae of the Clytrinae, of which there are many species in Africa, construct a protective case of excreta. The biology of the African species is unknown but elsewhere the larvae live in ants' nests where they feed on vegetable debris. Most adults of this subfamily show interesting sexual dimorphism; the males sport enlarged jaws and elongated forelegs.

The adults of both the subfamily Clytrinae (and the related Cryptocephalinae), are often coloured as a warning to predators ('aposematically coloured' is the technical term), being yellow or orange with black spots or bands. Although some seem to taste unpleasant, it is possible that others may be mimicking ladybird beetles and blister beetles, which are unpleasant tasting, and which occur on the same plants and flowers.

Members of the subfamily Eumolpinae are very common in Africa. Those larvae which have been studied live in the soil and feed on roots. Adults of the genera *Syagrus*, *Corynodes* and *Euryope* eat leaves. *Corynodes* and *Euryope* are associated with milkweeds (*Asclepias* species), which contain substances poisonous to many vertebrates, and it is quite possible that the beetles gain some protection from predators by ingesting these chemicals. *Euryope* species have, in addition, bright orange and black warning colours.

Halticinae, commonly known as 'flea beetles', constitute a large subfamily of generally small beetles. Their hind femora are enlarged and, as their common name suggests, they can jump very well – a feature which probably helps them to escape predators. Most species have larvae that feed in the stems and roots of herbaceous plants, while the adults often chew 'shot-holes' in the leaves. Some genera are specialised, feeding almost exclusively on a single group of plants, like *Phyllotreta* on the Cruciferae (cabbage family) and *Phygasia* species on milkweeds.

Certain Halticinae are of great interest as the source of Bushman arrow poison. One species of *Polyclada*, feeding on *Sclerocarya caffra* trees, and two species of *Diamphidia*, feeding on two species of *Commiphora* trees, have been discovered to be the species involved. Accurate identification is complicated, however, by the fact that each of the three flea beetles concerned is parasitized in the larval stage by the larvae of a host-specific *Lebistina* beetle belonging to the family Carabidae (ground beetle). Apparently, the Bushmen consider the *Lebistina* larvae to be a more destructive poison than the host larvae.

The larvae of the flea beetles feed on the leaves of the host tree, and when mature they drop off onto the soil below and burrow very deeply into the ground, some 50-100 cm below the surface. The *Lebistina* parasites attach themselves to the fully grown larvae, and penetrate the flea beetles' cocoons which are regular, rounded objects with a hard wall. It is these that the Bushmen dig up and then carefully open to extract the pupae which are used to poison the arrows.

Tortoise beetles, of the genus *Aspidomorpha*, often

attract attention because of their striking shape and colour. They belong to the subfamily Cassidinae, and many species feed on Convulvulaceae and Solanaceae. The adults are some 8 mm long, flattened and shaped somewhat like a tortoise, golden green in colour with a beautiful metallic lustre. This is not due to a pigment, but is structural and is caused by reflection and interference in light reaching the different layers of cuticle. Unless the beetles are kept in alcohol the colour fades soon after death.

The life cycle of *Aspidomorpha* is fairly typical of the other members of the subfamily. The female lays her eggs singly on the leaves, dotting them about indiscriminately. Each is yellow, oval and surrounded by a blob of transparent liquid that quickly hardens so that the egg seems to be enclosed in a tiny disc of glass attached to the leaf. Usually, but not always, the female disguises her egg by depositing excreta on top of it.

In ten to 12 days the egg hatches into a little green grub with a row of flattened, branched spines down each side of its body. On its hind end it has a two-pronged fork that sticks up jauntily in the air. It retains this tail which serves a most curious and important function throughout its larval stages. The newly-hatched larva at once proceeds to dig a pit in the fleshy leaf, eating away the tissues so as to form a shallow hole in which it can be comfortably lodged. It does not eat completely through the leaf but always leaves the epidermis on the opposite surface intact as the base of its home.

As it feeds the grub gives off thin black threads of excreta which are not dropped but become entangled in the fork on the tail and are retained there. When it is a few days old it stops feeding for a time and casts its skin. The moulted skin is not discarded but shrivels up and slips backwards along the body on to the fork and is held there, mingled with the excreta. So it goes on throughout its life until, by the time it is fully grown, it has a strange unsavoury burden on its tail consisting of four cast skins, one above the other, and a black, gluey mass of excrement. If disturbed, it waves this accumulation in the face of its enemy, as it were. The green colour of the larva harmonises well with that of the leaf, but the black shining lump feebly wagging to and fro is very conspicuous and attracts attention, diverting the predator from the insect itself. Besides serving a protective purpose, the quaint habit of carrying its excrement on its back may also be of sanitary value preventing the larva's food from being soiled with waste matter.

When the larva is fully grown it fixes itself firmly to the leaf by digging in the claws of its six short legs. As it takes no more food in this stage the lump at the back dries up and falls off, leaving only the bare fork with the two parallel prongs. Then the skin splits and reveals the flattened, green pupa. Finally, about a fortnight later, the adult tortoise beetle emerges.

Weevils The Curculionidae is the largest of the insect families – more than 60 000 species have already been named and doubtless thousands more await discovery

194. Bushman arrow poison beetle *(Polyclada* sp.), one of several species of leaf beetles whose larvae are used by the Kalahari Bushmen for poisoning their arrows. This species feeds on the leaves of the marula tree *(Sclerocarya caffra)*. 11 mm.

195. Cocoons and pupae of the Bushman arrow poison beetle *(Diamphidia nigroornata)* which have been excavated from sand at the base of the *Commiphora africana* tree on which the larvae developed. Cocoons about 12 mm.

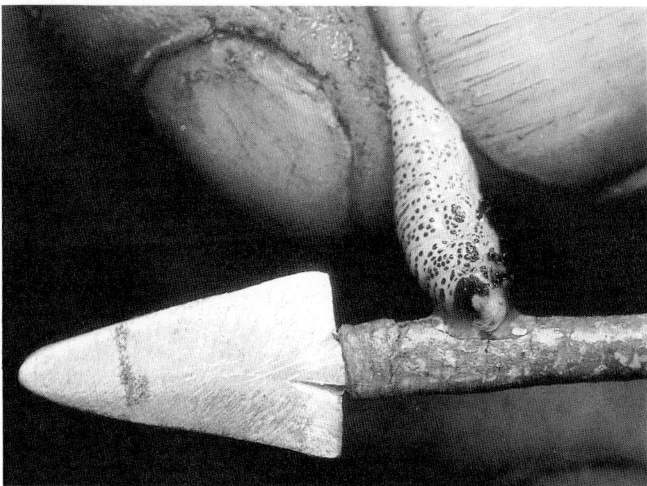

196. A Kalahari Bushman squeezes the body juices of an arrow poison beetle pupa onto the shaft of an arrow. A well-placed arrow will kill a fully grown giraffe in 30 minutes.

and description. These beetles are characterised by the prolongation of the front of the head into a snout, or rostrum, and the antennae are usually elbowed and clubbed. In some species the rostrum is short and broad while in others it is long and narrow and may even exceed the rest of the body in length. The mandibles are lodged at the tip of the rostrum and the females of many, but not all, species use it as a boring instrument for making holes in which they lay their eggs. The rostrum of the male is often shorter than that of the female and we do not know what function it serves in his case.

An extreme example of a long rostrum is found in the South African cycad weevil, *Antliarrhinus zamiae*: the female has a rostrum fully three times as long as the rest of her body. She lays her eggs in the cones of cycads.

All weevils feed on plants. Since the larvae are legless they cannot feed externally on plants as the leaf beetles do, and many of them live inside plant tissue.

Several genera of broad-nosed weevils are found in Africa: a number of species of *Systates* are minor pests of citrus and coffee, the adults feeding on the leaves. The females of the large genus *Protostrophus*, mainly found in southern Africa, apparently drop their eggs at random while feeding, and their larvae feed on roots or decaying vegetable matter in the soil. Sometimes the adults are of economic significance when they emerge in large numbers and destroy seedlings, crop plants or trees.

Another genus of broad-nosed weevil is *Brachycerus*, with numerous species in south and east Africa. They are medium to large, strongly sculptured and mostly brown or black in colour. The bulb weevil, *Brachycerus obesus*, is a striking member of this genus, about 25 mm long, with a black head and thorax and a dark red abdomen. The adult cannot fly, although most of its numerous relatives are excellent aviators. The round, hard back of the abdomen really consists of the elytra fused together to form a hard protective cover. So tough are the wing-cases that it is very difficult to drive a pin through them when a specimen is being mounted for the cabinet. If one of these beetles is trodden on it will not be crushed unless the ground is hard and stony – it will merely be pressed into soft soil and emerge quite unharmed.

This weevil feeds on the tender young leaves of bulbs just as they appear above the ground and in this way may do much harm to gladioli and other garden bulbs. If the beetle is disturbed while it is feeding or while walking with its slow, clumsy gait across a garden path, it will at once 'sham dead'. It falls on its side and holds its legs out stiffly and no amount of prodding will cause it to reveal any signs of life. This clever trick on the part of the insect probably deceives its enemies, but it must not be thought that this is a conscious or voluntary act. The insect has no reasoning powers and it is quite incapable of thinking out such a ruse. Its nervous system is so constituted that, whenever it is disturbed, it falls down automatically in a sort of cataleptic fit. If one of these beetles is observed until the fit passes and it begins to revive and move off, it can be made to fall down again immediately by touching it, and this can be repeated

197. Adult and larva of a tortoise beetle (*Aspidomorpha* sp.) feeding on the leaves of a morning glory creeper. Adult 15 mm.

198. A larva of a tortoise beetle (*Aspidomorpha* sp.), showing the characteristic accumulation of cast skins and excreta on its 'tail'. 10 mm.

199. Head-on view of a broad-nosed weevil, showing the snout that is characteristic of all members of this very large family of insects.

many times – the succeeding fits gradually becoming shorter until finally the insect no longer responds to the stimulus and only tries to escape. Most weevils act instinctively in this way, shamming dead when they are disturbed.

In the crowns of the bulbs, just beneath the surface of the soil, the female bulb weevil lays her eggs which hatch into creamy, white, legless maggots. The maggot feeds on the bulb, eating out a hole and eventually destroying it. If the bulb is big enough the larva remains feeding inside it until it is fully grown; if not, the larva burrows through the soil in search of other bulbs. Finally it pupates either in the hollowed bulb or in a cell excavated in the soil beside the bulb. The adult emerges when the first rains cause the bulbs to sprout the following season.

The long-nosed weevils are much more numerous and varied in their biology. Most species have specialised feeding habits, and only attack closely related groups of plants.

Members of the genus *Rhynchaenus* are leaf miners as larvae, each species mining the leaves of a particular family or genus of tree or shrub. The adults are small and have modified hind legs which enable them to leap away if disturbed.

There are many economically important weevils: *Alcidodes haemopterus* is a pest of cotton; the larvae bore into the cotton stems and induce the formation of a gall, while the adults feed on the succulent green shoots.

200. A bulb weevil flips over onto its back and 'shams dead' at the slightest hint of danger. 12 mm.

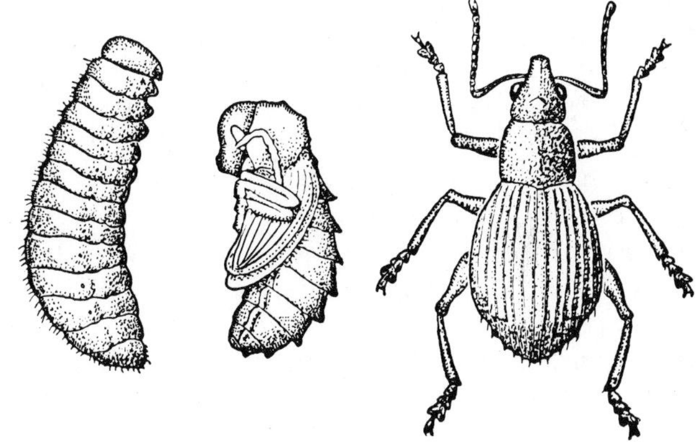

201. Larva (left), pupa and adult (right) of the vine weevil, *Phlyctinus callosus*. The adult is brown and about 6 mm long.

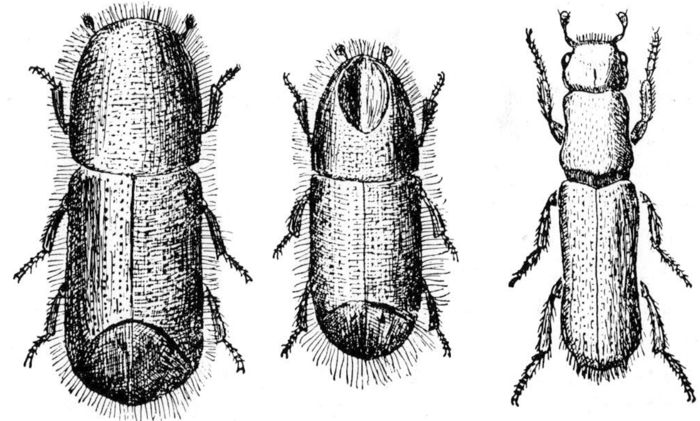

202. A female bark beetle (left) (6 mm) and a male (centre) of the genus *Xyleborus*, and an ambrosia beetle (right) of the genus *Platypus*.

Pinhole borers and ambrosia beetles These beetles used to be classified in separate families, but recent trends treat them as two subfamilies of the weevil family – the Scolytinae and Platypodinae. They are mainly wood borers: most species attack dead or dying trees, logs and moist timber, but they do not breed in seasoned timber, and so are not normally found in buildings. A few, however, live in seeds; *Hypothenemus hampei*, for example, lays its eggs in maturing coffee beans, on which the larvae feed.

These subfamilies display two distinct types of biology: the first is seen in most Scolytinae, which make galleries beneath the bark, or in the bark and the sapwood. In some species the female excavates a gallery and lays her eggs at regular intervals in niches on either side of the gallery. In other species the male excavates a nuptial chamber to which two or more females are attracted, and each female makes her own gallery, the galleries radiating out from the nuptial chamber. The arrangement of the galleries is often characteristic of a species.

The second type of biology is seen in some Scolytinae and in all the Platypodinae. Although they make tunnels in the wood, neither the adults nor the larvae feed on the wood itself, but on fungus found only in the galleries, which blacken as a result.

Some species of ambrosia beetle are communal, with all stages occurring together in the same brood chamber. Breeding may continue in a log for a number of generations, if it contains sap and is damp enough for the fungus to thrive. If the log dries out the beetles leave it and go off in search of a fresh one. They carry the spores of their fungus with them, on the hairs or in special sac-like receptacles on their bodies. As they bore into their new home the spores are deposited on the damp wood where they grow to provide a fresh supply of food.

These beetles bear some resemblance to the fungus-growing termites, and they show the beginnings of a social way of life as well. Some species make simple galleries in which all developmental stages live together. Others make compound tunnels with side branches along which there are small cells in which not only do the larvae develop, but they are fed by the adult female with wads of fungus that are thrust into their cells. Part of the larval excreta and sawdust from the wood borings are used by the female to make the fungus garden bed.

CLASSIFICATION

ORDER: **Coleoptera**

Forewings hard, horny or leathery, called 'elytra' and cover the membranous hind wings that are used for flying. Some beetles lack functional hind wings, and the elytra may be fused, or short in some groups. Mouthparts adapted for biting or chewing. Life histories variable, and size range considerable, from 0,5 mm to 15 cm. Larvae also quite variable in form, hardness of body and development of appendages. The beetles constitute the largest order of insects, and because of the great numbers of species and families, identification is often possible only by an expert on the group. In the account below, only the families mentioned in the text have been dealt with; readers should be aware that there are very many more. The suborders Myxophaga and Archostemata are rare and seldom seen by the average naturalist.

SUBORDER: **Adephaga**
Hind coxae dividing the basal abdominal sternite into two lateral pieces; prothorax with notopleural sutures. A small suborder containing mostly terrestrial beetles, or aquatic, predatory species.

FAMILY: Carabidae
Terrestrial beetles, hind coxae not extending laterally to meet the elytra. Antennae may be flattened or otherwise highly modified and conspicuous (ant nest beetles, subfamily Paussinae) or antennae threadlike (in other subfamilies). The ground beetles (subfamily Carabinae) and tiger beetles (subfamily Cicindelinae) are fast-running predaceous insects.

FAMILY: Gyrinidae
Aquatic 'whirligig' beetles, eyes completely divided into upper and lower parts; antennae short and thick, swim on the water surface, scavenging dead insects.

FAMILY: Dytiscidae
Aquatic, predaceous beetles, swim below water surface. Eyes not completely divided, antennae threadlike. A related family is the Noteridae.

SUBORDER: **Polyphaga**
Hind coxae do not divide the basal abdominal sternite into two lateral pieces; prothorax without notopleural sutures. The great majority of families (more than 135) belong to this suborder, and they are indeed a diverse assemblage, in size, appearance and habits.

FAMILY: Hydrophilidae
Maxillary palps elongated, usually longer than antennae. Antennae short and clubbed. Body generally oval or elliptical, hind legs flattened, usually with a fringe of hairs. A large family of beetles of diverse appearance, including both aquatic and terrestrial species. The larvae are carnivorous, adults vegetarian. Non-aquatic species occur in herbivore dung, and accumulations of decaying vegetable matter.

FAMILY: Histeridae
Antennae distinctly elbowed and clubbed; elytra shortened, exposing one or two abdominal segments at the tip. Hard-bodied, shiny, compact beetles, often black in colour. They usually occur around decaying organic matter.

FAMILY: Staphylinidae
Nearly always elongated, parallel-sided beetles with flexible abdomens. Elytra short, and expose three to six abdominal segments. Antennae threadlike or clublike. Staphylinids occur in all sorts of habitats, and are often associated with carrion or dung. They often run fast and fly well. The hind wings are folded and tucked under the forewings at rest.

FAMILY: Lucanidae
Elongated, robust beetles, mandibles of males very enlarged in some species; antennae more or less elbowed, clubbed towards end. Stag beetles are uncommon in Africa.

FAMILY: Trogidae
Dorsal surface strongly sculptured, with ridges and bumps; head deflexed below pronotum. Abdomen usually with five visible sternites; apical tergite of abdomen (the pygidium) concealed beneath elytra. Usually found in dried animal carcases, feeding on skin.

FAMILY: Scarabaeidae
Dorsal surface generally lacking sculpturing; head not deflexed beneath pronotum; abdomen usually with six visible sternites; apical tergite of abdomen usually exposed. The family is very large and contains many common and conspicuous members. These are placed into six subfamilies, which may be recognised by the following key.

1 Antennae 8-9 segmented; beetles associated with dung **2**
Antennae 9-10 segmented; beetles not associated with dung **3**

2 Elytra completely covering the abdomen; small, parallel-sided species; hind tibiae with two terminal spurs ....Aphodiinae
Elytra leaving the pygidium uncovered; broadly oval species; hind tibiae with one terminal spur ....Scarabaeinae (=Coprinae)

3 Head and pronotum usually without horns or outgrowths; metathoracic epimera not visible from above; labrum corneous, exposed **4**
Head and pronotum usually with horns or outgrowths, or metathoracic epimera visible from above; labrum membranous, concealed **5**

4 Hind tarsal claws equal, immovable, mainly brownish, yellowish or blackish nocturnal species ....Melolonthinae
Hind tarsal claws unequal, movable; mainly brightly coloured, often metallic, diurnal species ....Rutelinae

5 Head and prothorax usually with horns and other outgrowths, mainly stout, convex, black or brown nocturnal species ....Dynastinae
Metathoracic epimera visible from above, usually without horns and outgrowths; moderately flattened, mainly brightly coloured or metallic diurnal species ....Cetoniinae

FAMILY: Buprestidae
Nearly always metallic or bronzed, hard-bodied, elongated beetles whose larvae generally bore into wood or other plant material. Antennae short and serrate, head vertical and largely sunk into the thorax; tarsi with ventral adhesive lobes on at least segments two to four.

FAMILY: Elateridae
Shape distinctive; body narrow and elongated, somewhat flattened and parallel-sided; posterior corners of thorax prolonged backwards as points. Prosternum with an elongate lobe extending posteriorly into a mesosternal depression – this together with a loose articulation of the prothorax, enables these beetles to 'click'.

FAMILY: Lampyridae
Head concealed from above by the pronotum; luminous organs present on one or two abdominal sternites (visible as pale yellowish-white patches); eyes very large; females sometimes larvaeform. Fireflies and glow-worms belong to this family; the larvae are predaceous, feeding on various invertebrates.

FAMILY: Lycidae
Pronotum with well-marked ridges and depressions; elytra with conspicuous longitudinal ridges, often broadest posteriorly. Head usually

concealed from above; colour usually yellow or orange and black; live on vegetation.

FAMILY: Dermestidae
Body covered with dense hairs or scales; elongate to broadly oval in shape; colour blackish or brownish, sometimes patterned. A median ocellus frequently present; antennae short and clubbed, fitting in grooves below sides of pronotum. Larvae cylindrical, covered in long hairs, and feed on dried animal and plant material.

FAMILY: Bostrychidae
Elongate, cylindrical, wood-boring beetles; head bent down, largely concealed from above by pronotum which is very convex, with spiny sculpturing or tubercles; apices of elytra often excavated or flattened, armed with spines or projections.

FAMILY: Lyctidae
Narrow, elongate, flattened, parallel-sided beetles; head visible from above. Antennae with short 2-segmented club at the end; reddish-brown to black beetles, which bore into seasoned timber.

FAMILY: Cleridae
Body elongated, clothed with sparse, long erect hairs; pronotum usually much narrower than elytra at base, and head usually as wide, or wider than pronotum. Antennae usually clubbed; often blue, orange or yellow beetles that occur on foliage.

FAMILY: Lymexylidae
Elytra very short, not reaching the abdomen; wings folded fanwise over the body when at rest; tarsi as long, or longer than tibiae. Larvae live in tunnels in hardwood.

FAMILY: Nitidulidae
Antennae with swollen scape (basal segment) and a club composed of three transverse segments. Tarsi usually broadly dilated; elytra often shortened and exposing one to three abdominal segments. Shape variable, usually elongate, robust or broadly oval. Often occur on fruit, sap or flowers.

FAMILY: Coccinellidae
Distinctive shape, broadly oval to nearly spherical, flat underneath and strongly convex dorsally. Often shiny, brightly coloured with orange, yellow or red patterns on black; some species appear dull because of a fine coat of hairs. Antennae short, with 3-6 segmented club. Adults and larvae may be plant feeders; the majority are predators of aphids and scale insects.

FAMILY: Tenebrionidae
Antennae usually 11-segmented, threadlike, beadlike or slightly clubbed. Eyes frequently 'notched', sides of forehead usually shelf-like, covering the antennal cavities. Generally dull black or brown, but a very diverse group that includes pests of stored products ('meal-worms') and varied desert forms.

FAMILY: Mordellidae
Hump-backed, wedge-shaped beetles with deflexed head and pointed abdomen which extends beyond elytra. 'Tumbling' behaviour when disturbed is characteristic for the family.

FAMILY: Meloidae
Usually elongated, head often broader than pronotum, which is broadest posteriorly, but narrower than elytra. Tarsal claws usually serrate, with a sclerotised, blade-like process beneath each claw; legs long and slender; body soft, often leathery; elytra may be brightly coloured. Larvae parasitic on other insects, but adults may damage flowers; they contain poisonous cantharadin.

FAMILY: Cerambycidae
Antennae usually arise from pronounced tubercle, which is often situated in a 'notch' in the eye; they are at least two-thirds as long as body (usually longer) and can be flexed backwards over the body. Long-horn beetles often have bright patterns or markings; their larvae bore into dead or dying trees; a few live in roots.

FAMILY: Bruchidae
Small oval or egg-shaped beetles, head concealed from above, prolonged into a short, broad snout. Elytra usually short, exposing tip of the abdomen. Basal segment of hind tarsus longer than the other segments together.

FAMILY: Chrysomelidae
Body broad, oval, sometimes circular (tortoise-like); basal segment of hind tarsus not longer than other segments together, and tip of abdomen rarely exposed by elytra. Vegetarian beetles that are common on all kinds of plants; some are agricultural pests.

FAMILY: Curculionidae
Face prolonged into a snout; antennae clubbed and nearly always elbowed. The weevils constitute the largest insect family and are widespread and abundant. Many are agricultural pests.

FURTHER READING

Arnett, R. H.: *The beetles of the United States (a manual for identification).* The American Ent. Inst. Ann Arbor (1968). 1112 pp

Arrow, G. J.: *Horned Beetles, a Study of the Fantastic in Nature.* Ed. by Hincks, W. D.: W. Junk, The Hague (1951). 154 pp

Balachowsky, A. S. (Ed.): *Entomologie appliquée à l'agriculture.* Tome 1 Coléoptéres. Vol. 1 & 2. Masson et Cie, Paris (1962-1963). 1385 pp

Balduf, W. V.: *The bionomics of entomophagous Coleoptera.* J. S. Swift Co., New York (1935). 220 pp

Britton, E. B.: 'Coleoptera.' Ch. 30 in *The Insects of Australia.* CSIRO, Melbourne University Press (1970). pp. 495-621

Crowson, R. A.: *The Natural Classification of the Families of Coleoptera.* E. W. Classey Ltd. Hampton, Middlesex (1969). 214 pp

Duffey, E. A. J.: *A Monograph of the immature stages of African timber beetles.* British Museum (Natural History), London (1957). 338 pp

Ferreira, M. C.: 'Catálogo dos Coleopteros de Moçambique.' *Revista de Entomologia de Moçambique* (1963). 6 (1) and (2):1-1008

Ferreira, M. C. 'Catálogo dos Coleopteros de Angola.' *Revista de Entomologia de Moçambique* (1965). 8 (2):415-1317 (a useful source of references to recent works on African Coleoptera)

Ferreira, G. da V & Ferreira, M. C.: (Papers dealing with Cerambycidae, Scarabaeidae (Scarabaeinae) of Moçambique; some Buprestidae of southern Africa; Scarabaeidae (Dynastinae) of Africa). *Revista de Entomologia de Moçambique.* (1958-1967)

Hagen, K. S.: 'Biology and ecology of predacious coccinellidae.' *Annual Review of Entomology* (1962). 7:280-326

Halffter, G. & Matthews, E. G.: 'The natural history of dung beetles of the subfamily Scarabaeinae (Col. Scarabaeidae).' *Folia Entomologica Mexicana* (1966). No. 12-14. 312 pp

Hanström B., Brinck, P. & Rüdebeck, G. (Ed). *South African Animal Life.* (The following volumes contain useful revisions of South African or African species: Bostrychidae (VI); Carabidae (Pterostichinae) (V); Dytiscidae (XI); Elateridae (XV); Endomychidae (VI); Gyrinidae (I); Haliplidae (XIII); Heteroceridae (XI); Lycidae (XIII); Mordellidae (IV); (XI); (XII); Scarabaeidae (Dynastinae) (VII))

Hinton, H. E.: *A monograph of the beetles associated with stored products.* Vol. I. British Museum (Natural History), London (1945). 443 pp

Hodek, I.: *Biology of Coccinellidae, with keys for identification of larvae.* W. Junk, The Hague (1973) 260 pp

Koch, C.: 'Some aspects of abundant life in the vegetationless sand of the Namib Desert dunes. Positive psammotropism in Tenebrionid beetles.' *Journal of the South West African Scientific Society* (1961). 15:8-92 (Many other papers on Namib beetles by the same author).

Linsley, E. G.: 'Ecology of Cerambycidae.' *Annual Review of Entomology* (1959). 4:99-138

Thiele, H. U.: *Carabid beetles in their Environments. A study on habitat selection by adaptations in physiology and behaviour.* Vol. 10. Zoophysiology and Ecology. Eds. Hoar, W. S., Hoelldobler, B., Langer, H. and Lindauer, M.: Springer-Verlag, Berlin (1977). 369 pp

Scorpionflies 15

Mecoptera is a small order that includes only about 400 known species from all parts of the world. The common name is derived from the male of the family Panorpidae which holds the tip of its abdomen curled up over its back. As Panorpidae do not occur in the southern hemisphere the common term 'scorpionfly' is singularly inappropriate and African members of the order, all belonging to the family Bittacidae, are more appropriately called 'hangingflies'. They are slender insects, generally small in size with two pairs of narrow, membranous wings which accounts for the name Mecoptera meaning 'long wings'. The antennae are long and threadlike and the front of the head is prolonged to form a curious beak with the mandibles at the tip.

African hangingflies These are yellowish-brown, four-winged insects, with long, thin legs. The slender body is 20-30 mm in length and the characteristic beak or rostrum projects from the head. The 52 known African species all belong to the genus *Bittacus*, with the exception of a single species of *Anomalobittacus* – an unusual and wingless hangingfly unique to the south-western Cape Province of South Africa. The majority of known species are from the eastern parts of Africa where they are found in rank vegetation on the edge of forests, on the forest floor and in open grassveld. As the common name suggests, Bittacidae spend most of their time hanging by the front legs, waiting for suitable prey.

All African hanging flies are predatory, able to capture prey with their long, prehensile feet or tarsi. They are unique in that their hind legs are not used for walking at all, but are specialised for the capture of prey. When the hangingfly makes a successful catch, it bites its victim with its long, thin mandibles and injects saliva to break down the tissues which may then be sucked up in this partially digested form. Once the contents have been consumed, the hollow corpse is discarded.

The mating behaviour of the Bittacidae is both complex and fascinating. Since both male and female are predatory, the male must use an ingenious ploy to ensure that he is not eaten. Therefore prior to approaching the female, he captures some delicacy; only then does he emit a pheromone from special glands to attract her. When she is close enough, he distracts her with his offering and whilst she eats, he is able to mate.

The female hangingfly deposits her rounded eggs at random in her rank habitat. The larvae resemble caterpillars, but have in addition to the three pairs of legs behind the head, eight pairs of abdominal legs instead of the five found in true caterpillars. In addition, a caterpillar has only four to six simple eyes on each side of its head, while the scorpionfly larva has a group of 20 or

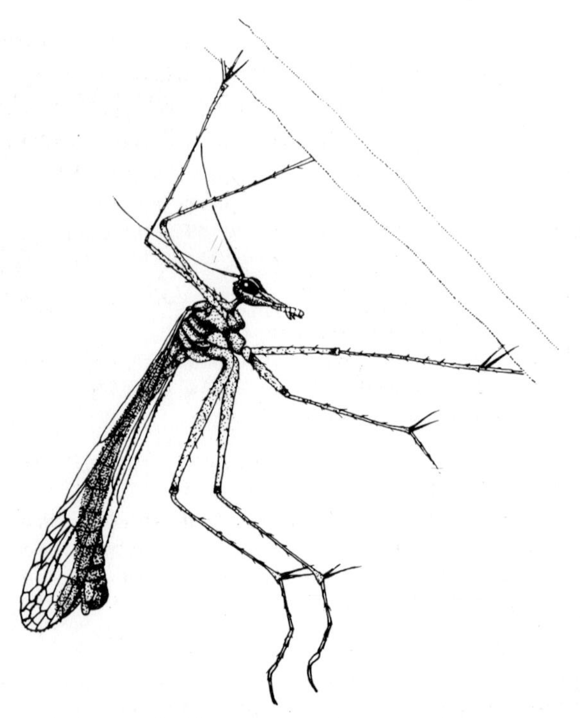

203. A male hangingfly, *Bittacus capensis*, waiting for prey, which it will capture by means of its hind legs. 30 mm.

more simple eyes on each side. Finally, the antennae of the scorpionfly larva are prominent and four-jointed, whereas those of a caterpillar are small and difficult to see.

Like the adults, hangingfly larvae are suspected to be predaceous, although experiments in North America suggest that they may consume dead tissue as well – a few species have been successfully reared on chopped earthworms and small pieces of steak.

When fully grown, the larva buries itself in the soil, forming a small underground cavern in which it pupates. It can move about if disturbed because its legs are not bound down to its sides as they are in the pupa of a moth or butterfly. When the adult is ready to emerge from the pupa, it exits from the pupal cell via a specially constructed lid at ground level.

CLASSIFICATION

ORDER: **Mecoptera**

Small to medium-sized insects with slender and soft body. Long-faced, the chewing mouthparts at the end of a long snout-like structure. Four membranous wings (absent in one species), very long and narrow. Antennae long and threadlike, legs long and slender, tarsi with one claw, fifth tarsal segment capable of being folded back on the fourth. Metamorphosis complete. One family in Africa, Bittacidae, with more than 50 described species, mostly from East Africa.

FURTHER READING

Byers, G. W.: An illustrated, annotated catalogue of African Mecoptera. *Kansas University Science Bulletin* (1971). 49: 389-436.

Londt, J. G. H.: (Various descriptions and records of Bittacidae.) *Journal of the Entomological Society of Southern Africa* (1972-1978).

Setty, L. R.: Biology and morphology of some North American Bittacidae. *American Midland Entomologist* (1940). 23: 257-353.

Fleas 16

Fleas belong to the order Siphonaptera and form a small group sharply divided from all other insects because their bodies are flattened from side to side and not dorso-ventrally, or from above downwards, as other insects are. The shape of the insects is an adaptation for slipping through the hairy coats or feathers of their hosts. Although the adult flea has no trace of wings, the pupa has wing-cases which indicate that the flea is related to or descended from one or other of the winged orders.

When not feeding on its host, the flea moves for the most part by means of powerful leaps, which may span 40 cm. This jump is not powered by muscle alone, but is assisted by the sudden release of energy stored in the metathorax in a rubber-like protein called resilin. Although fleas do not fly, they have several features peculiar to insects which do, such as the wing-hinge ligament, the starter muscle in the leg and some flight muscles – each of which has been modified to produce the flea's spectacular leap.

The hind legs of a flea are larger and stronger than the first and second pairs and they alone provide the power for the jump. When about to leap, the flea crouches down and various muscles in its body and hind legs contract, squeezing the stored resilin. Several catches on the body click into place to co-ordinate the combined energy of muscle and resilin. As these catches are released, the hind legs move down with considerable force and hurl the flea into the air.

Household fleas The fleas most commonly found in human dwellings are the human flea, *Pulex irritans*, the cat flea, *Ctenocephalides felis*, and the dog flea, *Ctenocephalides canis*. The cat flea also occurs on the dog and in fact in Africa is more often found on dogs than the dog flea. All three are similar in their habits and life histories.

Both male and female fleas are voracious bloodfeeders. When feeding, they inject an anti-coagulant saliva into the wound made by their lancet-like mouthparts, and it is this saliva that causes irritation and swelling. Fleas often leave a row of bites on their victim and there may be small dark spots on the sheets. These are the faecal deposits of adult fleas, which are such greedy feeders that they often expel undigested blood from their intestine whilst they are imbibing more through the mouth. The blood which has been ejected clots on the hairs of the host and finally drops off as tiny black lumps.

The female deposits her eggs, which are relatively large (5 mm long), glistening white and rounded at both ends, in small batches amid the fur of the animal on which she is feeding. A dog, giving itself a vigorous shake inside the house, will sometimes send a shower of eggs flying all around him. Alternatively, the female flea may drop off and lay the eggs on the ground. The dog's kennel or the favourite sleeping place of the cat usually has a large number of eggs lying about, but they are so inconspicuous that they pass unnoticed.

The eggs hatch into slender, cylindrical, active larvae, pale yellow in colour with segmentally arranged bristles. They move about in dirt and debris, in places such as between the cracks of the floorboards or on the floor of the kennel where they feed on any organic matter that provides the necessary protein, including epidermal scales, dried blood flecks and flea excreta. Depending on whether conditions and temperatures are favourable, the larval period may be as short as ten days or as long as 200. At the end of the active feeding period when fully grown, the larva spins a thin, silken cocoon around itself, which is soon coated with dust and debris and becomes inconspicuous.

Inside the cocoon the larva changes into the pupa, white at first but slowly turning brown. Just as the larval period is irregular, so the pupal period varies enormously, depending on the temperature. When the adult fleas hatch, they may lie quiescent in the cocoon for weeks or months until aroused by the vibration of footsteps or some other stimulus associated with the presence of a host. This accounts for the fact that people are often ambushed by hordes of ravenous fleas when they first enter a house that has been empty for some time.

In the absence of a host, adult fleas can survive prolonged periods of starvation – more so under humid than under arid conditions. Indeed, fleas flourish best in moderately warm, moist places.

Apart from the irritation caused by their bites, household fleas are significant as intermediate hosts of the cat and dog tapeworm, *Dipylidium caninum*. The eggs of the tapeworm are devoured by the larvae of the flea and they hatch inside the larvae where they reach a certain stage of development. The tapeworm larvae remain in the flea until it reaches adulthood and if swallowed by a dog or by a child, as so often happens, these immature worms complete their development into tapeworms in their new hosts.

Rat fleas and plague Plague is a disease of rodents caused by the bacteria, *Yersinia pestis*. It is transmitted by rodent fleas to both human beings and rodents and under certain conditions serious epidemics may occur.

Plague has been known since ancient times and has had a great influence on the course of history: epidemics have devastated entire cities, countries and even continents. The last major outbreak to ravage a continent (a pandemic) occurred in Asia towards the end of the nineteenth century. Today plague is endemic to parts of southern, eastern and central Africa: Uganda is believed to be an ancient focus of the disease.

Prior to 1899, plague was unknown in southern Africa, but the visit of a ship from Argentina to Cape Town in March 1900 introduced the disease. At the time, the second Anglo-Boer War was in progress, and plague quickly spread to all the major ports as well as along supply lines to the interior. Although there has never been a major epidemic in South Africa, many people have in fact died of the disease. The domestic rodent plague in the cities came to an end in 1912, but in 1914 it was discovered that the disease had become established in wild rodents where it remains to this day. Only the constant vigilance of health inspectors and medical entomologists prevents major outbreaks in urban areas. Regular collections are made of fleas from rodent burrows, and these are tested for plague: if plague is detected, teams move in and destroy the rodents in the affected area, at the same time controlling the fleas by the application of insecticides. The main reservoirs are gerbils of the genera *Tatera* and *Desmodillus*, while the multimammate rat, *Mastomys natalensis*, plays a key rôle in carrying plague from wild to domestic rodents. The most important flea vectors belong to the genus *Xenopsylla*.

Plague is transmitted by fleas from one creature to another in a curious manner. After feeding on an infected animal, the digestive tract of the flea becomes blocked with a solid mass of plague bacteria and partially digested blood. Such a 'blocked' flea cannot take any more food, and it becomes ravenously hungry. When the sick animal dies, the flea leaves its body and seeks out a new host. However, when the 'blocked' flea tries to suck blood from another animal, this cannot pass the plug of bacteria into its stomach and consequently is regurgitated into the wound along with infective bacteria. In this way the flea acts as a living hypodermic syringe, and infects its new host with the plague. In their restless search for food, 'blocked' fleas may infect a number of new hosts, until eventually they die of starvation.

When humans are infected by plague bacteria from flea bites, they suffer from bubonic plague, characterised by 'buboes' or swollen lymph glands. A second type of plague, called pneumonic plague, is transmitted from human to human by droplet infection and fleas are not involved in the disease cycle.

Jigger fleas The jigger flea, *Tunga penetrans*, introduced to Africa from tropical America in the seventeenth century, has since spread widely throughout most of the continent's tropical zones. The adults are similar in their habits to other fleas, and they will feed on the blood of a wide range of hosts, but human beings and pigs seem to be their favourites. The particular importance of the flea lies in the fact that the female, after she has been fertilised, but before her eggs develop, burrows into the skin of her host, generally in tender and easily penetrated areas such as between the toes and beneath the toe-nails.

The flesh around the flea becomes inflamed and swollen and encloses the insect, with only a small hole leading to the exterior through which the tip of the flea's abdomen projects. As the eggs develop, her body swells up to the size of a pea and, in about a week, she expels her eggs through the hole in the skin. The eggs hatch on the ground and the larvae feed on organic debris, developing and pupating in the same way as typical household fleas.

The wounds made by the burrowing females often become infected with bacteria and are very painful. Sometimes the distended body of the insect is broken in the wound with severe ulceration and complications resulting.

In parts of Angola it is common to see people with missing toes, following amputation because of infection and gangrene resulting from jigger flea ulcers. Walking barefoot in areas where jiggers occur is bound to result in infestation, and people who live in such areas regularly hold 'foot inspections' to remove any insects before they develop. The best way to deal with the pest is to enlarge the hole with a sterile needle or sharp blade and to remove the insect whole, afterwards treating the wound with an antiseptic.

Sticktight fleas Fleas of the genus *Echidnophaga* exhibit some of the evolutionary tendencies of the jigger flea, in that the females attach themselves tightly to the skin of the host by means of their mouthparts, causing inflammation and discomfort. Here they are fertilised by the males and lay their eggs within the ulcers that form around them. Most eggs drop to the ground before hatching. *E. gallinacea*, one of the six African species, is widespread in tropical regions and attacks poultry, clustering in dense masses around the heads of the unfortunate fowls. Another species, *E. larina*, occurs on wart-hogs and bushpigs and has also been found clinging to the ears of African elephants.

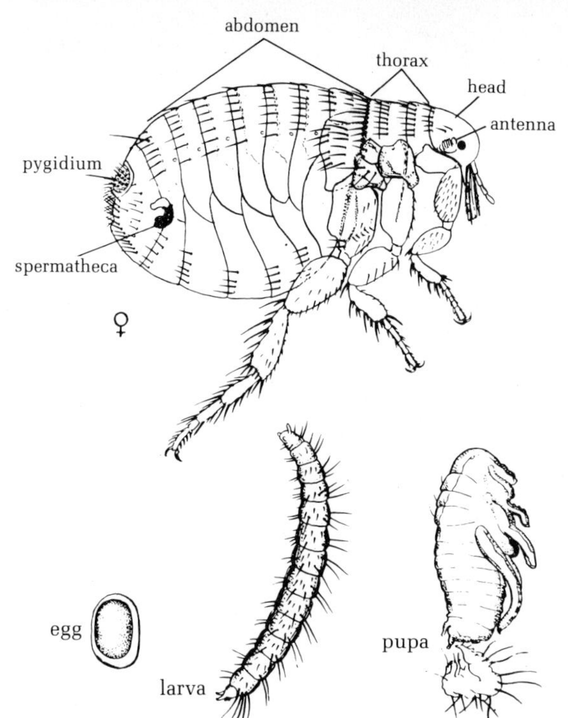

204. A typical rat flea of the genus *Xenopsylla*, showing the major features of the adult, and the development stages.

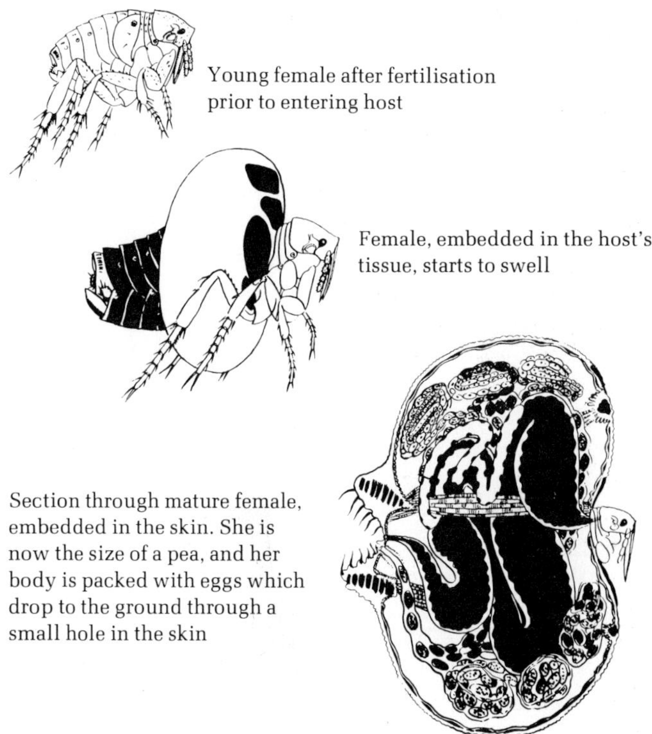

205. Stages in the development of the female jigger flea, *Tunga penetrans*.

CLASSIFICATION

ORDER: **Siphonaptera**

Adults small, wingless, laterally compressed, blood-sucking ectoparasites of mammals and birds, with distinctive morphological features. Head with characteristic groove dividing forehead from occiput; the antennae fold into this groove – they are sense organs, which are also used by the male to hold the female during copulation. Mouthparts consist of the sucking tube with maxillary stilettoes which are serrated. The eyes are large in some species, but in many they are reduced or absent. The thorax consists of three segments, each bearing a pair of legs. The last segment is highly developed to support the jumping mechanism of the hind legs. The abdomen consists of ten segments.

Features used to classify fleas include the shape and form of the female spermatheca, the male genitalia and the number and length of bristles on the legs. African fleas are classified into ten families. The three largest can be identified as follows:

1 Outer internal ridge of mid coxa absent . . . . .Pulicidae
Outer internal ridge of mid coxa usually present, sometimes short 2

2 Hind coxa with a row of spiniform bristles . . .Chimaeropsyllidae
Hind coxa without row of spiniform bristles Hystrichopsyllidae

FAMILY: Pulicidae
This large family has a world-wide distribution and contains the most important pests of man and domestic animals, as well as the principal vectors of plague. Four subfamilies occur in Africa. Of the Pulicinae, members of the genus *Echidnophaga* attach themselves firmly to the skin of their hosts. *Pulex irritans* is the human flea and the only member of the genus found in Africa. The Archeopsyllinae include *Ctenocephalides* of which the dog and cat fleas are well-known species. The subfamily Xenopsyllinae contains *Xenopsylla*, a very important genus of plague vectors. *Procaviopsylla* is specific to hyraxes, while *Pariodontis* is found only on porcupines.

FAMILY: Hystrichopsyllidae
The largest family of fleas, with three subfamilies in Africa, most of them rodent parasites. *Ctenophthalmus* is an important genus. *Dinopsyllus* are extremely large fleas, and one species is an important plague vector in central Africa.

FAMILY: Chimaeropsyllidae
This family is peculiar to Africa, and most species occur in southern Africa where one, *Chiastopsylla rossi*, is a plague vector. There are three genera which are specific to elephant shrews, *Chimaeropsylla*, *Demeillonia* and *Macroscelidopsylla*, while the genus *Cryptopsylla* occurs only on mole-rats.

OTHER FAMILIES

Tungidae. Only one species in Africa, introduced from America. Discussed in the text.

Ischnopsyllidae. Confined to bats, and thus not commonly encountered. Eight genera in Africa.

Ceratophyllidae. This family includes the bird-fleas, which for some reason are very rare in Africa. Migrant birds from Europe leave their fleas behind when they travel south.

FURTHER READING

Cloudsley-Thompson, J. L.: *Insects and History*. World Naturalist Series. Weidenfeld & Nicholson. London (1976). 242 pp

De Meillon, B. H., Davis, D. S. & Hardy, F.: *Plague in Southern Africa. Vol. 1. The Siphonaptera (excluding Ischnopsyllidae)*. Government Printer, Pretoria (1961). 208 pp

Hopkins, G. H. E. & Rothschild, M.: *An illustrated catalogue of the Rothschild collection of fleas* (Siphonaptera) *in the British Museum (Nat. Hist.)*. Five volumes, published in 1953, 1956, 1962, 1966 & 1971 by the British Museum (nat. Hist.) London.

Zumpt, F. ed.: *The Arthropod Parasites of Vertebrates in Africa south of the Sahara. Vol. III. (Insecta excl. Phthiraptera)*. Publications of the South African Institute for Medical Research Johannesburg, 1961. 283 pp

Flies

There are few places in Africa where one is not painfully aware of that most successful insect order, the Diptera. If they are not falling into our tea, crawling over our food or flying into our ears and noses, we are wincing in pain as a tsetse fly or horse fly strikes, or cursing as the whine of a mosquito keeps us from sleep. Flies are ubiquitous and abrasive, yet those that torment us constitute only a tiny fraction of the known species in this enormous order.

Flies have only one pair of well-developed wings, hence their scientific name, Diptera, which means two-winged. The second pair of wings found in other insects are represented in the flies by the halteres which are small stalks with club-shaped ends and project, one on each side, just behind the bases of the front wings. These are specialised organs which act as flight stabilizers. Flies are splendid aviators, and it is a pity that the limitations of human sight do not allow us to appreciate their airmanship.

It is thanks to modern high-speed photography that we have finally learned how a house fly can land on the ceiling, not only apparently defying gravity, but reversing the direction in which it had been flying a split second earlier. The forelegs, outstretched and raised, reach the ceiling and grip fast by their suction pads. The fly's body then pivots about the anchored legs and the remaining legs make contact with the surface – the intricate manoeuvre is complete.

There are so many different kinds of flies in Africa that a few introductory remarks about how they are divided up and classified should make the whole chapter less formidable. Firstly we must note a group of 'primitive' flies, or 'lower Diptera', which has multi-segmented, long and often threadlike antennae: it forms the suborder Nematocera. Examples are crane flies, mosquitoes and their related families. The next major category is the 'higher Diptera': all have short antennae and fall into the suborder Brachycera. This enormous group itself falls into two natural divisions and we may differentiate between a smaller group of more primitive families, the Brachycera proper, and a larger group known as the suborder Cyclorrhapha. The most familiar flies, such as the house fly and its relations, fruit flies and blue-bottles, belong to this suborder.

In fact the house fly group is so common and abundant that it is useful to call them 'muscoid' flies and divide them into two, the acalyptrates and the calyptrates. Calypters are a pair of membranous, wing-like structures at the base of the true wings. Blue-bottles and other Calliphoridae, for example, have well-developed calypters and they are considered highly advanced and successful. Amongst the acalyptrates, which are more primitive in their structure, we find the fruit flies and the vinegar flies.

SUBORDER **Nematocera**

Crane flies These slender, long-legged flies that look rather like enormous mosquitoes and are often called 'daddy-long-legs', frequently come into houses and flutter clumsily at the window panes or perch on walls behind basins and other damp places. They are among the simplest of flies and belong to the family Tipulidae. They have slender, threadlike antennae and very long, fragile legs that come away only too easily, as many an amateur entomologist knows!

Crane flies are common in the rainy season and are usually found in damp places because their larvae require moisture. The immature stages occupy a wide variety of habitats, from decayed wood to moss on dry rocks to soil, but invariably near water. The plump and fleshy larvae of the big daddy-long-legs are terrestrial and may be found in lawns and on playing fields where they eat the grass roots; they may cause substantial damage to lawns and young crops. Most of the large crane flies are vegetarian, but larvae belonging to the subfamily Limoniinae are aquatic and predatory, feeding on dragonfly nymphs, worms and other larvae.

Tipulidae are found throughout the world, and many thousands of species have been described. Apart from

206. A crane fly resting on the leaf of a forest tree; typically these flies seek damp places, out of sunlight. 7 mm.

207. Close-up of a crane fly showing the typical features of this primitive fly family, such as the multi-segmented antennae and the simple mouthparts. Like all flies, it has a single pair of wings, each hind wing being replaced by a balancing organ known as a haltere, which in this case can be seen as a thin stalk projecting horizontally from just below and behind the base of the wing.

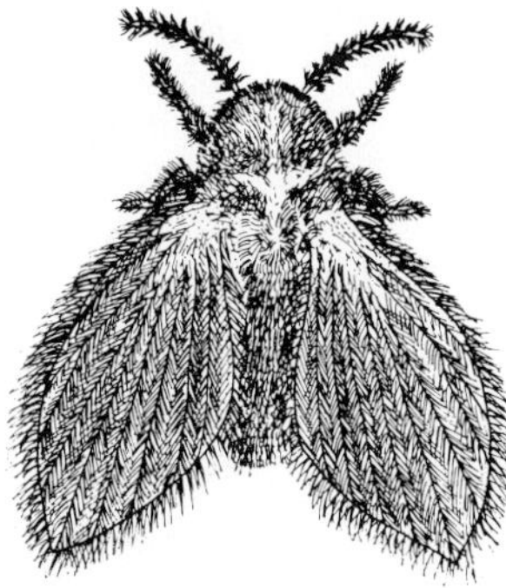

208. Moth flies are common in bathrooms and kitchens, and their dark, hairy wings are held rooflike over the abdomen at rest.

the large ones that we see in houses, there are hundreds of small, inconspicuous ones that hide in vegetation near water. Their mouthparts are both primitive and unspecialised, so that crane flies can neither chew nor bite, let alone pierce the human skin. The majority of adults appear to require little in the way of food, and obtain nectar from flowers by means of an elongated proboscis. Their slow and clumsy flight makes them easy prey to robber flies, spiders, ants and birds.

A striking feature characteristic of many crane flies is the rhythmical waving of a leg or the wings; sometimes the whole body bobs as if keeping time to some invisible metronome. This action is part of the mating ritual, but some crane flies carry the activity to extraordinary lengths, hanging from a spider web while performing; surprisingly they are neither caught in the web nor attacked by the spider. One theory accounting for this mating ritual is that crane flies, in the act of luring a mate by their conspicuous actions, also attract the unwelcome attention of predators such as robber flies; thus the spider web serves to protect the performing male from aerial attack while he, perhaps, acts as live bait for the spider.

Some small crane flies dancing in the air form dense clouds to attract females which are pounced upon as soon as they enter the swarm, and carried off to a nearby leaf or branch where mating takes place. Similar swarming habits are found among several of the various families of Diptera.

Moth flies and sand flies The family Psychodidae contains a number of small and rather inconspicuous flies, some of which are important vectors of human disease. The flies that belong to the subfamily Pyschodinae are tiny mothlike flies, with broad, hairy wings that meet like a roof over their bodies. They are attracted by the smell of urine and damp conditions and are encountered in public lavatories, stables and bat caves. Although they are feeble fliers and attract little attention because of their small size, moth flies are also often seen in the house, particularly in the kitchen and bathroom because they like the dampness at the sink and basin.

Moth flies belonging to the genera *Psychoda* and *Telmatoscopus* may occur in countless millions at sewage works where the activity of the larvae who feed on algae, fungi and bacteria that would otherwise clog the filters, plays a fundamental rôle in the purification process. Although they cannot bite, swarming moth flies may cause discomfort to people. Occasionally employees at sewage works suffer from asthma or allergies caused by the wind-borne scales and particles from the millions of insects.

The sand flies belong to the subfamily Phlebotominae and some are vicious bloodsuckers that make life out of doors in the evenings impossible in certain parts of Africa. The ancient practice of blood-letting is in fact known as phlebotomy, derived from the Greek 'phlebos' meaning vein. All sand flies are very tiny creatures of about 3 mm in length and unless they bite, are liable to pass unnoticed. Their larval habitats are dark, humid places where there is organic matter upon which to feed; animal burrows, termite hills and tree holes provide suitable breeding sites.

Sand flies of the genus *Sergentomyia* feed on cold-blooded vertebrates such as toads, snakes and lizards and have been found to transmit a trypanosome to the common skink lizard found all over Africa. Members of *Phlebotomus*, however, bite mammals and act as the vectors of the parasite *Leishmania*, which causes in man a variety of clinical diseases collectively known as leishmaniasis. Both cutaneous and visceral leishmaniasis occur in various regions of Africa, a serious threat to public health. Common names for the diverse forms of the disease include 'Oriental Sore' for the type that causes boils and lesions on the skin, and 'Kala-Azar' for the dangerous form that invades the internal organs.

In the Sudan, Kenya, Ethiopia and elsewhere, medical entomologists have worked for years to find the elusive sand flies and understand how they transmit leishmaniasis. In doing so, they have uncovered some fascinating disease relationships indicating that man, not normally involved in the disease cycle, is very often the accidental host of a *Leishmania* from a wild animal. In Ethiopia and in Namibia, the rock hyrax or dassie has a barely visible infection of leishmaniasis at the tip of the nose, the only place the sand fly can penetrate. When an infected sand fly subsequently bites a human, the organisms are transferred and cause a nasty sore at the site of the bite. Other animal hosts in Africa are gerbils and giant rats, and doubtless further interesting associations will be revealed in time.

Mosquitoes All mosquitoes breed in water. A common belief in parts of Africa that they can breed in pepper trees and gum trees is wrong, unless the trees happen to be hollow and contain accumulations of rain water. Furthermore, mosquitoes do not fly far from their breeding places; a range of 1-2 km is about their limit, as a rule, and many of them do not fly more than 200-300 m from the places where they were bred. Not even wind carries them long distances, for they are such frail creatures that they take shelter when a strong wind is blowing. The name 'mosquito' comes from the Spanish, and means 'little fly'.

The common household mosquitoes, such as *Culex pipiens* and *Culex fatigans* (called *Culex quinquefasciata* by some workers), will breed in almost any stagnant water. Rainwater barrels, septic tanks, tin cans, blocked roof gutters, anything, in fact, that will hold water for a few weeks serves these pests as breeding places.

It is only the female that sucks blood. In many species she requires a feed of blood before she can mature her eggs, but in other species this not essential, and the female is then said to be autogenous. This means that the first batch of eggs can be laid in the absence of a meal of blood, while subsequent egg laying requires the ingestion of blood.

A male mosquito cannot suck blood because his mouthparts are imperfectly developed and they are incapable of piercing the human skin; his food consists of the nectar of flowers and the juices of ripe fruits, food which the female will also take when there is no blood available. The male's antennae are feathery, like beautiful little plumes ornamenting his head, while the female's antennae are threadlike and armed with only short hairs scarcely visible to the naked eye. This difference in the antennae offers an easy means of distinguishing the sexes.

The female's proboscis consists of an elongated lower lip which is deeply grooved along the top. Six slender lancets lie in the groove and are the weapons by means of which she pierces the skin of her victim and sucks the blood. The lancets are the highly modified mandibles, maxillae, the hypopharynx and labrum-epipharynx. The comparatively thick lower lip, or labium, which constitutes the bulk of the proboscis, does not enter the wound; it is bent back out of the way as the lancets are thrust deeper and deeper into the flesh. Saliva is injected into the wound along a very fine narrow channel in the hypopharynx and this sets up irritation and produces a little local inflammation that draws a plentiful blood supply to the spot; it is also the means by which disease organisms are introduced by those mosquitoes that transmit malaria, yellow fever, dengue fever, and filariasis. Because of the widespread misery, suffering and death caused by these diseases, mosquitoes must be regarded as the greatest insect enemies of man.

The mosquitoes that commonly attack human beings may be divided into two types, the culicines (from the name of the principal genus of the group, *Culex*) and the anophelines (from the principal genus, *Anopheles*), and they are easily distinguished from one another in each of the stages.

Mosquitoes have scales, or flattened hairs, on their bodies and wings, much like those found in butterflies and moths; the moth flies and sand flies (Psychodidae) are the only other Diptera that have these scales. The scales on the wings of culicine mosquitoes are all of the same greyish tint, whereas many anophelines have patches of black scales among the grey ones. These anophelines, therefore, have black spots on their wings.

On the head of the adult mosquito there is a pair of palps projecting on each side of the proboscis. These palps are as long as the proboscis in all male mosquitoes, but they are much shorter in female culicines. Female anophelines, on the other hand, have palps as long as those of the male. Culicine mosquitoes, when at rest, hold their bodies parallel with the surface upon which they are resting, while anopheline mosquitoes rest with the body at an angle of about 45 degrees to the surface. Thus the patterns of the wings, the length of the palps in the females and the resting position are foolproof means of distinguishing between the two types.

Basically, the life histories of all mosquitoes are simi-

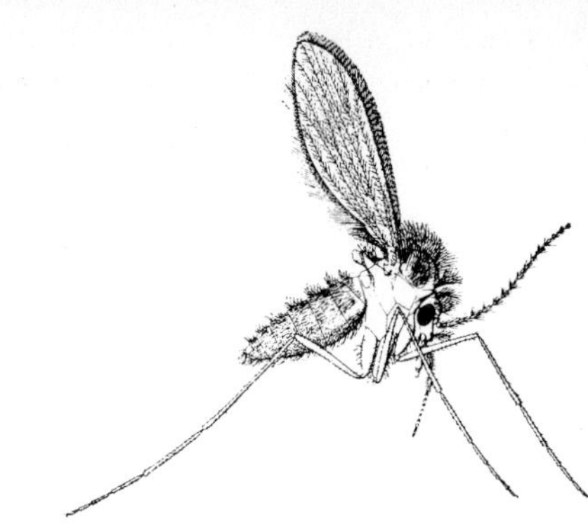

209. A sand fly (*Phlebotomus* sp.) showing its hairy appearance and the wings held together at an angle above the body. These flies are very small (2 mm long), and fly in short, fluttering hops from one spot to another.

210. Unlike their blood-sucking mates, male mosquitoes feed only on the nectar of flowers. This feeding mosquito is readily identifiable as a male, by his plumed antennae. 5 mm.

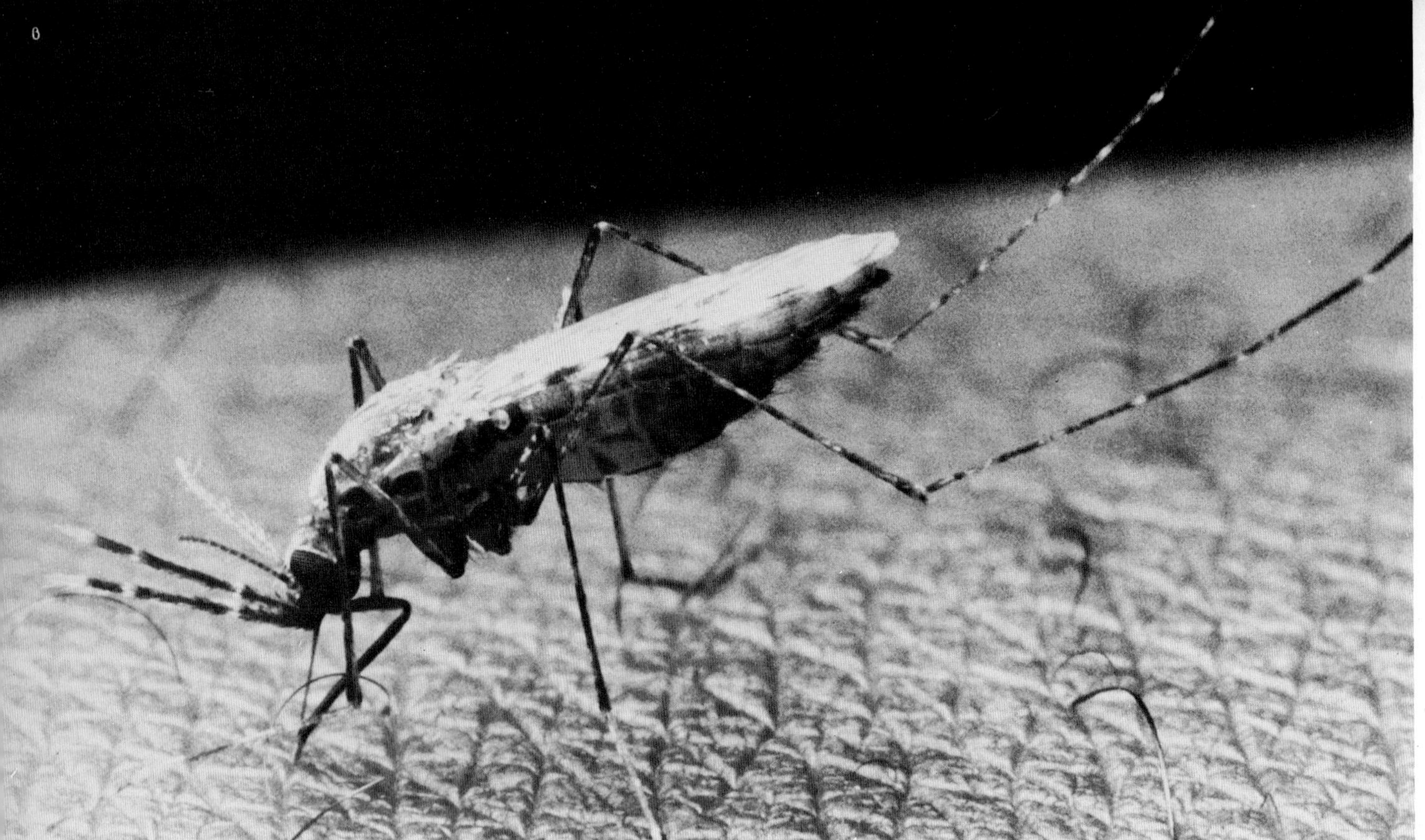

211. A female *Anopheles arabiensis*, one of Africa's main malaria vectors, enjoys a meal of human blood. Note that the sheath (the 'labium') that normally covers the needle-like proboscis folds backwards as the lancets are thrust into the skin. 4 mm.

lar, but there is considerable variation in detail. There is one constant: the eggs of mosquitoes never hatch except in the presence of water. Culicine females mostly lay their oval eggs, something like caraway seeds, glued together in the form of miniature rafts. These grey rafts may be found floating on stagnant water and cannot be upset or submerged.

A few culicines and all anophelines lay their eggs singly, not joined together, and the eggs of the anophelines may be recognised by the tiny air-floats, one on each side. A few species lay eggs that sink and some deposit their eggs in dry hollows where they lie dormant until the rains fill the hollows and form pools.

The larvae are always aquatic and are commonly called 'wrigglers'. Instead of legs, they have bunches of long bristly hairs on the body, and these serve to keep them steady in the water. The eyes and antennae are well-developed and on each side of the mouth there is a brush of stiff hairs – the mouth brushes that serve to sweep up into their mouths the microscopic organisms that form the food of most larvae. Some species have predaceous larvae that feed on other mosquito larvae and small water creatures. Members of the genus *Toxorhynchites*, for example, have larvae with prehensile mouth brushes and strong teeth on the mandibles. In confined habitats, they feed on all the other mosquito larvae, until they alone remain. Finding a single mosquito larva in a container is often a clue to its predaceous nature. Interestingly, *Toxorhynchites* adults do not suck blood!

Although aquatic, the mosquito larva breathes air and has two spiracles at the hind end of the body. In culicine larvae these spiracles are lodged at the tip of a prominent horn or breathing tube, which is very short or absent altogether in anopheline larvae. In addition there are flattened, leaf-like tracheal gills on the last segment of the abdomen so that the larva can survive for some time below water, but it must come to the surface from time to time to fill its tracheae with air through the respiratory horn. The body of the larva is slightly heavier than water so that it sinks slowly towards the bottom and the larva must jerk its abdomen from side to side to rise. It can hang suspended from the surface by opening the little pointed plates at the tip of its respiratory horn which form a tiny star but which close over the spiracles when the larva sinks. Anopheline larvae have star-shaped hairs along the back which also serve to hold them up when resting at the surface. Culicine larvae always rest at the surface with the body hanging down at an angle but anopheline larvae rest parallel with the surface.

The larva casts its skin four times and takes from a few days to two or three weeks to reach full size, the time depending on the temperature and the amount of food available. After the fourth moult it changes into a comma-shaped pupa. The 'head' of the pupa is really the combined head and thorax and the curved portion is the abdomen. Unlike the larva, the pupa is lighter than water and it rises to the surface as soon as it stops swimming. Instead of having spiracles at the hind end of the abdomen at the tip of a respiratory horn, the pupa has two breathing trumpets on the back of its thorax, so that as it rises to the surface, these automatically pierce the surface film and the little creature can breathe. The breathing trumpets of culicine pupae are usually long and narrow from the side view, while those of anopheline pupae are short and broad.

The pupae of most insects are inactive but mosquito pupae can swim about by vigorously jerking their abdomens. The pupal stage may last only a few hours in the case of those species that breed in rain pools liable to dry up quickly, while in other cases it may last two days to a week or more. The adults emerge rapidly from the floating pupae through a longitudinal slit in the back of the thorax. They rest for a few moments, using the old pupal skins as boats and then fly off.

Most anophelines breed in natural accumulations of water, such as swamps, vleis, the edges of streams and grassy ditches. They are not to be found, as a rule, breeding in blocked drains and gutters, tanks and pots, as culicine mosquitoes are.

Although a number of different species of *Anopheles* are found in Africa, from the Cape to Cairo, only a few of these are known to be carriers of malaria. The rest are comparatively harmless, either because the malaria parasites cannot survive and multiply in the insects, or because they do not enter dwellings and attack human beings but prefer the blood of animals.

The *Anopheles gambiae* complex contains the most important transmitters of malaria in Africa. For a long time it was thought that only one species, namely *Anopheles gambiae*, was the malaria vector. However, the application of the principles of population genetics, and a better understanding of the concept of biological species, has resulted in the discovery that '*Anopheles gambiae*' is a complex of at least six species, all identical in appearance, but totally different in their distribution, habits and malaria-transmitting capabilities. We call such groups 'sibling species'. When insects lack convenient external features, such as colour patterns and size or shape differences, other indicators of genetic discontinuity must be sought. In the case of *Anopheles*, there are giant chromosomes, known as polytene chromosomes, in certain tissues, and the study of these permits entomologists to sort out difficult problems like that of the *Anopheles gambiae* complex. A simple test to identify certain enzymes, which are different in the various species, is now used as a routine method by entomologists in Rhodesia and South Africa.

The importance of this work cannot be overemphasised. For instance in a typical African country like Rhodesia, where malaria is a major public health problem, '*Anopheles gambiae*' occurs over a wide area, and expensive spraying programmes are mounted to combat malaria. Entomologists trained in the skills of cytogenetics point out that three members of the *Anopheles gambiae* complex occur in Rhodesia. Of these, Species A (*A. gambiae*) is a minor vector, Species B (*A. arabiensis*) is a major vector, while Species C (*A. quadriannulatus*) is

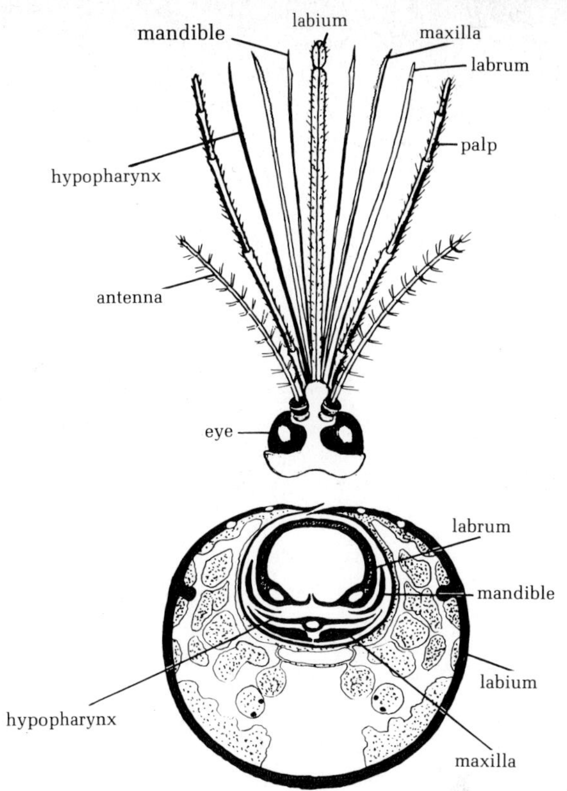

212. In this diagram of the mosquito's mouthparts, the upper picture shows all the various components separated for clarity. The lower picture is a cross-section of the mosquito's proboscis, to show how the labium forms a sheath around the other mouthparts which are thrust into the skin to suck up blood.

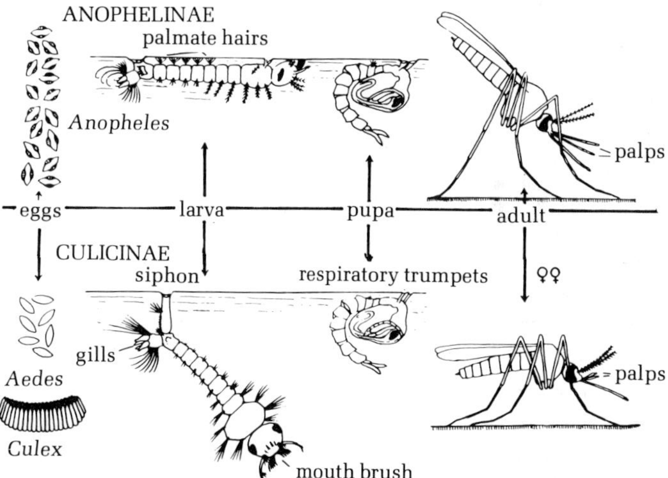

213. Diagrammatic differences between the two major groups of mosquitoes, the Anophelinae (above) and the Culicinae (below).

irrelevant since it feeds mainly on cattle and seldom enters huts. It is, therefore, a waste of both time and money to pursue malaria control operations in those parts of the country where only *A. quadriannulatus* occurs.

A similar situation exists in the case of the other important malaria vector in Africa, *Anopheles funestus;* also a complex of several biological species which lack convenient external features for their identification. *Anopheles funestus* breeds in slow-flowing streams and the larvae may be found along the edges of shallow pools where the grass and reeds afford shade and where the water is still. It is therefore found where there are permanent streams. As it enters houses freely and seems to prefer human blood, it is mainly responsible for the endemic malaria in regions where it is found.

Anopheles arabiensis and *A. gambiae* on the other hand, breed in shallow temporary pools that are fully exposed to the sunlight. When the rainfall is heavy and there are many pools about on the veld, these species can breed up rapidly and spread widely, and are therefore largely responsible for epidemic outbreaks of malaria. *Anopheles gambiae* and *A. arabiensis* enter dwellings to feed on humans and their habit of resting on walls led to the discovery, by Dr Botha de Meillon of the South African Institute for Medical Research, that spraying residual insecticides onto the walls effectively controlled the mosquitoes.

Some years ago a member of the *Anopheles gambiae* complex was carried accidentally from Africa to Brazil and there it established itself and multiplied rapidly, causing one of the worst and most widespread outbreaks of malaria ever known in that country. A determined campaign and the expenditure of large sums of money led to the extermination of the pest before it got entirely out of hand. It has never been discovered which species was responsible for the Brazilian incident.

The yellow fever mosquito, *Aedes aegypti,* belongs to the culicine group and has been widely spread throughout the world by man's commerce, and is found today in all tropical and sub-tropical regions. Its original home is believed to be West Africa. This small black mosquito, conspicuously marked with silvery white bands on its legs and abdomen and with a white lyre-shaped design on its thorax, is perhaps the most thoroughly domesticated species of them all, as it is seldom found except in the vicinity of houses and it shows a decided preference for human blood. It hides indoors and attacks stealthily, usually by day, crawling under clothing and biting silently and without warning. It breeds in almost any accumulation of water in and about the house, in barrels, tanks, tin cans, blocked roof gutters, vases, old tyres and so on.

As this mosquito is the principal carrier of the deadly yellow fever, and as it is common in many parts of the world where the disease does not occur, there is a constant danger that, in these days of rapid travel, visitors may bring in the virus with them and cause an outbreak of the disease. This explains why people going to tropical and sub-tropical parts must have the yellow fever inoculation and why aeroplanes on international flights are sprayed with insecticides.

214. The yellow fever mosquito, *Aedes aegypti,* showing the characteristic resting posture and the contrasting markings of silver and black. 4 mm.

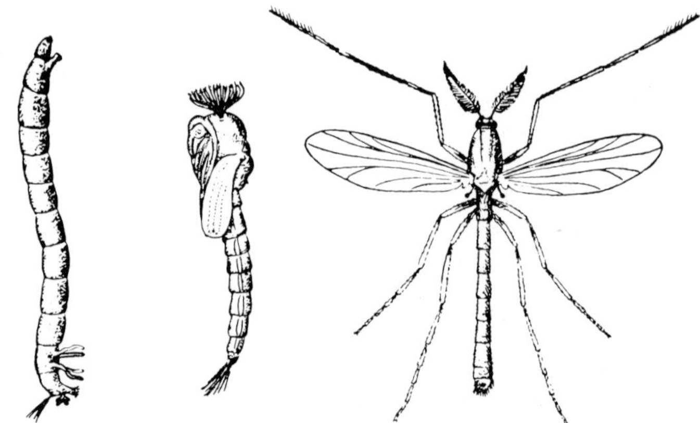

215. The larval, pupal and adult stages of a midge *(Chironomus* sp.). These harmless insects are of the same size and general appearance as mosquitoes, but they cannot bite. Sometimes they appear in vast numbers around their aquatic breeding places in lakes and pans.

Since the disease is endemic to West Africa as well as the warmer parts of the Americas, a constant watch has to be maintained against the possibility of its spread. There is no yellow fever in the south of Africa, although '*Aedes aegypti*' is common, and medical entomologists are now investigating the possibility that this group too may be a complex of sibling species, with the southern African species an ineffective transmitter of the virus.

Culicine mosquitoes are responsible for the transmission of a number of other viruses to man and domestic animals in Africa. After seasons of heavy rainfall in South Africa, extensive epidemics of West Nile and

Sindbis virus in humans have occurred. The virus is transmitted by *Culex univittatus* and affects birds as well as people. The infection is seldom fatal in man, its symptoms being fever, rash and pain in joints and muscles. Rift Valley fever is a serious disease of livestock, and epidemics occur after the rains when the population of *Aedes caballus* has been built up; the dangerous virus can cause blindness or even death in man.

The disease known as filariasis, or elephantiasis in its aggravated form, is also transmitted by mosquitoes. The tiny thread worms (which have the ponderous scientific name of *Wuchereria bancrofti*) are imbibed by the mosquito when feeding on an infected person and they go through certain developmental stages inside the mosquito's body. Later the worms make their way into the mosquito's proboscis and from there infect anyone bitten by the mosquito. The tropical house mosquitoes, *Culex pipiens* and *C. fatigans* and the yellow fever mosquito are the principal agents in the spread of this disease, but it is known that several other species are also able to transmit it. Filariasis occurs in some of the warmer parts of Africa as well as in other tropical regions of the world.

One of the most remarkable features about certain kinds of filariasis is the periodicity of the minute worms in the blood; they appear in swarms in the superficial blood vessels, just beneath the skin of infected persons at night, between say 2200 and 0400 hours, but disappear almost completely during the day, when they make their way into the deeper blood vessels. Thus, during the time when the mosquitoes are feeding, the parasites are in a position where they can enter the insect for the next stage in their development.

In addition to the above diseases, mosquitoes are the vectors of many other viral and protozoal diseases in a number of different animals.

Midges On a still day, just before sunset, swarms of gnats or midges resembling mosquitoes may often be seen flying low over water. In fact they are harmless flies with no mouthparts capable of piercing the human skin; most species do not feed at all in the adult state. These midges belong to the family known as the Chironomidae.

If a net is swept through a swarm of these midges and the captured specimens are examined they will be found to be all, or nearly all, males. Like the mosquitoes, the males can easily be distinguished by their feathery antennae; the females have threadlike antennae with only short hairs on them. The males assemble in swarms and for hours at a time dance at the edges of a pool. Females which are ready to mate are attracted to the swarm and they dash into the midst of the dancing males, are secured by a partner and then drop to the ground.

Midges are often attracted into the house and may be seen on the window panes, where they are often mistaken for mosquitoes. A glance is enough, however, to distinguish them from their blood-sucking relatives. A midge does not have a long proboscis on the front of its head, and it rests with front legs raised from the surface, whereas a mosquito always raises its hind legs. Furthermore, there are no scales on a midge's wings.

The female lays her eggs in stagnant water, in pools, barrels, storage tanks, ditches, blocked-up drains, and so on. The eggs are laid in strings, several hundred enclosed in a sausage-shaped rope of jelly about 25 mm in length. These strings of eggs are sometimes attached by short, slender stalks to pieces of stick or dead leaves floating in the water. The egg-masses are remarkably large when compared with the size of the insects that laid them, but the greater part of the bulk is made up of the jelly surrounding them and this at first consists only of a thin coating that later swells up enormously in the water, serving as a protective covering for the eggs.

The larva of the common midge is the well-known blood worm that can be found at any time of the year in the mud at the bottom of ponds and pools. The red colouring matter in the blood of the worm is the same as that in our own blood, haemoglobin. But whereas the haemoglobin in human blood is contained in corpuscles, and not in the fluid of the blood, in the case of the worm, the fluid itself is dyed with the substance, and not the corpuscles.

Most insects have colourless or bluish blood that contains copper, whereas haemoglobin contains iron. It is thought that the larva of the midge is a rare exception because it lives in stagnant water where oxygen is difficult to obtain; an efficient oxygen-carrier such as haemoglobin is, therefore, essential. The blood worm has two pairs of blood-filled slender tubes on its hind end which function as gills and serve to extract dissolved air from the water.

The worm spins a flimsy tube for itself on the mud at the bottom of the pool. The silk for this tube comes from its salivary glands and particles of mud and decaying vegetation are glued to it. The larva remains inside this tube for the greater part of its cycle, moving its body with a rhythmical wavelike motion that causes water to flow through the tube and over its gills. It feeds on organic matter in the mud and on decaying vegetation. Sometimes it will leave the tube and swim towards the surface with a lashing movement of the body, twisting itself into figures of eight. These occasional journeys to the surface seem to be made in search of air and the larva does not return to its original home, but makes a new tube for itself wherever it happens to sink back upon the mud.

When fully grown the larva is nearly 25 mm long and changes to a pupa inside the tube. It is still very slender and the head, legs and wings of the adult can now be seen through the skin. Instead of four gills on its tail, its breathing organ consists of dense tufts of threads on its thorax. When the adult is ready to emerge the pupa wriggles out of the tube and floats to the surface; it is lighter than water because its stomach is filled with air extracted by the gills from the water. At the surface the skin splits down the back and the fly emerges in the course of a minute or two, leaving the empty pupa case floating.

The larvae of some species of Chironomidae are found along the sea-shore, amid sea-weeds and in rock pools. Others live in the sap beneath the bark of trees or in decaying organic matter; while the larvae of some of those that remain near the surface of fresh water are green instead of red.

Chironomidae vary greatly in size, from tiny insects around 1 mm in length to large species bigger and stouter than most mosquitoes. At certain times when there is water which provides the optimum conditions of salinity and organic content, they emerge in countless millions to the annoyance of people living nearby.

They are attracted to lights at night and their persistent presence can make life intolerable, as well as cause severe asthma in allergic people. In the Sudan the midges from the Nile River are a notorious problem. When the Kariba Dam across the Zambezi River was completed, midges entered the electrical installations in such great numbers that they caused flash-over faults.

Control of Chironomidae by the application of insecticides is often unsatisfactory because most of the blood worms are protected by their tubes, and other aquatic organisms are adversely affected by the chemicals. Balancing the acidity and organic content of the water is the best way to deal with the problem.

In Africa one occasionally encounters the Chironomidae when a red worm descends from a tap into your glass of water – this may be disconcerting but is not dangerous. Invariably such incidents can be traced back to a storage tank that is not midge-proof, and in which the female has laid her eggs.

Biting midges The family Ceratopogonidae contains some of the smallest of flies, less than 1 mm in length. More than 500 species of biting midges are known in Africa south of the Sahara, although not all species bite. They have diverse habits in both the larval and adult stages – many species have aquatic larvae, others live in mud, manure or rotting vegetation.

Several biting midges are parasites specific to different insects and two genera in Africa are regular bloodsuckers on vertebrates. Certain *Leptoconops* species bite man and can be an effective deterrent to sitting out of doors on a warm summer's evening, for their bite is painful and may cause severe swelling and itching. All biting midge adult males and many of the females suck plant juices, often from flowers. The realisation in recent years that the Ceratopogonidae are important pollinators of crops has drawn the attention of agricultural scientists: for example members of the genus *Forcipomyia* are particularly significant as pollinators, vital to the propagation of cocoa and other plants.

Biting midges are of great veterinary importance because species of *Culicoides* transmit the viruses that cause African horse sickness and bluetongue in sheep. Early pioneers in South Africa soon realised that horse sickness was in some way connected with low-lying, marshy areas and built stone walls around the tops of nearby hills, making large camps in which the horses were kept in summer.

Today vaccines are available to protect horses and sheep from *Culicoides*-borne viruses. These flies also transmit tiny filarial worms to game animals and humans, although these filariae do not seem to cause serious illnesses. Thus the size of biting midges belies their potential threat to man and domestic animals.

Black flies or simuliids Commonly known as 'black flies', the small dark biting flies that belong to the family Simuliidae torment man and animals and cause a serious human disease, onchocerciasis, in tropical Africa. The irritation caused by the blood-sucking females can be intense. The males are rarely encountered and to obtain them it is usually necessary to rear them from the immature stages.

The life cycle of a common and widespread African species, *Simulium ruficorne,* is typical of most members of the family. As they all require water in which to breed, the female seeks out a shallow, shaded, slow-running stream when ready to lay her eggs and deliberately crawls down the side of a rock or other object into the water. Her body is enclosed in a bubble of air, which is captured in the hairs of her body so that she can survive under water. The eggs are small, white to brownish and glued together in a flat mass, which may be found adhering to the underside of rocks or branches in the water.

When the eggs hatch, they give rise to tiny larvae that are club-shaped, with the hind part of the body swollen. There is a sucker at the tail end by means of which the larva can adhere firmly to a stone, thus preventing the water from carrying it away. The larva hangs with its anterior end pointing downstream. On its head it has two prominent brushes, each bearing a fringe of about 50 long, dark bristles. These mouth brushes are constantly in motion, setting up currents which sweep food particles into the mouth. Jutting from the anal aperture are three or four short tubes, like small sausages; these are the gills by means of which it breathes. However, this breathing apparatus is effective only in aerated streams and the larva will die if placed in a jar of water; it can thus be reared only in running water.

When the larva is fully grown it is nearly 10 mm long and dark grey in colour. It spins a cocoon of brown silk attached firmly to a stone or any other underwater object. This cocoon is cone-shaped, open at the top, and inside this shelter the larva changes into a pupa. It now looks something like a tiny, pink moth chrysalis with two tufts of long filaments attached to the thorax. These tufts are the gills, and they protrude from the cocoon and wave about in the running water.

The adult fly emerges from the pupa in a remarkable manner. The problem it has to overcome is to avoid being swept away by the swift current or drowned in the crucial period when it makes the change from a helpless water-dwelling pupa to the six-legged two-winged fly adapted to life in the air. When it is ready to emerge, air is stored inside the pupal skin around the body of the adult fly. The pupal skin then splits dorsally and the adult, carried by the bubble of air, shoots up to the surface where it immediately takes to flight.

Some black flies have unique larval habits: for example, two species of *Simulium* from Zaïre have been found to attach themselves to the aquatic nymphs of mayflies (Ephemeroptera), while larvae of the *Simulium neavei* complex attach themselves to African freshwater crabs of the genus *Potamonautes*.

Simulium ruficorne feeds mainly on birds and seldom bothers man; it is a serious poultry pest in some parts of Africa. In South Africa, *Simulium chutteri* caused severe problems amongst livestock along the Vaal River.

In man the medical importance of simuliids arises from their rôle as transmitters of the parasitic worm *Onchocerca volvulus* which is injected by the bite of the black fly. The adult worms mature in the skin where they tend to congregate in nodules and although often painless they are extremely dangerous, especially if located on the head – the adult worms produce tiny microfilariae which move through the body, mainly along the blood vessels. They are able to penetrate the eyeball and when this happens cause various ocular lesions that finally result in blindness.

In large parts of West Africa many members of local populations are afflicted by 'river blindness' and vast areas are uninhabitable because of the threat of onchocerciasis. The most important vectors of the disease are members of the *Simulium damnosum* complex, and there are additional vectors in east and central Africa in the *Simulium neavei* complex. These two groups both contain species complexes – species that can be recognised only by microscopic examination of the chromosomes. The disease extends to the Sudan in the north and Angola, Zambia, Zaïre, Malawi and Tanzania in the south. It occurs also in southern Mexico, Guatemala, Colombia and northern Venezuela.

As is the case with sleeping sickness, the medical treatment of river blindness in man is both dangerous and unpleasant; as a result control is directed at the insect vector. In this sphere, the World Health Organisation has mounted a major research and control programme in the Volta River basin. The current method of attempting to eliminate the larvae is to apply chemicals to the rivers from the air. *Simulium damnosum* complex females present an even more complicated problem to the entomologist as they are extremely powerful fliers and can cover large distances, particularly when aided by wind. Flight distances of up to 79 km over a period of 24 hours have been reported for marked flies moving along a West African river, and flights of more than 150 km by individual flies seem quite possible.

SUBORDER: **Brachycera**

Horse flies Horse flies belong to the large and important family of moderate to large-sized flies known as Tabanidae. They are active on warm, sunny days. The females which locate their hosts by both sight and smell

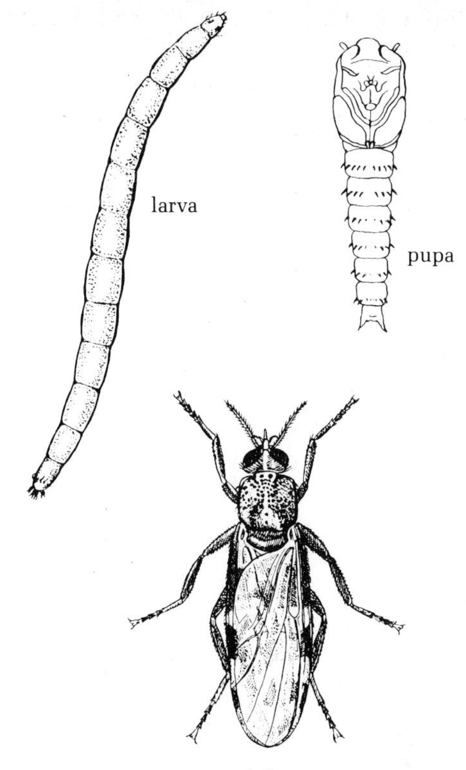

216. Life stages of the biting midge, *Culicoides*, which plays an important rôle in the transmission of blue-tongue virus to sheep. Adult is 3 mm long.

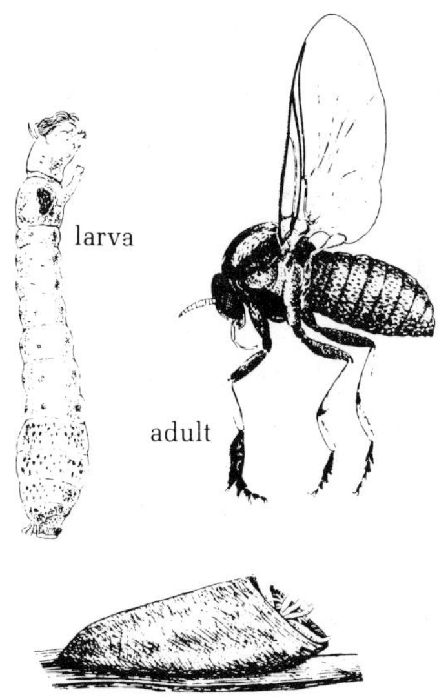

217. The black fly, *Simulium* sp. These insects have aquatic larval and nymphal stages, and the adults are a major health hazard in Africa as several species transmit parasitic worms responsible for 'river blindness' in man.

are well-known as irritating blood-suckers, but the males subsist mostly on nectar and are harmless.

The mottled horse fly, *Haematopota ocellata,* is a common African species and may be taken as our example of the group. In the male the eyes are so large that they occupy the greater part of the head, meeting at the middle line on top and shining with beautiful iridescent colours in the living insect. The facets or lenses on the upper part of each eye are larger than those on the lower half, as is the case in some other flies. The eyes of the female are also large and beautifully coloured but they do not meet in the middle line of the head.

As blood-suckers, the female horse flies are potential carriers of disease-causing organisms. In West Africa certain species of the subfamily Chrysopsinae are the carriers of the parasitic eye worm, called *Loa loa.* These minute thread worms live in the tissues of human beings and, when the eggs hatch, the tiny worms are set free in the blood. A horse fly sucking the blood of an infected person is in its turn infected and the worms go through certain developmental stages in its muscles. Eventually the parasites make their way into the mouthparts of the fly and enter the wound in the skin of the next person attacked.

There is evidence that horse flies are mechanical transmitters of protozoan parasites of animals: if disturbed while feeding on an infected animal, they may move immediately to a healthy host and continue their meal, carrying infected blood on their mouthparts and spreading the infection. The Tabanidae have considerable veterinary importance. Their persistent attacks torment livestock and can cause anaemia; they also transmit anthrax, a dangerous bacterial disease which affects game and livestock in Africa, and the trypanosomes which cause 'surra' in horses *(Trypanosoma evansi)* and nagana in cattle *(Trypanosoma brucei).*

Some horse flies have a very long proboscis that projects in front of the head and is more than twice the length of the body. The hovering male uses the proboscis for sipping nectar from deep flowers while the female, when sucking blood, bends her lower lip under the thorax, or to one side, and inserts only the short stabbing lancets. Like that of the mosquito, the lower lip is grooved along the top and the lancets lie in this groove. If one of these flies is caught and the tip of the proboscis bent down, the cutting mouthparts are displaced from the groove and it will be seen that they are only about one third the size of the whole proboscis. These long-tongued horse flies belong to the subfamily Pangoniinae, of which *Philoliche* is a common African genus.

Horse flies breed in water, damp soil or in moist organic matter in rot-holes in trees. We know little about the details of the life histories of the various African species. The female lays her eggs in masses on the leaves of water plants or on grass, twigs or stones close to the larval habitat and when they hatch, the larvae drop into the water or burrow into the damp soil. The larva is predaceous, its small head armed with sharp, curved jaws with which it spears the water insects, small tadpoles and worms, on whose juices it feeds. It is said that some of the larger kinds can inflict a painful bite.

When the larva is fully grown it forms a cell just beneath the surface of the soil, and there changes into a pupa which looks like a small moth chrysalis and can be recognised by the two ear-shaped spiracles on its back; the abdomen is armed with rows of spines. While the larval stage is long, the pupal stage lasts only two or three weeks.

Many species of horse fly in Africa have but one generation per year, the adults visible for only a few weeks at a time. In some species, the adults can be found throughout the year, but are most concentrated at a specific time.

The different species of horse fly normally emerge in a distinct sequence related to the incidence of rainfall at any particular place. In West Africa, however, adults of some species appear to move about according to rain patterns, their presence not necessarily indicating breeding in that locality.

Specialists on the horse flies believe that the various genera evolved along with the animals on which they feed. For example, the family Bovidae, which contains antelopes and cattle, has developed successfully in Subsaharan Africa; horse flies of the genus *Haematopota* feed on Bovidae and some 200 African species of this genus alone are known.

Snipe flies Snipe flies belong to the family Athericidae, one of the youngest families of African insects. Dr Stuckenberg of the Natal Museum created the Athericidae in 1973 to cover a group of flies that are related to the Tabanidae but had been included with the family Rhagionidae by earlier workers.

Snipe flies, like horse flies and mosquitoes, share the phenomenon of blood-sucking by the females. There are few records of which hosts are preyed upon and a fertile field of study awaits investigation. *Suragina bivittata,* a member of a genus of Athericidae that occurs all over the world, has been found feeding on blood from the eyelids of a Giant Eagle-Owl in South Africa.

Like horse flies, snipe flies lay their eggs in clusters in some place above the larval habitat; mass oviposition at favoured sites has been recorded for certain members of both families, the females, exhausted by their efforts, usually dying near the egg clusters. The larvae of athericids are aquatic and predaceous, and have poison ducts running inside the sharp mandibles used to capture their prey.

Rhagionid flies The family Rhagionidae is not very well-known in Africa, and even though the adults are quite large they are seldom recognised as members of this group. The remarkable larvae are also overlooked: any conical pits in the sand are assumed to be the homes of antlions (order Neuroptera, Chapter 13); but the Rhagionidae in fact have a subfamily called Vermileoninae, which means 'worm lions' and the larvae of these flies are predaceous, pit-digging carnivores that have developed the same method of trapping their food as the antlions have. These are the only Diptera that dig pits to capture their prey. The pit made by the worm lion is so similar to that of the antlion that it is impossible to distinguish one from the other unless the owner is dug out.

The most common Rhagionidae in Africa are members of the genera *Lampromyia* and *Chrysopilus*. Where the larvae do occur they are quite abundant if one knows where to look for them. The larvae, which dislike damp environments, usually make their pits in dry soil under overhangs or in caves where they are protected from wind and rain. If one digs some sand from the bottom of the pits and spreads it on a piece of paper, a larva will sooner or later be captured. It is about 12 mm long, grey and legless, the hind end of the body broader than the front end.

When removed from its home it will initially lie still and rigid, coiled in an S-shape on its back, for this strange creature lives and moves in the reverse of the normal position. When digging a pit for itself, the larva lies on its back just beneath the surface of the soil, and by continually jerking its head up as it moves slowly round, throws out the sand so that a circular groove forms. As it moves round and round the head jerking tirelessly, the circle becomes smaller and the hole gets deeper, until finally the larva is lodged at the bottom of a pit sometimes completely concealed, and sometimes with the head and the first two or three segments uncovered.

The larva lies motionless, for days if necessary, waiting for some creature, such as an ant or small beetle, to stumble into the pit. Then the worm lion springs into action – its head jerks up, striking blindly while it tries to coil its body around the victim. Several attempts may be necessary before it manages to get a grip and drive home the two pointed hooks in its mouth which inject poisonous saliva.

As soon as the victim is immobilised, it is pulled below the sand and devoured. This process is repeated many times. The period needed by the larva to reach full size depends on its luck in obtaining food. If victims are scarce the worm lion may take a year or more to mature, but if many creatures stumble into the trap, its development is speeded up. When fully grown, the larva stops feeding and allows its pit to fall into disrepair. Buried about 25 mm beneath the surface, it makes a roughly tubular cocoon, coated with sand grains, in which it pupates. After two or three weeks the pupa wriggles to the surface and the adult fly emerges. It is slender, long-legged, about 12 mm long and has smoky brown wings. The body is smooth and shiny, brown and yellow, and the head has two large eyes and a long proboscis.

Robber flies Members of the family Asilidae are attractive and fascinating Diptera, the favourites of many amateur collectors, but rather a difficult group when it comes to classifying them and describing the species.

218. Eye to eye with a female horse fly. Concealed within her mouthparts as seen here are the slender hollow lancets, with which she sucks the blood of man and other animals.

219. A female horse fly thrusts her lancets into a man's arm as she takes a blood meal – this will undoubtedly cause her victim some pain and may introduce disease organisms. 10 mm.

These extraordinarily active creatures go about their daily business in a single-minded and tireless manner. They are not really robbers, but assassins that slay and devour, even attacking insects much larger than themselves. Some species sit on a rock or a leaf waiting for likely prey to go past. The robber fly then takes off in hot pursuit, overtakes and swoops down upon the victim, scooping it up with its legs and stabbing it with its powerful proboscis. Other robber flies patrol a particular path, returning always to the same resting place after each sortie.

Robber flies are recognisable mainly by their large eyes which bulge upwards, separated at the top of the head by a very deep trough. As one might expect from such efficient aerial hunters these eyes are adapted to binocular vision. The head is very mobile, and it is characteristic of robber flies that their heads turn continuously while they watch out for prey.

Robber flies are generally very hairy, especially about the face where they have a bristly 'moustache' called the mystax. This seems to serve as a form of protection against the formidable insects which the robber fly attacks such as bees, wasps, beetles and dragonflies, which could damage the robber fly's eyes in their struggles to escape.

Its proboscis is generally straight and not particularly long, but it is often extremely rigid and covers the sharply pointed hypopharynx which slides out to pierce the victim. Some of the big species can inflict a painful bite if handled carelessly. Asilidae suck the body contents of their victims and drop the empty exoskeletons when they have fed. Their strong legs are armed with bristles, spines, stout claws and pads, which form a very effective grasping apparatus. The enlarged thorax houses the powerful wing muscles, giving most robber flies their characteristic hump-backed appearance. The abdomen is usually long and quite slender, but some species resemble very closely carpenter bees (genus *Xylocopa*), or other solitary bees; examples are the various species of *Hyperechia*, which closely mimic several different species of *Xylocopa*, and can often be seen sitting near the holes that the bees make in wood. The robber fly adults seem to concentrate on carpenter bees as prey, but it is doubtful that the robber fly larvae feed on the bee larvae, although they live in the same burrows.

Variations in size and appearance among the robber flies are greater than in any other family of Diptera. They range in length from 3-40 mm, and some of the largest have a spectacular wingspan of 80 mm. Morphologically they range from carpenter bee mimics to wasp mimics, and from tiny inconspicuous grey flies to the larger, more robust species that are familiar to most observers. Robber flies are found in a wide variety of habitats, from semi-desert to montane forest, although the majority occur in relatively open bushveld and grassveld.

The life histories of African Asilidae are little known, but there is undoubtedly tremendous diversity in egg-laying habits, from merely scattering the eggs on the ground, to covering them with soil, to ovipositing into flower heads or even into the stems of plants.

Most robber fly larvae are thought to be vegetarians, and they are normally found in soil or rotting wood. The larva is a cylindrical brown or grey maggot whose small pointed head bears a pair of sharp, curved jaws. When mature it develops into the pupa covered with spines and bristles; through the pupal skin, the legs and wings of the adult stage can be seen. When the adult fly is ready to leave its confined quarters, the strange creature inside its pupal skin works its way to the surface of the soil or wood until the front end projects far enough for the adult to burst forth.

Mydas flies The family Mydaidae is related to the robber flies and its members are sometimes mistaken for Asilidae. Mydas flies are rather wasp-like and fly swiftly in a way that has been likened to the 'rapid gliding flight reminiscent of partridges'. Usually they are encountered singly, resting on the ground in spaces between bushes or on paths, their wings either fully or partially open. They are difficult to collect, and seem to be strictly seasonal in their emergence. Most Mydaidae are fairly large, elongated flies, and in fact the biggest fly in the world belongs to this family – *Mydas heros* of South America which reaches a length of some 60 mm, about twice as long as the average African species.

Extremely little is known about the biology of Mydas flies, but unlike Asilidae the adults are certainly not predaceous, and probably feed from flowers. There is evidence, however, that the larvae may be both carnivorous and predatory. Apart from the southern African species, very little is known about the taxonomy of the African Mydaidae, and it seems certain that there are many species awaiting discovery. In a study of South African Mydas flies, it was found that many species are extremely restricted in their distribution, with a change in species composition occurring at roughly 80 km intervals.

Bee flies The bee flies (Bombyliidae) are well-named, both because of their bee-like appearance – short, plump and hairy – and because the larvae of many bee flies prey upon the pupae and larvae of solitary bees. However, there are many types of bee fly which do not look at all like bees. Some resemble robber flies, others wasps, some are tiny hump-backed insects and still others are gigantic black flies known only from a few specimens. Based on the number of species described, the Bombyliidae is currently the largest family of flies in Africa.

The species most commonly encountered are medium to large flies with a long proboscis projecting from the front of the head. Despite its fearsome appearance the proboscis cannot pierce the human skin, and is used to probe flowers for the nectar and pollen on which the adult feeds. Bombyliids are often seen settled on the ground or on stones in the blazing sunshine, taking short hovering flights from time to time, and returning always to the same spot. They frequently hover close to the ground looking for flowers, but the females also fly in this way when they are looking for a place to lay their eggs which they drop singly near the burrow of a solitary bee or wasp. When the egg hatches, the larva crawls into the host's nest, and proceeds to consume first the stored food supply, then the larva or pupa of the bee or wasp.

Bombyliidae do not confine their attentions to bees and wasps alone; certain species have larvae that attack army worm caterpillars, tsetse fly pupae and locust egg-packets, to name a few.

Bee flies of the genus *Systoechus* are responsible for the destruction of considerable numbers of grasshoppers and locusts. Before it starts feeding, the young larva casts its skin and undergoes a marked change of form, to become a fat, legless grub. It devours the locust eggs and grows to a length of some 12 mm by the time it is ready to pupate. Then it burrows into the soil beside the egg-pod, hollows out a cell for itself and changes into a pupa armed with stout spines on the head and rows of stiff bristles on the abdominal segments. It uses this armour to make its way up through the soil to the surface when the adult is ready to emerge.

Systoechus species help to control the number of locusts and grasshoppers in Africa, and are splendid examples of 'good' flies which effectively answer the frequently-asked question: 'What good are flies?'

Dance flies Until quite recently the family Empididae was little studied in Africa, and certainly nobody here has a common name for the group, so there is no harm in borrowing the American term, which is derived from their habit of flying in swarms, with a circular or bouncing motion. Like the crane flies, some male dance flies bring presents for the females. The gift, usually a tasty insect, may even be wrapped in silk, although some present their partners with a packet of silk that has nothing inside. The whole object of the exercise, of course, is to avoid being consumed while procreating.

The Empididae are often compared and confused with Asilidae because the adults bear a superficial resemblance to one another, are predatory, and tend to complement one another in distribution; the dance flies flourishing in cool, temperate regions and the robber flies in the hot tropics. The dance flies are agile and many species, in marked contrast to the jet-fighter robber fly which hunts from the air, run about on trees and shrubs, seizing and devouring small arthropods that come their way. Empididae also exploit the aquatic habitats of the sea shore and rivers, where they scavenge on insects trapped in the water.

The larvae of dance flies have been found in soil, rotting vegetation and in water, where they prey upon other insect larvae. The African Empididae hold potential for exciting research – it is known for example, from other parts of the world, that dance fly adults and larvae are important predators of adult and larval black flies (Simuliidae), and since we know how important

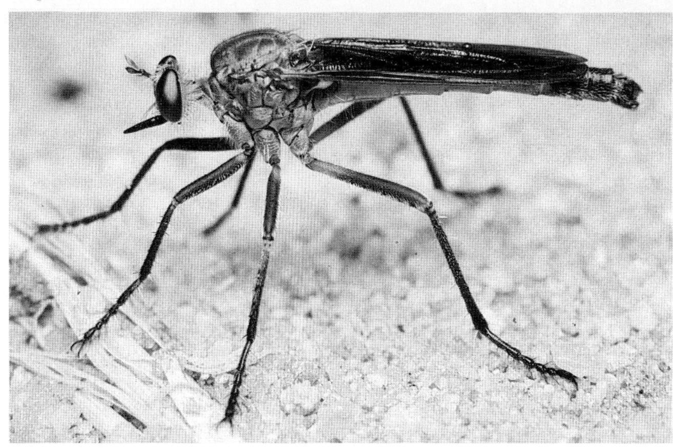

220. Robber flies can be recognised by their stout piercing proboscis, and their ability to move the head from side to side as they wait alertly for suitable winged prey to pass. 20 mm.

221. Robber flies of the genus *Hyperechia* are outstanding mimics of carpenter bees, near whose nest entrance holes they lurk; they pounce as the bees fly from their nests, overpowering them and devouring them. 18 mm.

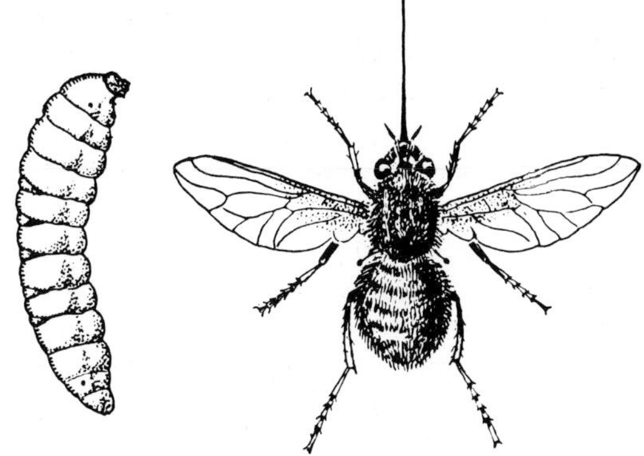

222. A larva (left) and adult bombyliid fly of the genus *Systoechus*, which plays an important part in keeping down the numbers of grasshoppers and locusts. The adult is about 25 mm long, including proboscis, and has a black body clothed with brownish yellow hair.

Simulium is in the maintenance of public health in Africa, it is clear that more research should be done on our Empididae to determine their importance as controlling agents of black flies.

SUBORDER **Cyclorrhapha**

Hover flies Hover flies, Syrphidae, form a large family of flies of varied habits and most are brightly coloured – striped, spotted or banded with yellow on a blue or black background. Frequently they may be seen poised in the air, their wings vibrating rapidly, and from this comes their popular name 'hover flies'. As they visit flowers for nectar and pollen they may be mistaken for bees or wasps, but can be readily distinguished by their single pair of wings.

One of the largest, commonest and best-known members of the family is the drone fly, so-called because it closely resembles a drone bee in appearance. This fly, *Eristalis tenax,* can often be caught in the hand, as it is rather slow-moving, and doing this will impress all sorts of people who will think you have caught a bee. However, mistakes do sometimes happen, so one should examine a 'drone fly' carefully before grabbing it!

The female lays her oval white eggs in small clusters at the edge of stagnant pools of dirty water, usually in a slight hollow in the mud where the eggs are sheltered from the direct rays of the sun. Any accumulation of foul water suits her, a blocked-up drain, a pool containing decaying vegetation and animal remains, a tub in which the gardener is preparing liquid manure or a puddle behind the stable in which horses or cows are kept. The eggs hatch into grey maggots, each with a slender tail, and they drop or creep into the water and feed on decaying organic matter, bacteria and protozoa.

Although the rat-tailed maggot, as the larva of the drone fly is called, lives in water, it breathes air and quickly drowns if it cannot obtain oxygen. Two spiracles at the tip of its tail lead to a pair of slender tracheae that pass down the tail into the body. As the larva creeps about on the mud at the bottom of the pool, it extends its telescopic tail until the tip just projects above the surface. This tail can be extended until it is a slender thread up to 16 cm long, but if the larva goes into water deeper than this it must come to the surface from time to time to breathe.

The larva has an elaborate filter in its pharynx, consisting of nine stiff Y-shaped plates parallel with one another. The arms of the Y are shredded so that they form an efficient strainer which retains particles of food as the water, kept moving by a pump in the pharynx, passes between them. Thus this tiny maggot may be said to feed in much the same way as the gigantic baleen whale.

When the larva is fully grown it leaves the water and buries itself in damp soil beside the pool. Here it changes into a brown pupa, easily recognised by its stump of a tail, and two or three weeks later the adult fly emerges. It is thought that the close resemblance of a drone fly to a honey-bee gave rise to the curious belief of ancient times that swarms of bees could be produced from the rotting carcase of a horse or ox. Many ancient writers, amongst them Ovid and Virgil, repeat this story. Someone probably noticed drone flies hovering over a dead, putrescent animal and later saw numbers of the flies emerging from the neighbourhood of the filthy liquid under the corpse and assumed they were bees. It has been suggested, too, that Samson's famous riddle, 'Out of the eater came forth meat, and out of the strong came forth sweetness', was based on his mistaking drone flies hovering over the dead lion for bees.

Many hover fly larvae are predaceous and through their activities play an important part in keeping down the numbers of aphids. These hover flies are mostly slender and have yellow markings on brown or black. The female lays her small oval white eggs among the aphids on infested plants. When the larvae emerge, they creep over the leaves and twigs, spearing the aphids and sucking their juices. Sluglike, and often marked with green or brown, the larvae are pointed at the front end and have two spiracles on a small, dark coloured prominence at the hind end. When fully grown they fix themselves in sheltered spots on the plant, change into oval pupae, and a few days later the adults emerge. A little searching during the spring and summer months will generally reveal the presence of the eggs, larvae and pupae of these flies on plants which are badly infested with aphids.

The larvae of still other species of hover flies, *Microdon* species, may be found in ants' nests. Small, oval, white and flattened, they look like small slugs – so much so that *Microdon* larvae were thought to be molluscs by early scientists! They can only move about very slowly. The ants tolerate the presence of these larvae in their nests because they apparently not only do no harm, but scavenge, feeding on dead and dying ant larvae and pupae and on any waste organic matter in the nest. The larvae pupate inside the nest and after they emerge, the adults make their way out into the open air.

SECTION **Acalyptratae**

Stalk-eyed flies The distinctive flies that constitute the easily recognised family of Diopsidae bear eyes and antennae on the ends of stalk-like projections on either side of the head. The stalks may be short (they are absent in the genus *Centrioncus*), medium, or very long, such as in the giant *Diopsis thoracica* (in which the eyes are about 12 mm apart). Stalked eyes are found in certain other families of flies, but in these the antennae are in a normal position and not close to the eyes, as they are in Diopsidae.

The peculiar arrangement of the eyes led earlier workers to presume that adult Diopsidae must be predatory, but there is certainly no evidence of this and they seem to feed on liquid exudates from flowers and decaying plants. The significance and function of the stalked eyes are questions that still await answers.

Adult Diopsidae are commonly encountered in swarms, especially in sheltered vegetation near marshes and water, or in forests. They seem to prefer warm, subtropical areas and are scarce on the South African highveld. Most species are rather slow and clumsy fliers, easily caught in a net. There is evidence that the adults are fairly long-lived.

The larvae either feed on decomposing plant material, or bore healthy plants. In certain parts of Africa they are minor pests of rice, sugar-cane and maize.

Fruit flies The Mediterranean fruit fly, *Ceratitis capitata*, the Natal fruit fly, *Pterandrus rosa*, and the Marula fruit fly, *Pardalaspis cosra*, are well-known in Africa because of the harm they do to ripe fruits of all kinds. They all belong to the family Tephritidae, which contains very many species. The Mediterranean fruit fly is rather curiously named for it is actually an African insect first recognised as a pest in the Mediterranean region, and one that has spread throughout the world.

The three species mentioned are pretty little insects, slightly smaller than the house fly, with striking colours, the wings patterned with bars of brownish yellow. They are seen in orchards, resting on the leaves of the trees, their wings held in characteristic drooping fashion, or running to and fro and taking short flights. Their life histories are similar.

The female uses her sharp ovipositor to pierce the skin of ripening fruit and then deposits her elongate white eggs in small groups just below the surface. The larvae that hatch from the eggs burrow into the pulp, causing soft patches which soon decay. When fully grown they are about 6 mm long, typical fly maggots with a pointed head end and blunt hind end on which two spiracles are lodged. If removed from the fruit and placed on a hard, flat surface they will try to move by wriggling for a time and then, one after another, they will bend into a circle, bringing their pointed mouthparts into contact with the hind spiracles; after a short pause they will straighten with a jerk that causes them to leap a few centimetres through the air.

The full-grown larvae leave the fruit and drop to the ground where they bury themselves as quickly as possible. On hard soil they jump erratically in the manner just described until they reach a suitable spot for burrowing. Once safely lodged in a cell beneath the surface, the maggot shortens and thickens, its skin hardens and forms a puparium inside which the pupa develops.

Some time later the adults emerge. Several generations may appear in a year, depending on how long there is fruit ripening in the orchard. The adults hibernate during the winter.

Many kinds of Tephritidae are known from Africa, and all their larvae feed on plant material of one kind or another. Several are found in the fruits and seeds of various kinds of wild plants; some feed in the flower heads of the daisy family (such as the Barberton daisy fly, *Craspedoxantha marginalis*); others burrow in stems and buds, while still others form galls.

223. Hover flies of the genus *Eristalis* are remarkably honey bee-like in appearance, having orange and black banded abdomens. Like honey bees, they feed at flowers, and may easily be mistaken for them. 12 mm.

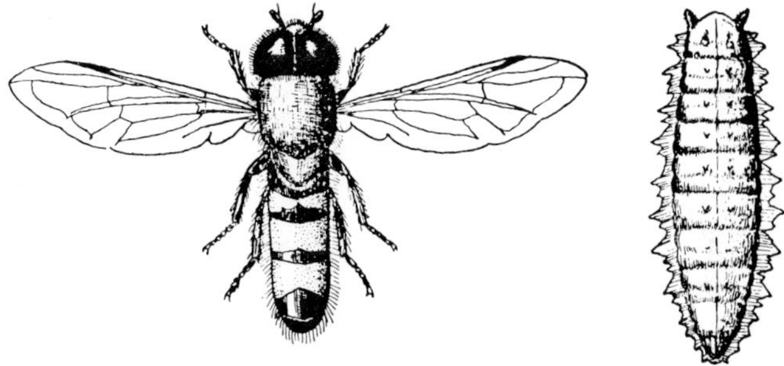

224. A yellow and black hover fly (*Syrphus* sp.) whose green larva (right) preys on aphids. 9 mm.

225. The green, slug-like larvae of hover flies may often be found on plants infested with aphids, where they consume great quantities of the pests. 10 mm.

The moderately-sized, wasp-like cucurbit flies cause much damage to pumpkins, melons, watermelons and other cultivated gourd plants. The smaller cucurbit flies, *Didacus ciliatus* and *Didacus vertebratus*, and the larger *Dacus bivittatus* are widespread in Africa. The olive fly, *Daculus oleae*, is the most serious pest of olives both cultivated and wild and consequently most important in the Mediterranean region.

Vinegar flies If you leave over-ripe and fermenting fruit exposed on a dish, a number of small flies about 2 mm long, pale brown in colour, with red eyes are soon attracted to it. They appear as if by magic when one uses acetic acid in a laboratory, or vinegar in a kitchen and they often fall into glasses of wine or beer. Tests have shown that vinegar flies, which form the family Drosophilidae, prefer a juice that contains about 20% alcohol and a little acetic acid, which is why rotting, fermenting fruit attracts them and they swarm around wine vats, wine presses and vinegar factories. Often one or more may hover about the mouth of somebody who has just taken an alcoholic drink.

A careful search on the bruised, wet surface of the fruit, after it has been exposed to the flies for a day or so, will reveal the very small oval white eggs, each with two filaments on it like a pair of slender horns. It is suggested that these filaments are breathing organs which enable the embryo inside the egg to obtain air even when it is submerged in liquid, as is often the case.

In one or two days the egg hatches into a blind, white, legless maggot which wriggles its way among the rotten fruit, feeding on the fermented juice. It has a pair of spiracles on its hind end which is lodged on a fingerlike process, which can be thrust in and out. It reaches full size in a few days and then seeks out a spot that is more or less dry and solid, where it can change into a pupa. Like the larvae of all the higher flies, it does not cast its skin when it pupates, but the last larval skin hardens to form an outer case, called the puparium, protecting the soft pupa inside. A few days later the adult pushes open a triangular lid on the front end of the puparium, and emerges.

There are numerous species belonging to the Drosophilidae in Africa, and they have varying larval habits. Aside from the majority, interested in fruit only after it has been damaged and has begun to ferment, some species breed in animal excrement or decaying vegetable matter or their larvae feed on fermenting sap oozing from trees. Other species are attracted by dregs of sour milk remaining in a bottle – within a few days the larvae pupate and stick firmly to the glass with a very powerful glue. Frequently these pupal cases are not dislodged by the dairy's automatic washing plants and housewives are horrified to find the insects sticking to the inside of a sealed bottle of fresh milk. Other species are 'leaf miners', the tiny maggots, emerging from the eggs, burrow between the upper and lower surfaces of the leaves. Some Drosophilidae have carnivorous larvae which prey on aphids and coccids, and there is a genus whose larvae are parasitic on the cottony cushion scale of citrus.

Vinegar flies have been extensively used in the study of genetics and heredity for they have giant chromosomes in their salivary glands and reproduce quickly and easily in the laboratory. *Drosophila melanogaster*, in particular, has been used by geneticists, and is probably the best-known insect in the world. By determining the loci or positions of genes in the chromosomes, it has been possible to work out how various characteristics of the flies are controlled by the actions of their genes. Variations that appear in the *Drosophila* breeding jars such as eye colour, wing shape and size, the number and arrangement of the bristles, and so on can be correlated with mutations and rearrangements of the genetic material in the chromosomes. Today principles of genetics and heredity that were first established by work on the tiny vinegar fly are being applied in studies on numerous living creatures, including man himself.

SECTION **Calyptratae**

The house fly and its allies The family Muscidae contains an enormous number of species of which a few are abundant in Africa – none more so than the ubiquitous house fly which is an important transmitter of several disease-causing organisms to man. Many muscid flies breed in dung and filth, although the larvae of some may be carnivorous. While several have developed biting mouthparts, most adult muscids mop up liquid and semi-liquid foods.

The Muscidae are divided into a number of subfamilies, but the taxonomy of these is complicated and a task for the specialist.

The lesser house fly, *Fannia canicularis*, is very common and widely spread. In spring and in autumn the males of this species may often be seen indoors, flying endlessly in circles below a light fitting, sometimes chasing one another in short flights, but always returning to their favoured spot. This behaviour is part of their mate recognition system, and the flight seems to require an overhead marker, such as a light or chandelier. *Fannia* adults can be mistaken for the common housefly, but they are recognisable by their smaller size and by the venation of their wings.

As a rule the female lesser house fly lays her eggs in batches in decaying vegetable matter, but she may also oviposit in excrement, in earth soiled with urine, in fungi or in rotting wood. The larva is very unlike the maggot normally associated with the Muscidae and can be recognised by the long, fleshy processes on its body. Apart from facilitating the identification of the *Fannia* larva, these fleshy processes help it to float in the semi-liquid, highly nitrogenous matter it favours as a breeding place. It is a dark grey colour, somewhat flattened, and about 6 mm long. As it becomes covered with debris and moves slowly, it is not easy to find. When fully grown it buries itself in the soil and there it pupates. The last larval skin, hardened and contracted, forms the puparium.

The latrine fly, *Fannia scalaris*, is very similar to the lesser house fly but is darker in colour and does not come into houses so freely. The female lays her eggs in decaying animal and vegetable matter and in excrement and the flies may breed in large numbers in privy buckets if these are not emptied often enough. The larva is very like that of the lesser house fly but the fleshy growths on its body are branched and have a feathery appearance.

The house fly, *Musca domestica*, is the commonest and most widely spread of all household pests. As it feeds on human food and excrement, it may act as the vector of many human pathogens such as bacillary dysentery, typhoid fever, cholera, salmonellosis, anthrax, leprosy, yaws, trachoma, poliomyelitis, infectious hepatitis and parasitic worms.

There are other kinds of flies that come into the house and that closely resemble this pest, but the true house fly can be recognised by the following combination of characteristics: a fleshy proboscis beneath its head, four dark stripes on its thorax, and the two veins that meet at a point on the wing tip enclosing a large cell. The male can be distinguished from the female by the size of his eyes: his almost meet on top of the head while hers are separated by a space about one third of the width of the head.

The house fly cannot swallow solid food; it can only feed on liquids or easily soluble substances. In feeding on sugar, the insect picks up a grain in its proboscis, turns it round and round at the same time dissolving the sugar by discharging saliva on to it. It then sucks up the sweet solution through its proboscis. The flies will feed on any liquid excrement they can find, the contents of the latrine bucket, the cess pool, a foul drain, sputum flecks and so on, and from these places they may fly into the house and settle on the milk jug, the sugar basin and the jam jar.

Inside its body the fly has a large crop in which it can store food not required immediately. In feeding, the fly satisfies its hunger by taking up a certain amount of food into its stomach and it then proceeds to fill its crop, which branches off from the gullet, as a reserve supply for future needs. Inside the house it may find food more to its liking and it empties the store in its crop on to the sugar, milk, butter, or jam, to make room for the tastier substance. Furthermore, the fly's feet, each with two sticky pads that enable it to crawl up the window pane, are always contaminated with bacteria, so it is not surprising that the house fly is a serious menace to public health.

The house fly's favourite breeding places include fresh, fermenting heaps of manure, but it will breed in almost any accumulation of garbage and rotting vegetable matter. The female seeks out a small cavity in the manure and deposits a batch of 100 to 120 white eggs, oval in shape and about 2 mm long. She may lay four or five batches of eggs before her ovaries are exhausted.

226. Like something from science fiction, the stalk-eyed flies are among the strangest of all African insects. They often occur in swarms in damp vegetation, and along the banks of forest streams.

227. The Mediterranean fruit fly, a native of Africa, is found wherever fruit is grown or stored. 5 mm.

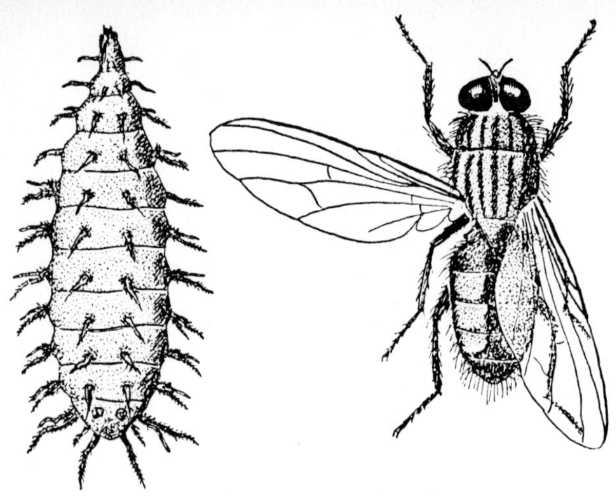

228. The lesser house fly, *Fannia canicularis*, looks very much like a small house fly in the adult stage, but its larva (left) is noteworthy for the fleshy processes which adorn it.

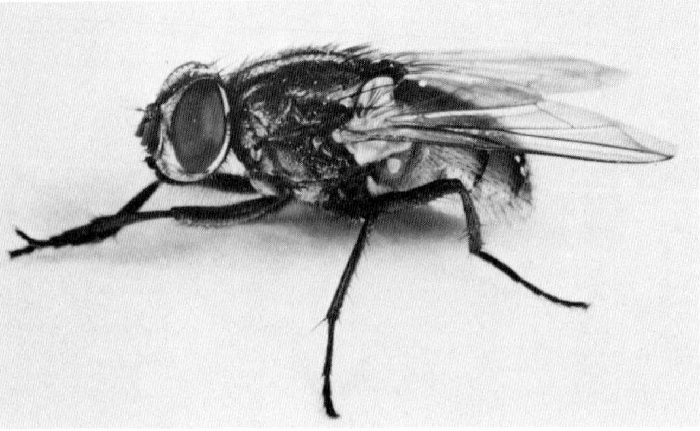

229. A house fly, *Musca domestica*, rubs its front pair of legs together as it preens itself. 7 mm.

The warmth generated by the fermentation hatches the eggs within 24 hours.

The larvae are white, legless maggots, with a pair of hooks in the mouth instead of jaws and two spiracles at the rear end. As soon as they hatch, they burrow into the manure heap to find favourable conditions of moisture and warmth. For about five days they feed on the liquid and easily soluble portions of the manure; then when fully grown, they leave the interior of the heap and seek out sheltered spots round the edge, where they burrow into the soil or creep beneath stones, loose rubbish or bits of old sacking.

The larva now contracts and takes on an oval form, its skin hardening and changing in colour first to red and then brown. This hardened outer skin is the puparium; no moult takes place at this stage, as is the case with the lower flies, butterflies, moths, beetles and so on. Inside the puparium the pupa of the fly forms. After five days the adult is ready to emerge, but it is a soft weak creature quite unable to struggle with sufficient violence to break open the hard puparium. To deal with this problem, a bladder, called the ptilinum, bursts through a slit on the front of the insect's head and pulsates in and out as blood is pumped into it. In this way the ptilinum acts as a miniature battering ram, striking the top of the puparium until it is pushed off and the fly is able to creep out. The fly also uses this bladder to push its way up through the soil to the surface. Once in the open air, the fly withdraws the ptilinum and the slit in the head closes up; the blood is now forced into the wings which expand and stiffen and the fly is able to take to the air. This method of escaping from the puparium is not peculiar to the house fly; it is common to all the higher flies and they all have a characteristic scar on the front of the head which marks the position of the slit through which the ptilinum protruded.

The tropical nest fly, *Passeromyia heterochaeta*, is widely distributed over Africa and the Orient. It is an example of a muscid fly whose larvae have evolved a parasitic habit, for they suck the blood of nestlings. The adult flies are about 9 mm long and look rather like house flies, with longitudinal stripes on the thorax. They are on the wing during the day, feeding on plant juices and the excreta of birds and mammals.

The female deposits batches of five or six eggs in birds' nests, close to the nestlings. When the larvae hatch, they crawl to the baby birds and suck their blood – and may, especially when there is a heavy infestation, cause their young hosts to die. The maggots grow to a length of 15 mm then pupate in the nest. In Africa, sparrows, swallows, sunbirds, starlings, weavers, mouse-birds and even eagles are amongst their victims.

The general term 'myiasis' is used to describe the infestation of live animals with fly maggots. All larvae involved in myiasis are either obligatory or facultative parasites. An obligatory parasite, of which the tropical nest fly is an example, has larvae which can develop only by feeding on living tissue. Other maggots are normally free-living, but may occasionally parasitize a living host, an example of 'facultative myiasis'.

Another muscid fly is responsible for the oft-repeated assertion that certain house flies can bite. This is the stable fly, *Stomoxys calcitrans*, which it must be admitted, bears a superficial resemblance to the house fly. However, a closer look reveals that it has a hard, black proboscis projecting in front of the head. It is a fierce blood-sucker, tormenting horses, cattle and dogs throughout Africa and the rest of the world. Mastiffs and labradors, for example, suffer greatly and their ears eventually become a mass of sores from fly attacks. *Stomoxys* can also inflict painful bites on people.

The stable fly breeds prolifically in horse and cattle dung mixed with straw bedding, commonly found in manure heaps on farms and at riding stables. The female lays up to 200 eggs, and the larvae develop in the manure in much the same way as those of the house fly.

Farmers suffer considerable economic loss each year as a result of the activities of these flies, for stable flies are potential transmitters of disease organisms as they suck blood from one animal and then move to another if disturbed. Experimental work has shown that several diseases can be transmitted under laboratory conditions, but there is little conclusive evidence of the importance of stable flies in a natural environment.

Among the many relatives of the stable fly, *Rhinomusca* is an interesting genus; it comprises two species, one associated with the black and the other with the white rhinoceros. The flies breed in the dung heaps or 'middens' of the rhinos and suck their blood during the day. We do not know whether *Rhinomusca* pierce the tough hides of their hosts, or whether they feed on blood from sores and scratches.

Tsetse flies All tsetse flies belong to the genus *Glossina*, and they are found only in Africa south of the Sahara. Formerly placed in the Muscidae, the tsetse flies are today considered as a separate family, the Glossinidae, which has certain affinities with the Gasterophilidae and Hippoboscidae.

The tsetse flies are drab, usually a yellowish or darker brown, sometimes with black bands on the dorsal surface of the abdomen. Their mouthparts project forward from under the head, and characteristically the wings are folded one over the other like the blades of a pair of scissors, their tips projecting beyond the end of the abdomen.

The flies are active during the day, but spend a large part of the time resting immobile in a place which is carefully chosen to satisfy various criteria of humidity and temperature.

Both sexes are blood-feeders, and the various species have particularised host preferences. It is interesting that man is not a favoured host, and we are bitten only as a poor second choice to a warthog or bushbuck! *Glossina longipennis* feeds mainly on the rhinoceros, with the elephant and the ostrich as alternatives. *Glossina morsitans*, a very important species, feeds mainly on warthogs and buffalo, while the bushbuck is favoured by several tsetse flies.

The female tsetse fly does not lay eggs, but retains them in her body where they hatch one at a time in the uterus. The three larval stages are nourished by secretions from a milk gland. When mature, the larva is deposited in a moist, shady spot where it immediately burrows beneath the surface to pupate; the outer layer of skin hardens and turns dark brown to form the puparium. If the larva is deposited on hard ground the puparium is formed above the surface where it may be vulnerable to predators and parasites. Apart from this one weakness, young tsetse flies are well protected against hazards, which explains why the female in her lifetime produces relatively few eggs (10 to 20), compared with the hundreds or thousands laid by some other flies.

The adult fly has enormous medical and veterinary importance in Africa as a vector of various types of *Trypanosoma* which affect man and domestic animals. Despite the eradication of the tsetse fly in many areas, it is estimated that at least ten million square kilometres of tropical Africa are still threatened by trypanosomiasis.

There are six main 'species' of tsetse-borne trypanosomes, of which four attack livestock and cause the disease called 'nagana'; these do have wild animal

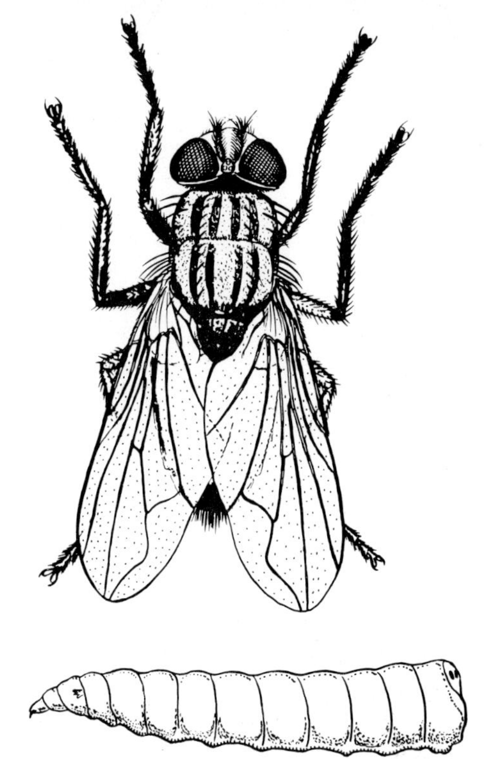

230. Larva (below) and adult of the house fly *Musca domestica*.

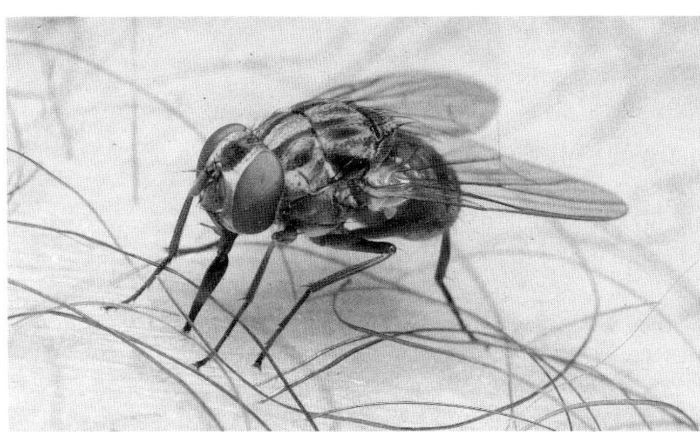

231. Similar in appearance to the house fly, the stable fly *(Stomoxys calcitrans)* is frequently mistaken for the former. However it is able to suck blood and inflicts a painful bite with its stout, piercing proboscis. 7 mm.

reservoirs, but do not cause any disease in them. The two species directly affecting man are *Trypanosoma rhodesiense*, found in cattle and game and which causes acute clinical disease in man and *Trypanosoma gambiense*, mostly restricted to humans, which causes the chronic and dreaded form of 'sleeping sickness'.

The drugs available to treat infected humans and livestock have unpleasant side effects and cannot be used to prevent infection, as is the case with chemicals used for malaria prophylaxis. Attention has centred, therefore, on control of tsetse flies rather than on the trypanosomes: the clearing of bush, the spraying of insecticides and the destruction of game are among the methods attempted to make areas available for human settlement.

The tsetse flies' enemies have also received close attention – among their predators are birds, ants, robber flies and spiders, while the puparia may be parasitized by a wide variety of insects including bombyliid flies and mutillids, chalcids and eulophids of the order Hymenoptera.

Of course it must be noted that the tsetse fly is responsible for preserving many of Africa's remaining wildlife sanctuaries, and as the medical entomologists succeed in opening up new areas for human settlement and agriculture, so the endemic animals and vegetation are destroyed and lost forever.

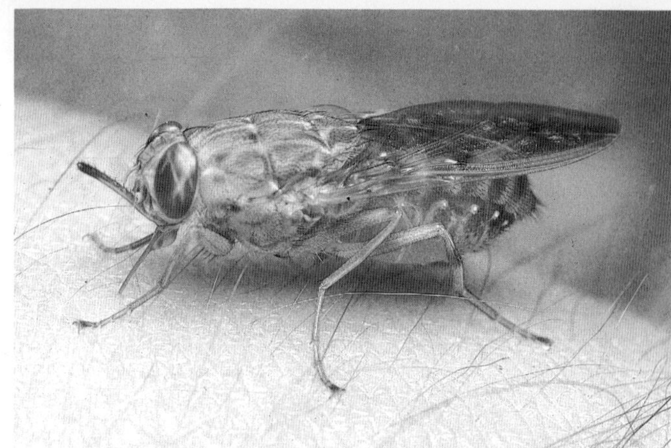

232. Sickness and death come to millions of Africa's people through the bite of the bloodsucking tsetse fly. Here a specimen of *Glossina morsitans* takes blood from the arm of a man in the Okavango River Delta of Botswana.

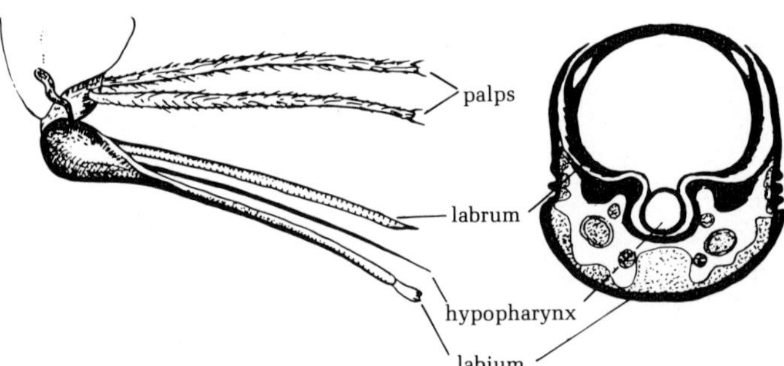

233. The mouthparts of the tsetse fly, showing the various parts (left), and a section through the proboscis (right).

Horse bot flies and their kin In summer one often sees horses constantly nodding their heads in the direction of their front knees, stamping their feet and swishing their tails. If you examine the area around the knees and the chest, you may see small yellow objects that look like grass seeds stuck to the hairs – these are the eggs of a fly called *Gasterophilus intestinalis*. The eggs hatch when they are moistened and rubbed by the animal licking itself, and the young larvae burrow into the tissues of the mouth cavity. The second and third stage larvae attach themselves by their strong mouthhooks to the wall of the pharynx, stomach or hind gut where they feed on blood and fluids, maturing over several months. When fully grown, they detach themselves and are carried through the intestine and finally ejected with the dung. They pupate in the soil where they give rise to adult flies which live for only a few days. The adults, pale yellow in colour, have much reduced mouthparts and do not feed, but they do drink water. When laying their eggs, they hover and dart around the horses which makes the animals nervous and excited.

The family Gasterophilidae contains several genera of truly amazing flies. In addition to *G. intestinalis*, there are another six *Gasterophilus* species in Africa, found in horses, donkeys and zebras. The genus *Gyrostigma* has giant wasp-like flies up to 25 mm long; their larvae, with a life cycle similar to that of the horse bot fly, are intestinal parasites of the various species of rhinoceros. Finally, there are the species of *Cobboldia* that live as parasites in the stomach of the African elephant. They do not pass through the alimentary tract but, when mature, collect under the elephant's tongue, and are ejected during feeding.

Louse flies and their relatives The Hippoboscidae are highly specialised blood-sucking flies adapted to life on the bodies of birds and mammals. The sheep ked, *Melophagus ovinus*, is a wingless member of the family that is found only on sheep; it occurs throughout Africa wherever these are kept, and spreads from sheep to sheep by physical contact. The fly is about 6 mm long, dark brown in colour and covered with short hairs. One large egg at a time is produced by the female; this is not laid but is retained inside the body and the larva is nourished by the secretions of special glands until it is fully grown.

The female deposits this fully-grown larva amid the sheep's wool and it is fixed in position by a sticky fluid which hardens rapidly. The skin of the larva hardens and turns brown to form a puparium, and after about three weeks the adult ked emerges.

It lives for four or five months and a female may produce about a dozen young during this time. This insect is an important sheep pest as not only does it cause considerable irritation – an animal may rub and scratch itself to such an extent that the fleece becomes ragged and the quality of the wool is affected – but anaemia may set in and the animal fall off in condition.

There are about 50 species of Hippoboscidae in Africa, and the majority are bird parasites. Interestingly, louse flies which feed on birds such as swallows and swifts that return to the same nest every year, often have absent or reduced wings. Conversely those flies which parasitize birds that build new nests each year usually have well-developed wings. The louse flies of birds do not attach their larvae to the feathers, but pupate in the nest and hatch the following spring.

Hippobosca rufipes, a tough, squat red and black fly, irritates the horses, cattle and antelopes on which it concentrates. A powerful flier, it may appear almost anywhere; if it lands on a person, its vicelike claws arouse an extremely unpleasant sensation as it crawls on skin and hair. A similar-looking fly, *Hippobosca struthions,* which normally occurs on ostriches, has been recorded as biting man.

Hippoboscidae play an interesting rôle in the transfer of other ectoparasites from host to host. If the host dies, as its body temperature drops, the flies leave and set off in search of a new source of food. Ectoparasites such as mites and lice are also stirred into desperate activity by the death of their host, and some attach themselves by their mouthparts to the wings, abdomen or legs of the nearest louse fly they can find. With a firm hold on this winged 'lifeboat', they are carried away to a new host!

Two closely related families are found exclusively on bats. These are the Streblidae and the Nycteribiidae, and anyone who studies bats will discover these parasites. Many of them are totally wingless and do not look at all like flies. It has been suggested that the presence of these two families of bat parasites may explain why bats are among the very few mammals which do not harbour lice; the bat flies have prevented lice from developing on bats, presumably because they occupy all the available niches.

Blow flies and their kin The large family of flies called the Calliphoridae contains some of the most familiar and unpleasant flies in Africa, many of them causing myiasis when their larvae develop in or on the living tissue of animals, including man. There are no blood-sucking adult flies in this family, and the parasitic way of life is restricted to the larvae.

Lucilia cuprina is a metallic green fly that is common and abundant throughout Africa. The female lays her eggs on carcases or on meat that is left uncovered. *Lucilia* and two other common African flies, *Chrysomya chloropyga* and *Chrysomya albiceps*, constitute a group of blow flies which do considerable damage to sheep flocks in southern Africa. *Lucilia* species are commonly called 'green bottles' and *Chrysomya* species 'blue bottles'. While all three species are primarily flies that breed in carrion, they will also lay their eggs on live sheep. The life history of these flies is as follows:

The female lays her small, white eggs in batches of 50 to 200. In hot weather they hatch in 12 hours, but take

234. Adult elephant bot fly *Cobboldia loxodontis*. These flies lay their eggs at the base of the tusks, and the resulting larvae enter the elephant's stomach by way of its mouth.

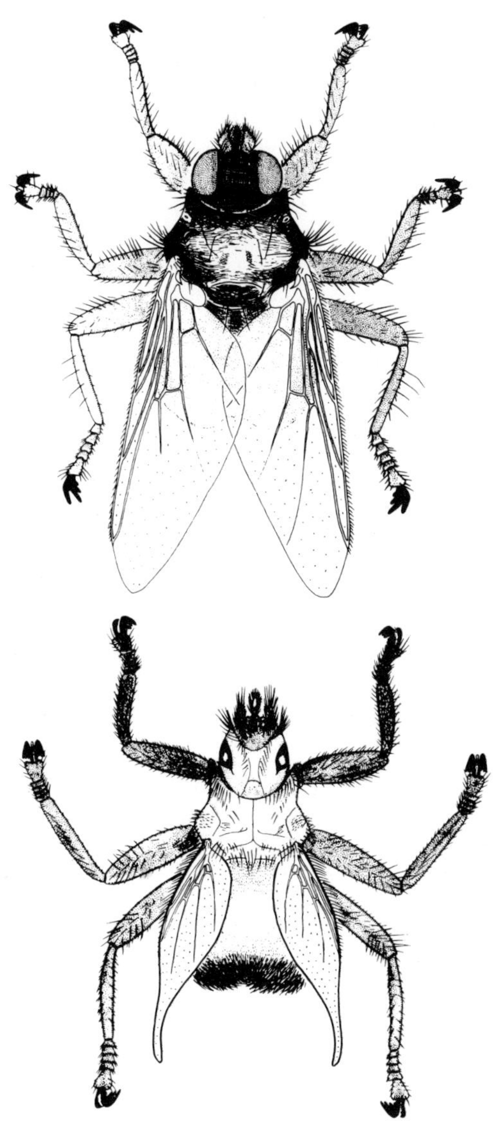

235. Two common African hippoboscid flies which parasitize birds. *Ornithoctona laticornis* (above) has well-developed wings, while *Crataerina acutipennis* (below) is a parasite of swifts and has reduced wings. 6 mm.

three days or more in spring and autumn. The larvae are white legless maggots, pointed at the head end, very much like the larvae of the common house fly. As they creep over the meat they thrust their mouth-hooks in and out of the small pores that are their mouths and at the same time they eject copious saliva that moistens the meat and digests it. Thus digestion takes place outside the body of these insects and a sort of meat broth forms which they can suck up.

A number feeding together will quickly dissolve the meat immediately around them, while the wool on the infected area of a sheep becomes wet and soiled and rots very rapidly. If the maggots are not destroyed or removed from the sheep, they will eat away the skin and produce an ugly sore, attracting more flies to lay their eggs, and eventually the animal may die.

The larvae may be fully grown in two days or they may take two or three weeks, depending on the temperature and the amount of food available. As soon as they have finished feeding, the maggots seek out a suitable spot where they may bury themselves in the soil or hide under cover of a stone or some other dark, sheltered spot. Those bred on living sheep simply drop to the ground and hide. They change into pupae and the adults emerge in the same way as the house fly. The pupal stage lasts for a week in summer but larvae that reach full size in autumn spend the winter either as larvae in the soil or as puparia.

During the First World War many wounded men who had to be left lying helplessly in 'no man's land' had their wounds infected with blow fly maggots. Surgeons noticed that such wounds often healed up more rapidly and cleanly than wounds not infected in this way. This led to the idea of treating deep-seated bone sores, known as osteomyelitis, with sterile maggots, but modern drugs have rendered this rather unpleasant mode of treatment unnecessary.

The action of the fly larvae in helping to clean up an infection is easily understood when one remembers their method of feeding. Groping restlessly inside the wound with their pointed heads and pouring out their digestive juice, they dissolve away the dead and diseased tissue and kill the bacteria at the same time, acting as a powerful antiseptic.

It should be remembered that the sheep blow flies normally breed in carrion and that they play an important ecological rôle in the natural breakdown of carcases. When Linnaeus declared that two flies can devour a dead horse more rapidly than a lion, he was referring to blow flies which breed prodigiously and with their offspring can demolish a carcase.

The three species mentioned above only attack sheep when the wool is soiled, particularly between the hind legs, or in spots where they have been wounded. Farmers in southern Africa have exterminated many of the carrion-eating creatures such as vultures and jackals; as a result vast sums of money must now be spent to protect sheep from blow flies – bred in the carcases of animals which would otherwise have been eaten by scavengers.

The three flies just mentioned are facultative parasites, as they can develop either in carrion or in living tissue. Another species, *Chrysomya bezziana*, is an obligatory parasite of living animals, and its larvae may cause a malign myiasis which leads to a quick death. This so-called 'Old World screwworm' (to distinguish it from the screwworm of America) is widespread in Africa and causes great veterinary problems in cattle. Unless the maggots are killed and removed, they can cause extensive and dangerous tissue destruction. The ears are especially vulnerable and become a living mass of maggots which destroy the tissue and can invade the eyeball and the brain. Sheep, horses and dogs may also be attacked, and there have been cases where people have been infested.

A very common but less dangerous fly whose larvae also attack humans is the 'tumbu fly' or 'putsi fly', *Cordylobia anthropophaga*. It is found throughout Africa, mainly in tropical and subtropical parts, but in wet years spreads extensively to arid areas, and has been noted even in the Namib Desert.

The female lays her eggs in sandy soil contaminated with urine or excreta, but sometimes on clothes hung up to dry or on bedclothes left to air. Infants are often attacked and it may be that the flies lay their eggs on the clothing, particularly in the region of the neck, while the child is lying in its cot. When the tiny larvae come into contact with human skin they burrow into the flesh just below the skin to develop, causing swellings similar to boils.

If one of these swellings is closely examined a small opening, usually darker in colour than the rest of the lesion and with moisture around it, is visible. This is the hole through which the maggot obtains air.

The natural hosts of these flies seem to be rats, small carnivores and other animals; dogs are also commonly infected. In their natural hosts the maggots develop to full size beneath the skin and then drop out on to the ground where they bury themselves for pupation. Man is not a natural host, and the larvae, usually removed as soon as they are detected, do not develop to maturity. If the boil in which the maggot develops is covered with some vaseline, the air supply is cut off, it then releases its hold and can be gently squeezed out of the skin.

The Congo floor maggot, *Auchmeromyia luteola*, is closely related to the tumbu fly and is also found throughout tropical and subtropical Africa. The female lays her eggs in the dust on the floor of huts; the larvae, when hatched, hide in cracks and crevices by day but creep out at night to feed on the blood of sleeping people. When the habit of sleeping on bedsteads rather than on the floor is adopted, the Congo floor maggot is unable to reach people and ceases to be a pest. Other species of *Auchmeromyia* occur in the burrows of warthogs and antbears.

The termite guest fly, *Termitometopia skaifei*, is another member of this family that has a peculiar life history. The soft white larva about 12 mm long is found in South Africa during the summer in *Amitermes has-*

tatus termite mounds, where it is fed and cared for by the termites, which seem to be fond of its fatty exudates. In the autumn, when fully grown, the larva burrows towards the outside of the mound and hollows out a cell for itself in which it pupates. The adult fly which emerges the following spring is about the size of a blow-fly, dark grey in colour and sluggish. Nothing is known of its egg-laying habits.

Flesh flies The large, grey 'flesh fly' with black stripes on its thorax and a checkerboard pattern on its abdomen is common all over Africa. A powerful flier, distinguished by its loud buzz, it is a member of the family Sarcophagidae. *Sarcophaga haemorrhoidalis,* as its name suggests, has a red tip to its abdomen and can be a loathsome and persistent nuisance on country picnics. The females are remarkable in that they give birth to batches of very mobile, active first stage larvae, which develop extremely fast. These flies normally breed in excreta, but the females also drop their larvae on decaying foodstuffs or meat. There are many other *Sarcophaga* species in Africa, some of which breed in decomposing organic matter and others which are specialised parasites of various invertebrates such as caterpillars and earthworms.

Tachinid flies Frequently, small, oval white eggs are seen attached to the sides of caterpillars. If such a caterpillar is kept and reared, instead of eventually becoming a butterfly or moth, a burly hairy fly will emerge from it. These are parasitic flies belonging to the family Tachinidae, whose larvae are all parasites of other insects – chiefly caterpillars, beetles, grasshoppers – and spiders and centipedes.

A typical example is the tachinid parasite, genus *Carcelia* of the wattle bagworm. This is a dark grey fly, marked with silver, measuring nearly 12 mm in length. The female lays her oval white eggs on the front part of the wattle bagworm's body whilst it is feeding. Although as many as five eggs may be found on a single caterpillar, only one fly can develop in each bagworm. The eggs hatch into tiny maggots very similar to those of the house fly and they burrow into the caterpillar's body where they feed on the liquids and the body fat, at first avoiding the vital organs. Eventually one of the fly larvae somehow gains a lead over the others and they die off, leaving the sole survivor to grow to a length of about 12 mm when it finally kills the caterpillar. The maggot leaves the dead body of its victim and may pupate inside the bag hanging from the tree, or it may creep out and drop to the ground where it buries itself before pupation. There are two generations of these flies a year and they destroy large numbers of bagworms.

Some tachinids lay a large number of very small eggs on the leaves of plants, so that caterpillars feeding on these leaves swallow the eggs which hatch inside the body of their host. The maggots burrow through the wall of the alimentary canal to get into the body cavity. In order to obtain air the parasite may pierce the skin of its

236. The calliphorid flies exhibit remarkably varied life styles. Here an ant-robbing fly of the genus *Bengalia* scrutinises a trail of driver ants passing beneath it, for any that might be carrying food, which it will steal from them. 8 mm.

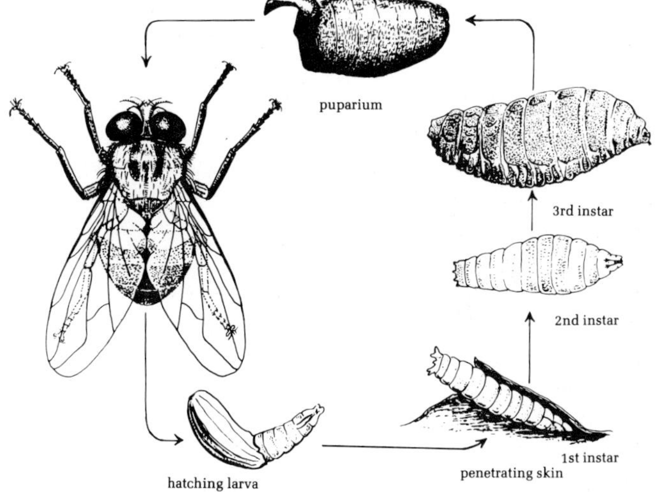

237. The life cycle of the tumbu fly, *Cordylobia anthropophaga.*

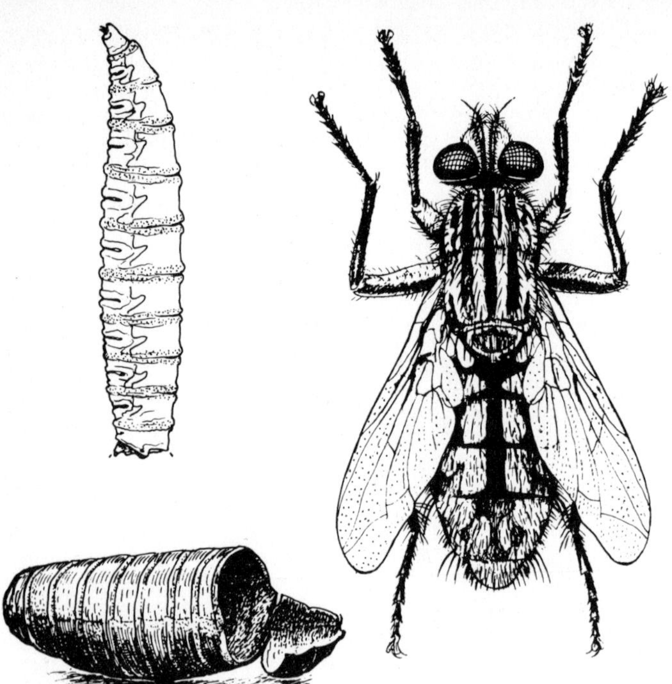

238. The larva, empty puparium and adult of the flesh fly, *Sarcophaga haemorrhoidalis.*

host and place itself in such a position that the pair of spiracles on its hind end are at the small hole, or it may pierce one of the larger tracheae inside the body and thus make use of the caterpillar's own air supply. There are a large number of different species of tachinid and they play an important rôle in keeping down the numbers of other insects.

The tachinid parasite of the honey bee, *Rondanioestrus apivorus,* is common in Africa but has not been recorded in any other part of the world. The adult flies may be found haunting beehives at almost any time of the year, but they are most prevalent in summer. Only the female, squat and grey with black markings and the same size as a house fly, is to be seen at the hive.

Close observation reveals a fascinating process: she rests, generally, just above the entrance to the hive with her head towards the entrance. From time to time she flies up and mingles with the bees returning to the hive. Her movements are difficult to follow amid the busy throng, but if you watch carefully you will see her swoop down and lightly touch a bee just as it is about to fly into the hive; after she has touched two or three in this way she settles once more on the side of the hive. She repeats the performance a few minutes later, and so it goes on. The bees that are touched by the fly do not falter in their flight but go straight into the hive as though nothing had happened to them and they show no hostility to the flies.

The fly does not lay eggs on the bees as she swoops down, for these have already hatched inside her body where a large number of tiny maggots are now packed like sardines in her oviduct. It is one of these newly-hatched maggots that she deposits on the bee as she touches it. The tiny larva which adheres to the bee because a little sticky fluid is exuded along with it, works its way between the segments of the bee's abdomen and burrows through the thin skin into the bee's body. Here it lives on fluids and, when fully grown, it occupies almost the whole of the bee's abdomen. It is a fat white maggot with two conspicuous black, circular plates on the hind end marking the site of the spiracles.

Despite the huge parasite it is carrying, the bee shows no signs of distress and works to the last. Death, when it comes, is very sudden. The bee drops to the ground, spins round furiously for a moment or two and then lies still. A few minutes later the larva breaks its way out of the dead bee's abdomen and proceeds at once to hide itself in soil, if it is soft, or beneath a stone, amid dead leaves and other debris, where it pupates. About two months later the adult fly emerges. There are two generations of the flies a year which overlap and the flies seem to be comparatively long-lived, hence they can be found at the hives during the greater part of the year. The harmless-looking parasites kill off hundreds of bees annually.

Bot flies and warble flies All members of the family Oestridae are parasitic on mammals in the larval stage, and as adults have rudimentary, non-functional mouthparts incapable of feeding. There are two main groups within the family, the first comprising those whose larvae live in the nasal and pharyngeal cavities of certain animals; and the second whose larvae develop in the skin of mammals, forming boils that have a breathing hole to provide oxygen.

Oestrus ovis, the sheep nasal bot fly, is a large, hairy yellowish insect whose eggs hatch inside the body of the female. She then deposits her tiny larvae in the nostrils of sheep and goats by hovering in front of the animal, and then darting forward to eject the larvae forcibly into the nostril. They wriggle their way up into the nasal passage and attach themselves to the mucous membrane. Here they grow very slowly, taking up to nine months to mature. When fully grown as stout, barrel-shaped maggots about 25 mm long, they loosen their hold inside the nose and wriggle out, or are sneezed out by the sheep and fall to the ground, where they pupate.

Oestrus ovis occurs throughout the world wherever there are concentrations of sheep and goats and pose a considerable veterinary problem. Sometimes the females mistake a human for a sheep or a goat (especially shepherds, who presumably take on the aroma of their charges) and deposit their larvae in the eye. This is an unpleasant experience for although the larvae do not develop beyond the first stage, they can penetrate the eyeball and affect vision.

There are also various African species whose larvae develop in different antelopes. Wildebeest are frequently infested, and may be seen sneezing incessantly, apparently oblivious of events around them. The blesbok is also tormented by nasal bot flies, and if a dissection is carried out, masses of large *Oestrus* or *Gedoelstia* larvae may be found in the sinuses that extend into the horns.

Of the Oestridae that develop in skin boils, only *Strobiloestrus* is encountered with any regularity in Africa, in several smaller antelope species. In other parts of the world, the 'ox warble flies', belonging to the genus *Hypoderma* attack cattle and cause considerable economic loss. Fortunately these flies have never become established in Africa, although they have been introduced on numerous occasions when livestock has been imported.

239. Tachinid flies are characterised by the stout bristles which clothe their bodies, particularly at the hind end of the abdomen. 11 mm.

240. The fully grown larva of a tachinid fly emerging from the body of a moth caterpillar, in which it has been developing for some weeks, prior to dropping to the ground and pupating in the soil.

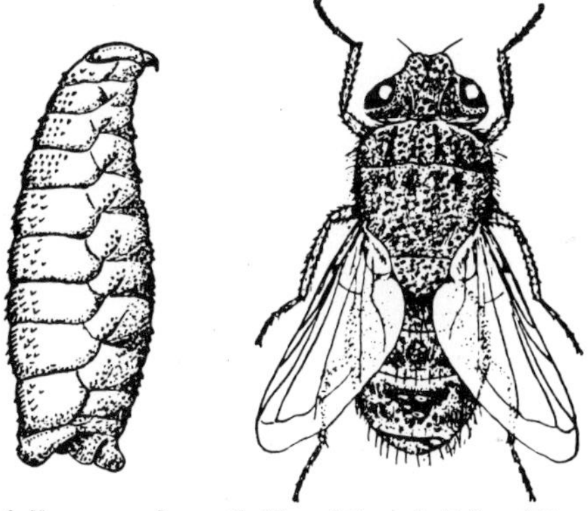

241. The fully grown larva (left) and the adult fly of *Oestrus ovis*. 20 mm.

CLASSIFICATION

ORDER **Diptera**

Insects with one pair of membranous wings on mesothorax (wings rarely reduced or absent), hind wings reduced to small knobbed structures (halteres). Antennae variable, but often short, inconspicuous and 3-segmented. Compound eyes usually very large. Mouthparts sucking, sometimes adapted for piercing, rarely vestigial. Tarsi 5-segmented. Metamorphosis complete, larvae usually legless and wormlike, commonly called maggots, develop in wide variety of habitats. Pupa either free, or enclosed in hardened larval cuticle, called puparium.

SUBORDER **Nematocera**

Antennae with six or more segments, often plumose in males. Palps usually 4- or 5- segmented. Wing venation variable, often greatly reduced. Mostly small, slender and soft-bodied flies with relatively long legs and antennae. Larvae usually with well-developed head and horizontally biting mouthparts, often aquatic or living in moist surroundings.

FAMILY Tipulidae

Mosquito-like, with very long and deciduous legs. Antennae long, 6- to many-segmented. No ocelli on head. Mesonotum with V-shaped transverse suture. Larvae aquatic or in moist soil. Crane flies are commonest near water and rank vegetation, but often enter houses.

FAMILY Psychodidae

Small, very hairy and moth-like flies, mostly 5 mm long or less. Wings usually broad, pointed apically and without conspicuous cross-veins. Two main subfamilies: Psychodinae are the non-biting moth flies, usually hold wings roof-like over body at rest and occur in damp places where larvae breed in water, sewage works, etc. Phlebotominae are the biting sand flies, hold wings together over body, very small and silvery in appearance. Important transmitters of various diseases; larvae develop in soil.

FAMILY Culicidae

Wings long and narrow, with scales along posterior margins and along veins. Distal part of wing has unforked vein between two forked veins. Proboscis elongate and piercing, ocelli lacking. Antennae densely plumose in males. Three subfamilies are recognised. Anophelinae have palps long in both sexes (clubbed in males) and at rest the hind part of the body is raised. Malaria vectors belong to this subfamily. The Culicinae have palps of the female short, those of the male long, and they rest with the body parallel to the surface. Many culicines transmit viruses. The Toxorhynchitinae comprise a single genus, whose larvae are predators of other mosquito larvae. The eggs of Culicidae are laid on the surface of the water, singly or in rafts. Some are laid in dry situations and hatch when flooded. Both larvae and pupae occur in water and are very active.

FAMILY Chironomidae

Wings long and narrow, lacking scales. Head small, mouthparts poorly developed, male antennae plumose, front tarsi usually elongated. Larvae aquatic, those of a few species called blood-worms. Midges sometimes emerge in enormous masses. They vary in size from very tiny (2 mm) to quite large (10 mm).

FAMILY Ceratopogonidae

Tiny flies generally less than 3 mm. Mouthparts biting, antennae short and front tarsi not lengthened. Larvae mostly slender, aquatic or semi-aquatic in rich organic matter. Biting midges are of veterinary importance as vectors of virus, and sometimes annoy man with their bites.

FAMILY Simuliidae

Small grey or black flies, generally 4 mm or less with short legs, stocky build and humpbacked appearance. Antennae short, though 11-segmented. Wings broad at base with anterior veins heavy. Larvae aquatic in running streams, attached to various objects. Some black flies are vicious biters and a serious medical problem in parts of Africa where they transmit onchocerciasis.

FAMILY Mycetophilidae

Slender, mosquito-like flies with elongated coxae; ocelli present. Fungus gnats are small to medium in size, rather resembling midges. They are very numerous in individuals and species, more than 2 000 having been described. They occur in damp or dark places where there is plentiful decaying vegetation or fungus growth. The larvae are slender and worm-like, living gregariously and producing slime; some species are luminous.

FAMILY Cecidomyiidae

Minute delicate flies, rarely over 3 mm, with long antennae adorned with conspicuous whorls of hair. Wings with venation reduced, no obvious cross veins. Larvae of most species are gall makers, some feed on plants without causing galls and others occur in decaying material. The gall gnats are a very large and important family, but little studied in Africa. A few species are economically important pests of crops. Members of the Cecidomyiidae exhibit the curious phenomenon of paedogenesis; some of the larvae develop simple ovaries and they produce eggs which develop without fertilisation into larvae. These consume the body of their 'parent' before escaping to pursue a vegetarian life.

SUBORDER **Brachycera**

Flies with eight or fewer (usually three) antennal segments, sometimes with terminal style, rarely with an arista (bristle). No frontal suture on head. Tarsi with two or three pads. Mostly medium to large, robust flies. Larvae with incomplete head, usually retractile, and with vertically biting mandibles.

FAMILY Stratiomyiidae

Third antennal segment annulated and elongated, scutellum (terminal part of thorax) often conspicuously developed, sometimes with spines. Soldier flies are medium to large, often found on flowers or in damp vegetation. They may fly rather weakly, fold their wings scissor-like over the abdomen, and may be metallic blue or green. Larvae may be aquatic or scavengers in decomposing material.

FAMILY Tabanidae

Third antennal segment elongate, but lacking a style, calypters large and body lacking extensive bristles. Medium to large flies, proboscis projecting and adapted for piercing in the female. Eyes large, often brightly coloured or iridescent. Larvae are found in water, wet soil or other damp places, they are carnivorous and have strong mouth hooks. Horse flies are well known in Africa, the females biting man and a wide variety of animals, transmitting the worm *Loa loa* to the former, and a variety of disease organisms to the latter. Of the three subfamilies present on the continent, the Pangoniinae are characterised by the genus *Philoliche*, which has a long, sharp proboscis, and the Tabaninae contains the majority of the commonly encountered species.

FAMILY Rhagionidae and Athericidae

Third antennal segment more or less rounded and bearing a long slender terminal style. Calypters small or vestigial. Bristleless flies. The athericids, commonly called snipe flies, are closer to the Tabanidae, and adults are blood sucking. Eggs are laid in massed clusters and larvae are aquatic. Rhagionidae of the genera *Chrysopilus* and *Lampromyia* have larvae which are predaceous, building pits into which their victims fall.

FAMILY Scenopinidae

First two antennal segments short, third elongate without style or arista. Narrow, oblong flies, robust and dark-coloured. Called window flies because a few species are often seen on the inside of windows. Larvae occur in wood, fungi or material containing infestations of insects such as clothes moths, on which they are predaceous.

FAMILY Asilidae

Top of head hollowed out between eyes, three ocelli present, third antennal segment usually elongate with a short style. Usually elongate and bristly flies, with bearded face and horny proboscis adapted for piercing. Legs powerful and prehensile. Larvae are predators or scavengers, living in soil, wood or decaying vegetation. Robber flies are predaceous as adults, catching other insects on the wing and sucking them dry.

FAMILY Mydaidae

Large and uncommon flies; antennae long, 4-segmented, last segment usually clubbed; one ocellus or none. Mydas flies are often dark coloured, with a yellow or orange band at the second abdominal segment. Adults predaceous, larvae in soil or decaying organic matter.

FAMILY Bombyliidae

Third antennal segment simple, style small or vestigial, not more than 2-segmented. Usually stout-bodied, densely pubescent with elongate slender legs and often a very long, tapering proboscis. Wings held outstretched at rest. Larvae are parasites of various insect orders. Bee flies are tiny to large insects, usually seen on flowers or resting on the ground.

FAMILY Empididae

Third antennal segment usually rounded, with a long terminal style. Moderately bristly flies with a proboscis adapted for piercing, thorax stout and abdomen tapering. Larvae are apparently predaceous and live in soil, decaying organic matter, or water. Dance flies are medium to very small, commonly occur in dancing swarms, and are rarely metallic in colour. Most adults are predaceous; may occur on flowers.

FAMILY Dolichopodidae

Small to medium bristly flies, often metallic green or blue, third antennal segment usually with conspicuous arista; proboscis short and fleshy. Male genitalia large, folded forward under abdomen. Larvae are found in damp situations and most are throught to be predatory. Adult long-legged flies are predaceous on minute soft-bodied insects.

SUBORDER **Cyclorrhapha**

Antennae 3-segmented, with arista. Frontal suture absent (division Aschiza) or present (division Schizophora). Larvae with vestigial head, pupation in puparium formed from larval skin.

DIVISION **Aschiza**

FAMILY Lonchopteridae

Third antennal segment rounded or globular, with long terminal or subdorsal arista; wings pointed at apex and lacking cross-veins except at base. Spear-winged flies are slender, bristly and pale, generally found in moist montane situations. Larvae occur in decaying vegetation.

FAMILY Phoridae

Antennae very short, appearing to consist of one large segment, which is actually the enlarged third segment that conceals the first and second; it bears a long arista. Small to minute dark flies with humpbacked appearance, hind femora flattened. Larvae live in decaying vegetable matter or carcases, some are termitophilous and others are parasitic. Coffin flies get their common name from the habits of certain species that live on bodies and emerge from graves. They are also called humpbacked flies.

FAMILY Syrphidae

Wing venation characteristic, with spurious vein, and false hind margin of wing formed by certain veins. Proboscis short and fleshy. Moderate to large flies, brightly coloured with yellow patterns, or bee-like, frequently seen around flowers. Hover flies get their name from their ability to hover motionless in the air; they are good fliers. Larval habits extremely varied, some are scavengers, others predators and a few live with ants.

FAMILY Conopidae
Venation as in Syrphidae but lacking the spurious vein. Proboscis long and slender, abdomen may be narrowed at base, or give that appearance by having transparent parts of the segments. Conopids are sometimes called thick-headed flies; they may resemble certain wasps and are parasites of bees or wasps. The adults lay eggs on the Hymenoptera, usually when they visit flowers, and the fly larvae develop inside their hosts.

DIVISION **Schizophora**

The Cyclorrhapha with a frontal suture consitute about a third of the whole order of Diptera, and may be conveniently referred to as 'muscoid flies'. There are many described families and species, and identification is usually a matter for the specialist. The muscoid flies divide conveniently into two groups – the Acalyptratae and the Calyptratae. The former have no calypters, or vestigial ones, and the second antennal segment lacks a longitudinal suture. The Calyptrates have well-developed calypters, and the second antennal segment nearly always has a longitudinal suture.

SECTION **Acalyptratae**

FAMILY Diopsidae
Head extended on each side into stalk-like process bearing the eye, and antennae widely separated (sometimes little or no extension of eyes, sometimes marked separation with eyes at the end of long, slender stalks). Front femora swollen. Stalk-eyed flies may be found in damp vegetation near water; larvae develop in decaying vegetation.

FAMILY Tephritidae
Small to medium flies, often brightly coloured with spotted and banded wings. Fruit flies are usually found on vegetation and flowers; some species move their wings slowly up and down while resting. Larvae are plant feeders and some are serious pests of fruit.

FAMILY Lauxaniidae
Small, stout-bodied flies, often with spots on the wings, occurring in vegetation in forests, grasslands and reedbeds. Larvae occur in decaying vegetable matter, leaf litter and birds' nests. Lauxaniid flies are common and abundant in Africa, but are generally overlooked by all but the specialist entomologist.

FAMILY Braulidae
Tiny (1,5 mm) wingless ectoparasites of the honey bee. Only one known species, *Braula coeca*, called the blind bee louse. Adults cling tightly to their hosts, but can move nimbly from one bee to another. They feed on honey regurgitated by the bee, and apparently cause no mortality. Eggs are laid on the comb, and the maggots feed on pollen and honey, burrowing along the cell caps.

FAMILY Ephydridae
Small, sometimes blackish flies found in marshes or near the sea, face somewhat bulging. Eggs attached to floating vegetation, larvae aquatic or living in plant tissue, some pupae puncture aquatic plants to obtain oxygen. Shore flies often congregate in enormous numbers near coastal pools. The larvae of *Psilopa petrolei* live in pools of crude petroleum in California.

FAMILY Drosophilidae
Small flies, 3-4 mm, usually yellowish or brownish with light red eyes, plumose arista (hair on third antennal segment), oral vibrissae present (bristles projecting forwards from mouthparts). Vinegar flies are common, usually found around decaying fruit or vegetables. Larvae develop in decaying fruit or fungi. *Drosophila* is well known as an experimental animal for genetic research.

FAMILY Chloropidae
Small to very small, colour variable, commonly encountered in vegetation. The genus *Hippelates* contains the 'eye gnats' which take secretions from eyes and sores of mammals and may spread disease organisms. Larval habits are extremely varied; many are plant feeders and may damage crops, some are predaceous on the eggs of spiders and mantids.

FAMILY Agromyzidae
Small to very small flies, blackish or yellowish, commonly found in vegetation. Leaf miner flies are inconspicuous; their larvae are leaf miners in a variety of plants, stem borers or sometimes gall makers.

SECTION **Calyptratae**

FAMILY Muscidae
Mostly medium flies, resembling the house fly. Mouthparts generally adapted for lapping up liquid food, sometimes modified for piercing and sucking. Most larvae develop in decomposing organic matter, but some are blood-sucking or parasitic.

FAMILY Glossinidae
Proboscis conspicuous, protruding from front of head, arista plumose, wings folded scissor-like at rest. Adults blood-sucking on a variety of animals. Larvae nourished within the body of the female and deposited singly when mature; pupate almost immediately. Tsetse flies have a great medical and veterinary importance in Africa as vectors of trypanosomes.

FAMILY Gasterophilidae
Mouthparts reduced and non-functional; some species yellowish and bee-like. Larvae are endoparasitic in the digestive tract of zebra, rhinoceroses and elephants.

FAMILY Hippoboscidae
Head sunk into thorax, antennae inserted into a depression, legs short and stout with strong hooked claws, wings developed, reduced or absent. Louse flies are specialised blood-sucking ectoparasites of mammals and birds. The female produces a fully-developed larva which pupates almost immediately.

FAMILY Calliphoridae
Robust, medium to large flies, often with metallic blue or green colouration. Adults attracted to decomposing organic matter in which the eggs are laid. Maggots may sometimes suck blood of living animals, form skin boils, or destroy healthy tissue.

FAMILY Sarcophagidae
Large robust flies, grey with black stripes on thorax and checkerboard pattern on abdomen. Flesh flies feed on filth and excreta, and many species deposit living first stage larvae. Some larvae are parasites of various arthropods.

FAMILY Tachinidae
Very bristly, medium-sized, often bee-like and yellowish in colour. Abundant and important, their larvae all being parasites of insects or sometimes other arthropods. A wide variety of life habits occurs among the larvae.

FAMILY Oestridae
Mostly stout, hairy flies, somewhat bee-like, distinguished by non-functional, undeveloped mouthparts. Adults are rare, larvae live in the nasal passages of various mammals, or form boils in the skin.

FURTHER READING

GENERAL

Greenberg, B.: *Flies and Disease Vol. 1.* Princeton University Press, Princeton (1971). 856 pp

Oldroyd, H.: *The Natural History of Flies.* Weidenfeld and Nicolson, London (1964). 324 pp

Stuckenberg, B.: 'Diptera'. In Coaton, W. G. H. (Ed.): *Status of the Taxonomy of the Hexapoda of southern Africa.* South African Department of Agricultural Technical Services. Entomology Memoir 38: 105-113 (1974). (Contains many significant references to the African Diptera fauna.)

Zumpt, F.: *Myiasis in Man and Animals in the Old World.* Butterworths, London (1965). 267 pp

PSYCHODIDAE

Abonnenc, E.: *Les Phlébotomes de la Région Éthiopienne.* Memoires ORSTOM No. 55, Paris (1972). 289 pp

CULICIDAE

Edwards, F. W.: *Mosquitoes of the Ethiopian Region. III. Culicine adults and pupae.* British Museum (Natural History), London (1941). 499 pp

Gillies, M. T. & De Meillon, B.: *The Anophelinae of Africa south of the Sahara (Ethiopian Zoogeographical Region).* Publications of the South African Institute for Medical Research No. 54 (1968). 343 pp

Hopkins, G. H. E.: *Mosquitoes of the Ethiopian Region. I. Larval bionomics of mosquitoes and taxonomy of culicine larvae.* 2nd edition. British Museum (Natural History), London (1932). 355 pp

Knight, K. L. & Stone, A.: *A Catalog of the Mosquitoes of the World.* The Thomas Say Foundation (1977). Vol. 6. 611 pp

Muspratt, J.: 'Research on South African Culicini (Diptera, Culicidae). III. A check-list of the species and their distribution, with notes on their taxonomy, bionomics and identification'. *Journal of the Entomological Society of Southern Africa* (1955). 18: 149-207.

Muspratt, J.: The Stegomyia mosquitoes of South Africa and some neighbouring territories. *Memoirs of the Entomological Society of Southern Africa (1956).* 4. 138 pp

Service, M. W.: *Mosquito Ecology. Field Sampling Methods.* Applied Science Publishers Ltd., London (1976). 583 pp

CHIRONOMIDAE

Freeman, P.: 'A Study of the Chironomidae (Diptera) of Africa South of the Sahara. Parts I-IV'. *Bulletin of the British Museum (Natural History),* London (1955, 1956, 1957, 1958). Vol. 4: 1-67; 287-368; Vol. 5: 321-426; Vol. 6: 261-363

SIMULIIDAE

Crosskey, R. W.: 'A Re-Classification of the Simuliidae (Diptera) of Africa and its islands'. *Bulletin of the British Museum (Natural History) Ent. Supp.* (1969). 14. 195 pp

Freeman, P. & De Meillon, B.: *Simuliidae of the Ethiopian Region.* British Museum (Natural History), London (1953). 224 pp

TABANIDAE

Oldroyd, H.: *The horseflies of the Ethiopian Region.* 3 Volumes. British Museum (Natural History), London. (1952, 1954, 1957). 226 & 341 & 489 pp

Travassos Santos Dias, J. A.: *Tabanideos de Moçambique* Estudos Gervais Universitarios de Moçambique (1966). 1 283 pp

Usher, P. J.: 'A review of the South African horse fly fauna (Diptera: Tabanidae)'. *Annals of the Natal Museum* (1972). 21: 459-507

RHAGIONIDAE/ATHERICIDAE

Stuckenberg, B. R.: 'Diptera (Brachycera) Rhagionidae.' *South African Animal Life* (1960). 7: 216-308

Stuckenberg, B. R.: 'The Athericidae, a new family in the lower Brachycera (Diptera)'. *Annals of the Natal Museum* (1973). 21: 649-673

ASILIDAE

Hull, F. M.: 'Robber Flies of the World; the genera of the family Asilidae'. *United States National Museum Bulletin* (1962). 224, 2 parts: 907 pp

Oldroyd, H.: 'An Introduction to the Robber Flies (Diptera: Asilidae) of Southern Africa'. *Annals of the Natal Museum* (1974). 22: 1-171

MYDAIDAE

Hesse, A. J.: 'The Mydaidae (Diptera) of southern Africa'. *Annals of the South African Museum* (1969). 54: 388 pp

BOMBYLIIDAE

Bowden, J.: 'The Bombyliidae of Ghana'. *Memoirs of the Entomological Society of Southern Africa* (1964). No. 9, 159 pp

Hesse, A. J.: 'A revision of the Bombyliidae (Diptera) of southern Africa.' *Annals of the South African Museum* (1938, 1956, 1967). 34 (1 053 pp); 35 (973 pp); 50 (p89-130)

EMPIDIDAE

Smith, K. G. V.: 'The Empididae of Southern Africa, (Diptera)'. *Annals of the Natal Museum* (1969). 19: 1-342

SYRPHIDAE

Curran, C. H.: Records and keys to Subsaharan hover flies. *American Museum Novitates* (1938-1939). 1009, 1010, 1025 & 1026

Vockeroth, J. R.: 'A revision of the genera of the Syrphini (Diptera: Syrphidae). *Memoirs of the Entomological Society of Canada* (1969). 62, 176 pp

DIOPSIDAE

Van Bruggen, A. C.: 'Diptera (Brachycera): Diopsidae'. *South African Animal Life* (1961). 8: 415-439

TEPHRITIDAE

Munro, H. K.: 'African Trypetidae (Diptera): A review of the transition genera between Tephritinae and Trypetinae, with a preliminary study of the male terminalia'. *Memoirs of the Entomological Society of Southern Africa* (1947). 1. 284 pp (Also numerous other papers by the same author in various journals.)

MUSCIDAE

Zumpt, F.: *The Stomoxyine Biting Flies of the World.* Gustav Fischer Verlag, Stuttgart (1973). 175 pp

GLOSSINIDAE

Buxton, P. A.: 'The Natural History of Tsetse Flies'. *London School of Hygiene & Tropical Medicine Memoir* (1955). 10. 816 pp

Ford, J.: *The Rôle of the Trypanosomiases in African Ecology: a Study of the Tsetse fly problem.* Clarendon Press, Oxford (1971). 568 pp

Mulligan, H. W. (Ed.): *The African Trypanosomiases.* Allen & Unwin Ltd, London (1970). 950 pp

Nash, T. A. M.: *Africa's Bane: the tsetse fly.* Collins, London (1969). 224 pp

GASTEROPHILIDAE, HIPPOBOSCIDAE, STREBLIDAE AND NYCTERIBIIDAE

Zumpt, F. (Ed): *The Arthropod Parasites of Vertebrates in Africa South of the Sahara.* Vol. III *(Insecta excl. Phthiraptera).* Publications of the South African Institute for Medical Research 13, Johannesburg (1966). 283 pp

CALLIPHORIDAE and SARCOPHAGIDAE

Zumpt, F.: *Calliphoridae (Diptera Cyclorrhapha). Exploration du Parc National Albert (des Virunga).* Mission G. F. De Witte, Bruxelles (1956, 1958, 1961, 1972). Part I, 200 pp; Part II, 207 pp; Part III, 137 pp; Part IV, 264 pp

Caddisflies 18

Caddisflies belong to the order Trichoptera meaning 'hairy wings' and not surprisingly their wings and bodies are densely clothed with hair. They are small to medium-sized insects, frequently dull in colour. The adults vary in size from species with a wing span of over 60 mm to tiny species that measure only 5 mm from wing tip to wing tip. They look very much like moths and might easily be mistaken for them, particularly as many caddisflies are active in the evening and some are attracted to light. A close examination, however, reveals that moths are clothed in scales, and their mouthparts modified to form a long, coiled proboscis for sucking nectar. Caddisflies by way of contrast have no proboscis and their mandibles are reduced to vestiges incapable of chewing solid food; they can only lap up liquids such as nectar from shallow flowers, or sap from a wound in the stem of a plant. Scales, if present, are few in number.

More than 5 000 species of caddisfly have been described, over 600 of them from Africa south of the Sahara, and undoubtedly there are many species still awaiting discovery. Adult caddisflies may be found in the vegetation along the banks of lakes and streams and most fly feebly for a short distance when disturbed, although some species may be relatively strong fliers.

The larvae and pupae of the caddisfly develop in water, where they are an important item in the diet of freshwater fish. Consequently hydrobiologists find these insects a useful gauge of the quality and level of chemical pollution in water.

The mountain streams of the western Cape Province contain a large number of species and *Dyschimus thrymmifer*, the largest found in the region, is a good general example. The adult measures 25 mm or more across the outspread wings, and its body is dark brown, clothed in blackish hairs. The wings are very hairy, mottled with different shades of brown. When at rest the insect folds its wings at a low angle over the abdomen which is unusual among the caddisflies as most of them hold the wings rooflike over their bodies. This species may be found during the warmer months, resting on bushes and trees along the banks of mountain streams at an altitude of 300 m or more. Being a nocturnal insect, it is sluggish during the day and only flies if disturbed, coming to rest after a very short distance. It is therefore seldom seen unless looked for.

The eggs of this species have not yet been found, but it is probable that the female, like other caddisflies, lays her small eggs in masses in the water or on overhanging foliage. They are enclosed in a kind of mucilage that swells rapidly when wetted.

The larva constructs a case in which to protect its soft body from the many predators it encounters in the wa-

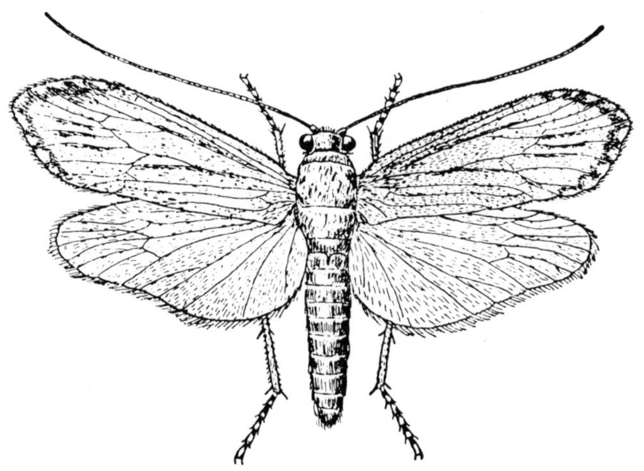

242. The large Cape caddisfly, *Dyschimus thrymmifer*, brown in colour and with a wing span of about 30 mm.

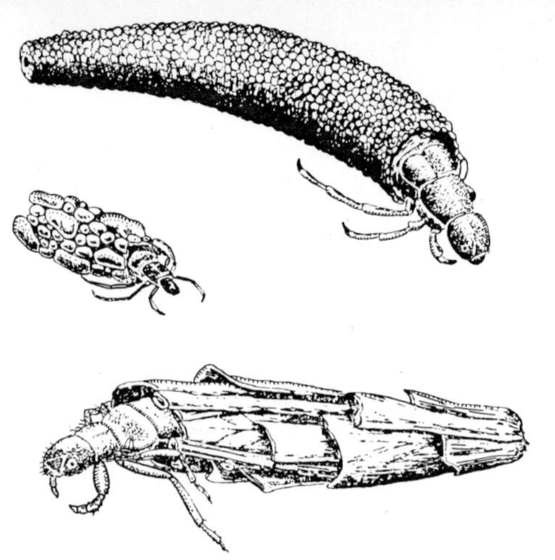

243. Three caddisfly larvae in their cases: *Rhoizema spinosum* (top), case about 25 mm long; *Sinion hageni* (centre), case about 8 mm long; *Dyschimus thrymmifer* (bottom), case about 25 mm long.

ter. Different kinds of caddisfly larvae use various materials for their cases, and *Dyschimus thrymmifer* constructs its home out of bits of dead sticks, leaves and other vegetable debris, bound together by silk that it produces from its specialised salivary glands and which issues as a thread from a spinneret below its mouth. *Dyschimus thrymmifer* feeds on dead leaves; other caddisfly larvae may be herbivorous, omnivorous or carnivorous according to the species.

The fully grown larva is 16-18 mm long. The head and the first two segments of the thorax which are exposed when the insect moves, are brown and protected by thick, tough skin. The rest of the body, enclosed by the case, is thin-skinned and white. The first pair of legs is stout and strong, the slender second pair is the longest, while the third pair is very short. At the hind end of the abdomen a pair of strong hooks enable it to hold securely to the silken lining inside the case. If you try to pull a caddisfly larva out of its case you will find that it hangs on so tightly by these hooks that you are liable to tear its body apart before it will let go. You can usually get it out without injury by poking a thin grass stalk or a pin into the back of the case. Then, if you put the naked worm into a jar of water and supply it with beads, or bits of coloured paper or wool or tiny shells, it may build itself an elegant case out of the materials supplied – although African species are less obliging than European species in this regard. In the case of caddisflies that live in running water, the jar should be oxygenated in some way or the insect will die.

On the abdomen of the larva there are slender white threads, mostly in groups of three – these are the gills, although not all caddisfly larvae have them. The insect renews the water inside the case by undulating its body, causing a slow current to flow in at the front end and out through the smaller opening at the back. Three swellings on the first segment of the abdomen, one at each side and one at the back, hold the larva in place inside the tube whilst allowing the water to flow past.

When ready to change into a pupa, the larva first anchors its case securely by silken threads in a crevice between stones, or amid heavy debris on the stream bed. Then it spins more silk across the back and front openings of the case to seal it. These barriers, reinforced by sand grains, keep out enemies but water still flows through them to carry oxygen to the pupa inside.

The compound eyes, the long antennae, the four wings and the six legs of the adult stage are clearly visible in the pupa; they are not attached to the sides of the case as occurs with certain butterfly pupae for example. The pupa also has gills on its abdomen, similar to those of the larva, to assist its respiration in the water. On its head are two prominent, long, sharp mandibles which it uses only once: when the adult is ready to emerge, the pupa becomes very active and using these mandibles cuts an opening in the top of the case. Then it wriggles out into the water and either crawls or swims to the surface. Once there, the skin splits and the adult emerges within a short time, casting off the mandibles and gills which it no longer needs.

Caddisfly larvae utilise various materials in constructing their cases which may differ in shape. Some build tubular homes out of slender bits of stick bound in bundles, others make neat little bivalve cases out of silk and green algae and still others build ovoid or cylindrical cases of sand grains. Some species use only their own silk as a protective covering and may make homes shaped like miniature elephant tusks or tiny flask-shaped cases. Finally there are species that do not make a proper case, but are either free-living or simply build a rough network of silken threads among stones and debris. These shelters sometimes have nets, beautifully constructed, to collect food. Several of the species that live in these silken shelters are carnivorous, feeding on mayfly larvae and other small aquatic creatures.

CLASSIFICATION

ORDER: **Trichoptera**

Small to medium-sized mothlike insects with long slender antennae, resembling Lepidoptera but lacking extensive scales and proboscis. Wings membranous, more or less densely hairy, held roofwise over body when at rest in majority of species. Tarsi five-jointed. Larvae aquatic, with three pairs of legs, a pair of anal prolegs, and a well-developed head. About half the species live in cases which they construct from various materials; the rest are free-living or use shelters, from which they emerge at times. Pupae with legs and wings free, always develop within a case of some kind, whether an altered larval case or a new structure.

The order is represented in Africa south of the Sahara by some 19 families of varying importance both in numbers of species, actual numbers of individuals, and rôle in the ecology of the waters in which they live. Of these 19 families, six have larvae of the free-living type, often dwelling in shelters of different kinds, and 11 are case-dwellers as larvae. The remaining two are intermediate in type, the family Hydroptilidae in particular having young stages which are free-living in the first four instars, only making cases in the fifth and final instar. It is a large and fascinating family, but not well-known owing to the very small size of both adults and larvae. Two families are of outstanding importance in Africa.

FAMILY: Hydropsychidae

The larvae belonging to this family are retreat-makers, spinning beautifully constructed catching nets; they are of great importance in fast-flowing water, particularly in places where there is an abundance of suitable food, as may be the case below the outflow of a large dam. The Hydropsychidae are of importance both as predators themselves and as food for fish and other large predators. This applies, of course, to the larval stages, though the pupal stage often serves as a meal for a roving fish, beetle or dragonfly larva as well.

FAMILY: Leptoceridae
While well-represented throughout the region, this family is of particular consequence in the acid waters of the west and southwest Cape, where the larvae form a very important component of the stream ecosystem. They are case-dwellers, and the cases constructed are extremely varied in shape and materials utilised, which include silk, sand grains, plant materials and even keratin from sponge spicules.

FURTHER READING

Barnard, K. H.: 'South African Caddisflies (Trichoptera).' *Transactions of the Royal Society of South Africa* (1934) 21: 291-394

Fischer, F. C. J.: 'Trichopterorum Catalogus.' *Nederlandsche Entomologische Vereeniging,* Amsterdam (1960-1971) Parts 1-12. (Catalogue of all the publications on Trichoptera produced between 1958 and the end of 1960, arranged systematically and giving all taxa described.)

Marlier, G.: 'Généra des Trichoptéres de l'Afrique.' *Annales Musée royale Afrique centrale (1962).* Ser. 8vo 109: 1-263

Ross, H. H.: *Evolution and Classification of the Mountain Caddisflies.* University of Illinois Press, Urbana (1956). 213 pp

Scott, K. M. F. & Scott, P. E.: 'A bibliography of literature on Trichoptera from Africa and adjacent islands.' *Journal of the Entomological Society of Southern Africa* (1969). 32: 399-411

Moths 19

The most familiar and easily recognised of all insects are moths and butterflies. Because of their beauty they are also the most popular with collectors and many are of great economic significance because they are serious pests of crops and various stored products. For these reasons this large group of insects has been more intensively studied than any other and as a result is the best-known; nearly 100 000 different species have so far been named and described from all over the world.

Moths and butterflies have two pairs of membranous wings that are covered with flattened scales. These scales are arranged something like tiles on a roof and give the wings their colours and patterns. However, they are easily rubbed off and specimens are quickly damaged if they are carelessly handled. Because of this scaly covering these insects are known as Lepidoptera, or 'scaly-winged' insects.

The distinction between butterflies and moths is superficial and from a structural point of view unsound.

The order Lepidoptera is divided into four suborders: the Zeugloptera, the Dacnonypha (not yet found in Africa), the Monotrysia, and the Ditrysia. By far the greatest number of species, about 98%, belong to the latter. These subdivisions are based upon rather obscure structural features. The non-ditrysians include the most primitive moths; they are often tiny insects found only with meticulous searching.

Primitive moths There are certain small moths (12 mm or less across the expanded wings), belonging to the family Micropterigidae, and the suborder Zeugloptera. These have bright, metallic colours, long slender antennae and fly by day. Usually found near damp spots on the outskirts of a wood, where sunlight and shade mingle, they seldom attract attention because of their small size and their short erratic flights from one patch of shade to another. These little moths are of great interest because they have a number of features considered to be primitive, and are believed to share a common ancestry with caddisflies.

Most butterflies and moths have either no jaws or at best, tiny, useless vestiges of jaws. However, they do have a long tubular tongue, with which they sip nectar from flowers. The Micropterigidae, by contrast, have no tongue for sucking, but biting jaws employed to feed on pollen, instead of nectar. They are known to occur in many parts of the world, although more prominent in temperate climes in the northern hemisphere.

So far only four species of this interesting family have been found in South Africa. The tiny caterpillars from which these moths develop are found in other parts of the world to feed on mosses; it is probable that the African species, although not yet discovered, do the same. Furthermore, it is likely that they have eight pairs of false legs on the abdomen, instead of the five pairs usual on the caterpillars of most moths.

Moths belonging to the suborder Monotrysia also have a structure that is considered primitive. However, some have developed quite specialised features. Among these, ghost moths or swift moths (Hepialidae), are very well represented in Africa – at least 80 species have already been described from south and central Africa. They have short antennae and fly swiftly, hence their name. Most are sombrely-coloured, usually a pale shade of brown, and they look like moth ghosts as they flit past in the twilight. Their mouthparts are very small and useless and the moths do not feed at all in the adult state.

The caterpillars of most of the ghost moths for which we have information feed on grass roots. The females simply drop their numerous small eggs on the ground as they fly just above the grass, and the newly-hatched caterpillars burrow into the soil to get at their food. As they grow, certain species make silken tubes above the surface of the soil and fix their droppings on the sides of these tubes. Some male ghost moths give off a scent and it is believed that the females thus locate the males at mating time, and not *vice versa* as is usually the case.

One of the most beautiful and striking of all ghost moths is the silver-spotted ghost moth, *Leto venus*, that has been found only in the Knysna forests in South Africa. About 14 cm across the outspread wings, it has orange-coloured front wings spotted with silver, pink hind wings, and a scarlet abdomen. The female lays her eggs in the soft soil at the base of a keurboom (*Virgilia capensis*), which is the only known foodplant of this insect. The caterpillars burrow into the tree and, like most wood-borers, take a long time to reach maturity: possibly two, three or more years. They pupate inside their burrows and the adult moths emerge in February or March. Being unable to feed, they are short-lived.

The caterpillars of some of the other families of monotrysian moths live between the two outer (epidermal) layers of leaves of trees and herbs. As they feed they make a characteristic channel or mine, from which their name, 'leaf-miners', is derived.

All the families of moths dealt with in the rest of this chapter belong to the suborder Ditrysia. Butterflies are also classified under this order but since they are so distinctive and familiar they are dealt with in the following chapter.

Carpenter moths The quince borer, *Cossus tristis*, is a greyish-brown moth that measures some 35 mm across the expanded wings. It is rarely seen as it hides during the day, flies only after dark, and is not attracted to light. As it has only rudimentary mouthparts it cannot feed and lives only for about a week as an adult.

The female lays her eggs in the spring in irregular masses on the bark of quince, apple and pear trees. She deposits them in cracks in the bark, in old burrows and in the angles where one branch joins another. Once deposited, she covers them with fluff from her body, and although the eggs are very small, the masses are easily seen as pink fluffy tufts. The eggs take about two months to hatch whereupon the young caterpillars feed at first on the bark before burrowing into the wood.

The presence of the caterpillars is revealed by the fragments of chewed wood, resembling sawdust, that is pushed out of the burrows. The bark surrounding the infested area becomes wet with sap, and the branch may die from the injury inflicted by the caterpillars. In about 18 months the caterpillars are fully grown, 30 mm long, with brown heads and pale, yellowish bodies mottled with irregular reddish-brown spots. Then, towards the end of March, in their second year, the caterpillars spin tough silken cocoons. These are mixed with sawdust and located about 25 mm from the entrance of the burrow. About a month later they turn into pupae in which state they pass the winter. Finally in October or November, the adult moths emerge.

The quince borer belongs to the family known as the Cossidae – moths that are often popularly spoken of as goat moths or carpenter moths. They are moderately large, or sometimes very large moths, some members of the family having a wingspan of 17 cm. Most lay their eggs on the bark of trees or in the tunnels from which they originally emerged, and the caterpillars which develop bore further into the wood, often doing serious damage to forest, shade and fruit trees.

Some cossid caterpillars make cases for themselves out of bits of grass which they neatly knit in a crosswise fashion. They live inside these cases and while carrying them about they may easily be mistaken for bagworms.

The large thorn-tree goat moth, *Xyleutes capensis,* is about 10 cm across its outspread wings, white, but mottled with small brown spots and lines. As might be anticipated the caterpillar of this moth is huge, dirty-white in colour, and has four rows of round brown spots along its body. It may be found burrowing inside thorn trees.

The codling moth and its kin The codling moth *(Cydia pomonella)* is the most serious pest of apples, pears, quinces and walnuts and also attacks apricots. The moth itself is not often seen, as it hides during the day and flies only at night, and, like the quince borer, is not attracted to lights. It is small (only about 20 mm across the outspread wings) and inconspicuous. It can most easily be recognised by the large bronze oval spot at the tip of each front wing; the remainder of the front wing is shaded grey, striped with darker grey stripes, and the hind wing is pale brown.

The female lays her eggs singly, depositing them on the leaves and fruit, and she may lay 50-100 eggs during her two or three weeks of life as an adult. The egg is white, round and flattened, and about the size of an ordinary pinhead. It hatches in four to 20 days, depending on the temperature, and the newly-hatched caterpillar at once seeks out a fruit into which to bore. Usually it enters at the calyx-end of the fruit, or at a spot where one fruit touches another or is in contact with a twig – locations where the fruit is both sheltered and well-supported.

The caterpillar feeds inside the fruit for four to six weeks, by which time it is fully grown (about 20 mm long), and white or pink in colour, with a brown head. Then it leaves the fruit (generally at night), and creeps down the branch to find a sheltered spot in which it can spin its silken cocoon. If the tree is young and there are no cracks in the bark, it will make its way to the ground and pupate under a clod near the base of the tree. On the bark of older trees, however, there are usually plenty of cracks and crevices into which it can creep.

It spins a white, silken cocoon, in which it rests for some days before changing to a pupa. After a fortnight or more the pupa wriggles its way partly out of the cocoon and then the moth emerges. The first moths of the year, the spring moths, appear in the orchards in September and October, just when the young fruit is forming. There are two generations a year, the second generation of moths emerging in December and January. There may be a limited third generation in March. These generations overlap and moths, eggs, caterpillars and pupae may be found simultaneously in the orchards during the greater part of the summer. The caterpillars that are fully grown towards the end of summer spend the winter resting inside their cocoons and they only change into pupae in the following spring, to become the first generation of moths of that season.

The codling moth belongs to a very large and wide-spread family of small moths known as the Tortricidae. The caterpillars live concealed in rolled or joined

244. The silver-spotted ghost moth, *Leto venus,* is about 14 cm across the outspread wings.

Adult moth

Caterpillar inside apple

Cocoons and pupae beneath bark

245. The life history of the codling moth, *Cydia pomonella.*

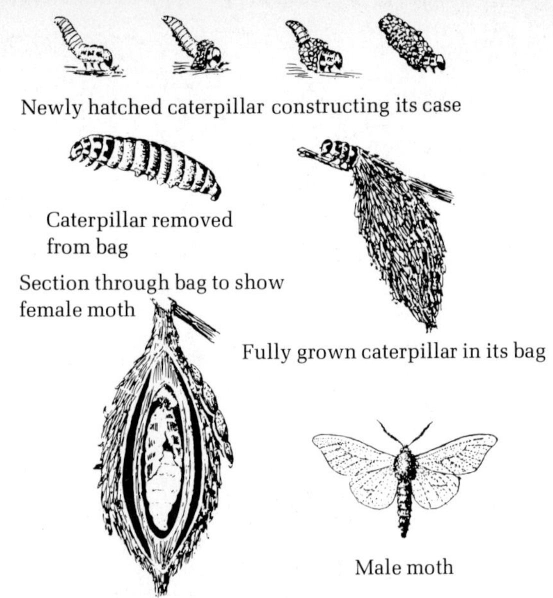

246. Features of the life history of the wattle bagworm, *Kotochalia junodi*.

leaves, in fruits, stems, roots or flower-heads and they are for the most part slender, slightly hairy and have the usual five pairs of abdominal feet. The pupae wriggle partly out of the cocoons before the moths emerge and the empty pupal cases are left projecting from the cocoons.

Bagworms Many insects construct portable homes for themselves, but perhaps the most remarkable and interesting are the caterpillars known as bagworms, or basketworms. These belong to a family of moths known as the Psychidae, which is very well represented in Africa. One of the most common and best-known members of the family is the wattle bagworm, *Kotochalia junodi*, which is found on thorn trees and which is also a serious pest in wattle plantations.

The transparent wings of the male wattle bagworm moth measure some 30 mm from tip to tip, are devoid of markings, and have few scales. As his mouthparts are imperfect and he cannot feed, his adult life is short. The female is quite different from her mate. In fact, most people would fail to recognise her as a moth because she has no legs, wings, or eyes, her body is fat and maggot-like, and she never leaves the bag in which she develops. The male, who flies about swiftly in the daytime, seeks out this bag in which she lies motionless, head downwards, inserts his long, extensible abdomen into the bag, and fertilises her. Soon after this he dies.

Shortly after this mating the female begins to lay her numerous, tiny eggs, some 1 500 in all. The eggs accumulate in the empty pupal skin behind her, mixed with the fluffy scales from her body, and finally, when the egg-laying is complete, only her dead shrivelled body remains, the mass of eggs and scales left behind in the bag. In cases where the male is very rare, or entirely absent, parthenogenesis (virgin birth) is known to occur among certain kinds of bagworms, including some African species; if a male fails to locate one of the maggot-like females, she will lay her eggs without mating and they hatch normally. All this occurs in the spring and the eggs hatch about a fortnight later, in the middle of September.

The tiny, newly-hatched larvae leave the bag and spin silken threads amid the twigs around them and they climb amongst these threads for two or three days before feeding. This apparently ensures the dispersal of the insects: strong winds blow them away or insects and birds, flying through the silken threads, may carry some of them away with the caterpillars still attached.

Before it settles down and begins feeding, the young caterpillar constructs a home for itself. It does this by biting off fragments of leaf and binding them together with silk to form a semi-circular girdle attached at each end to a leaf. The insect then puts its head through the loop, frees the two ends, and then joins them together so that a collar is formed just behind its head. By adding more silk and fragments of leaves the collar is extended until the whole body is covered and only then does the little caterpillar move and begin feeding. As it grows it adds more silk, leaves and twigs to its home until the familiar, ragged looking bag forms with the fat brown caterpillar inside. The caterpillars of the different species of bagworms found in Africa inhabit cases that exhibit great variety both of form and materials used in their construction; they cover their silken abodes with fragments of leaves, or sticks, thorns, pieces of grass, small stones and other objects. Only when feeding does the bagworm expose the front portion of its body.

By the end of summer the bagworm is fully grown, with a bag nearly 50 mm long. It now fixes its bag to a twig, binding it securely with a band of silk so that it will not be dislodged by the coming winds and storms. Then the worm withdraws into its bag and spins a snug inner tube of silk inside which it sleeps, head downwards, throughout the winter. With the advent of warmer weather the following spring, it changes into a pupa and finally into an adult moth; active and winged if male, sluggish and helpless if female.

Although we would expect wattle bagworms to be well protected by their bags, their mortality rate is very high. The large number of eggs laid by each female suggests that this must be so – if all the eggs matured, the bagworms would reach astronomical numbers. Bags containing dead caterpillars remain attached to the trees and it is easy to collect them and ascertain the cause of death. Of some 60 000 bags collected in Natal it was found that a total of 53% contained dead caterpillars: 1% were destroyed by birds and rats, 19% by insect parasites, 16% by fungous disease, and 17% by other diseases. However, this mortality rate pales in comparison with the destruction of the young, newly-hatched caterpillars, fewer than one quarter of 1% surviving the early perils of their lives; probably the great majority fail to reach a suitable foodplant and die of starvation.

Clothes moths Most of us are familiar with the damage done by clothes moths, but few people are able to recognise the moths that are responsible. Three species are common and widely spread in Africa: the common clothes moth *(Tineola bisselliella)*; the case-bearing clothes moth *(Trichophaga tapetziella)*; and the old-fashioned clothes moth *(Tinea pellionella)*. They belong to a family of small, dull-coloured moths called the Tineidae.

All three are small, yellowish or greyish moths, with narrow, fringed wings which rarely span more than 12 mm. The common clothes moth is a pale yellowish colour without any markings on its wings and the small, narrow insect (little more than 6 mm long) easily escapes the notice of the housewife when it is at rest inside a cupboard. The female lays her tiny eggs on woollen goods and furs, but not on cotton or linen fabrics. It is the little white caterpillars with dark heads that do the damage – they spin delicate silken tubes over the material and feed on the wool and fur. They pupate on the material inside thin white cocoons.

The case-bearing clothes moth may be recognised by its black and white front wings. The caterpillar feeds on wool, fur and any other dead, dry animal matter it can find. It makes a neat silken case inside which it lives and which it carries about: as this case generally has dust particles and fragments of food sticking to it, the insect is not at all conspicuous.

The old-fashioned clothes moth is grey and is speckled with indistinct darker spots on the front wings. The caterpillar also makes a silken case in which it lives and it is often found on the wall of a room, creeping slowly upwards to find a suitable spot where it can settle and turn into a pupa.

Clearwings The pretty little moths of the family Aegeriidae, known as clearwings, fly swiftly by day in the bright sunlight. They can be recognised by the absence of scales on the greater part of both wings – hence their popular name. Some resemble wasps and bees because of their clear wings, slender bodies and bright colours.

The caterpillars tunnel in branches of trees and bushes and in the roots, and pupation takes place inside the larval galleries. The pupae are armed with spines and hard, sharp cutting plates on the head which enable them to work their way to the surface before the moths emerge.

Cabbage moths The diamond back moth *(Plutella xylostella)* belongs to the family Yponomeutidae and is a well-known pest that has been distributed all over the world by man's commerce. It is very common in Africa on plants of the cabbage family, particularly during the dry season. Its wingspan is a little over 12 mm and it is ash-grey in colour. There is a wavy white line along the hind margin of each front wing and, when the insect is at rest, these wavy lines meet along the back to form the diamond-shaped patterns that give the moth its common name.

The female lays her tiny yellowish-green eggs on the upper surface of the leaves of cabbage and cauliflower

247. After emerging through the lower end of its 'bag', a male bagworm moth dries its wings before flying off to fertilise females of the species, which are wingless and never leave their bags. Bag length 55 mm.

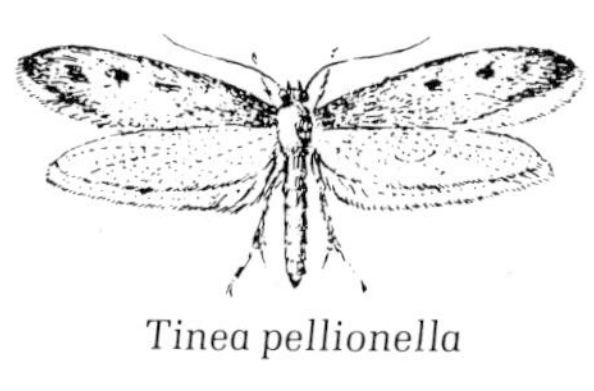

Tinea pellionella

Tineola bisselliella

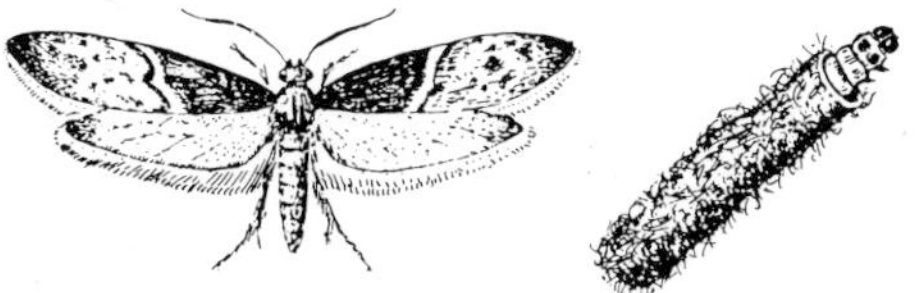

Trichophaga tapetziella

248. The three common and widespread clothes moths of Africa.

plants and these hatch in a few days into green caterpillars that feed on the under surface of the leaves; if there are many caterpillars the leaves are quickly reduced to a mere network of veins. The caterpillars spin a thin gauzy covering of silk beneath which they shelter and feed. They are about 12 mm long when fully grown and spin white silken cocoons on the underside of the leaves, inside which they change into pupae. After only a few days in this state the adult moths emerge; there may be as many as ten generations a year and, as each female may lay 50 or more eggs, it is not surprising that their numbers may increase very rapidly when conditions are favourable.

Potato moths The worst insect pest the potato-grower has to contend with in Africa is the potato tuber moth, *Phthorimaea operculella*. It is a member of the family Gelechiidae, and another insect that has been widely spread over the world by human activity. The moth measures about 20 mm across the expanded wings and is greyish brown, speckled with darker markings on the front wings. The female lays her tiny white eggs on potato plants in the field, and on the tubers in the ground or in the store-house. The caterpillar feeds on the leaves, mining between the upper and lower surface or joining two young leaves together with silk and feeding between them. If feeding on the tuber itself, it burrows below the surface. Besides potatoes, the caterpillars will feed on tobacco, *Datura* and other members of the potato family. When fully grown the caterpillar is about 12 mm long, greenish-white in colour, with a black head; at this stage it seeks out a sheltered spot, spins a silken cocoon, and changes into a pupa. There may be five or six generations a year.

Slug caterpillars In spring and again in the late summer, green caterpillars about 30 mm long, their flattened bodies covered with spines, may be found feeding on the leaves of oak and plum trees. As a result of their shape and the apparent absence of legs, they are often spoken of as slug caterpillars. A colourful creature, the slug caterpillar may be identified by the pale blue stripe which runs down the middle of its back, and the pair of black dots, bordered with white, which appear on each segment except the third and eighth; the sides of the thorax are deep red.

Each spine is hollow and terminates in a short, sharp point that can pierce the skin if the caterpillar is handled. At the base of each is a tiny poison gland which emits a secretion that can cause inflammation and swelling if it enters the wound made by the spines. At certain times of the year doctors and dermatologists have a busy time treating people, especially children, who have come in contact with slug caterpillars and are allergic to their poison.

When fully grown, the caterpillar spins an oval cocoon around itself on a twig. This brittle, egg-like cocoon is at first white but soon turns brown. After resting inside the cocoon for about ten days, the caterpillar changes to a pupa and about three weeks later, during February, the moth emerges. The moth is about 35 mm across the outspread wings; the front pair are pale green, with a light brown outer border, and the hind wings are pale yellow.

The female lays her flat oval eggs on the underside of the leaves of the foodplant, arranging them like the tiles on a roof, each egg partly overlapping the next. There are two generations a year, the first moths emerging in October and November and the second generation making its appearance in February.

The slug caterpillars belong to the family Limacodidae, and three species of the genus *Latoia* are commonly encountered in Africa, *L. latistriga*, *L. johannes* and *L. vivida*. These are mostly small moths, dull brown in colour and sometimes green, as in the case of *Latoia vivida*. The body is short and the wings are rounded. As the moth has no proboscis it cannot feed.

Meal moths and their kin The Mediterranean flour moth, *Ephestia kuehniella*, is a well-known and widespread pest that infests flour, bran and other cereal products. It is small – measuring about 20 mm across the outspread wings – dark and grey. It lays its eggs in the flour or meal in bins or on the sacks. The eggs are small, white when first laid, but turning brown before hatching some five to ten days later. The white caterpillars feed on the meal, spinning crude silken tunnels wherever they go and fouling the foodstuff with their strong silk threads and their excrement. They take three to five weeks to reach full size (about 12 mm). They spin silken cocoons inside which they pupate for about a fortnight, after which the adult moths appear. Each female moth lays about 300 eggs and, under African conditions, they continue breeding throughout the year, thus quickly increasing in numbers and doing serious damage in flour mills and pantries if left undisturbed.

The Indian meal moth, *Plodia interpunctella*, is related to *Ephestia* and is also often found in pantries in Africa. The moth is handsomely-marked, with front wings that are half creamy-white and half reddish-brown, and dusky-grey hind wings; the wingspan is some 20 mm. The female lays her eggs in meal, dried fruits, breakfast foods – in fact in almost any stored product that is edible. The caterpillars burrow through the food, fouling it with their webs and excrement, and quickly rendering it unfit for human consumption. During the colder months of the year they hibernate as caterpillars, but continue their activities as soon as temperatures start to rise.

The Karoo caterpillar, *Loxostege frustalis*, is a notorious pest in sheep-farming areas where it destroys the foliage of the valuable fodder bush, *Pentzia incana*. In some years it appears in vast numbers and does great damage to the veld, whilst in other years it is not nearly so common. The young caterpillar, green or almost black in colour, spins a silken web over the plant but ceases to do so as it grows older. It reaches full size (about 25 mm) in two to four weeks, depending on the weather, and then makes its way to the ground and buries itself in the soil, where it spins a cocoon. It may rest for some months as a caterpillar inside the cocoon or it may change into a pupa after only a few days' rest; whatever the case, the adult moth emerges about a fortnight after pupation – the speed of the change dependent again on the weather conditions.

The moth measures nearly 25 mm when the wings are spread and is brown with cream-coloured spots on the forewings. Active both by day and night, the moths are attracted in enormous numbers to light, particularly on warm moist evenings. The eggs are deposited singly or in small clusters on the underside of the leaves of food-plants, and they hatch in five to ten days.

Like other moths, the Karoo caterpillar is parasitized by a number of flies and wasps which generally keep its numbers down. However, when climatic conditions are favourable, the moth increases enormously in numbers and does great harm. Some 25 years ago in South Africa attempts were made to control the Karoo caterpillar 'biologically' by importing *Chelonus* wasps in the hope that they would breed; unfortunately this enormous project failed because the parasites never became established in the Karoo.

The wax moth, *Galleria mellonella*, is well-known to beekeepers in Africa as it is very common and widely dispersed. Dull grey, the moth ranges from 30-50 mm across its expanded wings. The female creeps into a beehive at night, particularly into a hive in which the bees have been weakened and reduced in numbers by disease and where the combs as a result are not well guarded. Combs that have been removed from the hive and stored also attract the female, particularly if the cells still contain pollen. She lays her eggs in crevices and cracks or inside the cells. The eggs hatch after about ten days and the caterpillars, dirty-white in colour, feed on the comb, boring their way through it in all directions and lining their tunnels with silk. A few of these caterpillars will quickly ruin a comb, reducing it to an unsightly mass of riddled cells from which silken tubes and excrement hang. A strong colony of bees can usually defend their home, but a weak colony may be overrun and the bees will desert the hive, leaving the caterpillars to complete the destruction of the combs.

The caterpillar is fully grown in about a month, whereupon it seeks out some corner in the hive to spin its cocoon of tough white silk. It frequently gnaws an oval hollow in the wood with its strong jaws, to form a snug resting place for itself. If the caterpillars are numerous their cocoons will be found piled in dense masses in a corner of the hive or on top of the frames, below the roof. There are three generations of the moths a year and the worst damage usually occurs during the late summer months.

The lesser wax moth, *Achroia grisella*, is a pale greyish brown moth with a wingspan of approximately 20 mm. The caterpillars of this moth are sometimes found destroying honeycombs in association with their larger relative, but they are not as common nor harmful.

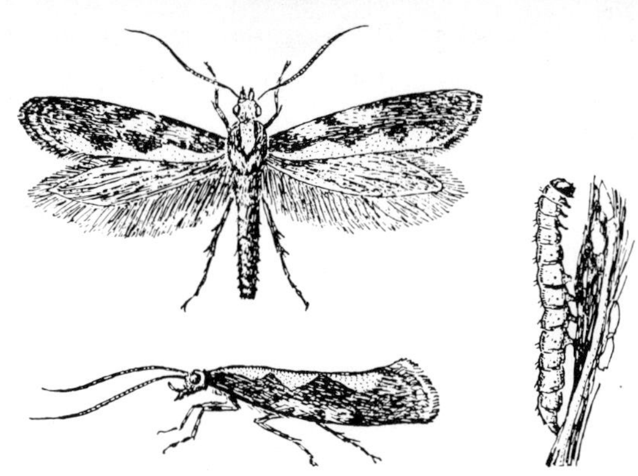

249. Caterpillar and adult of the diamond-back moth, *Plutella xylostella*.

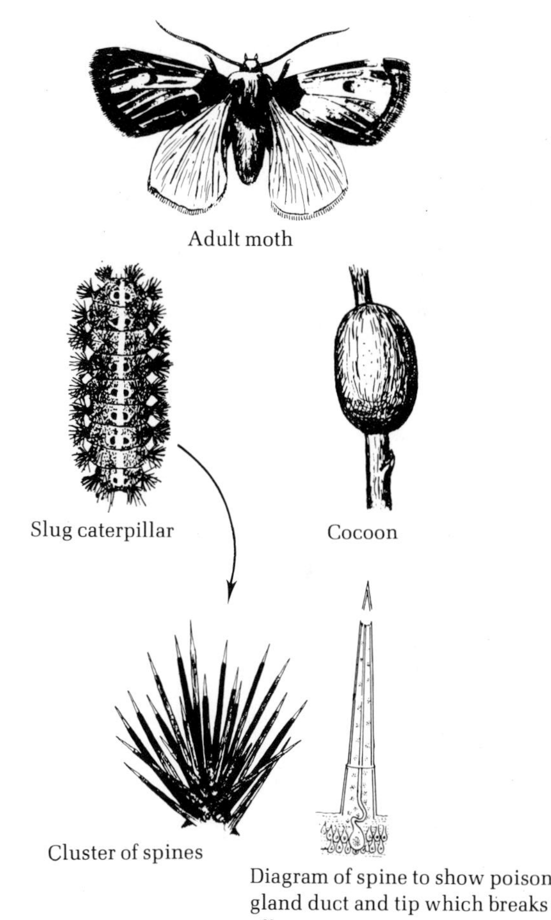

250. Features of the slug caterpillar, *Latoia vivida*.

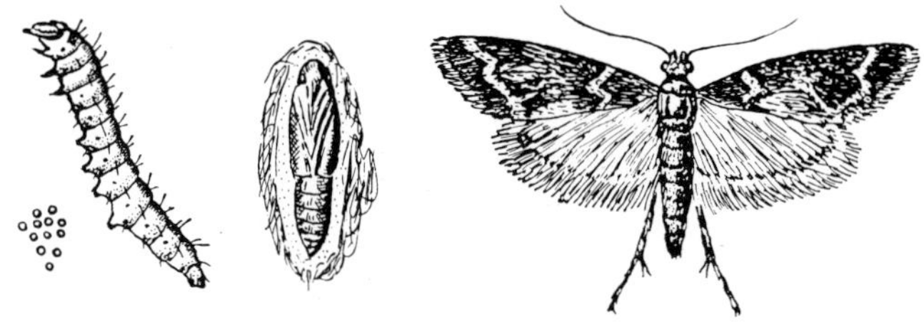

251. The Mediterranean flour moth, *Ephestia kuehniella*, showing (from left to right) eggs, caterpillar, pupa and adult.

Their galleries are smaller and the webs are finer and closer to the surface. Besides leaving debris in beehives, the caterpillars will attack dried fruit and other stored foods.

All the above moths belong to an enormous family of small to medium-sized moths called the Pyralidae, which is divided into a number of subfamilies. The caterpillars' habits vary, and many live in concealment; they are mostly slender, nearly bare, and have little or no colour pattern. Many wriggle backwards or forwards in their burrows when disturbed.

Although many moths of this great family are serious pests there is at least one species that is undoubtedly beneficial; this is the grey prickly pear moth, *Cactoblastis cactorum*. Some 30 mm across the outspread wings, it is greyish-brown in colour, with indistinct markings on the front wings and the paler hind wings. Like its foodplant the prickly pear, it is a native of America. However, it was introduced to South Africa nearly 50 years ago to help eradicate prickly pears that infested some one million fertile hectares, rendering them useless for any agricultural purposes. It had previously been introduced into Australia where it proved very successful in destroying prickly pears. Unfortunately, this was not the case in South Africa, although more than 500 million moth eggs were distributed during the project! This failure was due to several factors, including extremes of temperature, hail, and fungous and bacterial diseases. The severe conditions along with predaceous insects, baboons, monkeys, rodents and birds killed the caterpillars. As a result, other insects, such as the cochineal, *Dactylopius opuntiae*, had to be introduced to assist the moths in eliminating the prickly pears.

When adult, the moth has rudimentary mouthparts and does not feed. Consequently it lives for only about one week in this state. The female deposits her eggs end to end in the form of a chain called an egg-stick, one egg adhering to another by means of a brownish mucilaginous substance secreted by the moth. Each egg is shaped like a tiny flat cheese and there are about 100 in a stick 25 mm long. Usually she chooses the tip of a spine on the prickly pear pad as the site for her egg-stick, and the slender columns of eggs look like curved prolongations of the spines. The eggs hatch in 20-70 days, depending on the temperature.

The newly-hatched larvae congregate at the base of the spine and then burrow into the pad. Gregarious throughout their lives, they feed on the soft tissues as they tunnel through them, returning to their silk-lined retreat to rest. Their excreta are thrust out of the entrance hole where they form an untidy mass, held by sap that has oozed from the hole. At times the caterpillars may leave the interior of the pad and cluster on the outside, near the entrance hole, where they rest for some time before re-entering the pad to feed again.

The caterpillars moult five times and are fully grown in six or seven weeks in summer, but this process takes much longer in winter. They are then about 25 mm long and a rich, salmon colour, marked with black. At this stage they leave the pad, drop to the ground, and each seeks out a sheltered spot to make its cocoon, which is white, but stained red at one end by secretions of the larva; the pupal stage lasts three to ten weeks. Meanwhile, the prickly pear pads that have been attacked rot, and a badly infested plant may die. In this way the caterpillars destroy the plants and, under favourable conditions, may eradicate them altogether over large areas.

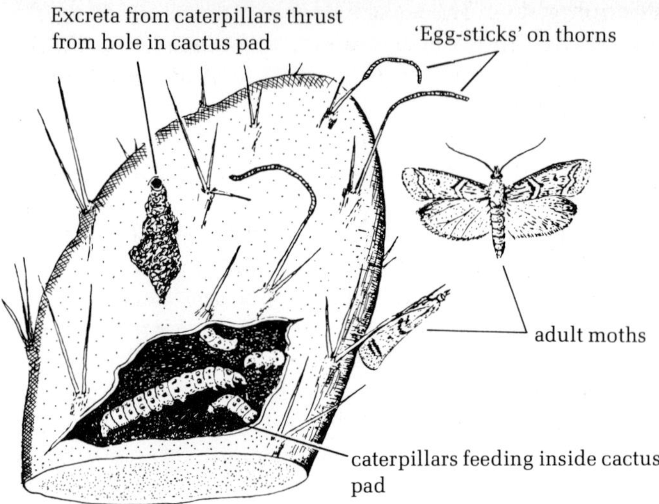

252. The prickly pear moth, *Cactoblastis cactorum*, showing important features of its life cycle.

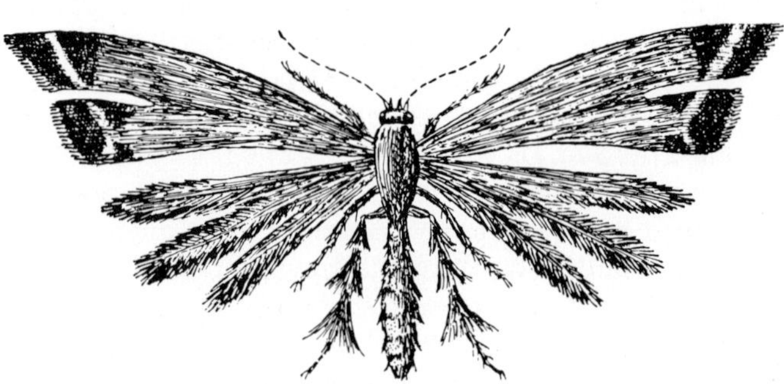

253. Plume moths of the family Pterophoridae are easily recognised by the division of the fore- and hind wings into a total of five to seven sections. Wingspan 15 mm.

Plume moths The beautiful little plume moths are readily distinguished from all others by their deeply fissured wings. They appear to have five or six narrow wings on each side as the front wings are split into two and, in some cases (although rarely), three or four sections, and the hind wings into three. A number of species are found in Africa but little is known about them. The small, slender caterpillars usually feed exposed on flowers and leaves but some bore into stems and seed-pods. Plants of the daisy family (Compositae) are their favoured food. Pupation takes place in light cocoons generally constructed above ground in a sheltered spot on the foodplant. The family is known as the Pterophoridae.

There is a family which superficially resembles the

Pterophoridae, but in fact is not related. This is the Alucitidae, the 'many-plumed' moths, in which the forewing is divided into six, and the hind wing into six or seven plumes.

Looper caterpillars Although they differ so widely in form and appearance, all caterpillars are built on the same pattern: each has a head and 13 segments, three thoracic, and ten abdominal. The simple eyes, usually six in number, are located near the base of the pair of very short antennae on the head. The jaws are large and strong, with a pair of maxillae behind them and the pointed spinneret projecting between them; these mouthparts are profoundly different from those of the adult and change completely when the larva turns into a pupa.

There are nine spiracles along each side of the body, one on the first thoracic segment and one on each of the first eight abdominal segments; spiracles are absent from the second and third thoracic segments, possibly because the wing-buds develop beneath the skin in these segments and spiracles and tracheae would get in their way. There is a pair of legs on each thoracic segment and these six are the true legs. In addition there are temporary legs, found only in the caterpillar stage on some of the abdominal segments; these are called prolegs, or false legs. Generally there are four pairs of these false legs, on the third to sixth abdominal segments, and a fifth pair of claspers on the last segment, but some of these are absent in certain caterpillars.

Most of us are familiar with those caterpillars that walk in a peculiar fashion, bringing their hind legs close up to the front legs, and arching their body before reaching forward again. These are called loopers, geometers, or earth-measurers because of this mode of walking. If one of these slender caterpillars is examined only one pair of prolegs will be found, on the ninth segment of the body, apart from the pair of claspers on the last segment. As they have no feet by which to support the middle part of their body, they loop it up out of the way as they move. These caterpillars are characteristic of the large family of moths known as the Geometridae.

From March to July a moth with grey wings, lined and marked with darker grey, may often be seen resting on the trunks of trees with its wings flat and spread out, matching the colour of the lichen-covered bark so closely that it is difficult to detect. This is the geometrid moth, *Ascotis selenaria*. The caterpillar resembles a twig and, if disturbed, will stretch itself out and remain motionless, stiff and straight, so that it too closely matches its surroundings. It feeds on the foliage of pepper trees and citrus and, when fully grown, buries itself in the soil to pupate.

Geometrid moths vary considerably in size but the majority are small with antennae of moderate length, often pectinate in the males. The wings are relatively large and when the moth is at rest they are not folded one above the other but are held open and pressed down against the surface on which the moths are settled; some

254. Looking for all the world like a twig, a geometrid caterpillar holds itself rigidly at an angle to maintain its disguise, using a thin strand of silk to brace itself against the wind. 25 mm.

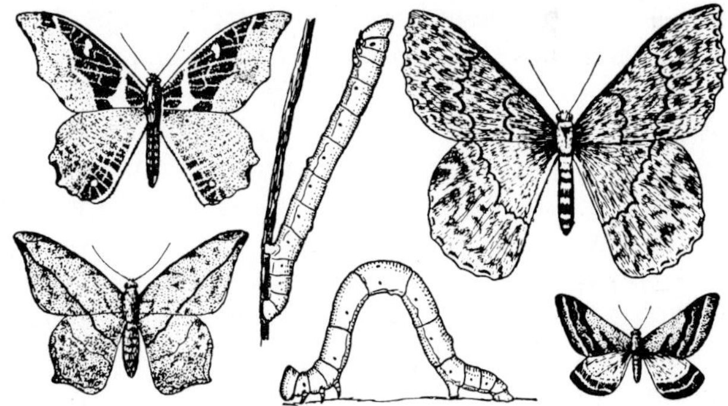

255. Some African geometrid moths: *Victoria fuscithorax* (top left, wingspan 40 mm) is white, heavily marked with dark green; *Semiothisa simpliciliņea* (bottom left) is pale brown mottled with darker brown; *Pingasa abyssinaria* (top right) is white with black and grey marking; *Ortholitha cryptospilata* (bottom right) is grey with brown markings. A typical 'looper caterpillar' of the Geometridae is shown walking (bottom centre) and resting (top centre).

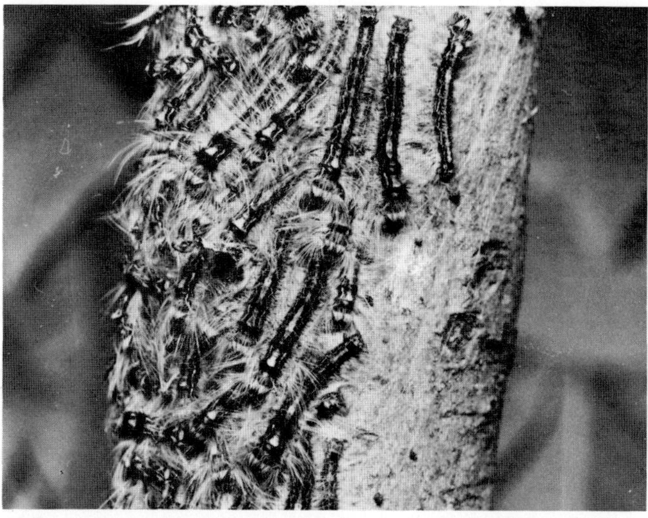

256. Lasiocampid caterpillars clustering on the trunk of a rose bush during daytime; after dark they will disperse to feed on the leaves. 40 mm.

species hold their wings above their backs like butterflies. The females of some species have degenerate wings or are completely wingless.

Lappet moths and tent caterpillars The family Lasiocampidae comprises moderate to large-sized moths with stout bodies and densely scaled wings. They do not feed in the adult state as their mouthparts are imperfect. The caterpillars are hairy and spin firm, oval cocoons of hair and silk. Many are gregarious and spin a community of silken webs on their foodplants – hence the name 'tent-caterpillars'.

In November and December, and again in February, March and April, hairy caterpillars, 25 mm long when fully grown, may be abundant on pepper trees. They are also found in fewer numbers feeding on the leaves of indigenous taaibos (*Rhus* species), for this is their natural foodplant, although the exotic pepper trees seem to be more to their taste. The body of the caterpillar, despite its yellowish appearance, is actually black, although there are two narrow yellow lines on each side; the yellow tinge comes from its coating of coloured hair.

The caterpillars feed together in small groups, and if the tree has been defoliated and they are hungry, they may resort to cannibalism, the larger caterpillars killing and devouring the smaller ones. They cast their skin four times during their growth, and reach full size in 50-60 days. When fully grown they crawl to the ground and swallow particles of soil which they first grind to a fine powder with their mandibles. Then they creep about, hunting for a suitable place to spin their cocoons; they may crawl back up the tree, onto fences or walls, or into cracks in the bark. Once fixed, they spin oval cocoons of dense silk, plastered on the inside with a paste made from saliva and the fine soil particles. The brown cocoons, some 20 mm long, are flattened on the side attached to the support. After resting for two or three weeks inside the cocoon, the caterpillar changes into a pupa and, if it belongs to the first generation of the year, the adult moth appears about a fortnight later. However, caterpillars of the second generation that reach full size in April or May, hibernate as larvae inside their cocoons and the moths emerge only the following October.

The female lays some 200 straw-coloured oval eggs in clusters which form a band about 25 mm long round a twig or petiole of a leaf; after about two weeks, just before hatching, the eggs turn blue-black in colour. At times a serious pest of pepper trees, this insect has been given the popular name of 'pepper-tree' caterpillar; its scientific name is *Bombycomorpha pallida*. The moth is pure white with a small round yellow spot on each front wing, and its wingspan is some 35 mm.

The brown pine-tree moth, *Nadiasa concolor,* is a member of the Lasiocampidae that sometimes does serious damage in pine plantations. The female moth, whose wingspan is 35 mm, is larger than the male, whose wingspan is only about 25 mm. Both are nut-brown, although the female has paler hind wings than the male. The moths appear in winter and the female lays her spherical white eggs in small batches on the tips of pine needles. The full-grown caterpillar is about 50 mm long, with long silky hairs along the sides of its body and its colour closely matches that of the pine bark. Before pupating it encloses itself in a spindle-shaped cocoon of brown silk, generally on the bark of the tree and in an angle where a branch forks. The second generation of moths emerges in November and December.

Towards the end of spring, in October and November, hairy caterpillars about 50 mm long are found feeding on the common 'Kannabas', *Passerina vulgaris,* on mountain slopes in the south western Cape; they are dark brown with yellow heads and thoraxes and yellow patches along their sides. The full-grown caterpillars may be seen scurrying restlessly over the ground, searching for suitable spots such as a hollow beneath a stone, a crevice between two stones, a hole amid exposed roots, or even a heap of debris in which to spin their cocoons. These are large, oval, compact structures of silk mixed with the hairs from the caterpillar's body; if carelessly handled, the sharp tips of the hairs may pierce the skin and break off, causing a mild irritation.

The light brown pupa inside the cocoon ranges in size from 20-35 mm; the smaller ones are males and the larger ones females. The male moth is a handsome creature measuring some 30 mm across its expanded wings and deep chocolate brown with a distinctive white oval spot on each wing. His mouthparts are reduced and he cannot feed. The female is very different from her mate, quite wingless, her head, eyes and antennae very small and her tiny, short legs are useless for any practical purpose. Consequently she never leaves her cocoon but awaits the male who seeks her out, mates with her and then dies. She lays about 100 oval, yellow eggs inside her cocoon, wriggling as she does so, so that the fine yellow scales on her body are rubbed off and form a soft bed for the eggs. Finally only her dead, shrivelled body remains, with the eggs wrapped in their dense, soft coat of scales. These lie dormant in the cocoon all through the summer, autumn and the winter, and hatch only the following spring – there is, therefore, only one generation of these moths a year. This insect has no common name, but is known to science as *Mesocelis montana.* Similar species are found in other parts of Africa.

The empty cocoons of certain Lasiocampid moths (*Pachypasa, Gonometa* and *Trabata* species) are used as ornaments by several tribes in Africa. They are strung together to form bracelets or anklets and small pebbles are placed inside the cocoons, producing a rattling sound when the ornaments are worn for a dance.

Sometimes, especially if there is drought, cattle swallow the cocoons of *Gonometa* – the silk, however, is resistant to digestive juices – and once in the rumen it is unwound from the cocoons, and forms great impacted lumps with the food mass. These cattle usually die unless the obstructions are removed surgically.

Silkworms The common silkworm, *Bombyx mori*, belongs to the family Bombycidae, and is so well known that it does not warrant detailed description here. What is not generally known, however, is that the eggs of this moth can be artificially hatched in a much shorter period than the usual ten months. Experiments show that one-day-old eggs dipped in concentrated hydrochloric acid for five minutes will hatch two to three weeks later. Eggs kept in the acid for ten minutes or longer are killed, as are newly-laid eggs, whose egg-shell is too soft.

Another interesting point about silkworm eggs is that some can be made to hatch even though they have not been fertilised, by gentle stroking with a soft camelhair brush. We do not know why this treatment should induce parthenogenesis. Silkworms that are fully grown and ready to spin their cocoons can be robbed of their silk in the following way: place the caterpillar in a tube just wide enough to receive it, with its head projecting; draw a silken thread from the spinneret and coil it around a drum. If the drum is turned at the right speed all the silk can be wound directly onto it. Apparently the silk then has a brighter colour and a more lustrous sheen than that resulting if the caterpillar spins its cocoon normally and the silk is then unwound.

Emperor moths The emperor moths, Saturniidae, include the largest moths in the world, the wing expanse of certain species being nearly 25 cm. They are characterised by these large, heavily-scaled wings, with a conspicuous eye-spot in the centre of each; by the strongly plumose antennae of the males; and by the atrophied mouthparts of the adults. Certain species of emperor moths yield silk of commercial value.

The large, handsome pine tree emperor moth *Imbrassia cytherea*, is well-known in timber-growing areas of South Africa, for in those years when it is abundant, its caterpillars do considerable harm to the pine plantations, defoliating the trees. The moth measures about 13 cm across the outspread wings; the female is larger and more stoutly built than the male and she also has simple, threadlike feelers which contrast with his feathery ones. None of the moths of this family can feed as their mouthparts are imperfect, and, despite their robust and strong appearance, they live only a few days in the adult state. Although pine trees are infested most often, the natural foodplant of this species is *Rhus angustiofolia*, 'taaibos'; the caterpillars may also be found feeding on the sugar bush, Cape beech, watsonias, and other native plants, as well as on wattles, eucalyptus, apples, guavas and quinces. The female is remarkably catholic in her choice of where she lays her eggs.

The moths appear in April, May and June, and the females lay their white, spherical eggs in small clusters on the twigs and foliage of foodplants. The substance with which the eggs are glued in position soon turns brown, giving the eggs a blotched appearance. A female lays from 150-200 eggs before her ovaries are exhausted and she dies. The eggs hatch after three to four weeks.

257. The pupa of a lasiocampid moth being removed from its cocoon (after the highly irritating spines have been rubbed off), by a Kalahari Bushman; the pupa will be cooked and eaten, and the cocoon, with a few small stones inside it, used as an ankle rattle.

258. A silkworm moth laying her eggs. The origins of these most notable of domesticated insects are lost in the history of ancient China; they are today unknown in the wild. Generations of selective breeding have resulted in silkworm moths having lost their power of flight.

259. Adult emperor moth (*Gonimbrasia belina*) showing the 'eye-spots' in both fore and hind wings which characterise this family. Wingspan 90 mm.

The newly-hatched caterpillars make their first meal of the empty eggshells, remaining clustered round them for two or three days. It seems that this preliminary meal of eggshell is essential for the young caterpillars, because if they are removed immediately after hatching they will wander about restlessly, refuse to feed, and consequently die. Having eaten all or part of the eggshell, the young larva begins to feed on the foliage. It moults six times in the course of its growth, is between 100-130 mm long when fully grown, and is striking in appearance: each segment of the body is striped with bands made up of tiny blue, green and yellow spots.

The caterpillars may be found on the trees from June to December. As soon as they are fully-grown they leave the trees and wander about on the ground, looking for loose soil into which to burrow. When a suitable spot is found, the caterpillar tunnels down to a depth of some 50 mm and hollows out a cell. After a week or so it changes into a pupa, red at first but soon turning black; the pupal stage lasts for five or six months and there is only one generation of these moths a year. In some parts of Africa the moths may be found on the wing from January to April.

A closely-allied moth that is also common at times is the willow-tree moth, *Gonimbrasia tyrrhea.* The adults are on the wing in October and the females lay their eggs on thorn trees (which seem to be their natural food-plants), wattles, pines, willows, poplars and oaks. The full-grown caterpillar, about 90 mm long, is a conspicuous insect with light blue and red markings on a velvety black background. Its life history is similar to that of the pine tree emperor moth.

Gonimbrasia belina is an interesting emperor moth; its caterpillars are often abundant on the mopane trees in the northern Transvaal, and these 'mopane worms' are collected for food by local African tribes. They are even sold in certain shops in Johannesburg.

The thorn-tree emperor moth, *Gynanisa maia,* is another large and handsome member of this family that is common and widely distributed. The moth measures about 13 cm across the outspread wings and is on the wing in November. The female lays her eggs on thorn-trees and the caterpillars are light green with rows of white and yellow points along the body. The cabbage-tree emperor moth, *Bunaea alcinoe,* can be caught during October. Its striking caterpillars may be found on the cabbage tree or kiepersol *(Cussonia)* during December – they are black with four rows of prominent white spines; the spiracles are orange, surrounded by scarlet.

If a virgin female of any of these moths is obtained – and this is easily done by rearing some of the caterpillars in captivity – an interesting phenomenon can be staged. When the stout-bodied female emerges from the pupa, and after she has spread and dried her wings, she should be placed in a box with a gauze cover. In the evening the windows of the room should be left open. Soon after dark, particularly if a warm evening, numbers of great moths of the same species as the imprisoned female will come fluttering into the room. The box containing the imprisoned female will attract them irresistibly. If the visitors are examined, they will all be found to be males (identified by their feathery antennae). Should one of them succeed in gaining access to the female and mate with her, the others quickly lose interest and depart.

This attraction of a number of males to a virgin female is described by entomologists as 'assembling', and is sometimes used to obtain specimens. If an enthusiast were to go out and hunt for the moths he might scour the neighbourhood fruitlessly for a long time whereas a single unmated female can draw males from far and wide. This assembling of the males does occur with other species of moths as well, but common to all the species where this happens are males with striking plumose antennae. Indeed, if these antennae are cut off, the male at once seems to lose all interest in the female. It is therefore assumed that the sense that enables him to find her is lodged in these feelers and that he is attracted by a subtle, far-spreading scent (a pheromone), given off by the virgin.

Hawk moths The hawk moths, Sphingidae, are a family of moderate to large-sized moths that are mostly very striking in appearance, with long, coiled tongues and narrow wings which enable the moths to hover in front of flowers as they feed and fly swiftly. The caterpillars are smooth and easily recognised by a curious horn, the function of which is unknown, on the penultimate segment of the abdomen. They usually pupate in the soil.

The death's head hawk moth, *Acherontia atropos,* is widely feared in South Africa as it is reputed to have a sting that can inflict a deadly wound. However, it is quite harmless. The so-called sting comes from the rather short proboscis, coiled up beneath the head when not in use, which is extended when the moth wishes to sip honey (as it frequently does). There are some slender, sharp spines on the hind legs that might prick the fingers slightly if the moth is handled, but that is the worst it can do. The alarm evoked by the moth is intensified by the rather sinister-looking yellow mark resembling a skull on its thorax. The popular name is derived from this mark.

The moth can also utter a squeak of protest when it is handled, and this is liable to startle a person not prepared for it. There is still some doubt as to exactly how the moth utters its peculiar call. Like all insects, it has no voice in the usual sense of the word. It was once thought that the moth made the sound by rubbing its two palps rapidly together, but nowadays it is believed that the insect trumpets like a miniature elephant when agitated – squeaking pulsatingly through its proboscis by a double sucking action, and blowing through a basal membrane. The death's head hawk moth can squeak even before it has emerged from the pupa.

Although not often seen, this moth which steals honey from beehives is fairly common in most parts of Africa; beekeepers and potato-farmers come across it most often. The death's head hawk moth has a very wide geographical range: from England, through Europe and

Africa, to the Cape. It is a powerful flier and can migrate long distances in search of food and plants on which to lay its eggs. In several instances, these moths were caught on ships far out at sea – both in the Mediterranean and off the coasts of France and Portugal. They are also found throughout Asia, although those in India and China differ slightly in colouring and are regarded as a separate species by some naturalists, while others view them only as varieties of the same species. They are not found in America or Australia.

The moth is some 10 cm across the outspread wings; the front wings are a deep brown, mottled with lighter brown, while the hind wings are yellow with two dark brown lines across them. The stout body is brown with yellow markings down each side. The male moth has a scent gland on each side of his abdomen, where it joins the thorax. Each consists of tufts of long, reddish scales lodged in a cavity and he can thrust these tufts out at will; at the same time the scent glands produce a liquid which gives off a musk-like odour. When the tufts are withdrawn and the openings to the cavities closed, there is no smell. Apparently the moth makes use of these organs only when courting the female.

The female lays her eggs on a variety of plants, but usually chooses plants belonging to the potato family. The eggs are small relative to the size of the moth, and light green in colour. They are laid singly on the leaves, scattered over a wide area, and take about a fortnight to hatch.

The full-grown caterpillar is a most striking insect. Some 15 cm long, its body is green or yellow with seven slanting purple stripes along each side; like the rest of the family, it has a curved tail on the end of its body. Although the caterpillars are so large and brightly-coloured, they are far from easy to find in a field of potatoes as they rest on the underside of the leaves and their colours and stripes blend with the colours and shadows of their surroundings. The destruction they wreak on the foliage and the large black droppings that litter the ground beneath infested plants reveal their presence.

If a caterpillar is disturbed it will draw in its head and sometimes make an audible clicking sound. The sound may be imitated by clicking the finger-nail under the thumb-nail and has been compared with the sound made by an electric spark. Sometimes the clicks are repeated so rapidly that they make a noise like a watch being wound. Apparently the insect produces the sound by clashing its mandibles together – by gnashing its teeth as it were.

When fully grown the caterpillar leaves the plant and seeks soft soil. Here it buries itself some 15 cm beneath the surface and makes a large, earthen cell by pressing back the soil with its head. It does not spin a cocoon but rests for a fortnight or so inside its cell and then changes into a pupa. During the summer the pupal stage lasts only two or three weeks, but if the caterpillar reaches full size late in autumn it spends the whole of the winter beneath the soil as a pupa, the adult emerging only with the advent of warmer weather in spring.

260. A moon moth *(Argema mimosae)*, newly emerged from its silvery silken cocoon. The cocoon silk from certain emperor moth larvae has been commercially exploited. Wingspan 100 mm.

261. Emperor moth caterpillars are but one of the many different kinds of insects eaten in Africa. Here 'mopane worms' (caterpillars of *Gonimbrasia belina*), which make a highly nutritious dish, are collected here by a Tsonga woman. 55 mm.

262. Head-on view of male emperor moth *(Argema mimosae)* showing the large, plumed antennae which are able to detect the scent of the female in incredibly low concentrations, over a great distance.

The convolvulus hawk moth, *Agrius convolvuli*, is another large hawk moth found throughout Africa. The caterpillars feed on the morning glory and an allied species of *Ipomoea*, and they are at times a serious pest, attacking sweet-potatoes. When fully grown they are up to 12 cm long, mostly brown in colour, with yellow or white slanting stripes along the sides and the typical tail on the end of the abdomen. They pupate in the soil like the caterpillars of the death's head moth. The moth itself is greyish-brown and its wingspan is some 12 cm. It is marked with pink and brown stripes on the abdomen and has a very long tongue which it carries coiled up like a watch-spring beneath its head when at rest.

The silver-lined hawk moth, *Hippotion celerio*, is another common and widespread species. Buff-brown in colour, it has white lines on the thorax and a prominent white band across each front wing; each hind wing is red at the base and has two black bands towards the outer margin; when extended, the wings span some 75 mm. The caterpillars of this common hawk moth often do damage to vines; they may also be found feeding on thorn trees and occasionally on tobacco and sweet-potato plants, as well as on *Ampelopsis* creepers. They are green at first, but usually turn brown as they age. They have an eyelike spot, black surrounded by a yellow ring, on each side of the head.

There are three generations of this moth a year; the first appears in the spring and gives rise to the second in December and January, which are followed by the third generation in March. The caterpillars of the third generation spend the winter as pupae in the soil. The moths deposit their spherical white eggs singly on the upper or lower surface of the leaves of the foodplants; pupation takes place in the soil.

Gregarious caterpillars Two members of the family Thaumetopoeidae, *Anaphe reticulata* and *A. panda*, have caterpillars that live in colonies of 200 or more. They are white moths with brown lines on the front wings and measure about 60 mm across the outspread wings. Found in Natal, the Transvaal and further north, the caterpillars construct a communal home of dense brown silk on their foodplant; this home is a conspicuous oval object and may be 30 cm or more in length. During the day the caterpillars remain inside their home but in the evening they leave it in a long procession, marching head to tail, to feed. As it walks, each caterpillar spins a silken thread so that a trail is laid which can be easily followed when the colony returns home after feeding. When full-grown, each caterpillar spins a thin white cocoon inside the communal home, and there may be 200 or more such cocoons lying side by side within the dense outer covering. When the moths emerge they separate.

Brown-tail moths and their kin Following the establishment of pine plantations for timber production in southern Africa, an indigenous moth turned from its native foodplants to attack these pine trees. Today *Euproctis terminalis* is called the pine brown-tail moth, and is a familiar pest. The female is about 35 mm across the outspread wings and deep yellow in colour, with a satiny lustre on the forewings and a dark-brown tuft on the end of the abdomen, which gives the moth its name. The male is smaller than the female and has plumose antennae; an active flier, with a rapid, zig-zag flight, he cannot feed as he has only vestigial mouthparts.

The female usually lays her eggs in a single, elongate cluster, near the end of a pine twig, on the bark of the main trunk, or on the pine needles. She covers her eggs with dark, buff-coloured down from her abdomen, but the spherical eggs themselves are yellow. Each cluster may contain up to 300 eggs and they are laid during February and March. The eggs hatch in three to four weeks.

When fully grown, the caterpillar is 25-30 mm in length and is black, with a narrow white line down the middle of its back and a buff-coloured band along each side. It has tufts of long white hairs on the side of each segment and down the middle of the back there is a row of tubercles that bear tiny poisonous hairs. These minute hairs are barbed and if a caterpillar is handled they can pierce the skin, setting up severe irritation. To a lesser extent the egg clusters, cocoons and adults are also armed with the poisonous, barbed hairs. All stages of the brown-tail moth should, therefore, be handled with care.

The caterpillars do great harm in the pine plantations, stripping the trees of their leaves during the winter and spring. They nibble through the needles so that the greater part falls to the ground. When fully grown they make their way down to the ground where they spin loose cocoons amid the fallen pine needles and pupate. Since the silk of the cocoons is interwoven with the caterpillars' hairs, severe poisoning may result from careless handling. The pupa is a dark, reddish-brown with groups of yellow hairs on the abdomen. The adults emerge in four to six weeks.

The thorn-tree brown-tail moth, *Euproctis fasciata*, is very similar to the pine brown-tail but has dark bands on the front wings. The caterpillar, about 30 mm long when fully grown, is found on thorn trees at midsummer and again in the autumn, as there are two generations a year. Black, with short white hairs between the segments, it has red tubercles and thick tufts of black hair along the back, and tufts of grey hair along the sides. The adults appear in January and October, having spent the winter as pupae in thin cocoons constructed amid the leaves and twigs of the foodplant. The eggs are deposited by the female in clusters on twigs of the foodplant and are covered with hairy, cream-coloured scales, the whole forming a cushion-like mass.

These stoutly-built moths belong to the family Lymantriidae, sometimes called tussock moths. They can also not feed as adults as their mouthparts are imperfect. They are mostly small to medium-sized and the males always have petinate, or comb-like, antennae. The female is distinguished by a prominent tuft of hairs on the end of her abdomen; in some cases she is wingless, but she does have functional legs and can walk about. The little brown moth, *Bracharoa dregei*, with feathery feelers, is the male of such a species; as his fat brown mate has no wings he has to seek her out in her cocoon where she remains and lays her eggs. The caterpillars of this moth may be found feeding on *Dimorphotheca* plants in May.

Tiger moths All caterpillars have short bristles, or setae, on their bodies. Even the smooth, greasy-looking larvae of the noctuids have seven short bristles on each side of each segment. But in addition to these inconspicuous primary setae, many caterpillars have long secondary bristles or hairs on their bodies. This hairy covering is believed to protect them from such enemies as birds, and apparently only cuckoos will eat them. Equipped as they are with such dense, hairy coats, these caterpillars are sometimes spoken of as 'woolly bears', and many, but by no means all, belong to the family of moths known as tiger moths, or Arctiidae.

The tiger moth owes its origin to large, brown hairy caterpillars which may sometimes be seen scurrying over the ground; each has a black body, with red spiracles and bears tufts of stiff brown hairs, amongst which are longer black bristles.

These caterpillars have no particular foodplant but seem to feed indiscriminately, travelling from one plant to the next. When fully grown and ready to pupate they are exceptionally active in their search for a suitable place in which to spin their cocoons. Having settled, the woolly bear spins a loose cocoon of soft silk, surrounded by a rough covering of soft earth and dead leaves; it then rests for about a week before changing into a short, blunt brown pupa, the cast-off caterpillar skin sticking to the hind end. After about six weeks a large moth emerges, its heavy red abdomen banded with black, yellow forewings spotted and lined with black, and dull yellow hind wings also marked with black. This is the Cape tiger moth, *Dionychopus amasis*.

Another very common and widespread tiger moth is *Diacrisia eugraphica* which may often be seen around lights. A pretty moth, about 50 mm across the outspread wings, it is white with two black wavy lines on each front wing. The hairy caterpillars may be found on various kinds of plants on the veld and in the garden in December and again in April. They pupate amid debris in loose silken cocoons on the surface of the soil. The moths are on the wing in November and again in March.

The Arctiidae are all small to moderate-sized moths and vary in their coloration and markings, but the majority are white or yellow with red and black markings on bodies and wings. The caterpillars are densely covered with a uniform hairy coat which is generally brown in colour. The pupa is always enclosed in a rough cocoon of silk and debris.

Window-winged moths Small, brightly coloured, day-flying moths, belonging to the family Ctenuchidae, are

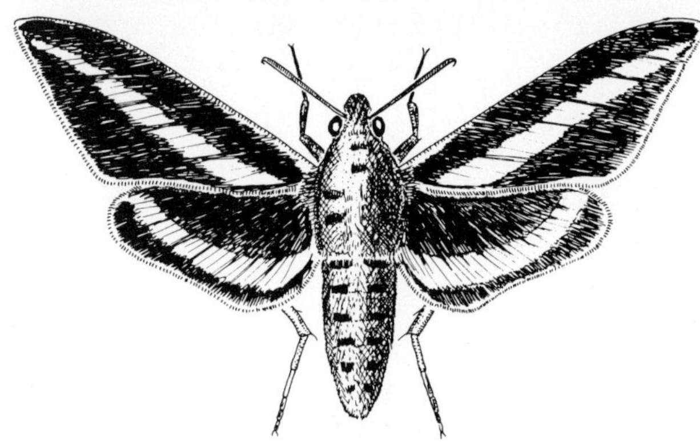

263. A typical hawk moth, showing the streamlined appearance characteristic of the family Sphingidae.

264. Second stage hawk moth caterpillar, showing the conspicuous 'tail' characteristic of caterpillars belonging to this family. 15 mm.

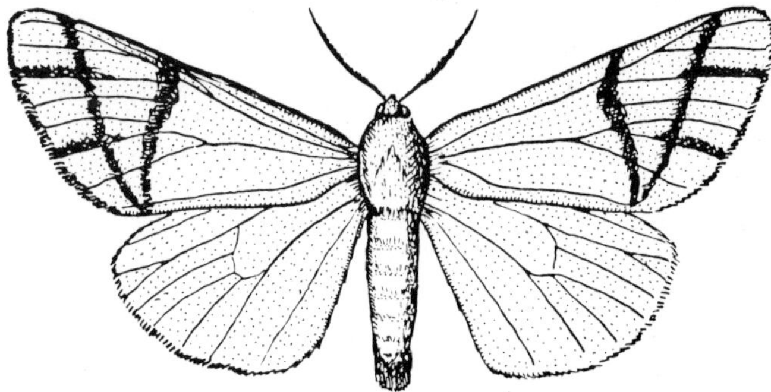

265. The communal moth, *Anaphe panda*, is white and measures about 60 mm across the wings. The caterpillars live in a communal home of brown silk and go out at night in a procession to feed.

266. A caterpillar of the tussock moth, showing the two forward-projecting tufts of black hair which are diagnostic of this group. This specimen has been parasitized internally by a braconid wasp, whose larvae have now left the body of the dying caterpillar and have spun their tiny silken cocoons on its back.

267. Tiger moths of the genus *Rhodogastria* are able to defend themselves by exuding a foul-smelling froth from glands on the thorax when threatened. 20 mm.

268. Danger passed, the frothing tiger moth conserves its body fluid by extending its proboscis and drinking the repugnant foam off its own back.

commonly seen in various places in Africa, feeding on flowers. Their common name is derived from the fact that their wings have characteristic translucent patches, devoid of scales. Some of the window-winged moths are almost wasp-like in flight. The hairy larvae feed on grasses, and the cocoons are formed principally of larval body hairs.

Cutworms and their kin Some of the worst and most persistent insect pests in farm lands and gardens are the cutworms, of which there are several species. In many parts of Africa their attacks on young maize plants, beans, cabbages, and other vegetables are so severe that crops have to be replanted two or three times. During winter the cutworms are present in the soil as full-grown caterpillars, and these pupate as soon as warmer weather arrives in spring. Two or three weeks later the moths emerge and lay their eggs in great numbers on the leaves of their foodplants; it is then that the cutworms develop to give so much trouble in September, October and November.

The moths belong to the very large and important family known as the Noctuidae, sometimes popularly called owlet moths. They measure about 30 mm across the outspread wings and are dull buff in colour, with the forewings darker than the hind wings; all of them look very much alike. A single female may lay as many as 1 000 eggs before she dies and these hatch after about a week into tiny black caterpillars which feed on the weeds for a few days but soon acquire their characteristic habit of lying hidden beneath the soil all day, coming out to feed at night.

When fully grown the cutworm is some 30 mm long, with a smooth body and a dull grey or brown colour. It lies coiled up in its lair beneath the soil during the day and crawls about on the surface at night to do the damage from which it derives its name. It bites off young plants at the base, leaving the top portion lying on the soil as though cut off by a knife. The caterpillar eats only a little from each plant it cuts down and it may destroy a good number of seedlings in one night's foray.

When a piece of ground is ploughed or dug over, the plants on it are destroyed and the cutworms in that area are temporarily deprived of much of their food supply. However, they can survive for some time on weeds or plant remains in the soil, and when the seedlings come up they are there, ready to strike. After it is fully grown the caterpillar buries itself 25 mm or so below the surface and there changes into a smooth, reddish-brown pupa; two or three weeks later the moth emerges. There are several generations a year.

A relative of the cutworms is the so-called army worm, the caterpillar of the moth *Spodoptera exempta*, which is found throughout Africa, in parts of Asia and in Australia. From time to time, generally towards the end of summer, there are massive outbreaks of caterpillars which can cause considerable damage to crops, pastures and gardens.

The full-grown army worm is a caterpillar some

30 mm long, variable in colour but usually velvety-black on top and yellowish-green underneath, with narrow pale-green lines along its sides. It feeds only on plants of the grass family, including maize, wheat, barley, sugar-cane, teff and so on. Feeding takes place during the day as well as during the night, with brief resting periods, but the larva is most active during the early morning and late evening. When fully grown the caterpillar buries itself about 25 mm deep in loose soil and there, by binding soil particles with silk, it forms an oval cell in which it changes into a brown pupa. The moth emerges after one to four weeks, depending upon the temperature.

The female usually lays her eggs on the underside of the leaves of the foodplant in masses of 200-300; they are covered with downy scales from her body. She may lay two or three such masses before dying. The eggs hatch two to 11 days later. As these insects do not hibernate at all, breeding goes on throughout the year. They are, however, very susceptible to cold and their natural habitat is therefore in the warmer parts of Africa.

In order to increase rapidly, the army worm needs a fairly high temperature, a humid atmosphere and an abundance of young grass. Consequently, if a farmer has burned his veld after rains and the weather is warm and the subsequent rains late, the moths find conditions eminently favourable and each lays a large number of eggs – perhaps 700 or more. These hatch in two to three days and the little caterpillars find abundant food in the succulent young grass that has sprouted over the burned areas. They are full-grown in a fortnight and the moths emerge a week or so later.

Under such circumstances the caterpillars increase very rapidly and the farmer, finding his veld suddenly invaded by great armies of pests, wonders where they have come from. Soon, however, with the onset of colder, drier weather, the food supply begins to give out and parasites and diseases multiply as so many victims are available and the horde of caterpillars dwindles just as rapidly as it grew. But they are not all wiped out: in suitable areas some survive and live unnoticed. Instead of a ravenous army devouring the veld there is only an occasional caterpillar here and there, and nobody pays them any heed. However, sooner or later – albeit years later – the combination of favourable conditions arises again and if natural enemies are absent the mystery worm swarms briefly in its millions once more. It is believed that the moths migrate in swarms at night from infested areas to lay their eggs in some distant area before they die, but this has not yet been proved.

All this is very similar to what happens with locusts, and it is interesting to note that the army worm also has gregarious and solitary phases. Caterpillars reared in cages under crowded conditions are nearly all velvety-black; this characterises the gregarious phase. If the caterpillars are reared in isolation, only one in each tube or jar, the great majority are green, or pink and green on the upper surface, and they are then said to be in the solitary phase. It seems highly probable that these phases occur in the natural state: the army worms swarming on the veld are nearly all velvety-black, but when they are few in number and scattered they are mostly green.

The lesser army worm, *Spodoptera exigua,* is very similar to *Spodoptera exempta,* but it is not as common. The caterpillar will feed on most cultivated crops, such as beans, potatoes, ground nuts and cowpeas, as well as members of the grass family, whereas the true army worm feeds only on grasses.

The maize stalk borer, *Busseola fusca,* is an African moth, apparently originally from the tropical and subtropical parts of the continent, but now widespread wherever maize is cultivated. The moth measures 35 mm across the expanded wings; its front wings are a dull coppery-brown, with inconspicuous markings; the hind wings are smoky-brown and without markings. The first moths of the season usually appear early in December when the maize plants are well-established. The female deposits her eggs in batches of 150 or more between the leaf sheath and the stem of the plant; the eggs stick to the underside of the leaf sheath, and if a strip is torn away the eggs come with it.

The eggs hatch in about a week and the young caterpillars feed at first under the leaf sheath, later leaving this shelter to migrate to the open top of the plant. In feeding on the rolled-up young leaves they bite holes right through them, and as they unfold the leaves reveal rows of holes that have been made by the caterpillars. After a few days the larvae burrow down into the stem; if there are too many of them on the plant some migrate to neighbouring plants.

In about 30 days the caterpillar is fully grown, lodged in its burrow in the stem. It prepares for its exit as a moth by burrowing towards the outer surface, leaving only a thin cap separating it from the air – a cap that can easily be pushed off by the adult moth. The larva then rests for a few days and turns into a pupa; three weeks later the moth emerges, generally towards the end of January.

The second generation of caterpillars complete their growth during March; some may pupate and produce another generation of moths before the winter, but the majority remain quiescent through the winter in the larval stage, as full-grown borers. These nearly always descend to the lowest part of the stem, at or below ground level.

The red bollworm, *Diparopsis castanea,* is a native insect that is attracted by the introduced cotton plant. It is found throughout Africa and is a serious pest wherever cotton is grown. The moth measures nearly 35 mm across its outspread wings; the forewings are pinkish-cinnamon, with a dark chocolate triangular patch at the base of each and a transverse olive-green band running parallel to the outer margin; the hind wings are dirty white.

The female lays her spherical grey eggs on almost any part of the cotton plant, usually singly, but sometimes in groups of two or three. The newly-hatched caterpillar makes its way to a young boll and bores into it. There it feeds for three to four weeks, by which time it is fully grown. It then leaves its burrow and makes its way to the ground where it pupates. There may be three generations of the moths a year if climatic conditions are favourable. Caterpillars that mature late in the season spend the winter in their cells in the ground.

The introduced American bollworm, *Heliothis armigera,* found throughout the world, is a common pest of cotton, lucerne, maize, tomatoes, peas, vines and fruit trees. It is known by several common names, amongst them tassel-worm or ear-worm of maize, tomato fruit-worm and tobacco bud-worm. The moth is about 35 mm across the outspread wings, with brown forewings and hind wings marked with a broad dark border. The female lays her small yellow eggs on the leaves, buds and flowers of the foodplant and she may deposit as many as 1 500 during her life of three or four weeks.

The eggs hatch after two to eight days. The caterpillars feed chiefly on the buds, flowers and fruits of their numerous food-plants and, when fully grown, are about 35 mm long, varying widely in colour from pale-green to almost black. Most have a yellowish white band along each side. The larval stage lasts two to four weeks, whereupon the caterpillars bury themselves in the soil to pupate; during summer the pupal stage lasts only two to four weeks, but caterpillars that reach full size late in the autumn spend the winter months under the ground as pupae.

Most moths that are pests do their damage as caterpillars and are harmless as adults, but it is just the opposite with the fruit-piercing moths. There are several species in Africa that do a considerable amount of damage to ripening fruits, particularly in orchards near wild trees and bush. They are large insects with greyish-brown wings measuring some 60 mm across when extended. They are strong fliers and are most active at night when most of the damage is done.

Unlike other moths, which feed only on nectar as they have mouthparts that are both degenerate and useless (indeed the majority do not feed at all in the adult state), the fruit-piercing moths have strong, sharp-tipped probosces, 25 mm long when extended, and equipped with sawlike cutting edges along the sides which enable the moths to pierce holes in fruit. They will attack apples, pears, grapes, peaches, plums, guavas and citrus fruits. Ripe fruit is preferred, but they will also feed on fruit that is still ripening.

A moth sucks the juice from the fruit by inserting its proboscis to full length after piercing a neat round hole in the skin; the proboscis is withdrawn at intervals and re-inserted at an angle, so the moth draws on the juice from a fairly wide area. In this way a dry spongy mass of tissue is left under the skin which later collapses and rots.

Three common species of fruit-piercing moths are *Achaea lienardi, Serrodes partita* and *Sphingomorpha chlorea.* The life histories of these moths have not been fully investigated, but we know that their eggs are deposited chiefly on indigenous plants. The caterpillars are nocturnal, feeding at night and hiding by day. Caterpillars of the most common and widespread of the three, *Achaea lienardi,* have been found on a wide variety of indigenous African plants.

The Noctuidae are one of the largest families of Lepidoptera, and from an economic point of view they

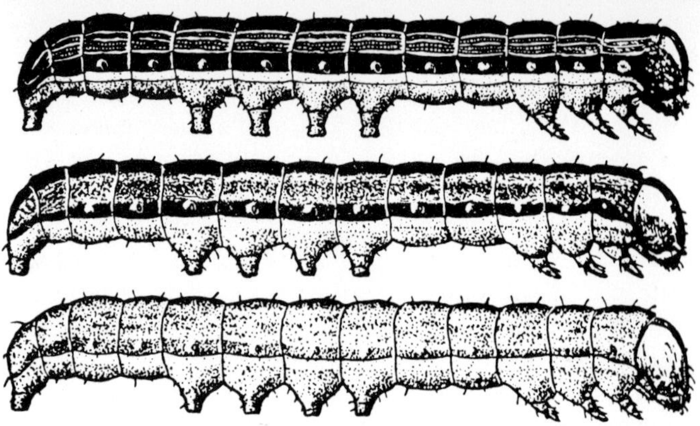

269. Army worm caterpillars have different coloration, depending on whether they are solitary or gregarious. The gregarious phase (top) is velvety black with green; transient phase (centre) is brown; while the solitary phase caterpillar (bottom) is green.

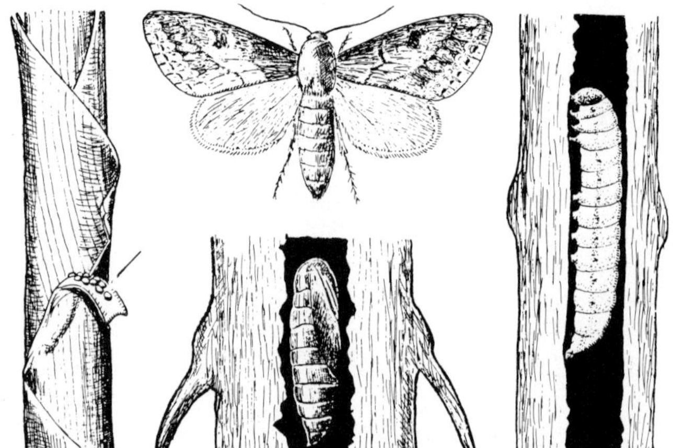

270. Features of the life history of the maize stalk borer, *Busseola fusca.*

271. American bollworm caterpillar *(Heliothis armigera)* having eaten out the inside of a cotton boll, now emerges and will make its way to the ground to pupate. 20 mm.

are certainly the most important. As shown above, they have a wide variety of life-styles, but perhaps the most remarkable of all the Noctuidae are those which feed on the eye secretions of mammals. Such moths have been recorded from Africa, Asia and South America, mostly in the tropics and subtropics. The caterpillars of these moths live on a wide variety of plants. The adult moths seek out mammals, sit at the lower edge of the eyeball and insert the proboscis into the conjunctiva; they are proven transmitters of certain eye diseases of cattle and sheep. Various species of the genus *Arcyophora* are common in Africa, with *A. longivalvis* one of the most widely distributed of eye frequenters.

CLASSIFICATION

ORDER **Lepidoptera**

The identification of moths and butterflies is to a great extent based on the venation of the wings. To see the veins properly, the wings have to be treated to remove the scales, or bleached. This damages the appearance of the specimen, and is only normally done by professional entomologists. For this reason no attempt has been made to give comprehensive descriptions of the moth families, although a simple key is provided to the butterflies. Readers interested in the more serious study of the Lepidoptera should refer to the extensive literature available on the group.

SUBORDER **Zeugloptera**

FAMILY Micropterygidae
Very small metallic moths that fly by day. They have functional mandibles with which they grind pollen grains. Larvae characterised by having eight pairs of abdominal legs, each terminating in a hook.

SUBORDER **Monotrysia**

FAMILY Hepialidae
Sometimes very small, sometimes large moths. Antennae very short, and mandibles lacking. Female genitalia unusual, with one, or two, genital openings on sternum IX-X.

SUBORDER **Ditrysia**
About 98% of all species of Lepidoptera are included in this suborder. The moths may be very small or very large. Mandibles are lacking, the mouthparts sometimes functional and very well developed, sometimes vestigial and not used for feeding. There are two genital openings on the female abdomen, one on sternum VIII, for mating, the other on sternum IX-X for egg-laying.

FAMILY Cossidae
Medium to large, heavy-bodied moths, dull grey or brown with spotted or mottled wings. Wings long and narrow, frequently with few scales. Larvae are long-lived, wood-boring and sometimes cause serious damage to trees.

FAMILY Tortricidae
A large family of small moths with wide and densely scaled wings of dull coloration. The majority fly at dusk with rapid darting flight. The caterpillars are small, slender, smooth and live in concealment; they burrow into the fruits, buds or other parts of their foodplant, or else roll leaves and tie them with silk for shelters.

FAMILY Psychidae
Small, mostly stout-bodied moths, the males with scales few or absent, dull coloured without striking patterns; swift fliers. The females are usually wingless, without legs, antennae and eyes and remain inside the cases, or bags, that are constructed by caterpillars ('bagworms') of both sexes.

FAMILY Tineidae
A huge family of small moths, usually with narrow wings bordered with long hairy fringes. Head with rough scales or bristles, antennae with a whorl of erect scales on each segment. Larvae are scavengers, feed on foliage or fungi, and a few species are economically important as they damage fabrics.

FAMILY Aegeriidae
Small to medium, wasp-like moths, with long, sometimes transparent wings with large areas devoid of scales. Body long and slender, often with red or yellow markings. Often sexually dimorphic. Active in the day and fly in the hottest sunshine. Larvae bore into stems and roots of their foodplants and may be economically important in damaging crops and trees.

FAMILY Yponomeutidae
Small moths, sometimes larger and brightly coloured in the tropics. Front wings usually with spots or other bold patterns. Larvae usually feed under webs they spin on the leaves of foodplants; a few species are leaf miners and some bore into fruit.

FAMILY Gelechiidae
A large family of small to minute moths, front wing often narrow and pointed at the tip. Larval habits vary widely, include leaf rollers, leaf miners, gall makers, grain borers and potato leaf and tuber feeders.

FAMILY Alucitidae
Many-plumed moths, both wings cleft into six or more narrow plumelike divisions, densely fringed with hairs along both margins. Larvae burrow into shoots and stems, and may cause galls.

FAMILY Limacodidae
A small family of small to medium-sized moths, stout-bodied with broad rounded wings, brown or green in colour. Larvae short, broad, 'slug caterpillars' with retractile head, minute legs and poisonous spines. Cocoon is brown, smooth, oval or rounded with a hard shell.

FAMILY Pyralidae
A very large family of small moths, its members occurring commonly everywhere. Often dull brown or grey in colour, slender-bodied, with long wings lacking fringes, and long slender legs. Frequently attracted to lights at night. Larval habits extremely varied, include many pest species of stored products, also attack beeswax, cactus leaves and various economically important plants.

FAMILY Pterophoridae
Forewings usually cleft in two or three divisions, hind wings into three; small and slender plume moths, grey, brown and other light colours are common. Caterpillars oval and short, often with rough hairs or spines; they feed openly on their foodplants, which are frequently members of the Compositae.

FAMILY Geometridae
A very large family of small to medium, slender moths with relatively large wings, often held horizontally at rest. Larvae are characteristic 'looper caterpillars' with only two or three pairs of abdominal prolegs, feed on foliage of wide variety.

FAMILY Lasiocampidae
Medium to large brown moths, densely scaled and stout-bodied, frequently attracted to light. Antennae pectinate in both sexes but more pronounced in male; proboscis absent. Caterpillars may construct shelters and sometimes live gregariously; they are armed with lateral tufts of hair that are easily detached and may cause skin irritation. Cocoon is firm, dense and comprised of silk and larval hairs, often in or below larval foodplants.

FAMILY Bombycidae
A small family of pale, heavy-bodied moths, typified by the silkworm which has been spread throughout the world. Antennae pectinate in both sexes, more pronounced in male.

FAMILY Saturniidae
Medium to large moths, often striking and brightly coloured, nearly always with an eye-spot in each wing. Antennae somewhat plumose, especially in males. Mouthparts reduced, and adults do not feed. Larvae are stout, smooth and often brightly coloured, sometimes with tubercles and spines. Feed on a wide variety of foodplants, and pupate in a firm, stout cocoon.

FAMILY Sphingidae
Moderate to large moths with stout bodies, narrow pointed wings, and strong smooth flight. Proboscis normally well developed, sometimes extremely long, used to probe flowers for nectar while hovering. Antennae thickened towards tips, often with small terminal hook. Caterpillars have a conspicuous dorsal projection on abdominal segment VIII, and often have bright zig-zag markings down their sides.

FAMILY Thaumetopoeidae
Moderately stout, pale moths, sometimes included in the family Notodontidae. Caterpillars gregarious, and leave silken trails when foraging.

FAMILY Lymantridae
Medium-sized moths, usually plainly coloured, mouthparts non-functional and adults do not feed. Male antennae conspicuously plumose, and extremity of female abdomen often with a prominent tuft of hairs. Caterpillars distinctive, having a pair of pencil-like hair tufts at each end, and four short thick tufts on the back. Hair tufts contain barbed spines which can cause severe irritation; cocoons occur above ground on foodplants (usually forest trees) and contain larval spines in their walls.

FAMILY Arctiidae
Small to medium, broad-winged, stout-bodied moths, often white, brightly spotted or banded. Common insects attracted to lights at night; generally hold wings roof-like over body at rest. Larvae usually very hairy, mostly feeding on grasses but eat other plants as well. The larval hairs are combined with silk for the cocoon.

FAMILY Ctenuchidae
Active, day flying moths characterised by translucent patches in their wings; formerly regarded as a distinct family, the African window-wings are presently regarded as a subfamily, Syntominae, within the Ctenuchidae.

FAMILY Noctuidae
The largest family of Lepidoptera, including many pest species. Found abundantly everywhere, mostly nocturnal. Antennae slender and thread-like, never plumose. Size and colour variable, mostly medium and dull coloured. Proboscis rarely vestigial, usually developed and sometimes stout enough to pierce fruit. Larvae smooth and dull coloured in browns and greens, include cutworms, boll-worms, army worms, stalk borers and other economically important plant feeders.

FURTHER READING

Common, I. F. B.: 'Lepidoptera (Moths and Butterflies)'. *In* J. M. Mackerras (Ed.): *The Insects of Australia.* Melbourne University Press (1970). pp. 765-866

Janse, A. J. T.: *The Moths of South Africa.* Transvaal Museum, Pretoria (1932-1964) Vol. I-VII

Pinhey, E. C. G.: *Some well-known African Moths.* Bundu Series, Longmans, Cape Town (1975). 116 pp

Pinhey, E. C. G.: *Moths of Southern Africa.* Tafelberg, Cape Town (1975). 273 pp

Butterflies

Formerly butterflies were regarded as a suborder, the Rhopalocera or 'club-horned', to distinguish them from the 'varied-horned' Lepidoptera – moths placed in the suborder Heterocera. Today we consider the differences between butterflies and moths so slight that this division is not justified.

Butterflies form two superfamilies, the Hesperioidea of one family and the Papilionoidea of ten families. As is well known, most butterflies are brightly coloured, the tips of their antennae are swollen and they fly by day. Their caterpillars are seldom hairy, although some are armed with spines, and the pupae are not enclosed in cocoons, except for some of the more primitive species. A more fundamental difference between butterflies and moths is that the wings on each side of a butterfly are not linked together by a jugum or a frenulum – except again in a few of the most primitive species. Certain skipper butterfly males found in Australia have a frenulum on each hind wing, like moths, but in all others the frenulum is absent; instead, the hind wing has a rounded lobe in front, known as the humeral lobe, which presses against the underside of the forewing when the insect is in flight.

Skippers These are the most primitive of butterflies and are popularly known as 'skippers' because of their irregular, darting flight. They belong to the family Hesperiidae.

The skippers are nearly all small but robust in structure. They may be recognised by their large heads with the antennae comparatively wide apart at the base; by their front legs which are fully formed and functional; by the two pairs of spines on each hind leg; by the unbranched veins on the wings, and by the way in which they hold their wings when at rest. Some of them hold their wings flat when settled, like a moth; others lift them above their backs, but hold them apart unlike other butterflies.

There are well over 500 different species of skipper in Africa. The majority fly by day, but some are on the wing late in the evening, even after dusk.

The eggs of the various skippers differ in form and structure. The more usual shape is approximately spherical, well-sculptured with a broad, flattened base. The caterpillars may be smooth, or finely hairy, green in colour and the first segments of the body so small that they seem to have a neck. They utilise a wide variety of foodplants, but records are generally scanty for tropical Africa. The caterpillars of the large skipper, *Coeliades forestan,* which occurs throughout Africa south of the Sahara, has been found to feed on as many as five different families of plants. Most of the skipper caterpillars join the edges of leaves together with silk to make shelters. Some – certainly those studied so far – keep their homes clean in a remarkable way: they have a small, comblike structure, just below the anus, with which they flick their excrement clear of their living quarters.

Pupation also occurs between leaves bound together with silk, or in a light cocoon. The pupae are usually attached by hooks on the hind end and a silken girdle around the middle, although these are often missing. The pupae are long and tapering, sometimes with an extended apex of the head.

One of the commonest skippers, to be found throughout East and South Africa, and on the wing at almost any time of the year, is the little brown, yellow-spotted butterfly known to science as *Metisella metis*. About 20 mm across the outspread wings, it can be recognised by golden-yellow spots on a dark purple-brown background, the underside being similar to the upper. The female lays her hemispherical white eggs, flattened on their underside, singly on blades of grass where they hatch in about a week.

The young caterpillar creeps to the tip of the blade and forms a tubular shelter for itself by binding the edges together with silk, where it remains hidden venturing out only to feed. In four or five weeks it is fully grown, about 30 mm long, tapering at each end, green in colour, striped with darker green along the back. It casts its skin four times in the course of growth and then leaves its foodplant to seek a sheltered spot to pupate. It may choose the underside of a leaf, or a twig, or the side of a stone, where it first spins a silken mat to which it fastens the hooks on the hind claspers and then spins a girdle around its middle. Supported in this manner, in an upright position, the caterpillar changes into a narrow, green pupa, pointed at each end. About a fortnight later the adult emerges.

272. A skipper butterfly *Kadestes macomo* takes a meal of energy-giving nectar. Length12 mm.

273. The common yellow-spotted skipper *Metisella metis.* From left to right: larva, pupa and adult.

Whites The predominant colours of the family Pieridae are white and yellow, variously marked with black, brown and other colours, and pierids are commonly known as 'whites', 'yellows' and 'orange-tips'. They are mostly of moderate size and may be recognised not only by their general form and colouring, but by the veins which form a closed cell on each wing, by their fully formed and functional front legs, and by their bifid claws.

The members of this family include some of the commonest and best-known butterflies. There are about 70 species found in South Africa alone and more than 150 species in the whole of Africa. Some are widely distributed and range from the extreme south to the borders of the Sahara. Although the pierids may be found in forests, they are especially abundant in the savanna. Many species are strong fliers and some, such as *Catopsilia florella,* have migratory habits; other species fly feebly and have to rest frequently, settling on the ground or on flowers.

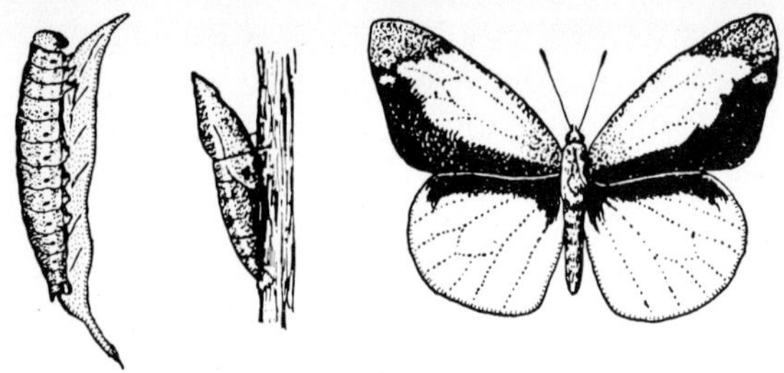

274. The banded gold tip, *Colotis eris*, showing the caterpillar (left), pupa (centre) and adult butterfly (wingspan 50 mm).

Often the sexes differ in colouring and markings. For example, in *Colotis eris*, the female lacks the golden-brown tip to the forewing found in the male and has instead a black tip marked with white spots.

In many species that fly throughout the year there may be further differences between the wet-season and dry-season generations. The wet-season forms are larger and show heavier pigmentation, whilst dry-season broods are small, and their dark markings greatly reduced.

The white or yellowish eggs are elongate with longitudinal ribs, and are either laid singly or in clusters on or near the foodplant. The caterpillars are cylindrical, and much elongated, tapering noticeably in some species especially towards the rear end which may have two short projections. The pupae are usually slender and are always held in an upright position by a series of hooks on the tail end (called the cremaster), and by the silken girdle about the middle. In this latter characteristic they resemble the swallowtails, but a pupa of the Pieridae can be distinguished from one of the Papilionidae by the single pointed projection at the head end, whereas the Papilionidae pupa always has two points.

The banded gold tip, *Colotis eris*, common in open bush country and savanna, is found from Ethiopia to the Cape. This butterfly varies in its markings: the male has golden brown tips on his forewings with a dark brown hind border, whereas the female usually has blackish-brown tips on her forewings with a narrower brown hind border. The general ground colour is white or pale yellow above with a deeper pinkish-yellow colour on the under-surface of the hind wings. The wings may span some 50 mm.

The female *Colotis eris* lays her conical white eggs singly on the underside of leaves of native shrubs known to botanists as *Capparis* species. In about a week it hatches and the newly-emerged caterpillar makes the empty egg-shell its first meal. In four or five weeks, after moulting four times, it is fully grown and is leaf-green in colour with a narrow white stripe down the middle of the back and another along each side; it is some 20 mm in length and has a forked tail end.

At this point it seeks out a sheltered spot on a leaf or twig and spins a small mat of silk to which it fastens the hooks on its anal claspers. Then it spins a girdle round the middle of its body, rests for a time and changes into a green pupa. The adult emerges from the pupa after two to three weeks. There are several generations a year.

Swallowtails The swallowtails, family Papilionidae, are amongst the most conspicuous butterflies in the tropics. There are two conspicuous swallowtail subgenera in Africa, *Papilio* (49 species) and *Graphium* (36 species). Members of the family include some of the largest butterflies in the world – some of them measuring 20-24 cm across the outspread wings. The largest butterfly in Africa is the Central African swallowtail, *Papilio antimachus*, with a wingspan of approximately 22 cm. The largest butterfly in the eastern parts, from Kenya to

275. The lucerne butterfly, *Colias electo*, newly emerged from its pupa. The caterpillars of these orange-coloured butterflies are sometimes a pest on lucerne. Body length 20 mm..

276. Mating pierid butterflies (*Pontia helice*). In this case the male is being carried by the female, although the opposite may occur with equal frequency in this family. Body length 25 mm each.

Natal, is the emperor swallowtail, *Papilio ophidicephalus*, which measures 10-14 cm across the wings. This species is found in forested regions and has the tail-like projections on the hind wings, from which this family derives their common name, very well-developed. Not all species of Papilionidae have 'swallowtails'. Several of these butterflies are mimetic and bear little resemblance to typical non-mimetic species of swallowtail until examined closely.

The swallowtails are nearly all large and slight in structure in relation to their size. As in the pierids, the cells of both the fore and hind wings are closed, but there are other differences in the venation of the wings. Similarly both sexes have fully-developed front legs. Most species are strong fliers, some flying high, others remaining close to the ground. Most species are forest or woodland insects and their foodplants are generally large shrubs or trees. When feeding from flowers they poise gracefully beside the bloom, their legs merely touching the flower while their rapidly vibrating wings maintain balance.

The eggs are spherical, smooth, and laid singly or in small lots on the leaves of the larval foodplant. The caterpillars are relatively thick, smooth and hairless, and vary in appearance. When irritated, this caterpillar bends back its head and shoots out a curious forked organ from the segment just behind the head. This osmeterium, as it is called, is yellow and is forced out both by muscular action and by pressure of the blood and gives off a sickly over-powering odour of lemons; the smell has also been likened to that of rotten pineapples. This means of defence is common to the caterpillars of all species of swallowtail – the combination of the menacing horn and the unpleasant smell deters enemies from interfering with the insect. The pupae are angular and are attached by the tail and supported by a silken girdle as are the Pieridae, but differ, as mentioned earlier, in having two points at the head.

In Africa the caterpillars of the Papilionidae feed primarily on Rutaceae (*Papilio*) and Anonaceae (*Graphium*). The various types of citrus such as oranges and grapefruit, which were introduced into Africa from Asia, belong to the Rutaceae, and a number of species of swallowtail now utilise them as foodplants. Among the species recorded using *Citrus* as a foodplant are *Papilio demodocus*, *Papilio nireus*, *Papilio ophidicephalus* and *Papilio menestheus*.

One of the commonest and most widely spread of all South African swallowtails is the citrus swallowtail, or Christmas butterfly, *Papilio demodocus*. Both sexes are alike but the male may have deeper yellow spots than the female. They have no 'tails' on the hind wings. Although they may be seen on the wing at almost any time of the year, these butterflies are most numerous at mid-summer, hence their popular name 'Christmas butterflies'. The caterpillars are sometimes abundant on citrus trees and can do considerable damage to the foliage – the larva's common name is 'orange dog'.

The female *Papilio demodocus* deposits her spherical, yellow eggs on the tips of tender young leaves of the foodplants. Besides citrus trees she may choose *Fagara* and other wild Rutaceae which were probably its original foodplants. The egg hatches in about a fortnight and the caterpillar takes about a month to reach full size. At this stage it is 50 mm long, smooth, green in colour with black and orange markings, and apparently protected from enemies by an unpleasant taste and smell; it feeds openly with no attempt at concealment.

The amazing process by which the full grown caterpillar prepares a spot for pupation can easily be

277. Swallowtail butterfly *(Papilio (Graphium) antheus)* drinking from moist earth on the forest floor. Body length 25 mm.

278. A citrus swallowtail *(Papilio demodocus)* sunning itself in the early morning in order to build up its body heat before commencing its daily activities. Most butterflies are unable to fly if their body temperature is below about 20°C. Wingspan 85 mm.

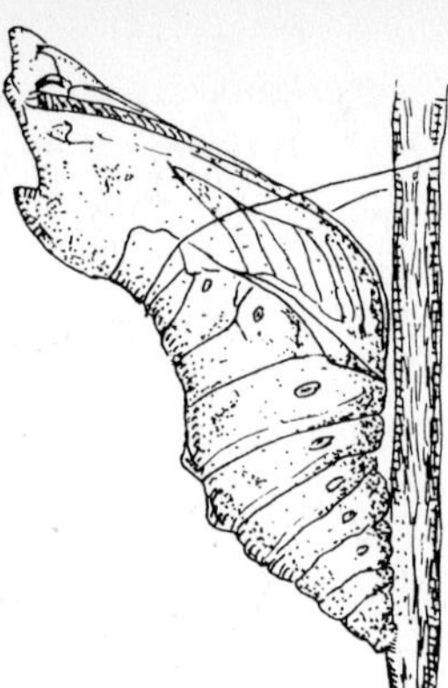

279. Pupa of *Papilio demodocus* showing the silken girdle which supports the pupa against the stem.

observed if some of these caterpillars are kept in captivity. First it spins a small silken mat on the twig, branch or other chosen spot and then carefully fixes the tiny hooks on its hind claspers into this mat so that it is securely held at the rear end. Resting, its head upwards, it now begins to move the front part of its body from side to side and, if you watch closely, you will see that it is weaving a silken loop, fixed at each end to the surface just below its front legs. The head is held bent well back so that the loop passes between its first and second pair of legs and is supported securely by them. After laying down several strands of silk which adhere together to form a strong silken loop, it stops and rests. Then by vigorous contortions it bends its head down and passes it through the loop, wriggling and writhing until the silken support passes to the hind edge of the thorax.

The caterpillar, securely held in position by the mat at the hind end and the girdle round the middle, now draws up its body, shortening and thickening, until finally it splits at the back of the thorax; by still more wriggling the skin is pushed back towards the tail end and the pupa is revealed. Now comes what is probably the most astonishing part of the whole performance. The shrivelled skin round the hind end is an encumbrance that must be discarded and the pupa does this in a remarkable manner. It bends the tip of its abdomen upwards so that the skin is gripped between two of the segments. Then it pulls the tip of its abdomen out of the skin and, holding on only by that piece nipped between the segments, it feels with the tip of its abdomen until the tiny hooks, called the cremaster, are fixed into the silken mat below. By a series of violent movements it ensures that its new hold is secure and then, with an upward jerk of the abdomen, it flings the cast skin of the caterpillar away.

In terms of colour, the pupa blends with its surroundings and is therefore difficult to see. Anybody who rears some of the caterpillars can experiment by placing fully grown larvae, just when they are about to pupate, in small boxes lined with paper of different colours.

Although the pupae cannot change colour as does a chameleon, the colour of their surroundings has a marked effect, for the pupa in a box lined with dark paper is much darker in colour than a pupa in a light box. This response to colour is found in the pupae of many butterflies and must be of value in helping them escape the attention of enemies. There are two or three generations a year of the citrus butterfly and the cold months are spent in the pupal state.

The mocker swallowtail, *Papilio dardanus,* offers what is probably the world's most striking example of the much-debated phenomenon of mimicry among butterflies. This butterfly is found throughout Africa south of the Sahara and occurs most commonly on the edges of forests and in clearings in wooded areas. The male is of the typical swallowtail form with a long tail on each hind wing, pale yellow with broad black bands round the margins of his wings. There are, however, several different forms of female and they are quite unlike the male; only by breeding them in the laboratory and by capturing them when mating has it been proved that these insects, differing so markedly from one another in colouring and marking, all belong to the same species.

The females do not have tails on their hind wings and they resemble other butterflies so closely that they may easily be mistaken for them. One form of female mocker is dark purplish-brown and has a large yellow patch at the base of each hind wing. It is very similar in appearance to *Amauris albimaculata* that belongs to quite a different family, the Danaidae. Not only is the mocker female similar in colour and markings, but also in her slow and deliberate manner of flying. Furthermore she is found in the same habitat as *Amauris albimaculata* – along the edges of forests and clearings.

A second form of female mocker is black with large white patches on each wing and closely resembles the friar butterfly, *Amauris dominicanus,* whilst a third form has brown instead of white patches and mimics the common African monarch, *Danaus chrysippus.* Still other forms are found in different parts of Africa and in each case they look very much like distinct species of butterflies that are found flying in the same neighbourhood; but everywhere the males are alike, sulphur yellow with black bordered wings and the characteristic tails on the hind wings.

Papilio dardanus has several different races or subspecies in various regions of Africa and each of these has several different forms of female which usually are close mimics of certain species of the unpalatable Danaidae. It is assumed that the butterfly called the mimic or imitator benefits from its close resemblance to the butterfly known as the model. The model is protected from the attacks of predators by its unpleasant taste and smell; in this case the Danaidae are all presumed to be distasteful to the usual predators such as birds and lizards. This is perhaps the most remarkable example of mimicry to be found anywhere in the world. The resemblance between the different types of female mockers and their models is so close that even the most experienced butterfly collector has to look very closely at the venation on the wings to determine which is which.

Almost all species regarded as unpalatable feed as

caterpillars on plants that contain in their tissues chemical compounds which appear to deter herbivorous animals. For example the caterpillars of Danaidae feed almost exclusively on Asclepiadaceae (milkweeds) and their relatives, a group of plants that contain toxic cardiac glycosides. These cardiac glycosides are stored in the body of the danaid butterfly and if it is eaten, for example by a bird, the chemicals will make the predator physically sick. After such an experience the predator will avoid eating any butterfly that looks like the one which made it sick and in this lies the value of mimicry. All models have bright warning colours which makes it easier for the predator to recognise it again. By the same token the mimic is presumably mistaken for the model by insect-eating enemies and is left alone.

Obviously the mimic must inhabit the same locality as the model and must have similar ways. Furthermore the mimic must be less numerous than the model, for if not, the particular colouring and markings of the pair would in time lose their association with unpalatibility and would no longer function as a warning to enemies.

The mimetic butterflies do not consciously imitate their models, of course; there is nothing voluntary about the phenomenon at all. However, in terms of the survival of the species, those females that look like the protected models have a better chance of surviving and so, over the course of time, mimics that look exactly like the models have evolved. The male is not protected in this way as he is swift flying and does not have to linger over egg-laying.

Lycaenids The Lycaenidae is a large and extremely complex family, containing some 1 400 species in Africa. It is divided into three subfamilies, the Lipteninae, the Liphyrinae and the Lycaeninae, which are considered by some authorities to constitute separate families in their own right. The lycaenids are small to moderate-sized butterflies, mostly blue in colour, although some are coppery-red, dark brown, orange, white and pale yellow. On the underside of the wings the colouration is usually more sombre, with dark centred eye-spots or slender lines and streaks; the hind wings frequently have delicate tail-like prolongations. The legs of the adults are all functional and used for walking, but in the males the front feet or tarsi are usually shortened and sometimes armed with a claw.

Members of the subfamily Lipteninae are usually orange, yellow, blue, brown or white, with elongated wings. The fore tarsus of the male is nearly always fused to a single clawless segment and the middle and hind tibiae of the legs are without spurs. Mimicry is a significant characteristic of some members of this group; species of *Mimacraea*, as the name suggests, are nearly all mimics of Acraeidae or Danaidae species. The eggs are spherical, flattened on the underside, with a sunken micropyle at the top and rings of indentations around the middle. The caterpillars bear numerous, slender, finely barbed setae or hairs; many of these are extremely

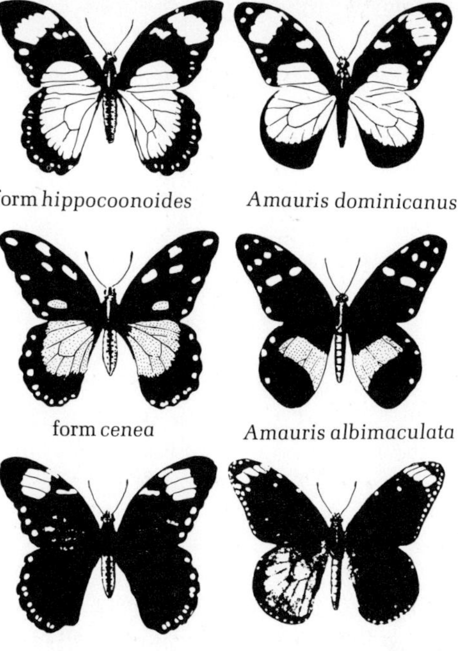

280. Examples of mimicry among African butterflies. The mimics (left) are all females of the mocker swallowtail, *Papilio dardanus*, while the models (right) are three different species belonging to the Danaidae, a family of distasteful butterflies.

281. A feeding lycaenid butterfly *(Spindasis natalensis)*, showing the fine extensions from the hind wing which resemble antennae and probably serve to deceive would-be predators into attacking the wrong end of the butterfly. Body length 15 mm.

long, and forming at the ends of the body, especially the posterior, a 'skirt' around the larva. The caterpillars feed on moss or lichen found growing on the bark of trees or on rocks.

The pupa lacks a girdle and is attached to the substrate by the cremaster alone. The adults are retiring in their habits, flying early in the morning and again in the evening from 1600 to 1700 hours, or on dull afternoons when the females may be seen laying their eggs on dead twigs and trunks of trees. A favourite habit is to sit at the extreme end of a twig with wings folded, displaying the undersides, which are often dull in colour and look like green or brown leaves. They are often found feeding on secretions from plant glands on the young tendrils of creepers and other plants, or among tree-hoppers sitting on vegetation.

A typical member of this subfamily is *Mimacraea krausei* which occurs in Central Africa. It is a small to medium-sized butterfly, some 50 mm from wing tip to wing tip, black in colour, marked by red and yellow and resembling closely some of the unpalatable Acraeidae. The female lays her eggs amongst lichen on the bark of trees. They are bun-shaped and very small relative to the size of the butterfly, yellowish-white, with the surface minutely ornamented with a network pattern and small central black spot. The caterpillar which emerges is dark sepia brown, almost black with a sparse covering of long blackish hair. The head is very small and the caterpillar looks very moth-like. The pupa is placed flat on the bark usually among moss, the larval skin enfolding the last few segments. It is dark blackish-brown with short thick hair arranged transversely across each segment, with an occasional longer hair.

Members of the subfamily Liphyrinae are generally drab butterflies whose males have the tarsus of the foreleg fully formed as does the female. The oval eggs are very small with a slight central depression. The larvae are flattened with a leathery skin, extending on each side down to the substrate so that the legs are hidden. Carnivorous, they feed on scale insects, tree-hoppers and leaf-hoppers. The pupae are secured to twigs, leaves or bark by the cremastral hooks and occasionally by a silken girdle.

One of the best-known butterflies in this subfamily is *Aslauga purpurascens*. It is small – its wingspan is only some 30 mm – a purplish-grey butterfly which inhabits grassy savanna. The males may occasionally be observed chasing one another on the tops of hills. The female lays her egg flat on the leaflet at the extreme tip of a branch near a colony of tree-hoppers (bugs of the family Membracidae). The egg is very small, white, and oval with a slight central depression.

In shape the larva is akin to a limpet shell, and coloured in mottled greys and greens to resemble lichen or moss on bark. The skin is rough and leathery, and the carapace is extraordinarily heavy, completely protecting the legs, head and undersurface. From above, the outline of the carapace is nearly oval with slight central indentations; from the outer edges, especially the front, it slopes very abruptly upwards to a broad dorsal ridge which has a central depression. At the extreme posterior end of the ridge are two small external tubercles. The head is small and black and protrudes from under the carapace, as does that of a tortoise, when the larva feeds or moves.

The larvae are carnivorous and feed on tree-hoppers. When catching a membracid it will move quietly until close enough, then the anterior portion of the carapace is raised slightly and lowered to capture the victim.

The brown pupa, mottled with black, is placed flat on bark or under it, and attached by the cremastral hooks. The abdominal segments are very broad and contracted, and slope sharply to the posterior extremity and more gradually to the head case. The pupa as a whole is squat and roughly oval in outline with a slightly ridged thorax and prominent shoulders. Low down on the sides are small, black depressions like eye-spots, which together with a small black line above the head case and a black spot in the centre of the posterior stalk, form a camouflage that makes the pupa appear to be another insect when seen from above.

The Lycaeninae is the largest of the three subfamilies in Africa and includes the blues and the coppers. In this subfamily the fore tarsus of the male is fused to a single clawless segment, the tip either blunt or extended to a ventrally curved point. The middle and hind tibiae each have a single pair of spurs. The predominant colours are blues, reds and browns, and many have intricate lines and spots, including eye-spots, on their underside. Occasionally there are long filamentous tails on the hind wings.

The Lycaeninae are found in all types of habitat, but many species are extremely localised – quite a few are restricted to the higher mountains in South Africa. They vary greatly in their habits, some are weak, slow-flying insects which remain near the ground whilst others have an extremely rapid and strong flight and live in high forest trees.

There is considerable diversity of form in the early stages of this subfamily. The most characteristic egg is spherical, flattened below, and beautifully sculptured either with fine reticulations or a honeycomb pattern. The caterpillars are short and thick, their small head and feet generally hidden beneath overhanging sides. The pupae are short and rounded, sometimes lying free, sometimes attached by tail-hooks or by tail-hooks and girdle. Most species of Lycaeninae are associated with ants, but the larvae generally feed on plants although in some species, plants and ant larvae and pupae are all eaten. A great many species feed on flowers and inside the green pods of the Leguminosae. There is a tendency in this subfamily for genera to be restricted to particular plant families, for example the *Iolaus* to Loranthaceae and *Myrina* to Moraceae.

The common copper, *Poecilmitis chrysaor,* which occurs in the Cape Province of South Africa, is a good example of this group. It is a small butterfly, only about 20 mm across the outspread wings, glittering golden orange in colour with a few small brown spots on each wing; the male and female are alike. The adults may be seen on the wing at almost any time of the year, although commonest in summer. They are active fliers but settle frequently on low-growing plants.

The female lays her small, white, bun-shaped eggs individually on the leaves of taaibos (*Rhus* species) and *Cotyledon* plants, and they hatch in about 14 days. The caterpillar is flattened, greenish-grey in colour with narrow brown lines down the back. It feeds on the leaves and sluggishly returns to the same sheltered spot each time it rests. It grows slowly, moulting seven times before it reaches full size and takes four or five months to do so. On the back of the tenth segment of its body behind a shiny, wrinkled area, is a gland with a small slit. This is the honey gland, and these caterpillars are eagerly attended by black cocktail ants (*Crematogaster* species) for the sweet secretion.

When an ant finds the caterpillar, it strokes the gland with its antennae and the caterpillar responds by protruding the gland slightly; a drop of liquid oozes from the slit and this the ant laps up. It is thought that the caterpillar benefits from this association as the ants protect it from parasites and other enemies.

On the segment behind the honey gland is a pair of tubercles that can be protruded at will, armed at the tip with bristles. The function of these tubercles is not known for certain but it seems reasonable to assume that they serve to protect the honey gland from unwelcome visitors. If you touch the honey gland with a hair, a small white piston-like protuberance shoots out of the opening in each tubercle and the stiff bristles at the tip sweep across the honey gland with a rapid, jerky motion which, apparently, would drive away insects trying to get at the sweet secretion; the visits of the ants alone are tolerated by the caterpillar. An alternative suggestion is that the tubercles give off a scent (pheromone) which attracts the ants and enables them to locate the gland.

When fully grown, the caterpillar seeks out a sheltered spot between two leaves, or amid dead leaves, or in the angle of a stem, and spins a light web. It then changes to a pupa, generally lying on its back held in position by the cremastral hooks at the hind end of the body, which are fixed in the web. The pupal stage lasts for 15 days or so.

The life histories of many of the Lycaeninae, as far as they are known, are similar to that described above, but there are some interesting variations. The beautiful blue butterfly, *Lepidochrysops trimeni,* for example, found in the Cape, is one of the bigger species, measuring nearly 50 mm across the outspread wings. The male is dark blue on top, with a short tail on each hind wing; the female is a dull brown. Both sexes are marked on the underside with a number of conspicuous dark brown and white spots on a paler brown background. These butterflies may be seen on the wing on the mountain slopes in the western Cape early in the summer.

The female lays her eggs singly on a common shrub that bears sweet-smelling mauve flowers; it has no

282. The larva (left), pupa (centre) and adult (wingspan 20 mm) of the common copper, *Poecilmitis chrysaor.*

283. An ant prepares to receive a glistening droplet of 'honeydew' from a special honey gland at the hind end of a lycaenid butterfly caterpillar. This probably serves as a reward to the ants for the protection they confer upon the caterpillar through their association with it.

284. A pair of mating lycaenid butterflies (*Syntarucus pirithous*). Body length 10 mm.

popular name but is known as *Selago serrata* (Selaginaceae) to botanists. It also uses *Selago spuria* as a foodplant. The eggs hatch into tiny sluglike caterpillars that feed on the flowers. The young larvae are attended at night by the large, nocturnal ant, *Camponotus maculatus*. The ant, upon finding a caterpillar, will stroke it with its antennae, usually in the vicinity of the honey gland. The larva responds to this treatment by remaining motionless and by exuding from the honey gland a drop of shiny, clear liquid which is imbibed by the ant. During the period of the first two instars (about two weeks) the caterpillars resist all attempts by the ants to carry them into their nests by holding fast to the substrate to avoid being taken away from their source of food before the end of the phytophagous period. While feeding on the plants the larvae are green.

After the moult to the third instar, however, the caterpillars, now pink, facilitate the ants' task: when the host ants in attendance try to grasp them somewhere around the middle, they roll themselves into tiny balls which are carried easily by the ant without being dragged along. In this manner the caterpillars are carried into the host ant's nest, where they spend the remainder of their life cycle, some ten to 11 months, being treated by the ants as their own young.

In the nest the *L. trimeni* caterpillar crawls around amongst the brood and the ants and has been observed feeding on the silken material of the ant cocoons. Occasionally three or four can be found clinging in a row on one cocoon. The larvae feed in this way until they are as long as the larger cocoons of the soldier ants (about 10 mm), some 15 days after being brought into the nest. The caterpillars now curl themselves around a cocoon, leaving no room for another larva and consume not only the silk cocoon, but the ant pupa inside as well.

Ant larvae are also eaten from this time onwards, and are attacked in the same way as the cocoons. The caterpillars are relatively active during the first six weeks of their life with the ants, but become more sluggish later on. Towards the middle of summer, about December, the ant brood becomes scarcer and the *L. trimeni* caterpillars become more lethargic and feed less often. They spend most of their time motionless on the floor of the nest, often surrounded by a few ants. During the greater part of April and May the caterpillars hang in a slightly contracted position from the roof of the tunnels where they have spun a silk mat. The *L. trimeni* caterpillars start feeding regularly again only from July when more ant brood becomes available. They pupate some time in September or October.

The *L. trimeni* caterpillar pupates secured by a girdle and cremastral hooks to a silk pad on the roof of a tunnel. Occasionally the pupating caterpillar is removed from the roof by the ants and must then pupate unattached on the floor of the tunnel. The pupa is amber-buff in colour and moderately thick in proportion to its length. There are small light coloured hairs over much of the body and pupae lying free in the tunnels are often dragged around by ants pulling on these setae.

Just before the emergence of the adults, the host ants show increased interest in the pupae. Once the adult butterfly has succeeded in breaking open the pupal case, the ants have been observed to seize a free edge and pull on it, apparently in an attempt to tear it apart so as to free the adult. After it has emerged the butterfly is ignored and with wings still folded it runs along the tunnels until it reaches the exit. Once in the open the butterfly expands its wings.

Lepidochrysops is a large genus consisting of some 150 species, all of which have a similar life history to that of *L. trimeni* described above.

Among the lycaenids and certain other butterflies, unlike moths, it is the males and not the females that are scented. The phenomenon of 'assembling' in moths is believed to be the result of a subtle scent (or pheromone) given off by the females, but this has not been observed among butterflies. On the wings of many male lycaenids, however, as well as other butterflies, there are patches of peculiar modified scales called androconia, or 'male particles'. These are associated with tiny glands on the wing that give off a fluid thought to have an odour agreeable to females. The scent patch is usually situated on the upper surface of the hind wing and the hairlike androconia are associated with it. The function of this is not known for certain, but it is generally believed that when the male is courting the female he scatters a scented dust as he flutters about her. On the other hand, it has been suggested that the scent patch is really an organ that enables him to find his mate by picking up the subtle odour she may give out when ready for the male. Further observations on the living insects are necessary before this question can be settled.

Riodinid butterflies The Riodinidae is mainly a tropical American family but with a few representatives in Africa and elsewhere in the world. There are only two genera in Africa, *Abisara* consisting of ten species and *Saribia* made up of three. The riodinids are small butterflies with short, broad wings and unusually elongate antennae. The wings are usually brownish with white or blue marks and eye-spots near the margin of the hind wings. They are closely related to the Lycaenidae, of which they are sometimes classified as a subfamily. The forelegs of the males are undeveloped and useless for walking, but in the females all six legs are well developed. In the genus *Abisara* the hind wing is strongly angled or has developed into a thick outward angled tail. They are relatively weak fliers, and can be recognised in the field by the characteristic manner in which they hold their wings when perched. Instead of closing them together above the body, as most butterflies do, members of most riodinid genera spread the wings laterally, flat against the substrate like many of the geometrid moths. Others keep their wings only half open.

The early stages of the African Riodinidae are not known, but in certain species studied in tropical Asia they are similar to those of the Lycaenidae. The eggs are laid singly on or near the foodplant. They are somewhat flattened, wider than they are tall, with either a broad, shallow concavity on top, or a somewhat conical rise with a small central depression in the micropylar area. The surface is uniformly reticulated with a network of fine ridges, but without the raised vertical ribs characteristic of many Lycaenidae.

The light green larvae vary but tend to be stout, with a large head, and are not as grub-like in appearance as lycaenid caterpillars. In the later instars the riodinid larvae bear a series of setae along the sides of the body which in some South American species are extremely long and may extend beyond the width of the body, brushing the substrate. The larvae of some *Abisara* species occurring in tropical Asia are light green and slug-like with numerous short, fine hairs and feed on Myrsinaceae.

The pupa is short and stout, although not as robust as typical lycaenids, with a flattened ventral surface. Most species bear at least a dorsal coating of fine hairs, which further distinguishes them from the Lycaenidae. Pupation usually occurs in debris on the ground or at the base of the plant, with the pupa attached by a frail median girdle and cremastral hooks. The pupa of the genus *Abisara* is light green and hairy with dorsal black spots.

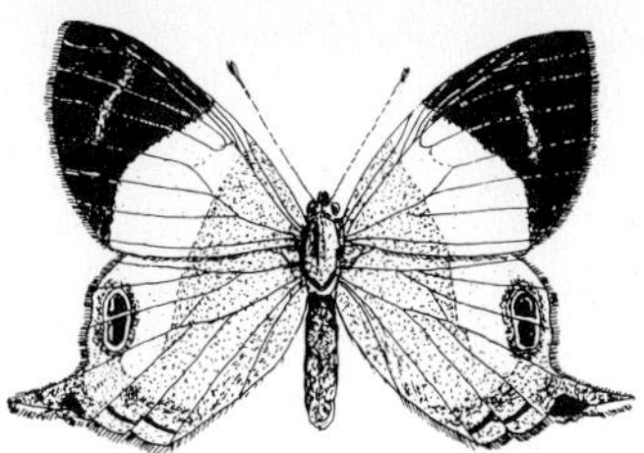

285. A riodinid butterfly, *(Abisara rogersi)*, showing the angled 'tails' on the hind wing that are characteristic of the genus.

286. The African 'snout' butterfly *(Libythea labdaca)* showing the conspicuous palps which project from the front of the head.

287. The autumn brown *(Dira clytus)* showing the caterpillar (left), adult (wingspan 50 mm) and the pupa lying among grass roots (right).

Snouts The Libytheidae are peculiar butterflies placed in a small family of their own, widely spread over the world and with only one species in Africa. Two other species occur near the continent – one on Madagascar and the other in Mauritius. The Mauritian species is known from only a single specimen and is now presumed extinct.

These butterflies are commonly called 'snouts', because the palps on their heads are much longer than those of other butterflies and project in front of the head like a snout. The 'snouts' are also characterised by their angular forewings. The front legs of the male are small, useless and without claws, but those of the females are fully formed and can be used for walking. The eggs are somewhat jar-shaped, with upright ribs and fine cross-ridges. The larvae are cylindrical and without spines, and the last segment is rounded and never bifurcate. The pupae are of an irregular shape, moderately thick, narrowing markedly toward the hind end; they are suspended head downwards.

The single African species, *Libythea labdaca,* is some 50 mm across the outspread wings, brown in colour with yellow markings and it is common in forested and wooded areas throughout the continent. It is often encountered in vast migratory swarms which settle in masses on roads and on damp mud or sand. In South Africa the snout is usually found in wooded areas where it can be seen flitting from flower to flower or flying low over the tops of bushes and small trees. When it settles it rests head downwards on the trunk of a tree.

The eggs are generally laid in batches, but occasionally singly. The emergent caterpillar is brownish-green, with greenish-yellow longitudinal streaks and reddish-brown marks along the sides. It may be green, with a yellow line on the abdomen or yellowish-grey, marked with dull yellow or dark brown.

Browns The butterflies described in this section and those following are characterised by the first pair of legs in both sexes being much smaller and more slender than the others, too short to be used for either walking or clinging. These front legs are usually even more reduced in the male than the female, without any joints or claws on the tarsi or feet; the tarsus in the female is jointed but short and not armed with claws. All these butterflies are sometimes classified as belonging to one large family, the Nymphalidae, which is divided into several subfamilies, or they may be regarded as belonging to distinct but closely related families. The first of these is the Satyridae of which there are over 250 species in Africa.

The Satyridae, or browns, are small to medium-sized butterflies – although large ones can be found – and usually a sombre brown colour. The main veins at the base of the forewing are thick and swollen and the cells of both fore and hind wings closed. In this family the eggs are usually spherical with a very slight reticulated pattern. The body of the larva is either smooth or covered with short hairs and is generally fairly long, slender and tapers towards each end. The hind segment is forked. The pupae which are broad and often rounded, rarely angular, are either attached at the tail end to some object, or rest loosely on the ground. Although some are quite swift the browns tend to be weak fliers, flying near the ground and settling frequently. In one genus, *Elymnias*, the butterflies are a striking black and white or black and orange, and mimic the unpalatable *Bematistes* (Acraeidae).

The browns occur at all altitudes and in different types of habitat, from grassland to rain forest, although in the larval stage most species appear to feed on grasses and related plants.

The autumn brown, *Dira clytus*, is a common species in the Cape Province of South Africa, and very similar closely related species are found in other parts of the continent. This butterfly is some 50 mm across the outspread wings, a rich chocolate brown colour with yellow markings on the front wings and five eye-spots (one very small) on each hind wing; the underside is a dull brown. It may be seen flying slowly and resting frequently over grassed open ground, from the middle of February to the end of May, but is most abundant in March.

The female scatters her eggs whilst she is settled on a blade of grass; they are smooth, yellow, round and slightly flattened on the underside. They hatch in about a fortnight and the caterpillars feed on grasses such as *Stenotaphrum glabrum* and *Ehrharta erecta*, hiding by day and coming out only at night to feed. They moult four times before fully grown when they are dull yellow in colour with brownish markings, about 30 mm long, thickened in the middle and narrowing at each end, with a largish head. The full-grown caterpillar seeks out a sheltered spot amid grass roots and dead leaves and stems and there it changes into a pupa, brown mottled with black, which is not attached in any way but lies loose on the ground. There is only one generation of these butterflies a year.

The evening brown, *Melanitis leda*, does not fly by day, but only in the evening and at dawn. During the day it frequents the darkest and shadiest spots in woods, resting on the ground or on leaves, where the colouring of the underside of its wings harmonises so well with its surroundings that it is difficult to see. If disturbed it takes a short, flapping flight before dropping again into some shady nook. After sunset it becomes active, seeking the open and flying about until after dark.

This butterfly is common in wooded areas from Natal in the south-east right up through Africa and it is also found throughout Asia. About 80 mm across the outspread wings, it is dull brown with a conspicuous black spot on a yellowish-red patch on each front wing, but the species varies greatly in its colours and patterns and also in the outline of its wings. There are two distinct seasonal forms, the summer one being smaller, duller and less plentiful than the winter form.

On grass blades the female lays her whitish eggs which hatch after a few days into caterpillars which are green or yellow-green, with darker green lines and a light lateral streak. The head is black or black and green and is finely hairy, with prominent 'horns'. The pupa is green and is suspended by its cremaster, feeding on grasses – including *Setaria sulcata* – as well as rice and sugar-cane.

The mountain beauty, *Meneris tulbaghia* is a large and handsome member of this family, some 100 mm from wing tip to wing tip, chocolate brown with yellow markings and with five eye-spots on each hind wing.

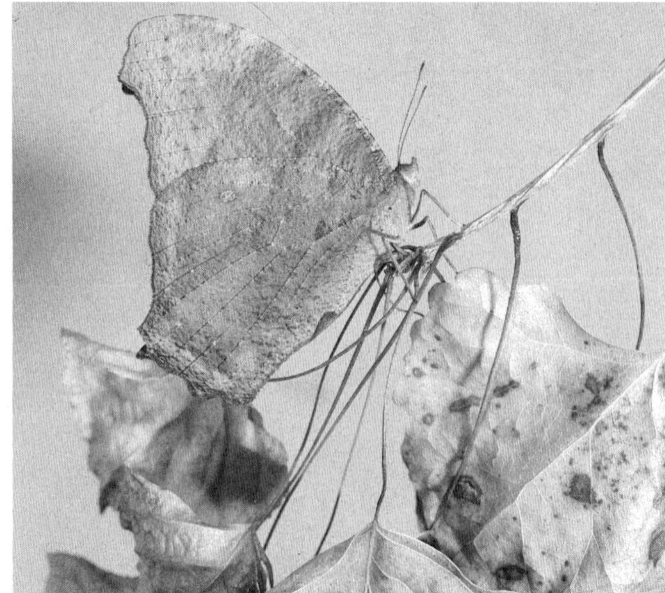

288. A satyrid butterfly (*Melanitis leda*) resting on a cluster of dry leaves, amongst which it is perfectly camouflaged. Length 40 mm.

During the summer months this swift and powerful aviator is found on mountains and rocky hillsides.

The pale yellow eggs are deposited loosely amongst the grass and take a week or two to hatch. The caterpillars vary considerably in colour and may be green, orange-brown or reddish-brown, with a black stripe down the back. The pupa is short and stout, suspended by its whitish, black-spotted tail.

The painted lady family The Nymphalidae is a very large family of medium to large butterflies, many of which are robust and colourful. A number of species exhibit striking sexual dimorphism which means that the male and female are quite dissimilar – in this case in colour; others such as *Precis octavia* exhibit extremes of seasonal dimorphism.

In this family the front legs of both sexes are degenerate and useless for walking; in the males they have two tarsal joints and are not brushlike. The cell formed by the veins on the forewing is usually closed but that on the hind wing is open – a feature which easily distinguishes the African species from butterflies in other families. This characteristic is often a useful guide to identification as some nymphalids are close mimics of the Danaidae and Acraeidae.

The eggs are usually oval and ribbed with a flat area at the top. The caterpillars bear either spines or tubercles, or may be smooth. The pupae vary in shape but are always suspended head downwards by the tail hooks.

There is considerable variation in the feeding habits of the nymphalid genera. While a large number feed from flowers, many feed only on rotten fruit, faeces and decaying organic matter. Some species also feed on the fermenting sap of wounded trees.

The painted lady, *Vanessa cardui*, is the commonest and most widely distributed butterfly in the world. It is found throughout Africa at all times of the year and is also an inhabitant of Europe, Asia and North America. It cannot survive the British winter yet in some years it is common in Britain which gives rise to the question: If this butterfly perishes in winter, how is the stock replenished in spring? The answer lies in the fact that this butterfly, like several others, is a migrant. Numbers of them fly across the English Channel from Europe every spring and they breed in England, giving rise to the autumnal generation of butterflies which are in their turn killed off during the winter. We do not know why butterflies migrate in this way, but it is assumed that they do so when they have increased so rapidly that food for the caterpillars is in short supply.

But this is only part of the answer. In the case of the painted lady the caterpillars feed on common wayside weeds, such as nettles, thistles and mallows, and there is rarely such a shortage of these foodplants as to cause a wholesale migration of the adults.

From various parts of Africa, reports have been received of swarms of these butterflies flying low and all in the same general direction. In Europe in the spring the species arrives from North Africa and in autumn flies south across the Mediterranean once more. The possibility exists that painted ladies cross the Sahara from the north to tropical Africa (and vice versa at the end of winter) for in 1969 they were exceptionally abundant in Britain, the year when numbers were also higher than normal in West Africa.

Their stout thoraces and large wing-muscles distinguish them as strong fliers, but we do not know how far they can fly or what the limits of their endurance are.

The painted lady measures some 60 mm across the outspread wings and is a rich tawny-red colour with black markings and some white spots. The underside of the wings is beautifully mottled with yellow, white and

289. The painted lady *(Vanessa cardui)* newly emerged from its pupa; the most widely distributed butterfly in the world. Body length 18 mm.

290. Caterpillar of the painted lady feeding on the leaves of a *Gazania* daisy. 28 mm.

brown. The red colour of the wings is unusual in that it is soluble in hot water and in that it dulls with age so that an old pinned specimen in a cabinet is not nearly as handsome as the newly emerged butterfly. The colour can be restored to a bright rosy red by exposing the specimen to chlorine gas.

The colouring and the pattern, as in all butterflies and moths, is lodged entirely in the tiny scales that coat the wings like tiles on a roof. A microscope will reveal that the red portion is coated with red scales, marvellously formed and arranged, whilst the white spots are covered with white scales, and so on. When the scales are rubbed off, the wing itself emerges as nothing but a colourless membrane.

The female lays her green eggs on the leaves of thistles and other weeds, usually one to a leaf. These hatch after about a fortnight into little black caterpillars coated with branched spines. Each caterpillar constructs for itself a shelter, in which it feeds, by binding a leaf to the stem with a few silken threads. After moulting four times, it is fully grown, nearly 35 mm long, dark brown, with a wavy light line down each side and the prominent branched spines along its back. It leaves the plant to pupate and seeks out a sheltered spot, where it can hang freely, head downwards.

First it spins a small silken mat on the underside of a branch or overhanging stone, or wherever it happens to be, and then fixes the hooks on its hind pair of claspers into this mat so that it can hang securely. Its body now thickens and shortens and the caterpillar curls the head and front part of its body upwards so that the skin splits across the back of the thorax and, by vigorous writhing and wriggling, is worked upwards and backwards off the body to reveal the greenish-yellow pupa, gilded on the back and wing-covers with three rows of golden spots down the back. It is this golden colour evident in the pupae of many different butterflies that has given rise to the word 'chrysalis'.

The shrivelled, discarded skin of the caterpillar still hangs round the top end of the pupa, where it is fixed to the support. In order to rid itself of this unwanted encumbrance the pupa has to let go its hold on the silken mat and it would seem that, as this is its only support, it must inevitably fall in doing so. But it does not fall. At first the pupa is held in place only by the tip of its tail still embedded in the cast skin, and this cast skin is held in its turn by the hooks of the claspers, the cremaster, fixed in the silken mat. However, the pupa has knoblike projections on its tail and it now grips the cast skin between two of these. Then it quickly disengages the cremaster and fixes it into the silk beside the cast skin. Finally, with a jerk, it flings away the skin and hangs from the mat securely with its new hold. This difficult performance has to be carried out by every caterpillar of the large family to which the painted lady belongs, because they all hang head downwards when they pupate. About a fortnight later the adult emerges. There are several generations a year and the painted lady may be seen on the wing at all seasons.

The diadem butterfly, *Hypolimnas misippus*, is another well-known and widely spread member of this family. It is of interest because of the striking difference between the sexes and because the female has several forms that mimic the unpleasant-tasting African monarch, *Danaus chrysippus*. The male, some 80 mm across the outspread wings, is violet-black with a large circular white patch on each wing. The female is quite different, closely resembling the African monarch, being brown with black borders to the wings. The brown caterpillars of this butterfly, armed with red and blackish spines and with two black horns on the head, may be found during the late summer months on *Portulaca* (Portulacaceae) and other plants.

In this family the gaudy commodore, *Precis octavia*, offers what is perhaps the most striking known example of seasonal dimorphism. It is a beautiful insect common right throughout Africa, but few people would recognise its two forms – one in the wet season and one in the dry – as being the same species. The dry-season form is blue, with darker blue wavy lines and a row of red spots parallel with the border of the wings; it is about 80 mm across the outspread wings and is popularly known as the blue commodore, and as *Precis octavia* form *sesamus* to entomologists. The wet-season form is utterly different in appearance and slightly smaller in size; it is red with blue-black margins and is called the red commodore, *Precis octavia* form *natalensis*.

When they were first found these two butterflies were naturally supposed to be quite distinct species, particularly as their habits are different: the red form prefers open grassy spots while the blue form favours a shady habitat. Furthermore they are found on the wing at different times of the year. They were named accordingly, *Precis octavia* the red form, and *Precis sesamus* the blue form. However, when specimens intermediate between the two in colouring and pattern were caught, as well as pairs of the two forms mating together, it was assumed that the two species hybridised and that the intermediate forms were hybrids. But more than 75 years ago the blue form was reared from eggs laid by red females, and vice versa, proving conclusively that the two are one and the same and that the striking differences between them are due in some way or other to climatic conditions. It has long been known that the colouring and markings of certain kinds of butterfly can be modified by exposing the pupae to abnormal conditions of temperature and humidity, and it seems reasonable to assume that the red commodore and the blue commodore are the result of climatic conditions during the wet and dry seasons of the year, although we do not know precisely how these conditions produce such striking differences. Several other species of African butterfly show seasonal dimorphism, but none is quite as remarkable as *Precis octavia*.

The handsome butterflies known as *Charaxes* belong to the subfamily Charaxinae. This subfamily is considered by some authorities to be a family in its own right but for the present purpose the arrangement as given is adequate. There are three genera in this subfamily in Africa, *Palla* (four species), *Euxanthe* (six species) and *Charaxes* (some 120 species).

They are medium to large-sized, their bodies thick and they usually have two pointed tails on each hind wing. These strong fliers occur chiefly in forested areas where they haunt the tree tops and descend to the ground to settle on muddy patches, on animal droppings, on carrion or decaying fruit. Collectors turn this habit to advantage when out butterfly hunting. They put up traps baited with fermenting fruit, usually bananas, mixed with brown sugar and sometimes rum, which attracts most species. The males are also fond of the droppings of carnivores and usually every pile of evil-smelling leopard or hyaena dung has several *Charaxes* upon it. *Charaxes* hardly ever visit flowers.

The eggs are approximately spherical, with a slightly flattened base and a flattened or concave top, which is radially fluted. The caterpillars have a smooth appearance and taper towards the rear end, with its two small projections. The head of this caterpillar is most distinctive and has four long horns, which vary in length and thickness from species to species. The pupae are thick in proportion to their length, though they taper somewhat towards each end and have a well-developed cremastral process by means of which they are suspended.

One of the commonest of this genus is the foxy charaxes, *Charaxes jasius saturnus* found from the Eastern Cape to Kenya in those localities where its foodplants occur. Measuring some 90 mm when the wings are outspread, it is brown with yellowish-orange and black markings and borders. The female lays her spherical yellow eggs singly on the leaves of the foodplant, which is usually *Schotia, Bauhinia, Burkea* or some other bush or tree belonging to the Leguminosae. The egg hatches in seven days and the newly-hatched caterpillar devours the egg-shell before starting to feed on the leaves. It moults four times over some six weeks until it is fully grown – 50 mm in length, green in colour with some ringed brownish marking on its back; the head is green with a yellow streak on either side and the horns are short and stout. The pupa, about 25 mm long, thick and bluish-green in colour, hangs by a well-developed cremastral process. The adult emerges after three weeks spent as a pupa.

Distasteful butterflies The members of the family Acraeidae are most distinctive and are readily recognisable by the shape of their wings, long abdomens and certain other typical features. They are mostly of moderate size, red and black in colour, the wings in some species almost transparent. The head and body of the adult are conspicuously marked with white and yellow spots. In both sexes the front legs are degenerate and useless for walking. The cell in both the fore and hind wings is closed.

The eggs, laid singly or in clusters, are usually oval or vase-shaped with numerous upright ridges and indentations. The larvae are cylindrical with longitudinal

291. Caterpillar (left), pupa (right) and adult butterfly of *Charaxes jasius saturnus*.

292. A charaxes butterfly *(Charaxes jasius saturnus)* joins a paper wasp for a drink of fermenting sap oozing from an acacia tree. 40 mm.

293. A typical acraeid butterfly *(Acraea natalica)* taking nectar at a flower. Note the long abdomen, the characteristic wing shape and the degenerate front pair of legs, held contracted against the body. Body length 18 mm.

rows of rigid branched spines. They are often gregarious, especially in the first or second instars. The pupae are long and slender and suspended by the tail end.

The Acraeidae have the conspicuous colours or pattern and leisurely flight normally associated with butterflies which are unpalatable and are regarded as being distasteful to predators. Almost all butterflies regarded as unpalatable feed as caterpillars on plants containing chemical compounds that appear to function as deterrents to herbivorous animals. These chemical compounds are stored in the body of the butterfly, making it in turn unpalatable.

Unpalatability is a relative concept: some species may be poisonous to some predators but not to others, while other species may simply be unpleasant tasting without actually being poisonous. Some of the African Acraeidae feed as caterpillars on the Passifloraceae, a family of tropical plants of which certain species bear fruits edible to man, while others contain a variety of toxic compounds. Thus *Adenia lobata*, a common West African member of this family of plants, and the foodplant of several species of *Acraea*, is a source of arrow poison.

The acraeids produce large quantities of yellowish, often foamy, fluid when handled, and it has been found that in *Acraea encedon* this fluid gives off hydrogen cyanide upon decomposition. Interestingly *Acraea encedon* does not feed on Passifloraceae but on *Commelina*, a common weed that is unlikely to contain toxic compounds. It is therefore believed that at least some of the toxic compounds found in butterflies are produced metabolically and are not obtained directly from the foodplant. Many of the acraeids are mimicked by butterflies belonging to other families, the Nymphalidae, Papilionidae and a few Lycaenidae, that are not actually protected by these unpleasant-tasting chemical compounds.

The Acraeidae in Africa consists of one large genus, *Acraea*, comprising some 150 species that includes both forest and savanna butterflies, and the smaller genus *Bematistes*, consisting of 20 species of mainly larger butterflies that are restricted to forest. Another genus, *Pardopsis*, consists of only one species, a small orange butterfly with black dots that lives in savanna.

One of the commonest butterflies in South Africa is the garden acraea, *Acraea horta*. The males are red with black markings and a partially transparent forewing, while the females are similar but paler and browner. The female can also usually be distinguished from the male by the presence of a small, black horny structure known as the sphragis at the end of her abdomen. The sphragis is found only in the females of this family and in a few females of the Papilionidae, and its function is not known, but it is suggested that the shield-like covering forms after she has mated in order to prevent other males from mating with her.

The female lays her eggs on the leaves of wild peach, *Kiggelaria africana*, or on related plants, including granadilla. The wild peach and the granadilla are quite dissimilar in appearance, but a female 'recognises' them from a distance by their characteristic odour borne on the wind. Having detected a possible foodplant on which to lay, other physical factors come into play for the *Acraea horta* female – and all other butterflies – such as suitable temperature, sunlight, shade, perhaps colour, and often the texture of the surface that will receive the egg and so on. Before the egg or eggs are laid, there must be appropriate chemical stimulation of special sense organs, known as chemoreceptors, found on the antennae, legs and tip of the abdomen. The appropriate stimulation is generally only produced by a very small number of closely related chemicals which may be effective singly or only in combination. Acceptable host plants for oviposition are, therefore, those that have the requisite chemical compounds. These host plants are often, but not always, closely related taxonomically. There are, however, many naturally occurring compounds that may actively result in the rejection of a foodplant. In some instances it appears that the absence of a repellent is even more important a factor than the presence of an oviposition or feeding stimulant. The reason for this selective egg-laying behaviour is not really understood, as the majority of plants are not toxic to larvae and, indeed, most of them contain all the basic factors required for larval nutrition.

The feeding action of the larvae, both biting off and swallowing, has also been found to be controlled by these same chemicals. The larvae have a variety of sense organs on the three-segmented antennae, the mouthparts and at the beginning of the digestive tract. Probably the most important chemoreceptors occur on the maxillary palps since, if these are surgically removed, the larva is unable to recognise many plants that it normally rejects.

The caterpillars of *Acraea horta* are dark brown and covered with branched spines, which together with an unpleasant taste, protect them and make it unnecessary for the caterpillar to conceal itself on the plants. There is a parasitic wasp, however, which attacks and destroys numbers of them; often a dead caterpillar may be found with little grey, barrel-shaped objects, barred with black – the cocoons of the parasites – hanging on silken threads below it.

The pupa of the garden acraea is a conspicuous object, white and black with small yellow dots. It is found hanging head downwards in extremely exposed positions on tree trunks, rocks, palings and walls. The adult emerges from the pupa in about a fortnight and the butterflies may be seen on the wing at almost any time of the year.

The African monarch and its kin The Danaidae is a small family of conspicuous, medium or large-sized butterflies that are all highly unpalatable and some of them even toxic to potential predators. Butterflies of this group are characterised by the toughness of their integument, which makes it almost impossible to injure them by squeezing the thorax. Distinguishing features are wings large for the size of the body, the head and thorax marked with white dots, the first pair of legs greatly reduced, the presence of a patch of scent scales on the hind wing of the male and closed cells on both the fore and hind wings. The eggs are more or less oval in shape, with longitudinal ribs connected by cross-ridges. The caterpillars have a smooth skin and bear several long fleshy filaments. The pupae are short and thick, often with metallic patches and are suspended by the tail.

The Danaidae derive their unpalatable qualities from chemical compounds which occur in the plants on which they feed as caterpillars. They feed almost exclusively on Asclepiadaceae (milkweeds) and their relatives, a group of plants that contain toxic cardiac glycosides. Chemical analysis has shown that *Danaus plexippus*, the American monarch, contains several of the cardiac glycosides that are found in *Asclepias curassavica*, the plant upon which the caterpillars feed. When *D. plexippus* caterpillars are fed on cabbage the resulting butterflies are readily eaten by birds, in marked contrast to those that have been reared on *Asclepias curassavica*, which are rejected. The danaids are mimicked by many species of other families.

Members of this family are particularly long-lived and some species are known to take part in migrations. The North American *Danaus plexippus* flies south from the northern United States and Canada to Mexico and Central America in autumn and some of the same individuals make the return flight the following spring. In these butterflies breeding takes place in the northern summer, but these populations cannot survive the harsh winters and the adults move southwards to warmer climates. The southward flight is therefore undertaken by the offspring of those that came north in the spring.

There are two genera in Africa, *Danaus* (three species), and *Amaurus* (20 species) and one genus confined to the Malagasy area, *Euploea* (five species).

The African monarch, *Danaus chrysippus*, is common throughout Africa – in fact, it is one of the most widespread butterflies in the world, being found from southern Europe to the Cape and from West Africa to the Far East. It is a conspicuous insect with reddish-brown wings, bordered with black and white and measuring 80-100 mm across the outspread wings. Like all unpalatable butterflies, it is a slow, lazy flier. The male and female are alike, except that he is distinguished by a velvety black spot in the middle of each hind wing. This black spot is of considerable interest and well worth a little attention.

It consists of a shallow pocket or pouch with a small slit on the upper surface. A thick ridge covered with black scales overhangs this opening. If the patch is dissected with the aid of a pair of needles and examined under the microscope, it is seen to contain innumerable tiny black scales, oval in shape and different from the scales that cover the rest of the wings. The function of this gland is not fully understood, but on the basis of its histology it seems to be secretory. There is considerable

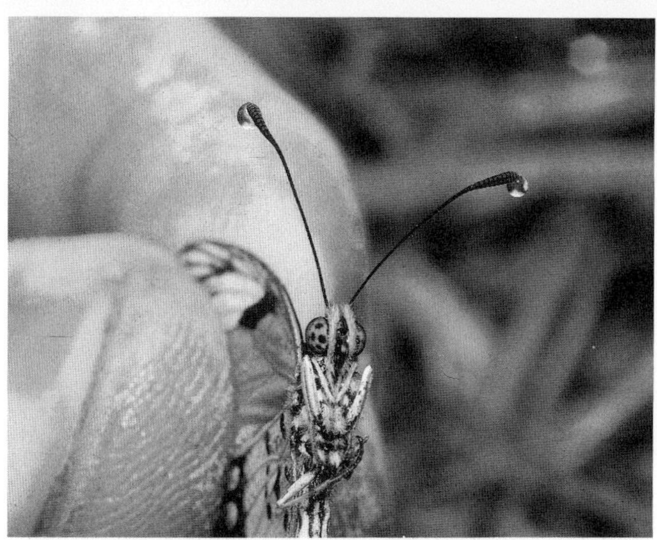

294. Noxious yellow fluid oozing from the antenna tips of an acraeid butterfly, a defense reaction to being handled.

295. Typical acraeid caterpillars, protected by their spiny armour and unpleasant taste, feed openly on their food plant. 24 mm.

296. The African monarch butterfly pauses to drink water from moist sand. The large wings and spotted thorax are diagnostic features.

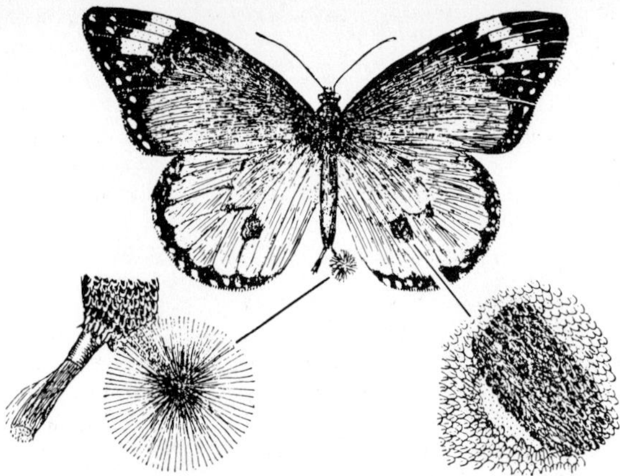

297. The male African monarch *(Danaus chrysippus)*, showing enlarged views of the hair pencils (left) with one open and one closed, and the wing gland (right).

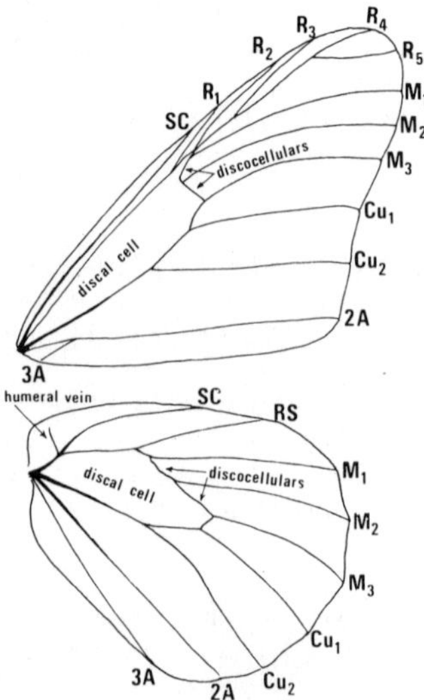

298. Wing venation in the African monarch, showing how the various veins are identified by letters and numerals.

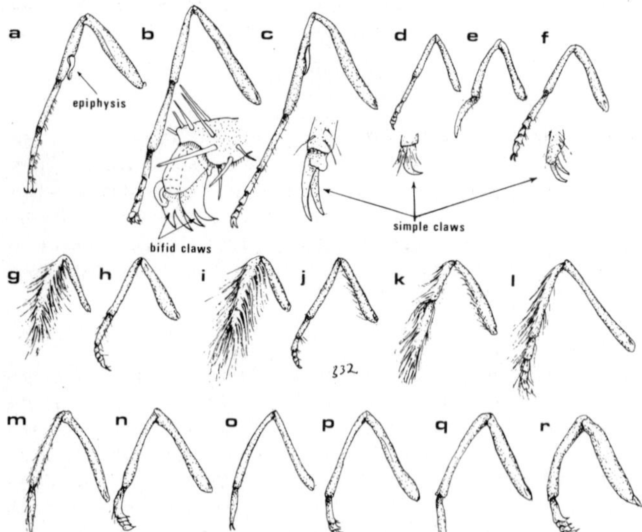

299. The front legs of butterflies provide key features for the identification of the various families. a. Hesperiidae; b. Pieridae; c. Papilionidae; d & e. male Lycaenidae; f. female Lycaenidae; g & h. male and female Riodinidae; i & j. male and female Libytheidae; k & l. male and female Satyridae; m & n. male and female Nymphalidae; o & p. male and female Acraeidae; q & r. male and female Danaidae.

variation in the structure of this wing gland in the different genera of Danaidae, but in all species of *Danaus* it appears, as described above for *chrysippus*, as a pocket.

If you capture a male monarch and hold him with his wings folded over his back and gently squeeze his abdomen, what appear to be two miniature shaving brushes protrude from the tip. These are the hair pencils. Each is about 3 mm long, as thick as a stout pin and easily visible to the naked eye. If you now increase the pressure of your fingers very slightly the two tufts of hair will suddenly explode, as it were, and instead of two tiny brushes you will see two powder puffs protruding from his tail. On the hair pencils are particles of pheromone, identified as a crystalline ketone and also a viscous terpenoid alcohol. A pheromone is a chemical substance released by an animal in interactions with another animal of the same species. The males push their hair pencils into the wing glands when by themselves and it has been suggested that the hair pencil and wing gland secretions combine to form the functional pheromone used in the courtship of the species.

The male, when courting the female, pursues her, thrusts out his hair pencils and induces her to alight by lightly brushing her antennae with them. The dust particles of crystalline ketone from the hair pencils stick to the female's antennae by means of the second compound, the viscous terpenoid alcohol. It appears that the production of the pheromone by the male prevents the female from escaping and makes her quiescent. The male at first hovers about the female displaying his hair pencils before alighting beside her and copulating. Once joined the pair move off on their post-nuptial flight with the male carrying the female.

The females lay white or pale yellow eggs singly on plants belonging to the family Asclepiadaceae, including *Asclepias* and *Stapelia*. The caterpillars, mainly bluish-white marked with yellow and black streaks, are easy to recognise because each has three pairs of black, threadlike filaments on its back, the use of which is unknown. They are hardy insects and feed freely exposed as though they have no enemies to fear. When fully grown, the caterpillar hangs itself up by its tail end and changes into a pupa marked with golden spots; the colour of the pupa varies and may be green, blue, pink or yellow. In about a fortnight the pupa turns black and soon afterwards the adult emerges.

CLASSIFICATION

ORDER **Lepidoptera**

SUBORDER **Ditrysia**

The superfamilies Hesperioidea and Papilionoidea constitute the butterflies and formerly made up the suborder Rhopalocera. The relationship to the remaining Lepidoptera is controversial, but it is now usually agreed that they deserve no more than superfamily status within the suborder Ditrysia.

KEY TO FAMILIES OF AFRICAN BUTTERFLIES

1 Antennae set widely apart at base; veins arising separately from discal cell in both wings, thus the peripheral veins are never stalked .... Superfamily Hesperioidea .... Hesperiidae

Antennae set close together at base; at least some of the peripheral veins of the wings are stalked .... Superfamily Papilionoidea ... 2

2 Hind wing with two well-developed anal veins (2A and 3A) present 3

Hind wing with a single well-developed anal vein (2A) present .... Papilionidae

3 Forelegs of male useless for walking 4

Forelegs of male well-developed 9

4 Forelegs of female well-developed 5

Forelegs of female useless for walking 6

5 Labial palps extremely long (about as long as thorax), third joint hairy .... Libytheidae

Labial palps not very long, third joint smoothly scaled .... Riodinidae

6 Lower discocellular (vein between M_2 and M_3) of both wings well-developed 7

Lower discocellular of both wings, or of hind wing alone, obsolete .... Nymphalidae

7 Vein 3A of forewing absent 8

Vein 3A of forewing present and forms a fork with 2A .... Danaidae

8 Subcostal vein (Sc) of forewing swollen at base; forewing short and broad, not markedly longer than hind wing .... Satyridae

Subcostal vein (Sc) of forewing not swollen at base, forewing rather narrow and elongate, distinctly longer than hind wing .... Acraeidae

9 The tarsi of the forelegs of the male more or less reduced, or with one or both claws absent .... Lycaenidae

The tarsi of the forelegs of the male normal, with both claws developed .... Pieridae

FAMILY Hesperiidae

The most moth-like of butterflies, nearly all small, dull in colour and with a distinctive darting and rapid flight. They are unique among butterflies in that all the veins arise direct from the cells, none branching subsequently. The head is wider than the thorax, with large eyes, and the bases of the antennae are wide apart. The first pair of legs are functional in both sexes, while the tibiae of the hind pair are usually armed with two pairs of spines, as in many moths. The caterpillars taper at both ends and spin leaves together to form a shelter. The pupae are long and tapering, often without cremastral hooks or girdle and they are often enclosed in a crude cocoon of silk and grass.

FAMILY Pieridae

Butterflies that are predominantly white or yellow in colour. The first pair of legs are functional in both sexes. The claws of the feet are bifid or toothed. The eggs are elongated, bottle-shaped and ribbed. The caterpillars are smooth, without tubercles or spines. The pupae are angular, supported in an upright position by cremastral hooks and girdle, characterised by only one point on the head.

FAMILY Papilionidae

In many species the hind wings have conspicuous tail-like prolongations. The prevailing colours are black and yellow or black and blue. This family includes the largest butterflies in the world. Front legs fully developed in both sexes with a flattened spur on the tibia. Claws large and simple, not bifid. Eggs rounded without distinct sculpturing on the surface. Caterpillars smooth and hairless, with a protrusible forked appendage, the osmeterium, just behind the head. Pupae differ from those of the Pieridae in having two points at the head end; they are supported by cremastral hooks and girdle in an upright position.

FAMILY Lycaenidae

Small or medium-sized butterflies, many with slender tails on the hind wings. Mostly blue, orange or red in colour. The front legs of the males often reduced in size, usually with only one segment in the tarsus and a single claw. The forelegs of the females are not so reduced and are armed with two claws. Eggs hemispherical with sculptured surface. Caterpillars short and thick, with small head and legs generally hidden beneath overhanging sides. Some caterpillars remarkable for their association with ants. Pupae are short and rounded, sometimes lying free, sometimes attached only by cremastral hooks or by cremaster and girdle.

FAMILY Riodinidae

Small butterflies with short, broad wings and unusually elongate antennae. The wings are usually brownish with white or blue markings and eye-spots near the margins. The forelegs of the males are reduced and useless for walking, while those of the female are well-developed. Eggs hemispherical or somewhat conical with sculptured surface. The caterpillars are stout with a large head and a series of setae along the sides of the body. The pupa is short and stout, usually with a covering of fine hairs and attached by cremastral hooks and girdle.

FAMILY Libytheidae

This is the smallest family of butterflies with only one species in Africa. Brown with yellow spots. The labial palps on the head are very long and project in front like a beak. Forelegs of males slender and reduced and without claws, while those of the females are well-developed. Eggs bottle-shaped and ridged. Caterpillars slender and smooth. Pupae suspended by the tail only, without girdle.

FAMILY Satyridae

Inconspicuous butterflies, brown being the prevailing colour, with eye-like spots on the wings. One or more of the veins of the forewings are dilated at the base. The forelegs of both sexes are degenerate, the tarsi of the male having one joint only, those of the female several joints, and they are not armed with claws. The eggs are rounded, marked with grooves. The caterpillars taper at both ends, smooth or coated with very fine hairs; usually feed on grasses. Pupae short, thick, rounded, lie free on the ground or held by cremastral hooks.

FAMILY Nymphalidae

Medium-sized or large butterflies, stoutly built, often with brilliant colours. Forelegs reduced in both sexes. The cell formed by the veins on the forewing is usually closed but that on the hind wing is open. The forelegs in both sexes are degenerate and useless for walking; in the male they have two tarsal joints and are brush-like, while in the female they have four joints and are not brush-like. The eggs are generally ribbed, with a flat area at the top. Caterpillars often bear spines or tubercles. Pupae are always suspended head downwards by the cremaster only.

FAMILY Acraeidae

Small to medium-sized butterflies with narrow wings. Forelegs degenerate and useless for walking. Red and black are common colours. They are poisonous and are mimicked by species of other families. Their flight is slow and deliberate. Wings thinly scaled. Females develop an abdominal structure called a sphragis after mating. Caterpillars armed with branched spines. Pupae suspended head downwards by cremastral hooks only.

FAMILY Danaidae

A small family of conspicuous butterflies with slow flight, protected from predation by poisonous chemicals sequestered from various plants. Mimicked by many species of other families. Forelegs greatly reduced in both sexes. Male with scent patch on each hind wing and scent brushes in end of abdomen. Cells of the wings closed. Eggs conical and ridged. Caterpillars smooth but most have one or more pairs of slender tentacles on their backs. Pupae are suspended head downwards by cremaster only.

FURTHER READING

Aurivillius, C.: 'The African Rhopalocera'. *In* Seitz, A., *The Macrolepidoptera of the World. 13.* Alfred Kernen, Stuttgart (1925). 613 pp

Clark, G. C. & Dickson, C. G. C.: *The Life Histories of the South African Lycaenid Butterflies.* Purnell & Sons, Cape Town (1971). 272 pp
Dickson, C. G. C. & Kroon, D. M. (Eds): *Pennington's Butterflies of Southern Africa.* Ad Donker, Johannesburg (1978). 670 pp
Evans, W. H.: *A Catalogue of the African Hesperiidae in the British Museum.* British Museum (Natural History), London (1937). 212 pp
Fox, R. M., Lindsey, A. W., Clench, H. K. & Miller, L. D.: *The Butterflies of Liberia.* Memoirs of the Entomological Society of America (1965). 19: 438 pp
Gifford, D.: *A List of the Butterflies of Malawi.* Blantyre, Malawi (1965). 151 pp
Owen, D. F.: *Tropical Butterflies.* Clarendon Press, Oxford (1971). 214 pp
Pinhey, E. C. G.: *Butterflies of Southern Africa.* Nelson, London (1965). 240 pp
Stempffer, H.: 'The Genera of the African Lycaenidae (Lepidoptera: Rhopalocera).' *Bulletin of the British Museum (Natural History), Entomology Supplement* (1967). 10:322 pp
Swanepoel, D. A.: *Butterflies of South Africa: Where, When and How they fly.* Maskew Miller, Cape Town (1953). 320 pp
Van Someren, V. G. L.: 'Revisional notes on African *Charaxes* (Lepidoptera: Nymphalidae).' Parts I-X. *Bulletin of the British Museum (Natural History) Entomology* (1963-75). 13: 197-242; 15: 183-235; 18: 47-101, 279-316; 23: 77-166; 25: 197-249; 26: 181-226; 27: 204-215; 29: 415-487; 32: 67-135
Van Son, G.: 'The Butterflies of Southern Africa.' part I. Papilionidae and Pieridae (1949); part 2. Danainae and Satyrinae (1955); part 3. Acraeinae (1963).' *Transvaal Museum Memoirs* (1949-63). 3, 8, 14
Williams, J. G.: *A Field Guide to the butterflies of Africa.* Collins, London (1969). 238 pp

Wasps 21

Wasps, bees and ants form an enormous order of over 100 000 species, known as the Hymenoptera, or membranous-winged insects. They vary enormously in size, habits and life histories, but all the winged members of the order have two pairs of membranous wings, the hind pair smaller than the front pair and the two linked by minute hooklets on the hind wings that fit into a fold in the front wing when the insect is in flight. The mouthparts are adapted for biting and chewing, and often for lapping and sucking as well. The ovipositor of the female is adapted for sawing, piercing or stinging. Male Hymenoptera cannot sting. Metamorphosis is complete, the larvae of the great majority of the order being legless, blind grubs.

The classification of the Hymenoptera is a somewhat difficult undertaking, partly because many of the wasps are very tiny creatures. We divide the order into two suborders: the Symphyta are the most primitive, and their abdomen is broad where it joins the thorax. All other Hymenoptera have a narrow constriction between the thorax and the abdomen, and belong to the suborder Apocrita. This group is further divided into a number of superfamilies which include all the most familiar wasps, as well as the bees (superfamily Apoidea) and the ants (superfamily Formicoidea). As the two last groups are so large and have such interesting social habits, they are dealt with in separate chapters.

SUBORDER **Symphyta**

Sawflies The most primitive Hymenoptera are the insects known as sawflies. As previously stated, they differ from all the others in that the abdomen is not separated from the thorax by a narrow constriction; the connection between the two is broad, and sawflies lack the narrow waist so characteristic of the higher Hymenoptera. Furthermore, the ovipositor of the female is not modified to form a sting but is a double-bladed saw with which she bores holes in plant tissue to hold her eggs. The habits of these insects are simple and they do not exhibit the remarkable instincts of the higher wasps, bees and ants. The larvae feed on plants, some in galls, some by burrowing in the stems, but the majority feed like caterpillars on leaves.

A common species in South Africa is the pelargonium sawfly, *Arge taeniata*, which belongs to the family Argidae, which is widely spread throughout Africa. The adult (so far only the female has been found) is about 10 mm long, black and yellow. The male is so rare that it is possible that such a creature does not exist, as is the case with many other species of sawflies.

When laying her eggs the female settles on the underside of a pelargonium leaf and, applying her saw to the surface, draws the blades alternately to and fro until she has made a slit in the leaf just large enough to receive an egg. The hole does not penetrate the upper side of the leaf so that the egg, when deposited, is encapsulated between the upper and lower epidermis of the leaf.

After it is laid the egg swells up to nearly three times its original size. We do not know what causes this, but possibly the drop of liquid which the female injects into the hole along with the egg may have something to do with it. In about 12 days the egg hatches into a larva which makes its way out of the chamber by biting a small round hole in the upper surface of the leaf where it feeds for three or four weeks, moulting five to seven times before it is fully grown. About 20 mm long, it looks very much like a small, green caterpillar, but it has 20 legs instead of the caterpillar's usual 16. As well as the six true legs on its thoracic segments, the pelargonium sawfly larva has seven pairs of prolegs, which lack the tiny hooks that are found on the prolegs of a caterpillar. Furthermore, the sawfly larva has only one eye on each side of its head whereas a caterpillar has five or six.

The fully grown larva seeks out a sheltered spot on the plant, or amid dead leaves at the base, where it spins a neat, silken cocoon, some 12 mm long, oval in shape and yellow in colour. After resting for several days, it pupates and ten days or so later the adult emerges. As the males are so rare, it is obvious that the majority, if not all, of the eggs of this species must develop parthenogenetically – without being fertilised.

The pear slug, *Caliroa cerasi*, is a member of the

300. The pelargonium sawfly, resting on top of the silken cocoon from which it has just emerged. 10 mm.

301. The pear slug, feeding on the upper surface of a plum leaf. 10 mm.

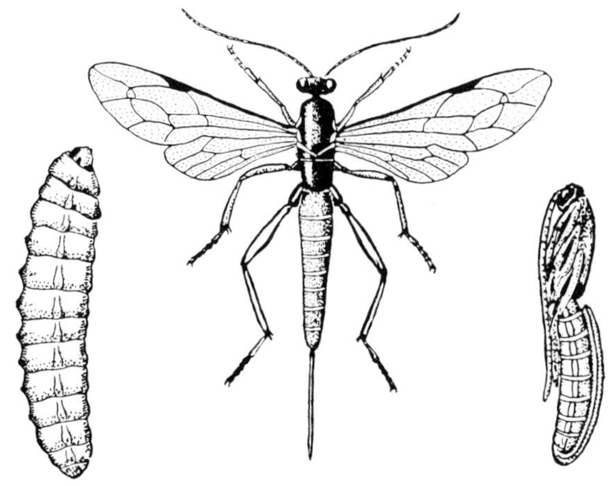

302. The ichneumonid parasite *(Sericopimpla sericata)* of the wattle bagworm, showing the larva (left), adult female (20 mm including ovipositor) and pupa (right).

family Tenthredinidae that has been introduced to Africa. In some years its larvae do severe damage to the foliage of pear, quince and plum trees. A black, slimy, slug-like creature, about 12 mm long, the larva feeds on the upper surface of the leaves. When fully grown it descends from the tree and buries itself in the soil at the base, creating a hard, dark cocoon around itself and then pupating. The adult is black and about 6 mm long. There are two generations of these sawflies a year in southern Africa, the adults of the first generation appearing in the spring and those of the second generation about mid-summer. The larvae of this summer generation spend the winter in their cocoons beneath the soil.

SUBORDER **Apocrita**

Ichneumonid wasps Parasitism is very common throughout nature and many people find this aspect of the study of the outdoor world cruel and repellent. What they do not realise is that parasitism is essential in maintaining an ecological balance: all living things, left unchecked, would reproduce so fast that they would soon exhaust their food resources. Parasites, by destroying their hosts, not only diminish pressure on food resources but also help control insect populations by affecting the death rate.

There are many families of Hymenoptera that parasitize other insects and they are the principal agents in keeping down numbers.

Members of the very large family of parasitic wasps, the Ichneumonidae, mostly prey upon caterpillars, but some are parasites of beetles, flies, wasps, bees and spiders. They are slender insects, varying in size from very small to comparatively large wasps of 25 mm or more in length. Some species are wingless, but the majority are winged, and the venation of the wings serves to distinguish them from their close relatives belonging to the family Braconidae. The female is armed with a long, slender and threadlike ovipositor.

The ichneumonid parasite of the wattle bagworm, *Sericopimpla sericata*, is common wherever its host is found and it plays an important rôle in keeping this pest in check. The adults vary in size but the males are usually about 12 mm long and the females about 20 mm, including the ovipositor; the head, thorax and hind legs are black, the abdomen red, and the forelegs are yellowish white. The female, when attacking a bagworm (for further details see Moths Chapter 19), settles on the outside of the bag, thrusts her ovipositor through it and lays her largish yellow egg within, attached to the side of the bag.

It hatches in about three days and the larva feeds as a parasite upon the bagworm caterpillar. It can move about in the bag with the help of the short, sharp spines on its back, which catch in the silken sides of the bag and hold the larva securely in position whilst it feeds. It has a pair of sharp mandibles with which it punctures the skin of its victim to obtain its juices. When fully grown the larva pupates inside the bag, beside the shrivelled remains of the caterpillar. The larva does not spin a cocoon but binds itself against the side of the bag by means of a few silken threads. In the female pupa the ovipositor can be seen curved over the back, but in the adult this appendage always points backwards. In some seasons ten to 20% of the bagworms may be destroyed by this parasite of which there are two generations a year.

The egg sacs of the black widow spider, *Latrodectus mactans*, are parasitized by a small ichneumonid called *Gelis latrodectiphagus*. The male is black, only about 5 mm long and has two pairs of wings; the female is about the same size and looks very much like an ant as she is wingless, but she can be recognised by the ovipositor at the end of her abdomen.

As many as 17 of these parasites have been reared from one spider egg-sac, which may contain about 170 eggs. Therefore it seems that each parasite needs about ten spider's eggs to bring it to maturity. The fully grown larvae of the parasite spin elongate cocoons inside the egg-sac in which they pupate; the adults emerge through small holes they make in the silken covering of the egg-sac. Several species of this genus, *Gelis*, with winged males and wingless females, are known to parasitize egg-sacs of spiders in other parts of the world but the above species is the only one so far recorded from Africa.

Of the many different species of ichneumonids, the reddish brown, slender wasp, *Enicospilos* species, that is often attracted to lights at night, is a parasite of the cutworm. Other ichneumonids that attack the caterpillars of butterflies make striking oval black and white cocoons, which are suspended by a thread near the dead body of the victim. The females of certain species that parasitize caddisfly larvae enter the water in search of their prey and can remain below the surface for a long time.

All the members of this large family show remarkable instincts in their ability to find their hosts and to provide for their offspring as well. Although they are parasites, many have to work hard to find suitable hosts and to distribute their eggs; for example, the species that parasitize wood-boring insects have first to locate their victims hidden in the timber and then have to bore laboriously through the wood with their slender ovipositors in order to reach the larvae and lay their eggs on or in them. How they ascertain the exact position of the borers in their burrows remains an enigma.

Braconid wasps The parasitic wasps of the large family, Braconidae, are closely related to the ichneumonids, differing from them mainly in the venation of the wings. Their hosts include caterpillars, fly larvae, beetle larvae, aphids and other insects. The species that prey upon aphids are very common and widely spread and the results of their work may be seen on almost any plant that is infested. Careful observation reveals numbers of aphids that are swollen and have a neat, round hole in the skin; these have been killed by parasite larvae and the holes are the exits made by the adults when leaving the dead bodies of their hosts.

The female *Lysiphlebus* lays her eggs inside the bodies of the aphids, generally a single egg in each host. When attacking a victim she stands just behind it and bends her abdomen forward, under her thorax, so that the tip projects in front of her head. Then, with a quick thrust of her ovipositor, she pierces the skin of the aphid and inserts her egg. Before she dies, she may lay 300 – 400 eggs.

The egg hatches into a tiny, blind, white, legless maggot with an appendage like a tail on its hind end. This tail-like appendage is found in many parasitic larvae belonging to the Hymenoptera and it is thought to have a respiratory function; it disappears when the young larva's tracheae are fully developed and it moults. It feeds for two days on the body fluids and body fat of the aphid before casting its skin. It is now a fat white maggot lodged near the hind end of the aphid. It feeds again for two days and then casts its skin once more. When it is a week old and fully grown, the host aphid dies. The parasite now cuts a small slit in the skin on the underside of the dead aphid and cements it, through this slit, to the leaf or stem with a little silk, so that the dead body, with the larva inside, cannot fall off or be blown away. The parasite pupates inside the swollen, hardened skin of the aphid and the adult cuts a neat, circular hole to emerge a few days later.

The tiny parasites of the genus *Lysiphlebus* play an important part in keeping down the numbers of aphids. Not only do they cause the premature death of the pests but they prevent them from multiplying too rapidly because the parasitized aphids produce few or no young. The *Lysiphlebus* larvae are themselves kept in check by hyperparasites – tiny wasps that lay their eggs in or on the parasitic larvae inside the aphids.

Anybody who has tried to rear moths and butterflies from caterpillars will know that the caterpillars frequently die before reaching maturity, killed by various kinds of parasites. Often the dead body of a caterpillar is surrounded by small white cocoons from which slender black wasps emerge. The commonest of such parasites are members of the braconid genus, *Apanteles*. One of these is an important parasite of the pine brown-tail moth, *Euproctis terminalis*. At times numbers of the caterpillars of this moth may be found dead on the pines, small, dirty white cocoons heaped in a mass around them; these are the cocoons of *Apanteles euproctidis*, a tiny (about 3 mm), black wasp with red legs. Another species, *Apanteles halfordi*, attacks the caterpillars of the diamond-back moth and its small white cocoons may be found fastened to the cabbage leaves on which the caterpillars are feeding. A third species, *Apanteles ruficrus*, preys upon the army worm; there are many others.

The Karoo caterpillar parasite, *Chelonus texanus*, is a small wasp about 10 mm long and dark brown in colour. It was introduced into South Africa from America in the 1950's to help control the Karoo caterpillar, *Loxostege*

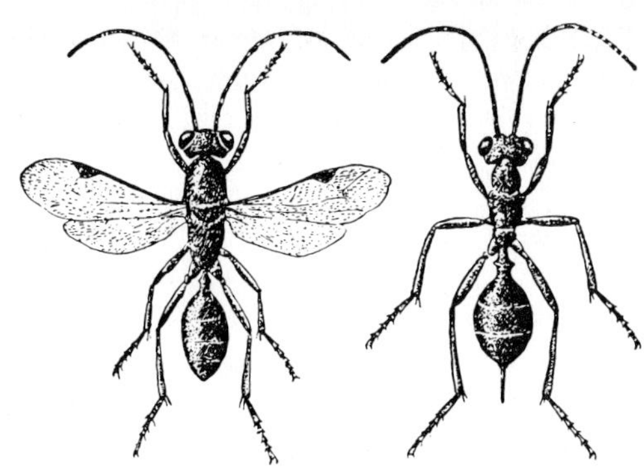

303. The ichneumonid parasite *(Gelis latrodectiphagus)* of the black widow spider, showing the winged male (left) and the wingless female (6 mm including ovipositor).

304. The cocoon of an ichneumonid wasp parasite of butterfly caterpillars, showing the typical thin silken suspension thread and the black and white markings.

305. The ichneumonid wasp *Osprynchotus* sp. is a common parasite of the mud wasp *(Sceliphron spirifex)*. Here it is seen using its ovipositor to 'drill' through the casing of the mud wasp nest in order to deposit her eggs within the developing mud wasp larvae. 26 mm.

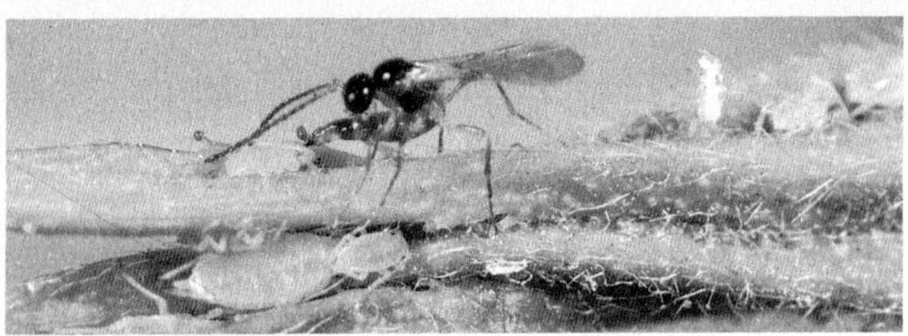

306. A braconid wasp (*Lysiphlebus* sp.) brings her abdomen under her body in order to lay an egg within the body of an aphid. 3 mm.

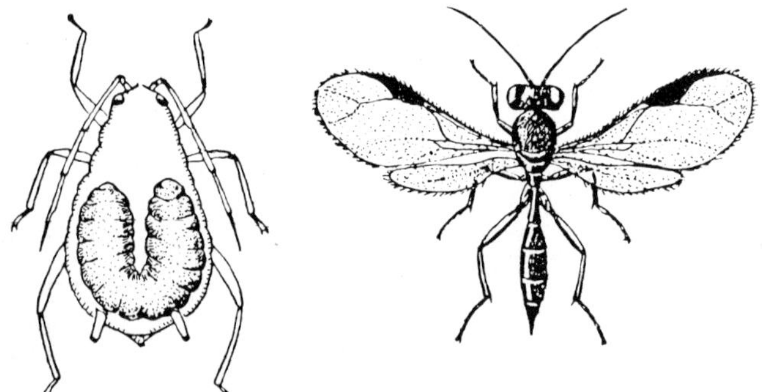

307. The aphid parasite (*Lysiphlebus* sp.) showing the female wasp (right) and the larva developing inside an aphid.

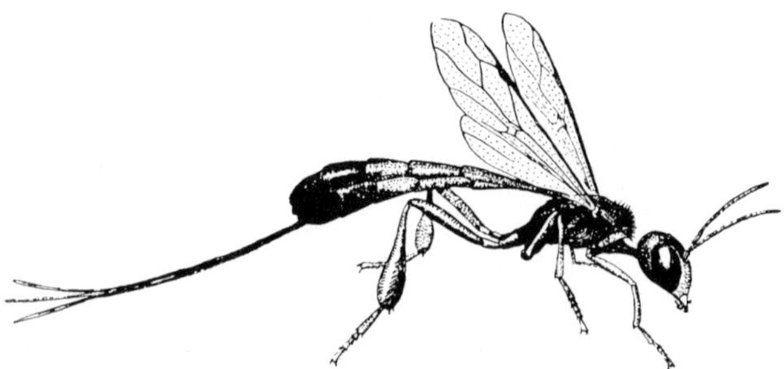

308. The ensign wasp, *Gasteruption punctulatum*, a parasite of solitary bees. Note the curious position of the junction between the abdomen and the thorax.

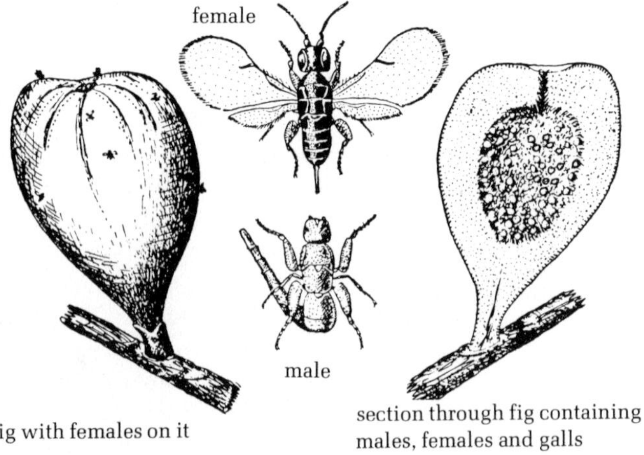

309. Some features of the Capri fig insect, *Blastophaga psenes*.

frustalis, which in some seasons does immense damage to the chief fodder plants of sheep in the Karoo. The female wasp lays her eggs in the eggs of the moth. Such parasitized moth eggs hatch normally and the caterpillars feed and grow and pupate as though nothing was the matter with them. Meanwhile, the parasitic larvae feed and grow inside the caterpillars, one in each, and they pupate inside the pupal skin of their victims. Although many thousands of the *Chelonus* wasps were bred in the laboratory (using caterpillars of the common meal moth as hosts) and then released in the Karoo, they failed to become established and the project was a failure.

Ensign wasps Members of the superfamily Evanioidea are sometimes called ensign wasps as a result of their curious habit of carrying the abdomen raised. This arises because the slender base of the abdomen is joined to the thorax high up on the back, and not in a straight line, as is the case with other insects. The tiny wasps that belong to the family Evaniidae are most welcome around our homes, for their larvae are parasitic upon the egg cases of cockroaches, and help keep down the numbers of these obnoxious insects.

The family Gasteruptiidae is found all over Africa; it contains only one genus with a number of species whose larvae are parasitic on the larvae of other wasps, or various kinds of bees. A common species, *Gasteruption punctulatum*, is a slender wasp, about 12 mm long and reddish brown in colour. The female has a long, thread-like ovipositor that is longer than the rest of the body, and black with a white tip. She flies slowly and deliberately, her abdomen in the air, closely examining holes in walls, fencing posts, tree stumps and similar places where her victims make their nests. She preys upon primitive bees of the family Colletidae and she seeks nests that contain freshly completed cells, containing the mixture of honey and pollen so laboriously gathered by the bees, and an egg floating on top of the semi-liquid food. She seems to be able to detect through her sense of smell when a hole contains a nest and, having found such a nest, she at once plunges boldly inside to investigate. Should the owner of the nest be at home she backs out, followed by the bee which drives her off, but there is no quarrel or fight. The parasite simply settles near the hole and waits until the bee leaves to hunt for food. Then into the hole the wasp goes again to make a brief inspection after which she comes out and, if satisfied, backs into the hole once more, tail first.

Her ovipositor consists of three threads, the two outer ones forming a protective sheath for the slender tube in the middle. When she re-enters the hole backwards she holds the two halves of the sheath bent up out of the way over her back, and only the slender tubular, central thread of the ovipositor is thrust down into the bee's cell. Her long, white egg passes down this capillary tube and is stuck on to the side of the cell, just above the mass of honey and pollen. Then, her work at the nest completed, she leaves the hole and flies away to repeat the process elsewhere.

The bee returns to her home, quite unaware of what has happened in her absence, and proceeds to build and stock more cells on top of the one that has been parasitized. Three days later the parasite's egg hatches. As the bee's egg takes eight days to hatch, the parasitic larva has a head start. A tiny maggot, it creeps down the side of the cell and makes its way across the sticky surface of the honey and pollen until it reaches the fat, sausage-shaped bee's egg lying on top of the food, whereupon it proceeds to devour the egg which is much bigger than itself. At the end of 24 hours the bee's egg has disappeared and the parasite is considerably enlarged as a result of its huge meal. It now looks like a small, white flat-fish lying on top of the honey. Having despatched its rival, it changes its diet and turns its attention to the honey and pollen. This lasts for about a week, by which time the parasite is about 6 mm long, only about half grown.

In the meantime, the bee's egg in the cell above has hatched and the bee larva is feeding on the meal provided by its mother. The parasite now breaks into the cell from below and feeds on honey and pollen there. As soon as this is finished, it turns on the bee larva and kills and devours that as well. Thus the parasite destroys two cells in the bee's nest before it is fully grown, changing its diet three times, first an egg, then honey and pollen, and finally a larva. In 16–18 days it is fully grown and pupates inside the two ravaged cells.

All the while it is feeding the larva does not pass any excrement. Its stomach is a blind sac which does not link with the hind intestine; therefore the waste matter from its food accumulates in its stomach. When it is fully grown and has stopped feeding, the stomach and intestine join and the larva cleanses itself by passing all the excrement at once. It then turns white in preparation for pupation. Through this remarkable provision of nature the larva in its confined quarters and in close contact with its food, does not soil its surroundings until its growth is complete. This is characteristic of nearly all the larvae of the higher Hymenoptera that live in cells amid their food supply.

There are two or three generations a year of these parasites. When the autumn arrives the parasitic grubs lying in their cells do not pupate but pass through the winter months as larvae, pupating only when the warmer weather arrives. Then, when the solitary bees are active once more, the adult parasites emerge, the females to find new nesting sites and repeat the cycle – in the process helping maintain the balance of nature. The male adult is easily distinguished from his mate as he does not have the long ovipositor on his abdomen.

Several other ensign wasps are very common in Africa, and may be seen wherever their hosts make their nests. *Gasteruption robustum,* for example, may regularly be found in association with carpenter bees.

Chalcid wasps The superfamily of small wasps called the Chalcidoidea contains a bewilderingly large number of species placed in several families. They are mostly small, black, metallic insects with elbowed antennae and wings that are devoid of veins, except for the stout vein along the edge of the front wing. Nearly all of them are parasites of other insects, but there are some that feed on vegetable matter, in the stems of plants, inside seeds, or in flowers. An example of the latter is the interesting little fig insect.

There are many different species of wild fig found in Africa; some are forest giants, whilst others are smaller and grow on rocky mountain sides under harsh conditions. All of them bear fruits similar to the cultivated fig – a thickened, hollow, juicy stem with a large number of tiny flowers inside it. Since the only entrance to the fig is a narrow opening at the top, surrounded by a ring of small bracts, it is clear that insects such as bees and butterflies cannot possibly get inside the figs to pollinate them, nor can the wind carry pollen from one flower to another, because they are hidden in the deep cavity in the fig. The question therefore arises, how are the figs pollinated?

The answer is that they have associated with them certain peculiar insects, tiny wasps called fig insects that belong to the family Agaonidae. The females are black and have four wings and are much more active than their wingless mates which never leave the figs in which they were born and bred. The female fig insect is fertilised inside the fig soon after she emerges from the pupa. Then she creeps out of the small opening at the top of the fig and, in doing so, passes over the male flowers in the fig and becomes well dusted with pollen. She subsequently flies to younger, smaller figs on the same or on neighbouring trees and creeps into them, thus pollinating the young figs. The female wasps lay their eggs in the ovaries of the female flowers and the larvae develop inside them to produce the next generation.

If some ripe figs from wild fig trees are collected and cut open it is usually quite easy to find the galls made by the larvae inside. Each is about the size of a large pin's head, and often the little brown males and the black, winged females may also be found in the cavity. Apparently most species of wild fig have their own species of fig insect associated with them and already many different species of fig insects have been described and named.

The best known is the Capri fig insect, *Blastophaga psenes,* which was introduced into California in 1899 from the Middle East to assist in the cultivation of Smyrna figs. Smyrna figs produce no pollen themselves and they must be pollinated with pollen from the Capri fig, which is inedible. The little fig insect does this work and it was only after the introduction of the insect that Smyrna figs could be successfully grown in California. In 1908 it was brought from California to South Africa and established in Capri figs growing at the Cape. For many years the Capri fig insects were distributed to fruit growers in South Africa free of charge, to encourage the cultivation of Smyrna figs, but this was discontinued when it was found that this type of fig was not a commercial success.

The families Encyrtidae and Aphelinidae contain a great many species that are parasites of insects such as citrus red scale, soft brown scale, black scale, pernicious scale, citrus psylla and various aphids, which cause considerable economic loss. As a result, agricultural entomologists in Africa have experimented with importing various of these tiny wasps to combat the pests, and in so doing, reduce reliance on expensive and often dangerous insecticides. These experiments have met with varying degrees of success, with some of the parasites failing to become established, while others have proved extremely successful.

The woolly aphid parasite, *Aphelinus mali,* is a small chalcid wasp belonging to the Aphelinidae that was introduced into South Africa in 1923 from the United States to help combat that major pest of the apple grower, the woolly aphid. It has become established in South Africa and widely spread in other parts of Africa as well and plays an important part in keeping this serious pest in check.

The wasp is very small, smaller than the aphid itself, black with a pale band across the base of the abdomen. The female, when about to lay an egg in an aphid, first approaches it from behind, examines it with the tips of her antennae and then turns quickly and jabs it with her sharp ovipositor. If she succeeds in piercing the skin of her victim her tiny egg is deposited inside its body. This hatches into a typical parasitic larva, white, legless and blind, that feeds on the juices of its host. The parasitized aphid swells, turns black and eventually dies, leaving the larva to pupate inside the dead body. About three weeks to a month after the egg was laid, the adult wasp emerges through a round hole it bites in the skin of the dead aphid.

Some members of the Encyrtidae exhibit the extraordinary phenomenon known as polyembryony, or the development of several individuals from one egg. One of the commonest examples of this is to be found in caterpillars that burrow in the stems of shrubs belonging to the genus *Aspalathus.* The action of the caterpillar causes a swelling on the stem of the plant and, if this is cut open, the caterpillar inside may well be parasitized. What remains of the caterpillar looks like a bundle of tiny white sausages, enclosed in a translucent skin. A hundred or more tiny black chalcid wasps may emerge from such a caterpillar and all are of the same sex.

It is not known how the parasite attacks the *Aspalathus* borer but, from observations made on similar parasites in Europe, it is probable that the attack begins with the moth egg. The female wasp seeks out the egg of the moth attached to the stem of the *Aspalathus* plant, punctures it and deposits her own minute egg inside. The moth's egg develops normally and hatches, despite the presence of the parasite's egg. The latter then begins to grow inside the young caterpillar into a long string of what look like microscopic sausages which separate and give rise to a number of larvae, all from the one original egg. They feed on the body fluids of the caterpillar and eventually kill it when it is nearly fully grown. As many as 50 or more larvae may arise from the one egg which, if the egg has not been fertilised, will all develop into males, whilst if the egg was fertilised all will be females.

Sometimes the bloated skin of a cutworm may be found in the garden, pierced with innumerable small holes like the lid of a pepper-pot. Such a caterpillar has been killed by a polyembryonic parasite and the holes in the skin are the exits made by the numerous progeny from the parasite's egg or eggs. More than a thousand have been counted from one caterpillar.

The tiny wasp, *Mormoniella vitripennis,* a member of the chalcid family Pteromalidae, is a widespread parasite of blow flies in Africa and elsewhere. The adult is black and only about 3 mm long and it may often be seen walking about among the larvae and puparia of blow flies under carcases on the veld. The female lays her eggs only in the puparia, ignoring the maggots, and she may lay 30 or more minute eggs in one puparium. The parasitic larvae feed on the pupa inside the puparium, kill it and then pupate inside the case, beside the shrivelled remains of their host.

Some of the smallest of all insects are egg parasites belonging to the chalcid families Mymaridae and Trichogrammatidae. A member of the latter group is the codling moth egg parasite, *Trichogrammatoidea lutea,* which despite its lengthy name is so small that four or five of them can reach maturity in one of the moth's eggs which is itself only about the size of a pin's head. This minute insect is indigenous to Africa and renders valuable service to the fruit grower by destroying large numbers of the eggs of various pests such as the codling moth, the American bollworm and many others.

An insect which originally came from Australia and which has now spread throughout Africa wherever eucalyptus trees are grown is *Patasson nitens,* which belongs to the Mymaridae. It is a tiny egg parasite of the eucalyptus snout beetle, and helps to keep this serious pest in check.

Cuckoo wasps The cuckoo wasps, or ruby wasps, are small insects with stout bodies that are brilliantly coloured, metallic green, blue and red, and they form the family Chrysididae. They are parasitic on solitary bees and wasps; on bright, sunny days they may be seen running about, their wings quivering and antennae vibrating, on walls, stumps and on the ground where the nests of their hosts are to be found. It is very easy to recognise members of this family because of their distinctive colouring and appearance and because only three or four abdominal segments are visible from above. The upper side of the abdomen is rounded and densely pitted, whilst the underside is flat or concave; this allows the insect to roll itself into a ball when it is alarmed, protecting the vulnerable underside, and leaving only the hard, dorsal surface exposed.

The female seeks out the nests of other bees and wasps. Having found one she waits until the owner is away and then slips inside to lay her egg in a cell. Her larva feeds on the larva of the host insect or on the food supply provided for it. When fully grown it spins a dense silken cocoon inside the cell, empties its alimentary canal of waste matter and then settles down for a long sleep until the following season; it then changes into a pupa and a fortnight or so later the adult emerges.

There are a large number of different species of

cuckoo wasp found in Africa but little is known about their habits and life histories. One of the commonest, the green cuckoo wasp, *Chrysis lyncea*, is about 12 mm long and preys on mason wasps and mud wasps. A smaller species, banded with green, blue and red, *Chrysis concinna*, parasitizes leafcutter and carder bees.

Spider-hunting wasps The spider-hunting wasps form a very large family, the Pompilidae, that is well represented in Africa. They may be recognised by their long hind legs, curled antennae and smoky wings, and they can be seen running on the ground at great speed, wings and antennae vibrating as they search for the spiders with which they provide for their young.

One of the largest and most striking wasps is the black spider-hunter (or, strictly speaking, huntress, as it is only the female that seeks out the spiders), *Hemipepsis capensis*, about 35 mm long, with a black body and legs, and smoky brown wings. Other species have wings of a dark metallic blue and some are quite small but they are all very similar in their ways.

The big black pompilid wasps hunt the formidable brown and hairy baboon spiders, with red round the mouth and a stout body about 35 mm long, or the large ground spiders, *Palystes* species, with the dark bars on the underside of their legs. The female wasp may be seen running tirelessly amid the undergrowth, looking under dead leaves and beneath fallen logs, under stones, and similar places that are the usual haunts of her prey.

When she finds a spider large and bulky enough for her purpose – usually a female like herself, because the male spiders are too small for her needs – she at once attacks it boldly. The French entomologist, Fabre, in describing the habits of a closely related wasp found in southern France, says that the wasp first stings the spider in the front of the head, in this way paralysing the fangs and rendering them harmless. Then, according to Fabre she goes into close attack and wrestles with her disarmed foe until she can sting it on the underside of the body, between the bases of the legs. Here, just below the surface, is lodged the large nerve centre that controls the spider's movements and, by stinging it in this spot, the wasp paralyses the spider, but does not kill it.

Fabre's observations, made more than 85 years ago, have been queried by later observers and it seems that the hunting wasps do not sting their prey precisely in the nerve centres, as he thought, but that stinging in almost any part of the body will produce the required paralysis. It can easily be shown that the victim is not killed, for if a spider after being stung is taken away from one of these wasps, it will show signs of life by feeble movements of its legs for some days and it may even recover sufficiently to be able to walk; alternatively it may die after a week or so.

After the fight the wasp cleans herself and then goes off to look for a dry sheltered hole or crack or crevice big enough to hold the bulky spider. Having found such a place, she may do some digging and scraping to enlarge the cavity, but she generally tries to conserve as much

310. Many species of parasitic wasps possess ovipositors several times their own body length such as this species, which uses its ovipositor to lay its eggs into the larvae of fig insects, deep within the fruit of the Sycamore fig. 25 mm including ovipositor.

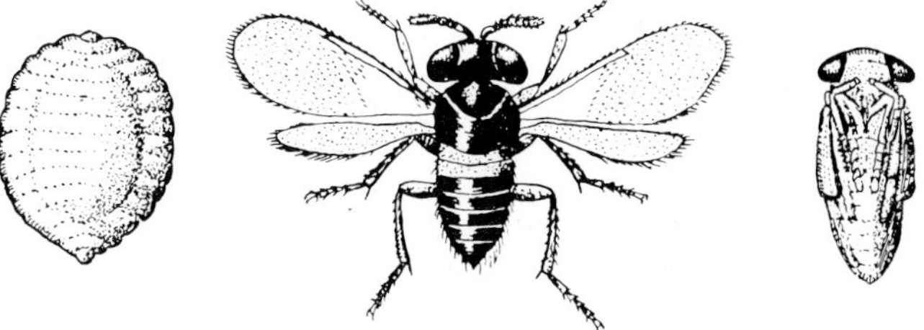

311. The woolly aphid parasite *(Aphelinus mali)*, showing larva (left), pupa (right) and adult.

312. Chalcid wasp (inserting its ovipositor) parasitizing the larvae of braconid wasps within their cocoons. This is a case of 'hyper-parasitism', since the braconid wasp larvae have themselves been parasites of a caterpillar. 2 mm.

313. A brilliant metallic green cuckoo wasp emerging from a nest cell of the mud wasp, *Sceliphron spirifex*, after laying her own egg in the nest.

314. Spider hunting wasp *(Hemipepsis capensis)* about to attack a large baboon spider, prior to paralysing it and dragging it off to her underground nest. 35 mm.

315. Female mutillid wasp, wingless and with conspicuous pale spots on her black abdomen; the thorax is reddish brown. Their powerful sting presents a nasty hazard to anyone walking barefoot in areas where they occur. 14 mm.

316. A scoliid wasp larva feeding on a fruit beetle larva within a compost heap. 10 mm.

energy as possible by finding a ready-made hole of correct proportions. If the selfsame spot where she herself was reared is reasonably near, she will return to it and prepare her nest there. Often she will return again and again to the same spot and make her cells close together in the soil.

Having chosen the site for her nest she flies back to the paralysed spider and, in doing this, she shows the remarkable memory and sense of direction that is characteristic of most of the higher Hymenoptera. She flies without hesitation back to the spot where she left the stunned spider and then, walking backwards, she drags her heavy burden over the rough ground to the hole, even though it may be many metres distant. From time to time she may leave the spider and fly back to the hole, as though refreshing her memory of its location. Once finally arrived at the hole she drags the spider down into it and lays her large, oval white egg on its abdomen. Her laying completed, she comes out and fills in the hole by scraping soil into it, levelling off the surface carefully and dragging small twigs and dead leaves over it so that no trace of her nest is visible on the surface. Finally she flies off to repeat the whole performance; she may bring her next victim back to this spot, burying it close beside the first, or she may make her next nest some distance away, particularly if her hunting takes her far afield.

The egg hatches in about ten days and the larva feeds on the paralysed spider, which provides enough food for the whole of the larva's life. By the time the spider is consumed, only the legs and the skin remain uneaten. By now the larva is fully grown and it begins to spin a dense cocoon of brownish silk. It now cleanses its alimentary canal of waste matter, the stomach opening into the intestine for the first time. It then lies motionless inside its cocoon for months, all through the winter, until the arrival of warmer weather the following summer triggers pupation which lasts two or three weeks at which point the adult wasp emerges.

Mutillid wasps Small insects that look like ants, about 6 mm long, mostly with a dark red thorax and black abdomen marked with white spots or bands, may often be seen running about restlessly in hot sunshine. These female wasps of the family Mutillidae, whose velvety, antlike appearance has led to their being called 'velvet ants', do not live in social communities and they are only distantly related to the true ants. These females are armed with a strong, curved sting and can inflict a painful wound if handled carelessly. The males are larger still and stronger and have two pairs of wings; their colouring is as a rule similar to that of the females, but in some species the two sexes differ markedly.

The female can stridulate by rubbing the narrow joints between the thorax and abdomen together and it is said that a male will sometimes be attracted to a spot if a female is held down and made to stridulate in protest. It is also said that the big, strong males of some species literally abduct the females, picking them up off the ground and flying away with them when about to mate.

Many mutillid wasps are parasitic on other bees and wasps, while some attack beetles and flies and three species of *Smicromyrme* have been reared from the puparia of tsetse flies. *Dolichomutilla guineensis* has been bred from the nests of the mud wasp, *Sceliphron spirifex*. It is about 12 mm long, with a red thorax and a black abdomen with a white band. Like the rest of the mutillids, its thorax is so hard that it is difficult to pierce it with an entomological pin.

For the rest, very little is known about the life histories of African mutillids. It seems that most lay their eggs on larvae in the nests, and when the eggs hatch the mutillid larvae feed as external parasites upon their hosts.

Scoliid wasps The family of solitary wasps known as the Scoliidae is well represented in Africa. They are mostly hairy, black and marked with bands of yellow or red. They include in their number some of the largest of wasps, although some are small and slender. Both sexes are winged and frequently the female is much larger and stouter than the male. Members of this family may be recognised by the constriction between the first and second segments of the abdomen.

Scoliid wasps prey upon the larvae of beetles belonging to the scarab family, the females seeking out their victims in the soil and in heaps of decaying leaves and vegetable debris. Having found a suitable beetle larva, the wasp stings, paralysing it, but a spark of life remains in the body so that it does not decay or dry up. She does not carry the larva away to a nest but leaves it just where she found it and she lays her egg on its ventral surface, just behind the legs. She then goes off to find other beetle larvae and repeats the process.

The egg hatches into a white legless maggot that feeds, never shifting its position, as an external parasite upon the beetle larva. When it is fully grown it spins a dense, oval cocoon of silk beside the shrivelled skin of the beetle and pupates.

Mason wasps The mason wasps of the family Eumenidae fold their forewings longitudinally when at rest, reducing them to half their normal width, and this characteristic, shared with the social wasps (Vespidae), enables us to recognise them easily. These are slender-waisted wasps that nest in holes in the ground and in hollow stems, or build mud cells on twigs, stones and walls; the only material they use in building their partitions and cells is clay moistened with saliva. They are mostly black or black and yellow and they prey only upon caterpillars.

One of the commonest and most widely spread species is the yellow and black mason wasp, *Delta caffer*, that is about 25 mm long, conspicuously marked with black on a yellow background. The female constructs beautiful little hemispherical cells of mud, with the circular opening at the top surrounded by a neatly curved rim. As soon as she has completed her cell she lays her egg inside; this is the reverse of the usual practice, as most solitary bees and wasps lay their eggs only after the cells have been stocked with food. The egg of this wasp is also peculiar in that it is suspended from the roof of the cell by a thread so that it hangs in the air like a tiny sausage on a string. It is suggested that this is a precaution to ensure the safety of the young larva when

317. A mason wasp (*Delta* sp.) arrives at her partly constructed nest, carrying a pellet of mud in her jaws.

318. Her rapidly vibrating jaws produce a buzzing sound as the mason wasp fashions her nest from the fluid mud.

319. Once construction is completed, she lays a single egg in the nest and proceeds to stock it with several paralysed caterpillars.

it first hatches and starts to feed. The caterpillars stored in the nest by the mother are only partially paralysed and can still wriggle about, so that if the newly-hatched larva were to lie in their midst, it might be crushed. For the first few days of its life it hangs from the thread, with its tail end still in the egg-shell; in this position it can reach its food but it is out of the way of the writhing caterpillars. When it is bigger and stronger it drops from the thread, as it is no longer in danger of being crushed.

The female stores a number of caterpillars – a dozen or more – in a cell, after which she breaks down the rim round the entrance and plasters the whole cell with a protective coating of clay. Having completed this task she leaves the cell, never to bother about it again, and goes off to start another one elsewhere; she may complete ten or a dozen such cells before her life's work is finished.

The mason wasps of the genus *Delta* have a long, slender waist, but other members of the family, such as *Odynerus* species, have very short waists scarcely visible between the thorax and abdomen.

Social wasps These slender brown wasps, about 25 mm long, that make their paper nests beneath verandah roofs and are often spoken of as 'hornets', are very well known in most parts of Africa. They are primitive social wasps of the genus *Belonogaster,* and there are several species, one of the commonest and most widely spread being *Belonogaster junceus*.

A fertilised female starts her nest by making a tough stalk of fibrous material under the shelter of a roof or an overhanging stone or bank, or some similar spot. On this she constructs her first cell of papery material, hanging with the opening downwards; she adds cells round it in concentric circles. Frequently she is joined by one or more females who assist in the labour of nest-building and a small colony forms. As soon as the cells are deep enough, the females lay their eggs in the bottom of them and, when the larvae hatch, they are fed with pellets of chewed caterpillars, brought to them by the females.

When a larva is fully grown the cell in which it lies is capped with papery material. The larvae pupate, developing within the cells into sexual individuals, males and females; there are no sterile workers among these wasps. The daughters stay with their mothers and assist with the nesting. There may be a certain division of labour, as it seems that the older females devote themselves to egg-laying whilst the younger hunt for food. The males remain in the nest but they do no work and are fed by the females. The nests never grow very large, mostly consisting of about 50 cells, although sometimes larger nests of 100–200 cells are found. When a nest reaches this size small groups of females leave it to found new nests elsewhere.

The smaller social wasps, *Polistes* species, are also very common and widely spread in Africa. They build their paper nests, consisting of a single comb with the openings of the cells pointing downwards, suspended by a central stalk in a sheltered spot, on the twig of a bush, or on the underside of an over-hanging rock, beneath a roof, and so on. The nest is usually started by a single female, the queen, who works alone, feeding her young on pellets of chewed insects. Her offspring may be fully developed females, like herself, or they may be workers, capable of laying eggs that develop only into males.

A particularly interesting point about these social wasps is the relationship between the larvae and the females that feed them. The hungry larvae protrude their heads with open mouths from their cells, like young nestling birds. It is said that they may even, when very hungry, scratch the sides of their cells to attract the attention of their nurses. When a larva is touched, a drop of clear liquid trickles from its mouth and this the attending female eagerly laps up. The liquid is sweet saliva and it is obvious that the adult wasps relish it enormously. All the adult wasps, males as well as females, are extremely eager for this salivary secretion and they are often observed on a *Belonogaster* nest soliciting the young for a sip. It is said that a nurse may even ill-treat a larva that does not give up the desired secretion quickly enough; she will seize the larva's head in her jaws, draw it towards her and then suddenly jam it back into the cell; this treatment, observers report, usually produces the desired result.

The social wasps belong to the family Vespidae and they, like the mason wasps, fold their wings longitudinally when at rest. *Belonogaster* and *Polistes* belong to the subfamily Polistinae; the subfamily Vespinae is, happily, not represented in Africa – the hornets and 'yellow jackets', (genera *Vespa* and *Vespula*) of Europe and America are dangerous insects whose stings cause the deaths of a number of people each year. Unfortunately, however, *Vespula germanica* has been introduced to South Africa from Europe where it appears to have become established in the Cape peninsula. It has bright yellow and black markings and builds a large nest of grey paper-like material. This may be fairly large, but it is usually subterranean, or at least concealed in some way. The original nest is constructed by the queen, but after the first brood she devotes her time to egg-laying. The larvae are fed on insects or pieces of meat and these wasps are therefore attracted to decaying carcases and even to bee hives. There is a real danger that *Vespula germanica* will spread to other parts of the continent in the future.

Sphecid wasps The family Sphecidae is a very large group of wasps, many of which are common and familiar insects throughout Africa. The family is divided into a number of subfamilies, each with varied habits and life histories.

Sand wasps and mud wasps

Among the solitary wasps that are found in our gardens there are none more deserving of the gardener's interest and protection than the slender-bodied black and red sand wasps of the subfamily Sphecinae. Several species are quite common and they vary in length from 20–25 mm or more. All have a black head, thorax and hind tip of the abdomen, with a long, slender, red waist.

The female sand wasp may often be seen digging her nest at the side of a path or in a sunny bank. If undisturbed, she will sink a tunnel in the hard soil to a depth of about 50 mm and at the bottom she hollows out a chamber about 20 mm in diameter. The soil and sand particles are carried up between her head and front legs and then swept away by vigorous kicks of her hind legs. Small stones and other obstacles are dragged out in her jaws and she flies 30 cm or so to drop them away from her dwelling, where they cannot hinder her.

When she has finished digging, she rests for a time, basking in the hot sunshine, carefully polishing her body and wings and sweeping the dust off her feelers by means of the tiny brush and comb she carries on each front leg. Certain species of *Ammophila* carefully cover the entrance to the nest with a small, flat stone before leaving, a truly remarkable instinctive action that seems to indicate intelligence – but they do not all do this.

Her nest ready, she now sets off to hunt, running quickly over the ground, searching amid the dense undergrowth, under clods of earth and amid dead leaves for the big, smooth caterpillars known as cutworms. When she finds one she immediately falls upon it and there is a short fierce struggle. Eventually, despite the wild writhings of the caterpillar, the wasp swings her slender abdomen round and stings her victim several times on the underside of the body, paralysing it.

It is too big for the wasp to carry through the air so she drags it along the ground to the nest. Once at her tunnel she drags her victim down into the chamber and lays her oval white egg on it, usually fixing it across the body about a third of the way back from the head, where there are no legs. She then returns to the surface and sweeps sand into the nest, sealing the entrance. When the spot is smoothly concealed she flies away never to return or to bother about that particular nest again. She repeats the whole operation about a dozen times before her labours are completed and she dies.

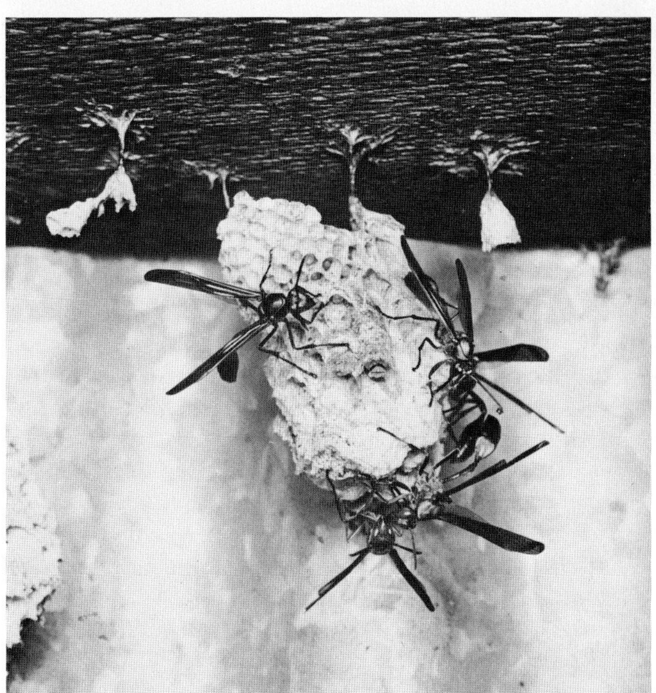

320. Watch out! Large paper wasps (*Belonogaster junceus*) raise their wings in alarm at the photographer's presence. This species will use its powerful sting at the slightest provocation. 35 mm.

The egg hatches in two or three weeks into a larva which feeds on the paralysed caterpillar. By the time it has consumed its huge meal it is fully grown and it spins a silken cocoon in which it sleeps for several months. Finally, the following spring or summer, it changes into a pupa and then about a fortnight later the adult wasp emerges.

The majority of the Sphecinae have habits similar to those described above, but there are some that build nests of mud and capture spiders instead of caterpillars. One of the commonest of these is the black and yellow mud wasp, *Sceliphron spirifex,* that makes its mud nests beneath verandah roofs, and in outhouses where it has free access to its nesting site. The nest is easily distinguished from that of the mason wasps, *Delta*

321. A sand wasp (*Ammophila* sp.) drags a large lump of soil backwards as she excavates her burrow. 25 mm.

322. In the nest chamber some 80 mm below ground, a sand wasp larva feeds on a caterpillar paralysed by the mother wasp.

species, for the entrance is at one end, not in the middle with a neat rim as is the case with the nests of *Delta*.

The female, after stocking her nest with a number of small, paralysed spiders, lays her egg on one of the spiders when the nest is about half filled. Once she has brought enough spiders to feed her young, she plugs the entrance to the cell with mud and then proceeds to construct a second cell alongside the first. So she goes on and, if undisturbed, she may make a group of half a dozen or more cells side by side. Finally she coats them roughly with a thick layer of mud as an extra protection. Frequently incomplete nests may be found that consist of only one or two cells without the thick protective coat; these are apparently the work of females that have been disturbed and either forced to desert the nest or killed.

Simple experiments to show the limitations of instinct can easily be carried out with these wasps. For example, if the spiders are removed from a cell, as they are brought by the female, she will – provided that her victims are removed during her absence so that she is not disturbed or frightened – go on bringing spiders until she has brought the required number. Then, even though only the last spider she has brought is in the cell, and her egg has been removed on one of the purloined spiders, she will seal the cell as though nothing untoward had happened and all was in order inside. Furthermore, if the cells themselves are removed, just before she begins the final plastering with mud, she will on her return plaster over the spot where the cells should be, again as though nothing had happened to ruin her work.

Bee pirates Every beekeeper in Africa knows the banded bee pirate *Palarus latifrons* that belongs to the subfamily Larrinae. About 12 mm long, with a dark brown head and thorax and brown bands on its yellow abdomen, the female may be seen haunting hives during the summer; the male is smaller and darker in colour and is not usually seen about the hives.

The female bee pirate settles on the ground or on the front of the hive during the hottest hours of the day and there she waits until a worker bee leaves to forage for food. Then the pirate sets off in pursuit, swooping down like a miniature hawk. They fall together to the ground, the pirate's abdomen curled round so that the tip is close to the underside of the bee's neck. Here she stings the bee and it is at once paralysed or killed. Then the wasp sometimes does a seemingly ghoulish thing; she stands astride her prostrate victim, which is lying on its back, legs in the air, and presses her abdomen to that of the bee and applies her mouth to the bee's mouth. The pressure makes a drop of honey ooze from the bee's mouth and this the wasp laps up. She then grasps her prey in her legs and flies away with it to her nest, which is a long tunnel, 30 cm or more in depth, that slants steeply in the side of a sunny bank.

Usually a number of pirates nest in the same vicinity; like other solitary bees and wasps they seem to like the company of their kind although they do not co-operate or work together in any way. At the bottom of her tunnel she has excavated a small chamber and here she stores the dead bee and lays her egg on it. The larva feeds on the bee but it needs more than one to bring it to maturity, therefore the mother visits the nest two or three times, bringing more bees to her young as they are needed. She does not stock a cell, lay her egg and then close up the cell, as do most solitary wasps, but she has several cells at the bottom of her tunnel, containing young at various stages of growth and she brings the bees to them from day to day.

The harm done by these pirates to the bees is not so much the number killed, which is comparatively small and insignificant, but the bees are so intimidated by the presence of even one or two pirates in the vicinity of the hive that they do not go out foraging for food. The whole colony may be rendered almost completely idle as far as food-gathering is concerned for days on end when the pirates are about. The few bees that do venture out generally fall victim to the waiting wasps.

A second species of bee pirate that is most common but never seen at the hives is the yellow bee pirate, *Philanthus triangulum*. This wasp, with its pale yellow abdomen, may be seen lurking amongst the flowers where it swoops on the bees that are collecting nectar and pollen and treats them in much the same way as does the banded bee pirate. Members of the genus *Cerceris* make nests in the ground, and prey on beetle larvae, solitary bees or wasps. *Philanthus* and *Cerceris* are common throughout Africa and belong to the subfamily Philanthinae.

Fly-hunting wasps The fly-hunting wasps of the subfamily Nyssoninae are all very similar in appearance and habits, and a description of one will serve for all. A common and widely spread species is *Bembix capicola*, about 20 mm long, its abdomen conspicuously marked with yellow and black bands. The front legs are armed with stiff spines which form efficient rakes. The females make their nests in sandy soil and, although they never co-operate one with another, often a number of them may be found nesting close together in one spot.

When digging her nest, the female stands high on her four hind legs and uses the rakes to scrabble vigorously in the sand, sending a shower shooting out behind her. Soon she disappears beneath the surface but the jet of sand continues to spurt out of the hole to show that she is hard at work. After a time she reappears, backing away from the hole and sweeps energetically to remove the heap of sand that has accumulated at the mouth of the burrow. Then she re-enters her shaft and the work proceeds at a great pace, the insect setting up a constant shrill buzz, until the slanting burrow is about 15 cm in depth. At the bottom she hollows out a chamber about the size of an acorn and her work is complete for the time being.

She always chooses spots for her nests where the sand is cool and moist a few centimetres below the surface, although above in the blazing sunshine it is quite dry and may be so hot that you cannot bear to touch it. When she leaves her nest after the digging is complete, the dry sand runs into the hole obliterating it, and she assists in the concealment by smoothing the sand with her feet to remove all traces of her work. Then away she flies and there is no sign at all on the surface to reveal the presence of the tunnel and the chamber beneath. Whilst she is away the footprints of animals or people may change the appearance of the sand but that does not confuse her. When she returns she drops down unhesitatingly at the precise spot where the entrance to her burrow is hidden, locating it by means that remain a mystery. After a few scrapes with her 'rakes', the hole is opened once more and she dives below.

Tucked away below her body and held securely by her middle legs, she carries a small fly down into the chamber with her. This fly she has captured and stung whilst on the wing, hunting it in very much the same way as a hawk hunts and catches a smaller bird. She deposits this fly in the cool chamber below and then lays an elongated, white, sausage-shaped egg on it.

She may go off and start another nest, but it is not certain whether she does this or not. It seems probable that she restricts her attention to one nest at a time, for if one of these nests is carefully excavated, a small side tunnel leading off the main tunnel will be found 25 mm or so down. In this the female spends a great deal of her time, resting. After bringing the first small fly to the nest, she lays her egg on it, and then probably waits until the egg hatches before going off to hunt for more food for her young, this time choosing a larger fly. Any sort of fly will do provided it is moderately large, and the *Bembix* wasps do considerable good by capturing such harmful flies as horse flies, flesh flies and tsetse flies.

From now on she has to provide her ravenous larva with ten or 12 flies every day for four or five days, some 50 or 60 altogether. Much in the same way as the parent bird feeds her nestlings, so does the *Bembix* wasp provide her larva with fresh food as it is required. The flies are devoured almost as quickly as they are brought, only the wings and harder parts of the skin being discarded. When the larva is five days old and fully grown the wasp stops bringing food and for the last time closes up the entrance to the burrow. She scrapes sand into the tunnel until it is blocked for the greater part of its length and then she carefully smooths the sand on the surface so that there is no external evidence of the nest below. Finally she flies away, never to return to that particular nest.

The fully grown larva leaves the heap of debris in the chamber and creeps into the lower end of the tunnel where it spins a dense cocoon of silk round itself, coated on the outside with a layer of sand grains, each grain placed in position as carefully as a stone-mason lays stones in a wall. How the larva forms this strong protective coat to its cocoon we do not know. Although the larva is inside, the coating of sand grains is continuous over the whole outer surface of the cocoon. Near the middle of the cocoon, round its widest circumference,

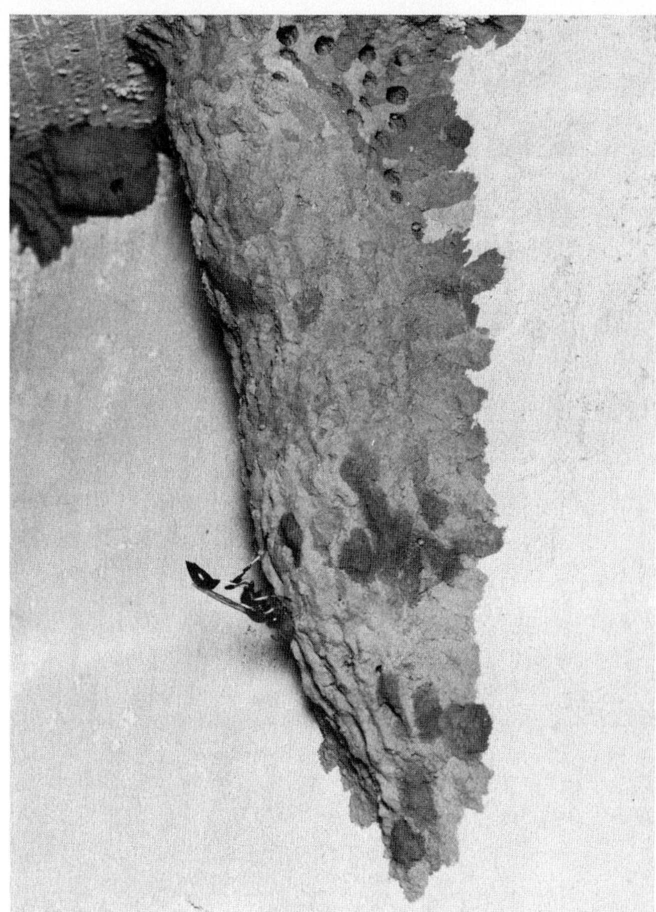

323. Large nest of mud wasp *(Sceliphron spirifex)*; the female wasp is seen applying an overall covering of mud to the nest, the darker patches being mud that is still damp. The holes at the upper end of the nest have been made by her emerging offspring. Such a large nest comprises several dozen cells, each stocked with a number of paralysed spiders.

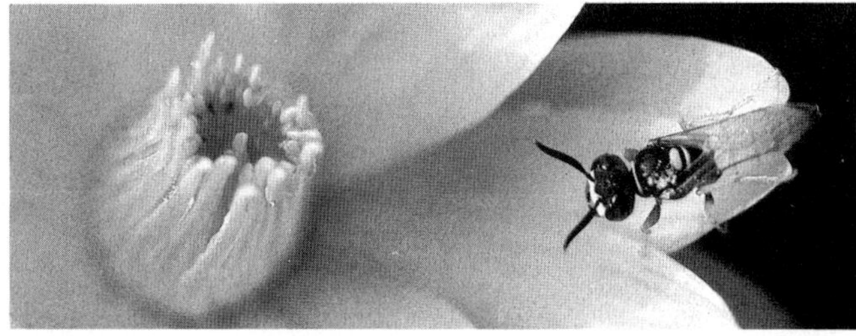

324. Waiting at a waterlily for honey bees to arrive, this yellow bee pirate *(Philanthus* sp.) will seize a victim as soon as it settles. 16 mm.

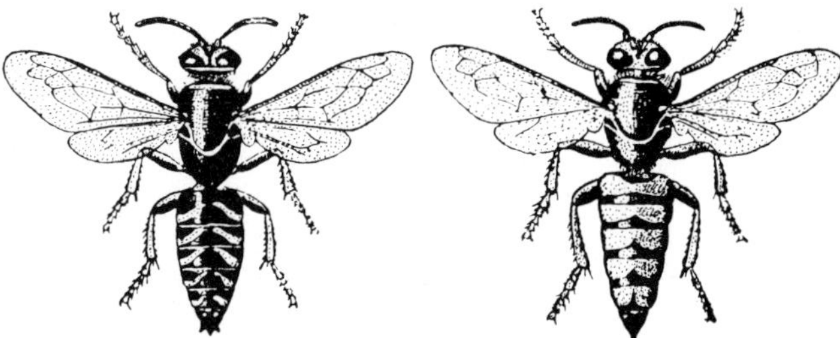

325. A male (left) and a female of the banded bee pirate, *Palarus latifrons.*

there are between three and seven black dots which are thought to be ventilation pores, constructed by the larva to allow air to circulate between the outside and the inside of the dense cocoon, but here again we have no idea how these neat little flask-shaped pores extending through the silk and between the sand grains are made.

Although each female *Bembix* makes only some half a dozen nests during her brief life, she must capture and kill 300–400 flies in order to feed her offspring. The majority of her victims are harmful flies, such as those mentioned above, therefore these little wasps must be counted among our friends and allies. There are a number of different species found in Africa and they are quite common where conditions are favourable.

Crabronid wasps The large subfamily of small sphecid wasps known as the Crabroninae includes many species that make their nests in hollow stems and that prey upon flies. Some burrow in the ground and others prey upon small caterpillars and other insects. As an example of the group we shall take the little watsonia wasp, *Dasyproctus bipunctatus*, some 12 mm long, with four yellow spots on the abdomen and red legs; it has a large square head and short antennae.

When she is ready to lay her eggs the female bores a hole in the side of a watsonia flower stalk, or the stem of some similar plant with soft pith in the centre. She chooses fresh green stalks for this, not dry stems as do so many of the solitary bees and wasps. She tunnels inside the stem, both above and below the entrance hole. As a rule the tunnel above the entrance is only about 25 mm in length, whilst the lower portion may be 75–100 mm long.

Having completed the construction of her nest she flies off to hunt for a fly which she captures by swooping down on it like a miniature hawk and stinging it. She then flies back to her nest, packs the fly inside and lays her egg on it.

The egg is large, white and curved in shape and is invariably fixed across the neck of the fly, between the head and the thorax. Then off the wasp goes once more in search of another victim. Five to ten flies are needed to nourish one larva, the number of flies depending on their size, for she attacks all kinds that are convenient for her to carry. Having stocked a cell with enough food, the wasp constructs a partition across the tunnel, chewing fibres from the inside of the wall of the stem to use as building material. Then she stocks a second cell above the first and lays her second egg, and so on up the tunnel. She is not prolific, eight or nine cells being the usual number, of which the last few may be lodged in the upper part of the tunnel, above the entrance.

When fully grown the larva spins a silken cocoon, pale brown in colour and two or three weeks later the adult emerges. There are a large number of crabronid wasps found in Africa but they have been little studied and there is still much to be learned about their ways.

CLASSIFICATION

ORDER **Hymenoptera**

Wings, when present, four, membranous, front wings slightly larger than hind wings and interlocked by means of tiny hooks. Wings with relatively few veins, nearly lacking in some small forms. Antennae usually fairly long, with ten or more segments. Female with well-developed ovipositor, sometimes longer than body and sometimes modified as a sting. Tarsi normally 5-segmented. Mouthparts chewing, sometimes adapted for sucking. Larvae caterpillar-like (suborder Symphyta) or maggot-like (suborder Apocrita).

SUBORDER **Symphyta**

Base of abdomen broadly joined to thorax. Trochanters 2-jointed, usually two apical spurs on front tibiae, females do not sting. Larvae with three pairs of thoracic legs, and 6-8 pairs of abdominal legs without crochets; mostly plant feeders. Some larvae slug-like, and may damage fruit trees. This suborder contains the most primitive of the Hymenoptera, and is usually divided into five superfamilies, with the Tenthredinoidea the largest. Important African families are the Argidae and Tenthredinidae.

SUBORDER **Apocrita**

Base of abdomen constricted, sometimes distinctly stalked. Thorax has an apparent fourth segment which is actually the basal abdominal segment, fused to thorax. There are many different morphological types in this suborder, which is divided into a number of superfamilies. Characters used to identify superfamilies include the form of the pronotum, antennae, ovipositor or sting, the number of trochanter segments and wing venation. Many of the Apocrita are very small, and many are parasitic or predatory on other insects or various arthropods. Others are medium to large wasps.

SUPERFAMILY **Trigonaloidea**

FAMILY Trigonalidae

A small family of stoutly-built, medium-sized, rarely encountered, wasps, often brightly coloured and with 16 or more segments in antennae. Larvae parasitize larvae of social wasps; sometimes eggs are laid on foliage, swallowed by a caterpillar and then attack dipterous or hymenopterous parasites inside the body of the caterpillar.

SUPERFAMILY **Ichneumonoidea**

An enormous group containing two families that are difficult to separate without examining details of wing venation. Antennae threadlike, with 16 or more segments. Ovipositor arises in front of apex of body, cannot be withdrawn and is often very long. Larvae are parasites of insects, less commonly of other Arthropoda, and they commonly spin silken cocoons in which they pupate after leaving the body of the host.

FAMILY Braconidae

Often dull and not brightly coloured, ovipositor often fairly short, second recurrent vein in forewing absent. Parasitic on a wide variety of insects, including many economically important species, especially caterpillars, but also fly maggots, aphids and plant bugs.

FAMILY Ichneumonidae

Second recurrent vein in forewing present, often brightly coloured and with exceptionally long ovipositor. Common and abundant, parasitic on a wide variety of insects, especially caterpillars (including economically important species), also syrphid and flesh fly larvae, and one species has been reared from spider eggs.

SUPERFAMILY **Evanioidea**

Members of this group are known as 'ensign wasps' because the abdomen is carried in a raised position, due to its being attached to the thorax in a very dorsal position.

FAMILY Evaniidae
Small, dark spider-like wasps, with short stout abdomen set high on thorax above hind legs, very short ovipositor. Larvae are parasitic on egg cases of cockroaches, and adults are likely to be seen wherever cockroaches occur.

FAMILY Gasteruptiidae
Similar in appearance to Ichneumonidae, but head carried on a slender neck, and the abdomen attached high on the thorax. Abdomen long, often swollen terminally, ovipositor long, often as long as the rest of the body. Larvae are parasites of wasps and solitary bees, while adults are often seen around flowers.

SUPERFAMILY **Proctotrupoidea**

A large group containing many species, but poorly studied in Africa. Most are small, often minute wasps, sometimes shining black, and all known larvae are parasites of other insects.

FAMILY Proctotrupidae
Antennae slender and threadlike, arising from middle of face, abdomen spindle shaped with short cylindrical petiole. Larvae parasitize beetle larvae, with one species recorded from a tsetse fly pupa.

FAMILY Diapriidae
Small to minute, black and shining, antennae threadlike and slender, arising from a shelf-like protuberance in middle of face. Larvae are parasites of the larvae and pupae of various Diptera, Coleoptera and Lepidoptera.

FAMILY Scelionidae
Minute insects, usually about 2 mm, black or brown. Antennae elbowed, arising low on face. Abdomen flattened with sharp lateral margins, wing venation greatly reduced. Larvae are parasites inside the eggs of various insects and spiders. *Scelio* parasitizes locust and grasshopper eggs, *Trissolcus* the eggs of the green stink bug *(Nezara viridula)* and *Tolenomus* the eggs of various Lepidoptera.

FAMILY Platygasteridae
Similar to scelionids, minute shining black wasps with almost no wing venation. Most larvae are parasites of gall midges (Cecidomyiidae). Females lay eggs in the host eggs, but they do not hatch until the fly larvae emerge and then the wasp larvae live inside the fly maggots.

SUPERFAMILY **Cynipoidea**

FAMILY Cynipidae
Pronotum triangular in lateral view, antennae threadlike, wing venation much reduced, thorax rough textured, abdomen oval and shining, usually black. These insects are called gall wasps; they are very common and either make galls on plants, or live in galls made by other organisms.

SUPERFAMILY **Chalcidoidea**

This is an enormous group of small to very small Hymenoptera, being the largest superfamily in the order. Its members are either parasites or hyperparasites of other insects (both harmful and beneficial) or else vegetable feeding forms that make galls or infest seeds. Eight of the largest families are listed here.

FAMILY Agaonidae
Very small black fig wasps, males wingless and vermiform, females winged, with deep longitudinal groove in top of head, middle legs slender, front and hind legs stout. Important in the pollination of figs.

FAMILY Trichogrammatidae
Minute insects with long hair fringes on the wings and 3-segmented tarsi (all other Chalcidoidea except Eulophidae have 5-segmented tarsi). Larvae develop in the eggs of a wide variety of insects (including pest species), some adults even going underwater to parasitize the eggs of aquatic insects.

FAMILY Eulophidae
Small, often metallic or black wasps, with 4-segmented tarsi. They have diverse habits, and attack eggs, larvae and pupae of various insects (including many pest species); some are hyperparasites of other wasps. *Euplectrus* species attack caterpillars, and up to seven larvae may develop in one host; pupae enclosed in cocoons, apparently unique in Chalcidoidea.

FAMILY Aphelinidae
Small to minute species with 5-segmented tarsi, mostly parasites of scale insects and aphids. Several species have been introduced into Africa to assist in the biological control of economically important aphids and scales.

FAMILY Mymaridae
'Fairyflies' are among the smallest of all insects (one species only 0,21 mm long), with narrow, almost linear hind wings. Wing margins fringed with long hairs, readily separated from Trichogrammatidae by 5-segmented tarsi. All known species are egg parasites, some of economically important species like weevils and Hemiptera. One fairyfly species swims under the water to parasitize eggs of water beetles.

FAMILY Chalcididae
Fairly large, dark coloured wasps up to 7 mm, with characteristic, greatly enlarged hind femora, toothed below. Larvae are parasites of various insects, especially solitary bees and carpenter bees. Also recorded from antlion larvae, ladybird beetles, caterpillars and tsetse fly pupae.

FAMILY Pteromalidae
A very large family of fairly large, black or metallic wasps up to about 4 mm; larvae parasitic on a wide variety of other insects including pupae of Lepidoptera and Diptera. *Mormoniella vitripennis* commonly hatches from pupae of blow flies.

FAMILY Encyrtidae
A large family of very small, stout bodied wasps which parasitize the eggs, larvae or pupae of a wide variety of insects and rarely other Arthropoda. Many species are polyembryonic, i.e. up to 1 000 larvae may develop in the single larva of a host which hatched from a parasitized egg. Important parasites of scale insects, mealybugs, aphids and psyllids are included in this family; other species attack Lepidoptera, carpenter bees, ladybird and buprestid beetles, while *Hunterellus* is an egg parasite of ticks.

SUPERFAMILY **Chrysidoidea**

FAMILY Chrysididae
Cuckoo wasps are conspicuous, abundant, with many species in Africa. They are metallic green, blue or purple and can roll the abdomen into a ball under the thorax when attacked. Body usually coarsely sculptured. *Chrysis* is the largest, cosmopolitan genus of over 1 000 species. Cuckoo wasp larvae are parasitic on the larvae of other wasps and solitary bees.

SUPERFAMILY **Pompiloidea**

FAMILY Pompilidae
Small to very large, usually dark coloured wasps with long legs and abdomen lacking a conspicuous petiole. Antennae often very long. A large family containing several thousand species, all of which are hunters of various kinds of spiders, which are immobilised or killed and serve as food for the larvae. *Hemipepsis* wasps are very large and hunt baboon spiders; some species make a noisy, rattling sound in flight.

SUPERFAMILY **Scolioidea**

This group contains some of the most primitive members of the order, and are considered to be representative of the ancestral group from which sphecoid wasps, vespoid wasps, bees and ants arose. They are mostly stout-bodied, hairy, ground-dwelling and all are parasitic.

FAMILY Mutillidae
'Velvet ants' are very hairy, often brightly coloured in reddish brown, black and white patterns. Females wingless, with potent sting, males winged. Parasitize solitary and social bees and wasps, also beetles and flies, with several species known from pupae of tsetse flies.

FAMILY Tiphiidae
Medium-sized wasps, mostly dark-coloured, usually distinguishable from next family by mesosternum having two conspicuous posterior lobes. Larvae parasitic on larvae of beetles, solitary bees and wasps; one species recorded from mole crickets.

FAMILY Scoliidae
Very large (up to 30 mm) hairy black solitary wasps, often with yellow or reddish bands; mesosternum without posterior lobes, wings with numerous wrinkles in membranous areas beyond closed cells. Adults may be found around flowers. They immobilise the larvae of scarabaeid beetles, lay an egg on the underside, and the larva feeds as an external parasite, spinning a cocoon when ready to pupate.

SUPERFAMILY **Vespoidea**

FAMILY Eumenidae
This family contains very many solitary wasps which are black, or black with yellow or reddish brown markings, and many of them construct mud nests (hence 'mason' or 'potter' wasps). Mandibles are elongate and delicate. They immobilise caterpillars or beetle larvae and seal these in the nests as food for the larvae.

FAMILY Vespidae
The subfamily Vespinae is represented in Africa only by *Vespula germanica*, introduced to the Cape Province. The Polistinae are common and abundant social wasps, which build paper nests and feed their larvae on pieces of chewed-up caterpillars. *Belonogaster* (large) and *Polistes* (small) are the common African paper wasps, both being reddish brown, sometimes with bands on the abdomen, and females have a fiery sting.

SUPERFAMILY **Sphecoidea**

FAMILY Sphecidae
A very large family of medium to large wasps, most of which dig nesting holes in the ground, a few nest in stems and a few make mud nests or use natural cavities. They prey on a wide variety of insects and Arthropoda, usually paralysing their victim and storing their bodies in the nest as food for the larvae. The family is divided into a number of subfamilies, a few of the most important of which are listed below.

Astatinae: nest in ground and prey on the nymphs of the Hemiptera, especially stink bugs (Pentatomidae), also lantern flies (Fulgoridae).

Larrinae: nest in hollow twigs or old wood or in the ground, and prey on aphids, spiders, Orthoptera or bees.

Trypoxyloninae: build mud nests, often on trees, prey exclusively on spiders.

Philanthinae: nest in the ground and hunt honey bees, solitary bees or wasps around flowers.

Nyssoninae: the genus *Bembix* nests in sandy soil, the nest being left open and the larvae fed with fresh Diptera.

Sphecinae: either make burrows in the ground (e.g. *Sphex*, *Chlorion* and *Ammophila*) and provision them with caterpillars, or build mud nests *(Sceliphron)* and provision them with spiders.

Crabroninae: nest in living stems of flowers, or in the soil and prey on flies or caterpillars.

SUPERFAMILY **Apoidea**

There are nine families of bees in Africa, dealt with in Chapter 22.

SUPERFAMILY **Formicoidea**

The ants all fall into a single family, Formicidae, which is dealt with in Chapter 23.

FURTHER READING

Annecke, D. P.: Various papers on Encyrtidae, Aphelinidae, Mymaridae and biological control in: *Entomology Memoirs, Department of Agricultural Technical Services, South Africa* and *Journal of the Entomological Society of Southern Africa* and elsewhere (1964-1978).

Arnold, G.: Various papers, especially on Sphecidae and Pompilidae, in *Annals of the Transvaal Museum*, and elsewhere (1913-1944).

Bischoff, H.: *Biologie der Hymenopteren.* Springer Verlag, Berlin (1927). 598 pp

Evans, H. E.: *The Comparative Ethology and Evolution of the Sand Wasps.* Harvard University Press, Cambridge, Massachusetts (1966). 526 pp

Krombein, K. V.: *Trap nesting Wasps and Bees; life histories, nests and associates.* Smithsonian Press, Washington DC (1967). 570 pp

Matthews, R. W.: 'Biology of Braconidae'. *Annual Review of Entomology* (1974) 19: 15-32

Prins, A. J.: 'Hymenoptera'. In *Biogeography and Ecology of Southern Africa.* M. J. A. Werger [Ed.]. W. Junk, The Hague [1978] 825-875

Richards, O. W.: 'The Biology of Social Wasps' [Hymenoptera Vespidae]. *Biological Review* [1971] 46: 483-528

Riek, E. F.: 'Hymenoptera'. In *The Insects of Australia*, I. M. MacKerras (Ed.) CSIRO, Melbourne University Press, (1970) 867-959

Spradberry, J. P.: *Wasps.* Sidgwick and Jackson, London (1973). 408 pp

Sundholm A.: 'Hymenoptera: Proctotrupoidea'. *South African Animal Life* (1970) 14: 306-401

Townes, H. and M.: 'Ethiopian Ichneumonidae'. *Memoirs of the American Entomology Institute* (1973) 19: 1-416

Vesey-Fitzgerald, B.: *The World of Ants, Bees and Wasps.* Pelham Books, London (1969) 117pp

Previous page: 1. Elegant grasshoppers (*Zonocerus elegans*)

2. Leaf-mimicking katydid (*Zabalius* sp.)

3. Eumastacid grasshopper (*Thericles* sp.)

4. Bush locust (*Phymateus* sp.)

5. Bladder grasshoppers mating

6. Short-horned grasshopper (*Cyrtacanthacris* sp.)

7. Pamphagid grasshopper (*Lamarckiana* sp.)

8. Katydid showing ear-slits on legs ▸

Previous page:
9. Predatory cricket-grasshopper eating aphids
10. Katydid changing its skin

12. Pyrgomorphid grasshoppers congregating ▶

11. Foam grasshopper (*Dictyophorus spumans*)

13. Elegant grasshoppers (*Zonocerus elegans*)

4. Tree cricket (*Oecanthus* sp.) using leaf-hole to amplify call

5. Long-horned antlion resting on stem

16. Praying mantid devouring day-flying moth

Overleaf: 17. Praying mantid nymph (*Pseudocreobotra wahlbergi*) 18. Praying mantid (*Empusa* sp.

19. Praying mantid displaying *(Popa spurca)*

20. Praying mantid laying egg-mass

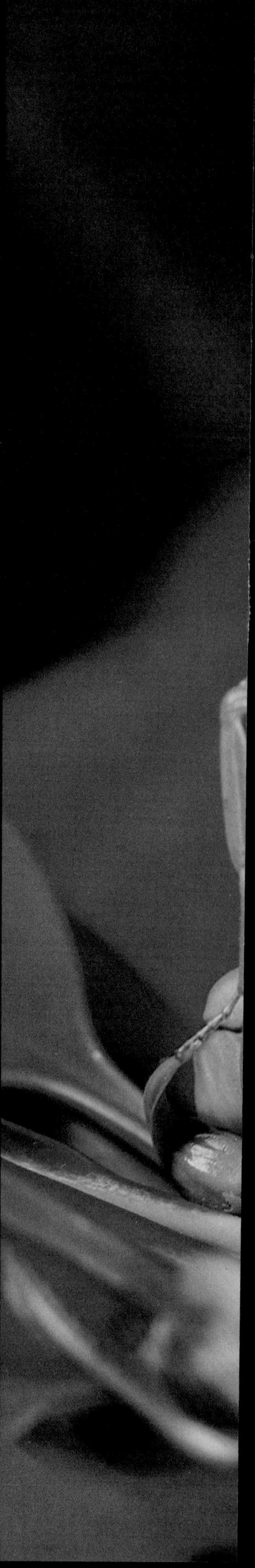

21. Praying mantid feeding on moth

22. Praying mantid *(Sphodromantis gastrica)* eating honey bee ▶

◀ 23. Giant stick insect *(Palophus reyi)* in threat display

24. Giant stick insect *(Palophus reyi)*

25. Giant stick insect, showing bark-like camouflage

26. Dragonfly (*Trithemis* sp.) awaiting passing prey

27. Dragonfly (*Brachythemis lacustris*)

28. Male damselfly (*Enallagma glaucum*) grasps female behind head

29. Emperor dragonfly (*Anax imperator*)

30. Termite queen, with workers and soldiers in attendance *(Macrotermes michaelseni)*

31. Termite queen being tended by workers

32. Termite nymph in fungus garden

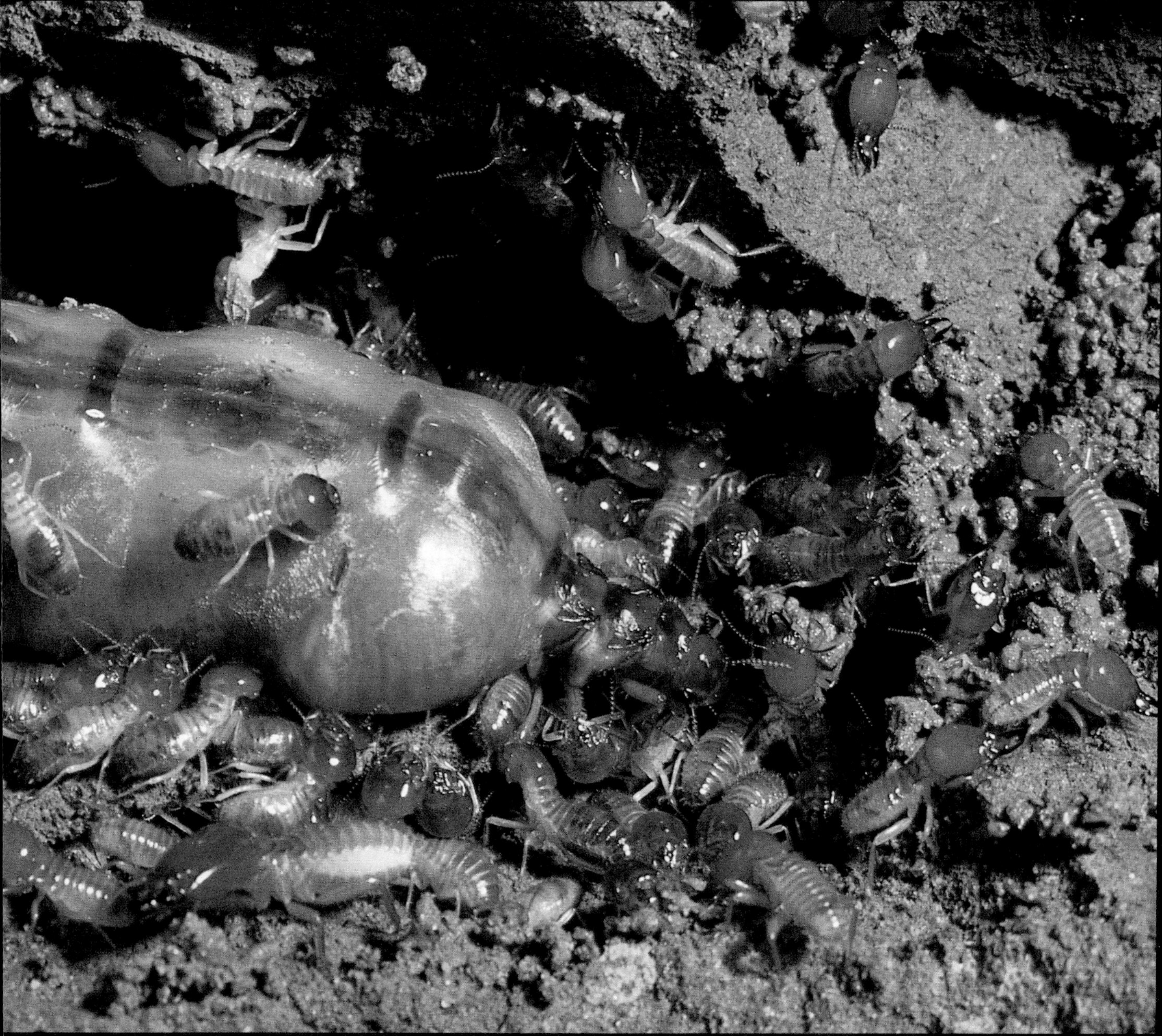

33. Termite soldier being overpowered by ant

34. Winged termites emerging from mound

◆35. Spiny coreid bug (*Pephricus livingstonei*)

36. Shield bug, showing simple and compound eyes

37. Shield bug on grass blade – note matching colours

38. Scutellerid bug nymph (*Calidea* sp.)

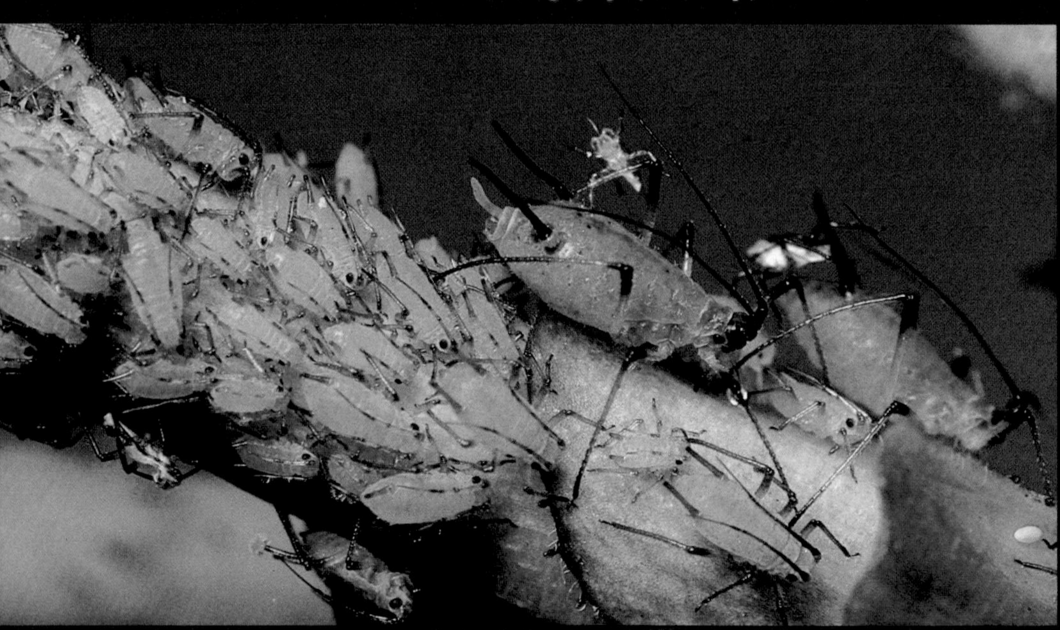

39. Adult aphids surrounded by their offspring

40. Scutellerid bug sucking plant juice

41 Pyrrhocorid bugs in various stages of development sucking sap

42 Spittle bugs (*Ptyelus* sp.) clustered on branch of 'rain tree'

43. Fulgorid bug nymphs with wax filament tails

44. Tree hopper laying eggs, while ant solicits honeydew

45. Eggs of a shield bug

46. Twig-wilter bug (*Anoplocnemis* sp.)

47. Assassin bug feeding on flower spider

48. Shield bug shedding its skin

49. Tiger beetle with fly victim

50. Fearsome jaws of ground beetle (*Anthia* sp.)

51. Water strider bug resting on lily pad

52. Ladybird beetle larvae, aphids and ants on flower bud

53. Spotted maize beetles (*Astylus* sp.)

54. Clerid beetle taking nectar

55. Ladybird beetle (*Chilocorus* sp.) devouring scale insects

56. Ladybird beetles (*Cheilomenes lunata*) eating aphids

57. Ladybird beetle (*Cheilomenes lunata*) laying eggs

58. Blister beetle (*Mylabris* sp.) taking off ▸

59. Tortoise beetles mating

61. Weevil beetle

60. Blister beetle feeding on flower

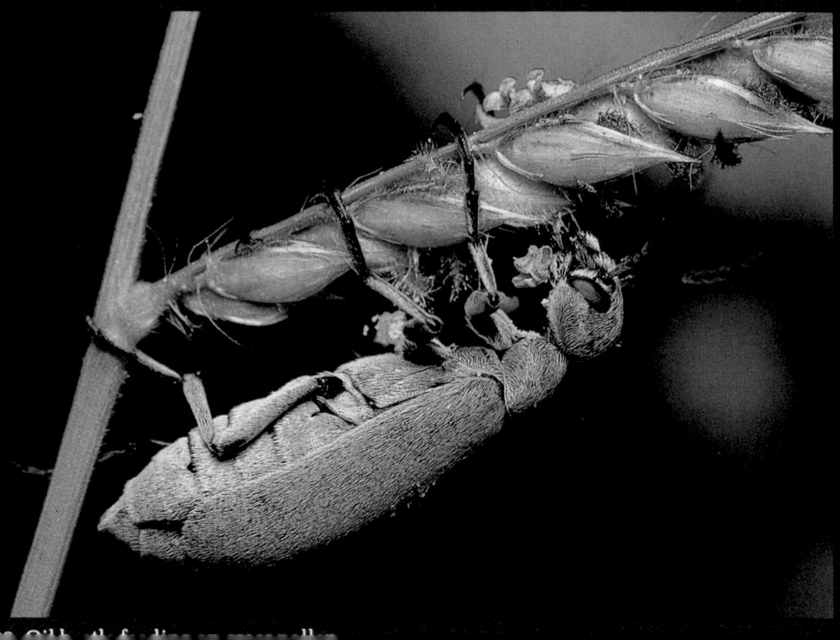

64. Cetoniid beetle feeding in Protea flower

65. Leaf beetle (*Macrocoma* sp.)

66. Tenebrionid beetle (*Onymacris unguicularis*) drinking condensed fog

◀67. Click beetle, showing the antennae

68. Female glow-worm beetle

69. Long-horn beetle laying eggs in dead wood

70. Long-horn beetle *(Litopus latipes)*

▲71. Tachinid fly feeding on nectar

72. Conopid fly mimicking a wasp

73. Hover fly larva eating aphids

74. Moth caterpillar with egg of parasitic tachinid fly laid behind its head

75. Stalk-eyed fly

76. Hatching fly with inflated ptilinum

77. Robber fly with hover fly victim 78. Alert robber fly awaiting prey

79. Blow fly feeding on nectar

80. Blow flies hatched from a crocodile carcase

81. Male horse fly feeds on nectar

82. Hover fly, showing large compound eyes

83. Male horse fly, showing upper and lower division of compound eyes large and small elements ▶

Overleaf: 84. Mimosa moon moth *(Argema mimosae)* laying eggs

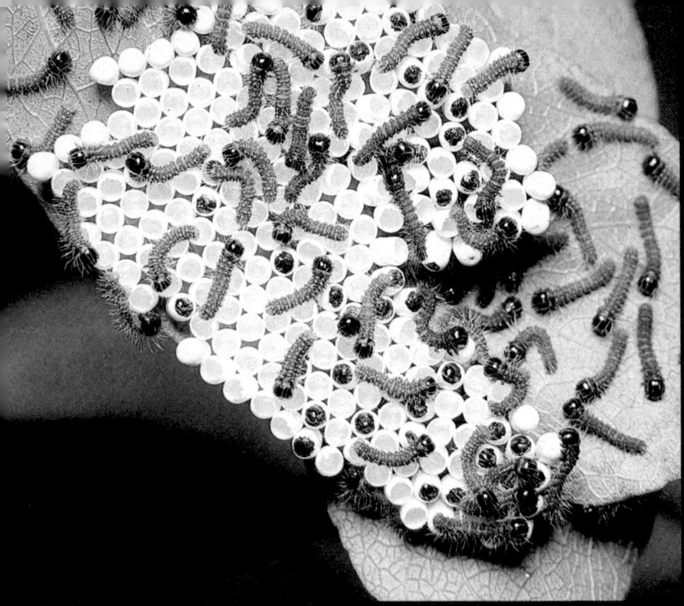

35. Emperor moth caterpillars hatching

86. Hawk moth caterpillar, showing false 'eye'

37. Emperor moth caterpillar reacts to being disturbed

88. Convolvulus hawk moth *(Agrius convulvuli)*

89. Window-winged moth (*Syntomus cerbera*)

90. Peach moth (*Egybolus vaillantina*)

93. Cape tiger moth (*Dionychopus similis*)

91. Hornet moth *(Euchromia formosa)*

92. False tiger moth *(Heraclia superba)*

94. Bagworm caterpillar (*Eumeta hardenbergi*)

95. Mopane worm caterpillars (*Gonimbrasia belina*) feeding

96. Burrow of leaf miner caterpillar (*Phyllocnistis* sp.)

97. Fruit-piercing moth (*Achaea* sp.) feeding on mango

98. Caterpillars and pupa of butterfly *(Acraea zetes acara)*

99. Nymphalid butterfly *(Byblia ilithyia)* sunning itself

100. Caterpillar of citrus swallowtail butterfly *(Papilio demodocus)* in defense posture with osmeterium extended behind head

Overleaf: 101. Blue pansy butterfly *(Junonia oenone)*

African monarch butterfly *(Danaus chrysippus)*:

102. Caterpillar hatching from egg

103. Eating egg-shell

104. Feeding on milkweed

105. Preparing to pupate

106. Skin being shed as pupation starts

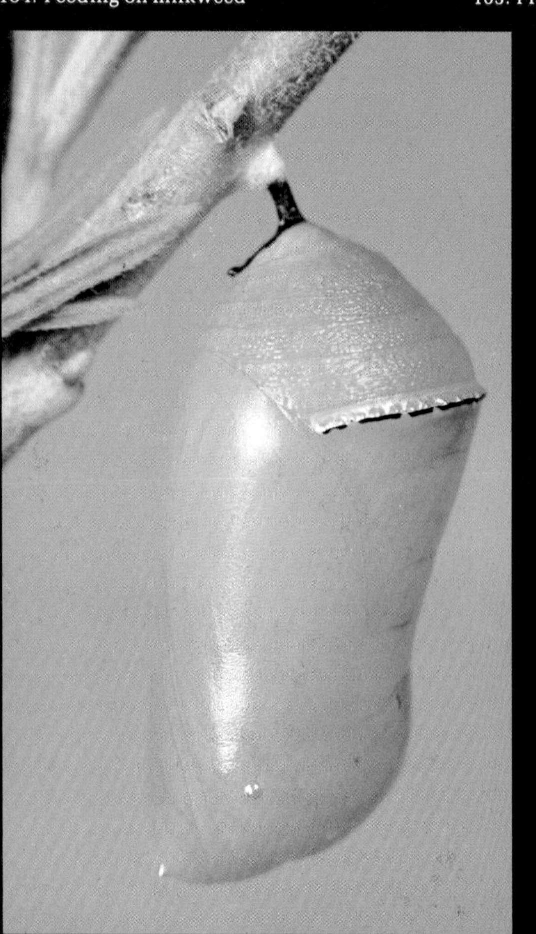

107. Pupa fully formed a few hours later

108. Butterfly emerging after a few weeks

109. The butterfly hangs suspended as its limp and crumpled wings unfold prior to hardening ♦

Previous page: 110. Migratory butterfly *(Belenois aurota),* showing coiled proboscis, scales and compound eye

111. Dry-leaf butterfly *(Precis archesia)*

112. Migratory butterfly *(Belenois aurota)* feeding

113. Charaxes butterflies *(Charaxes jasius saturnus)* feeding on dung

114. Acraeid butterfly feeding *(Acraea zetes acara)*

115. Dry-leaf butterfly *(Precis tugela)*

116. Marsh butterfly *(Henotesia perspicua)* sleeping ▸

17. Parasitic braconid wasp laying eggs in
ewly-hatched African monarch butterfly caterpillar
18. Growing caterpillar feeding, outwardly
naffected by wasp grubs developing within
19. Mature wasp larvae bursting from the body of the
ully-grown caterpillar
20. Wasp larvae spin cocoons alongside their now
lead host
21. After several weeks, adult braconid wasps
merge from their cocoons

122. Mason wasp (*Delta caffer*) stocking her nest with a paralysed caterpillar

123. Sphecid wasp dragging captured cricket to nest

124. Male braconid wasp courts female while she preens antenna

125. Mud wasp stocking her nest with spider

126. Pollen-covered scoliid wasp feeding on nectar ▸

◆127. Paper wasp *(Polistes smithi)* about to feed chewed caterpillar to larvae

128. Paper wasps attend nest with eggs in cells

129. Large paper wasps (*Belonogaster* sp.) on the alert

130. Parasitic cuckoo wasp investigates mud wasp nest

131. Section through nest of mud wasp, showing paralysed jumping spiders and mud wasp larva

132. Eumenid wasp guards entrance to her nest

133. Mason wasp (*Odynerus* sp.) on the mud-tube entrance to her nest ▶

134. Minute stingless bee (*Trigona* sp.) foraging for pollen

135. Male carpenter bee (*Xylocopa* sp.) hovering at mating site

136. African honey bee (left) and stingless bee (*Trigona* sp.) visiting flowers of marula tree

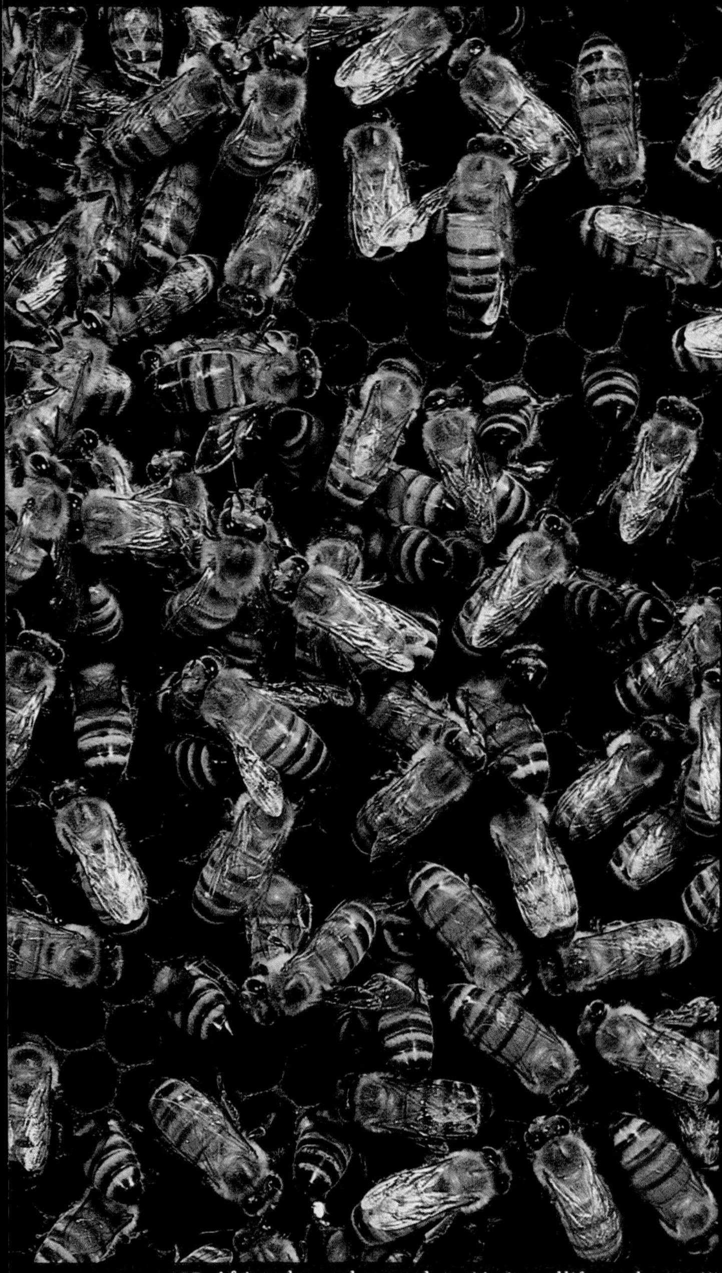

137. African honey bee workers (*Apis mellifera adansonii*)

138. Megachilid bee on her nest of fibres, soil and resin

139. African honey bee worker foraging

140. Using silk from a larva held gently in its jaws, a worker tailor ant binds leaves together to form its nest

41. Tailor ants carry pupa of winged male to safety after their nest has been opened

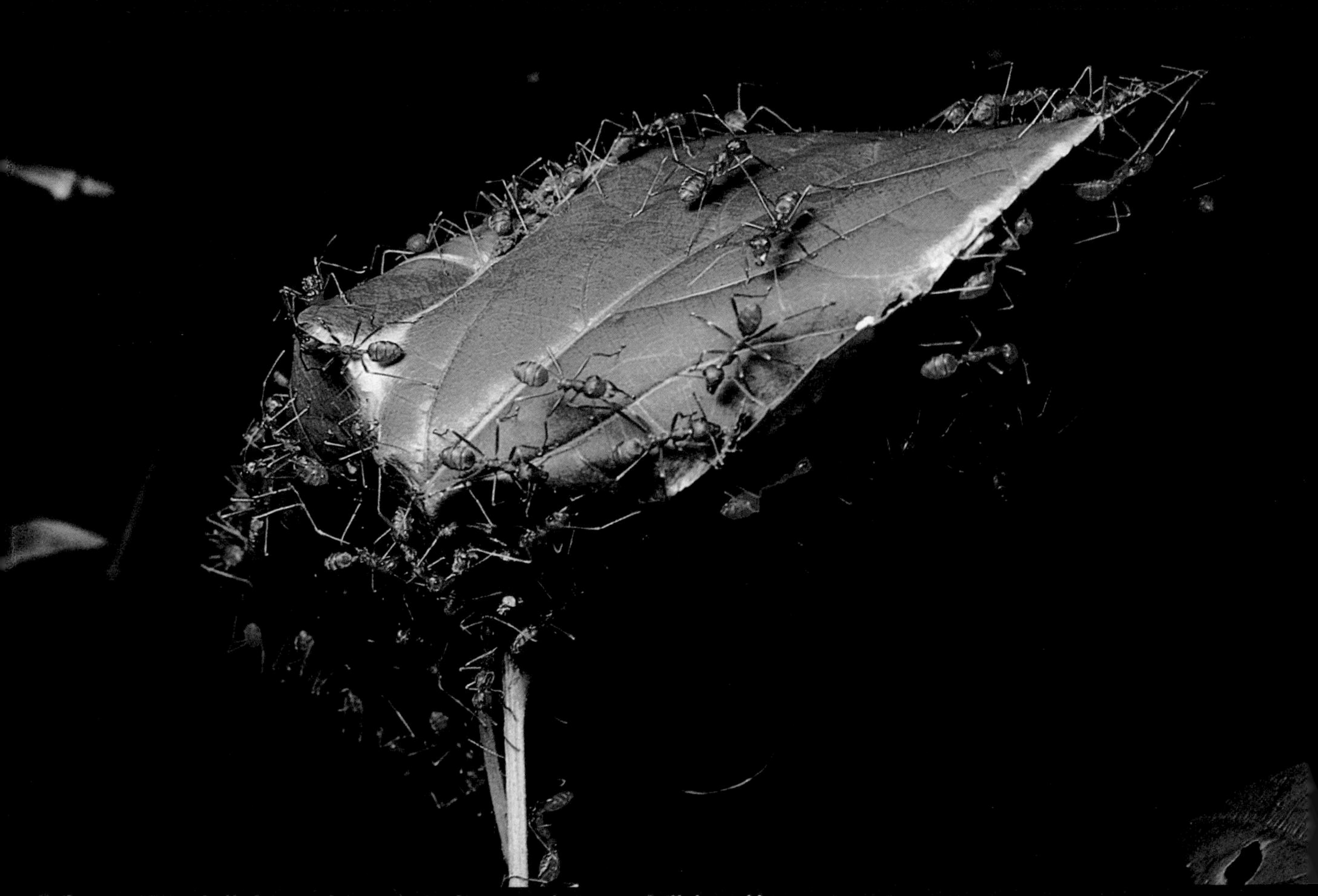

42. Tailor ants (*Oecophylla longinoda*) swarm in alarm over their nest of silk-bound leaves

143. Cocktail ants (*Crematogaster* sp.) moving pupa of a reproductive

144. Male driver ant (*Dorylus* sp.)

145. Formicine ants (*Polyrhachis* sp.) feed on fermenting tree sap

146. Sectioned nest of slender ants (*Sima* sp.) in hollow thorn contains ant brood and guest scale insects

Overleaf: 147. Formicine ants (*Polyrhachis* sp.) tend scale insects for their sweet secretions

CAPTIONS TO THE COLOUR PLATES

Note: Sizes given refer to the distance between the front of the insect's head (excluding antennae) and the hind tip of the abdomen where this is visible, or to the hind tip of the folded wings in cases where they obscure the abdomen.

Grasshoppers

Plate 1. In contrast to most grasshoppers the elegant grasshopper makes no effort to conceal itself, or flee, when approached. Instead, these garishly-coloured insects flaunt themselves openly, often in clusters, on the many wild and cultivated plants upon which they feed. Natural selection has endowed the elegant grasshopper with foul-tasting body juices and the ability to give off a nauseating smell when alarmed. Its bright colours advertise this fact to would-be predators and are therefore called warning colours. Only about 5% of adult elegant grasshoppers ever develop full-length wings; in most specimens the wings never grow beyond mere stubs. Found from Zaire across the continent to Kenya and southwards to the Cape, these striking insects are reported to be eaten by at least one tribe of African people (the Pedi of the northern Transvaal of South Africa). The photograph shows both winged and wingless individuals, as well as others in earlier growth stages. Longest individual: 50 mm.

Plate 2. Anyone who has ever camped beneath or near the giant Sycamore fig trees that deeply shade the banks of many African rivers in the southern parts of the continent will almost certainly have heard the katydids of the genus *Zabalius*. Few female insects possess sound producing organs and it is usually only the males that sing; their songs being frequently so high in pitch as to be well beyond the range of human hearing. The shrill chirping of the male *Zabalius* can be heard from the time that darkness falls until the early hours of morning from amongst the dense foliage of the Sycamore fig on which these insects feed. They mimic the colouration and markings of the leaves to a remarkable degree, even to the point of possessing false insect 'chew holes'. 52 mm.

Plate 3. The eumastacids are closely related to the short-horned grasshoppers and are relatively common in the tropics. They are all wingless, do not seem to produce any call, and vary greatly in size and colouration. The garish colours of this specimen possibly indicate that it is inedible. 21 mm.

Plate 4. Many people mistakenly refer to any large grasshopper as a locust, but in fact the only true locusts are the half-dozen species that multiply into the notorious swarms that periodically ravage parts of Africa. The bush locust shown in the photograph is really a large, solitary short-horned grasshopper, well protected by its disgusting taste and smell. When approached it makes no effort to fly but simply raises its wings to reveal a large area of bright colour and contrasting tones ('warning colours'). If one of these insects is handled it releases a revolting odour that clings to the hands for days in spite of repeated washing. 65 mm.

Plate 5. These mating bladder grasshoppers present something of a mystery. Whilst the female is quite typical in appearance, the male in the photograph lacks the bloated, hollow abdomen for which these grasshoppers are well known (and from which the species derives its common name). It has been suggested that male bladder grasshoppers occur in two distinct forms: in the one it develops wings, the characteristic bladder-like abdomen, and the stridulatory apparatus with which to produce a call. The other form is wingless, lacks the bladder-like abdomen, and is fertile. It is further suggested that the rôle of the winged form is simply to summon the females and wingless males to a common area where they would meet and mate; the females being fertilised by the wingless males. As is the case with by far the greater number of African insects, very little is known about the life-cycle of the bladder grasshopper. The urgent need to increase food production in today's overcrowded world means that entomologists have little time to spare for research into insects that are of no economic importance. Female: 48 mm.

Plate 6. This large short-horned grasshopper (*Cyrtacanthacris* sp.) is enjoying the succulent bud of a canna flower. Though widespread in Africa this insect is nowhere abundant and is seldom a pest. By lashing out with its sharply spined legs – even bringing them forward, right over its head, *Cyrtacanthacris* gives a good account of itself to any bird, lizard or other would-be predator. 70 mm.

Plate 7. Day and night grasshoppers of the genus *Lamarckiana* may be heard calling periodically in areas of open woodland. The call of these cryptically-coloured insects is a rather rapid and nasal 'rat, rat, rat, rat, rat', repeated by the male every few minutes or so. In between calls he usually flies to a new site (usually a tree trunk or a branch) and seems to confine himself to a territory of about 30 m square. As with all grasshoppers of this group (the Pamphagidae) the female has no wings, but in common with the male she does possess a hearing organ on either side of her thorax. Presumably the male's call serves to attract the pedestrian female into his territory, where in turn she attracts the male by odour. The male produces his call by rubbing a tiny 'spur' on each of his hind legs over a corrugated area of each adjacent wing. By very slowly approaching a calling *Lamarckiana* one is able to get within a few centimetres and observe it quite closely. 40 mm.

Plate 8. Using a pair of hearing organs located on its front legs (the openings of which can be seen quite clearly as vertical slits) this katydid can, if female, easily pin-point her calling mate and accurately home-in on him. If a male, it can locate the whereabouts of competitive males and either displace them from its own territory or remove itself from theirs. Most insects' songs are very high in pitch and consist in part of sounds that are in the ultrasonic region. In fact, the voices of many insects are totally inaudible to man. High frequency sound waves tend to be very directional, with the result that the source of such a sound is easy to locate. The structures hanging from the katydid's mouth are organs of taste and touch, known as palps. 52 mm.

Plate 9. Having emerged from its daytime retreat (a leaf rolled up and stitched with silk from its mouthparts), this cricket-grasshopper (superfamily: Gryllacridoidea) has climbed a *Cotyledon* plant and is feeding on the aphids that infest it. The rewards are many for those naturalists prepared to spend an hour in the garden or bush after dark observing insects by torchlight. 18 mm.

Plate 10. Few moments in the life of an insect are more critical than that when the old skin is shed for a new and larger one. At such a time the insect is quite helpless, for its new skin (in other words its exoskeleton – its whole framework) remains soft and rubbery for up to several hours until it hardens through the action of hormones in the blood. By shedding its old skin after dark, this katydid is able to carry out the delicate process of moulting free from the menace of predators such as birds and lizards. In the photograph the grasshopper hangs upside down with only the very tip of its abdomen still within the old skin; the now empty feet of that skin still grip the grass stalk on which the moult was begun an hour earlier. As the insect waits for its new skin and wings to swell to their full size, and then to harden, it cleans its long antennae. 28 mm.

Plate 11. Accompanied by a sound rather like that of escaping air, vile-smelling foam issues from behind the head of a foam grasshopper after it has been prodded. Like all pyrgomorphid grasshoppers, *Dictyophorus spumans* obtains the repugnant and poisonous substances it uses for its defence by way of its food plants: principally members of the large family Asclepiadaceae, or milkweeds. Its red and black markings are typical warning colours. Overall length: 58 mm.

Plate 12. A feature of most species of repugnant grasshopper is that they live in congregations. From the hopper to the adult stage they move about slowly in a group, feeding first on one plant or shrub and then moving on to another; an entire congregation has even been seen moulting simultaneously. Grasshoppers massed like this are very conspicuous, and this behaviour, in conjunction with their contrasting warning colours, probably serves to heighten the warning message of their inedibility. Here massed pyrgomorphid grasshoppers ascend a new host plant, a tree trunk in the Tsitsikama forests along the extreme southern coast of Africa. Average length: 35 mm.

Plate 13. Elegant he certainly is! The elegant grasshopper (*Zonocerus elegans*) is almost impossible to overlook in his coat of many warning colours and contrasting patches of dark and light tones. As well as possessing body juices containing several powerful poisons, which in some cases induce vomiting or even cardiac arrest, these short-horned grasshoppers also exude repugnant fluids from glands along the thorax.

Crickets

Plate 14. Having gnawed a pear-shaped hole in the centre of a large leaf, a delicate, 16 mm long male tree cricket (*Oecanthus* sp.) places his head and forelegs through it and proceeds to produce a chirping call. At first his call is audible only a few centimetres away, but then he carefully adjusts his position so that his wings are a perfect fit in the hole, whereupon the acoustic power of his call increases tenfold – audible for over 30 m. This effect is brought about by the leaf acting as a baffle, which prevents sound waves from the front of the wings from interfering with those coming from the back. The principle is well known to acoustic engineers, who use baffles to increase the efficiency of Hi-Fi loudspeakers. 18 mm.

Antlions

Plate 15. Like most adult antlions, the long-horned species spend the hours of brightest daylight resting motionless on vegetation, apparently trying to look as unlike an insect as possible in order to avoid the attentions of predators. Here a crab spider, in the hope of catching visiting bees and flies, spins threads of silk onto the antennae of the motionless antlion, quite unaware of its presence on the flower. 19 mm.

Mantids

Plate 16. Lurking amongst flowers frequented by nectar-seeking insects, this praying mantid (*Sphodromantis* sp.] has caught a small day-flying moth [*Utetheisa pulchella*], which it will rapidly devour. 50 mm.

Plate 17. Like all immature praying mantids this young specimen of *Pseudocreobotra wahlbergi* carries its abdomen curved over its thorax. Numerous flattened projections and its general body profile make its camouflage near perfect as it waits for prey. In their adult form these mantids possess striking eye-marking on their wings, which are remarkably realistic when the wings are raised. 24 mm.

Plate 18. Praying mantids of the genus *Empusa* can easily be recognised by the projection from the back of the head. Unlike most mantids this species has comblike antennae. 35 mm.

Plate 19. Many praying mantids are able to put up very impressive threat displays when in danger: the wings and forelegs are raised in order to increase the apparent size of the insect. Though such antics are most amusing to watch, they must be of significant survival value as protection against small lizards and birds. 40 mm.

Plate 20. Late at night, an hour after she started, a praying mantid *(Sphodromantis gastrica)* completes her egg-mass. It is a complex structure, consisting of an inner portion containing approximately 100 tiny chambers, each of which has an egg in it, and an outer covering of hardened white foam. If one watches the egg mass being laid all that is visible is the foam emerging, frothy and liquid from the hind end of the mantid's body. The foam soon hardens. Presumably the inner, egg-carrying portion is exuded from her body complete during the laying process, having formed inside her during the weeks previous to laying. In spite of the protection offered by the foam covering, mantid eggs are frequently parasitized by tiny wasps. Mantid: 50 mm.

Plate 21. Besides the strange projection from the back of the head, mantids of the genus *Empusa* usually possess an extremely long thorax and leaf-like projections from their legs. This specimen has caught a window-winged moth *(Syntomis cerbera)*. 55 mm.

Plate 22. A praying mantid *(Sphodromantis gastrica)* makes a meal of a honeybee, whose sting was useless against the mantid's grasping front legs, well armoured by a heavy layer of sclerotin, the substance that provides rigidity to an insect's body. Lower in the photograph an ant makes off with one of the honeybee's wings. 48 mm.

Stick insects

Plate 23. Though few species of stick insect are able to fly, many have rudimentary wings which they use for threat display and which produce a clacking sound to further frighten the enemy. As well as use its wings for display, which it is seen doing here, this giant stick insect *(Palophus reyi)* is able to fly. 18 cm.

Plate 24. Just about impossible to see amongst the woodland vegetation it inhabits, the giant stick insect *(Palophus reyi)* feeds mainly after dark and spends the daylight hours rigid and motionless against the twigs and branches it resembles so perfectly. 20 cm.

Plate 25. The bark-like camouflage of this giant stick insect is exact right down to the smallest detail, as this close-up of its head shows. The 'ears' are nothing more than projections to assist camouflage. Notice that even the insect's eyes are patterned with bark-like markings.

Dragonflies and damselflies

Plate 26. The compound eyes of dragonflies possess more elements (ommatidia) per square millimetre than any other insect and it is probably for this reason that these active and handsome creatures are able to see their prey up to a metre or more away. Although some species of dragonfly remain in flight whilst on the lookout for the tiny flying insects that form prey, many, such as this member of the genus *Trithemis*, prefer to perch on a stem or branch from which they have a good all-round view of passing insects. After pursuing a victim a dragonfly will usually return to its same perch. 52 mm.

Plate 27. The dragonfly *Brachythemis lacustris* is frequently found on rocks near rivers, from where it hunts mosquitoes and other aquatic flies. 35 mm.

Plate 28. Damselflies, like their close relatives the dragonflies, can often be seen paired ready to mate. The male uses a clasping device on the tip of his abdomen to grip his mate just behind the head. Note the far more slender build of a damselfly when compared with a dragonfly, and the way the wings are held closed when at rest. *(Enallagma glaucum.)* Each 35 mm.

Plate 29. The emperor dragonfly *(Anax imperator)* is one of Africa's largest species and, like many dragonflies, may be seen hunting across the open veld, far from water. This specimen was photographed in the early morning amongst the low vegetation where it had spent the night, waiting for the ambient air temperature to rise sufficiently before it could begin to use its flight muscles. 72 mm.

Termites

Plate 30. Perhaps as many as 20 years have passed since this queen termite *(Macrotermes michaelseni)* and her royal partner founded the enormous nest of which they are now the focal point. Over the years since their brief wedding flight her abdomen has grown to several hundred times its original size, now containing enormous ovaries that produce eggs continually. Her head and thorax have remained their original size, and the four stumps of the wings that once carried her high in the air can still be seen just behind her head. Her partner, the king, hid behind his wife's enormous body whilst the photograph was being taken. In the photograph some pincer-jawed soldiers may be seen, as well as many worker termites licking the body of the queen for certain odorous secretions that will be passed on to other individuals in the nest. 80 mm.

Plate 31. A worker termite feeding the queen by regurgitating food from its own stomach. Another worker can be seen licking the queen's body.

Plate 32. An immature termite worker amongst the galleries of the fungus gardens deep within the nest. The white blobs are fungi growing on compacted termite excrement, and are eaten by the termites. 4 mm.

Plate 33. Ants are some of the worst enemies of termites; they will seize almost any opportunity to enter a termitarium, and carry off large numbers of the inhabitants. In the photograph a pugnacious ant (*Anoplolepis custodiens*) fearlessly attacks a powerfully jawed termite soldier (*Macrotermes* sp.) many times its size, which it soon kills. Termite: 12 mm.

Plate 34. Winged termites (*Macrotermes* sp.) emerging through an opening made in the nest wall by workers. This is the only time that termites will deliberately open their nest to the outside world, and as soon as the winged individuals have left the hole is closed over. This event usually takes place after the first good rains of the year have fallen and almost invariably after dark. Always, at such times, great numbers of worker termites mill about the area; possibly to serve as bait for the frogs and toads that so often prey upon emerging termites – in this way they distract the amphibians from the winged individuals whose rôle is the important one of founding new nests. Worker termites: 8 mm.

Bugs

Plate 35. Just what benefit the spiny coreid bug (*Pephricus livingstonei*) receives as a result of its bizarre form is hard to decide. Perhaps this sap-sucking bug presents a painful beakful for any bird, or perhaps its profile renders it inconspicuous on its food plant. 11 mm.

Plate 36. Just above the pair of compound eyes of the shield bug may be seen a much smaller pair of simple eyes. The latter are constructed quite differently from the compound eyes and although they are almost certainly unable to resolve much detail, they possibly serve as general light sensors to control the insect's activity according to the prevailing light level. 10 mm.

Plate 37. Coloured to match the blue grass upon whose sap it feeds, this shield bug shows the typical shield shape from which these insects receive their popular name. Anyone handling one of these insects very quickly comes to appreciate the reason for their other popular name, 'stink bug', for they are quick to defend themselves by exuding sickly-smelling, highly volatile fluids. 10 mm.

Plate 38. A bug of the family Scutelleridae, approximately two instars (growth stages) before the adult form, as seen in plate 40. The flying wings and their outer protective wing cases have not yet fully formed. The striking metallic colours are the result of light being diffracted through the many microscopically thin layers of material comprising the outer covering of the insect. 6,5 mm.

Plate 39. Few insects can match the fecundity of aphids: in mid-summer some African species give birth to three live young per day. The photograph shows several adult female aphids surrounded by their offspring born during the previous few days, all of them with their probosces embedded in the tissue of the host plant as they suck its sap. Adults: 2,5 mm.

Plate 40. With its proboscis piercing the vein of a leaf, a scutellerid bug (*Calidea* sp.) feeds on sap, a food rich in sugars. The family name of these bugs is derived from the Latin *scutum*, or shield, in reference to the similarity of the upper part of the insect to the shields carried by the soldiers of ancient Rome. Commonly they are known as shield-backed bugs. 12 mm.

Plate 41. Pyrrhocorid bugs are seen here in various stages of development as they feed on sap of the common milkweed. The individual in the lower part of the photograph will pass through one further growth stage before it is fully grown, at which time the wings, seen here as mere stubs, will have developed fully, enabling it to fly. Largest individual: 11 mm.

Plate 42. A number of African trees are commonly known as 'rain trees' due to their strange habit of weeping copious quantities of water from their branches at certain times of the year, often forming pools on the earth below the tree. The cause of this 'rain' is nymphs of the cercopid bug, *Ptyelus grossus,* clustering in thousands along the branches as they suck sap. The water component is exuded as a spittle-like froth that covers the clustering insects and drips continually to the ground. Commonly they are known as spittle bugs in their nymphal stages and as froghoppers when adult due to their somewhat frog-like appearance. In England the exudate of the spittle bugs is called cuckoo-spit. 12 mm.

Plate 43. These fulgorid bug nymphs have tufted 'tails' of fine wax filaments which they are able to open out in umbrella fashion when alarmed. The visual effect when several hundred of these nymphs, clustered on a plant stem upon which they are feeding, suddenly and simultaneously snap open their white tails is striking to say the least; even the slightest tap anywhere on the host plant, such as might be caused by a small bird alighting, is enough to produce a sudden 'explosion' of white. It seems most probable that the effect of this display is to frighten off prospective predators. Nymph excluding tail: 4 mm.

Plate 44. It seems that all bugs as they suck sap must in some way cope with the ever-present ants and avoid falling prey to them. Many bugs, such as this tree hopper (family Membracidae), appease the ants with sweet secretions of honeydew and are therefore left unmolested. A pugnacious ant is seen soliciting honeydew by gently tapping the tree hopper with its antennae. At the same time the bug is laying a mat of eggs behind her, partly embedded in the tree branch upon which she is feeding. Bug: 10 mm.

Plate 45. The eggs of shield bugs can frequently be found on the walls and windows of houses, as well as on various garden plants. The hatching nymphs pop open the circular 'escape hatch' (more correctly called an operculum) seen on top of each egg. Notice the beautifully detailed sculpturing on the surface of the eggs. Each egg 1,5 mm diameter.

Plate 46. A twig-wilter (*Anoplocnemis* sp.) feeding on plant sap. Perhaps the name stink bug would have been a more suitable common name for these 'super-stinkers' of the bug family, whose malodorous secretions when alarmed can only be described as utterly revolting. In some areas these insects feed on the climbing ivy that covers old buildings and often inadvertently enter the building through open windows, much to the annoyance of the inhabitants. 22 mm.

Plate 47. Predator becomes victim as an assassin bug (family Reduviidae) sucks the juices of a crab spider that only moments before had been lying in wait for insects visiting the daisy on which the drama now takes place. Assassin bug: 23 mm.

Plate 48. Here a shield bug slowly eases itself out of its previous skin to reveal the new, but as yet soft, skin beneath. The old skin, rendered thin and flexible through the action of moulting hormones, is shed in its entirety; every leg, antenna and even microscopically fine breathing tubes (spiracles) are moulted. A spiracle is visible in the photograph as a fine white thread being pulled from the side of the insect's abdomen. Bug overall; including moulted skin: 24 mm.

Beetles

Plate 49. This tiger beetle has caught a small fly along a sandy river bank where hundreds of these predatory beetles hunt throughout the day. They are invariably found near water. These beetles always take to the wing as danger approaches and then settle again a few metres away. Along African sea shores they are often found in the vicinity of the strand-line hunting prey such as kelp flies. 12 mm.

Plate 50. Theme for a nightmare are the formidable jaws of a ground beetle, *Anthia* sp. (family Carabidae). These generally large beetles can often be seen hunting after dark for various insects that occur on the surface of the ground. Distance between tips of jaws: 14 mm.

Plate 51. Even though this water strider bug is resting on the edge of a lily pad, one of its legs (the rear left) is still in contact with the water surface in order to sense vibrations that will keep it informed of the activities of its fellows, or of approaching danger or prey. Notice the short pair of front legs that these insects use for grasping their prey in praying mantid-like fashion. Their other common name, 'pond skater', more accurately describes the way these insects move across the surface of the water. 14 mm.

Plate 52. Probably to protect themselves against attack from ants, these ladybird larvae have evolved a body covering of fluffy wax tufts. The photograph shows the ladybird larvae feeding on aphids while ants 'milk' other aphids for honeydew on a poinsettia flower bud. Longest ladybird larva: 4,5 mm.

Plate 53. The spotted maize beetle (*Astylus* sp.) was accidentally introduced into Africa from South America and is today a pest of many crops and garden plants. It feeds on pollen. 12 mm.

Plate 54. A clerid beetle taking a meal of nectar from a Mesembryanthemum flower in the arid Karoo of South Africa. 6 mm.

Plate 55. Its jaws firmly clamped onto a scale insect, a ladybird beetle (*Chilocorus* sp.) extends its six legs as it strains to pry its prey off a citrus leaf. Behind the ladybird lie the upturned remains of scale insects it has already eaten. 8 mm.

Plate 56. A pair of lunate ladybirds [*Cheilomeres lunata*] make a meal of aphids. Predatory ladybirds, such as these, are a blessing to farmer and gardener alike. 9 mm.

Plate 57. Having chosen a site sheltered amongst foliage, a lunate ladybird [*Cheilomeres lunata*] proceeds to lay a batch of approximately 20 eggs. She will repeat the process at intervals of about a day until her ovaries are exhausted; the eggs hatch into tiny six-legged larvae within a week or two. 9 mm.

Plate 58. All set for take-off, with its wing-covers [elytra] raised and wings beating, a blister beetle [*Mylabris* sp.] lifts off from a daisy upon whose petals it had been feeding. Protected by poisonous body juices, these slow-flying beetles seem to have little need for a quick getaway when danger approaches. 27 mm.

Plate 59. Looking like miniature flying saucers a pair of tortoise beetles (*Aspidomorpha* sp.) mate on a leaf of the *Ipomea* creeper that they and their offspring will feed on. 9 mm.

Plate 60. The pollen grains on the face of this blister beetle (*Mylabris* sp.) reveal the second favourite food of these insects; their principal food is the coloured petals of flowers, upon which this specimen is seen feeding. Frequently they are attracted to the printed flowers on women's dresses, which can make out-of-doors social functions a problem at times! 16 mm.

Plate 61. A weevil shows the forward-projecting head that characterises most members of this the largest of all beetle families. 11 mm.

Plate 62. An oil beetle makes a meal of grass pollen, a food rich in proteins. Notice the beetle's covering of fine hair. 16 mm.

Plate 63. A species of tiny dung beetle rolls a ball of fresh cow dung many times its own weight as it seeks out a patch of soil where it can bury the ball and lay an egg into it. The beetle itself is covered in dung. 10 mm.

Plate 64. Deep within a protea flower a cetoniid beetle feeds on the stamens of the bloom. The various species of these beetles are all brightly coloured and often do great damage to roses; their fat white grubs can frequently be found in compost heaps. 20 mm.

Plate 65. A leaf beetle of the genus *Macrocoma* climbing a grass blade. 7 mm.

Plate 66. Of the many species of tenebrionid beetles unique to the Namib desert of Namibia (South West Africa) *Onymacris unguicularis*, like several others, has evolved a way of life that enables it to survive in the waterless 'sea' of sand. Somehow sensing the presence of early-morning fog drifting over the dunes from the nearby Atlantic Ocean, the beetle emerges from beneath the sand, climbs to the highest ridge of a dune, and orientates its body into the wind. Fog begins to precipitate on the insect's body, as the photograph shows, and runs down into its mouth to be drunk. 18 mm.

Plate 67. A click beetle (family Elateridae) hurrying on its way along a branch. Its antennae, like those of all insects, are principally organs of smell and in this case are of a construction known as lamellate. Overall length of each antenna: 20 mm.

Plate 68. A female glow-worm beetle clinging to a grass blade after dark emits a greenish glow in the hopes of attracting an airborne male of her species. The light is emitted from the tip of her abdomen, which she moved during the 30 second exposure necessary to take the photograph, making the glow appear slightly displaced from her body. 19 mm.

Plate 69. In order to lay their eggs deep within cracks in dead wood most long-horn beetles have ovipositors that can be extended to considerable length. Here *Litopus latipes* probes a section of fissured timber for egg-laying sites. Length of ovipositor: 15 mm.

Plate 70. Its common name well-warranted, a long-horn beetle *(Litopus latipes)* shows its 55 mm long antennae; they are more than twice the length of its body.

Flies

Plate 71. Most tachinid flies are easily identified by the very thick bristles covering their bodies. This specimen is busy taking a feed of energy-giving nectar. 9 mm.

Plate 72. Many flies of the family Conopidae, such as this one, bear a striking resemblance to wasps. This specimen was photographed resting on a flower and a moment later parasitized a solitary bee gathering pollen there. The fly grappled with the bee briefly, laying an egg on it which would subsequently hatch into a tiny maggot and feed on the bee. 15 mm.

Plate 73. A hover fly larva grasps an aphid; it will suck the aphid's body dry of its contents before discarding the empty skin. These beneficial fly larvae can usually be found on aphid-infested plants during the warmer months of the year. 11 mm.

Plate 74. Destined for a living death, this moth caterpillar continues to feed on its foodplant, as yet unaffected by the tiny white egg that a tachinid fly (see plate 71 opposite) has laid just behind its head. Within hours the egg will hatch into a grub that will burrow into the caterpillar's body and begin to feed upon it, avoiding eating any part of its host that might kill it. Only when full grown does the tachinid fly larva kill its host, whereupon it emerges and pupates in the soil. 32 mm.

Plate 75. Some of the weirdest of African flies are those of the family Diopsidae, whose eyes are located on the ends of stalks which gives them the appearance of miniature Martian monsters. Besides the compound eyes on the stalks a cluster of three simple eyes is visible on the top of the head between the stalks. Midway along the stalks is a pair of antennae. Eyes: 8 mm apart.

Plate 76. In order to break their way out of their puparia many types of fly possess an inflatable, bladder-like organ called a ptilinum on the front of the head, which operates as a sort of battering ram. The photograph shows a fly, its ptilinum inflated, emerging from the puparium. This is the only occasion the ptilinum is ever used and it will now be permanently withdrawn into the fly's head.

Plate 77. Having pursued and caught a hover fly in mid-air this robber fly *(Promachus vagator)* has settled to eat its victim, whose eyes bear strange map-like patterns. The robber fly is using its piercing mouthparts to suck the body fluids of its prey. Note the hump on the upper thorax of the robber fly which accommodates the powerful flight muscles. The overall length of robber fly: 24 mm.

Plate 78. Ready for instant lift-off a robber fly watches for passing flying insects by means of its large compound eyes. Once airborne it will close in on its victim and seize it from above by means of the long and spiny legs seen in the photograph. Notice the piercing and sucking mouthparts projecting through the dense hair beneath the insect's head.

Plate 79. Although blow flies are normally associated with meat and carcases, they need, as do many insects, occasional feeds of nectar in order to provide them with the energy necessary for their daily activities. Here a blow fly takes his fill of nectar at a daisy. 10 mm.

Plate 80. Whilst blow flies are frequently a pest to man, they also do immense good by bringing about the rapid decomposition of dead animals; in this way breeding sites for dangerous germs are reduced and they help to re-cycle the organic materials from which all living things are made. The photograph shows a few of tens of thousands of blow flies emerging from the carcase of a crocodile that has been killed by fire in the Okavango swampland of Botswana. Longest fly: 8 mm.

Plate 81. Unlike their female counterparts, male horseflies do not feed on blood but on the nectar of flowers. This male horse fly makes use of the copious nectar of an Acacia bloom. 13 mm.

Plate 82. Insect eyes are some of the most remarkable of all structures in the animal world. Here we get a close-up look at those of a hover fly, the micro-structure of whose compound eyes creates a prismatic effect.

Plate 83. The compound eyes of this male horse fly can be seen to meet along the centreline of the head, whereas in the case of the female the eyes are distinctly separate. It is clear that the individual elements are larger in the upper part of the eye than in the lower. Notice also the forked antennae (one of which is not clearly visible due to its proximity to the camera).

Moths

Plate 84. A mimosa moon moth lays her eggs. These large moths of the family Saturniidae are found over an area from southeastern to central and eastern Africa. One of the favourite food plants of the larvae is the Marula tree (*Sclerocarya caffra*).

Plate 85. Caterpillars of the emperor moth *Gonimbrasia belina* hatching from eggs laid on a leaf of a mopane tree. Within three to four weeks these larvae will have increased their weight several hundred times and will resemble those seen in plate 95. 9 mm.

Plate 86. The caterpillars of many hawk moths possess remarkably realistic eye-like markings. Should they sense any vibration of the plant upon which they are feeding (which might indicate the presence of a bird or other potential predator) these caterpillars retract their heads, so that the eye-spots become conspicuous, and begin to jerk the forward part of the body from side to side. The result of all this is to create a frighteningly snake-like effect. Overall length of larva: 70 mm.

Plate 87. In contrast to the hawk moth caterpillars, some, such as this emperor moth caterpillar, 'freeze' when danger threatens and remain motionless for several minutes. Like many other caterpillars this species also relies on colouration and shading to render itself less liable to be seen. The specimen in the photograph was found feeding on a mopane tree and 'froze' in this posture as soon as the branch upon which it was feeding was tapped. 65 mm.

Plate 88. Of all Lepidoptera the hawk moths have probably the swiftest powers of flight. Often at dawn and dusk hawk moths can be seen flying silent and ghostlike in the dim light as they flit from flower to flower, hovering in front of deep-throated blooms and sipping nectar with their long probosces. In the photograph a convolvulus hawk moth (*Agrius convolvuli*) hovers at Nicotiana flowers as it takes nectar through a proboscis that can extend up to 200 mm. Length of moth: 42 mm.

Plate 89. Although by far the majority of moths fly only at night there are a few species that are active in the brightest sunlight. Such an insect is the window-winged moth (*Syntomis cerbera*). Judging by the bright colours and rather ponderous feeding habits of this moth as it visits flowers, it is probably protected by distasteful body juices. Notice its somewhat wasp-like appearance. The 'windows' are simply areas of wing that are free of scales. Wingspan: 27 mm.

Plate 90. The peach moth (*Egybolis vaillantina*) is another day-flying moth and occurs particularly in tropical lowlands and coastal plains. It is the only member of the huge family Noctuidae active by day. Length overall: 30 mm.

Plate 91. Mating hornet moths (*Euchromia formosa*). Like the window-winged moth they are members of the family Ctenuchidae and resemble wasps in appearance, as well as being day flyers. Their larvae feed on the leaves of morning glory creeper. Wingspan: 45 mm.

Plate 92. 'You have been warned' say the colours of this false tiger moth (*Heraclia superba*) as it flies about in broad daylight advertising its distastefulness to any would-be predator. Wingspan: 60 mm.

Plate 93. A Cape tiger moth (*Dionychopus similis*) at rest on a leaf. When these moths are handled they give off a yellowish repugnant fluid. Wingspan: 55 mm.

Plate 94. A bagworm (*Eumeta hardenbergi*) climbs a twig in order to reach a new leaf on which to feed. Once it reaches the leaf it will spin silk between its bag and the twig in order to secure its mobile home whilst it leans out and feeds. This specimen was living on a pussy-willow tree in a Johannesburg garden, from whose twigs the caterpillar has made its bag. Overall length of bag: 90 mm.

Plate 95. Wherever it grows in its wide tropical African range the mopane tree hosts caterpillars of the emperor moth *Gonimbrasia belina* during summer each year. They are commonly known as mopane worms, though each tribe has its own name for these much relished insects which are gathered in great quantities when fully grown and sun-dried for use throughout the year. Length: 70 mm.

Plate 96. Like some miniature batik, the meandering trail left by a leaf miner caterpillar [*Phyllocnistis* sp.] lies etched within a wild ebony leaf. As the tiny caterpillar grew, so its trail widened, until eventually it pupated at the point where the trail stops dead along the lower edge of the leaf. Length of leaf: 65 mm.

Plate 97. Lovers of fruit juice and alcohol, the fruit-piercing moths are a pest at almost any time. Besides piercing cultivated fruit with their powerful probosces and causing it to rot, these pesky moths quickly find their way into an opened can of beer or a glass of wine, much to the annoyance of many a party-goer or camper in the tropics. The specimen in the photograph is feeding on a mango. Wingspan: 35 mm.

Butterflies

Plate 98. Caterpillars and a pupa of the butterfly *Acraea zetes acara*. One of the caterpillars has suspended itself from the twig in preparation for pupation. Pupa: 20 mm.

Plate 99. A nymphalid butterfly (*Byblia ilithyia*) spreads its wings in order to receive maximum warmth from the rays of the early morning sunlight. Butterflies, like most other flying insects, are unable to use their flight muscles when their body temperature is low. Wingspan: 50 mm.

Plate 100. Alarmed, a caterpillar of the citrus swallowtail butterfly (*Papilio demodocus*) rears up the front part of its body and everts its osmeterium from just above its head. This bifurcated, inflatable organ is covered in a foul-smelling highly volatile fluid which no doubt serves to repel would-be predators; its effect on man is quite nauseating. Notice the false eye marking on the insect's side. Length: 35 mm.

Plate 101. A blue pansy butterfly (*Junonia oenone*) suns itself as it feeds on nectar. Wingspan: 48 mm.

Plate 102. A caterpillar of the African monarch butterfly (*Danaus chrysippus*) begins to emerge from an egg laid on a milkweed plant. Note the micro-sculpturing on the egg surface.

Plate 103. Once it has emerged from the egg the monarch caterpillar makes a meal of its eggshell. This behaviour is common among Lepidoptera and probably serves to provide the developing caterpillar with chitin, the stiffening substance of insects' bodies. Caterpillar: 4 mm.

Plate 104. An almost fully grown monarch caterpillar, still feeding non-stop on the leaves and stalks of milkweed. Length: 34 mm.

Plate 105. Once fully grown the African monarch caterpillar spins a pad of silk on a stalk and suspends itself from it by means of its hindmost pair of larval legs. Now chemical changes within the insect's body set the process of pupation in motion.

Plate 106. Twelve hours later the caterpillar begins to flex its body and jerk from side to side. Suddenly its skin splits and, aided by even more violent jerking of the body, is gradually forced towards the hind end. For the first time the developing wings are visible. In a very tricky operation the caterpillar exposes a special hooked organ (the cremaster) from beneath its almost shed skin and embeds it in the silk pad, allowing the skin to drop away.

Plate 107. A further 12 hours later the pupa has now fully formed, complete with a hard waxen coating and firmly suspended by the cremaster. The developing wings can be clearly seen through the transparent pupal case. Length including cremaster: 22 mm.

Plate 108. A month later, perhaps several months during winter, the adult butterfly splits open the pupal case and begins to emerge. At this stage its wings are still unexpanded.

Plate 109. Ten minutes later the African monarch butterfly is free of its pupa; it clings to the plant stem as it fits the two halves of its proboscis together and gradually inflates its wings with blood. Within an hour its wings will be at their full size, after which the wing veins will be made rigid through the action of hormones and the butterfly will be ready to take to the air for the first time. Length of body: 25 mm.

Plate 110. Eye to eye with a pierid butterfly (*Belenois aurota*), we are made aware of the absolute perfection to be found in all of nature's creations. The coiled proboscis through which the butterfly sucks nectar and water and the various structures of scales and hairs that protect the body and sense air-flow over its surface, enabling the butterfly to fly most efficiently, are visible. The pattern of dark areas seen in the compound eye is an optical effect brought about by the complex structure of the organ, which amongst other of its functions is responsive to the polarisation of skylight and thereby enables the butterfly to navigate.

Plate 111. *Precis archesia*, one of several nymphalid butterflies whose underwings resemble dry leaves. Overall length of wings as seen in photograph: 48 mm.

Plate 112. *Belenois aurota* is a butterfly well known to most people living in the southern parts of Africa. Every few years millions upon millions of them fly northeastwards in a continuous flood of white, pausing only to feed on energy-giving nectar at flowers (as shown in the photograph), or to spend the night clinging to vegetation in low-lying areas. Day after day the fly-past continues, through the busiest towns and the remotest countryside, only tailing off after a fortnight or so. Though little research has been done it appears that *Belenois aurota* suffers periodic population explosions and flies northeast in order to populate new breeding grounds. Wingspan: 48 mm.

Plate 113. *Charaxes* butterflies are well known for their habit of seeking moisture from fresh mammal dung. Very likely they obtain food from this source too. The photograph shows several *Charaxes jasius saturnus* (as well as some harvester ants) feeding on steenbuck droppings. Length from front of head to rear tip of wing: 46 mm.

Plate 114. Common in the woodland areas of eastern and southeastern Africa *Acraea zetes acara* is seen here feeding from the flowers of a pussywillow in a household garden. Length from front of head to tip of wing: 38 mm.

Plate 115. Of all African leaf-mimicking butterflies *Precis tugela* is one of the finest examples. It frequents tropical and sub-tropical forests, blending superbly with the leaf litter on the forest floor. Length from front wingtip to rear wingtip: 44 mm.

Plate 116. Although butterflies do not sleep in the strict sense they do rest amongst vegetation at night. The photograph shows a satyrid, *Henotesia perspicua*, clinging to a grass blade where it is spending the night. Like all members of the family Satyridae this butterfly is only able to use its middle and hind pair of legs for clinging or walking, the front pair being very reduced in size and probably, as in the family Nymphalidae, they are used as organs of taste. Length between front and rear wingtips: 30 mm.

Wasps

Plate 117. Taking no more than a second or two a braconid wasp thrusts its ovipositor into the side of a newly hatched monarch butterfly larva, injecting several dozen tiny eggs. The caterpillar exudes a blob of defensive fluid at its mouth, which the wasp carefully avoids. Length of caterpillar: 4 mm.

Plate 118. Three weeks later the caterpillar is growing normally and still feeding avidly on milkweed. Outwardly it appears quite healthy, but within its body several dozen wasp larvae are growing as they feed on tissues and blood, carefully avoiding eating any vital organ the loss of which might kill their host.

Plate 119. At about the time the monarch caterpillar would normally pupate it ceases all activity and lies quiet. Within its body the developing parasitic wasp larvae now begin their final meal, consuming all remaining tissue and killing their host. After a few hours the wasp larvae simultaneously chew their way through the caterpillar's skin and wriggle free, beginning at once to spin silken cocoons for themselves. Length of each wasp larva: 5 mm.

Plate 120. Their cocoons complete and secured to the milkweed stem, the wasp larvae now pupate. It often happens at this stage that an extremely small species of chalcid wasp arrives on the scene and parasitizes the braconid wasp larvae by injecting its own eggs through the wall of each cocoon.

Plate 121. Several weeks later the braconid wasps begin to emerge from their cocoons alongside the now shrivelled body of their former host. Within a few days they will mate and begin searching out further monarch butterfly caterpillars to parasitize.

Plate 122. A mason wasp *(Delta caffer)* places a paralysed but still living moth caterpillar in her newly constructed mud nest. In all she will stock her nest with three or four paralysed caterpillars as food for the single larva that will develop from the egg she has already laid in the nest. Length of wasp: 28 mm.

Plate 123. Having overpowered and paralysed a cricket several times her own size, this sphecid wasp is struggling to drag her still living victim to a nest hole she has dug in the soil. Though unable to move the cricket will live for several days and provide a source of fresh food for the wasp's young as they develop. Length of wasp: 20 mm.

Plate 124. Whilst a female braconid wasp *(Iphiaulax* sp.) cleans her antenna a male taps her gently with his. This species is parasitic on wood-boring beetle grubs, whom the female braconid wasp reaches by drilling with her long ovipositor into the burrows of the beetles in dead wood. Overall length of female (excluding antennae): 15 mm.

Plate 125. Having just completed the first cell of a new nest, the mud not yet dry, a mud wasp *(Sceliphron spirifex)* clutches a small spider she has paralysed. She will stock her nest with several such paralysed spiders, which will live for a fortnight or more and provide her developing larva with a continuous supply of fresh food. Length of wasp: 25 mm.

Plate 126. As this scoliid wasp feeds on the nectar of a poinsettia flower it inadvertently receives a covering of pollen grains. In this way wasps can act as pollinators performing an important function in the life of plants. Length of wasp: 27 mm.

Plate 127. A paper wasp *(Polistes smithii)* female pulverising a section of a caterpillar before feeding it to her developing larvae, whose heads can be seen protruding from their cells in the lower part of the picture. Like all paper wasps this species hunts caterpillars as food for its young, stinging them to death and cutting them up on the spot. Those nest cells that can be seen covered over with domed caps contain pupating larvae, which have spun the caps with their silk. Wasp: 18 mm.

Plate 128. This pair of paper wasps have only recently begun construction of their nest, which like all paper wasp nests is made from plant fragments chewed into a crude paper. Several eggs can be seen in the upper cells, which will be extended upwards as the larvae hatch and develop. Lower wasp: 19 mm.

Plate 129. Although paper wasps are generally feared by householders most species vary rarely sting, even when their nest is approached closely. However, those of the genus *Belonogaster* will often attack anyone within several metres of their nest, administering painful stings about the victim's head and neck. In the photograph *Belonogaster* females raise their wings in alarm at the photographer's presence. Length: 25 mm.

Plate 130. A cuckoo wasp of the family Chrysididae using its antennae to locate the nest cell of a mud wasp, into which she will deposit her own egg. The mud wasp to whom the nest belongs was away hunting spiders at the time. Length: 11 mm.

Plate 131. A nest cell of the mud wasp *Sceliphron spirifex* opened along its length reveals the ghostly sight of a dozen or so paralysed yet still living jumping spiders, each awaiting its turn to be eaten alive by the developing wasp grub (seen at the left-hand end of the picture). Length of nest cell: 27 mm.

Plate 132. Taking no chances against parasites a eumenid wasp guards the entrance to her nest built in a disused wood-borer hole. She has surrounded the entrance to the hole with a sticky substance, which probably helps to keep out parasites. Diameter of hole: 5 mm.

Plate 133. A mason wasp (*Odynerus* sp.) clinging to the mud entrance tube of her nest. Often these wasps will take over old *Sceliphron* nests, adding on such a curved entrance tube. Length: 15 mm.

Bees

Plate 134. The tiny stingless bees of the genus *Trigona*, such as this foraging 4 mm specimen, are important pollinators of many wild plants. Unfortunately they can be a thorough pest on hot dry days as clouds of them fly about and land on one's face in their quest for moisture. 4 mm.

Plate 135. Male carpenter bees such as this *Xylocopa* sp. can sometimes be seen hovering in the same small area hour after hour awaiting the arrival of a female. Should another male show up at such a mating site the two of them immediately begin an airborne head-butting contest – all of which is very amusing to watch – until the weaker one is forced to retire. Length: 14 mm.

Plate 136. Both seeking nectar and pollen from the flowers of a marula tree are an African honeybee (*Apis mellifera adansonii*) and a much smaller stingless bee (*Trigona* sp.) that makes its nest underground. Honeybee (left-hand side of picture): 12 mm.

Plate 137. Workers of the African honeybee (*Apis mellifera adansonii*) within their nest. Although they have the reputation of being ferocious they appear to cause few problems for the many tribal peoples who frequently raid wild nests in hollow trees, rock crevices, and disused aardvark holes, amongst other sites. Average length approximately 11 mm.

Plate 138. This megachilid bee has just emerged from its pupa within the orange-sized nest of mud, resin and fibre, built by a solitary female high in the branches of a tree. In all, eight such bees hatched from this nest, which must have taken its builder several weeks to complete. Diameter of nest: 60 mm.

Plate 139. An African honeybee worker foraging for pollen and nectar. These honeybees thrive far better than the European subspecies in African conditions. Length: 11 mm.

Ants

Plate 140. Tailor ants (*Oecophylla longinoda*) are seen 'sewing' living leaves together as they build their nest in a tree. The worker on the left holds his body in tension as he draws the edges of the leaves together, whilst the worker on the right holds a silk-spinning larva gently in its jaws, shuttling it between each leaf in turn as it spins silk between them. Each worker: 10 mm.

Plate 141. Deep within their arboreal nest a colony of tailor ants move the large naked pupa of a winged male to safety after their nest has been disturbed. Winged males and females are released from the nest during the rainy season each year, flying off to mate with winged tailor ants from other colonies and found colonies of their own. Workers: 10 mm.

Plate 142. Tailor ants (*Oecophylla longinoda*) swarm agitatedly over their nest of silk-bound leaves, having sensed the photographer's presence. These ants are well known for their aggressive nature and painful bites, as anyone who regularly picks mangoes along the East African coast will verify!

Plate 143. Cocktail ant workers (*Crematogaster* sp.) co-operate to move the pupa of a reproductive. When alarmed these little ants cock their 'tails' (abdomens) over their heads. Worker: 4 mm.

Plate 144. Male driver ants (*Dorylus* sp.) such as this are frequently attracted to lights during the rainy season. Buzzing loudly, they fly about, crashing into walls and falling to the ground where they curl their abdomens in a most threatening manner, but are in fact quite harmless. Due to the secretive ways of driver ants these winged males are all that most people ever see of them. 32 mm.

Plate 145. Ants are attracted to anything containing sugars. The photograph shows formicine ants (*Polyrachis* sp.) feeding on sap that has oozed from a wounded tree and is fermenting. 9 mm.

Plate 146. The hollow thorns of certain Acacia trees provide nesting sites for small colonies of ants, such as the slender ant (*Sima* sp.). The photograph shows a 'V'-shaped pair of thorns that has been sectioned to reveal the slender ant's nest within. Two of the ants are carrying larvae, and several scale insects (seen covered in whitish wax powder) can be seen living within the nest. The latter provide the ants with sweet honeydew in exchange for the protection they receive. Ant: 10 mm.

Plate 147. Practically all scale insects provide ants with sweet secretions in exchange for a measure of protection. Here we see formicine ants (*Polyrachis* sp.) tapping wax scales (*Ceroplastes* sp.) with their antennae as they solicit honeydew. Lower ant in photograph: 9 mm.

Bees 22

In general it may be said that bees differ from wasps in the nature of the hairs on their bodies and in the nature of their food. A wasp's hairs are simple, without side branches, whilst many of the hairs on a bee's body are plumose or feathery, particularly those on the head and thorax. It is thought that the plumose hairs on the bee assist in collecting pollen. Bees feed on nothing but honey and pollen throughout their lives, whereas wasps in their larval stage are carnivorous. Bees have two pairs of membranous wings, linked together with tiny hooks on the hind pair that fit in a fold on the front wing when the insect is in flight; in this they resemble the majority of wasps, but whereas there are wingless species of wasps there are no wingless species of bees.

The tongue of a bee is well-developed and adapted for lapping nectar; in the more primitive bees it is short and blunt but in the higher bees it is long and slender; the jaws are well-developed in all bees. The larvae are all blind, white and legless, and the females provide them with food.

There are a large number of species, most of which are solitary, each female working alone to construct her nest and provide for her young, but some are social and live in highly organised communities. Bees are classified as forming a superfamily of the Hymenoptera known as the Apoidea. There are nine families of bees in Africa, and we will deal here with the six largest.

Primitive or membrane bees These bees are placed in the family Colletidae, which is divided into two groups which have very similar habits.

The first comprises the plumed bees, which are medium-sized to large, and extremely hirsute, especially on the face and thorax. Some of the more common plumed bees belong to the genus *Colletes*, and they resemble Cape honeybee workers in shape and colour, except for their antennae which are longer.

The bees in the other group are smallish insects, not more than 12 mm long, wasp-like in appearance because they have few hairs on the body, and generally brown and red in colour. The tongue is short and broad and they have no special pollen-collecting apparatus as is found in the higher bees.

A common species is the brown membrane bee, *Hylaeus heraldicus*, of which the female is about 9 mm long, and the male a little bigger. She is reddish brown and black, with red antennae and legs, a yellow front to her head and a small yellow stripe across each side of the abdomen. She makes her nest in any suitable dry tubular opening she can find, in hollow stems, in the deserted burrows of wood-boring insects, holes in walls, and so on. The only materials she uses for lining the nest and dividing it into cells is her own saliva, which she applies with her tongue.

The female starts building her nest by licking the inside of the tube with her gummy saliva which dries to form a thin, transparent pellicle or membrane. After she has coated the inside of the tube with this waterproof varnish she makes a transverse partition of the same substance near the mouth of the tube, with a small round hole in the middle, just big enough for her to fit through. This is a long, laborious process that entails several hours licking with her broad, short tongue that she uses as her trowel. It is from this method of nest-building that the group takes its common name – membrane bees.

When she begins to stock her first cell at the bottom of the tube the reason for the water-proofing becomes evident. As she cannot carry pollen home on her legs or on the underside of her abdomen, as the higher bees do, she swallows it and brings it home in her crop together with the clear, watery nectar. The two are mixed with saliva and she regurgitates the mixture, which has the consistency and usually the colour of the yolk of an egg, in the bottom of the cell. It is much more liquid than the food provided by most solitary bees and were it not for the preliminary coating of varnish, it would soak into the walls of the nest.

When she has accumulated enough food for her larva she lays her large, sausage-shaped egg in the centre of the mass of food, where it floats. Then, leaving sufficient space for the larva when it is fully grown, she makes a transparent partition across the tube, sealing off her first cell, which is about 10 mm in depth from back to front. And so she continues, constructing and stocking cell after cell, one above the other. Finally she seals up the mouth of the tube with another membranous partition that looks much like a thin sheet of transparent mica. If her egg-laying is not yet complete, she goes on to find another tube where she can nest. The limit of her capacity is about 12-15 eggs. However a female will often go on working after her ovaries are exhausted and she has no more eggs to lay. In this case she constructs more cells, stocks them with food and seals them off, but all this effort is in vain because the cells contain no eggs.

The egg hatches in five to 11 days, depending on the temperature, and the larva, coiled like a letter 'C', feeds whilst floating on the mixture of nectar and pollen. It grows rapidly and devours its huge meal in six to 12 days. As is the case with the larvae of most Hymenoptera that feed on a store of food in a confined space, the stomach of the larva is blind – that is, it has no connection with the intestine; it is like a bag, open in front and closed behind. As a result the larva cannot evacuate and contaminate its food. The waste material accumulates as a dark mass at the hind end of the stomach and this is visible as a discoloration through the translucent body-wall of the larva. Only when it is fully grown and has stopped feeding, and whilst it is resting motionless in its cell for a week or ten days prior to changing into a pupa, does the larva's stomach join with the intestine and open at the hind end. Then, and then only, can it evacuate, and all the waste material is expelled at once. There is not much of it because of the nature of the food and the excreta is pushed out of the way to the end of the cell, where it dries as small yellow granules.

The larva, now pure white and ready to pupate, does not make any sort of cocoon but lies loose in its cell. After about two weeks the eyes of the pupa turn brown and then black. Slowly the body darkens until it, too, is brown and finally, after three to four weeks, the skin is cast for the last time and the adult emerges, about two months after the egg was laid.

There are two generations a year of these bees in the Cape Province of South Africa, the first generation nesting during the latter half of October and November, and the second during January and February. The larvae of this second generation reach full size in April and they rest motionless in their cells all through the winter, changing to pupae in the spring and giving rise in October to the first generation of the new season. These bees are heavily parasitized by the ensign wasp, *Gasteruption punctulatum*.

Burrowing or mining bees Many solitary bees dig tunnels in the ground, often in paths or in banks where the soil is compact and dry. Although solitary in the sense that each works alone, some are communal in their choice of a nesting site and frequently a large number of tunnels will be found close together. The shiny, dark-coloured bees, many with banded abdomens, are *Lasioglossum* and *Halictus* species of the family Halictidae. Over 70 species have been described from Africa, and they all exhibit this habit of living in colonies to a marked degree. Sometimes a small area on a path will be seen dotted with little heaps of earth, like miniature mole-hills, and each marks the spot where a bee is burrowing below the surface.

The females of some species of *Halictus* dig a common burrow; several females work together at the excavation, but a little way below the surface the tunnel branches and each female has her own particular branch with her own cells at the end; the only communal part of the nest is the main entrance and passage-way. We know little of the habits and life histories of the African species but some of their nests have been studied. In general, on flat ground the main burrow goes down vertically, in a bank it is horizontal. Isolated cells radiate into the soil from the main tunnel, and if the cells are numerous the nest structure is rather like a slender bottle brush. The slightly constricted nest entrance may be closed with soil at night, or during adverse weather, or it may be guarded by a bee or even left open.

Each cell is lined with a thin, shining layer of waxlike material, secreted by a gland at the tip of the bee's abdomen and spread over the cell wall with a special brush on the hind leg. Within each cell there is a firm, rounded loaf of pollen, on top of which a curved egg lies, only its two ends touching the pollen mass. The cell is then sealed with a plug of soil, tamped into place by the female bee.

It is said that among certain European species there are two generations a year. The spring generation consists of females that mated the previous atumn and that have survived the winter. The males die soon after this mating, before winter begins. The offspring of the spring generation are all females whose eggs develop parthenogenetically (without being fertilised) and it is they who constitute the summer generation. Their offspring, in turn, are the males and females which mate the following autumn.

In other species of *Halictus* the female of the spring generation survives after her egg-laying is completed and guards the nest. When her daughters emerge they return to the nest and form a small community: the old female acts as sentry at the entrance, whilst the young females go busily in and out, foraging for food and stocking their cells.

Small bees with black heads and thoraxes, coarsely pitted, and red abdomens, belonging to the genus *Sphecodes*, may often be seen in the vicinity of the *Halictus* colonies. Close relatives, they belong to the same family yet they parasitize *Halictus*. The females enter the host's nest, open the completed cells and replace the egg lying on the pollen with one of their own. The *Sphecodes* then either leave the nesting burrow, or else remain inside to deposit further eggs on subsequent days.

In addition to the members of the Halictidae already mentioned, there are a large number of species of small bees belonging to the genus *Nomia* that also make their nests in the ground. A group of mining bees which lap up the perspiration from the human skin in hot weather, have come to be called 'sweat bees'. The females sting if they become entangled under clothing.

Leafcutter and carder bees Leafcutter bees, *Megachile* species, are very well known because of their habit of cutting neat circular or oval pieces out of the leaves of rose bushes and other plants. There are a large number of different species, varying in size from that of a house fly to that of a honey-bee, and they are common and widely spread. They are stoutly built, brown or black, hairy bees with a conspicuous yellow tuft of hairs on the underside of the abdomen, where the pollen grains are collected. Many bees collect pollen on their hind legs, but all the members of the family to which the leafcutter bees belong, Megachilidae, have this special pollen-collecting apparatus on the underside of the abdomen.

Megachile is a large and common genus found throughout Africa, and most of these bees have habits similar to those of the southern African *Megachile venusta*. When the female leafcutter bee is ready to lay her eggs she seeks out any sort of tube of the right dimensions that is sheltered, dry and that will serve as a home for her young. It may be a hollow stem, a hole in the wall, an abandoned mud wasp's nest, a burrow left in a fallen log by a wood-boring beetle, even a key-hole. Having decided on the site, she begins by cutting an oval piece from a leaf of some suitable plant; as she needs

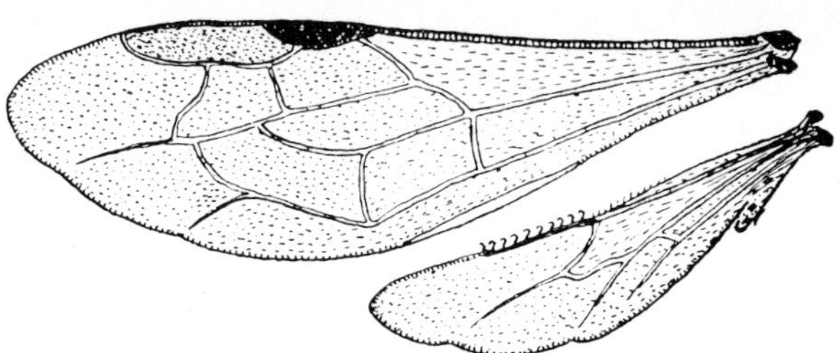

326. The left wings of a bee (*Allodape* sp.) showing the small fold on the hind margin of the forewing, and the tiny hooks on the hind wing that fit into it.

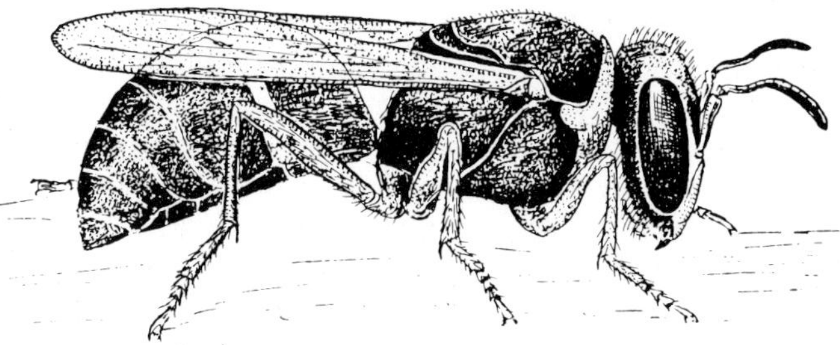

327. A female membrane bee (*Hylaeus heraldicus*).

328. A female leafcutter bee (*Megachile venusta*).

fairly thin, smooth leaves, the young foliage of rose bushes and certain kinds of gum trees are favoured sources of building material. Some species use the petals of flowers and a few cut pieces from the papery bark of particular trees.

She tucks the freshly-cut oval segment into the base of the nesting tube, pressing it into position with her broad head and using her saliva as a cement. Several of these oval pieces form the base and side-wall of her first cell. They overlap in three or four thicknesses and form a receptacle like a small cup or thimble about 10 mm deep. This she fills to about three-quarters of its depth with a thick yellow paste of pollen and honey. On top she lays a white, sausage-shaped egg. Then she closes the thimble with a lid made of three or four circular pieces of leaf, cut to size with amazing accuracy.

After the lid has been fitted, the bee proceeds to make another cell, the lid of the first forming the base of the second. This is in turn stocked with food and an egg, and so construction continues until the tube is nearly filled with thimbles. To finish off her work the bee brings a number of pieces of leaf of assorted shapes and sizes which she pushes in at random, to form a barrier at the mouth of the tube. Finally she seals off the entrance with a plug of chewed leaf cemented with saliva.

There seems to be only one generation a year of these bees. The fully grown larva spins a cocoon, lining the inside of its cell, and then, after it has emptied its alimentary canal and coated the inside of its cocoon with a thin brown layer of excrement that dries to form a water-proof varnish, it sleeps in its snug cell for months until the following season, when it pupates. Two or three weeks later the adult emerges.

The little carder bees of the genus *Immanthidium* also belong to the Megachilidae. They are mostly black with white markings on the abdomen, and with a white pollen brush on the underside of the abdomen. In some species the males are bigger than the females, an unusual feature among insects. Most of them make their nests in tubular openings, in sites similar to those chosen by the leafcutters, but their cells are lined with cottony fibres which they strip with their mandibles from various hairy plants. As an example of the group we can consider the widespread species, *Immanthidium junodi*.

The female carder bee arrives at her home carrying a little bundle of white fluff between her front legs. She takes this into her nest and cards the fibrous material by pressing it with her head and working it with her jaws until it forms a thin, uniform, thimble-shaped lining to the bottom of the tube. It takes several journeys before her beautiful white thimble is complete, ready to receive its store of food. She carries the pollen back to the nest on the underside of her abdomen and the nectar in her crop and stocks the cell with the mixture. It takes her about two days to construct and stock a cell; she then lays an egg on top of the food and closes the cell with a pad of fluff, well carded and felted. She fills the tube with cells within 10 mm from the entrance and then seals it off with a thick pad of fibres, pressed down firmly by her head and jaws to form a protective barrier to keep out enemies.

The egg hatches in seven to eight days and the larva eats all the food provided by its mother. In ten days it is fully grown. From the time it is about half-grown it begins to excrete waste matter in the form of flattened yellow pellets which it pushes behind it and arranges neatly in a single layer lining the inside of the cotton wallet. By the time it is fully grown these pellets of dry excrement form a layer which covers almost the entire inner surface of the cell and the larva now proceeds to spin a cocoon of brown silk, with the yellow pellets adhering to its outer surface. The cocoon is dense and smooth, almost spherical, only slightly longer than it is broad; at the head end there is a curious little nipple which, when examined under the lens, is seen to have a tiny circular opening – it is probably constructed by the larva as a ventilation hole. The adult bee emerges two or three weeks after pupation. There are one or two generations a year and the larvae that reach full size late in the summer spend the winter months as larvae resting inside their cocoons.

Some species of this family make remarkable nests of matted plant fibres, attached to leaf blades or to branches of trees and shrubs. If such a nest is broken open it is found to consist of a number of cells embedded in a thick, warm, protective coat of fibres.

Such nests made by *Serapista* species may be as big as a large orange. Besides plant down and animal hairs, small downy feathers may sometimes be used to build the tough outer layer of the nest. These large nests contain up to 15 cells, and are probably built by a single female. They are sometimes found under the eaves of houses, or in big concrete stormwater pipes.

Still other species, of the genus *Chalicodoma*, make their nests in tunnels which have been made by wood-boring insects, in hollow stems, in holes in walls or in the mud cells of sphecid wasps. They use soil particles glued together with their saliva, or with resin, to form the partitions between the cells, and they do not cut pieces of leaf to construct their cells.

Hoplitis species do not nest in ready-made cavities, but excavate in bare soil single cells which are lined with petals or with resin. In the dry western regions of southern Africa, *Hoplitis globicola* builds a remarkable spherical nest of small pebbles and resin. The nest is about 15 mm in diameter and attached to twigs of bushes.

A number of species of the Megachilidae have become 'cuckoo bees' – they do not construct and stock nests for themselves but lay their eggs in the nests of related bees, their larvae feeding on the honey and pollen stored by the host and starving out the legitimate occupants of the nest. Some of the commonest of these are the striking black and white bees, with pointed abdomens, *Coelioxys* species, that are parasitic on leafcutter bees.

Anthophorid bees Over 100 species of stoutly-built, hairy bees with striped abdomens, belonging to the family Anthophoridae, have been described in Africa. They are well-represented in other parts of the world as well. Some of them look like small carpenter bees, they are very swift on the wing and their flight – accompanied by a shrill hum – is erratic.

All African species, as far as is known, nest in the ground, digging deep burrows, generally in the sun-baked side of a bank. At the end of the burrow, short side tunnels lead to the cell chambers which are lined with a waxlike material and stocked with a yeasty-smelling mixture of nectar and pollen.

Some species construct a curious curved tube at the mouth of their burrow, made from grains of sand cemented together with saliva.

A large number of anthophorids are parasitic or 'cuckoo bees'. The larvae of some cuckoos are active and have elongated, curved mandibles with which they kill the anthophorid larva.

So-called 'sleeping clusters', consisting of a group of male bees which gather in certain places to pass the night, are found among the anthophorids as well as among other non-social bees. Occasionally a cluster of anthophorid males may be discovered on cool mornings in a small bush where they cling to the twigs with their large mandibles. The males of many of the Anthophoridae have unusually long antennae, from which they derive the name of 'long-horned bees'.

329. A leafcutter bee inserting a piece of rolled up leaf into her nest hole, which is the disused burrow of a wood-boring beetle. 9 mm.

Carpenter bees and allodapine bees There are no bumble bees in Africa south of the Sahara; instead we have a number of species of the big burly bees, known as carpenter bees, that form the family Xylocopidae. These include the largest of all bees and they are mostly black, marked with bands of yellow or white hairs. They are all very similar in their life history and habits and the common and widely spread species *Xylocopa caffra* serves as an example of the group.

This carpenter bee varies in its colouration in different parts of Africa. In the southwestern Cape the female is black, about 20 mm long, and she has two prominent bands of yellow hair, one on the hind half of her thorax and one on the front of her abdomen. The male is about the same size as his mate, but he is completely covered with a dense coat of yellow hair. Her wings are a dark smoky brown, his are paler in colour. In the eastern coastal areas of southern Africa, *Xylocopa caffra* is smaller and several generations occur during the year, as against a single generation in the Cape. In the interior of southern Africa this species is equally small, also with several generations a year, but here it is banded with white instead of yellow.

In the Cape the female starts nesting in spring – at the end of October or the beginning of November – and she may choose the dead flower stem of an aloe, pine timber in a building or, more usually, a dead branch of a tree that has partially rotted so that the wood is soft and easy to tunnel through. Whatever her choice, the material

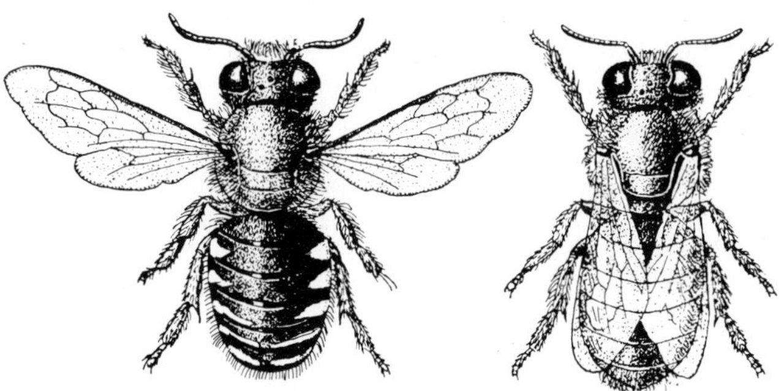

330. A pair of the widespread carder bees, *Immanthidium junodi*, with the male on the left.

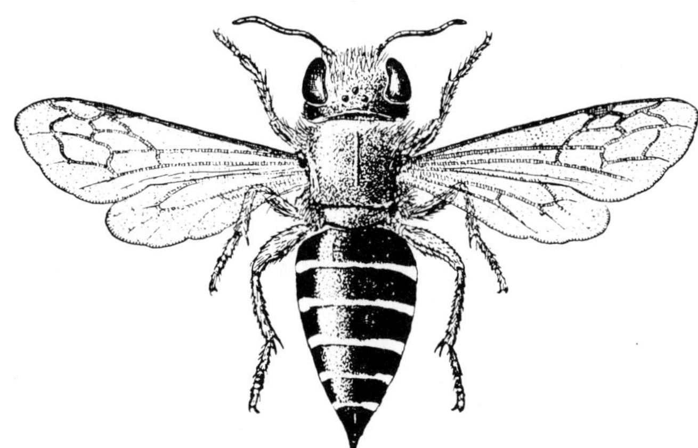

331. The female cuckoo bee (*Coelioxys* sp.), a parasite of leafcutter bees.

must be dry, for dampness is one of the chief enemies of these bees, many of which die of fungous disease if moisture penetrates into their homes.

She bores a neat tunnel in the wood, about 10 mm in diameter and around 15 cm deep, rasping away the wood fibres with her powerful jaws. Several bees may bore tunnels side by side in a dead branch, but they do not, as a rule, co-operate in the work; each female has her own home from which she jealously excludes all intruders, buzzing loudly in protest and butting vigorously with her head if any other bee should enter her tunnel.

Having prepared her nest, with the walls of the burrow carefully smoothed and polished, she sets about collecting food; she limits her attentions mostly to flowers of the pea and bean family, the Papilionaceae, and those of the sage family, the Labiatae. She brings back the pollen on her hairy hind legs and mixes it, inside the nest, with nectar regurgitated from her crop, to form a thick, dull yellow paste that is barely moist. On top of this mixture she lays her astonishingly large egg, white, curved and 12 mm long. Then she closes the cell with a seal made of sawdust chewed from the side of the tunnel and mixed with saliva.

In the course of about a month she constructs six or seven such cells, at which point her work is complete. After this she rests in the tube guarding her nest from any intruders and leaving it only occasionally for a little food. The eggs hatch in about a fortnight and the larvae take three or four weeks to consume all the food and reach full size. They pupate in their cells, without spinning a cocoon, and the adults of the new generation emerge at the end of January or the beginning of February. In the meantime the old bee dies or flies off.

The young adults break down the partitions between their cells soon after they emerge, so the tube contains not only the six or seven brothers and sisters resting amid it but debris as well. After a few days they become active and sweep the rubbish out of the nest. They continue to live in the nest amicably as a family party, the various individuals only leaving occasionally to go out and find food; by far the greater part of their time is spent in the nest, even on bright sunny days. In this way they spend the autumn and the winter. When the spring arrives, the bees are about ten months old and they become more active. The females begin to show hostility towards the males who are eventually driven out and take up bachelor quarters in an abandoned tunnel; early in the spring tunnels can be found crowded with males only. Later the females show hostility to one another and finally only one, apparently the boldest and most aggressive among them, retains possession of the original nest, whilst the others go off to make new tunnels for themselves elsewhere.

In the winter rainfall area at the southern tip of Africa there is only one generation of these bees a year and, unlike most other bees, the greater part of their comparatively long life of about a year is spent in the adult state. They can easily be induced to nest in bamboo tubes, about 30 cm long and from 10-18 mm in internal diameter, if they are taken from their natural homes on a cold day in winter and put into the tubes. The bamboo must be placed in a box which is completely dry, as the bees quickly desert a damp home. It was from bees nesting in such tubes that the observations recounted above were obtained.

Although carpenter bees are large and strong, their sting is not as painful as that of the honey bee; it is not barbed and is not left behind in the wound.

Some of these bees have remarkable mites associated with them. *Xylocopa caffra* and allied species are all infested with strange large mites, of the genus *Dinogamasus*, that are found only on the bees and in their nests, but nowhere else. If a female *Xylocopa caffra* is carefully examined, a small hole will be seen at the base of the abdomen, on the dorsal side, just where it touches the hind end of her thorax. This hole leads to a chamber in her abdomen, lined with chitin, and about the size of a lentil. The mites live in this special compartment in her body, packed together like sardines and up to 18 on one bee. She carries them about with her wherever she goes and occasionally one or more of the mites may creep out of the hole and wander over her body, before returning to its retreat.

When she constructs her nest, two or three mites leave her body and enter each cell so that, by the time she has completed her egg-laying, the chamber in her abdomen is empty. These mites lay their eggs on the food mass in the cells and their young grow up side by side with the larvae of the bee. Apparently they feed on a fatty exudation from the skin of the bee larva but they do not seem to harm their host in any way.

When the young bees emerge from the pupal state the mites in the cells with them creep into the abdominal pockets of the female bees (the males do not have such pockets and therefore never carry mites). We do not know precisely the relationship between the bees and the mites. It has been suggested that the mites feed on pollen grains they pick off the hairs on the bee's body, but this is highly improbable because of the nature of the mites' mouthparts. Another suggestion is that the large dinogamasid mites feed on smaller mites that pester these bees, but this, too, is improbable as one frequently finds a bee badly infested with the small mites and yet with a number of dinogamasid mites in its pocket. Much remains to be explained in this remarkable symbiosis between certain species of carpenter bees and the dinogamasid mites.

A number of species of much smaller bees, ranging in size from about 3–12 mm, with few hairs on their bodies and generally black or metallic green in colour, belonging to the genus *Ceratina*, are sometimes called lesser carpenter bees. They make their nests in hollow stems, such as the dry flower stalks of aloes or watsonias. On a much smaller scale, their nests are very similar to those of the carpenter bees, each cell stocked with a mass of the rather dry mixture of honey and pollen and each cut off from the next by a partition of fragments chewed from the wall of the stem and glued together with saliva.

Some remarkable and very interesting little bees, informally called the allodapine bees, are also included in the family Xylocopidae. The largest is about 15 mm long, brown or black as a rule; the others are much smaller. Almost without exception, they have yellowish facial markings, which serve to identify them, either thin lines or a patch in the lower centre of the face. They are common and widespread throughout Africa, except on the southern African highveld.

Allodapine bees nest in simple burrows in hollow or pithy dead stems, especially where these stems have been cut, broken or burnt to expose the pith. Favourite nesting sites are stems of lantana, khaki weed along railway lines or the edges of cultivated fields, or coarse grass used as thatch. The nest entrance, a neat round hole constricted by a collar built by the bees, is defended by a female, either with her head or with her tail end, which contains the sting.

These bees are unique in that their nests have no partitions; the young are reared together even though they may be at different stages of development. In most nests inhabited by more than one mature female, there is usually one which appears more physically worn than the others, has enlarged ovaries, and it is she with whom the male mates. She is the egg layer and could be regarded as the queen. The other females, often smaller than the queen, may lay a few eggs or none at all and in some allodapine colonies they are the workers.

This kind of behaviour makes these allodapines 'subsocial' insects. As our example of this group we may take one of the largest as well as one of the most common species, *Allodape mucronata.*

The female is easily recognised by her size – about 14 mm – and by the three pointed projections at the end of her abdomen. She makes her nest in dry flower stalks similar to those chosen by the lesser carpenter bees (*Ceratina* species). Usually she chooses a stalk that has been broken and she burrows down into it from the top, chewing out the pith to a depth of about 15 cm. Then she lays two or three large oval white eggs which lie loose at the bottom of the burrow. She now spends most of her time in the tube, guarding her eggs until they hatch. She does not attempt to collect a store of food for her young but, as soon as the first egg hatches, she goes out to collect nectar and pollen. Returning to the nest, she scrapes the pollen from her hind legs into a heap on the floor of the nest, regurgitates some nectar on to it and then mixes the two into a stiff paste. Using her jaws, she places the paste on the larva just behind its head. The larva lies on its back and by bending its head, it can reach the food lying on its chest, as it were. As soon as this food is finished, the mother fetches more and, when the other eggs hatch, she feeds those larvae in the same way. She always arranges them so that the oldest is near the entrance, the next in age a little lower down, and so on, while the newly-hatched larva and any eggs that may be present are at the bottom of the tube. Usually she must feed a family of six or seven at any one time.

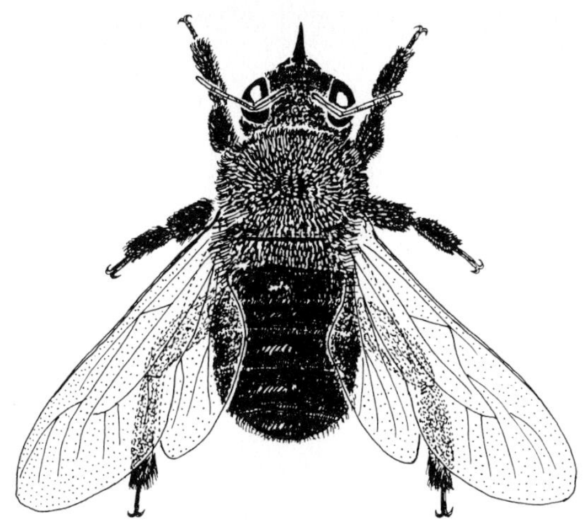

332. This hairy carpenter bee (*Xylocopa* sp.) is a metallic blue-black colour, with a yellow thorax and first abdominal segment.

333. Development of the carpenter bee, *Xylocopa caffra,* showing the different stages found in one nest, with the egg on the left and the pupa on the right.

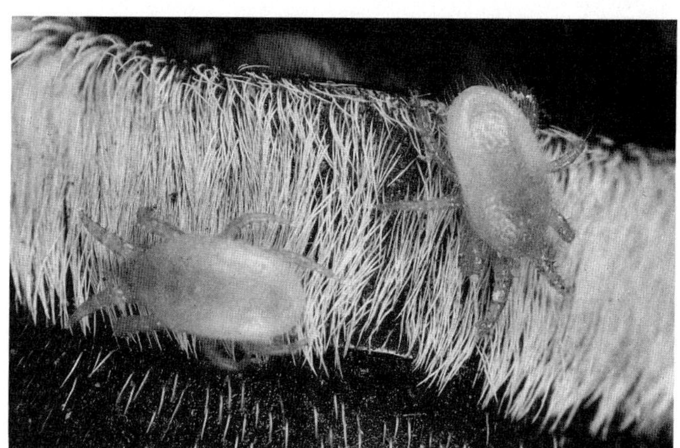

334. Mites which live in a special chamber on the body of the female carpenter bee.

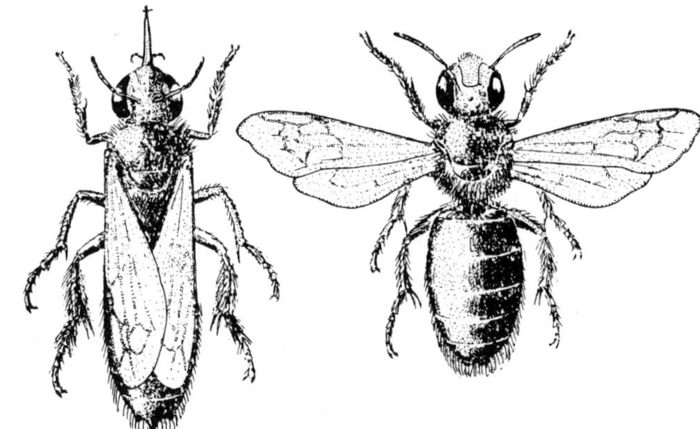

335. A pair of subsocial bees, *Allodape mucronata,* with the large female on the left (14 mm, with three pointed projections at the tip of her abdomen).

When she is not occupied caring for her young, the mother rests at the mouth of the tube, the tip of her abdomen at the entrance, ready to sting any intruder. Her other duties include keeping her nest spotlessly clean and she carefully removes the excrement, passed by the growing larvae. When the larvae pupate she spends practically all her time in the nest, waiting patiently a fortnight or more for her sons and daughters to emerge. The family may remain together, mother (now with tattered wing tips) and her sons and daughters (their wings as yet undamaged), if the tube is commodious enough. Usually the young bees will leave their home to go and seek nesting sites elsewhere, but one or two of the males and females remain with their mother. In this way small colonies form but they never grow beyond three or four individuals. The females work together in caring for the young, the old female spending the greater part of her time in the nest, guarding the entrance. The presence of males in the nest is tolerated, although they do not assist at all in rearing the young. In other *Allodape* species the males, although shorter-lived than females, may stay in the nest for months.

Here, among these bees, we see the primitive beginnings of social life. They are comparatively long-lived, each female surviving for nearly a year as an adult; it is not known how long the males live, but they also live longer than do most male bees. The females are actively involved with their young and they see them grow up into adults. With the great majority of other solitary bees, the females never come into actual contact with their young as they seal off the cells after stocking them with food and they die before their family reaches adulthood.

Allodapine bees exhibit these interesting social habits, and they are well worthy of further study. They display striking differences within the species as well. For example, the small species *Allodapula acutigera*, that is very common and nests in dry flower stalks, has quite a different method of arranging her eggs from that seen in the *Allodape mucronata* discussed above.

The female *Allodapula acutigera* lays her eggs, which are comparatively small, on the wall of the nest, gluing them in an upright position in a circle, jutting towards the centre of the burrow like the spokes of a wheel. She lays half a dozen or more in a short period and when they hatch (which may take five to six weeks in cool spring weather), each larva remains attached to the wall of the nest by its hind end, which is fixed in the egg-shell. Thus the larvae all rest with their heads towards the centre and are all at the same level. The mother brings in pollen which she piles in a heap just in front of her young. To feed them, she regurgitates some nectar on the heap, mixes it with the pollen to the desired consistency, and then picks up the sticky mass and thrusts it between the heads of her young, effectively supplying her entire family with food at once.

As the larvae grow bigger they eventually lie side by side, with their heads up, pointing towards the entrance, still all at the same level. Therefore throughout their larval stage the mother can feed her whole family at once by thrusting a lump of food paste in between the heads of the larvae. When they are fully grown she drags the larvae apart and arranges them in a row along the tube; she now spends most of her time in the nest, with her tail at the entrance to keep out intruders. When the adults of the next generation emerge they remain with the mother for a time but soon, to prevent overcrowding, some members of the family depart to found new nests elsewhere.

These little subsocial bees, that are so abundant in Africa, offer a fruitful field of study. They can be induced to nest in glass tubes, and watched throughout their fascinating breeding cycle. Further details are given in Chapter 24.

Social bees There are about 20 000 species of bees known all over the world, but of these only about 500 are 'social' bees; all the rest are solitary – they do not form colonies and the females work alone. Excluding the subsocial bees described above, and the bumble bees (which do not occur in Africa south of the Sahara), all social bees are placed in the family Apidae, and in Africa these include the well-known honey bees and the little stingless bees.

The stingless bees, also known as 'mopane bees' or 'mocca bees', belong to the genus *Trigona*. They are tiny; indeed some of them, at only about 3 mm long, are among the smallest of all bees. They cannot sting, because their stings are vestigial and useless as weapons of defence; so instead they swarm out of their nest if disturbed and buzz about in front of one's face in a very irritating way, settling in the hair and on the eyebrows and forehead, crawling into eyes, mouth and nose and generally being very unpleasant. On some occasions they bite freely.

They nest in hollow tree trunks and in holes in walls or rocks. The ground-nesting species also use ready-made cavities, such as termite nests. An unusual nesting site of one African *Trigona* species is in the nest of a cocktail ant.

The nesting material, usually dark coloured, is called cerumen. It is a mixture of light wax and large amounts of resin gathered by the bees. The wax is produced between the dorsal segments of the abdomen, unlike the honey bee which produces it from the underside. The cerumen is used to block up cracks and crevices and also in the construction of the curious spout or funnel that marks the entrance to the nest. It has been suggested that the sticky funnel at the entrance prevents ants and other unwanted visitors from entering. Sentries remain on guard at the entrance during the day, as is the case with the honey bee, but at night the stingless bees close up the funnel with a temporary plug of wax and gum.

The interior of the nest of stingless bees consists of a brood section and a section for the storage of food. In the nest of *Trigona gribodoi*, a well-known, minute, tree-nesting species of Africa, the brood portion consists of irregular clusters of oval-shaped cells and cocoons, supported by slender pillars of cerumen. The cells, vertical and open at the top, are first filled with food and then closed after an egg has been laid erect on top of the food supply in each one. Therefore these little bees, although they are social, rear their young in very much the same way as the solitary bees do. The large storage pots, which contain pollen and honey are up to 7 mm in diameter, and made from soft cerumen, yellowish to brownish in colour.

Both the honey and the brood of stingless bees are relished by Africans. The honey is usually sourish and thin compared to that of honey bees, but it can be just as tasty, depending on the species of stingless bee and the source of the nectar. On rare occasions they may make honey from *Euphorbia* flowers, and since the plant is known to be poisonous, Africans regard this honey as poisonous too.

The Zulus in Natal find the nests of *Trigona gribodoi* by placing a freshly cut branch of a tamboti tree in the sun in a clearing. The bees gather the latex welling from the cut and bruised parts of the branch, and use it to make their cerumen. They return again and again to collect more latex, and their flight path betrays the location of their nest.

As an example of an African ground-nesting stingless bee, we shall take *Trigona denoiti,* whose nest may be 1-2,5 m below the surface. The bees do not excavate the nest themselves, but use natural hollows in the ground, such as termite nests. Entrances at ground level are usually vertical cerumen funnels, but sometimes they are simple holes.

At the top the nest, which is lined with a mixture of cerumen and mud, is connected to the outside by a more or less vertical passage. Below the nest is a second passage like a pipe, half a metre or more in length and which simply ends in the ground. This acts as a drain pipe for any water that may reach the nest. Within the nest cavity the brood area is enclosed in laminated sheets of cerumen, separate from the storage pots. The brood cells are arranged in layers, to form a more or less spiral comb.

The bees make a store of sticky cerumen in the nest chamber near the entrance tunnel. This is to trap any insects that attempt to invade the nest, and puts them out of action.

Dactylurina staudingeri is unique among the stingless bees in that it makes vertical, double-sided combs, like those of the honey bee. It is found in Central and East Africa, where it makes cerumen-covered nests under the branches of large trees. When disturbed the bees attack in large numbers, carrying lumps of very sticky cerumen which they glue onto their foe, biting at the same time. Even determined humans are soon demoralised by this treatment!

The number of individuals in *Trigona* colonies varies very widely, from a few hundred to several thousand, depending on the species and on the age of the colony. The inhabitants are nearly all sterile females, or work-

336. Section through nest of a subsocial bee, (*Allodape* sp.), made in a piece of thatching reed, showing how the youngest larva is located at the bottom of the nest, and the largest nearer the entrance (right hand side of picture). Still nearer the entrance is a pupa.

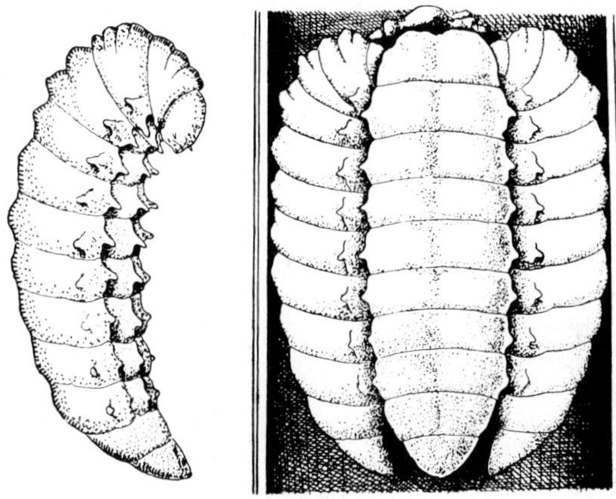

337. The larvae of *Allodapula acutigera,* showing a single larva (left) and a group of larvae feeding inside the nest (right).

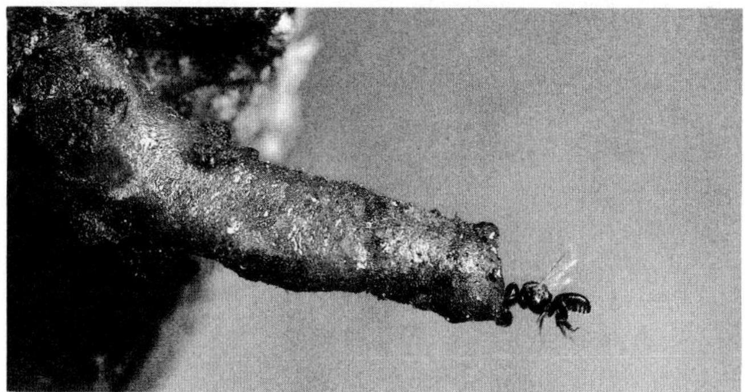

338. Stingless bee (*Trigona* sp.) arrives at the waxen entrance tube to its nest in a hollow mopane tree (*Colophospermum mopane*).

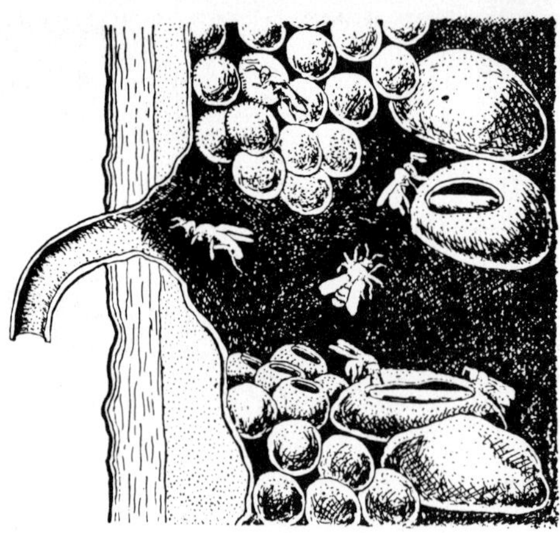

339. A section through a *Trigona* bee nest showing the entrance spout (left), the round brood cells, and the large, flattened cells used for the storage of pollen and honey.

340. Swarm of African honey bees (*Apis mellifera adansonii*) clusters in a shrub while scout bees search for a suitable nest site in which the swarm can take up residence. Frequent swarming is a feature of the African honey bee.

ers, although many males may be present in the nest as well. They often form swarms near their nest, where they probably mate with virgin queens.

The queen differs little in appearance from the workers; her abdomen is slightly more portly because of her active ovaries. There is only one mother queen in a colony, but a number of daughter queens may be present as well, to assist the old queen. From time to time swarming, young queens leave the nest accompanied by a detachment of workers, to form new colonies. This again is somewhat different from the honey bee, where it is the old queen that relinquishes her nest and leads the first swarm to create a new colony. The old queen of the stingless bees is too fat and heavy with eggs, and her wings too tattered, to fly out with a swarm.

The honey bees form a group that differs considerably from the stingless bees. There are four species of honey bee in the world, and of these three are found only in the Indomalayan region and further east, while the fourth is the well-known hive bee, *Apis mellifera* of Africa, the Middle East and Europe, that has been carried all over the world by man. Several different subspecies of the hive bee have been named, no less than six of these from Africa south of the Sahara. Of these the two best known are the yellow-banded African bee, *Apis mellifera adansonii*, and *Apis mellifera capensis*, the black Cape bee that is less aggressive and usually has less populous colonies than *adansonii*.

One point of special interest about the Cape honey bee is that the workers, during a queenless period, will lay eggs that can develop into workers or even queens. It is well known that workers of other races of honey bees lay eggs that develop into infertile drones. It is thought that this phenomenon of the Cape workers laying fertile eggs developed as an adaptation to the heavy losses of queens on mating flights. These losses are probably due to the very strong winds in the southwestern Cape, and also to predation by Alpine swifts. These birds are present throughout the year, and prey voraciously on the bees which they swallow whole during their fast, swooping flights.

The African honey bee has attracted much attention in recent years, mainly as a result of its importation into Brazil in 1956, and its subsequent successful establishment in vast areas of the South American continent, where European races of the honey bee had not settled permanently in the wild, despite repeated attempts to introduce them. Because of their aggressive nature, the *adansonii* bees caught the imagination of the media in America, and were named 'killer bees'. This reputation is no longer valid, for the figures available indicate that today the African bees are responsible for less than a dozen attacks (only a few of which are fatal) each year in all the areas of South America where they occur. People who spend much time out of doors in Africa are well aware of the dangers of attack and stories of lucky escapes are legion.

European races of honey bees were imported on a fairly extensive scale into Africa from the turn of the century onwards, because of certain 'undesirable' characteristics of the African *adansonii* honey bee (from a beekeeper's point of view). These include its aggressiveness, the readiness of colonies to leave their hives, and the weakening of colonies through queens repeatedly leaving at the head of swarms. All traces of the introduced European bees, however, soon disappeared, and the African bees seem unaffected.

It is now clear that the *adansonii* bee is better adapted to, and consequently more successful in, the harsh African environment, with its many predators, its irregular supplies of nectar and its long dry season. The adaptations by the African bees include a rapid build-up of the colony due to increased egg-laying by the queen, shorter development period of the workers, drones and queens (known to entomologists as 'castes'), foraging in the cool of dusk or in moonlight, migration to areas with plentiful food, and the ability to occupy successfully almost any nesting site, even if only temporarily.

When a bee scout finds a likely source of food he returns to the hive and performs 'the dance of the bees' – one of the most extraordinary phenomena in natural history. Karl von Frisch was the first to describe this 'dance' by which the scouts inform the other workers of the find. This amazing communication takes place in the dark of the hive, the scout performing on the vertical honeycomb. According to the duration and enthusiasm of the dance he imparts details of the amount of food. Depending on whether these ritualized movements take the form of a 'round' or 'tail-wagging' dance and depending on the emphasis, the scout specifies the direction (relative to the sun) and the distance (based on flying time) to the source. The scent left on his body indicates the quality of the food. When other bees have received the information, they find the spot and when they return, they too dance. Within a short time most of the workers in the hive are out gathering the food.

We usually associate honey bees with their stings, and these can be very painful indeed, and extremely dangerous to those people who are allergic to components in the chemical mixture injected when the bee stings. In some cases, a single bee sting can lead to rapid death, and it is vital that anybody who supects that he or she may be allergic to insect stings should consult a doctor, and if necessary undergo a course of desensitisation as insurance against the possibility of a fatal sting. For most of us the sting of the honey bee worker is no more than a painful experience which can be relieved by putting ice on the affected area after removing the sting as quickly as possible.

CLASSIFICATION

ORDER **Hymenoptera**

SUBORDER **Apoidea**
Tarsi of hind legs usually more or less enlarged and flattened. Pronotum short and collar-like, with rounded lobe on each side that does not reach to the base of the wing. Body usually hairy, the hairs branched or plumose. Food consists of honey and pollen.

FAMILY Colletidae
Primitive, solitary bees that line their nests with saliva that dries to form a transparent membrane. They partition off the cells in the nests in the same way.

SUBFAMILY Hylaeinae
Small, wasp-like almost hairless bees (e.g. *Hylaeus* species), often with yellow or white markings on the face. Females swallow pollen and carry it to the nest in their crops.

SUBFAMILY Colletinae
More robust and hairy than those of the first subfamily (e.g. *Colletes* species).

FAMILY Halictidae
A large family of small to medium-sized bees of varied habits, but most construct nests in the ground, with short branches at the lower end giving access to the cells. Some better-known African genera are *Nomia, Lasioglossum* and *Halictus.* Some species nest in colonies. Some members of the family are parasitic in the nests of other bees, *Sphecodes* being an example.

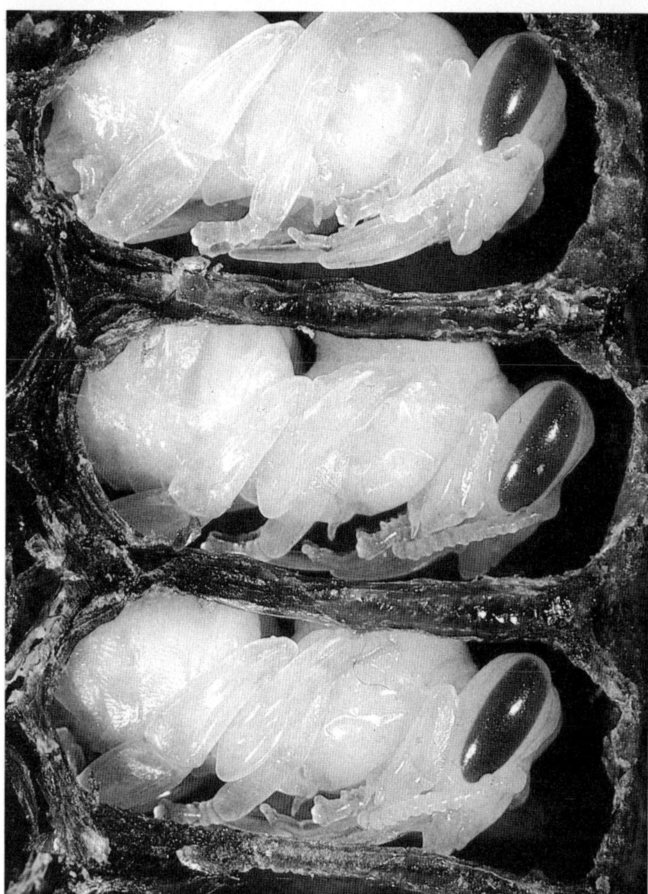

341. Pupae of the African honey bee revealed in a section of the brood cells.

342. 'Wild honey' is a nutritious delicacy eagerly sought by people throughout Africa. Here a Bushman in the northwestern Kalahari enjoys a meal of comb honey that he has just gathered from a baobab. Skilfully using smoke as a weapon, he avoided even a single sting.

FAMILY Megachilidae

A large family of moderately-sized bees, the best known of which are the leafcutter bees like *Megachile* species. Other members of the family, such as *Immanthidium* and *Chalicodoma* species, make their nests or the nest partitions out of plant fibres, resin or mud. Some nest in the ground, others in holes in wood, walls, hollow stems and so on. Some, like *Coelioxys* species, are parasitic on other bees.

FAMILY Anthophoridae

SUBFAMILY Anthophorinae

Burly, hairy bees with a swift, erratic flight. They nest in the ground, making deep tunnels and constructing their cells at the bottom. Examples are *Anthophora* species, some of which look like small carpenter bees.

SUBFAMILY Nomadinae

All members of this subfamily live as parasites or 'cuckoos' in the nests of other bees. *Nomada* species have pointed abdomens which are usually marked with white, blue or yellow.

FAMILY Xylocopidae

SUBFAMILY Xylocopinae

The carpenter bees, *Xylocopa* species, include some of the largest of all bees. They are mostly black with bands of white or yellow, and make their nests in dead branches, dry aloe stems and pine timber used in buildings. They mostly prefer to feed on flowers of the Papilionaceae and Labiatae.

SUBFAMILY Ceratininae

The lesser carpenter bees are all *Ceratina* species. They are mostly black, slender and almost hairless. Their nests are very similar to those of carpenter bees. The other bees in this family are called allodapine bees, common genera being *Allodape, Allodapula* and *Braunsapis.* They nest in stems and twigs, make no partitions in their nests, and the larvae are fed one after the other according to age.

FAMILY Apidae

The true social bees of Africa all fall into the subfamily Apinae, which includes the little stingless bees of the genus *Trigona,* and the well-known honey bee, *Apis mellifera.* The bumble bees (subfamily Bombinae) do *not* occur in Africa south of the Sahara, and carpenter bees are often incorrectly called bumble bees.

OTHER FAMILIES

Three small and less important African families have not been dealt with: they are the Andrenidae, Fideliidae and Mellitidae.

FURTHER READING

Butler, C.G.: *The World of the Honey Bee.* Collins, London, (1974) 226 pp

Fletcher, D.J.C.: 'The African bee, *Apis mellifera adansonii,* in Africa'. *Annual Review of Entomology* (1978) 23: 151-171

Michener, C.D.: *The Social Behaviour of the Bees. A Comparative Study.* Belknap Press, Harvard University Press. Cambridge, Massachusetts (1974). 404 pp. (The same author has published many other important papers in various journals)

Smith, F.G.: *Beekeeping in the Tropics.* Longmans, London (1960). 265 pp

Watmough, R.H.: 'Biology and behaviour of carpenter bees in southern Africa'. *Journal of the Entomological Society of southern Africa* (1974) 37: 261-281

Ants 23

Ants form one very large family, the Formicidae, which constitutes the superfamily Formicoidea in the order Hymenoptera – thus conceding a close relationship to bees and wasps. The family is subdivided into 11 subfamilies, of which seven occur in Africa south of the Sahara. As most ants lack common names, it is sensible to refer to them by the names of the subfamilies, hence in this chapter we will talk about ponerine ants, doryline ants, myrmicine ants, and so on. All ants are social insects, none lives alone. Two narrow waists – between the thorax and the abdomen – distinguish them from other Hymenoptera; in ants, the first, or first and second abdominal segment, forms a small pedicle, or petiole.

There are at least 8 000, but probably as many as 14 000 species of ant in the world, in over 250 genera. Without doubt they are the most successful social insects, if one measures success in terms of sheer numbers and geographical distribution. Through a variety of life histories unparalleled in the insect world, this single family has spread out from its original home in the tropics to inhabit all but the polar circles, the peaks of the highest mountain ranges, and the most barren desert regions of this world; they occupy the entire African continent, although they become scarce in the alpine and subalpine areas of central Africa and the Sahara desert.

A colony of ants may consist of less than a dozen individuals, or it may reach enormous proportions, numbering several million. Most ants build permanent nest structures, the doryline ants being the only exception (these merely form temporary clusters of workers about the queen and brood). A large percentage of ants nest in the soil, either excavating the entire nest, or making use of existing crevices and cavities under rocks and among roots. Other species nest above ground in rotting wood and humus, while some dwell in trees in nests built of soil particles and chewed wood, or of live leaves spun together with silk produced by the larvae.

A colony comprises a queen, or queens – the only individuals in the nest that are fertile and capable of laying eggs – and a large number of workers, all of whom are sterile females. Workers may differ morphologically but if they differ in size only, we refer to them as major and minor workers. However in a number of species, the major workers have massive heads and powerful jaws and are known as soldiers. The only time that males are encountered in the nest is when they have been reared for mating flights. However, they die soon after mating, and are not found in the nest as kings, as is the case with termites. Only males and virgin queens have wings, and these are retained for the duration of the nuptial flights. Once this is over, the males die and the queens shed their wings before starting new colonies.

The ant brood consists of eggs, larvae and pupae, which are kept either in groups or singly in the nest's brood chambers. They are not reared in specially constructed cells, as are the young of some bees and wasps. The larvae are blind, legless and quite helpless: workers feed and clean them and should the nest site be changed, transport them. In most species the larvae spin silken cocoons when fully grown; however there are some which do not, and the pupae of these species lie naked in the brood chambers. No myrmicine or dolichoderine larvae spin cocoons, while in other subfamilies this trait is absent only in certain species. The silk of *Oecophylla* larvae appears to be expended during nest construction, but this is not a rule among nest-spinning species; the larvae of *Polyrhachis* all spin cocoons before pupating, despite the fact that their silk is used in the construction of the nest.

Larvae periodically emit a clear fluid from the mouth which is attractive to workers; they also produce an equally attractive clear fluid from the anus and workers often solicit these fluids by stroking the heads and abdomen tips of the larvae with their antennae. It is likely that there is some communicative purpose behind this behaviour, as it appears to encourage care of the brood by attendant workers. Those insects which live in close association with ants (technically called myrmecophilous insects) appear to mimic the ant brood in that they too produce glandular secretions that not only calm the ants, but encourage them to feed the mimics.

The larvae of the lycaenid butterfly, *Euliphyra mirfica*, are tended by *Oecophylla* workers; the ants feed and care for the larvae within their nests, despite the fact that the caterpillars feed on the coccids from which the ants obtain honeydew. Some beetles, and in particular the staphylinid beetles, appear to be highly-advanced myrmecophilous insects. These beetles are found above ground by the ants who, after licking the secretions produced by the beetles, pick them up and carry them down into the nest to the brood chambers.

Precarious relationships of this kind can only occur if the guest is able to mislead the host regarding the nature of its activities, for the ant – a normally aggressive creature – would not tolerate hostile strangers within its nest without some form of disguise. Numerous other less precarious relationships have been found to exist within ant nests; these include flies, moths, cockroaches, silverfish, spiders and isopods. In almost all these relationships some form of communication occurs between guest and host.

It has been found that many myrmecophilous insects 'tune into' the communication system of their host outside the nest. The staphylinid beetles detect the trail made by ants and by waiting on the trail, are assured of making contact with the colony. The properties associated with such a trail are purely chemical: if foraging ant workers find food that is too large to be carried back to the nest without help, they will first feed, and then immediately return to the nest – depositing a chemical substance along the way on the ground. These chemicals are appropriately called trail pheromones. (A pheromone is the chemical component of a glandular secretion produced by an individual, which elicits a specific response from individuals of the same species once they receive it). Pheromones are generally produced by glands on the abdomen, but in some species may also be produced by tarsal glands.

Close observation of ants on an ant trail will reveal that certain individuals trail or dab the tips of their abdomens on the substrate, whether it be the ground, a wall or the branch of a tree. All the ants can be seen hurrying along the trail, their antennae bent forward, following the pheromone odour; ants that have filled themselves at the food site strengthen the trail when they return to the nest. Provided that there is food in plenty, a large number of workers are recruited to the site and a broad trail is established. However, as the food supply is depleted, fewer ants pass along the trail and as a result the odour diminishes and fewer and fewer ants visit the site until eventually the food is finished.

The foraging scout, however, has no pheromone trail to follow back to the nest, yet after wandering about outside the nest in search of food, always finds the way home without retracing its path. The scout uses the pattern of polarised light in the sky as a light compass to show the way home. In fact all ants, regardless of whether they are following a trail or not, use the light of the sun whenever they leave the nest. The workers of the harvester ant, *Messor barbarus*, which form some of the most impressive trails in dry savanna, can be induced with the use of mirrors and by shielding the sun, to turn about and return to the foraging area – despite the fact that they were busy carrying grass seeds back to the nest.

Generally, ants do not have good eyesight, although this can only be asserted in a relative sense. Their degree of vision is closely related to their life habits. Thus most dorylines are totally blind, as they spend most of their lives underground, whereas the more time a species spends above ground, the better its eyesight. The arboreal tropical ants *Oecophylla* and *Santschiella* have exceptionally good eyesight, and this not only makes them efficient hunters, but also particularly aggressive. If, in general, ants have poor vision, they compensate for this deficiency with an acute sense of smell and sensitivity to ground-borne vibration: few will respond to a movement or an object unless they detect a vibration or an odour. While many remain motionless upon detecting a vibration in the substrate, *Oecophylla* and *Crematogaster* respond aggressively, swarming about in alarm, trying to locate the cause. An object brought near an ant will elicit little response until its odour is detected, after which the ant will begin to wave its antennae through the air in an attempt to fathom the source, and, having done so, will become alarmed, either adopting a threatening posture or running about aggressively.

Ants have also developed glands for use in other spheres of communication. They are able to distinguish one another from members of other colonies in that they bear a unique and complex odour; this 'colony odour' is thought to be a mixture of chemicals derived from the nest material, objects in the immediate vicinity of the nest, and especially from the food that members of the colony consume. The identity of workers is also maintained by trophallaxis – the exchange of liquids both from the mouth and anus by processes of regurgitation and defecation. This lively exchange of food from what has been termed the 'social stomach', is encouraged by workers, who both beg food and offer theirs to others. However, while in the myrmecioid subfamilies workers frequently engage in the exchange of regurgitated food, in the poneroid subfamilies exchange is either poor or totally absent. It is apparent, therefore, that other mechanisms ensure a uniform odour within a colony, and that these may involve not only odours of the nest and its surroundings, but also the composition of pheromones in each colony.

A most important group of glands are those which produce alarm pheromones: if attacked or harassed, an ant, walking along a trail, foraging for food, or merely within the confines of the nest, will release the contents of its glands and any ants in the vicinity detecting the odour will immediately become alarmed. An alarmed reaction can take a number of different forms: often a very high concentration of the pheromone makes the ants flee from the source; a lower concentration, however, will attract the ants, arousing aggression and attracting assistance.

Alarm can be induced by crushing an ant, and often the striking smell of pheromones remains on one's fingers. In its lowest concentration an alarm pheromone acts as an attractant, and the first response shown by other ants is an orientation towards the source. But immediately thereafter they show alarm and typically open their jaws in an aggressive fashion. *Oecophylla* workers raise their abdomens and continue their approach with a somewhat stiff-legged gait, alert and attentive to every movement. *Crematogaster* also raise the abdomen, but behave quite differently: instead of a cautious approach they become frenzied, rushing about in search of the disturbance. *Odontomachus* workers, who hold their jaws wide open when alarmed, readily snap them closed with an audible click, the force capable of severing the limbs of other insects. A different attitude is adopted by the workers of *Polyrhachis*, who lower the abdomen between the legs. These, and other formicine species, spray mixtures of formic acid and pheromone from the tip of the abdomen, and the mixtures have a dual purpose, serving both as defensive substances and as alarm pheromones.

The actual defensive mechanisms used by ants are equally diverse. All but the dolichoderines and formicines have stings, although many species do not readily use them. All have large mandibles, and these are used as all-purpose tools. The dorylines are capable of stinging and yet defend themselves effectively with their bite – overpowering their enemies and victims by sheer numbers. Almost all ponerines use their stings readily, especially the workers of *Megaponera* and *Odontomachus*, and in view of their size their sting is a most efficient weapon. Although dolichoderines and formicines lack stings, they do have equally effective defensive mechanisms: the dolichoderines produce scented chemicals from anal glands which not only have repellent and insecticidal properties but are also sticky or oily. Most formicines spray formic acid from a modified sting gland, the spray reaching up to 50 cm. *Oecophylla* not only sprays formic acid, but also administers it with its bite, cocking its abdomen forward over its head and releasing the acid onto its jaws.

Ponerine ants The ponerine ants are regarded as the most primitive of the family in Africa and may be recognised by the postpetiole, formed by a slight constriction between the second and third abdominal segments. Many species are found throughout Africa, although they flourish chiefly in the tropics and subtropics. The smallest species are found in the genus *Apomyrma*, in which the minor workers are barely 2 mm long; however most ponerines are considerably bigger and workers of the South African species *Streblognathus aethiopicus* are the largest ants in Africa, measuring up to 22 mm. Colonies are generally small, numbering a few dozen, but may be larger, those of *Paltothyreus tarsatus*, *Odontomachus haematoda*, *Megaponera foetens* and species of *Leptogenys* numbering several hundred.

343. A column of Matabele ants (*Megaponera foetens*) return from a raid on a termite colony, each worker's jaws crammed with termites. 12 mm.

All are carnivorous, hunting other insects and arthropods and preying to a large extent upon termites. The queen and workers look alike, differ little in size and are armed with powerful stings; thus equipped, some of the larger species can inflict a painful wound. A number of ponerines stridulate by rubbing the post-petiole against the rough surface of the gaster. The sound made by *Megaponera* workers whilst raiding is quite audible to humans even from some distance. The larvae are fed by the workers on scraps of insects and, when fully grown, they spin cocoons round themselves.

Megaponera foetens, one of the largest members of this subfamily, is distributed throughout Africa. It is well-known because of its aggressive ways, its painful sting, and its distinctive stridulation. The workers were once regarded as two different species: the larger, measuring up to 17 mm long, is dull black with fine yellow hairs all over its body; while the smaller is only 10 mm long and seems to be more shiny than the major worker. The queen, though a little bigger than the major worker, looks very much like it but for a stouter abdomen.

These ants feed exclusively on termites and make well-organised raids to secure their prey. Before the raid, a lone major worker scout locates the termite nest and immediately returns home, laying a pheromone trail behind her. Once back in the ant nest she arouses the colony and then leads them to their quarry. If she is located by an observer and removed before the column reaches the termite mound, the attackers mill about in confusion and then return to the nest without achieving their objective. A successful raid, however, is conducted with military precision: the ants march in a wide col-

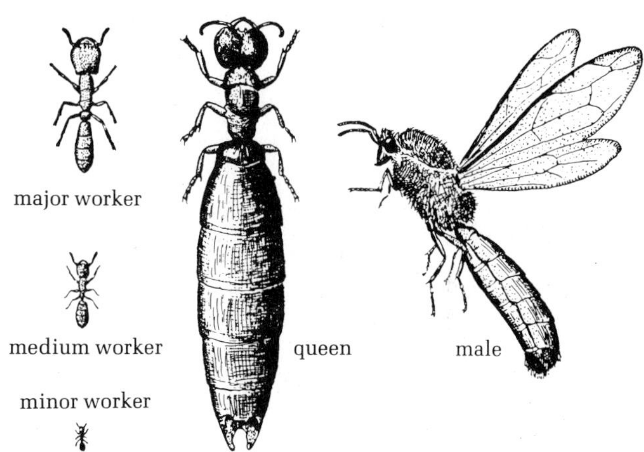

344. The various castes of the driver ant, *Dorylus helvolus*.

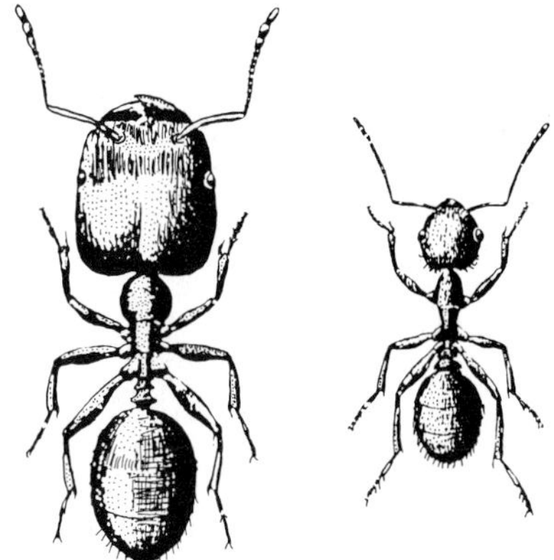

345. The major (4 mm) and minor worker (right) of the brown house ant, *Pheidole megacephala*.

umn, five to ten abreast and, upon reaching their target, pour into every hole and crevice that gives access to the galleries below. Once inside the galleries, the workers seize and sting termites and bring them to the surface, where they are left, severely maimed. The workers then dive below again in search of further victims. Later, the army reassembles at the surface and each worker picks up as many paralysed termites as it can carry in its jaws and returns to the nest along the same path. If the termite nest is nearby, workers may return to the mound for further victims, so that a shuttle service is established between the nest and the mound. Workers can be seen strengthening the pheromone trail by periodically dragging their gasters on the ground. It is these raids that make this species so well-known, and earn for it the name 'Matabele ant'. The species undoubtedly plays an important part in checking the numbers of termites in Africa, and for this reason alone, can be regarded as one of the most beneficial ants we have.

Other ponerines are less well-known. The majority nest in the ground, some to a depth of a metre or more, and the entrances to the nests are often marked by mounds of excavated earth, although that of *Megaponera foetens* is a simple hole without a mound. The remainder nest under stones or in leaf litter, rotting wood, and hollow logs. The most impressive mound builders are members of the genus *Platythrea*. One species constructs mounds of up to 20 cm high and 30 cm wide from hundreds of small, even-sized pebbles, which are deposited about the entrance. Originally they were thought to mine the pebbles from within the nest and bring them to the surface, but it has since been established that the majority are collected in the vicinity of the nest and carried back to the entrance.

Doryline ants The members of the subfamily Dorylinae, commonly known as 'driver ants' because of their legionary and nomadic habits, are found throughout Africa, from the southern Cape to the Sahara. They are rarely seen because of their secretive, subterranean ways. However, when on the march they appear in dense columns: countless hordes may suddenly appear in a garden, on a lawn, or the manure or compost heap, moving along in slow, never-ending streams just beneath the surface of the soil and under piles of dead leaves. They stay for a time and then disappear as silently and unexpectedly as they came. Occasionally a colony may take up temporary abode in hollows in the wall of a house, but normally they dig holes in the ground where some protection from extremes of temperature and humidity is offered. Gardeners sometimes complain about the damage done by these insects to plants, but as their stay in any particular spot is short, and as they are entirely carnivorous, they can do little harm to plants. In fact they provide a beneficial service, for their presence is undoubtedly due to pests such as cutworms, lawn caterpillars and root-eating beetle larvae. In central Africa stories are told of great armies invading houses, driving every living thing before them as they swarm everywhere in a ceaseless search for prey. These stories, however, are exaggerated as their columns move only a few metres an hour so that any healthy large animal is capable of escape and only the maimed and immobile succumb to the ants' advance.

The most common and widespread of the driver ants in Africa is *Dorylus helvolus*. Workers, reddish-brown in colour, range in size from midgets of less than 2 mm to others as long as 8 mm. All are completely blind, yet when on the march they move with uncanny precision, disciplined, orderly and purposeful. Whereas ponerine raids are led by individual ants, *Dorylus* columns are leaderless. The swarm moves forward as ants in the van press ahead excitedly for a short distance then retreat back into the mass, giving way to others.

The nest, a temporary resting place, is probably deep below the surface of the ground, at the base of some rock or tree trunk. From this central point the marauding columns radiate, hunting for any living creature they can overcome, cut up and carry back to the nest as food. When the surrounding area has been thoroughly cleared of all available food, the colony moves away to seek fresh hunting grounds, carrying their brood and their enormous queen with them. The queen is a remarkable insect: huge and clumsy, she is the biggest of all ants, measuring up to 50 mm long. She is quite blind, has no wings, and her enormous abdomen is distended by her ovaries, which are capable of producing up to four million eggs a month! She can hardly walk, and it is for this reason that we assume she is carried by her workers when the nest site is changed.

When on the move, even the ants' insect guests go with, for despite their ferocity these ants have numerous beetles and other insects living with them. Because they are hunters, and because they live in communities consisting of as many as 20 million individuals, these ants are forced to live a nomadic life, for no one place is capable of supplying a constant source of food large enough to meet their needs.

Male driver ants are commonly encountered in Africa, and are called 'sausage ants'. They reach some 30 mm in length, and have brown, fluffy heads and thoraces, and brown cylindrical abdomens. If picked up, they wave their abdomens around in a threatening manner but, like the males of all the Hymenoptera, they have no sting, nor are they able to inflict a bite, although they have sharp jaws. They have large wings and are strong fliers; drawn by the light, they will frequently enter a room on a hot summer's night after rain, flying about noisily and crashing heavily to the floor. Their flights are made in search of virgin queens from other colonies. These clumsy ants are the only dorylines which have eyes. As the females cannot fly, it is obvious that the males must seek them out. Foreign males are readily accepted into nests containing virgin queens and, after mating, these queens then leave the parent colony to begin new colonies, taking numerous workers with them.

Myrmicine ants The Myrmicinae are the most numerous ants in the world, and in Africa they probably outnumber all the other subfamilies together. As might be expected, they show a greater diversity of habits and structure than any other subfamily, and while some may be regarded as rather primitive, others are highly specialised. Most myrmicines are catholic in their diet, but many are either carnivorous or granivorous. Some feed to a large extent on nectar, or the sugary liquids excreted by aphids, coccids, psyllids and leafhoppers.

Myrmicines have a two-jointed petiole between thorax and abdomen, and although all have stings, many do not use them. Some of the most common and widespread are members of the genus *Pheidole*, which are found throughout Africa. The little brown house ant, *Pheidole megacephala*, is very widely distributed throughout the southern and central regions, and is typical of the form which has become a serious household pest in the tropics of the world. The workers are small, a little less than 3 mm long, and brown in colour; in a large colony several thousands may be present. The major workers are over 4 mm long, and have large, square heads armed with powerful jaws. It is misleading to speak of these large workers as soldiers as they do not play an important part in the defence of the nest. Indeed, if a stone is upturned and a nest exposed, these so-called soldiers run away and hide, whilst the more aggressive minor workers attack in hordes, stinging and biting. Apparently the large-headed workers function chiefly as labourers: they remove material from the nest that is too heavy for the minor workers, cut up hard-bodied insects and perhaps crush seeds with their powerful jaws. The queens are a dark reddish-brown, and about 7 mm long; there are usually several in a nest.

These ants nearly always make their nest in the soil, but they may also live in humus and in the cracks of walls. Many nests can be found under stones. These are shallow – never more than a few centimetres deep – and the entrances are often marked by small heaps of loose soil excavated from the irregular, shallow cavities of the nest. The ants are most active in the evening and at night, visiting aphids and coccids for their honeydew excretions, capturing and cutting up insects, and foraging for any other food they can find.

Little breeding occurs during winter, but early in the spring the queens begin to lay prolifically. The tiny white eggs hatch in two or four weeks depending upon the temperature, and the larvae, which pupate without spinning cocoons, are fed by the workers for about the same length of time. Larger larvae, destined to develop into winged males and females, are found in the nests in early summer. The sexual individuals that develop from these larvae appear by midsummer and are gone by autumn. Nuptial flights are thought to occur at night, for there are no records of such flights by day. Males and females emerge in the early evening and many may be attracted by the lights of houses where they remain until the morning. Young mated queens shed their wings and often start new colonies without the assistance of workers as is the case with dorylines. In a number of other myrmicines however, young queens leave the parent colony with an attendant group of workers, many carrying brood, to begin new colonies elsewhere and as *Pheidole* are polygynous (having more than one queen in a colony), it is quite likely that single queens may leave in this way once colonies become too large.

Closely allied species of the brown house ant are the well-known harvester ants. A common and widespread harvester ant is *Messor barbarus*, with large-headed soldiers, or major workers, a little over 10 mm long, and small-headed minor workers about 6 mm long. Both are brown. These ants form large nests in the soil and feed mainly on the seeds of different kinds of grasses. The husks removed from these seeds are deposited in a circle around the entrances to the nest and, in the case of large colonies, heaps may be over 50 mm deep and cover a considerable area of ground. The workers have remarkably well-trodden pathways, which they regularly use in passing to and from their harvesting grounds.

Frequently, if a nest is opened in the autumn or winter, heaps of the heads of major workers will be found piled in chambers at one side of the nest. This phenomenon, which is also found in *Pheidole* and other myrmicines, possibly occurs towards the end of the season during periods of inactivity when there is a dearth of food and minor workers slaughter the major workers for food.

The thief ant, *Carebare vidua*, is a remarkable myrmicine ant common throughout the Subsaharan Region. Its tiny yellow workers, just over 1 mm in length, with black heads and thoraces and reddish-brown abdomens, contrast with the giant queens, which measure up to 25 mm. The queen's mandibles are so large that she cannot care for her eggs and feed her tiny young when she begins a new colony. As a natural compensation she is equipped with dense tufts of hair on her legs, onto which, during her nuptial flight, several tiny workers cling tenaciously. The fellow-travellers aid her in founding the new colony, although we know nothing of how this is accomplished.

The queens are regarded as a delicacy in Africa, and during the nuptial flights they are caught in large numbers, their gasters torn off, and eaten either raw or fried.

These ants are found nesting only in termite mounds: the tiny workers make very narrow tunnels through the mound, large enough for them to pass through, but too small for the termites. It is believed that the thief ants creep into the chambers of the termite nest and carry off the eggs and young as food, secure from pursuit and harm once they reach the confines of their narrow tunnels.

Another well-known myrmicine genus is *Crematogaster*. The many species of this genus are easily recognised because of their habit of raising the abdomen when alarmed or disturbed, hence the name 'cocktail ants'. The petiole is joined posteriorly to the dorsal surface of the abdomen and this joint is very flexible, enabling the ant to cock its gaster. If disturbed, many

346. The harvester ant, *Messor barbarus*. An ant at the upper left of the picture has a seed in its jaws which it is carrying into the nest. 5 mm.

347. Cocktail ants (*Crematogaster* sp.) co-operate to transfer the cocoon of a reproductive from one part of their nest to another. 4 mm.

exude a sticky, white fluid, which has a strong unpleasant odour, from glands in the tip of the abdomen. Their sting is spatulate in shape and, while they do not sting with it, they do use it to wipe the poisonous fluid onto the object causing the disturbance. This wiping action is evident as a lateral twisting of the abdomen, and is accompanied by frenzied biting; it is this combination that makes these ants rather unpleasant (despite their small size).

Most cocktail ants are arboreal (tree-dwelling), nesting under bark, in hollow branches, or in carton nests attached to the branches of trees. The carton nest is more or less spherical in shape and black in colour, its size varying according to the size of the colony inhabiting it. They are made of chewed vegetable fibres mixed with a secretion of the maxillary glands of the workers, which blackens the material and acts as a cement. The walls are thin and papery and the interior consists of irregular cells like those on a coarse sponge. If the wall of one of these nests is broken open, or if the branch bearing the nest is banged, the workers swarm out with their gasters raised in alarm and their repugnatorial glands exposed.

Cocktail ants are fond of sugary substances and they attend aphids, coccids or any other member of the Hemiptera for the honeydew they excrete. Frequently the ants secure this food supply by building small carton shelters over these insects to protect them from the elements and from their enemies, although the ants are able to reach them through small holes.

The *Crematogaster* queen is similar to her workers in shape and colour but she is larger and her gaster is more swollen. The queen of *Crematogaster peringueyi* is almost 10 mm long, while her workers vary from 3-6 mm. The males are about the same length as the workers, but are noticeably more slender. The carton nests of this species are usually built in low bushes or among reeds with the stems of the plants running through them. The ants adapt readily to artificial nests built of cork lino and glass, as described in Chapter 24, and provided that they are supplied with an adequate amount of food and an area in which to forage for it, they may be kept for considerable periods of time.

Dolichoderine ants The ants belonging to the subfamily Dolichoderinae are small and soft-bodied. They are very similar in appearance to the formicines and may at first be confused with them.

The petiole of the dolichoderines is single-jointed. The workers cannot sting, as their sting is vestigial or absent. Instead special glands at the hind end of the abdomen produce a secretion that hardens on exposure to the air and has an unpleasant smell. Since its stickiness immobilises enemies by clogging up their legs, this secretion serves as an effective means of protection.

The Subsaharan Region contains only four indigenous genera, three of which: *Semonius, Technomyrmex* and *Tapinoma* are widespread, whereas the fourth, *Engramma* is restricted to equatorial Africa. All are shy, inconspicuous ants that live in small or moderate-sized colonies under bark, in dead wood, under stones or in soil. With one exception, they are not well-known as none are pests. However, by way of contrast, the introduced dolichoderine, the 'Argentine ant' or *Iridomyrmex humilis* is abundant and harmful in the south-west Cape. This ant was introduced to southern Africa at the beginning of the twentieth century during the Anglo-Boer War and has since spread from the Cape Peninsula throughout the southern region as far afield as Lesotho and the Orange Free State, and has recently been recorded from the Witwatersrand. In some regions it has become the dominant ant species, totally replacing the ant fauna of the area. In Cape Town, in particular, it is a serious pest in houses and is injurious to fruit trees and vines.

Little is known of the habits of indigenous African species of these genera, but it can be assumed that they bear little resemblance to those of the Argentine ant, which forms huge compound colonies under stones, in compost heaps and in logs. As a rule, colonies are polygynous and large communities may have as many as 50 or more queens. Workers do not restrict themselves to a single nest, but go to and fro between the nests in the neighbourhood, the workers from each nest coexist without any form of antagonism. However, their fierce intolerance of other ants, and their extraordinarily catholic tastes in food, ensure the extermination of competitors. Whereas their colonies may grow to enormous sizes, with hundreds of thousands of workers, the indigenous African species seldom have more than a few hundred, and may number fewer than a hundred.

A number of dolichoderines are arboreal, and some are closely associated with certain plants. Of the six species of *Engramma*, only *E. wolfi* is ground-dwelling, living in leaf litter on the forest floor. The others live in the cavities and swellings of various plants, except *Engramma zimmeri okiavoensis*, which builds nests of silk and vegetable matter against the trunks of trees. Most *Technomyrmex* and *Tapinoma* species are ground-dwelling too, but some are arboreal, living in hollow stems or carton nests. Ground-dwelling *Tapinoma* form fairly large colonies, and the introduced species *T. melanocephalum* can become troublesome as a household pest in West Africa. *Tapinoma gracilis* lives in light, sandy soils and because of its ochre colour and its quick, erratic movements, is extremely difficult to detect as it forages on the ground. The only *Semonius* species, *S. schultzei*, nests under the bark of trees and is widely distributed throughout Africa. It is a timid dolichoderine ant and when disturbed will readily emit a white sticky fluid from its anal glands.

348. A typical tree nest of cocktail ants. It is 20 cm in diameter and made of chewed vegetable fibres.

Formicine ants The ants of the subfamily Formicinae are commonly regarded as the most advanced members of the family – the formicines are advanced not only in their morphology, but also in their social behaviour and their habits, which are both diverse and highly specialised. Like the dolichoderines, they have a one-jointed petiole. The workers have no sting although the poison gland is still present and functional, and instead of a transverse anal opening, the orifice is circular. They are represented in Africa by 15 genera: *Acantholepis*, *Plagiolepis* and *Camponotus* being very widely distributed throughout the continent.

Perhaps one of the most common and best-known formicine ants of dry savanna regions is the pugnacious ant, *Anoplolepis custodiens*. It is an active, aggressive species that will attack fiercely if its nest is disturbed. The workers, brown in colour, vary in size, the smallest being less than 5 mm long, whilst the largest are almost 10 mm. They are clothed with yellow hair, the hairs of the abdomen being directed at different angles, which gives the ant a striped appearance in sunlight. The queens are darker in colour and are some 13 mm long.

These ants usually nest in large colonies in the ground, but may frequently be found living in the walls of termite mounds. The nest entrances are small round holes, rarely surrounded by any material that the ants have excavated as such material is usually spread out thinly some distance from the entrances. The ants are mainly carnivorous, living on any other insects they can capture, and are useful in keeping down the numbers of

349. Hollow swellings at the base of the thorns of the 'whistling thorn' Acacia (*Acacia drepanolobium*) are the nesting-sites of cocktail ants (*Crematogaster* sp.) that tend numerous plant bugs on the same tree.

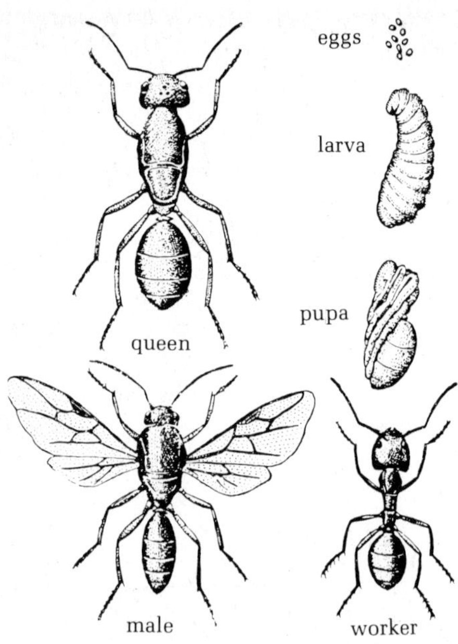

350. The various life stages and castes of the Argentine ant.

351. Many times the size of the pugnacious ants (*Anoplolepis custodiens*), a winged driver ant male falls prey to them having accidentally landed in their territory. Active and aggressive pugnacious ants swarm over the ground in the vicinity of their nests, attacking man or any creature that they find. 6 mm.

termites and other noxious insects. However, they also attend aphids and coccids for honeydew and, as the ants are so fierce, the enemies of these insects keep away and as a result the aphids and coccids multiply much more freely. For this reason *Anoplolepis custodiens* is regarded as a serious pest in gardens and orchards and must be controlled. Another troublesome habit of this species is that it rushes about in frenzied hordes on hot sunny days, climbing up and biting one's legs whenever one stops for a moment. It can become impossible to stand on a footpath, or any bare area where they are nesting, without suffering considerable discomfort.

Like the dolichoderines, the formicines frequently engage in trophallaxis. They favour liquid foods, and often workers can be seen hurrying back to their nests, their abdomens distended and translucent because of nectar and honeydew in the swollen crop. As ants have no cells in their nests in which to store liquid food, they cannot build up large reserves as bees do. However, certain formicines have solved this problem by converting some of the workers in the nest into living honeypots. Although these honey ants, or repletes as they are called, are not common in Africa, they do occur in *Anoplolepis trimeni,* a close relative of the pugnacious ant, and may occur in other species of *Anoplolepis* and *Camponotus.*

Anoplolepis trimeni is common in the southeastern regions of Africa. It is an active insect which moves erratically, much like the pugnacious ant, and nests in sandy soil. The workers are straw-yellow in colour. If a nest of these ants is carefully opened, the repletes will be found in a chamber about 20 cm below the surface; they are major workers whose abdomens have been swollen by the large quantity of nectar and honeydew stored in their crops. They can hardly walk about, and are incapable of leaving the nest while in this state. However, should their crops be emptied they return to normal. Workers returning with liquid food go to these repletes and give it to them by regurgitation. The repletes lap up the liquid until their crops are full almost to bursting. In this manner the ants are able to store food and use it as required, for the repletes readily surrender it when needed.

Another remarkable member of the Formicinae is the tailor ant, *Oecophylla longinoda,* which is common in most parts of tropical Africa. Further south it may also be found along the east coast, and colonies have been discovered nesting in coastal vegetation throughout KwaZulu and northern Natal. The ant makes its nest between the leaves of trees, which it fastens together with larval silk. Workers range in size from 7-11 mm and show distinct polymorphism. Although many are of intermediate size, the majority are either large or small, forming two distinct castes. Colonies are polygynous and may occupy a number of trees, building a dozen or more leafy nests. Whether these are close to the ground or higher up, all are in the outer foliage where the rays of the sun can warm the brood. Their populous communities number hundreds of thousands. Most individuals are major workers, and these yellowish-red ants can be seen wandering about on the branches and leaves in search of food. They are very aggressive creatures with exceptional eyesight and will attack at the least provocation, if necessary launching themselves at the intruder. During such an attack, the ants grip tightly with spreadeagled legs and bite with ferocity, injecting formic acid from their cocked gasters into the wounds.

The rôle played by each caste is not clear; the minor workers are not seen as frequently as the major workers, and this has led to speculation that they are involved in brood care. However, as they are less numerous than the major workers this may not be so. Furthermore the minor workers do tend colonies of coccids with the major workers and can be seen on branches outside the nest. An additional complication is the fact that the major workers are known to feed and carry the brood, and if a nest is tapped, hordes rush out and cover the outside, running about with jerky movements, jaws apart. The major workers are in the main, however, responsible for all prey captured and brought back to the nests, and they are also responsible for building the nest. The part played by the minor workers is unknown as they neither capture prey nor help in nest building, and any task they do participate in is shared with the major workers. Recently we have learnt that they have a different alarm pheromone to that of the major worker, and this indicates that they do have a specific, albeit unknown, rôle to play in colony life.

The construction of a nest by *Oecophylla* workers is a remarkable feat of co-operation. As existing nests dry out, the ants explore the tree for suitable alternative sites and then congregate at the new site during the evening to build the nest overnight. Groups of workers pull leaves together, and when the gaps either between the leaves or between the leaf and its stem is too great, the workers form chains – some up to 12 individuals long – to bridge the gap. For some hours they pull the leaves this way and that until they are arranged into a tight bag, and then, while a group of workers hold the leaves in position, others hurry back to the old nest and return with the larvae. The larvae then act as animated shuttles, spinning the leaves together.

The entire process can be seen by slightly tearing the leaves of an established nest. Workers will at once rush out to defend the nest, but after some time they begin pulling the leaves together again. Once in position, others appear from within the nest with larvae and the spinning begins. The workers hold the larvae in their jaws and wave them from side to side across the tear so that the mouths of the larvae touch each edge. They give off fine silken threads from their large silk glands and a white web forms, binding the edges together.

Another unique element in their behaviour is that *Oecophylla* colonies have been found to establish territories in the vicinity of their nests. This they do by first dotting a colony-specific gut pheromone all over the trees they occupy, and thereafter actively patrolling this area to prevent intrusion. These areas are fiercely defended so that a kind of 'no-ant's-land' is established between colonies, where no ants dare to venture. Foreign ants encountered within the territory are quickly overpowered in the same manner that prey is captured and killed: workers hold the intruder by its legs, stretching the victim until it is paralysed, after which it is carried back to a nest as prey, or dropped to the ground and abandoned.

The sugar ant, *Camponotus maculatus,* active in the evening and at night, is very common and widespread throughout Africa, and indeed throughout the world. In fact it represents one of the largest genera in Africa. It is

352. Tailor ants (*Oecophylla longinoda*) co-operate to draw the edges of adjacent leaves together, while a larva, held by a worker ant in its jaws (at upper left) spins silk to bind the joint. In this way tailor ants make large nests from the living leaves of various trees and shrubs in the tropical eastern areas. 6 mm.

353. Spotted sugar ants (*Camponotus maculatus*) carrying cocoons containing pupae to a safe place after their nest under a stone had been disturbed. 9 mm.

354. Turning to face danger, a formicine ant (*Camponotus detritus*) of the Namib Desert curves its abdomen under its body in order to spray formic acid at the enemy. 11 mm.

355. Carrying a doubled-up caterpillar heavier than itself, a formicine ant (*Camponotus fulvipilosus*), returns to its nest. 12 mm.

often a nuisance in houses, where it is attracted by sweet foodstuffs in the kitchen and pantry. These ants nest in the soil under a stone or log, the entrance to the nest often surrounded by a low crater of excavated earth. The workers are of various sizes; the minor caste being about 8 mm long, pale-brown in colour, with still paler spots on the abdomen; while the major caste is about 12 mm long, with black heads and thoraces and paler abdomens which are also spotted.

Most species, like *Camponotus maculatus,* nest in the soil under stones, but others nest under bark, in dead wood, hollow branches and galls (a swelling on a branch or stem caused by a fungus, a virus or an insect); while others build carton nests or use their larvae to spin silken nests in soil or vegetable matter. The subgenus *Colobopsis* nests in tree trunks and its workers have sharply truncated heads which are used effectively to plug the entrance tunnels. While most *Camponotus* workers are timid, or at least apathetic, the major workers of larger species are somewhat belligerent and can inflict painful wounds with their strong jaws.

A large number of other formicines are found in Africa and they differ widely in their habits. Some are active only by night, while others may be seen foraging by day. A number are mainly carnivorous, but most obtain their sustenance chiefly from honeydew and nectar.

The large genus, *Polyrhachis,* is common throughout Africa, and the habits of its species are as diverse as those of *Camponotus.* They are very timid ants and can often be seen walking alone along the branch of a tree or tending coccids and other Hemiptera for their honeydew. They are attractive, medium-sized, black ants and are usually covered with a dense coat of fine hair, the colour varying from silver to gold and bronze. Their nesting habits vary greatly, some species being arboreal, but most nesting in the ground. Many use larval silk and paperlike matter in the construction of the nest, but unlike *Oecophylla,* whose pupae are naked, *Polyrhachis* larvae always spin cocoons before pupating.

A simple key to subfamilies of Subsaharan ants (workers only)

1 Petiole two jointed **2**
Petiole one-jointed **3**
2 Elongate, slender ants; eyes very large; frontal carinae do not cover bases of antennae; tibial spurs pectinate .... Pseudomyrmicinae
Frontal carinae large, often covering bases of antennae; tibial spurs simple or absent .... Myrmicinae
3 Eyes absent; promesonotal suture weak or absent; maxillary and labial palpi 2-3 jointed .... Dorylinae
Eyes usually present **4**
4 Sting present and extensible in dead specimens **5**
Sting absent or very small and atrophied **6**
5 Antennal fossa encircled by a distinct ridge; pygidium flattened, with rows of spines laterally .... Cerapachyinae
Antennal fossa not encircled by a ridge; pygidium simple .... Ponerinae
6 Anal aperture transverse .... Dolichoderinae
Anal aperture circular .... Formicinae

CLASSIFICATION

ORDER **Hymenoptera**

SUPERFAMILY **Formicoidea**

FAMILY Formicidae
First, or first and second, abdominal segment constricted to form a 1 or 2-jointed petiole between thorax and abdomen. Antennae 6-13 segmented, strongly elbowed, first segment usually long. The family is divided into two major taxonomic branches. The poneroid complex contains the subfamilies Ponerinae, Cerapachyinae, Dorylinae, Leptanillinae (only known from Barbary coast of North Africa), and Myrmicinae. The myrmecioid complex comprises the subfamilies Sphecomyrminae (entirely fossil), Myrmeciinae (restricted to Australasia), Pseudomyrmecinae, Dolichoderinae, Aneuretinae (restricted to Sri Lanka) and Formicinae.

SUBFAMILY Ponerinae
All workers armed with a powerful sting. Petiole 1-jointed, but a distinct postpetiole present. Mostly black in colour; many are among the largest ants of Africa. They are carnivorous, many species preying exclusively on termites. Most live in small colonies. Certain *Leptogenys* species are nomadic. Most ponerines rely on their sting for defence, but *Opthalmopone berthoudi* scurries under grass tufts and hides.

SUBFAMILY Cerapachyinae
A small subfamily of only four genera in Africa. Workers small, seldom exceed 5 mm. They are legionary and probably nomadic. Known species feed on the brood of other ants, secured by group raids into brood chambers. Little is known about the African species.

SUBFAMILY Dorylinae
Polymorphic, reddish-brown or black shiny ants called legionary or driver ants. Species are nomadic and do not construct permanent nests. They are entirely carnivorous, and workers search for food in populous columns through leaf litter, or just below the surface of the ground.

SUBFAMILY Myrmicinae
The most numerous ants of Africa, and the most diverse subfamily; the brown house ant is a well-known species. Workers armed with a sting, petiole distinctly 2-jointed; larvae do not spin cocoons before pupation.

SUBFAMILY Pseudomyrmecinae
Slender, elongated ants, with long petioles and postpetioles. Three African genera, *Sima*, *Viticicola* and *Pachysima*. All have good eyesight, with *Sima* species having especially large compound eyes. They are generally fast-moving and have powerful stings. *Pachysima aethiops* is greatly feared where it occurs, the *Barteria* trees used for nesting being left standing in clearings or forest paths. All are arboreal, *Sima* nesting in various trees, *Pachysima* in *Barteria* and *Viticicola* nests exclusively in the hollow stems of *Vitex* creepers, restricted to equatorial Africa. Larvae of Pseudomyrmecinae unique in having a special feeding pouch, the trophothorax, into which the workers place regurgitated food pellets.

SUBFAMILY Dolichoderinae
Closely related to the next subfamily, but clypeus more pronounced and anal orifice transverse. The gizzard, or proventriculus, in dolichoderines has become elaborate, probably related to the frequency of trophallaxis and to withstand fluid pressure in the crop. They have anal glands producing secretions with strong, characteristic odours repellent to other ants. Pupae never enclosed in cocoons. African species poorly known, but the introduced Argentine ant is a serious pest in parts.

SUBFAMILY Formicinae
Highly advanced and specialised ants, widely distributed and successful. No sting, but poison glands well-developed and functional. No anal repugnatorial glands; anal orifice circular. Species spray formic acid and many are capable of inflicting painful bites. Pupae usually in cocoons, but sometimes naked.

FURTHER READING

Arnold G.: 'A monograph of the Formicidae of South Africa.' *Annals of the South African Museum* (1915-1926). 14: 1-766, 23: 191-295
Skaife, S. H.: *The Study of Ants.* Longmans, London (1961). 178 pp
Sudd, J. H.: *An Introduction to the Behaviour of Ants.* Arnold, London (1967). 200 pp
Wheeler, W. M.: *Ants: their Structure, Development and Behaviour.* Columbus University Press, New York (1910). 663 pp
Wheeler, W. M.: 'Ants of the American Museum Congo Expedition. A contribution to the myrmecology of Africa.' VII 'Keys to the subgenera of ants.' VIII 'A synonymic list of the ants of the Ethiopian region.' *Bulletin of the American Museum of Natural History* (1922). 45: 631-1004
Wilson, E. O.: *The Insect Societies.* Belknap Press, Harvard University Press, Cambridge, Massachusetts (1971). 548 pp

24

Entomology as a hobby or career

Insects are so abundant that you can usually collect large numbers without affecting the overall populations in the slightest. For this reason there are few restrictions placed on insect collecting compared to the regulations and laws relating to the collection of birds' eggs, reptiles or plants, for example, where the activities of collectors may constitute a threat to the survival of certain species. Sometimes over-zealous collecting of rare or particularly attractive insects such as butterflies has been blamed for the near extinction of a few species, but generally it is the deterioration or destruction of habitat containing the essential food plants or breeding sites that causes insects to decline to dangerously low levels.

By collecting and preserving insects you learn about their habits, and for young people it is a first class introduction to natural history and a training in orderly thinking. As a healthy outdoor activity, entomology is a fine and fascinating hobby for everyone, young and old, and a box of well-mounted specimens, identified and labelled, not only brings lasting pleasure but happy memories of time spent in the field as well. You need not be a trained or full-time entomologist to make a worthwhile contribution towards our knowledge of insects, and many amateurs have done excellent work and have contributed fine publications on various aspects of their hobby, from taxonomic papers to life history descriptions and ecological studies. School teachers who show their pupils examples of preserved insects, or better still, live specimens, will find their lessons on biology far more exciting and the impact of this knowledge may well influence the future of their students.

Since a number of reference works are available to guide the amateur collector, only the essential aspects are discussed here. If you live near a large centre with a museum, university or research institute, a visit to look at their insect collections, and to meet and talk to an entomologist will be worth many hours of reading. Provided that you are genuinely interested and enthusiastic about your hobby, you can be sure that the professional entomologist will help and encourage you in every possible way. What is more, if the professional is a specialist in a particular group of beetles, for example, you may well be able to help him in his work by collecting material for him, according to his needs and requirements. He will also be able to tell you where to get equipment, pins, forceps and chemicals, for in many countries of Africa these items are not easy to obtain. But remember that your local entomologist is probably very busy at most times, and may spend days away in the bush collecting, so do telephone or write to make an appointment beforehand!

If your interest in entomology develops to the stage at which you require access to more specialised reading than that available in general textbooks on insects, you may consider joining an entomological society, or subscribing to some of the many regular journals on entomology that are published throughout the world. Most professional entomologists belong to one or more entomological societies, but they usually have access to libraries containing many journals as well. The amateur worker, or the professional posted to some isolated spot, does not enjoy such facilities, and obtaining essential literature may be a major problem.

Where to find insects Because insects occur in every conceivable habitat, the more places you examine, the more different insects you are likely to find. They vary in size, and the majority are small or very small, so if you restrict your collecting to large specimens only, you will miss a great many kinds. Depending on the climate of the country you live in, insects may be abundant all the year round, or more so in wet, warm months than cold, dry months. Out of doors at night you can set up bright lights which will attract many different insects, and you may find a number of specimens by examing different kinds of plants, fruits, flowers and dead logs. Any stream or dam will have its own aquatic insects, and each bird or mammal will have *its* kinds of parasitic insects, so there is one simple answer to the question of where to look for insects: Look anywhere and everywhere!

How to catch and kill insects To catch insects is largely a matter of ingenuity and patience, although one or two gadgets do make things a lot easier and some of the strong fliers such as butterflies and dragonflies will evade capture unless you are skilled at using a net.

A net is the basic tool of the entomologist. You can buy one ready made, if you have a supplier of such things nearby, or else you can easily make one to suit your own requirements: cut a wooden handle about a metre long and 20 mm in diameter and fix a circular, thickish wire frame with a diameter of 30-40 cm to one end by binding it with fine wire or strong cord. A groove and a hole on either side of the handle, into which the bent ends of the frame can be fitted will ensure that the whole assembly is good and strong. Now you need to make up a bag of muslin, bolting cloth, mosquito netting or other suitable material, which must be stitched and then sewn onto the wire frame. A strip of heavier material around the rim will reinforce the fine mesh of the net and protect it when catching insects in vegetation. The type of material you use for the bag will largely depend on what you can get hold of in your area – it should have a small mesh, but one through which you can see the insects, and which passes easily through the air.

To use your net, first locate the sitting or flying insect and then smoothly swing the open mouth over your quarry. To prevent an active insect from escaping, quickly twist the handle to fold the bag over the rim. With a bit of practice you will soon develop the necessary skill to pluck a swift-moving robber fly out of the air! Another way to catch a number of small insects is to walk through grass or other vegetation, systematically swinging the net from side to side so that it just sweeps the tops of the plants – look out for thorn bushes, though, or your net will soon need repairs.

Once caught, insects, especially fragile ones, should be removed from the net speedily to prevent damage. In the case of biting or stinging ones, some care will be needed to avoid injury to yourself. The insect can be grasped in a fold of the net, and then the rest of the bag turned inside out. Another method is to use a small tube and slip it over the insect, or pick it up with a pair of forceps. Butterfly collectors usually grasp a specimen by the body and stun it by quickly pinching the thorax between the fingernails of thumb and forefinger, before dropping it into the killing jar. This prevents damage to the delicate scales of the butterfly by its fluttering in the net or the jar.

This brings us to the problem of killing insects, and the next essential piece of equipment for the collector is a suitable killing jar. Various types of chemicals can be used as killing agents, but the best and safest general-purpose killing jar makes use of ethyl acetate fumes. Choose a suitable size and shape of glass bottle with a wide mouth and a good, tight-fitting screw top (one or two bottles of different sizes are useful for handling different insects). Then take some plaster of Paris (most chemists will be able to obtain this and the ethyl acetate for you), make up a thin paste with water, and pour about 25 mm into the bottom of your bottle. Let it dry thoroughly. Now pour in some ethyl acetate which will be absorbed by the plaster of Paris, and give off fumes that will kill insects placed in the bottle. Do not put in so much ethyl acetate that the surface of the plaster is wet – this will damage your specimens. Depending on the tightness of the lid, and on the frequency with which it is opened, the killing bottle will remain effective for a week or two. It should be recharged with ethyl acetate before each collecting expedition, and you should take a small bottle of the chemical into the field with you in case the bottle runs out of vapour at a critical time.

Some insects take longer to die than others, but one advantage of the ethyl acetate killing bottle is that insects can be left in it for a long time without damage. Leave larger beetles in the bottle for at least 12 hours – they often take a long time to succumb, and it is disconcerting to have an insect start moving after you have pinned it, believing it to be dead. Other tips about using the killing bottle are to keep the inside clean and dry by periodic wiping with tissue paper, and to use a separate jar for moths and butterflies, because they are easily damaged by other insects, which in turn become coated with an unsightly layer of scales.

A suitable carry bag or haversack is useful in the field; into this place your killing bottles, a few small plastic or glass tubes with tops, a bottle of ethyl acetate, a pair of forceps, a hand lens, and any other odds and ends that you find useful in your pursuit of insects. Flat tins or boxes, filled with several layers of tissues, are good for storing and transporting specimens until you reach home, because you do not want your killing bottles to become overfull.

Mounting and preserving insects Small, soft-bodied insects are best preserved in small tubes containing 70% alcohol (or methylated spirits if alcohol is not available). Preservatives such as formalin are *not* suitable for insects. The tubes should have tightly-fitting tops, but even the best tubes lose alcohol through evaporation, and must be topped up from time to time. Other small insects should be mounted on microscope slides, and a method for doing this appears later in the chapter.

Most medium and large insects are preserved dry on pins and, once properly mounted and dried, they will last virtually for ever provided they are stored under good conditions. The setting of dead insects so that they dry in a symmetrical, lifelike position takes time and effort, but the end result is worth the trouble and a well-mounted specimen is always a tribute to the care and patience of its collector.

Before an insect is pinned it must be in a relaxed state so that its limbs and wings can be manipulated into the desired position. If a specimen has become stiff and dry, put it back into an ethyl acetate killing bottle overnight, or for several days, until it becomes relaxed.

Proper 'insect pins', long and specially made for the purpose, are the only ones suitable for mounting insects. They are usually black, or made of stainless steel, and

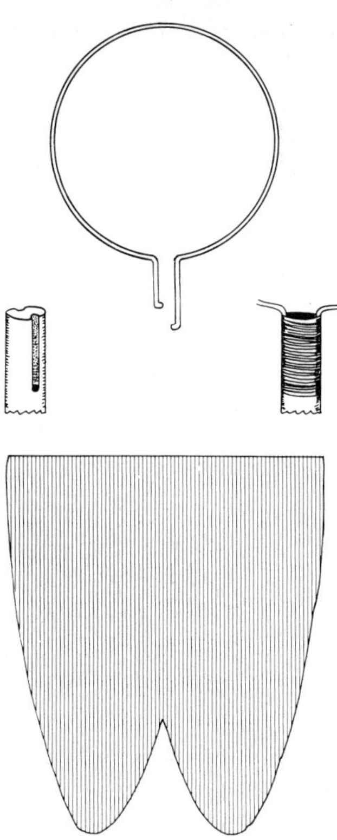

356 Details of the construction of an insect net: the wire frame (top); the method of cutting grooves into the wooden handle and binding the frame onto the handle (centre); the pattern to which the netting or material should be cut prior to stitching.

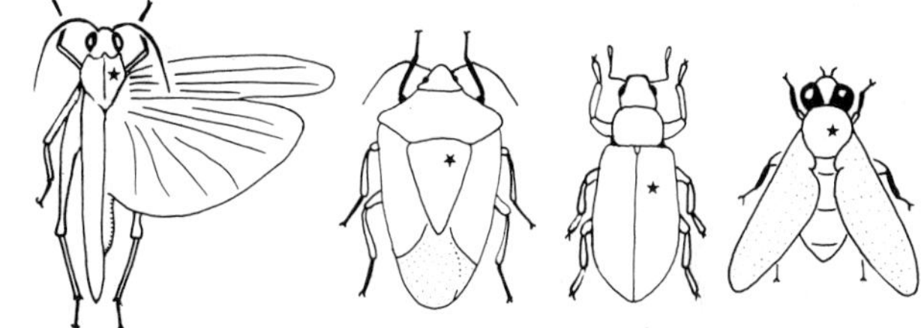

357 The position where the pin should be inserted in the major groups of insects (from left to right): grasshoppers and locusts, bugs, beetles and flies.

come in several thicknesses, from very fine for the smallest flies to very stout for the biggest beetles. You may experience some problems in obtaining the correct insect pins, and you might even have to write to an overseas supplier. Your local entomologist will probably be able to tell you how to obtain a supply of insect pins – but don't be tempted into using ordinary sewing-type pins to mount insects with – they rust and are too short.

Entomologists follow certain conventions in pinning insects, based on the need to examine them later for diagnostic features that could possibly be obscured or damaged by the pin. Most insects are pinned vertically: beetles through the front part of the right wing; bugs through the scutellum if it is big enough, otherwise as for beetles; grasshoppers through the hind part of the pronotum on the right hand side; and flies through the thorax, just to the right of the midline. Certain insects are pinned in non-standard manner, from the side, or on very tiny pins called 'minutens' or else are glued onto triangular cardboard 'points' which are then fixed onto standard insect pins. You should check with your local museum or entomologist as to which method is preferred for each particular group of insects.

The easiest way to pin an insect in the standard way is to hold it between the thumb and forefinger, align a pin of the correct diameter in the other hand in such a way that it will pass vertically through the body without contacting any of the legs on its way out, and then push it through the insect with firm pressure. A block of polystyrene foam is a very useful working surface, as the pin is able to pass into it while you hold the insect in place. All specimens should be placed at a uniform height on their pins, and you will be able to achieve this either by working on a piece of polystyrene of uniform thickness, by marking the pins at a uniform distance from their heads, or by using a pinning block that has a series of steps, or a series of holes of different depths.

Once the insect is satisfactorily impaled, you can now go about setting the legs, wings and antennae of the insect so that it will dry in a symmetrical and lifelike position. Begin with the legs, gently extending them with a pair of forceps and then fixing them in place with a pin thrust into the styrofoam at a low angle to hold the limb in place. Do this with all the legs and the antennae, but do not ruin the specimen by over-zealous arrangement of its appendages. It is better to have a slightly lop-sided insect than one with no legs at all! The wings may be extended and supported on strips of cardboard held in place with pins. The antennae and abdomen are likewise arranged and held in place to dry with carefully placed pins. Look at specimens in your local museum for ideas on how insects can be mounted.

Butterflies and moths receive special treatment to spread their wings and reveal their patterns. You will need to make or buy some proper spreading boards if you intend concentrating on the Lepidoptera. These boards have a narrow channel down the middle to take the body, and two lateral pieces set at an angle to take the wings. The angle is quite small and is intended to compensate for any sag the wings may suffer after removing the butterfly from the board. The lateral pieces have sheets of cork glued to them to take pins, and the central channel also has a cork base to receive the pin through the butterfly.

After piercing the thorax and setting the specimen on its pin in the channel, spread the wings carefully and then hold them in place with strips of paper attached by pins pushed into the cork, but not through the wings. The hind margin of the front wings should be at right angles to the body, and the hind wings placed in a lifelike position in relation to the forewings. Arrange the antennae in a symmetrical position with pins to hold them in place, and fix the abdomen likewise with pins so that it cannot twist or curl up as it dries.

The time needed for pinned insects to dry depends on their size, and the weather as well; hot, dry conditions result in hard insects in a short time. You can speed up drying times to a few hours by placing mounted specimens in an oven or hotroom.

Once the specimen is quite dry (touch the abdomen with a pin – if it moves or bends the insect is not ready), carefully remove all the pins used to hold the various parts in position, and carefully lift the specimen by the pin through its body. It is often convenient to use a pair of stout forceps for moving pinned insects and for arranging them in cabinets or boxes. Grasp the pin just above the insect, and do not bring any pressure to bear on the specimen, otherwise it will become loose on its pin.

Every specimen must be labelled if it is to be of any use at all, and the minimum information required is the locality and date of capture. The name of the collector is useful, as well as supplementary information on habitat, food, altitude or host (in the case of parasites). Labels for pinned specimens should be made of stiff white paper, about 10 x 12 mm in size, fixed at a uniform height on the pin and parallel with the specimen. The best way to attach the collecting label is to place it on the second step of the pinning block, and pass the pin through the centre of the label as far as it will go.

You can write your labels with waterproof black ink, or else if you use a great many you can have them printed, or made by a photographic process. The latter work very well: a typewritten page of labels is photographed and then printed at a reduced size onto photographic paper. These small labels are then cut and used.

If the specimen is identified to genus or species, a second label bearing this information should be set on the pin below the label with the collection data. The name of the person who performed the identification should be given, too, and the year in which the insect was identified. This information is often very useful to later workers who may need to sort out taxonomic problems based on preserved specimens.

How to store pinned insects Depending on your needs, you may store your insect collection in home-made boxes, in commercially-made insect trays, or in a cabinet with glass-topped drawers if you are really serious about your entomology. Home-made boxes may be of a variety of materials such as cardboard, masonite or plywood; strong, shallow boxes made for other purposes can be modified as insect storage boxes as well. Whatever the design, the boxes should have tight-fitting lids, and a layer of cork sheet or polystyrene foam in the bottom to receive the pins. The inside can be lined with white paper glued to the bottom and sides to finish it off. Arrange the pinned insects neatly in rows. Labels for orders or families may be typed, and glued or pinned to the floor of the box. There are many different ways to organise and arrange insect collections attractively, and you will find many excellent ideas by looking at existing collections.

It is vital to protect the collection against museum beetles and other pests, for they enter any boxes or cabinets containing dry insects, regardless of the apparently tight-fitting lids.

Naphthalene flakes, or paradichlorobenzine (available in the form of 'mothballs') may be placed inside the box, but the chemical must be in a cloth bag, a compartment in a corner or otherwise firmly contained so that it does not spill and damage the specimens. Remember that the chemicals evaporate steadily, and have to be replenished regularly, so any collection should be checked from time to time to see that it is adequately protected.

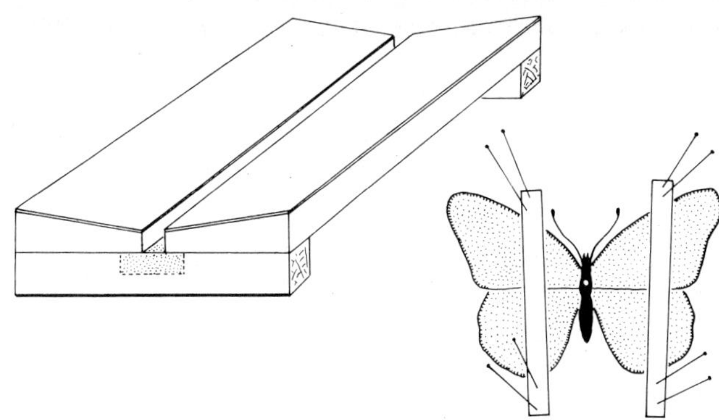

358 Beneath the central groove, the butterfly spreading board must have a cork or polystyrene strip to take the pin through the insect. The side pieces must either be made of soft wood or have a layer of cork glued onto them to take the setting pins. While the wings dry, strips of paper and pins hold them in position.

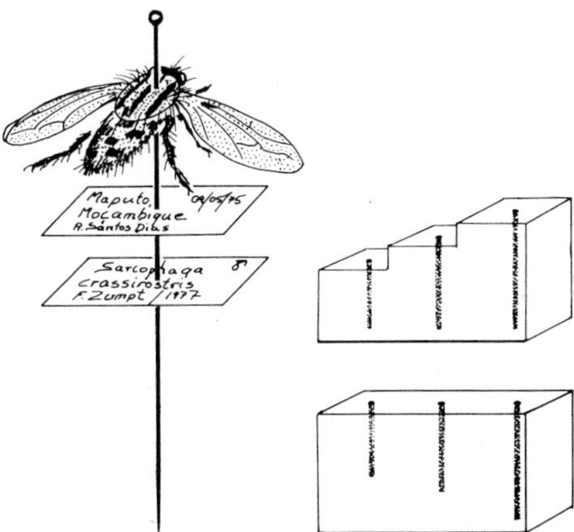

359 A specimen of a fly near the top of the pin, with collection and identification labels at fixed distances below. This neat arrangement is best achieved by using a pinning block – two possible designs are shown at the right. Convenient depths for the three holes are 25, 15, and 10 mm.

Mounting insects on slides Small insects such as fleas and lice should be mounted on microscope slides in order to see details of their structure. A number of chemicals are needed but, once mastered, the technique is quite straightforward and the mounted specimens will last indefinitely.

One needs a number of small dishes ('syracuse dishes', available from laboratory supply firms), fine pins in wooden or metal holders, glass slides (25 x 75 mm), cover slips, and the following chemicals: 5% potassium hydroxide, 10% acetic acid, alcohol in concentrations of 40%, 70%, 96% and absolute alcohol, oil of cedar wood, Canada balsam and xylene.

Place the specimens in the potassium hydroxide, which softens and dissolves the body contents. Remove the contents by making a small hole with a pin in the insect, and gently squeezing the body with another pin bent into the shape of a loop. When the specimens are sufficiently 'cleared', transfer them to acetic acid for five minutes, then place them in dishes containing increasing concentrations of ethyl alcohol, through absolute alcohol and into oil of cedar wood (five minutes in each). Now dry the insect briefly on a piece of clean, smooth paper, and place it in the centre of a slide which has a little sticky Canada balsam smeared onto it with a small glass rod.

Arrange the specimen neatly by moving its limbs with a pin, then add a few drops of fluid Canada balsam (xylene is used as a solvent), place a coverslip over the insect, and put the slide in a warm place to dry for about a week. It should then be labelled and placed in a specially made box with grooves to hold the slides.

Looking at insects Because insects are so small we are usually obliged to use some sort of magnifying device to see details of their structure. The simplest and cheapest device is a hand lens or magnifying glass which enables one to see considerable detail on larger insects. The next step up is to the binocular stereoscopic microscope which permits magnifications of around 10x to 100x. Compound microscopes, magnifying from 100x to 1000x, are used by entomologists specialising in very small, slide-mounted insects.

Unfortunately few of us can afford our own microscopes, although it is also true to say that many instruments are reasonably priced and cost about the same as a single lens reflex camera, so there is no reason why the serious amateur entomologist should not strive to buy himself a microscope. You can often buy second-hand ones from universities or research institutes when they replace their equipment, so keep a lookout for bargains.

Professional entomologists and research workers generally have access to very sophisticated equipment, including powerful compound microscopes that may be used to photograph banding patterns on the chromosomes of mosquitoes or black flies. At the top of the scale is the scanning electron microscope which is capable of producing photographic images with unbelievable clarity and depth of field at very high magnifications, of surface features of insects.

Studying living insects If you restrict yourself to catching, killing and pinning insects you will miss many interesting and fascinating things best observed in the living creatures. Observations in the field are very fruitful, and you will learn a great deal merely by watching insects – perhaps with the aid of a hand lens. Find an aphid-infested plant, and watch ladybird beetles and their larvae feeding on the aphids, hover fly larvae creeping about and likewise making a meal of the plant pests, or braconid wasps piercing the aphids to lay eggs inside them. At flowers you will see the comings and goings of bees and flies, and the activities of ambush bugs, assassin bugs and spiders which prey on the visitors. You can make tape recordings of insect sounds, or take photographs – there is no end to the variety of things one is able to do with living insects.

Another way to study insects is to make artificial homes for them, in which they live and breed while you observe them at close quarters. Many important facts about the biology of termites, ants, solitary bees, carpenter bees and other insects, have been learned by the use of articial nests.

A very successful artificial nest for termites may be constructed as follows: take a sheet of cork about 6-8 mm thick (or cork lino if you can find such material) its area depending on the number of termites to be kept in the nest. A convenient size for quite a sizeable colony of termites is 25 x 37 cm. Punch, or cut out with a sharp blade, holes 30 mm in diameter in the cork; make seven rows with nine holes in each. Then glue the cork with cold glue quite flat on one half of a sheet of three-ply board or masonite measuring 40 x 50 cm. Glue strips of wood (15 mm square) around the edge of the base so that it forms a tray.

Now cut grooves about 3 mm wide and the same depth in the cork to form runways for the termites, connecting the cells with one another. Cut a deeper groove from the middle cell in the front row to the exterior so that the termites may enter and leave the nest.

Fix four 20 mm screws to each corner on the underside of the tray, to form short supports on which the tray stands. To keep the termites in the tray and ants out of it, each screw should be stood in an inverted crown cork containing an insecticidal powder such as malathion or 5% carbaryl. This forms an effective barrier that the insects soon learn to avoid.

In order to make the termites enter the nest and take up residence, take a little of the material of their mound and grind it to a fine powder. Moisten this with water to form a paste, a little of which is put into the bottom of each cell and pressed down firm and flat. When the nest is baited in such a way the termites go in readily enough, seeming to recognise the smell of the material from their original home.

The next step is to collect and break up a small mound and shake out the termites into the tray beside the cork nest, which must now be covered first with a sheet of glass of the right size, and then with a piece of felt or other dark cloth to exclude the light. For food, put some decaying sticks and leaves in the open half of the tray and cover them with a thin layer of humus. Keep this damp, and the termites will soon come out of the nest and burrow into it quite freely in search of food and moisture. A little sugar added to the water used to dampen the soil makes the food more attractive.

The black mound termite, *Amitermes hastatus*, has been kept alive in such nests for several years, and the account of the life history of this species as given in Chapter 5 is based on observations of such a captive colony. Interesting physiological experiments may also be carried out in such artificial nests, for example to determine the effect of temperature on termite activity. Two cells, one at each end of a piece of cork, are connected by a long, straight groove through which the termites are able to run from one cell to another. A thermometer is also embedded in the cork so the temperature can be read, and the cork is then covered with a sheet of glass. At 0 °C the termites do not move at all, at 10 °C they move at a speed of about nine metres an hour; at 20 °C at 18 metres an hour and at 30 °C at 27 metres an hour. In this way one is able to reach the conclusion that termite activity is directly related to temperature.

An identical artificial nest is a most suitable home for a colony of cocktail ants (*Crematogaster* sp.). If a carton nest of ants is broken up and the ants shaken onto the tray, they soon find their way into the darkness of the nest and carry their young stages inside and settle down. They will eat honey, scraps of meat, dead insects and, if a plant with scale insects or aphids is placed on the tray, the ants will visit them eagerly. They never attempt to construct any carton cells in the artificial nests, possibly because the necessary raw material is not available, but in every other respect they behave normally and their habits and the rearing of the different stages can be studied with ease. They develop obvious odour trails to feeding sites on the foraging table and may be induced to follow artificial paths of trail pheromone extracted from glands in the third pair of legs.

Sometimes young cocktail ant queens just commencing a new nest are found in hollow stems; if they are removed with their young and placed in a small artificial nest they will also settle down and you will be able to watch the new colony being established. It is a slow process, for at the end of a year the colony consists only of the queen and perhaps a dozen dwarf workers, together with some eggs, larvae and pupae. The study reveals the difficulties and dangers facing the young queen in her endeavour, and one soon comes to appreciate that in nature many do not succeed.

Carpenter bees may be induced to nest in bamboo tubes, about 30 cm long and 10-15 mm internal diameter, if they are taken from their natural homes on a cold day and put into the tubes. The bamboo tubes must be placed in a box where they are quite dry, as the bees will quickly desert a damp home.

The primitive social bees (*Allodape* sp.), so abundant in Africa, offer a fruitful field of study at close quarters. They can be induced to nest in glass tubes, about 6 mm in diameter and 15 cm long, plugged at the rear end with a piece of cotton-wool, and lined along the lower half with a strip of paper to give the bees a foothold. If such tubes are pushed into holes in the side of a box so that only the mouths protrude, and if pupae collected from nests in the field are put into them, the bees that emerge will remain in the tubes and nest in them. All that goes on inside the glass nest is easily observed.

With a bit of imagination and ingenuity, almost any type of container may be converted into a cage in which to keep insects. A glass jar with a gauze top is a simple but effective cage; a box with panels cut out and fitted with gauze or glass will work well; if you have a food plant growing in a pot, put it in the cage as well, or else build up a screen cylinder with a glass top around the pot. Plastic buckets make good insect cages – a hole cut in the side may be fitted with a netting sleeve for introducing and removing insects, food containers, or receptacles for eggs laid by the females. The plastic top may be modified by cutting out a circle and replacing it with netting. Many household adhesives can be used with success to glue netting or gauze to plastic, and cages of this type are successfully used to maintain mosquitoes indefinitely in an insectary.

Sometimes the best way to confine insects for observation under natural conditions is to cage them right where they occur in the field. Plant feeders can be con-

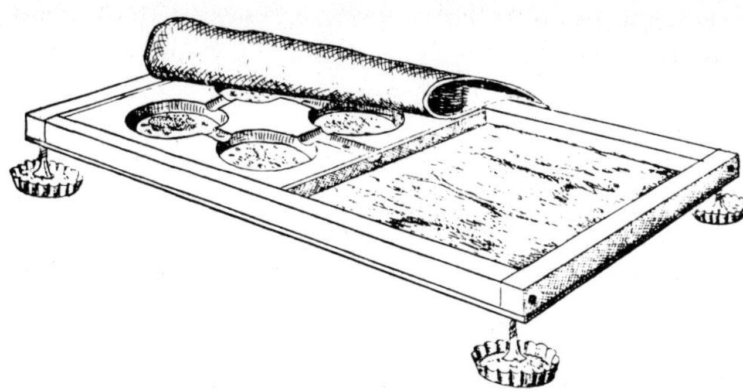

360 An artificial nest for termites and ants. Details for construction are given in the text.

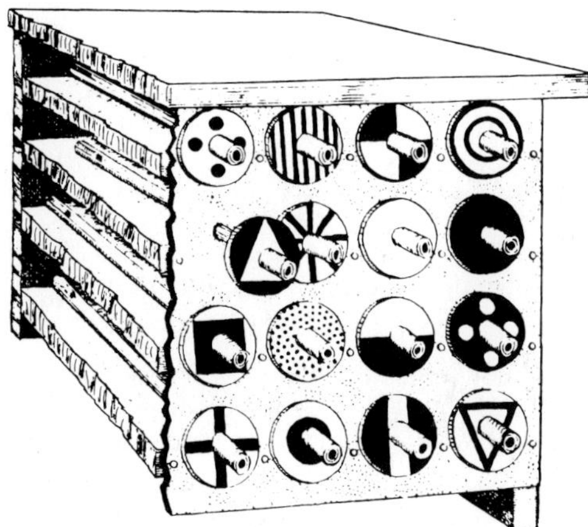

361. This cutaway view of the holding box reveals artificial nests for primitive social bees (*Allodape* sp.). The glass tubes have black and white patterned discs to help the bees find their homes.

tained in a cylinder or sleeve placed over the part of the plant they are feeding on, and in the case of a plant infested with aphids, for example, one can experiment by introducing predators to some cages (leaving others as predator-free 'controls') to see what effect they have on the aphid populations. Caged insects are also invaluable for studying life histories, from egg through immature stages to adulthood.

Photographing insects

With their tremendous diversity of size, colour and behaviour, insects present an exciting challenge to any photographer. In these days of soaring motoring costs it is worth remembering that insects are the most readily accessible wildlife photographic subjects, never further away than the garden, the vacant plot down the street, or the nearest patch of undeveloped countryside – and guaranteed to be every bit as exciting as the larger animals of national parks and wildlife reserves.

Today, more than ever before, the range of photographic equipment available brings high quality close-up photography within reach of just about anyone able to handle a camera. Assuming that you have some experience in using a camera we can proceed to look at just what is required in order to photograph living insects successfully.

The Camera: Whatever make or size of camera is chosen for photographing insects it should be a single lens reflex (SLR), and be able to take interchangeable lenses. A built-in through-the-lens (TTL) exposure meter and a shutter that can synchronise an electronic flash up to a 1/125 second or higher are also valuable features when photographing insects. Most modern 35 mm cameras in the medium and upper price ranges offer all these features, as well as some useful additional ones such as electronically controlled shutter and automatic exposure control.

Although a 35 mm camera is ideal for most people wishing to photograph insects, there are one or two SLR cameras available that take larger transparencies on 120 size film. These include the sizes 6 x 6 cm and 6 x 7 cm all of which require heavier and more cumbersome cameras than the 35 mm types, but do offer the advantage of extra sharpness when the photographs are enlarged.

Lenses and close-up devices: Almost any 'standard' focal length lens will work well for close-up photography. In the case of a 35 mm camera the standard lens is one that has a focal length in the region of 50 mm. Telephoto and wide-angle lenses are not often used for photographing insects, although a short telephoto lens may be valuable when working with exceptionally shy species, or ones that present a hazard to the photographer, such as honey bees and certain paper wasps.

The great majority of lenses do not focus nearly close enough for a subject the size of an insect to appear sufficiently large on the film. For this reason it is usually necessary to insert extension tubes or extension bellows between the camera body and the lens; the longer the extension used the closer the camera will be able to focus and hence the larger the subject will appear on the film. Most camera manufacturers offer extension tubes of various lengths to be used singly or in combination to obtain the required closeness of focusing. It is important that any extension tube should be of the automatic (sometimes called 'auto') type; that is they permit the diaphragm of the lens to be actuated by the camera when they are in position.

Extension bellows provide a way of varying the distance between a lens and a camera body – they can be considered as a sort of continuously variable extension tube. The better extension bellows are fitted with a focusing rail on which the entire assembly of bellows, lens and camera can be moved forwards or backwards by a vernier adjustment in order to achieve very accurate focusing. Their main use is where higher magnification is required than extension tubes can conveniently provide. Their drawbacks are that they usually need to be mounted on a tripod, and their high cost – especially when fitted with an automatic lens diaphragm facility.

A decided boon to the insect photographer are the so-called 'macro' or 'micro' close-focusing lenses which are offered by several manufacturers. With these lenses it is possible to focus on subjects ranging in distance from infinity right down to those only a few centimetres away, all with a single turn of the lens's focusing ring, and without any extension rings or bellows being necessary. Such lenses work well for general photography too and are therefore valuable as a general purpose lens in place of the 'standard' lens that most cameras are supplied with.

Also of interest to the insect photographer are the 'macro-focusing' zoom lenses that have made their appearance on the market in recent years. Some of these zoom lenses (a zoom lens is one whose focal length can be continuously varied) are able to focus sufficiently closely to make them useful for photographing insects, as well as retaining their advantages as good all-round lenses because of the multiple focal lengths they offer. One problem with them, however, is that they tend to be rather heavier than fixed focal length lenses, both in mass and on the wallet.

Loss of light and depth of field: An inescapable law of close-up photography is that the greater the magnification the more light is lost in the optical system and the less the depth of field. This loss of light must be compensated for either by using a slower shutter speed, or by using a wider aperture, or by using a faster (i.e. more sensitive) film, or by increasing the amount of light falling on the subject. Most built-in exposure meters automatically take into account any such loss of light when close-up photographs are being taken, and therefore still give an accurate reading.

The loss of depth of field may be compensated for by using a smaller lens aperture (i.e. by 'stopping down' the lens), and also to some extent by arranging that one's insect subject and camera are positioned in such a way that as much of the subject is in sharp focus as possible.

In many ways these compensations to offset the loss of light and loss of depth of field tend to interact adversely with each other. The result of this in practice is that the insect photographer all too frequently finds himself requiring more light than is available from the sun for his live, active, close-up subjects.

'Camera shake' is often a problem with close-ups and a tripod is sometimes valuable in preventing, or lessening this. However a tripod can be irritatingly difficult to adjust quickly and is no equal for the versatility of a steady hand for holding the camera.

Using daylight: Fortunately our African sunlight is relatively strong, and provided the subject is in direct sunlight there is sufficient light for most insect photography provided you use a film with a speed of at least ASA50. A piece of white cardboard is useful for reflecting light into the darker shadows. Overcast conditions provide pleasantly soft light for photographing insects, but then its strength is a good deal less than that of direct sunlight. All in all, in spite of the various difficulties in using daylight to photograph insects, these photographs look the most natural.

Using electronic flash: Electronic flash provides a powerful and conveniently portable source of illumination for photographing insects. Even the smallest units provide sufficient light when you hold them within a few centimetres of the subject, allowing a relatively small aperture to be used and therefore a good depth of field. Another advantage of electronic flash is that it provides a very rapid burst of light (between 1/500th and 1/50 000th of a second) which has the effect of eliminating subject movement and camera shake.

Many of the newer electronic flash units offer automatic exposure control by way of a photocell that measures the amount of light falling on the subject and then adjusts the burst of light to give the correct exposure. Unfortunately, however, few of these so-called 'computer' units are of much use to the insect photographer due to the fact that their photocells scan an area very much larger than that seen by the camera when being used in a close-up situation. One or two of the latest models that have a photocell whose field of view can be varied may work well with insects. Some of these same 'computer' flash units offer manual adjustment of the burst of light, and this feature is a decided advantage in insect photography as it enables the subject to be lit by the exact amount of light required. The usual methods of mounting the electronic flash onto the camera will not generally work well in a close-up situation since the flash is aimed too far ahead of the subject. For this reason it is often necessary for the insect photographer to either hand-hold the flash unit in order to aim it at his subject, or else to engineer a special bracket to do the job for him. Again, a square of white cardboard may be very useful for reflecting light into deep shadows. Alternatively use a second flash unit for this purpose.

Technique: This is without doubt the most difficult part of insect photography to master. Be prepared to invest heavily in time and film to begin with, keeping accurate notes on how you took each photograph, then critically examining your results and noting them too. There are quite a number of useful publications available at the larger camera shops and booksellers which offer much sound basic advice on close-up photography, a great deal of which is applicable to photographing insects.

If you intend simply to photograph insects as things of beauty (which they certainly are!) and not capture them engaged in any sort of activity then it is possible to photograph them indoors under controlled conditions. Because insects become inactive at low temperatures it is quite practical for you to capture an insect in a bottle and place it in a refrigerator (not a deep-freeze!) for a few minutes. After this it will remain sluggish for a while and allow you to pose and photograph it with ease against the background of your choice. This is a useful way in which to begin insect photography as it enables you to familiarise yourself with your equipment and lighting. But beware, insects photographed in this way seldom look more natural than do pinned specimens.

Photographing insects out of doors in their natural habitat brings with it a level of satisfaction that is probably unbeatable in the whole field of nature photography. Within every patch of grass, each tree and shrub, every flower and forest glade you are likely to find insects: courting, mating, laying eggs, being born, being eaten, lying in ambush and being ambushed, and all there ready to be captured on film. Most people's reaction to being shown a good series of photographs of living insects is to remark on the patience the photographer must have had. How right they are! Patience is not only a virtue, it is a prerequisite of successful insect photography.

Stalking insects in the field is invariably a difficult business, and takes its toll on the nerves. You may use a variety of techniques in order to approach a free-living insect to within photographing distance, but most of all it is important that all your movements are slow and steady; watch a chameleon stalking an insect and you will get a good idea of what is required of an insect photographer.

Assuming that you have seen an insect that you would like to photograph, that the prevailing light is strong enough and coming from the right direction (or that you

362. In the insectary of a large citrus estate, this entomologist is transferring predaceous ladybirds to a melon covered with scale insects, on which they will feed and breed. When large numbers of the beetles have been reared in the insectary they are released into the orchards, where they control the citrus scale insects, saving the estate the large sums of money which would normally be spent on dangerous insecticides.

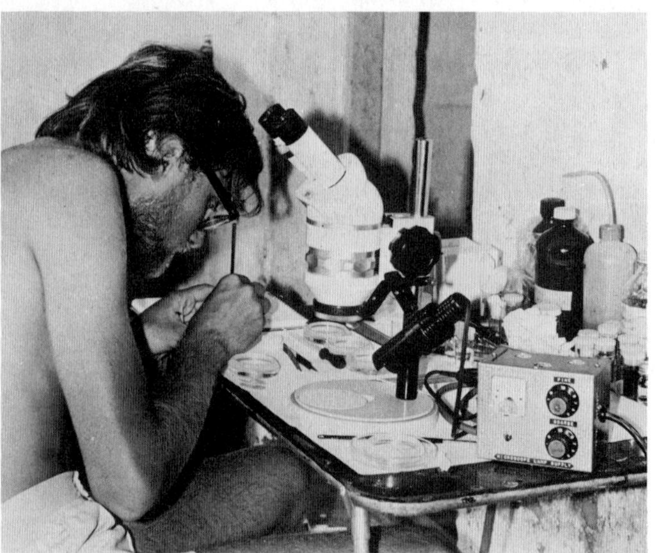

363. Research entomologists often spend long periods in the field, working under uncomfortable and difficult conditions. Here, far from the comforts of the laboratory, sand flies are examined under an expensive microscope for leishmaniasis.

have an electronic flash unit), and that you have prepared your equipment for action, the method would be something as follows: set the magnification of your camera to accommodate the size your subject appears to be as best you can judge at the distance you now stand from it; now begin to move forward, slowly and steadily until you are close enough to focus on your quarry. At this stage the insect may well have perceived your movement and taken off in fright – or perhaps moved off of its own accord. If so begin stalking it once more. Once you are close enough, raise the viewfinder to your eye and gently move the camera forwards and backwards until the subject is at sharpest focus, then gently press the shutter release. If the insect has not moved off you might care to attempt a second exposure. If so you must remember to wind on the film with those same slow movements in order not to disturb the subject. In fact the nearer you are to the insect, the more important it is not to make any rapid movements at all; adjust your equipment, change extension tubes, alter your shutter speed in a way reminiscent of someone in a barrel of treacle. Friends might laugh watching you from afar going through this slow-motion routine – but it is necessary.

Success comes slowly to the insect photographer, but the thrill and satisfaction of producing a well exposed, well composed photograph of an insect 'in action' in its natural surroundings makes insect photography one of the most worthwhile of all pursuits in the field of natural history, and through it one's eyes are opened wider.

Entomology as a career

A career in entomology is usually interesting and constructive. While not particularly well-paid, most entomologists seem to enjoy a high level of job satisfaction and indeed many of them live to a ripe old age! The fascination of working with an endless variety of insects, solving systematic or evolutionary problems and describing species new to science, keeps some entomologists happy for most of their days. Others achieve satisfaction through contributing towards the quality of human existence, by controlling agricultural pests or by preventing insect-borne diseases.

You will find people with extremely diverse backgrounds working as entomologists throughout the world today. Some have no formal training in entomology, yet have succeeded because of their enthusiasm and talent; engineers, chemists and agriculturalists sometimes find themselves working as entomologists because of various circumstances and opportunities. In general, however, most professional entomologists have a background of university training in biology, and this may be regarded as the normal way in which you enter the field.

Biology as a school subject is recommended for the aspiring entomologist, but this is not taught in all schools and other science subjects such as physical chemistry or geography may be the only courses available. Mathematics is important, and in some countries it may be difficult to be accepted for a science course at university unless a satisfactory mark is attained in school mathematics. The important thing to remember is that if you eventually wish to become a professional entomologist you need to study the sciences.

Once you have finished your secondary schooling, the would-be entomologist should move on to university. Courses offered by universities in Africa and overseas are so diverse that it is difficult to generalise, but a sound procedure is to register for a three-year course for the Bachelor of Science degree, with zoology or biology as a major subject, and physics, chemistry, geology, botany, geography or mathematics as ancillary subjects. Such a course provides a good general biological education, from which one can proceed to a further year's study in a more specialised field. However some universities do offer a four-year degree in entomology.

The pressures to leave university and go out to earn a living may often be irresistible, depending on individual circumstances. However, if you are to reach the top in your chosen career of entomology, you should stay at university until you are sufficiently qualified to be able to continue obtaining further degrees while employed. Many Masters' and Doctorates are obtained by entomologists working full-time in research posts. Of course, if you are able to afford it, or able to obtain bursaries and study grants, you may decide to stay at university to do research there for higher degrees.

Once on the labour market, the entomology graduate is faced with a wide variety of job prospects, some of which are more attractive than others. At times there may be a scarcity of posts, but this situation is not unique to entomology. In general, there is a dual choice of either entering a commercially orientated entomology career, or an academically orientated one. Chemical companies, pest control firms, large agricultural organisations and others employ entomologists, whose main duties are to promote their employers' products. Although well paid, these positions can sometimes suffer from the pressures of commercial expediency.

In the non-commercial field there are many openings for entomologists in agriculture, medical and veterinary research institutes, universities and colleges. Quite often opportunities arise that you would never have dreamed of while you were studying at university!

The fragility of the earth's ecosystems, the pressing need to improve living standards and food production throughout most of Africa and the frightening lessons learned about the misuse of insecticides, make it imperative that future generations of entomologists should be well educated, in the broadest possible sense, so that they will appreciate the long-term implications of badly-conceived projects aimed at short-term entomological solutions.

FURTHER READING

Oldroyd, H.: *Collecting, Preserving and Studying Insects*, Ed. 2. Hutchinson, London (1970). 336pp.

364. As part of an experiment on the ecology of the sand dunes these tenebrionid beetles have been marked by research workers at the Namib Desert Ecological Research Unit.

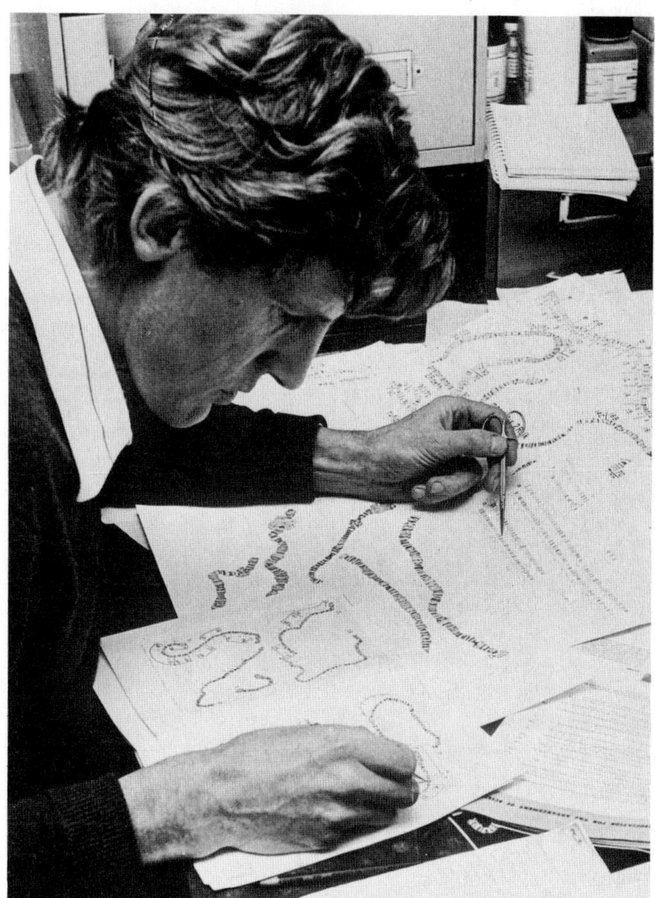

365. After taking highly magnified microphotographs of the polytene chromosomes of *Anopheles* mosquitoes, this medical entomologist is now sorting out the banding patterns that will enable him to identify morphologically indistinguishable species.

Index

All numbers in **bold** type refer to the plates, those in *italics* to the black and white illustrations, and those in roman to the text

C

D

E

F

G

H

I

J

K

L

M

N

O

P

Q

R

S

T

U

V

W

X

Y

Z